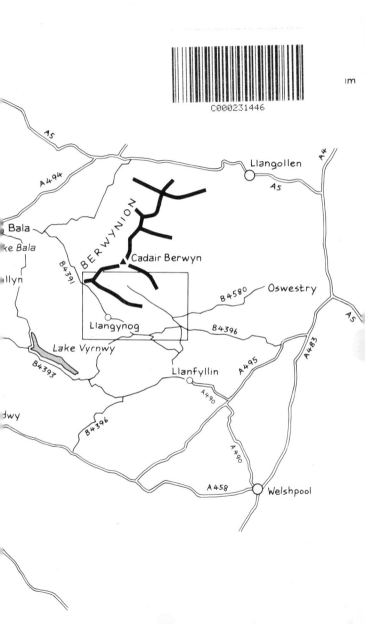

Climbers' Club Guides
Edited by John Willson

Meirionnydd

by

Martin Crocker, Elfyn Jones, Mike Rosser
John Sumner, Terry Taylor, Dave Wrennall

Artwork
by
Simon Cardy, Phil Gibson, Don Sargeant

Front Cover: *The Emperor's New Toes* (VS), Simdde Ddu, Arennig Fawr
Climber: Norman Clacher
Photo: Terry Taylor

Rear Cover: *Sci-Fi* (E7 – first ascent), Tap y Gigfran, Craig Cywarch
Climber: Martin Crocker
Photo: John Sumner

Frontispiece: *Blame It on the Gods* (E5 – first ascent), Craig Cau, Cadair Idris
Climber: Martin Crocker
Photo: Don Sargeant

Reverse Frontispiece: *Gwern Pillar* (VS), Gwern Craig Rock, Cadair Idris
Climber: Simon Bailey
Photo: John Sumner

Published by The Climbers' Club

Craig Cowarch (The Mountain Club 1958)
by R E Lambe

Moelwynion (The Climbers' Club 1962)
by J R Lees

Craig Cowarch (The Mountain Club 1964, & revision 1966)
by R E Lambe and A B Knox

Snowdon East (The Climbers' Club 1970)
by A J J Moulam

Central Wales (West Col 1973)
by John Sumner

Dolgellau Area (West Col 1975)
by John Sumner

Tremadog and the Moelwyns (The Climbers' Club 1978)
by Mike Mortimer

Tremadog (The Climbers' Club 1983)
by Leigh MaGinley (Moelwyn section co-author: Mel Griffiths)

Mid-Wales (The Climbers' Club 1988)
by John Sumner

Tremadog and Cwm Silyn (The Climbers' Club 1989)
by Mark Pretty, Dave Farrant, Geoff Milburn

Meirionnydd (The Climbers' Club 2002)
by Martin Crocker, John Sumner, et al.

© The Climbers' Club 2002

Crocker, Martin   Sumner, John   Meirionnydd
(Climbers' Club Guides)

British Library Cataloguing in Publication Data

A catalogue record for this book is available from the British Library

796.552

ISBN 0-901601-63-2

Typeset by the Editor
Produced by The Ernest Press, Glasgow G46 6AQ
Distributed by Cordee, 3a de Montfort Street, Leicester LE1 7HD

Contents

Maps and Diagrams

[1] Photo: Don Sargeant
[2] Photo: Terry Taylor
[3] Photo: Martin Crocker
[4] Photo: John Harwood
[5] Photo: Mike Lewis
[6] Photo: Simon Cardy

[1-5] Photodiagrams prepared by Don Sargeant
[6] Photodiagrams prepared by Simon Cardy

Climbers' Club Guides

The Climbers' Club

The publisher of this guidebook is The Climbers' Club, which was founded in 1898 from origins in Snowdonia and is now one of the foremost mountaineering clubs in Great Britain. Its objects are to encourage mountaineering and rock-climbing, and to promote the general interest of mountaineers and the mountain environment.

It is a truly national club with widespread membership, and currently owns huts in Cornwall, Pembrokeshire, Derbyshire, Snowdonia, and Argyll. Besides managing seven huts, The Climbers' Club produces an annual Journal and runs a full programme of climbing meets, dinners, and social events. Club members may also use the huts of other clubs through reciprocal arrangements. The club publishes climbing guidebooks (currently 20 in number) to cover most of Wales and Southern England. The club is a founder-member of, and is affiliated to, the British Mountaineering Council; it makes annual contributions to the Access and Conservation Trust, as well as to volunteer cliff and mountain rescue organizations. In 1999, the Climbers' Club Colin Kirkus Guidebook Fund was established as a means of distributing some of the profits earned from guidebooks to assist climbing-related projects that are in keeping with the aims of the club, though they need not be confined to the club's guidebook areas.

Membership fluctuates around 1,200, and at present there are no limits on growth. Members of two years' standing may propose a competent candidate for membership and, provided that adequate support is obtained from other members, the Committee may elect him or her to full membership; there is no probationary period.

Climbing Style

The following policy statement on climbing style was agreed in principle at The Climbers' Club Annual General Meeting on 25th February 1990:

The Climbers' Club supports the tradition of using natural protection and is opposed to actions which are against the best interest of climbers and users of the crags. This applies particularly to irreversible acts which could affect the crags and their environs.

Such acts could include: the placing of bolts on mountain and natural crags; retrospective placing of bolts; chiselling, hammering, or altering the rock appearance or structure; excessive removal of vegetation and interference with trees, flowers, and fauna.

The Climbers' Club policy is that guidebooks are written to reflect the best style matched to the ethos and traditions of British climbing.

The Climbers' Club Hut in Cwm Glas Mawr   Photo: Ian Smith

Guidebook Disclaimer

This guide attempts to provide a definitive record of all existing climbs and is compiled from information from a variety of sources. The inclusion of any route does not imply that it remains in the condition described. Climbs can change unpredictably: rock can deteriorate and the existence and condition of *in-situ* protection can alter. All climbers must rely on their own ability and experience to gauge the difficulty and seriousness of any climb. Climbing is an inherently dangerous activity.

Neither The Climbers' Club nor the authors and editor of this guidebook accept any liability whatsoever for any injury or damage caused to climbers, third parties, or property arising from the use of it. Whilst the content of the guide is believed to be accurate, no responsibility is accepted for any error, omission, or mis-statement. Users must rely on their own judgement and are recommended to insure against injury to person and property and third party risks.

The inclusion in this guidebook of a crag or routes upon it does not mean that any member of the public has a right of access to the crag or the right to climb upon it. Before climbing on any crag in this guidebook, please read the access and conservation notes in the Introduction (from page 19), and detailed guidance given in the area introductions, especially with regard to the Aran (page 35).

www.climbers-club.co.uk

Editor's Note

This guide has had a painful and protracted gestation. By 1996, the 1988 *Mid-Wales* and 1989 *Tremadog* guides were at the end of their runs, leaving the whole vast area of North and Mid Wales south-west and south-east of Snowdon to be redocumented. Various combinations were discussed, but fresh development in what had previously been regarded as something of a quiet backwater repeatedly upset the balance, and plans had to be revised more than once. At one stage it was proposed that the region should be published collectively in a three-volume *Snowdonia South*. In the end, pragmatic considerations such as script readiness and consumer demand led to *Tremadog* being fast-tracked.·

What was left closely co-incided with the ancient county of Meirionnydd (though it does bleed off the edges in places), and so this became the selected title for this guide. Early in 2001, no sooner had Ian Smith been elected President of the club than he was promptly precipitated into handling the serious consequences to the club, its workers, members, and finances, of the foot-and-mouth disease crisis, and he had to relinquish most of his guidebook editorial work. His designated successor was unable at that point to pick up the reins, and so what I had thought was a well-earned retirement after ten years as South-West Editor was hijacked in order to see this title through to publication. I set an outrageously rigorous schedule for completion of the work, and it is a magnificent tribute to all involved that this was met.

At the centre of those illustrious workers was **John Sumner**, author of the previous *Mid-Wales* and universally regarded as the area guru. His task was to update the text of his earlier guide to the Aran, Cadair, and Berwyn ranges, incorporating the developments that he had continued to make and that others, attracted by the prospect of exploring a tranquil and little-known area the book had revealed, sustained.

One of these was **Martin Crocker**, who had over a few months trans-formed Craig Cau on Cadair Idris into one of the great high-mountain crags of Britain and had throughout the decade developed dozens of gritstone crags in the Rhinogau where no one seemed ever to have thought of going before. He was appointed joint author with John Sumner with a brief to compile a script for the Rhinog main areas and to rewrite the Craig Cau section, while John retained Craig y Cae, Craig y Merched, and the Barmouth crags.

By this time the exploits of **Terry Taylor**, a GP who had settled in Tywyn, also loomed large. He had played the leading part in the exploration of the also completely new crags on Arennig Fawr, and seemed to be intent on mopping up every small crag and quarry to be found in the region. The Arennig script is his, as are those of many of those lesser crags and quarries that are too numerous to list, though they include the other Rhinog outliers and the remaining slate quarries and sea-cliffs.

The Moelwynion script is by **Elfyn Jones**; Cwm Lledr has been covered by **Mike Rosser**; and the Betws-y-coed crags are described by **Dave Wrennall**. These areas are on the homegrounds of the writers, who have all done sterling work in unearthing information on crags, climbs, and ascent details long thought lost or never before come to light.

A number of others have made smaller but still important contributions to the text: Mike Lewis provided scripts for Moelwyn Bach and Carreg y Saeth; Lindsay Griffin supplied an account of his own development of Moel yr Hydd; John Appleby researched and wrote up the Craig Dinas section; and the unique bouldering on The Tubes is described by Nick Dixon. After work on the Lledr had got well under way, a draft script for the valley by Bob Wightman turned up unexpectedly; although it was by then not possible to use this, ideas and information it contained proved very helpful to the section author.

The Introduction is a co-operative effort, with sections by John Sumner (Winter Climbing), Terry Taylor (Sea-Cliffs and Slate Quarries), and Martin Crocker (Geology). The Conservation Notes were kindly written by Barbara Jones of the Countryside Council for Wales.

The Historical has been compiled from various sources, including: Geoff Milburn's Historical in the 1988 *Mid-Wales* guide; various notes, essays, and chronologies by some of the above-mentioned authors and also Harold Drasdo; and some original research by Vivienne Smith.

It has been our aim to make this the most lavishly-illustrated guide ever published by the club. Fortunately, we had a headstart with the superlative diagrams **Phil Gibson** drew for the 1988 *Mid-Wales*, which must rank amongst the finest collections of crag drawings ever made. **Simon Cardy** has patiently overseen the revision of the line-dropping on all of these to take account of the important new climbs and of the errors that crept into the 1988 guide; and he has produced the fine photodiagrams for the Moelwynion and Cwm Lledr. The remaining maps, diagrams, and photodiagrams are all the work of the ever-stalwart **Don Sargeant** who, having moved to the area in the mid 90s, became a regular partner in Martin Crocker's exploits. I cannot praise their work too highly or thank them adequately for their efforts.

We are very grateful to all who submitted action photographs.

I must also thank: Iwan Arfon Jones for his guidance on the spellings and translations of the Welsh names – his book **Enwau Eryri** ~ *Place-names in Snowdonia* should be on the bookshelves of all who love the crags and mountains of Wales; Mike Vetterlein, David Hope, and Mark Hounslea for proof-reading the book, an unspectacular and sometimes thankless, but nonetheless essential task; and finally Terry Taylor and Martin Crocker who, in addition to writing their own sections, have provided invaluable advice and information about most of the other areas covered, and lent much support and encouragement to me personally.

JW ~ New Year 2002

Acknowledgements

My love of climbing in this beautiful and unspoilt region grew very quickly after acquiring John Sumner's *Mid-Wales* guidebook in 1990. His work provided the helping hand for me to start exploring a land rich in mysterious great places and atmosphere. Thanks, John, for showing me around, and (co-author or not) for keeping going through times of change with such vigour and dedication – always personifying, to me, the set of core climbing values that reassure and inspire.

In preparing my script for the Rhinogau and Craig Cau, I should like to thank stalwart companions of a like generation and spirit, Don Sargeant and John Harwood, for some long, hard days on the hill. (It is somewhat amusing that The Rhinogau should treat these two so disparately: Don would always get the sunny weekends, while John the wet ones!) The Carreg y Saeth script belongs to Mike Lewis who also supplied descriptions of his climbs on Craig y Groes; I don't know who was more surprised – he or I – when we crossed paths on Carreg y Saeth in September 1997. I must thank Iwan Arfon Jones for admitting an Englishman (though with a Welsh wife as a ticket) into staunch Welsh literary territory, and providing me with some advice on how not to upset the Welsh – too much. My colleague Terry Taylor merits an acknowledgement for climbing just about everywhere save the Rhinogau – until 1999 that is, when he saw the light, and started bombarding me with endless descriptions of new routes being established right across the range.

Thanks are also due to Raymond Roberts and Dr Bob Matthews for checking my Geological Notes. And once again it has been a pleasure working alongside editor John Willson, even though he may not care to admit to muscling in on time that I should have spent on my *Avon and Cheddar* guidebook. Finally, words aren't enough to record my acknowledgement of the understanding and spiritual and practical support of my wife, Beverley, and my children, Jonathan and Emily.

Martin Crocker ~ 2001

I should like to thank everyone who has helped in the production of this guidebook script, especially: my old friend Alex George, who has always been a willing helper over many years of the area's new-route scene; Martin Crocker, who rekindled the old fires on my flagging enthusiasm with his tremendous energy, great talent, and genuine passion for Meirionnydd; Don Sargeant for his excellent maps and photodiagrams and his time spent hunting down obscure crags; and Ian Smith, who with great patience guided me through the intricacies of the computer. Not least, my wife Jill still encourages me with my guidebook work and has been my second on countless first ascents, pulling me out of many a gripped state with a few well-chosen words.

John Sumner ~ 2001

Thanks to Mel Griffiths and Elfyn Jones for lifting my ambitions and pointing me at unclimbed lines. Thanks also to Martin Crocker, whose extensive exploits hereabouts lifted my ideals and my spirits. All my climbing partners in the last ten years deserve praise for allowing themselves to be seduced by the wonderful crags of Meirionnydd, in particular Norman Clacher, who is prepared to go almost anywhere in any weather if a good line is promised, and Paul Jenkinson for similar enthusiasm. The rollercoaster ride on the Arennig was due to Jayson Cooper, who opened up the possibilities there for me in 1990. And for all those days away from home, thank you, Chris.

Terry Taylor ~ 2002

The astute will notice that much of the text of the Moelwynion section remains essentially unchanged from previous editions. This is testimony to all the tremendous and detailed work done by previous authors, in particular Johnny Lees and A J J Moulam. I have received many useful comments and suggestions on the text from many people, and in particular from the following: Malcom Davies, David Bailey, Mel Griffiths, Derek Johnston, Steve Mayers, Terry Taylor, Lindsay Griffin, Mike Turner, and Tony Shelmadrine. I should also like to thank my partner Rosie for her tolerance and patience as I avoided domestic and other duties while I typed away at the keyboard or dashed off to some obscure part of Meirionnydd to check (yet again) on one of Terry Taylor's most recent esoteric discoveries.

Elfyn Jones ~ 2002

My thanks must go: to Harold Drasdo for providing historical data and valuable local knowledge; to Nick Dixon for his work on The Tubes and encouragement throughout; to John Appleby for undertaking the Craig Dinas section; and to Mark Hedge, Phil Blain, and Chris Shaw for suggestions.

Dave Wrennall ~ 2002

Introduction

Five mountain ranges form a great ring around southern Snowdonia, the peaks and valleys of which together provide one of the most richly diverse climbing-grounds in Britain. Each range in turn is encircled by its own compact road-system that gives good access to all the climbing areas.

The starting-point in the south is Dolgellau. Running north-east from hereabouts are the Aran, with Cwm Cywarch at their south-western foot. Although the cwm does not have a *Cenotaph Corner*-dominated road running through it and will doubtless never achieve the popularity of the Llanberis Pass, its fine crags are as truly 'mountain-type', and just as easily reached. From the far end of the chain, a north-west arc will take you across the Arennig to Blaenau Ffestiniog, the key northern base. On the north and east flanks of Arennig Fawr are a series of terraced crags, again quite quickly reached, that have been developed almost entirely in the last decade. Despite the mountain setting, the routes tend to be single-pitch, mostly clean and sound, and, though not entirely, in the middle and higher grades.

The tourist knows Blaenau for its slate-tips, but immediately adjacently the climber has the friendly rough and juggy slabs of the classic Moelwyn crags. The two peaks here are linked by a broad, tarn-dappled ridge/plateau to their dominating partner to the north, Moel Siabod, and from the eastern watershed falls the Afon Lledr, which is trailed by the A470 to Betws-y-coed, where it joins the Afon Conwy on the final stages of the latter's journey to the sea at Llandudno. Along Cwm Lledr and around the confluence are to be found several small crags offering climbing in all grades as well as the novelty of bouldering in a river-gorge setting on the recently-developed 'Tubes'.

Running south from Blaenau to Barmouth are the Rhinogau, perhaps the least known and visited of all the main Welsh hills. Two of the most blatant crags had been climbed on before the 1990s, but the mass of them, hidden away in the heather and contours of the rolling hills, lay undisturbed until five years ago; yet this section is now the largest in the book. Some of the routes here require a walk in (with the use of map and compass); this may no longer be to many climbers' taste, but, especially combined with a heathery bivouac, will provide rewards of its own as well as a perhaps essential spiritual preparation for the true appreciation of the climbing. This is mainly on gritstone outcrops and in the middle and upper grades, but the traditional mountaineer will still find a fine choice of climbs to combine with traverses of the peaks.

Back east, its summit less than five kilometres from Dolgellau, towers Cadair Idris, where, especially on the magnificent Craig Cau, are to be found some of the finest big, mountain rock-climbs in England and Wales, many topping out at an altitude of between 600 and 800 metres.

Lying just outside the north-eastern quadrant of this circle are the Berwynion. They never made it into Poucher's *The Welsh Peaks*, and to the northbound

A5 commuter they just appear as distant grassy hills away to the left between Llangollen and Corwen; but on the steep, hidden southern slopes, set amongst a discreet blend of woods, grass, and rocks is the largest waterfall in Wales. And this, in turn, is contained within a complex of pleasant and easily-reached crags sporting a good selection of middle-grade climbs together with a few modern desperates.

The technical geology of the region is explained below but, except for the Rhinog gritstone and the quarried slate, the rocks are of volcanic types and will appear reasonably familiar to mainstream North Wales climbers; limestone is nowhere to be found. The weather is, of course, just as fickle as in the main northern Snowdonia peaks but, being a few metres lower and a few kilometres further south, the area may just escape its most extreme manifestations of harshness. The corollary, though, is that vegetation finds it that much easier to thrive, and some of the older and less-frequented climbs may no longer seem the 'classics' they were once 'destined to be'. Most of the more recent development, however, has taken place on the steeper and cleaner walls or followed discreet preparatory cleaning. To what extent the condition is maintained will depend upon such imponderables as the course of global warming and the amount of traffic the routes attract.

Geology

The crags of Meirionnydd fall into three main contrasting geological types. The first, and oldest, are the Cambrian grits of the Rhinogau; the second are the slates of the Lower Ordovician (Tremadoc) and Upper Ordovician (Ashgill), represented by the quarries of the Tonfanau to Dolgellau and Tywyn to Corris areas respectively; and the third, responsible for the majority of crags in the region, are the igneous rocks of the Ordovician Period which are widespread across the principal mountain ranges of Cadair Idris, the Aran, the Moelwynion, and, to a lesser extent, the Berwynion.

During Cambrian times a marine basin in the area of the Rhinogau was the site of some 5000 metres of deposited sediment, the thickest succession of Cambrian rocks to be seen in Britain. These sediments were subsequently uplifted and folded during a major phase of mountain building (the Caledonian Orogeny) which took place in late Silurian to early Devonian times. The main zone of uplift, known as the Harlech Dome, is dominated by major folds including the north-to-south-trending Dolwen Pericline and the Caerdeon Syncline. Ultimately the dome was eroded to reveal some of the oldest rocks in its central core, namely the Rhinog Formation and the slightly younger Barmouth Formation, which make up all of the crags of the Rhinogau. The Rhinog Formation, which forms the higher hills of the massif (including Rhinog Fawr, Rhinog Fach, and Craig Wion), comprises tough greywacke, with thin beds, lenses, or multiple units of coarse sandstone or quartz pebble conglomerate. The Barmouth Formation is well exposed in the south of the Harlech Dome where it makes up the crags at Craig Bodlyn, Llawlech, and Craig y Merched. The lithologies, which are similar to those of the Rhinog Formation, are dominated by slightly coarser greywacke turbidites, but with fewer mudstone intercalations. Some coarser beds occasionally grade into conglomerate bands containing striking pebbles of white and rose-coloured quartz. To the climber these coarse greywackes and grits, when clean, provide some of the highest-friction rock in Wales. And the coarser units of the Barmouth Formation, especially those with a purple hue, are perhaps the most beautiful grits in Great Britain. Typically the crags are short, rectangularly and massively jointed, and weathered into frequent steep escarpments across the dissected, rugged plateau of the Rhinog massif.

Higher in the Lower Palaeozoic succession are shales and mudstones belonging to the late Cambrian Ffestiniog Flags and Dolgellau formations, and the early Ordovician Dol-cyn-afon Formation. Some of these sequences are of interest to climbers. Strong compression during the Caledonian Orogeny resulted in the formation of slate, a lithology characterized by the development of a finely spaced cleavage. These slates crop out along the southern flank of the Mawddach Valley, to the north of Cadair Idris, where they have been quarried in places to provide worthwhile climbing sites such as Friog, and Cae-du.

Following a period of uplift and erosion of some of the Cambrian succession of North Wales, the sea advanced again at the beginning of the Ordovician Period. However, the deposition of marine sediments in the area was interrupted by major phases of submarine and subaerial volcanic activity from independent centres located about Cadair Idris, the Aran, Arennig, Moelwynion, and Berwynion. These volcanoes erupted intermittently and at different, but sometimes overlapping periods throughout the Ordovician Period. The larger ones emerged above sea-level as islands. The volcanic rocks, which consist mainly of extrusive ashes (tuffs), agglomerates, lavas, and various types of intrusive igneous rocks, form large erosion-resistant tracts of upland across the area. The extrusive lithologies are characteristically interbedded with marine sedimentary rocks, especially mudstones, which were deposited during phases of volcanic quiescence.

The crags of Cadair Idris fall into two igneous rock-types, namely extrusive and intrusive. Craig Cau, Craig yr Aderyn and Craig y Llam largely comprise pyroclastic material of the Aran Volcanic Group which is dominated here by rhyolitic tuffs. These tuffs were erupted as great clouds of ash from a nearby volcano before settling into distinct layers, the layering being most obvious at Craig Cau. Commonplace in these rocks, and so useful to the climber, are the cavities (vesicles) that were once bubbles of trapped gas produced as the hot ashes settled and compacted. These are very pronounced on the top walls of Craig Cau, while lower down the crag the tuffs are coarser and highly textured. Contrastingly, the whole of the northern escarpment of the mountain and the crags of Cyfrwy, Twr Du, and Mynydd Moel comprise a microgranite (or granophyre) which was intruded into the mudstone and volcanic formations at a later time in the Ordovician. Of lesser significance, from the climber's point of view, are the spilitic lavas of the Pen y Gadair Volcanic Formation that form the ridge and crags of Craig Cau and Waun Bistyll. Here rounded pillow-like shapes typify the effects of basaltic lavas being extruded into seawater.

Rhinog Grit ~ Lechau Mawr (Rhinog Fawr)
Climber: Martin Crocker   Photo: Don Sargeant

The Rocks of Cadair Idris
Above: Craig Yr Aderyn   Below: Cyfrwy in the evening sun
Photos: Don Sargeant

The chief crags of the Aran, Craig Cywarch and Gist Ddu, consist entirely of rhyolitic ash-flow tuffs, also of the Aran Volcanic Group. These are hard and brittle in places, especially on the high western faces of Cywarch, and can fragment to glass-edged flakes and interwoven complexes of conchoidally fractured blocks. Care is required in their handling.

The swathe of volcanic rocks continues northwards into the Arennig mountains. Here too, rhyolitic, and to a lesser extent andesitic, tuffs make up the major crags, though these are distinct from those at Cadair Idris which originated from a different volcanic centre.

Volcanic material, but of a younger, Upper Ordovician age, dominates the crags of the Moelwynion, the most northerly of the mountain massifs represented in this guidebook. These make up the bulk of the Moelwyn Volcanic Formation, a unit which is a precursor to the major phase of volcanic activity responsible for the rather more celebrated volcanic cliffs of Snowdon to the north. On the south-eastern slopes of Moelwyn Mawr, resistant bands of rhyolite, extruded as lavas, form the principal crags of Clogwyn yr Oen, Craig yr Wyrsgan, and Craig y Clipiau. Here, in places, the volcanic rocks are at their most vesicular, thanks to countless trapped gas bubbles, one of the endearing characteristics of the Moelwyn climbing experience. The crags of Moelwyn Bach are of a pyroclastic nature and consist of breccias, tuffites, and tuffs. To the east of Blaenau Festiniog an older centre of volcanicity, lower in the Ordovician succession, is represented by the Rhiw Bach Volcanic Formation and its rhyolitic lavas that form, for example, Carreg y Frân.

Volcanic rocks make less of an impression on the Berwynion. The bulk of the massif comprises mudstones of the Llangynog Formation, with sporadic tuffs, tuffites, lavas, and limestones evident, for the most part, as bands of outcrops. The tuffs which are acid, and sometimes welded (ignimbrites), form most of the area's climbing crags, like those which give rise to the great waterfall of Pistyll Rhaeadr, Craig y Mwn, and the majority of crags on Craig Rhiwarth. On a few of the crags, like Pistyll Rhaeadr and Rocho Crag, a crude columnar jointing is evident which was caused as the ash layers slowly cooled. Elsewhere on Craig Rhiwarth, an intrusive quartz felspar porphyry is present. The massif, known in structural terms as the Berwyn Dome, is another product of Caledonian earth movements: a complex pericline. So too was the Central Wales Syncline, a major structure that introduces a north-south strip of Silurian grits and shales between the Berwynion and the Aran.

Late Ordovician sedimentation also gave rise to the youngest rocks of interest to the climber in the area. Following the cessation of volcanic activity during Upper Ordovician (Caradoc) times the sea covered much of the region and thick successions of mudstones were deposited during the Ashgill. The slate quarries at Abergynolywn and Corris, a few of which offer sites for climbing, have been hewn from sedimentary rocks of this age; again like the older slates in the region, they were cleaved by Caledonian earth movements.

The final, rugged form of the mountain crags and their environment owes much to the effects of the massive ice sheets and glaciers of the Ice Age which culminated approximately 18,000 years ago in North Wales. Cirques, the hollowed-out feeding grounds of mountain glaciers, are no more finely exemplified than at Cwm Cau; they abound in North Wales. Large glaciers powered over the mountains scouring out U-shaped valleys, their over-steepened sides forming lines of steep crags. Rocks embedded in the lower surface of glaciers left scratch marks in outcrops across the region, and, as arctic conditions waned, material dumped by melting retreating glaciers dammed many valleys and cirques within which lakes were to form. Thousands of years later, man took over.

The Corris Slate District Quarries

The area of slate mines in southern Meirionnydd lies between the rivers Mawddach and Dyfi, extending from the coast of Cardigan Bay eastwards for some thirty kilometres to Dinas Mawddwy. Just north of Tonfanau at Cae-du Farm Caravan and Campsite is a coastal quarry, past which the Cambrian railway runs. Facing west, and just above some of the best bouldering sea-cliffs in this region, it has three worthwhile long slabby routes. Further north at the village of Fairborne the quarry of Hed-dol (Friog), visible from the road, provides some bolted steep and fingery lines on good-quality slate. Abergynolwyn Quarry has only three routes, but in a fantastic setting, a huge hole by the path into which even the winter sun streams. The other site worth visiting is Minllyn at the eastern extreme of the slate vein, where the excellent *Zone of Totality* follows a bolt ladder up a long steep slab.

Anyone scouring a map will find other old workings which appear attractive, notably Abercwmeidaw north of Corris and Llwyngwern south of the village. The first is undeveloped (at time of writing) but has possibilities on its 25-metre walls. Some excellent lines have been explored at the second, and there is great potential for more, but the owners here are adamant that climbing is not to be permitted. This, though for different reasons, is also the sad case at Barmouth Quarry, which was well developed in the 80s.

Sea-Cliffs

An area that has never fully publicized its many coastal attractions is, for the climber, studded with easily-accessed short cliffs that catch the afternoon sun and are a delight at any time of the year. At Fairbourne beach, low-tide allows an approach to a wonderful array of rocks that is perfect for bouldering, although there is also scope for leading. The rock is poor in places but the possibilities are many.

Further south along the coast road to Tywyn is Llwyngwril and Alan's Sunbeach Caravan Park. On the beach just south of the park is another stretch of cliffs, again rising to 15 metres in places and which is popular with outdoor centres. Routes here have been led and there is plenty of bouldering.

Five miles to the south, below Cae-du Caravan park, lies the next cliff, also used by outdoor centres. There are routes of 8 to 12 metres, some equipped with belay stakes; but of greater interest is the superb bouldering above a sandy beach on west-facing, solid, clean, water-worn rock. Many of these problems rate (British) 6a or 6b and there are long difficult traverses a metre above the sand. The cliffs are accessible four hours either side of low-tide.

To find more cliffs it is necessary to travel a long way south, across the Dyfi estuary, to Borth. The beach here has massive cliffs at the southern end, but the quality of the shale is woeful. Notwithstanding this, there are some 40-metre lines at V Diff that may attract a certain type of explorer. There is more bouldering on the beach itself. Further south again, the shale cliffs at Clarach Cove provide good bouldering and a handful of bolted lines which are forced to stop half-way by the deteriorating upper bands.

More detail about the existing sea-cliff lines and further possibilities can be found by visiting www.midwalesclimbing.co.uk.

Winter Climbing in Meirionnydd

If cold winters ever return, some excellent snow and ice climbing will be found on Cadair Idris and the Aran. In the right conditions possibilities are numerous, but routes constituting a must include: *East Gully Direct* (IV) on the east face of Aran Benllyn directly below the summit (OS Ref 868 242); *Sloose* (V) on Gist Ddu (OS Ref 872 255); *Pistyll Gwyn* (III) at the head of Afon Pumryd (OS Ref 885 195); and *Maesglasau Falls* (IV) on Craig Maesglase at the head of a little valley close to Dinas Mawddwy (OS Ref 826 141).

On Cadair Idris there are three all-time classics: *Great Gully* (III) on Craig Cau; and *Trojan* (V) and *Colonial Virgin* (VI) just to the left of *Trojan*, both on Cyfrwy (OS Ref 702 735).

Access

Please note the statement in boldprint at the bottom of page 9. In such a large and diverse area, it is beyond the resources of a guidebook team to establish full acceptability to landowners and other authorities of the use of every crag and approach described. Suffice it to say that the generally fairly low level of use and discreet conduct by activists has meant that very few problems have so far come to light. There is, however, the potential for difficulties to arise if patterns of use change.

There is a general presumption that once open ground (i.e. uncultivated land) is legitimately reached (by right-of-way or permitted path) it is all right to wander anywhere provided no damage is caused or threatened to livestock or constructions. However, this is not a statutory right, and in the Aran at least its application is firmly rejected. The conditions on which climbing on Craig Cywarch and elsewhere in that range is permitted are set out in detail on page 35 and *must* be adhered to if the limited access that has been negotiated is to continue.

Trespass on private (including open) land, even where there is no evidence of prohibition, is a civil offence and anyone asked to leave by a landowner or official in authority should be prepared to do so. Please report such an incident promptly to the BMC's Access Officer, who will know best how to resolve the matter.

The Countryside and Rights of Way Act (known universally as CRoW) has already passed into law, but its provisions are unlikely to take significant effect before c.2005. From then, the 'right to roam' (which includes the climbing of rocks) on much open land (but not, of course, cultivated farmland) will become statutory, though still subject to various conditions and limitations (which in certain circumstances could be *more* restrictive than the current de-facto position). At that stage, climbers are strongly urged not to make any general assumptions without obtaining precise clarification of individual circumstances. It is expected that the BMC will publish very full information and guidance, and The Climbers' Club will endeavour to publish on its website the ways in which individual crags or climbing areas covered by its guidebooks will be affected.

The foot-and-mouth disease crisis of 2001 has highlighted for the first time how interdependent we all are, landowners and land-users, commercial, recreational, and conservationist; and the objects of CRoW (though framed earlier) were to strike the right balance between the potential conflicting interests. The reputation of climbers was enhanced during that crisis; it is important that we build on it by going about our activities with restraint and consideration for this balance and thus our own (and future generations') continuing opportunities to enjoy them.

It should scarcely be necessary to enjoin climbers to obey the **'don'ts'** of the Country Code: leave litter; damage walls or fences; leave gates open; light fires; fail to control dogs; park inconsiderately; harm wildlife or vegetation; disturb sheep, especially in the lambing season (February to April). Now go the extra step, read the suggestions about walls and litter in the Rhinogau introduction, and ponder whether there are further, similarly-positive gestures that could be made.

Conservation   (by Barbara Jones)

Some climbers may still imagine that Meirionnydd climbing was appropriately summed up by O G Jones in 1895 when he wrote of the Aran, 'The mountain face is so broken up that we have no gullies or arêtes separated by impossible walls… From the enthusiastic shin-scraper's point of view the architecture of the Aran face is defective.' This guidebook will no doubt banish that view, with its descriptions of classic lines on the 'traditional' cliffs and modern test-pieces on more recently developed crags. However, O G Jones's appraisal is significant in that many of the fine, steep, clean walls, arêtes, and tiers throughout this area are divided or bounded by damp gullies and ledges that break up the crag and allow vegetation to spread profusely.

Vegetation to a climber is a nuisance, but to a botanist it is an obvious delight, particularly on cliffs and crags – some of the few places where natural habitats have managed to survive away from the all-consuming grazing animals, particularly sheep. This is why steep ground, including rock-faces, are so important for conservation. Here we find not only the arctic-alpines on the high cliffs, but also heaths, ferns, and trees. How many trees do you see in the uplands of Britain other than those planted or fenced as small oases in a desert of cropped grassland? Herein lies the basis of the climbing–conservation debate. The consequences of climbing activities may appear insignificant in relation to the numerous and more substantial pressures on the countryside, but the fact that we undertake our sport in these special areas – some of the few remaining 'near-natural' habitats – can dramatically magnify any impact we have.

Vegetation abounds on sections of many cliffs in Meirionnydd. Much of it consists of relatively widespread species – heath, ferns, bramble, and scrub – which attain a greater luxuriance out of the reach of grazing sheep on cliffs composed of relatively acidic rocks, but it also includes important colonies of tiny lichens and mosses. However, base-rich rocks do occur in the area covered by this guide and these provide nutrients for the less common but more demanding species, some of which are important and either locally or nationally scarce. Craig Cau and the northern cliffs on Cadair Idris, for example, Craig Bodlyn in the southern Rhinog, Daear Fawr on Arennig Fawr, outcrops in Cwm Cywarch, and scattered outcrops on most sites including the Aran and the northern Rhinog all support areas of such vegetation; and some of it, particularly on Cadair Idris, is of international importance. So, how do we ensure that climbing can continue while avoiding damage to the plants and their habitat?

This vegetation is usually distinguishable from the ubiquitous heather and grasses of the acidic rocks, as it includes a number of flowering plants such as roseroot, meadowsweet, great wood-rush, angelica, globeflower, welsh poppy, ferns, and saxifrages: wonderful to see in summer, and easily recognizable, so damage can be avoided. It is best anyway to steer clear in winter as it likes the shaded, damp, dripping rocks, which provide moisture and nutrients for the plants but not good friction for boots. Gardening should always be limited to the absolute minimum, but crucially so where this vegetation grows. Consider the advice in some sections about abseiling in to your route rather than thrashing through vegetation from below. Isn't climbing in Meirionnydd largely about exploration and appreciating some of the wilder parts of Wales anyway? Anyone bold and determined enough to get to some of these crags should surely be prepared to cope with some vegetation.

Large areas of the Rhinogau and Cadair Idris are National Nature Reserves. Many of the rest of the crags in the guide are within Sites of Special Scientific Interest or in internationally important Special Areas of Conservation. The grounds for designation are varied and can include breeding and feeding birds, of which Meirionnydd has many, nesting on crags as well as in heaths and woodlands. If a situation arises where nesting birds are found close to climbing routes, the situation will be investigated by climbers and conservationists working together, and a temporary restriction will be agreed if considered necessary. As happens in many other parts of the country, this will be removed if nesting in the location ceases. Craig yr Aderyn south of Cadair Idris (Eastern Face and Central Buttress only) is an example of where current restrictions exist. It is unlikely that there will be many others, but please watch out for signs close to the bases of the crags during the spring and early summer months.

Recent development of the Merionnydd cliffs has generally been less damaging to important vegetation than the earlier development here and in northern Snowdonia, with thankfully fewer tales of the removal of acres of 'green caterpillars'. However, climate change (especially the recent milder and wetter winters), coupled with the waning enthusiasm of climbers for visiting the more remote mountain crags, has resulted in a vigorous regrowth of vegetation. Be kind to it. Even lichens are far more than just a second rock skin and can take years to recolonize if removed. There is, of course, more than enough climbing in the areas covered by this guide to challenge even the most ardent 'shin-scraper'. Have a marvellous time, and see for yourself the wonderful wildlife the cliff environment supports, but remember that it *needs* this environment to survive into the future.

If you have any queries about the development of, or wildlife on, any of the areas covered in the guide, or if you have any interesting plant, bird, or animal records to report, then do contact the Countryside Council for Wales in Bangor on 01248 672500, or the Dolgellau office on 01341 423570.

Equipment

A standard rack of cams, chocks, and micro-wires will be adequate for almost all climbs; additional or special requirements can be expected to be specified in the descriptions. New-routers may carry pegs in to the crag and preplace them, but this will not for the most part be necessary for the ordinary climber. However, a few descriptions specify that a peg has been used but removed; and a number of the older pegs on Cywarch and Cadair may have deteriorated beyond usefulness or vanished altogether. It is often the case that modern equipment will provide a more than adequate substitute, but where pegs are mentioned in situations that could be serious, climbers may find it advisable either to avoid such routes until they have had time to familiarize themselves thoroughly with the surroundings, or to carry hammer and a small selection of pegs, or to abseil in and inspect first. Except for the quarries, the whole region is, of course, designated bolt free.

Though most of the crags described in this guide can be approached and quitted easily and safely in 30 minutes or less, the high cliffs of Cadair Idris and the more remote outcrops in the Rhinogau are a different matter. Many of them are some way from popular walkers' paths, and here, while locating your crag in the morning sun may be simple, getting back home again in a misty dusk could be a problem. For such outings, a map (preferably 1:25,000 to help cope with the myriad walls and fences) and compass and the ability to use them are essential; trainers may well not be adequate to cope with the terrain; and provision of protective clothing, food, first aid kit, and a torch are sensible precautions.

The 1:50,000 OS Landranger map 124, Dolgellau, covers the whole guidebook area except for the Berwynion (for which 125 is needed) and Cwm Lledr and Betws-y-coed (115). The 1:25,000 Outdoor Leisure map 23 covers Cadair Idris and the Aran, and map 18 covers Arennig Fawr, the Rhinogau, the Moelwynion, Cwm Lledr and the southernmost Betws crags.

The Guidebook

Every effort has been made to render this huge book as user-friendly as possible, notably by the fullest provision and careful placement of maps and diagrams, and the insertion of many cross-references. A map or diagram can generally be expected to be found within two pages of the start of the section to which it is a guide; where that has not been practicable, the page number is noted.

The grades used are the standard ones, and every effort has been made to supply technical grades (4a and above) for Severes and Hard Severes, for the first time on a number of crags, though a few still elude.

A dagger symbol † is used to show that a route is not known to have had a second ascent (in a style comparable with or better than the first). The proliferation of daggers in this guide represents not the authors' unwillingness to check routes by climbing them, rather the fact that they themselves have been responsible for the first ascents of so many.

[R] on a route-title line indicates that a seasonal restriction applies; [r] that a seasonal restriction may be required in some years.

Left and right are always used as if facing the crag, even in descent, unless otherwise stated.

The usual three-star system has been used to denote route quality, though its application may be found uneven, an inevitable result of the size and diversity of the area. For unrepeated routes, the star-rating (if any) given by the first ascensionist is shown by hollow symbols; these are invariably and in principle unmodified by the author.

Where Welsh names for the crags are known they are used, and translations are generally placed after them on the heading lines. Often, the literal translations can appear cryptic or meaningless in the context and some imagination is needed to supply the metaphorical link; and a few arbitrary decisions have had to be taken in the choice of alternatives. Grammatically, too, the languages are sometimes difficult to correlate, and the 'of' that begs to be supplied to make sense in English is not part of the Welsh construction and therefore appears in brackets.

New routes and whole new crags will continue to be found in this region, probably in an abundance as great as anywhere else in England or Wales. The normal repository for North Wales new-route descriptions is the Pete's Eats log book in Llanberis, email info@petes-eats.co.uk; and details of new routes etc. can be found on the Pete's Eats website www.petes-eats.co.uk. Alternatively (or additionally), Meirionnydd new routes may be sent to Dr Terry Taylor, email terry@mid-walesclimbing.co.uk and, as mentioned elsewhere, much information and many photographs can be viewed by visiting the website www.mid-walesclimbing.co.uk. A handsome new-routes book also resides in The Mountain Club hut, Bryn Hafod, in Cwm Cywarch. Finally, Martin Crocker would be very grateful to receive details of any developments in the area, especially in the Rhinogau or on Cadair Idris: 23 Ryecroft Rise, Long Ashton, Bristol, BS 41 9NQ.

Historical

The ascents described in this guidebook include some of the earliest recorded mountain climbing in Britain; yet the subsequent patterns of climbing in Meirionnydd rarely mirror that in other areas. Partly the result of the location, partly suffering inconsistent recording and publishing of routes, but also reflecting climbing fashion, the history of the area is unable to portray an uninterrupted line of development. Instead, it owes much to certain individuals' persistence and exploring spirit.

Slow Beginnings

Cadair Idris, the chair of the legendary giant, is likely to have attracted many travellers long before the first recorded ascent in 1767, with its striking image dominating the surrounding valleys, its relative ease of access, and the stupendous summit panorama, and it quickly became the most popular Welsh mountain after Snowdon.

The early years of British rock-climbing, towards the end of the nineteenth century, tended to focus on the ascents of gullies and arêtes, and it was on Cadair, too, that the first Welsh rock-climbs south of Snowdon were completed. The obvious central gully of Penygadair was probably climbed before 1880 and appears for a while to have achieved some status as a route, but the first recorded climb was Owen Glynne Jones's solo ascent of *Cyfrwy Arête* in May 1888. Seven years later to the day, he partnered W P Haskett-Smith on an ascent of *Great Gully* on Craig Cau, a line the latter had been eyeing for some time and about which both climbers were to gain a reputation for waxing lyrical. Later a section of the gully collapsed, which may have changed the nature of its difficulty, but both it and its near neighbour, *East Gully*, which the same pair climbed the next day, now rate a good Severe grade.

In 1900, Cyfrwy's *North Arête* was added, and on consecutive days (again), in August 1902, the two gullies on Tŵr Du followed. A year later the Dalton brothers, better known for their exploits in the Lake District, climbed *Pencoed Pillar*, the striking sentinel of Craig Cau. Then, inexplicably, after this auspicious start, interest dried up abruptly and totally, and it would be forty years before Cadair extended its repertoire.

Haskett-Smith and O G Jones were markedly cooler about prospects for the Aran, and it was not until Easter 1907 that a Rucksack Club party, led by C H Pickstone, visited Craig Cywarch and climbed the three big gullies. They spent some time also on indiscriminate scrambling, but if they covered any ground that later became 'routes' they failed to record it, and this enterprising weekend's work failed to inspire further exploration of the crag.

The first recorded route in the Moelwynion remains one of its most famed and popular, *Kirkus's Climb* on Clogwyn yr Oen in 1928, but even this failed to draw the interest of mainstream climbers. However, one local adventurer, R Elfyn Hughes, set out from his grandfather's house to explore several of the crags, certainly Craig Fach, Clogwyn Holland, and Craig y Clipiau, and without a climbing partner he was forced to ascend alone such routes as *Septentrionale* and *Betimes*, noting the quantities of bilberries and ash and oak saplings which could aid or inhibit climbing depending on their position. He also climbed and scrambled on Clogwyn yr Oen (only later discovering that one of 'his' lines was *Kirkus's Climb*), and several of the post-war routes included at least sections that he must have covered twenty years earlier.

Two remaining ascents of the 30s are of note. Typical of their generation and, though unfortunately unfashionable now, still worth seeking out for their unique flavour, both are on real mountain-summit ridges. In 1935 Showell Styles reached the top of Rhinog Fach by *The South Ridge*, and in 1939 Wilfred Noyce climbed *Lone Buttress* (alone) on Moel Siabod.

Charles Evans, like Noyce, was a member of the 1953 British Everest team and two years later led another British team to success on Kanchenjunga; but as a young medical student in 1941 he somehow found himself on the Aran and climbed three routes, the most significant being *Devious*, on the crag that became known as Gist Ddu. Apart from *Steric Slab* on Cyfrwy in the summer of 1942, these were the only recorded climbs in Meirionnydd of the war years, indeed of the whole 40s decade.

Post-War Revival

The end of petrol rationing in the early 50s, and thus the increased accessibility of climbing to more people, saw major developments in many British climbing areas. At the same time, equipment designed for the commando war-time effort resulted in the introduction of nylon ropes, Vibram soles, and slings and karabiners. Much energy was focused on the Peak and Snowdonia, and large tracts of Meirionnydd remained untouched for several more decades. However, activity soon spilled south to the Moelwynion. Tony Moulam had for a year or so been touring the peripheral crags of Snowdonia that offered better prospects when foul weather ruled out the higher cliffs, and finally alighted at Clogwyn yr Oen in December 1952 to climb *Chic*, an acronym that set a precedent for the series of monosyllabic route-names that followed: 1953 Moelwyn routes alone outnumbered the total existing Meirionnydd tally to that date. Moulam remained foremost (and also discovered Carreg Alltrem in the Lledr), but climbers who were later to achieve fame in various spheres, such as Chris Bonington, Chris Brasher (the two teaming up for *Double Criss*), and Ian McNaught-Davies were involved; and G Williams, D H Jones, and others struck blows for the home team and the Welsh language.

Development in the Moelwynion and Lledr continued steadily, if unspectacularly, over the next fifteen years until Moulam finally gathered the strands together in the long-awaited *Snowdon East* guide of 1970. That book also included some small crags in the Conwy Valley, most significantly Clogwyn Cyrau. The first main phase of routes here, in the 50s, was the work of activists from the North Wales Mountaineering Club and the RAF Valley Mountain Rescue Team, amongst whom Johnny Lees was prominent. A second phase was spearheaded by a Llanrwst climber, John Kerry, who raised the standard to the HVS/Mild Extreme level. Soon a number of local climbers were contributing, including Joe Arthy, Harold Drasdo, and Moulam himself.

The Mountain Club

At the opposite end of the region, things were slower to get under way, though once they did the acceleration was greater. After reading old Rucksack Club journals in the local library, Norman Horsfield travelled in 1950 to Craig Cywarch with Peter Harding and, although disappointed at the amount of vegetation, they attempted lines on Maen Hir, a pinnacle they named the Shark's Fin, and cleared a way to the top with *Kurzweg*.

A couple of years later, the study of a W A Poucher photograph of Cywarch attracted members of the Stafford-based Mountain Club to the crag and this resulted in routes by R E 'Larry' Lambe, Eric Byne, and Ernie Marshall, most notably *Oread* and *Central Route*. A lack of accommodation in the vicinity encouraged the club to acquire a farmhouse, Tyn-y-twll, at the head of the valley, in 1954. Since routes often required several visits to clean and complete, this acquisition aided a minor explosion of activity by many members of the club. John Sumner, Barry Knox, and Dave Adcock began extensive exploration, the big breakthrough being the creation of routes on the impressive Sawdl y Graig (then known as North-East Buttress) including *Stygian Wall* and *Styx*. The ubiquitous Moulam was soon on the scene, too, leading Lambe up *Acheron*, the hardest route on the crag to that date. Artificial climbing was much in vogue at the time, and the big overhanging crack on Tap y Gigfran was an obvious candidate; thus *Purge* (A2/3) was climbed in stages and various combinations by Sumner, Don Chisholm, Knox, and Adcock. (It was a nice touch that Sumner himself made the first free ascent over twenty years later!)

At the end of 1957 the lease on the farmhouse was terminated and, though activity had subsided somewhat, with now a total of 50 routes in the valley it was time for a guidebook, which was written by Lambe and published in 1958 by The Mountain Club. In 1960 the club started construction of their own hut on the site of a previous mine building at the head of the valley. Indeed, some members, many of whom were engineers, spent more of their time building than climbing. The official opening was an excellent party, to which all the local farmers were invited, a gesture establishing a relation-ship, sustained largely by Sumner's patient work over several decades, that has permitted more or less unfettered climbers' access to the crags in an area notorious for its general access problems. Bryn Hafod, as it was named, contained a special hardback book for recording new routes, which provided an excellent record, especially as the hut was available for bookings by other clubs and groups. Lambe remained a driving force throughout this time and wrote a new guide in 1964, reprinted with minor additions two years later.

Interlopers

At last, other climbers took an interest. One such visitor to Sawdl y Graig was Bonington, who climbed an already cleaned line to create *Hades*, not knowing that Knox and Adcock had prepared it for their next session. He was soon followed (inevitably?) by Joe Brown, who with various partners climbed five routes, including the classic *Sloose*, on Gist Ddu (an interesting choice of crag – homage to his leader on Kanchenjunga, perhaps?). However, he did not tackle the superb arête, *Aardvark*, which fell later to Martin Boysen.

The minor route explosion on Cywarch was not matched on Cadair Idris, though here visitors had included Ray Handley and Bowden Black who put up two classics, *Obsession* on Cyfrwy and *Triad* on Twr Ddu, and Nat Allen and Derek Burgess, who created several climbs including *Route 2* on Cyfrwy. It appears that Allen and Handley (and Boysen, too) also explored crags on Arennig Fawr but chose not to record the results.

No doubt this activity was made possible by the increased opportunity to go away for weekends as the need to work on Saturdays decreased. More climbers had their own motorbikes and beat-up bangers, and the 60s saw the growth in the number of higher education students who had the time and the opportunity to join clubs that provided transport. Mo Anthoine was to pioneer development of Craig Bodlyn, the largest crag in the Rhinogau, ascending several routes including the steep *Strictus* and, with Boysen, the intimidating *Tenuous*. He also added a route on Craig y Cae, a vegetated crag on the eastern fringe of the range towering above the valley just north of Dolgellau, which had had just two climbs previously.

Around the same time, climbers from the University College of North Wales and the Rimmon Mountaineering Club visited Craig yr Aderyn (Bird Rock), reputed to be Britain's furthest inland point for nesting seabirds. Some of their fine ascents included *The Beak*, *The Gizzard*, and the bold line of *Daisy Belle*.

Sumner Makes His Mark

Members of The Mountain Club continued to dominate the climbing in the Aran for the next decade. Major achievements, many involving Sumner, included *The Gem* and *The Grafter* on Tap y Gigfran, *Keel Haul* on Ffenestr y Graig, and *Scimitar*, *Obvious* and *Moai Man* on Gist Ddu. The classic *Will-o'-the-Wisp* on Tap y Graig is also a product of this time, cleaned and climbed by Sumner and his climbing partner, soon to be wife, Jill. Sumner's prodigious activity combined with his meticulous recording of the detail of all development made him the obvious candidate to write a new guide, which was published by West Col in 1973, and illustrated by Robin Thorndyke, who had also become active on the new-route scene. Two years later the same team filled an even more pressing void with the first ever guide to Cadair Idris. Here, in addition to Sumner, two other names had kept cropping up: Dave Shaw and Keith Bentham. Their finest route was *Darker Angel* on the West Wall of Pencoed Pillar, but there were many other classics, such as *Crack of Cau*. On Aderyn, too, they climbed the bold and striking line of *The Diamond*, which had repulsed an attempt by Bonington many years earlier.

The late 70s and early 80s saw a new generation of climbers push standards on Craig Cywarch, though old hands were there too. The big north-end cliffs produced *Strobe* and *Hard Rain* for George Herus and Sumner, and *Heretic* for John Codling. On Tap Mawr, the young Gary Gibson found *Bear Cage* and his brother Phil climbed *Crozzley Wall* with Sumner. Sumner continued to have a hand in many ascents on Tap y Gigfran such as *Rolair, Heist,* and *Beggars' Banquet,* while Herus and Bob Bradley climbed *Tumblin' Dice.* Codling was also responsible for two of the earliest E5s in the area – *Messiah* and *Rabble Rouser* on Cadair Idris. The year 1984 saw the addition of two of Gist Ddu's finest climbs: *Voie Suisse* by Sumner and the E5 *Hungry Hearts* by Andy Grondowski

By now Sumner's sights were adjusted from focus on the mere discovery of new lines to the opening up of whole new crags. Craig Rhwyddfor and Craig y Llam on the south side of Cadair came first, and then Craig y Mwn in the Berwynion. Nearby Craig Rhiwarth had gained a handful of routes in the 60s, but it, too, was now subjected to a thorough update. Another guide was planned, but West Col backed out and The Climbers' Club ventured onto this territory for the first time to publish *Mid-Wales* in 1988, Sumner pulling together the strands of his two earlier guides and all the new development.

Moelwyn Renaissance

A small flurry of activity in the Moelwynion after the publication of *Tremadog and the Moelwyns* guide in 1978 had been inspired largely by the arrival on the scene of Mel Griffiths, who has remained at the cutting edge of development here (and, of course, elsewhere in North Wales) for a quarter of a century. His 1978 tally, much of it made in the company of Martin Crook, tended to hover around the E1 mark, but by 1980 the standard rose several grades with *The Emerald* on Craig y Clipiau. The comfortable complacency that being local encouraged had led to an assumption that there was no rush to climb the remaining major lines: this was somewhat rudely shattered when, in the same year, Ron Fawcett with Paul Williams stole the spectacular *Crimson Cruiser* and *Non Dairy Creamer,* also on Clipiau. Next year, Griffiths was joined by a very young Elfyn Jones, and honour was salvaged with the *Non Creaming Dairy Start* to the latter route, converting it into one of the finest climbs in the Moelwynion. The partnership produced a number of routes climbed in fine style that year, though perhaps most notable of its period was Griffiths's audacious solo of *Louis Wilder.*

Some small new crags were opened up in the Lledr as well, most importantly Clogwyn yr Adar and Pont-y-pant, and blitzed by Llanberis-based climbers George Smith, Ed Stone, Steve Howe, and later, to produce some very technical test-pieces, Nick Dixon. A new Tremadog guide was needed, too, and duly appeared a year after *Mid-Wales,* again including the Moelwynion and Lledr, though the Conwy crags were, not for the first time, scarcely accorded the treatment they deserved.

Pivotal

The publication of new guidebooks may reveal a variety of possibilities for those who have an eye to see. In more 'established' climbing areas this can result in mere gap-filling. Other lines become possible by developments in equipment or, as had become the case by the late 80s, improved fitness and training. The 1988 guide provided tantalizing hints of what was to come, with its inclusion of the new crags, slate quarries at Barmouth and Dinas Mawddwy, and diagrams and photographs of the two Rhinog crags (Bodlyn and Craig y Cae). The exploration of these areas and the hitherto unknown Arennig Fawr, along with further development of existing areas, can be attributed largely to the tenacity and vision of a few, mainly the irrepressible Sumner, newcomers Martin Crocker and Terry Taylor, as well as local activists such as Griffiths and Mike Lewis.

A Force in the Wilderness

Martin Crocker, that whirlwind of new-route activity, was attracted to the area by the publication of the guide. Since then few crags in the area have escaped his influence as the draw of the wild, open, uncrowded spaces increasingly inspired him. This resulted in the pushing of standards and the creation of numerous climbs of both great difficulty and outstanding quality. A glance at the First Ascents List for the 90s might lead one to assume that Crocker went nowhere else. This is far from the truth, as for most of the decade he spent at least as much time climbing on the equally tranquil and under-explored yet dramatically-situated cliffs of the south-west coasts of England and Wales. Nor should one assume that he was interested only in first ascents – the time he spent making early repeats and exploring meant that he almost always became immersed in the physical and spiritual aura of a crag's environment.

His exploration began in April 1990 with three big climbs on Craig y Mwn in the Berwynion, and continued a month later with *Basil Brush Stroke* on Cywarch, the area's first E6. Two more weekends followed over the next few weeks and ten major climbs resulted. On most of these Crocker was helped by his wife Beverley, but in August he made the acquaintance of guru Sumner, who partnered him on two more powerful routes, *Blood of an Englishman* and *The Doghouse*, the latter based on the line of an aid route Sumner himself had put up many years earlier. The pair climbed another three routes together here the next year, and in 1994, only a year after suffering a horrendous climbing accident in Cornwall, Crocker brought along his trusty partner, John Harwood, for more. A week's family holiday in Bryn Hafod, climaxed in the most prodigious day in Cywarch's history: six big routes scattered on several crags were climbed, the highlight being *Quartizone* on Ffenestr y Graig, which with two sustained E6 6b pitches set a new standard for bold and irreversible climbing on this crag. Yet, in difficulty stakes, this was soon superseded on the huge overhanging prow of Tap y Gigfran, which succumbed to the all-out stamina test of *Sci-Fi*, at a pumping E7.

Crocker and Harwood had also climbed on Cadair's showpiece, Craig Cau, in 1992 and their brilliant *Brass Butterfly*, in particular, illuminated the potential quality of routes that would follow later. In 1996 he spent one weekend after another here, mostly with an equally enthused Don Sargeant, and transformed the cliff into one of the very great high mountain crags of Britain. You may well be convinced you will never venture onto an E7 (of this kind anyway); nevertheless, turn to page 394 and read Crocker's description of *Time Is the Fire in Which We Burn*.

Taylor Moves In

The other dominant figure of the decade was Terry Taylor, a GP who had settled in Tywyn with his family and so had plenty of opportunity to explore the open spaces and virgin rock for which he had an insatiable appetite. One of his early gems was *Turquoise Lady* on Cyfrwy, and a string of new routes appeared on Aderyn. Most importantly, Taylor was to be made aware of the potential of Arennig Fawr following Jayson Cooper's rediscovery while out walking in 1990. This led to routes such as *Gyllion* and *Madryn* on the South Buttress of Simdde Ddu and, with Jones, Taylor opened up the little dome of Craig Bryn y Dyfrgi with *Mohican* and *War Cry*. Unaware of this, John Appleby with various companions also explored Daear Fawr, producing *Rapscallion* and *Scorpion*. Both parties found evidence, such as peg stubs, of earlier activity, yet explored without any contact with each other. In 1993 Taylor managed the Arennig's hardest route to that date, *Shamanic Voices* on Dyfrgi.

Strangely, neither Taylor nor Appleby returned in 1994, but in stepped Drasdo, for whom the mountain had held a long but unfulfilled fascination. More important than the four routes that he then climbed was his subsequent tracking down of the recent protagonists (and unearthing some of the vague prehistory) and sorting out just what had been done (all the subject of an entertaining article later published in *High Magazine*), thus paving the way for the maelstrom that ensued. Next year Taylor was back and introduced Norman Clacher, who raised the standard a grade further with *The Jump over the Shadow*. They were there again throughout 1996 with a newcomer Richard Hudson, and so were Drasdo and Appleby. The number of routes on the mountain doubled, and the former team worked out Daear Fawr, while the latter discovered the amazing tumbled blocks and arêtes of Pen Tyrau and the lovely clean rock of Craig yr Hyrddod. By September 1997 there were a hundred routes ranging up to E5, almost all climbed by Taylor, Appleby, Clacher, or Drasdo.

Meanwhile, if Sumner had had any thoughts about resting on his laurels, the amount of paper from Crocker, Taylor, Drasdo, and others swamping his house must have persuaded him otherwise. He discovered the Craig y Merched complex above a remote valley in the south-east Rhinog, and opened up two new crags on Cadair (Gwern Graig Rock and Gau Craig), and two more at Craig Rhiwarth in the Berwynion. At each he was hotly pursued by Crocker, or Taylor, or both!

Meirionnydd boasts various types of rock including slate, a medium that received little attention until the burst of activity in Llanberis in the 80s. Taylor, armed with a local geological map, researched the Corris vein and sorted out the possibilities. Friog Quarry had the benefit of being close to the road and boasted the Blue Lagoon (a flooded opencast pit) as well as a variety of climbs, most of which Taylor equipped with staple bolts. Two special gems were *Zone of Totality* on the superb slab at Minllyn Quarry, providing technical F7a climbing, and *Choose Life* at Abergynolwyn.

The 90s in the North
Less spectacular results in the Moelwynion followed the 89 *Tremadog* guide, but Griffiths continued to find hard and worthwhile lines, often partnered now by the ubiquitous Taylor. Their most important contribution was the development of Chwarel Manod, with the E5 *Steel against the Sky* and the E7 *Tears in Rain* being outstanding. At Carreg y Frân, Griffiths and Jones continued to push standards, inspiring the best in each other: after Jones led *Wee Laddie* at E6 Griffiths followed with *Big Boy!* at E7. Following a party at the end of an International Women's Meet, an impressive team gingerly ventured onto the crag and, despite some decking-out, dropping of equipment, and painful heads on a hot day, Andy Cave climbed the photogenic *Sack Thrower's Association*. Nearby, Dixon added *Parsimony*. He also completed unfinished business at Pont-y-pant in Cwm Lledr with some short, very technical lines on perfect rock, and, along with Llanberis-scene stars such as Smith, Paul Pritchard, and Crispin Waddy, developed a novel type of bouldering in the Afon Conwy – The Tubes.

Meanwhile, a completely new crag to the west of the main area had been discovered by Lewis in 1990 and two classics were rapidly established, *Igam Ogam* and *Maen Tŵr Og*. Lewis continued to work away quietly over the years without anyone taking any interest until he let Crocker in on the secret. A single weekend in May 1998 with Sargeant was enough for him to take the dozen pickings that still challenged. A couple more crags at the head of Cwm Lledr were found, too, and developed by Appleby, Drasdo, and others who, together with Dave Wrennall, also kept things ticking over at the traditional Conwy crags. Further north, Cae Coch Quarry yielded two tremendous bolted slab routes to Smith and Dixon.

The Dénouement
The only crag in the heart of the Rhinogau described in the 1988 guide was Craig Bodlyn, but in fact Lewis had climbed several routes on Carreg y Saeth in Cwm Bychan in the mid 80s. Around the time of his foray onto Arennig Fawr in 1990, Cooper made a similar one into the Rhinog and climbed a couple of routes, but here no publicity followed. Lewis found Craig y Groes in 1992 and added routes on Saeth in 1994. It was not for another two years that Crocker arrived to discover 'a whole new Peak District of gritstone outcrops'. Throughout the summer of 1997 he spent much time climbing on the crags that he and Sargeant had found during a walkabout reconnaissance the previous year. Initially he had the support of Sargeant, but increasingly he found himself climbing alone, often ropeless, or using his new Soloist self-belayer. He would occasionally see passing walkers, but no other climbers crossed his path until a chance encounter with Lewis occurred at Saeth. In November he wrote up a full

account of all he had done in preparation for publication in the next guidebook, whenever it should come.

In September of that year two events of note occurred: Taylor ventured into the Rhinog and Crocker set foot on Arennig Fawr, but whereas the former got caught in a severe storm, became ill, and did not return for two years, Crocker set about Arennig Fawr in his customary manner. The first weekend, with Sargeant, produced some good climbs on Simdde Ddu; the second, with Harwood, was devoted to Dyfrgi, and especially to the solving of its stunning *Brubeck's Cube*. Taylor and Clacher also added a further sixteen routes in the month. The main protagonists were all there next year, and activity continued in a similar vein, with Crocker and Taylor recording excellent routes such as *Cosy Powell*, *Drive Like You Drum*, and *Charlie Spitkid* on Y Castell. Crocker, frequently climbing alone, created many more, including the nerve-wrenching *Black Power Salute* on Simdde Ddu. This was followed in 1999 by the heinously fingery *All Fingers and Thumbs* on Y Castell, which brought E7 to the Arennig. By now the mountain was largely worked out and new finds soon dwindled to a trickle.

The same was not true of the Rhinogau, and after a break in 1998, Crocker was back in full swing in 1999. Taylor's second foray was more successful and soon, mainly with Clacher, Gary Morgan, and Mark Hedge, he was matching Crocker's high energy. The bonanza continued right through 2000 and, apart from the enforced break during the foot-and-mouth disease closure, 2001; and Taylor continued to find numerous small new crags, both in the heart of the range and on its periphery. But the fulfilment of this intense four-year period of development in the Rhinogau undoubtedly came with Crocker's partnership with Harwood (somewhat in contrast to his earlier 'isolationist' activities) back on the range's largest and original crag, Bodlyn, now specifically upon its Silver Screen, where they established a series of high-standard and brilliant-quality climbs.

Despite Crocker's note in this section that 'there is still scope for an E9 or two' on this wall, and despite the publication of this guidebook, Merionnydd may remain largely outside the mainstream of fashionable climbing. It will, nevertheless, certainly continue to provide opportunities for local groups and individuals who relish the open wilderness experience and the chance to be alone on the rock rather than queuing with others in crowded spaces that are more akin to climbing-walls. It embodies the spirit of an earlier century and provides another dimension to the varied experience that is climbing.

Stygian Wall (VS ~ first ascent) Craig Cywarch
Climber: John Sumner   Photo: Dave Adcock

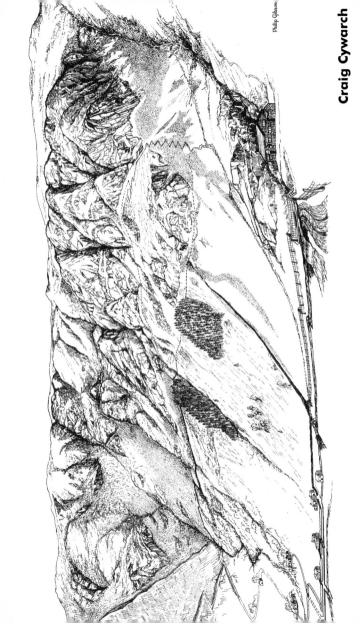

Craig Cywarch

Philip Gibson

Craig Cywarch
Crag Nomenclature

The pioneers of this crag gave names to the buttresses and gullies mainly to accord with their character, features, and locations.

However, for the 1988 guidebook the author had available a collection of the true Welsh names. The two were then used side by side but, as the Welsh ones have now become established and accepted, the older ones have been dropped. A further complication has arisen as the literal translations of the Welsh names often conflict with these.

To avoid any possible confusion, it has been decided not to place the traditional names in brackets after the headings as was done in the 1988 guide, or the translations as has become the norm in CC Welsh guidebooks and as has been done elsewhere in this guide. Instead, the comparative table here will provide at a glance any such information required.

Traditional name	Current name	English translation
Craig Cowarch	Craig Cywarch	
	Pant Lygog	Lygog Hollow
	Tapiau Geifr	Masses (of the) Goats
	Tap Pant Cae	Mass (of) the Hollow Field
	Cwm yr Ychen	Valley (of) the Bullocks
The Fortress	Maen Hir	Long Rock
Craig Tyn y Fedw	Craig Maen Hir	Long Rock Crag
Cwm Rychain	Craig y Gornel	Corner Crag
Shark's Fin	Tap Rhygan Ddu	Mass (of the) Black Hood
	Tap y Gigfran	Mass (of) the Raven
	Tap Mawr	Big Mass
Far South Buttress	Tap Mawr Pella	Far Big Mass
Sheep Run Buttress	Tap y Graig	Mass (of) the Crag
South Buttress	Tap Dwyren	Eastern Mass
Upper South Buttress	Esgair Felen	Yellow Spur
Central Buttress	Hafn Mawr	Big Gully
North Gully	Tap Isa Hafn Mawr	Lower Big Gully Mass
Lower North Gully Buttress	Tap Ucha Hafn Mawr	Upper Big Gully Mass
Upper North Gully Buttress	Sawdl y Graig	Heel (of) the Crag
North East Buttress	Craig Llywelyn	Llywelyn's Crag
North Buttress	Dinas Llywelyn	Llywelyn's Fort
	Ffenestr y Graig	Window Crag
North Face	Creigiau Sawdl Efa	Crags (of) Efan's Heel
Far North Buttress	Creigiau Camdwr	Crags (of) the False Water

Tap means mass or lump; buttress might be nearest to what is intended

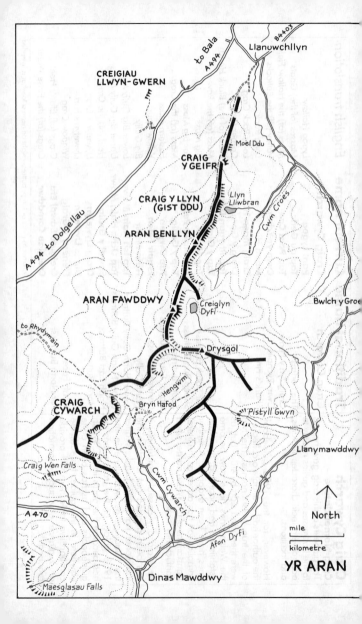

CREIGIAU
LLWYN-GWERN

to Bala
A494

Llanuwchllyn

B4403

A494 to Dolgellau

Moel Ddu

CRAIG
Y GEIFR

CRAIG Y LLYN
(GIST DDU)

Llyn
Lliwbran

Cwm Croes

ARAN BENLLYN

ARAN FAWDDWY

Creiglyn
Dyfi

Bwlch y Groes

to Rhydymain

Drysgol

Hengwm

CRAIG
CYWARCH

Bryn Hafod

Pistyll Gwyn

Llanymawddwy

Craig Wen Falls

Cwm Cywarch

North

mile

A470

Afon Dyfi

kilometre

Maesglasau Falls

Dinas Mawddwy

YR ARAN

Yr Aran The Heights

To mix statistics, Aran Fawddwy, at 907 metres, is only ten metres short of being classed with the fourteen 'three-thousanders' of the Snowdon, Glyder, and Carnedd ranges and is thus the highest point in Wales south of them. It stands in the centre of the fifteen-kilometre ridge extending from Dinas Mawddwy northwards to the shores of Bala Lake. The western slopes are gentle and grassy but, seen from the north-east, almost the entire ridge appears to be buttressed with crags and seamed with gullies on its eastern side. Unfortunately, for most of the way the rocks are broken and scrappy, and only a few places yield worthwhile climbing. However, the magnificent and majestic Craig Cywarch at the southern foot, some isolated walls on the eastern faces of the two main peaks, and two smaller crags at the northern end present a wonderful, tranquil, yet spectacular environment in which to climb.

Although the range lies within the Snowdonia National Park, practically all the land, right up to and including the summit ridge, is privately owned and is managed by The Aran Society. Over the years, a permitted path along the summit ridge has been conceded, and patient negotiation has resulted in access agreements for at least Craig Cywarch, Gist Ddu, and Craig y Geifr; these are described in detail under their respective headings. The routes near the summits of Fawddwy and Benllyn have no formal access, though it may be possible with discretion to descend to them from the summit ridge; on no account try to reach them from below.

The main ridge is gained from the south either by the right-of-way shown on the map from near the start of the approach path to Craig Cywarch, or by following the Rydymain path up past the crags (see maps opposite and overleaf). The south-west and south-east ridges meet at Aran Fawddwy summit, and the ridge path then runs north to descend, joining a bridleway, to Llanuwchllyn.

It is essential that not only the formal agreements but also the highest standards of general conduct continue to be observed, in the interests of both conserving the hill and crag environment and maintaining a spirit of good will between climber and landowner. In particular, please adhere to the code printed in the main Introduction on page 20.

Craig Cywarch   OS Ref 845 190

Lying on the eastern slopes of Glasgwm, the highest point on the southern end of the main ridge, and standing sentinel over Cwm Cywarch, this fascinating cliff complex has the largest concentration of rock-climbs in

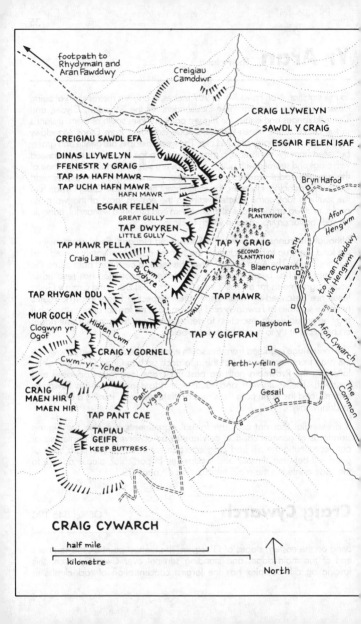

footpath to
Rhydymain and
Aran Fawddwy

Creigiau
Camddwr

CRAIG LLYWELYN

SAWDL Y CRAIG

ESGAIR FELEN ISAF

CREIGIAU SAWDL EFA

DINAS LLYWELYN

FFENESTR Y GRAIG

TAP ISA HAFN MAWR

TAP UCHA HAFN MAWR

HAFN MAWR

ESGAIR FELEN

GREAT GULLY

TAP DWYREN

LITTLE GULLY

TAP MAWR PELLA

Craig Lam

TAP RHYGAN DDU

MUR GOCH

Clogwyn yr
Ogof

Cwm-yr-Ychen

CRAIG Y GORNEL

Hidden Cwm

CRAIG
MAEN HIR

MAEN HIR

TAP PANT CAE

TAPIAU
GEIFR

KEEP BUTTRESS

Cwm
Bydyre

TAP Y GRAIG

FIRST
PLANTATION

SECOND
PLANTATION

Blaencywarch

WALL

TAP MAWR

TAP Y GIGFRAN

Pant
Llyog

Bryn Hafod

Afon
Hengwm

PATH

to Aran Fawddwy
via Hengwm

Plasybont

Perth-y-felin

Gesail

Afon Cywarch

The
Common

CRAIG CYWARCH

half mile

kilometre

North

Meirionnydd. The Cywarch crags extend for more than two and a half kilometres and sport a variety of buttresses, walls, and ridges – some of which are well hidden up in cwms and deep gullies. The longest routes, some well over 120 metres, are found at the northern end of the cliffs where such magnificent brooding classics as *Acheron* and *Doom* are located. The crags face mainly south-east and north-east.

The igneous rock is in places sound and compact, but in others rather unstable. Vegetation is more prolific than on crags in, say, Llanberis, but this may reflect the level of climbing traffic. Protection is on the whole good for routes graded up to E2; in particular, carry a plentiful selection of small nuts.

Approach
From Dinas Mawddwy on the A470 Dolgellau to Machynlleth road, take the minor road to Aber-Cywarch and follow the sign-posted road up the Cywarch valley. Approach the crags (on foot) by taking the track marked to Rhydymain which bypasses the last farm in the valley at Blaencywarch. Follow this track for another 500 metres to where a sheep track leads up to the small crag of Esgair Felen Isaf. Tracks then lead to the various parts of the crag (see map opposite).

Pant Lygog
The hanging valley of Pant Lygog has many broken buttresses, the best of which is Tapiau Geifr. To the left of these, at the south-west end of the crags where the rock deteriorates, there are some overlapping slabs. **S & D** (76 metres Very Difficult 31.5.58) takes the largest of the slabs.

Keep Buttress
The small steep and vegetated buttress starting from the scree to the left of the gully which contains the overlapping slabs of Tapiau Geifr. **Portcullis** (43 metres Severe 4.11.56) is a vegetated line up cracks in the buttress.

The Black Tower
A rather menacing name for what is merely a 12-metre-high leaning buttress at the very top of the Keep. Approach, visibly, by scrambling direct from the base of the cwm or, invisibly, from your best guess at the crest of the ridge. (A lot of leg power for the choice of two micro-nasties.)

The Cywarch Finger Flake   12 metres   E5 6a †   (18.6.94)
The unmistakable hanging flake in the left arête. Start from a good thread belay at the underlying break. Climb the flake, with interest, to the top.

Kangaroo Moon   12 metres   E6 6b †   (18.6.94)
Fingery and sequential climbing on the leaning wall right of the hanging flake. Start as for *The Cywarch Finger Flake*. From the break, mantel onto the sloping ledge on the right. Follow a thin crack in the wall (peg runner and tiny spike), bear left to a large sloping handhold, and finish quite out of breath.

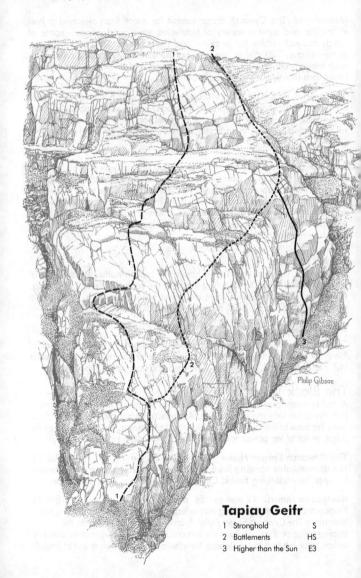

Philip Gibson

Tapiau Geifr

1	Stronghold	S
2	Battlements	HS
3	Higher than the Sun	E3

Tapiau Geifr[1]

The striking V-shaped buttress in the first gully encountered on entry to the hanging valley.

Stronghold   99 metres   Severe   (11.4.70)

A delicate slab with a well-maintained standard throughout. Start at the lowest point of the buttress.

1 27m. Climb an easy slab until it steepens; then trend rightwards to a bracket on the arête. Climb the arête for a short way to a ledge on the left, go back right to the arête, and follow a crack just left of it to a long narrow ledge under a short steep wall. Go left along the ledge to a heather ledge.

2 12m. Return right a metre or so to a weakness in the short steep wall. Climb it and a slab above to a large heather ledge.

3 27m. 4a. From the left-hand end of the heather ledge, climb a subsidiary slab and make a delicate exit onto the main slab above; then climb the main slab direct to another heather ledge on the left.

4 12m. Return right and continue up the slab to a ledge; then traverse right and go up easily to a large grassy ledge.

5 21m. An obvious chimney and a crack in the slab above provide the finish.

Battlements   106 metres   Hard Severe   (19.4.70)

Quite a good slab route, but with greater exposure than *Stronghold*.

1 40m. Follow *Stronghold* to the long narrow ledge under a short steep wall. Return right along the ledge to the arête, and climb the groove to steep heather and a tree; continue to a large heather ledge. Good spike belay on a steep wall.

2 30m. 4a. Crux. Climb a steep broken groove just right of the spike belay to the slab above, and make an airy traverse right for 6 metres to another groove. Climb this to a heather ledge and continue to another heather ledge and a tree.

3 15m. Take a little wall directly behind the tree, climb another slab, and exit right to a large grassy ledge.

4 21m. Finish up the right edge of the slab above.

Higher than the Sun   27 metres   E3 6a †   (18.6.94)

A worthwhile direct line through the overlapping slabs in the upper right-hand end of the crag. Start towards the top of the gully, below prominent twin leftward-leaning cracks in the headwall. Step left and pass a short but tricky arête to reach a rising break. Take the wall above, just left of a wide crack, and move up a slab to the twin cracks. Climb the left-hand crack to a grassy platform.

Tap Pant Cae

Wet in places, and rather vegetated except for an area near a greenish wall on the East Face and an obvious smooth wall on the North Face.

1 Named *Tapiau Gwlybion* in the 1988 guide.

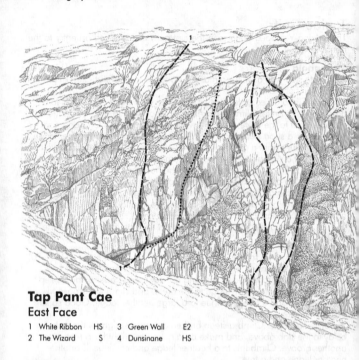

Tap Pant Cae
East Face

1	White Ribbon	HS	3	Green Wall	E2
2	The Wizard	S	4	Dunsinane	HS

East Face

★White Ribbon   42 metres   Hard Severe   (5.8.63)
A good route, varied and exposed. Just left of the green wall a grass
terrace runs out onto the face. Below its right-hand end is a small block
and cairn above a hawthorn tree. Start on the block.
1 21m. 4a. Make a short rising traverse right before moving up left into
a groove. Climb the groove for a short way; then traverse left into the base
of a narrow chimney and climb it on reasonable holds. The top of the
chimney is choked with vegetation, so a bulge on the left is taken to reach
a ledge.
2 21m. A reasonably clean slab is climbed fairly directly on small incut
holds to the top.

The Wizard   36 metres   Severe   (31.8.68)
A good line, though often wet. Start as for *White Ribbon*.
1 12m. From the block, traverse right to a slab, and move rightwards
across the slab to a tree.

2 9m. Move up just to the right of the tree and climb a ramp to another tree and grassy ledges.
3 15m. Climb a short chimney; then go slightly leftwards up to a large spike. Climb over the spike and finish up the wall above.

Green Wall   37 metres   E2 5c   (18.4.81)
A direct way up the obvious green wall, the outstanding feature of the crag; its lower half has become a vertical rock garden. Climb with increasing difficulty via cracks directly up the steep wall. Gain a ledge on the left beneath a steep little corner and move left to enter a scoop; then go straight up from the scoop, using a good pocket hold to reach easier ground.

Dunsinane (46 metres Hard Severe 4a 7.7.68) has a vegetated first pitch starting 9 metres right of *White Ribbon*. The second takes a hidden chimney on the right of the green wall.

The Sting   55 metres   Hard Very Severe (1 pt aid)   (16.4.74)
About 25 metres down and to the right of the conspicuous green wall is a steep wall that is rather vegetated in the upper section. Start directly beneath the steep wall, at the crack in its centre.
1 24m. 5a. Climb the crack to a little groove below a steepening. Use the peg above to reach good holds up on the left and gain a slab. Climb the corner to the slab above, move right, and continue to a grassy ledge with a block belay.
2 11m. 4a. Climb the wall on the left of the block to a bulge, which is overcome by spike holds on the right, and so reach a heathery ledge.
3 20m. 4c. Climb the wall between two towers to the overhang, and take the wide crack in the centre. Above the overhang, move right to an arête, and go up to easier ground.

Gryptych (52 metres Hard Severe 4b, 4a 27.5.73) is a vegetated route right of *The Sting*. **Clubs** (32 metres Severe 27.11.55) is further right at the lowest point of the buttress, and starts to the left of a wall. A broken slab and an overhanging block on the right are taken to a ledge, after which the climb deteriorates.

North Face
Above and right of the lowest point of the buttress is a smooth, steep wall with an obvious corner-crack on its right overhung by a large capstone. *Room at the Top* takes this corner. To the left of the steep wall are two diagonal cracks, the left-hand of which is *Paper Back*.

Paper Back   27 metres   Hard Very Severe 5b   (24.5.69)
Climb the clean, fine-looking, diagonal crack with increasing difficulty to a pinnacle on the right. Step off the pinnacle top and climb a short wall to a ledge; continue up the short steep wall above.

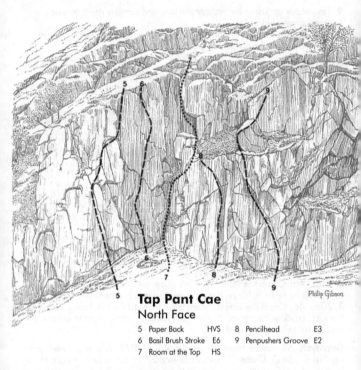

Tap Pant Cae
North Face

5   Paper Back   HVS
6   Basil Brush Stroke E6
7   Room at the Top   HS
8   Pencilhead   E3
9   Penpushers Groove   E2

Philip Gibson

☆**Basil Brush Stroke**   21 metres   E6 6a †   (5.5.90)
A deadly serious pitch which takes a central line, the cleaned strip, up the
smooth wall between *Paper Back* and *Room at the Top*. Excellent rock,
beneath a regrowth of lichen, doubtless. Follow a central line of weakness
trending slightly leftwards to a good spike at 11 metres (first runner; 5c up
to this point). Bear rightwards on better holds (peg runner) and then make
committing moves in the same line (peg runner) until it is possible to climb
directly to the top.

Room at the Top   27 metres   Hard Severe   (24.5.69)
Climbers of small frame will find it easy for its grade. Start at the
corner-crack.
1 18m. Climb the wide crack on good holds to a ledge beneath the
capstone.
2 9m. Climb the wide crack above by the through route.

Pencilhead   15 metres   E3 5c †   (18.6.94)
The fine wall between *Room at the Top* and *Penpushers Groove*; high in the
grade. From a pedestal, climb the centre of the wall (peg runner) to
pockets (crucial *Rock 4*). Bear slightly leftwards to a diagonal crack and
horizontal slot above. Climb the finger-crack above to a jug just above the
heather; then traverse left to a straightforward exit onto the arête.

Penpushers Groove   27 metres   E2 5c †   (17.6.90)
The climb follows another diagonal crack, to the right of *Room at the Top*.
Start from the large block below the line. Step right from the top of the
block and climb a short rib to join the crack. Follow the crack leftwards on
jugs and then the continuation corner with more difficulty to a
straightforward exit onto heather. Walk right and finish up a short arête
above a block. Tree belay. Abseil off.

Cwm yr Ychen
Maen Hir
The short side of the pinnacle gives **Kurzweg** (6 metres Difficult 1950).

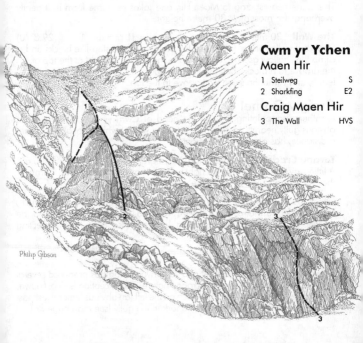

Cwm yr Ychen
Maen Hir

1 Steilweg   S
2 Sharkfing   E2

Craig Maen Hir

3 The Wall   HVS

Philip Gibson

Steilweg   18 metres   Severe   (13.6.53)
Start on the east side of the pinnacle, a short distance down the gully from
the neck. Climb diagonally right to a quartz bulge, and then gain a small
ledge above it. Move delicately right and pull onto a bilberry ledge on the
front of the pinnacle. Move round onto the other face and gain the sharp
edge above, which is followed to the top.

☆**Sharkfing**   21 metres   E2 5b †   (7.6.95)
The edge of the fin in its entirety. The crux section could be better protected
(*RP1* or nothing). Clamber into a niche immediately left of the arête, and
make bold moves to get established on the edge. Climb the edge, now
supplying a thin crack for wires, to ledges on *Steilweg*, which is followed to
the top.

Schnellweg   15 metres   Severe   (29.8.70)
Start by a traverse out below the neck on the western side of the pinnacle.
Traverse horizontally left on good handholds to reach a small ledge, move
up and left to the arête, and climb it to finish.

Craig Maen Hir
This is the nearest crag to Maen Hir, and takes its name from it. It gently
overhangs for most of its 30-metre height.

The Wall   30 metres   Hard Very Severe 5a (1 pt aid)   (29.8.70)
Steep but well protected. Traverse left on the obvious step-like blocks and
climb the shallow groove running up to the left. Move right at the top of
the groove to a block; then use the peg above for aid to traverse right to a
ledge, and climb the steep wall above to the top.

Craig y Gornel
A rather disappointing crag at the head of Cwm yr Ychen. There is an
obvious gully near its centre, the right-hand wall of which, not obvious from
a distance, has one worthwhile route.

Taranu Crack   27 metres   Hard Very Severe 5a   (4.6.69)
A little way up the gully on the right wall is an overhanging crack. Climb
the crack. The crux is in the centre where the crack constricts.

Other routes have been done on the lower section of the crag. One such,
Flashback (46 metres Hard Severe 4b 4a 31.7.76), takes a line up the
middle of the slabs, finishing by a long traverse right to a projecting
pedestal.

Hidden Cwm
A cwm between Craig y Gornel and Tap Rhygan Ddu has produced several
short routes, mostly of a rather scrappy nature. The exception is *Knockdown*,
which takes an arête line on Mur Goch on the left (an obvious feature) just past
the narrow entrance to the cwm at a fork in the gully (see map page 36).

Knockdown   60 metres   Very Difficult   (26.7.57)
Start 5 metres to the right of the lowest point of the crag.
1 27m. Move up on flakes and climb the slab above until it is possible to
step out right onto the nose of the arête. Climb this on good holds to a
small ledge and spike belay.
2 9m. Move right into a corner; then climb diagonally left across a slab to
join the arête again at a small ledge.
3 12m. Climb the arête to a small corner, move round to the left, and
climb the slab above to a heather terrace. Large belay block on the left.
4 12m. Surmount the belay block and climb up left to the top of the crag.

Tap Rhygan Ddu
This wildly steep crag offers some of the most sensational positions on Craig
Cywarch. Its most obvious feature is a horizontal break, which has a large
overhang above and an overhanging wall beneath it.

Shady Saunter   52 metres   Severe   (23.6.57)
A 'shady saunter' along the ramp under the lower overhanging wall. Some
bad rock. Start at the lowest point of the buttress, below and just left of a cave.
1 15m. Traverse easily left round an edge to gain the ramp below the
overhanging wall. Nut belays.
2 37m. Continue along the ramp to a bulge. Surmount this and the slab
above to a steep corner. Climb the corner on dubious rock to the sloping
ledge above. Nut belay well back.

Darkness on the Edge of Town   24 metres   E3 6a   (30.5.82)
Start at the sloping finishing-ledge of *Shady Saunter* and *The Girdle*, at the
left-hand side of the crag, below a rust-coloured wall. Climb the wall for 3
metres; then traverse left on side-pulls to a peg. Step left to a bottomless
V-groove and climb it with difficulty to good holds. Step left to a ledge, and
climb the wall above, passing hollow flakes, to the top. Belay on big hexes.

Shouts in Space   40 metres   E3 6a †   (25.5.98)
An airy and atmospheric pitch up the wall right of *Darkness on the Edge of
Town*. An appropriate introduction to the harder routes. Start as for
Darkness..., and pull up and right to the break beneath a bulge. Extend
through the bulge via a short diagonal crack and reach jugs above (*in-situ*
sling on small spike), and the large spike on the traverse of *Baptême de
l'Air*. Climb straight up to an overhanging flake crack above; then trend
right beneath ledges across a hanging slab to finish up a clean rib.
Scramble to belays.

★Chariots of Fire   37 metres   E2 5c   (10.6.84)
A worthwhile pitch taking the main break through the overhangs above
the traverse-line of the girdle. From the huge nest on the last pitch of the
girdle, where a small pillar bridges the overhangs, climb the steep
overhanging corner above the pillar (peg), and exit left to a ledge.
Continue up a flaky crack; then climb the wall above to the top.

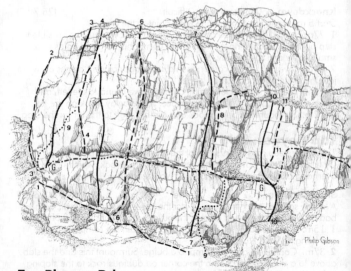

Philip Gibson

Tap Rhygan Ddu

1	Shady Saunter	S	5	Sulphur Mountain	E5	9	Baptéme de l'Air	E1
2	Darkness on the Edge of Town E3		6	The Devil Within	E6	10	The Stud	E5
3	Shouts in Space	E3	7	Tithing Man	E4	11	Tobias	E5
4	Chariots of Fire	E2	8	Barbarism	E5	12	Girdle Traverse	VS

☆☆**Sulphur Mountain**   46 metres   E5 †   (27.7.91)
A stunning climb sizzling above the gross exposure typical of this crag.
Start from good nut belays on a large ledge 18 metres along the *Shady
Saunter* traverse, and above the first steep awkward step.
1 9m. 6a/b. From the right-hand end of the ledge, attack the leaning
wall to gain good holds in an overhanging corner-scoop. Climb the scoop
(peg runner) and pull over the bulge to a good stance at the girdle break.
Thread belays.
2 37m. 6b. To the right of the stance an alarming roof protrudes; launch
out over it (peg runner with sling and *in-situ* wire) and continue on
reasonable holds up the wall to a thin break (good wires). Move up to a
flake (*in-situ* thread), step left, and climb thin cracks and then the easier
groove above to the top.

☆☆**The Devil Within**   46 metres   E6 6b †   (16.6.90)
A spectacular climb making a direct assault on the overhanging central
section of the crag. A bold pump-out up the leaning groove immediately
right of the one-third-height roofs makes the grade just warranted if the

route is climbed in one pitch (E5 in two pitches). Start from nut belays 15 metres along *Shady Saunter* and below a 2-metre step formed by a block. From the top of the step, launch rightwards via a flake onto the overhanging wall (peg runner) and proceed strenuously on surprising holds to a large spike and the ledge-system of the girdle. Pull straight over the right-hand end of the massive roof past a peg runner, and continue up the leaning groove on awkward sloping holds to a slot taking a crucial *Rock 9*. More strenuous climbing up the groove leads eventually to easier ground (peg runner), and a thin crack is followed to a step right into a grassy bay. Belay here; then scramble up easy rock on the left to the top.

☆Tithing Man 45 metres E4 † (17.6.90)
An intriguing second pitch that takes the sharp V-groove in the overhanging arête above the start of *Baptême de l'Air*. Start as for *Shady Saunter*.
1 15m. 5c. From the first block-ledge, pull straight up overhanging cracks and continue up a shallow groove (from which *Baptême de l'Air* traverses right) to reach good finishing-holds. Step right and move up to a tree belay below the grooved arête.
2 30m. 6a. Tackle the groove (peg runner), and bridge directly up it (*in-situ* thread on the left) to surmount the final bulge on good holds. From a heather ledge above, step left and climb a system of pleasant cracks through bulges to finish up a clean slab on the right. Continuously good climbing.

Barbarism 35 metres E5 † (25.5.98)
The seriously overhanging corner above the left-hand end of the forested terrace in the right-hand part of the crag (between *Tithing Man* and *The Stud*). The name tells all.
1 20m. 5c. *Tithing Man* pitch 1; then walk right to the corner.
2 15m. 6b. Struggle up the unforgiving corner to a ledge at its top. Move up and right, and then traverse right to good tree belays.

★Baptême de l'Air 107 metres E1 (16.6.84)
A rather wandering route, but with some good climbing. Start from a cave at the lowest point of the crag, beside *Shady Saunter*.
1 23m. 5b. Step left onto a nose of rock, move left again to a crack, and climb it to gain a ramp on the right. Traverse right along the ramp to a crack in a corner and climb this to join the girdle-line.
2 44m. 4b. Traverse left along the sensational last pitch of the girdle to its end at the sloping finishing ledge of *Shady Saunter*.
3 40m. 5a. Move right; then go up to a traverse-line above that of the girdle. Traverse right along this to a big spike on the edge, make an awkward move right, and then follow a rising traverse right on good holds to a ledge. Take the wall above and finish up the easiest line.

☆The Stud 30 metres E5 † (17.6.90)
Fine climbing throughout but with an especially rewarding top pitch that takes the left-hand of two leaning cracks in the rectangular wall in the right-hand side of the crag. Start at the foot of the evil wet chimney.

1 15m. 6a. Climb the clean arête immediately left of the chimney, starting on wet jugs and passing a difficult move at half height. Tree belays on the terrace.
2 15m. 6b/c. Go up a short open groove at the back of the terrace to a sloping ledge. Reach the crack above and follow it – on superb holds at first but finally with a hideously powerful move – to reach jugs just below the heather. Pull out to the top and a tree belay. Excellent gear.

☆**Tobias**   35 metres   E5 †   (25.5.98)
The right-hand of the twin cracks in the overhanging wall above the forested terrace in the right-hand part of the crag. An equally fine companion to The Stud.
1 15m. 6a. The Stud pitch 1 (or approach by abseil from the tree above).
2 20m. 6b. Climb the initial awkward groove of The Stud; then traverse right along a break into the right-hand crack (in-situ thread) and make desperate moves slightly right to reach a fine jug on the rib. Pull up and swing right to land on the terrace at a young hazel tree.

★**Girdle Traverse**   75 metres   Very Severe   (11.5.68)
The brilliant final pitch is worth all of its star; unfortunately, the first two pitches are in poor condition. The obvious horizontal break from right to left. Start at an easy-angled vegetated groove 12 metres right of the wet chimney. (The break starts above the wet chimney and was originally gained via the chimney – not recommended.)
1 27m. 4a. Climb the vegetated groove to gain the traverse-line and follow it leftwards to an in-situ wedge and sling in a horizontal crack. Abseil from these to the holly bush.
2 24m. 4a. Traverse left to a corner, descend 3 metres, and traverse the pleasant slabs to their end. Nut belays under the overhang.
3 24m. 4b. A sensational pitch. Follow the break, starting with an awkward move round a wedged block, and carry on in the same line round an exposed pillar to a gigantic nest. Continue leftwards, making some final thin moves to the sloping finishing-ledge of Shady Saunter. Nut belay well back.

General Galtieri   18 metres   Hard Severe 4a   (13.6.82)
A rightward-diagonal line on the clean right edge of the buttress, starting 2 metres left of its undercut base. Make a rising traverse right to a ledge on the edge. Climb a slab for 1 metre and step right to a groove. Climb the groove; then move right and climb a slab to a niche. Move left to a small tree. Stance. Exit right to vegetation.

Tap y Gigfran
The crag has faces to the south and east and forms the division between Cwm yr Ychen and Cwm Bydyre.

Sci-Fi (E7 ~ first ascent) Craig Cywarch
Climber: Martin Crocker   Photo: John Sumner

Tap y Gigfran

South Face

Philip Gibson

South Face

The impressive South Face overlooking Cwm yr Ychen is one of Cywarch's better cliffs, giving routes among the best in the valley, and some of the harder climbs have the unique merit of staying dry in showery weather. Its most obvious feature is the great overhanging crack of *Purge*.

The maximum height of the face is 90 metres; unfortunately, the lower half is very broken and vegetated. From a small sheep-track passing below the face just above the scree, the broken lower section rises to a wide grassy ramp crossing the whole face diagonally from the bottom right-hand corner to roughly mid height. This is known as The Ramp and has sections of Very Difficult climbing. Above The Ramp a very steep wall rises to the top of the crag. This wall is split at mid height by a large ledge; and from its left-hand end rises the overhanging corner of the second pitch of *Purge*. The Ramp affords an approach to *Dream Racer, Purge, The Grafter, Heist*, etc., and is easily gained from the right at about one-third height by a grassy terrace.

The best way off the top of the South Face is to scramble up heather and rock leftwards to a hidden short gully. Descending to the left, continue traversing leftwards across scree and grass slopes until beneath the crag of Tap Rhygan Ddu. Descend steep grass to the small track beneath the face. Descent from routes ending on the large midway ledge, i.e. *Tumblin' Dice, The Crab, Heist*, etc., has traditionally been by making a 23-metre abseil from a steel spike on the large sloping ledge under pitch 2 of *Purge*; this has become increasingly worrying and the safest bet is to continue to the top by pitch 3 of *The Grafter*.

It is also possible to make a single 45-metre abseil from the top of the crag to the ramp. The anchor is a chockstone in the extension of the *Purge* crack (*in-situ* slings will need back-up), which is easily accessible, if somewhat exposed.

High on the extreme left side of the South Face is a steep grassy gully leading up to a steep headwall. Cutting across this from left to right is another ramp-line: this is **Concorde** (37 metres Severe 2.5.70) in 2 pitches. **South West Arête** (41 metres Very Difficult 23.8.70) is a vegetated climb on a broken rib forming the left edge of the south face, and starts from the bottom of the gully leading to *Concorde*.

★Concorde Direct   30 metres   E1 5c   (9.9.90)

A fine-looking thin crackline goes through the apex of the triangular headwall above the ramp-line of *Concorde*. (A good approach is by doing *The Clilverd Line*, from the top of which an easy traverse left leads to the start.) Start up and to the right of the bottom of the ramp-line of *Concorde* at a weakness in the undercut base. Step left from a little corner and climb a short wall onto the ramp. Continue up it to the top of a huge spike directly below the thin crackline. Climb steeply to gain good holds and the crack, make an awkward move left, and continue directly to the apex of the wall. Good protection when needed.

The Clilverd Line   24 metres   Very Severe 4c   (9.9.90)
Start just left of the overhung corner pitch of *Beggars Banquet*, below a
pear-shaped clean wall. Surmount two vegetated ledges beneath jammed
blocks. Gain a flake on the left; then step back right and go up steeply to a
groove/flake-system. Climb this until an obvious traverse left over a steep
wall leads to easier climbing. Climb straight up to finish in a groove. Huge
block belays.

★★Beggars Banquet   50 metres   Hard Very Severe   (4.7.81)
Start beneath the square-cut corner topped by a triangular roof, best
approached from the left via a grassy rake. A very good second pitch.
1 20m. 5a. Climb the corner; but before reaching the roof, step right to a
foothold on the right edge. Move round this and go up to a ledge. Continue
moving up right to reach the big grassy ledge under a steep wall.
2 30m. 5b. Starting 5 metres left of the spike/block in the centre of the
ledge, climb the ragged vertical crack above and then an overhung slab,
keeping to its right edge at the top.

★★Buzzard's Balcony   46 metres   Severe   (4.6.55)
A climb of character, finding the easiest line through some intimidating
ground at a surprising standard. Start as for *Beggars Banquet*.
Alternatively, climb The Ramp (V Diff) to its highest point at some blocks.
1 14m. From the corner, traverse right to a line of weakness trending up
right; or, from the blocks at the top of The Ramp, make a short traverse left
to this point. Climb the weakness and make a short traverse right at the
top to reach a large ledge on the right. Nut belays behind a substantial
block below a corner.
2 8m. Climb the corner above to another large ledge on the left.
3 18m. Move onto the end of the projecting rock on the right; then make
a long stride onto a rightward-slanting slab and climb to its top via some
cracks. Small stance with good nut belays and a spike above.
4 6m. Go up a short easy wall above to the large terrace. Block belays
well back.

★Little Red Rooster   57 metres   E2   (4.10.81)
An interesting climb – the quickest-drying route on the crag. Start as for
Dream Racer.
1 27m. 5a. Climb the wall of *Dream Racer* to the ledge. Continue up the
corner above to the large ledge on the left with a huge spike/block in its
centre.
2 30m. 5c. Climb the overhanging wall just right of the spike/block to a
short ramp on the left; then go right to a slab (rest place). Climb diagonally
leftwards to a large foothold on the prow, and continue up the prow to the top.

★★★Dream Racer   54 metres   E2   (21.6.81)
Superb. Start a few metres below the top of The Ramp, just left of a tree
and right of blocks beneath a wall.
1 24m. 5a. Make a short rising traverse right and then climb the wall
direct to its highest point.

2 30m. 5c. Above on the right is a huge prow: the pitch follows its edge. From a flake just right of the corner, step onto the wall, and climb rightwards to a peg. Make a difficult move to a crack, and then gain a ledge above on the edge of the prow (peg runner). Climb diagonally right into a niche above the overhang. Step up left to an arête leading to an easy slab. Belay at the top of the slab.

Lucy in the Sky 67 metres Hard Very Severe (28.6.75)
Start 3 metres left of the belay block of *Purge*, beneath a steep wall bounded by a slight corner to its left and an arête to the right. Good small thread at the base of the corner.
1 21m. 5a. Good handholds to start lead up the steep, strenuous wall to a resting-place at 6 metres. Step right and follow a narrow exposed slab to a large ledge. Nut belays in a corner up to the left.
2 8m. *Buzzard's Balcony* pitch 2.
3 21m. 5a. Climb onto the projecting rock on the right and then gain a ramp on the left. Follow it until it is possible to make a move to a steep crack trending rightwards beneath the overhangs. Follow the crack with a final difficult move to reach the stance.
4 17m. Climb the steep groove above and exit left to a grassy area and a tree belay.

☆☆**The Doghouse** 57 metres E6 † (26.8.90)
A powerful free version of *Alecto* (which this route supersedes) is followed by a walk-in-space along the very lip of the huge hanging prow. Just worth the grade for excitement value. Start as for *Purge*.
1 23m. 5b. From the belay block, climb directly to a crack. Step left to a sloping ledge in the corner, and climb this for a short way to an undercut flake. Traverse to the right-hand end of the flake (peg runner) and climb a very steep broken crack above to a large ledge.
2 34m. 6b. Just left of pitch 2 of *Purge* is a system of cracks in the overhanging prow; start below these. From the dubious flake, gain the large spike. Climb even more steeply (peg runner) to big block jugs from where another jug over the lip on the left enables the *Dream Racer* niche to be entered. Step right into the crack on the lip of the prow and follow it intrepidly right to its end and a few final steep moves up a short rib. Scramble up a short wall to belays.

☆☆**Sci-Fi** 27 metres E7 6b † (5.8.95)
[Photo rear cover and page 48a.] An outstanding climb which takes on the full height of the wildly overhanging prow of the Gigfran: one of the most impressive pieces of mountain rock in Wales. Expect to get pumped in a big way. Start from the large ledge below the corner at the start of the second pitch of *Purge*. Pull up onto the pedestal of *The Doghouse* and make a hard move (peg runner) to the first of a line of sinking jugs (rock-spike runner), which are followed rightwards to their end and an *in-situ* thread. Bear slightly rightwards (bomber *Rock 3 in situ* on left) and then power direct up a slight left-facing groove (three peg runners) to a glorious square-cut jug. Span left to another good hold (peg runner); then

make a final hard move, from pockets, to reach holds on the left arête, which enables the lip to be passed. Finish easily.

★★★**Purge**   60 metres   E3   (1956/1969/1979)
The classic of the crag. Start at a large block on The Ramp, about 25 metres above the ash tree at the start of *The Grafter*.
1 24m. 5c. Make a long step right off the large detached block; then move up and right to a good ledge below a steep triangular wall formed by two cracks which merge in an overhanging groove. Climb the triangular wall and the overhanging groove (two pegs) to the niche above. Move out left above the niche to a large ledge under an imposing corner.
2 21m. 5c. Climb the steep crack in the corner to a bulge. Go right to a peg and then up to a good hold. Move delicately right again to reach the large sloping ledge. Move back left and climb the corner to a grassy ledge and block belay.
3 15m. Easy rock leads to the top.

★**Sveinstock**   67 metres   Hard Very Severe   (13.9.68)
Start at a crack 9 metres right of the large detached block at the foot of *Purge*.
1 24m. 5a. Step up right onto a block. Make an awkward move up left to gain a sloping ledge below a groove. Climb the groove to a platform on the left (junction with *Purge*). Traverse right for 6 metres to a right-slanting slab and climb it to a large spike in a corner.
2 43m. 4b. *The Grafter* pitch 3.

★★★**Crozzley Wall**   46 metres   E4   (30.8.80)
A direct, sustained, and brilliant route. Very small wires are needed for protection on pitch 1, which takes the abseil line from the steel spike under pitch 2 of *Purge*. Start 3 metres right of *Sveinstock*, below a thin overhanging crack.
1 23m. 5c. Climb the crack with difficulty to a flake and reach the ledge above. Climb the next short steep wall to another ledge; then climb the wall direct to the big ledge under pitch 2 of *Purge*.
2 23m. 5c. From 2 metres right of the abseil spike, climb the wall above to a peg runner under a little overlap. Step left and climb on up the wall to the peg on *Purge*. Continue, taking the crux of *Purge*, to the sloping ledge on the right. Move back left and climb the crack in the corner to a grassy ledge and a block belay.
Right-Hand Finish
2a 23m. E2 5c † (30.10.82). Climb *Crozzley Wall* pitch 2 to the peg in the horizontal break; then go up the wall directly above to a final bulge.

★★★**Rolair**   30 metres   E3 6a   (24.4.82)
A stunning pitch, which follows the steep slab above the diagonal line of *The Grafter*. Start by a small stunted tree a short distance up left from the start of *The Grafter*. Climb the steep wall just right of the tree, past a peg, to a shallow niche. Traverse right from the niche to a sloping ledge. Step round a rib on the right and climb diagonally up right, passing pegs, to good underpulls below and to the right of the last peg. Follow these

rightwards round a shield of rock to reach the ramp on pitch 2 of *The Grafter*. Continue up the ramp up left for a few metres; then go straight up via a crack to reach a big sloping ledge.

☆☆**Fleet Air Arm**   27 metres   E5 6c †   (19.5.90)
An excellent route on superb rock, featuring high-powered climbing up the slanting crackline and thin, right-facing corner which bisects *Rolair*. Start 3 metres to the right of the tree at the base of *Rolair* from a good grass ledge. Gain and follow a diagonal line of jugs leading rightwards to a sloping ledge. Reach left to the overhanging thin crack and tackle this desperately (crux) to reach good holds on the left and a large ledge. Climb cracks and the right-facing corner directly above (peg runner) until a jug on the right enables the overhanging ramp to be belly-flopped. Continue up the easier crack above to the large terrace and nut belays.

★★**The Grafter**   87 metres   E3   (29.8.68)
A good route, taking the rightward diagonal traverse-line under the overhangs. Start at an ash tree growing against the overhanging wall roughly three-quarters of the way up The Ramp.
1 21m.   6a.   Shin up the tree to a ledge. Move left into a niche at the start of the diagonal traverse-line. Follow this to a short groove with a peg, and continue moving right to a niche and a large spike belay.
2 23m.   5a.   Climb the steep gangway on the left to its top; then move up to a large spike belay in a corner.
3 43m.   4b.   Climb the wall via the crack; then continue as for pitch 3 of *The Gem*. A better alternative to this pitch is pitch 2 of *Crozzley Wall*.

★★**Heist**   35 metres   E2 5c   (9.5.81)
The excellent middle section of *Tumblin' Dice* can be enjoyed with an easier start and finish. Start at the ash tree, as for *The Grafter*. Climb the ash tree; then traverse right via a large green flake to a sloping ledge with a peg. Move up and right to a broken flake (good tape). Two metres above the flake, reach a hidden jug and step right to a short groove, using good little pockets. Reach a good hold up right and gain a small ledge beneath a large spike. From the top of the spike, climb directly up on good side-pulls until stopped by a short steep wall. Traverse left past a peg to a short crack, and climb it to a large sloping ledge. (This pitch could be split at the large spike. Pitches would then be 5c, 5a. Finish up *The Grafter* or abseil from the steel spike under pitch 2 of *Purge*.)

Tumblin' Dice   41 metres   E2   (8.78)
Start 9 metres right and down The Ramp from *The Grafter*, at an undercut crack.
1 24m.   5c.   Layback rightwards up the undercut crack to a small bramble ledge beneath an overhang. Pull over on dubious holds and gain a sloping ledge above by some technical moves (peg runner). Move up and right across the wall to the bottom of a short groove, and follow the groove to the first spike belay on *The Grafter*.

2 17m. 5c. From the top of the spike, go straight up to attain a position at the bottom of a very small groove/pod on the right. Exit awkwardly right (peg on the left) onto a slab. Nut belays.
Way off: go easily up the short slab on the left, and traverse leftwards over large sloping ledges to the steel abseil spike under pitch 2 of *Purge*.

The Crab   47 metres   Hard Very Severe   (10.8.80)
The leftward-slanting gangway above the very steep wall of *The Grafter*'s first pitch. Poor protection on pitch 1. Start just below the start of *Tumblin' Dice*, beside a vegetated slab that goes off right.
1 24m. 5a. Climb the ramp until a line can be taken up to the start of the ramp-line. Follow this to the large spike belay on *The Grafter*.
2 23m. 5a. *The Grafter* pitch 2.
Continue up *The Grafter* or abseil from the steel spike under pitch 2 of *Purge*.

★Thyme   35 metres   Hard Very Severe 5b   (13.5.84)
Lower down The Ramp, well below and right of *The Crab*, are two very steep grooves. Start to the right of the left-hand one. Go easily up a slab to the left-hand groove, which is overhung (peg at its foot). Climb the right wall of the groove to good jugs below a holly bush. Traverse right to a short arête under a V-notch, climb through the notch, and take a slab and arête on the right to the top.

Nicht Schlafen Trauma   27 metres   E5 6b   (19.5.90)
Overlooking the initial section of The Ramp, where it is disjointed by a grassy ledge with a tree (below *Thyme*), is an overhanging pod-shaped groove, which is taken by this route. A very dynamic problem requiring a little innovation to protect initially. With protection from the lower tree in the vegetated groove on the left, clip a peg runner at 5 metres from the left and then reverse. That done, attack the bulge from the right via the obvious underclimb to reach good holds and a peg runner in the pod above. Bridge up and then escape rightwards onto a rib. Ascend an easy ramp above to a break and pull up and left into a short angular groove leading to easier ground and tree belays 9 metres higher. Abseil off.

★★Lanchester   38 metres   Very Severe 4b   (7.3.82)
A quality route, starting from the lowest point of The Ramp. Scramble up a vegetated corner for 7 metres to a huge block on the right wall and start from its top. Step left across a slab to reach a spike. Climb left again to reach jugs on the right; move right and go up to a niche. Traverse the slab up left below an overhang to a wide crack. Go left again to the end of the slab and step left onto the front of the wall; climb this, trending slightly right to a scoop and the base of a left-trending groove. Climb the groove to the top.
Descent: from 2 metres above the top of the route, descend a ramp to the left into an overhung corner; then go down a groove.

Eastern Slabs

The east face of Tap y Gigfran consists of vegetated slabs and walls cut by gullies. The largest area of slabs consists of those sweeping down to the lowest point of the crag, and is known as the Eastern Slabs. Their left edge drops away to form the South Face. Right of the Eastern Slabs a vegetated gully rises the full height of the face, and right of this, two slabby buttresses, one above the other, form the North Wing. The steeper Lower Buttress is split on its right-hand side by *Square-Cut Gully*.

Ways off the Eastern Slabs and the upper North Wing are as for the South Face. Descent from the North Wing Lower Buttress is by grassy slopes to the right of the crag, i.e. towards Cwm Bydyre, or by descending *Square-Cut Gully*.

The vegetated arête at the junction of the South Face and Eastern Slabs is **Incapability** (90 metres Moderate 14.6.53). It finishes on a grassy terrace where *Jack o' Diamonds* starts. This terrace, above the lower scrappy section, can also be reached from the shallow gully on the right.

★★**The Gem**   76 metres   Hard Severe   (27.8.68)
The big right-angled corner topped by a square overhang high up on the left-hand edge of the Eastern Slabs. A leftward traverse from the overhang gives an exposed finish above the steep South Face. Start from the left-hand end of a ledge, directly below the corner, to the left of the top of pitch 1 of *Jack o' Diamonds*.
1 18m. Climb the corner to a holly tree at 6 metres. Continue up the slabby corner to a large rock ledge beneath an overhang. Nut belay in overhang, small spike above.
2 18m. 4a. Make an awkward move over the overhang to reach the upper slab. Climb delicately up the slab to the large square overhang; then traverse left to the arête.
3 40m. 4b. Traverse leftwards on big holds for 6 metres to a rightward-slanting crack. Climb this to a niche, pull out to the right, and go more easily up to the arête. Climb easily up the arête to the top of the crag.

★**Jack o' Diamonds**   105 metres   Very Difficult   (22.9.56)
Start in the middle of the grass terrace reached by climbing *Incapability*, or from the shallow gully on the right.
1 18m. Climb a short slab to a ledge below a steeper slab. Climb this to a grassy ledge.
2 18m. Climb the undercut slab taking a line of weakness diagonally up right to a ledge in a corner beneath a steep wall; traverse right for a metre or so to another ledge with spike belays above.
3 24m. Climb diagonally back left across the steep wall on good holds to continue by the slab above to a ledge on the left. Spike belay.
4 30m. Easy slab work to a large heather ledge.
5 15m. Scramble to the top.

North Wing Upper Buttress

This is the wedge-shaped buttress high to the right of the Eastern Slabs, framed by two gullies.

Hot Pants   91 metres   Very Difficult   (2.5.71)
A line up the centre of the buttress. Start at the toe of the buttress, above a rowan in the gully.
1 30m. Climb directly up the wall via cracks for 24 metres. A heather terrace then leads to the start of the slabs (nut belay).
2 27m. A rising traverse to the left leads to a spike. Move up the open slab to an overhanging nose. Climb this on the right; then go back left into a corner (nut belays).
3 34m. Climb the broken slab on the right of the corner and continue direct to the top of the buttress.

North Wing Lower Buttress

Best examined and approached from the ruined hut in Cwm Bydyre. It is cleaner and steeper than the upper buttress and has a square-cut gully on its right-hand side. A corner near the left-hand side of the buttress, formed by a large leaning tower, marks the start of **Wright's Route** (40 metres Severe 3.7.65): take the corner for 6 metres; then traverse left under an overhang and finish up the arête.

Sifta   39 metres   Severe   (3.4.56)
Start 1 metre right of the corner.
1 30m. Climb the wall and small groove above until a step left can be made into the crack in the corner. Climb the crack to the overhang, traverse left to the arête, and follow it to a stance and a small tree belay.
2 9m. Easy slabs lead to the top.

Salt Free   40 metres   Hard Very Severe 5a †   (5.9.93)
Start immediately left of *Cerebos*. Climb the slab to twin cracks in a bulge on the left. Pull through on the left and continue directly to the V-shaped overhang. Pull directly through the overhang to an awkward exit on heather, and continue up the slab.

★Cerebos   39 metres   Severe   (4.12.55)
Start roughly in the centre of the slabs.
1 21m. Climb the steep slab to a small ledge (thread runner in the crack above). A slight overhang above is climbed using the crack on the left, and an obvious line is followed to a pinnacle up on the right. Belay further right.
2 18m. Move back left above the pinnacle onto an exposed slab and climb it to a steep heather finish.

Square-Cut Gully (90 metres Moderate 10.7.56): normally used as a descent.

Square Chimney (50 metres Very Difficult 10.7.56) starts on the right-hand side of the gully where a large block forms the side of a square chimney: two pitches, following the chimney-line.

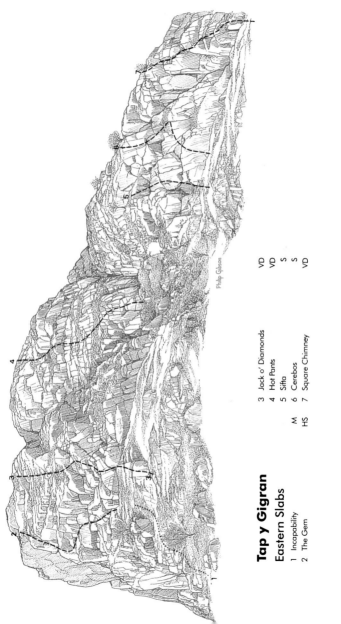

Tap y Gigran
Eastern Slabs

1	Incapability	M	3 Jack o' Diamonds	VD
2	The Gem	HS	4 Hot Pants	VD
			5 Sifta	S
			6 Cerebos	S
			7 Square Chimney	VD

Philip Gibson

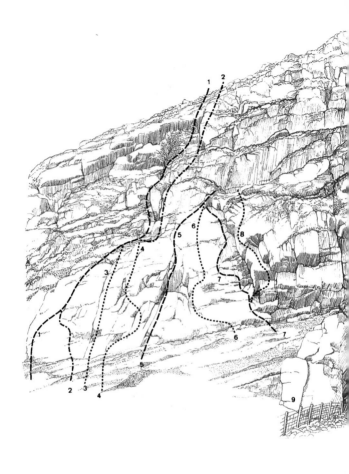

Tap Mawr

Philip Gibson

The Overlap (E2) Craig Cywarch
Climber: Nigel Turner   Photo: John Sumner

Tap Mawr

Lying between Cwm Bydyre and Little Gully, and above the second fir tree plantation, is a large triangular-shaped buttress. Its upper and lower tiers are separated by a large grassy terrace extending all the way across the buttress, and from it two grassy rakes cut diagonally down leftwards, ending above overhanging rock. The lower tier is very steep, with roofs and overhangs, though unfortunately the grassy rakes tend to spoil the continuity. The most commendable feature is a steep and relatively clean central slab and wall which provide a clutch of good-quality climbs in an open and quite sunny location. Left of the clean area is a heavily vegetated section with a line trending left following trees; this is *Sheep's Climb*. Left of this the crag steepens with an area of wet black overhangs before the buttress again degenerates into vegetation.

Descent from routes on the lower tier can be made from either end of the large horizontal terrace via Cwm Bydyre or Little Gully. From routes going to the top, descend into Cwm Bydyre.

Migraine   51 metres   Hard Very Severe   (6.6.76)
Start 18 metres left of *Black Wall* below an obvious steep chimney just left of the black overhangs.
1 15m. 4c. Climb the crack to the steep chimney; ascend this, move out left, and then go up a steep wall to a ledge and belay.
2 30m. 5a. Climb the crack behind the belay to a ledge and tree. Move up to a huge flake and gain the scoop above (crux). Steep climbing from the scoop, trending slightly right, leads to a ledge and belay.
3 6m. The steep wall above leads to the top.

Black Wall   66 metres   Very Severe   (31.3.56)
Start at the right-hand side of the large dark overhangs. A band of black rock runs up vertically. The climb follows this black band, starting where an easy-angled slab and a steep wall meet.
1 12m. 4b. Climb the small black slab to a corner, and the corner for 1 metre; then traverse 3 metres right on good holds, and move up to a stance and poor tree belay.
2 18m. 4c. Surmount the chockstone in the wall behind the stance, climb awkwardly up, and trend left to a small ledge below a quartz corner. Avoid the corner by a delicate traverse left for 5 metres; then climb to a large grassy rake.
3 18m. 4b. Walk up the rake for 12 metres and climb an arête, still on the black rock, to another good stance.
4 18m. A short black wall and a slab above lead to grass and a large tree belay.

Delli (67 metres Hard Severe 14.6.70) is a vegetated route, starting approximately 2½ metres right of the corner taken by *Black Wall*. Climb a steepening slab to a ledge-line full of trees. Walk along this to its right-hand end and climb the left side of a corner to finish on vegetation. **Sheep's**

Climb (60 metres Moderate 1966) follows a line of trees up a leftward chimney/groove-line.

Jungle 57 metres Very Severe   (26.5.56)
Sparse protection. Start from the huge block with a tree growing out of it just right of *Sheep's Climb*, on the left extremity of the clean central wall.
1 27m. 4b. Step right from the top of the block and move right to a rib; climb this and then move into and up a short corner on the right. Move out right above the corner and climb a short wall to trees.
2 30m. Climb the vegetated corner behind the trees until it is possible to move onto the right-hand wall at some cracked blocks. Traverse right for 1 metre and go up to the large grassy terrace.

★Short Circuit 50 metres Very Severe   (17.5.82)
Start at the lowest point of the wall 5 metres right of the huge block with a tree growing out of it.
1 26m. 4b. Climb the wall, on good incuts, trending left to a light-coloured ramp, and follow this left and go up to a short corner. Move right above the corner and climb a short wall to a ledge with large dead trees.
2 24m. 4a. Go to the right-hand end of the ledge, past a hawthorn tree in a corner, and step down and round the arête; then climb straight up the front of the buttress to the top.

The Graveyard 50 metres Hard Very Severe   (27.4.75)
A crackline midway between *Scourge* and *Jungle*. Start directly beneath the crack.
1 26m. 5a. Ascend easily to the first bulge; then go awkwardly over this to a resting-position beneath the second steeper bulge. Climb this (crux) to a small ledge and an easier-angled section; continue, following the vague crackline, to vegetation and trees.
2 24m. 4a. *Short Circuit* pitch 2.

Frigid Pink 27 metres E1 5b   (11.80)
A devious line between *Scourge* and *The Graveyard*. Start 1 metre right of *The Graveyard*. Climb the slab to a good nut crack in the wall above, traverse right, and gain a sloping ledge beneath a quartz wall. Make a move up the quartz wall (good nut crack high on the right); then traverse back left to a niche with a downward-pointing fang of rock. Climb the groove just left of the fang and then an easier-angled wall above to a niche. Pull out of the niche to a stance with a tree on the left. Either continue as for pitch 2 of *The Graveyard* and *Short Circuit* or abseil from the tree.

The remaining routes take only the lower tier and finish on the grassy rakes, which lead easily to the terrace.

★Scourge 34 metres E1 5c   (24.5.69)
Start at the crack to the left of the overlap line. Climb the crack to a niche, starting at a short overhung corner. Continue up the overhanging crack (peg runner) to a sloping ledge. Go up and right to the ledge directly above *The Overlap*. Escape right on easy ledges.

★The Mind's Eye   34 metres   E4 5c   (23.8.80/5.5.90)
Start 4 metres left of *The Overlap*. Sparse protection. Pull over the bulge and immediately tiptoe traverse left to a rounded spike hold. Move over it, and climb a small quartz ramp to a good hold at its top below a bulge. Step right and go over the bulge leftwards to a spike. Climb another bulge direct to join *The Overlap*. Move right as for that route to ledges.

★★The Overlap   34 metres   E2 5c   (1.5.71)
[Photo page 56d.] The obvious overlap line trending left. A powerful line and a Tap Mawr classic. Climb the corner to a horizontal flake crack in the overlap (good *Friend 2*). Traverse left and move up to gain another overlap, and traverse left again to a good foothold below a crack. Climb straight up on good holds to a bulge, pull over it on the right, and climb the wall above. Move out right above the last roof to a ledge (nut belays). Escape right on easy ledges.

★Old Glory   30 metres   E4 6a   (8.9.79/5.5.90)
Start as for *The Overlap*. From the shelf at the start of *The Overlap*, traverse right at a low level. Climb to the overhang and take the roof direct on good holds. Go up the ramp on the left past a peg and a wire (*in situ*). Difficult moves on awkwardly-spaced holds allow the crux overhang to be breached. Climb the right-slanting crack to a grassy ledge and belays.

China Shop   24 metres   Very Severe 4b   (23.7.67)
Everything is concentrated in the first 8 metres. Start at the break in the overhangs directly below a small tree at 8 metres. Climb the steep wall on big holds, and move left onto the lip of the overhang on the left. Take the steep crack above to the tree. Easier vegetated climbing in the same line leads to a large grass rake.

☆Live Like a King   12 metres   E5 6b †   (9.6.95)
Short but superb Bachar Ladder climbing. Start as for *Wedgewood*. Step off an embedded flake and, from a good crack, reach the first of a series of good holds in the overhanging wall on the left (crucial *Rock 2*). Stretch left powerfully; then continue up the 'ladder' past a thin crack (*Friend ½*) to easier ground and an optional abseil spike at the top of a scoop on the right.

Wedgewood   26 metres   Hard Very Severe 5a   (3.9.70)
Start beneath the inverted V-chimney. Climb strenuously up the chimney until the angle relents at a good thread runner, and continue to a ledge below an overhang. Pull rightwards over the overhang; then climb a steep slab, which becomes less steep and then steepens again. Move left at this point and finish up the grassy groove to small trees.

★Loon Plage   30 metres   E5 6b   (27.5.90/9.6.95)
Start 3 metres right of *Wedgewood*, below a thin slanting crack. Pull up past the crack and step left. Intricate climbing straight up leads to good holds in a break. Reach left to a thin crack and climb up to huge holds. Go diagonally right to join *Bear Cage* on the upper wall.

★Bear Cage   27 metres   E4 5c   (17.5.80)
A fine sustained pitch with sparse protection, more so now that the peg has deteriorated beyond usefulness, and high even in this grade. Start 5 metres right of *Wedgewood* below a clean steep wall, Pull over the initial overhang and climb a short faint groove to a good flake. Pull blindly over the bulge (crux) to a ramp (rotted peg). Make a move right up the ramp to another faint groove and climb this to a break. Make a long reach for a good jug and move right into the centre of the face. Follow a thin crack and edges to the large ledge with small trees.

Tapdance   24 metres   E5 6a   (9.6.95)
A committing excursion onto the face right of *Bear Cage*. Start, as for *Peacekeeper*, 2 metres left of *Soldier*. Climb to the good finger/wire-slots at 5 metres, traverse horizontally left for 2 metres on tiny crozzley pockets, and then pull up to a sloping ledge. Make a long, protectionless stretch to the main break. Continue direct up the short steep headwall and step left to join and finish up *Bear Cage*.

★Peacekeeper   24 metres   E3 6a   (9.6.95)
A deceptively strenuous climb up the leftward-arching crack left of *Soldier*. Start 2 metres left of *Soldier*. Climb the thin crack on good but spaced slots until hard laybacking, aided by poor holds on the left, gains the main break. Bear leftwards up the *Soldier* ramp to join and finish up *Bear Cage*.

Soldier   27 metres   E1 5b   (24.8.80)
Start 3 metres left of the corner of *Delft*, below a vertical crack. Reach the crack and climb it, using some good face holds in places, to a niche. Foot-traverse left along the good ledge to a short ramp. Go up this to an overhang and pull over it rightwards; then go direct to the top on good holds.

Delft   21 metres   Hard Very Severe 5a   (8.73)
Start below a shallow corner topped by an overhanging block. Climb a crack directly under the corner to a sloping ledge at 3 metres. Climb the corner above to reach a second ledge at 12 metres. Keeping left of the crack, pull over the block to easy ground.

Flanker   30 metres   Very Difficult   (5.6.66)
Start at the right-hand side of *Tap Mawr*, at a point where the grassy ramp below the face narrows and goes round an edge just before the gully. Block belay.
1 18m. Stand on the belay block and move up to the ledge above. First traverse down left to a tree in a niche and then go up to a ledge.
2 12m. Make a layback move up left and continue left again to gain a ledge. Traverse left to a group of trees on a grassy rake. Scramble off to the right.

Upper Tier

The Steeple   63 metres   Very Severe   (18.5.75)
Start above and 6 metres to the right of the large perched boulder above
The Overlap.
1 6m. Ascend by a leftward-rising ledge to gain a sloping ledge. Take a
stance in a corner with a smooth right wall and a cracked back wall,
below and left of the prominent recess in the face.
2 37m. 4b. Climb the cracked wall and chimney to gain the top of a
block on the left. Move up left and reach the bottom of a leftward-leaning
crack, and climb this to the top of the tower. Spike belay.
3 20m. Go up heather above the belay to finish up a wall leading to a
grassy ledge. Belay on the tree 3 metres right.

Some 30 metres right of a large perched boulder, an obvious arête right of a
tree in a corner gives **The Perishers** (64 metres Severe 9.70), a vegetated
climb in three pitches.

Old Man of Cywarch

A little tower situated below the right-hand end of Tap Mawr and just left of
the fence running up from the left-hand end of the plantation.

There are a number of short routes, ranging from Difficult to Very Severe (on
the right). The longest on the front face is **Frontal Crack** (8 metres Very
Difficult).

Little Gully

Little Gully (Difficult) gives mainly steep vegetated scrambling with the odd
jammed boulder.

Tap Mawr Pella

Well up Little Gully is a crag with an obvious horizontal vegetated ledge at
mid height. The lower section has a wall on the right with a tower on the left.

Barad d'Ur   57 metres   Severe   (5.8.69)
Start in the corner between the tower and the wall.
1 18m. Climb the corner and move over a bulge; then go left into the
middle of the face. Climb directly upwards over an overhang block to a
steep crack, and follow it to good belays.
2 18m. Go up right over shattered pinnacles; then climb a short corner to
a ledge.
3 21m. Climb an overhanging chimney, and go up right below
overhanging blocks. Move back left on them to gain the base of a
chimney and climb it to the top.

Tap y Graig

This is the large buttress between Little Gully and Great Gully. From the track
above the first plantation, the most obvious feature is a shallow gully running

diagonally up from right to left, starting above the chimney/cave pitch of *Central Route*. The left-hand edge of this gully (*Diagonal Arête*) forms the right edge of a relatively clean triangular section of rock that gives several good climbs over 60 metres long.

To the right of the shallow gully the buttress is, though steep, more vegetated. A large heather terrace (known as Bed of the Yellow Policeman) cuts across this part of the buttress and can be gained fairly easily from the Very Difficult *Tower of Babel* on the right. *Ring Wraith* and *Quartzberg* both start from the terrace.

The way off from the top of the buttress is by a sheep track descending left below Tap Dwyren, then down a gully leading into Little Gully, and thence to the base of the crag.

Little Gully Wall

[Diagram page 64a.] The first routes start on the section of the buttress overlooking the bottom of Little Gully.

Fritz the Cat (30 metres Very Difficult 24.7.76) starts 9 metres up to the left of *Flu '69*, below the last groove-line close to the descent gully. The groove leads to a tree (belay) and then a corner with good holds.

Flu '69   45 metres   Hard Severe   (26.12.69)
Start by a little step in the gully, level with a tree on the right.
1 15m. Traverse right to the tree; then climb the slab on the right to a slab and spike belay.
2 12m. 4b. Climb the left wall of the corner and move left to a grassy ledge; climb the steep slab (awkward) to a tree.
3 18m. 4a. Follow the groove on the right, which trends left to a short steep wall with a tree above. Continue above the tree in the same line to the top.

Tappers Arête   54 metres   Very Severe   (9.5.76)
The arête just to the left of *Porcupine*. Start 6 metres left of *Porcupine*, below a clean corner directly under the arête.
1 17m 4a. Climb the right wall of the corner on good holds, continue up the steep wall above the corner to a ledge, and move left to the ledge on *Flu '69*.
2 17m. 4c. Climb the thin crack directly above a block to gain a good flake hold. Traverse right, and then climb the arête a little more easily to its top. Nut belay on the right.
3 20m. 4b. Move back left; then go up vegetated rock to gain a small tree below a steep corner. Finish awkwardly up the corner.

Porcupine (64 metres Very Severe 25.8.70) starts 6 metres left of a large triangular overhang and makes for an obvious overhanging corner about 24 metres up.

★★Sweet Baby James   43 metres   Hard Very Severe 5a   (9.5.76)
A delicate slab climb taking the overlapped wall between *Porcupine* and *Mud Slide Slim*. Start, as for the latter, at the ramp below the overhang. Go

up the ramp to a steepening (as for *Mud Slide Slim*). Pull left over the steepening to gain an upper short ramp, move left again to avoid an overhang, and move up to the slab above. A delicate move up right gains a large hold. Continue delicately up to an overlap; then go left via a ramp into the corner of *Porcupine*. Traverse out right between two overlaps, climb a groove more easily, and finish by a crack to the stance on *Will-o'-the-Wisp* with a tree belay.

★Mud Slide Slim 63 metres Very Severe (2.1.72)
Start from the leftward-sloping ramp under the large triangular overhang. There is a distinctive white water-mark at its base.
1 18m. 4c. Climb the ramp to a steeper section, move right, and go up to the overhang. Traverse right under it to the arête and move easily right to a small ledge (nut and spike belays).
2 21m. 4a. Move back left; then go diagonally left and climb the arête to an overlap. Pull over on good holds to a slab and go up to the stance on *Will-o'-the-Wisp* beneath a steep wall.
3 24m. 4a. Climb the steep wall to a large tree; the wall above leads easily to the top.

Will-o'-the-Wisp Wall
[Diagram page 64b.] This is the most popular area on Tap y Graig, and the cleanest. Rock and protection are generally good.

Oread 90 metres Very Severe (26.9.53)
Start at a large block with a short steep corner directly behind, 6 metres down from and to the right of the large triangular overhang.
1 15m. Climb the corner to a ledge below a small overhang. Take the overhang by an awkward wide crack; then climb a slab to a small stance.
2 23m. 4b. Traverse easily right to a spike after 5 metres. Climb the wall above the spike for 3 metres; then traverse delicately right and climb a groove to a ledge.
3 15m. 4a. Move up and left to an obvious break in the steep wall. Climb this for a few moves before traversing left to a tree.
4 37m. 4a. Gain the rock ledge on the right and move right again to the foot of a buttress. Climb a steep corner on the right until it is possible to move round onto the face. Climb this to easier ground and scramble up vegetation to the top.

Derwent 73 metres Very Severe (8.5.76)
Two vague cracklines run up the centre of the buttress; this route takes the left-hand one. Start beneath a lower vegetated band, 15 metres below the foot of the crackline.
1 17m. Ascend rock and heather to below a small overhang at 14 metres. Traverse 1 metre left on vegetation; then go up to a small stance below the crackline.
2 17m. Follow the vague crackline to a ledge on *Will-o'-the-Wisp*.

3 24m. 4b. Continue up the crackline directly above, over a bulge at 10 metres, to a block below and left of a heather ramp. Gain a small tree at the top of the ramp below the final tower of *Bluebell Babylon*.
4 15m. Exit easily leftwards.

Electric Rail 46 metres   Hard Very Severe   (7.80)
The wall sandwiched between *Derwent* and *Raindrop*.
1 12m. 4b. Move left as for *Raindrop*, but continue traversing to the middle of the wall. Climb this in the centre.
2 34m. 5b. From a belay on *Will-o'-the-Wisp*, climb the wall 6 metres left of *Raindrop*. Take the bulges direct, the last being the hardest. Step left to a crack, avoid a block on the right, and finish up mixed ground.

★Raindrop 58 metres   Very Severe   (16.4.79)
The right-hand of the two vague cracklines. Start from the ledge below pitch 2 of *Bluebell Babylon*.
1 17m. 4b. Gain the crack by a move left from the left end of the ledge, and climb it to a junction with *Will-o'-the-Wisp* just under its second Tea Ledge. Peg belay.
2 26m. 4c. Go directly up above the peg, following the vague crack. Move awkwardly over a bulge and continue in the same line to a ledge; then climb a crack direct to a small tree and belay below the final tower.
3 15m. 4c. In the centre of the tower is a thin crackline. Climb this and exit left to the arête. Easy ground then leads to the top.

★Bluebell Babylon 78 metres   Very Severe   (27.5.56)
The classic VS of the crag.
1 27m. Climb pitch 1 of *Will-o'-the-Wisp*, but move left above the final short wall to a stance under an overhanging wall.
2 15m. 4b. From a corner-crack on the right, climb diagonally left up the overhanging wall on good holds; then take the delicate slab above to a ledge. From the ledge, climb direct and go delicately left into a corner. Small thread belay.
3 18m. 4b. Move onto the left edge of the corner and climb up to a ledge on a steeper section of wall. Gain the ledge by an awkward move and then climb diagonally left. Move up to a sloping ledge and traverse right along it to a groove. Climb the groove to a stance.
4 18m. Above is the final tower. Climb its right-hand edge via a small tree until an escape left can be made to the edge. Go up over the large blocks to the top.

★★Will-o'-the-Wisp 95 metres   Very Difficult   (4.4.72)
Justly popular. A rising traverse left leads across the left-hand triangle of the buttress. Start at a left-trending weakness in an easy-angled wall.
1 29m. Follow the weakness towards a small tree and a large block. Climb the rightward-slanting slab above the block to a short wall and take this to a good stance on the right.
2 8m. Climb the short crack above to a bulge; then traverse right up a ramp to gain the big ledge above – the First Tea Ledge (nut-slot belay).

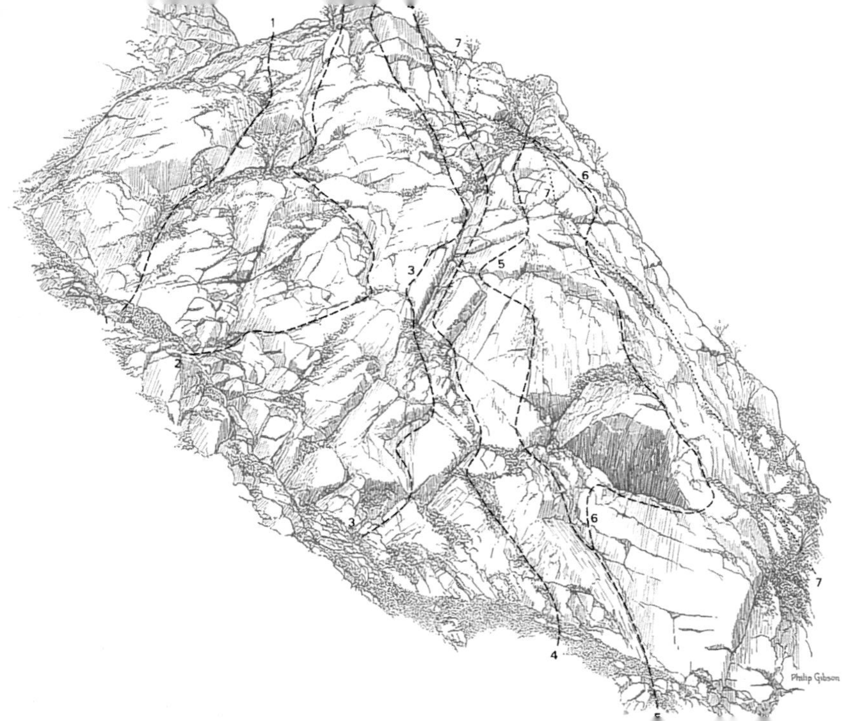

Tap y Graig

Little Gully Wall

1 Fritz the Cat — VD
2 Flu '69 — HS
3 Tappers Arête — VS
4 Porcupine — VS
5 Sweet Baby James — HVS
6 Mud Slide Slim — VS
7 Will-o'-the-Wisp — VD

Philip Gibson

Tap y Graig

Will-o'-the-Wisp Wall

Philip Gibson

1	Sweet Baby James	HVS
2	Mud Slide Slim	VS
3	Oread	VS

4	Derwent	VS
5	Electric Rail	HVS
6	Raindrop	VS
7	Bluebell Babylon	VS
8	Will-o'-the-Wisp	VD
9	Pear Treee Blues	VS
10	Katmandu	HVS
11	A Touch of Class	VD
12	Diagonal Arête	D
13	Tombstone Blues	HS
14	Baskerville	HVS

3 15m. Go left along the ledge, passing a small spike, and continue left to gain a short ramp. Go up this easily to a good small nut-slot; then make a delicate traverse horizontally left across a slab to a crack, which is climbed to another big ledge – the Second Tea Ledge (peg belay).
4 17m. Walk along the ledge and step across a gap to a ledge under a small overhang. Continue traversing horizontally left for 3 metres until a long stride left is made to a sloping foothold. Go left again and slightly down to good holds; finally, move up to a ledge close to the arête under an overhanging wall.
5 8m. Move round the arête on the left, climb up on good holds to a fine position on the arête, and move right at the top to a large tree.
6 18m. From the top of the large square block on the left, climb the corner on its right and continue easily up to the right until a traverse left can be made to a small tree in a crack. Finish up the crack.

★Pear Tree Blues   55 metres   Very Severe   (23.4.78)
Pitch 1 takes a shallow groove just left of the obvious square-cut overhangs. Start from the First Tea Ledge on *Will-o'-the Wisp*, i.e. the top of the latter's second pitch.
1 23m. 4c. Move left and climb the wall above to an overlap where it is at its narrowest (nut-slot in the overlap). Pull over the overlap and gain a niche. Climb the shallow groove above on good holds until a step out right to a big heather ledge can be made. Belay as for *Touch of Class*, 6 metres along the ledge.
2 32m. 4c. Climb the groove and leftward-leaning ramp to the foot of a corner (as for *Touch of Class*). Climb the corner direct. Move out right beneath a bulge and gain a niche. Leave this awkwardly on the left, and climb a steep groove to easy ground and the top.

Katmandu   66 metres   Hard Very Severe   (3.9.78)
Pitch 1 takes the right-hand corner of the obvious square-cut overhang above the start of the *Will-o'-the-Wisp* traverse. Start at the nut-slot belay on the First Tea Ledge.
1 21m. 5a. Move 1 metre right from the belay and climb up to the steep overhung corner. Climb this to the overhang and pull out right. Continue up the wall above and move left to the large heather terrace.
2 21m. 4c. Follow *A Touch of Class* to the start of the ramp; then traverse out right for 1 metre at a weakness in the right wall to a crack. Climb the steep slab above the crack to the traverse-line of *A Touch of Class* and move into the corner on the right.
3 24m. 4b. Climb the steep groove directly above the stance on big holds and finish up heathery slabs.
Direct Start
1a 21m E1 5c (1.9.79). Climb straight up the bulging wall until under the centre of the square overhang. Pull over direct on widely spaced holds and move left to a crack, which is followed to the terrace.

★A Touch of Class   78 metres   Very Difficult   (4.2.78)
Exhilarating climbing in its upper section. Start from the top of pitch 2 of
Will-o'-the-Wisp.
1 5m. Move right and go up to a small tree (flake belays).
2 14m. From the end of the ledge right of the flake belay, climb the wall
above for 2½ metres until a slightly rising traverse to the left can be made
to a big spike. Swing left round the spike and climb up to the large heather
terrace. Nut belay below a broken groove.
3 12m. Climb the groove to gain a left-trending ramp, which is followed
to a belay under a big corner.
4 17m. Climb the corner for 2 metres to gain ledges. Move right along
these until a move can be made up the wall to gain a higher traverse-line,
which leads right to a huge block in a corner. Make a move round the
base of this to a stance with a chockstone belay.
5 30m. Climb the steep corner above a spike for 2 metres and step right
to a slab. Traverse the slab to a ramp on the right; then follow the ramp to
the arête. Finish up the arête.

Oh Calcutta   79 metres   Very Severe   (24.8.70)
A rather vegetated route but with *some* good rock. Start at the foot of a
shallow chimney 9 metres left of a rowan.
1 23m. Climb the chimney to a ledge. Move right and go up vegetation
to reach a large heather ledge.
2 18m. Follow the vague chimney-line; then break back right. Move
easily left to a large heather terrace and a small tree belay.
3 27m. 4a. Climb delicately rightwards up slabs to the right of a
square-cut overhang to reach a groove, and climb it to an oak tree. Follow
an easy ramp to belays.
4 11m. 4b. Gain the base of an overhanging chimney. Move onto its left
arête; then continue moving up left to easier ground.

Elephant Walk   82 metres   Severe   (13.4.71)
Sustained climbing higher up but with much vegetation between pitches.
Start at the rowan (9 metres right of *Oh Calcutta*'s shallow chimney).
1 27m. Move right to a little chimney; then go right again to a slab above
on the right. Climb this to a heather ledge, move right into a little corner,
and climb the arête on the right. A slab leads to below an overhanging
wall. Go up and left on heather into a corner.
2 18m. Ascend vegetation to a small tree below a clean, left-leaning
buttress, bounded on its right by *Diagonal Arête* and on its left by the
ramp-line on pitch 3 of *Oh Calcutta*.
3 37m. 4a. Climb rightwards by a line of holds; then go left under
steepening rock to an arête on the left and climb it to a small ledge. Move
2 metres left above a tree; then go diagonally left until a break can be
taken onto the crest of *Diagonal Arête*.

Diagonal Arête (99 metres Difficult 17.5.53) follows the heavily-vegetated
arête on the left of the prominent shallow gully. The arête forms the right edge
of the triangular section of rock that gives the best climbing on Tap y Graig.

Baskerville Wall

Slightly down from and further to the right of Will-o'-the-Wisp Wall. It is fairly steep and reasonably clean, though it suffers from a certain amount of seepage.

Baskerville 40 metres Hard Very Severe 5a (19.5.79)

A line on the left of the smooth wall located just left of the top of the large broken pinnacle (start of *Central Route*). Start about 40 metres right of *Will-o'-the-Wisp*, on the left side of a huge boulder. Traverse 3 metres left; then move up to the top of a flake and delicately right to a thin crack. Climb this to a jutting hold, gain its top with difficulty, and move delicately left to a scoop at the foot of the upper slab. Take a fairly direct line up this to an overhanging wall, traverse right to a small tree, and finish straight up to a large tree. Abseil from the tree.

Dancing Man 30 metres Hard Very Severe 5b (6.7.79)

A vertical crack just right of *Baskerville*. Start from the huge boulder and reach the crack by stepping off its top; move up strenuously until good holds arrive above the steep section. Continue up the slab above to the large tree. Abseil from the tree.

The Fortifier 43 metres Very Severe 4c (16.9.79)

An obvious diagonal crackline left of *Central Route*'s diagonal chimney pitch. Start beneath slabs just left of the fallen pinnacle at the start of *Central Route*. Climb the cleaned slabs, trending right to a small tree at the base of the diagonal crack. The crack is climbed, with difficulty at first, to good footholds; the climbing then becomes less strenuous. Continue, following the now vague crackline, to a small tree; then go up left to a cleaned corner, which is taken to the large tree and ledges. Abseil from the tree.

Thung Wall

An area of vegetated, wet walls and terraces, and the two routes here are for veggie lovers only. They finish on the central terrace – known as Bed of the Yellow Policeman. Escape is down to the right into Great Gully.

Central Route 66 metres Severe (30.8.52)

At the right-hand extremity of Baskerville Wall is a large pinnacle which has broken into blocks and fallen against a steep wall. Start below the pinnacle.

1 9m. Gain the top of the pinnacle by the crack on its right.

2 18m. A long traverse right leads to a ledge at the foot of a crack sloping up left. Climb the crack and move right to a cave.

3 12m. Climb the cave's left wall and then another crack. Over the heathery edge, move right to a stance in a small chasm.

4 27m. The next wall is over 6 metres back. Climb a steep break to the right of small overhangs. Finish up slabs to trees on the central terrace.

Tap Dwyren

| 11 | The Dome | VS |
| 12 | Alicia | HVS |

Upper Wall

5	Tombstone blues	HS
6	Ring Wraith	HVS
7	The Yellow Policeman	VS
8	Quartzberg	HVS
9	Surrealistic	S
10	Tower of Babel	VD

Tap y Graig
Thung Wall

| 1 | Cental Route | S |
| 2 | Thung | VS |

Bric-a-brac Wall

| 3 | Georg Machine | VS |
| 4 | The Comedians | HVS |

Thung 87 metres   Very Severe   (5.8.56)
Start 15 metres right of *Central Route,* by a short chimney with a steep wall on the right.
1 18m. 4a. The 3-metre chimney leads to a grassy ledge on the right with a square block on its right. Go 4 metres right to a crack and jam this to a large heather ledge.
2 15m. Trend right and go up to a small tree to belay in a recess.
3 15m. The left edge of the recess and then a steep slab lead to another large ledge between two small trees.
4 18m. Scramble rightwards; then trend up right to a steep buttress with a crack in a recess just right of a small tree. Spike belay 3 metres up a crack.
5 21m. 4b. Climb 6 metres up the crack to where the wall bulges; then step left to a small ledge below an overhanging rib. The right of the rib is awkward until a delicate escape left can be made. Mossy slabs lead to the central terrace.

Bric-a-brac Wall
On the right-hand corner of the buttress, close to the bottom of Great Gully, is a steep wall. The wall itself is hidden from the valley by a small triangular-shaped buttress. Approach by a rightward-slanting gully which joins Great Gully on top of the triangular-shaped buttress. Descent is made on the right into Great Gully. The wall has the following six routes.

Bric-a-brac 41 metres   Very Severe   (7.9.86)
On the left-hand side of the wall is a narrow cracked slab, the only real weakness to breach the lower section of the wall.
1 11m. Climb the cracked slab to ledges on the left-hand end of a line of overhangs.

2 30m. 4b. Climb directly up (peg) to an oak tree. Traverse horizontally right on good foot-ledges with increasing exposure to a groove. Climb this to an overhang; then traverse right across a slab to a broken groove, which is climbed to the top. Good nut belays a long way back.

★**Brick Wall**   37 metres   E1 5b   (14.9.86)
A steep line up the overhanging wall left of *Georg Machine* to gain the obvious groove of *Bric-a-brac*. Start midway between *The Comedians* and the slab of *Bric-a-brac*. Climb just to the right of an overhanging vegetated groove and step left to a niche directly above it. Make a difficult move left to gain good holds and a peg directly below the exit groove. Move up into the groove of *Bric-a-brac* and finish as for that route.

Georg Machine   27 metres   Very Severe 4c   (31.1.81)
Start at a rib just above the boulder in the gully. The rib is also directly below a tree at the top of the wall. Sustained climbing. Climb the rib to an overlap with an inverted-V cut out. Move left over the overlap to some big holds. Step back right to gain a groove directly below the tree at the top of the wall. Climb the groove direct, over a bulge, to the tree.

★**The Comedians**   21 metres   Hard Very Severe 5a   (30.8.68)
The overhanging chimney just right of *Georg Machine*. Start beneath the overhanging arête on the right edge of the wall. Climb a little groove on the right-hand side of the edge for about 3 metres; then move left onto the wall below the chimney-line. Climb the wall to a ledge beneath the chimney and then the chimney itself to easier ground. Large block belay on the heather terrace above.

Second Foundation   23 metres   E2 5c   (26.10.85)
The overhanging arête right of *The Comedians*. Lichenous. Start right of the edge. Climb up into the corner below the first overlap and traverse left to an obvious sloping foothold on the arête. Climb the arête, with some very steep moves at first, after which it relents slightly, to an obvious ledge.

Auto-Man   23 metres   Hard Very Severe 5a   (26.10.85)
As for *Second Foundation*, climb up into the corner below the overlap. Go straight over the overlap to make some quite technical moves up a little slab and over the next overlap. Finish up a final short wall.

The Upper Wall
The next five routes all start from the large central terrace (Bed of the Yellow Policeman). Either scramble up vegetation from *Diagonal Arête*, or climb *Central Route* or *Thung*. See page 62 for descent.

Tombstone Blues   48 metres   Hard Severe   (18.10.70)
On the left-hand side of the upper wall a clean groove can be seen high up on the right. The climb takes this groove and starts 12 metres below it from the left-hand end of the central terrace.

1 12m. Trend first left, then right to gain a niche below the overhang. Climb over the overhang and up a corner to a heather ledge.
2 21m. 4a. Climb the groove, then an arête on the right. After a move left across the smooth wall of the groove to a square-cut detached block, continue up the arête to a heather ledge and spike belay.
3 15m. Finish up a steep little yellow wall.

Ring Wraith   39 metres   Hard Very Severe   (4.8.68)
At the left-hand end of central terrace are some smooth walls. The route takes a line up the walls following the thin obvious crack. Start in a groove beneath the crack, about 10 metres right of *Tombstone Blues*.
1 24m. 5a. Climb the groove to a ledge at 6 metres. Climb the thin crack above (crux at the top) to a small ledge. Move into the groove left of a slight arête and climb it until it is possible to step right to a stance and belays.
2 15m. Climb leftwards to easier ground.

★The Yellow Policeman   53 metres   Very Severe   (27.3.71)
On the right-hand side of the Upper Wall is a smooth slab above an overhanging wall. The climb takes the only weakness in the smooth slab. Start beneath an overhang on the right-hand side of the wall.
1 9m. Move easily up a corner to the overhang; then traverse left below it to a grassy ramp. Scramble a few metres up this, passing an obvious overhanging, greeny-yellow groove.
2 9m. 4b. Climb the wall and the steep groove above to a niche. Nut belays.
3 35m. 4c. Traverse 1 metre right and gain the slab above. Climb this, taking a thin crack trending up right, to a diagonal break going back left. Follow the break below a steep wall to an escape leftwards; then move easily up slabs to the top.

★Quartzberg   35metres   Hard Very Severe 5a   (5.7.80)
A very fine pitch. Start in the greeny-yellow groove, just right of pitch 2 of *The Yellow Policeman*. Swing immediately out right across a steep wall and climb a thin crack to a ledge and a cleaned niche. Move diagonally left across the overhanging wall to a small ledge at the foot of a slab. Take a thin crack trending slightly right to a diagonal break, step right, and pull over the overlap; then go up a quartzy crack above.

Surrealistic (55 metres Severe 6.4.69), a chimney-line to the right of the overhanging wall of *The Yellow Policeman* and *Quartzberg*, gives three vegetated pitches.

The final route on Tap y Graig starts back at ground-level and takes the full length of the right edge of the buttress, overlooking Great Gully. Descent is made via a sheep track down to the left, crossing a gully, and traversing left over the top of the crag to the top of *Will-o'-the-Wisp*; then follow the descent given on page 62.

★Tower of Babel   133 metres   Very Difficult   (13.2.82)
Vegetated between pitches. Start at the lowest point of the buttress, just left
of Great Gully, at a corner with a tree just to its right.
1 12m. Climb the crack in the left-hand side of the arête, which is just left
of the corner, to a ledge. Alternatively, climb the corner with an awkward
chimney exit to the ledge.
2 12m. Climb the steep crack on the left to grassy ledges. Nut belay at
the base of the arête above.
3 23m. Climb the pleasant arête to the top of a subsidiary buttress.
Boulder belays. Walk across a saddle and move up to an undercut corner
with a large quartz ledge on its right.
4 24m. Crux. From piled blocks, make a difficult move up the corner
and gain the quartz ledge on the right. Return left to some jammed flakes,
which are used to gain the tree above. Go up easily right to a quartzy
corner-crack. Nut belays.
5 24m. Climb a clean rib above to a tree on the left. Gain a left-slanting
ramp and follow it to a short corner with a tree above. Ledge and nut
belays above and to the left of the tree.
6 15m. A wall above has three cracks in it; gain the left-hand one and
step into the centre crack. Climb this and then move left to a niche.
Continue direct to finish at a large tree.
7 23m. Gain a groove on the right of the arête and follow it to a poised
chockstone. Climb above the chockstone for a few metres; then traverse
left and take the arête to a vegetated groove and boulder belays.

Tap Dwyren
This is the dome-shaped buttress high above the left-hand end of Tap y
Graig, and it overlooks Little Gully. It provides a pleasant continuation to the
climbs on Tap y Graig, especially as it gets most of the afternoon sun. The
rock is good.

The Dome   27 metres   Very Severe   (20.12.70)
An obvious steep groove in the middle of the buttress. Start from a grassy
ledge directly beneath the groove.
1 15m. 4b. Climb the cracked overhanging wall to a ledge at 5 metres,
and go diagonally up left to a large spike. From 1 metre above the spike,
traverse right on good holds into the groove and climb it to a stance on
the left.
2 12m. 4a. On the right is a steep wall. Climb the wall on good holds
and move right at the top.

★Alicia   40 metres   Hard Very Severe   5a   (25.6.83)
A sustained pitch taking a direct line up the steep wall right of *The Dome*.
Start 1 metre right of *The Dome*. Go rightwards up a ramp, then back left
to a large flake in the centre of the wall. Climb directly up the wall,
trending slightly left near the top.

Philip Gibson

Esgair Felen

1 Shade of Pale   E1
2 Lone Ranger   HVS
3 Grimbarian   VS
4 The Mekon   S
5 The Worm   HVS

Great Gully

Great Gully (150 metres Difficult 1907) is heavily vegetated, but there are no serious difficulties and the pitches are short.

Esgair Felen

This buttress, lying between Great Gully and North Gully, is very broken and heavily vegetated except for an area of rock at the bottom left-hand corner at the start of Great Gully. Descent from *Shade of Pale, Lone Ranger, Grimbarian,* and *The Mekon* is down to the left into the gully, and across this to a saddle on the left. Descent from the remainder is by a sheep track to the right.

★★**Shade of Pale**   53 metres   E1   (5.5.83)
[Photo page 80a.] A memorable second pitch, with exhilarating jug-pulling on a steep wall. It dries quickly after wet weather. A short distance up Great Gully is a light-coloured overhanging wall about 30 metres high. Start well down and to the right of the light-coloured wall.
1 12m. Climb a short crack on the left out of the gully; then traverse left up an obvious ramp until directly below the overhanging wall. Old peg belay.
2 41m. 5b. Climb steeply just left of the peg to gain a niche. Go straight up on widely-spaced jugs to reach a sloping ledge under an overhang. Move up to a thread in an undercut flake and pull over it to the left to reach good holds. Step right onto the lip of the overhang to gain easier ground, and finish leftwards up easy rock.
Variation
Shade of Pale Right-Hand   E1   (4.4.81)
2a 41m. 5c. Move down and right from the thread into a groove (peg runner). Climb the groove to join *Shade of Pale* at the easier ground.

Lone Ranger   50 metres   Hard Very Severe 5a   (13.9.81)
The big curving groove just right of *Shade of Pale*. Start as for the latter. Climb a short crack on the left; then traverse left to beneath the groove-line. Take this easily at first to a bulge, surmount the bulge, and continue up the groove above until another groove on the overhanging left wall can be entered. Follow this to join the final easy section of *Shade of Pale*.

Grimbarian   65 metres   Very Severe   (12.8.84)
The arête to the right of *Lone Ranger*.
1 17m. 4b. Climb the crack to the top of a block (as for *Shade of Pale*); then move up to a small roof. Traverse right under this to the arête and climb it to a ledge. Thread belay.
2 11m. 4b. Climb the steep corner on the right to another ledge. Large block belay.
3 37m. 4b. Step out airily left and climb the broken arête to slabs; continue easily straight up to the top. Tree belay.

The Mekon   52 metres   Severe   (7.5.72)
The vegetated groove 3 metres right of the arête of *Grimbarian*.
1 37m. Climb the groove for 3 metres and then the slab on the right until
it meets a ramp trending leftwards. Take the ramp back into the corner
and climb it for 5 metres; then move out onto the right-hand wall. Climb
for 3 metres to a ledge which leads right to an arête. Gain the arête and
follow it to a stance on a large ledge. Thread belay.
2 15m. Climb steeply behind the stance to gain a ledge at 3 metres.
Move up left to below a small overhang, climb up to the right, and then go
left and climb flakes and spikes to the top.

The Worm   24 metres   Hard Very Severe 5b   (11.83)
The left-hand arête of the clean pillar which makes the bounding edge of
Great Gully. There is an overhang at 6 metres. Climb the wall below the
arête to a small tree under the overhang and move left to a ledge. Move
back right to gain the arête directly above the overhang. Climb the arête to
a small overhung groove and pull over this to the easier stepped arête
above.

The Arch (49 metres Severe 24.9.66) is a vegetated route which starts
below the huge natural arch. After climbing a crack, traverse left across a
slab below the arch to another crack. Above this, a break in the overhanging
left wall leads to a holly bush. Traverse left across the wall to a corner and a
final arête.

★Lectern Direct   46 metres   Very Severe 4c   (24.9.67)
Sustained. Start at a steep groove 5 metres right of *The Arch*. Climb the
groove for 6 metres; then make a move left onto the arête. Move up
trending left; then go straight up (oak tree in a corner on the left) to
another arête. Climb the arête to another tree. Continue straight up
vegetated slabs to a large ledge.

Esgair Felen Isaf
A rather vegetated buttress, but its easy angle and low position on the hillside
make it an ideal beginner's crag. The buttress is passed on the main
approach to Tap y Graig. Descent is easy via a sheep track on the right.

Yggdrasil (55 metres Very Difficult 4.8.68) is a vegetated route starting at
the left-hand end of the crag to the right of the wall which runs up the north
side of the first plantation. Climb a steep little nose of rock, partly hidden by
a fallen tree, then various short walls above.

Peal   43 metres   Hard Severe   (3.9.66)
Start on the left-hand side of the main buttress, part way up a grassy ramp
by a crack.
1 20m. Climb the crack and a slab; then move right above the steep
section and go up a crack on *Recuperation* to a grassy ledge in a corner.
Move left to a tree below a rib.

Philip Gibson

Esgair Felen Isaf

1	Peal	HS
2	Recuperation	D
3	Restoration	VD
4	First Anniversary	M

2 23m. 4a. Climb the right-hand side of the rib for 6 metres, move left awkwardly, and climb the arête. Step right and finish up easier ground.

Recuperation 54 metres Difficult   (3.9.66)
Vegetated. Start at the lowest point of the crag below a vague crack.
1 6m. Ascend easy-angled, vegetated rock to a small ash tree on the left.
2 21m. Move right to the crack, and climb it to where the wall steepens. Make a slightly rising traverse left to a crack, which leads to a grassy ledge in a corner.
3 27m. Move right and go straight up to another small ash, then to a hawthorn bush. Finish up a short steep groove behind the bush.

Restoration   48 metres   Very Difficult   (25.5.68)
The best route on the crag takes the middle of the buttress, making for a
small inverted V-chimney. Start 6 metres right of the lowest point of the
crag.
1 24m. Easy slabs lead to the foot of a rib. Climb the rib for 9 metres and
then trend slightly left up a shallow chimney. Move right to a huge wedged
block belay.
2 24m. Move up left to the inverted V-chimney; take this direct to a slab
above. Step right and climb a short steep wall on good holds to another
slab and then the top.

First Anniversary   32 metres   Moderate   (2.4.56)
The arête forming the right edge of the buttress. A good, safe, introductory
route for the youngest of climbers. Start at the extreme right-hand end.
1 9m. Climb the right-hand edge, moving first right then left, to a big
ledge and block belay.
2 18m. Go straight up the rib to another ledge. Thread belay low down
on the right.
3 5m. Finish up the steep corner. Steel spike belay.

Above and to the right of the top of the arête of *First Anniversary* are two
small buttresses, easily reached and quitted by the main Esgair Felen
descent track. The first is overhanging and has a green watermark down it.

The Archer   18 metres   Very Severe 4c   (8.8.70)
Start at the bottom of a diagonal fault on the left of the buttress. Pull up
onto the fault-ramp and follow it to a niche. Step down, go round the
bulge on the right, and climb up to a tree. Step left to the top of the wall
and finish at a good hold. Poor protection at the top.

★**Lincoln Green**   18 metres   Very Severe 5a   (4.4.82)
Start directly below the greenish wall in the centre of the buttress. Climb
the wall to a niche below an overhanging groove. Climb the groove and
move out left at the top.

Inclination   20 metres   Hard Severe   (8.8.70)
The obvious arête on the small buttress to the right of *Lincoln Green*
buttress. Start at the base of the arête. Poor protection. Step up, move right
onto the arête, and climb it on big holds to a small tree. Continue up the
arête, more broken, to finish with a pull over a little overhang. Nut belays
well back. The arête can be avoided by moving right onto the face forming
the right-hand wall (this wall takes some time to dry out).

Hafn Mawr
North Gully   180 metres   Hard Severe   (1907)
Vegetated lower pitches can be avoided by scrambling to the right or left.
The gully asserts itself only at the Tombstone Pitch, where the walls
converge some 65 metres up.

1 14m. Tombstone Pitch: the gully closes to form an overhanging chimney. Awkward to start but the holds improve, and the left wall is climbed until it is possible to move right and finish direct.
2 8m. The crux is just above: a short pitch, undercut at the base. Struggle awkwardly up the overhanging chimney.

On the right wall of North Gully are two short, steep, and fairly clean buttresses: They lie roughly one above the other, separated by the upper of two right forks in the gully. The lower buttress, sandwiched between the two forks, has a smooth slab on its left and large overhangs on the right.

Tap Isa Hafn Mawr
Rolling Stone   48 metres   Severe   (9.7.67)
On the left edge of the smooth slab is a rightward-leaning chimney-line. This can be gained by climbing vegetated rock at about Difficult standard from the gully on the right. Start on the left edge of the smooth wall, where it meets the gully.
1 18m. Climb the steep edge; then move right into the chimney, follow this, and continue to the ridge.
2 6m. Traverse right easily along the ridge to a large flake belay.
3 24m. Move left to the arête and finish up slabs.

The next two routes follow lines up the smooth convex slab which is taken by pitch 3 of *Mother's Pride* further right. Both are worthwhile, safe, technical test-pieces on superb rock.

All in a Day   15 metres   E2 6b †   (9.6.95)
Start 6 metres from the left-hand end of the slab. Make very thin moves up leftwards to gain the base of a broken crackline, and follow it more easily to a spike belay on the ridge above.

Time after Time   15 metres   E2 6a/b †   (9.6.95)
Start 12 metres from the left-hand end of the slab below the foot of the obvious rightward-curving crack. Make a hard crank to reach the crack; then climb it and the wall above to the spike belay.

Mother's Pride   76 metres   Hard Severe   (6.64)
A line up the middle of the smooth wall. Start at the lowest point of the buttress, where the gully branches.
1 34m. Go over vegetated slabs to a small overhang; then move right to a stance with a large spike belay.
2 9m. Move left and go straight up vegetation to a wide terrace below the smooth slab.
3 18m. 4b. Climb the slab by a steep crack just left of centre (the first few moves can be avoided by coming in from the right); then follow the line of weakness, trending right.
4 15m. Finish up easy vegetated slabs.

Tap Isa Hafn Mawr

1 Rolling Stone   S   5 Big Boy   E3
2 All in a Day   E2   6 Sickle Wall   S
3 Time after Time   E2   7 The Scythe   VS
4 Mother's Pride   HS

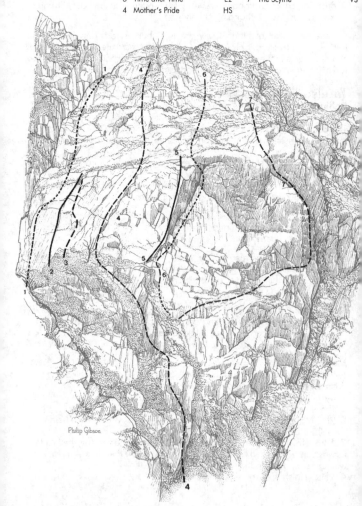

Philip Gibson

☆**Big Boy** 18 metres E3 6a † (9.6.95)
A really dramatic pitch for its length: it climbs the acutely-leaning arête overlooking the crack of *Sickle Wall*. From the right-hand end of the grass terrace beneath the smooth slab, follow *Sickle Wall* to the foot of the arête. Pull up onto the left side of the arête and climb it with exhilarating moves between jugs to finish on its edge. Perfect wire protection should guarantee enjoyment.

★**Sickle Wall** 57 metres Severe (14.9.68)
The striking rightward-rising crackline under the overhanging arête below a big roof. Start half-way up the lower right fork at a corner with a cracked left wall.
1 11m. Move right and climb a steep little wall onto slabs above. Move right again, and then go left into a groove that leads to the ledge below the smooth slab.
2 12m. 4b. Right of the slab is an overhanging arête which finishes 4 metres above. Climb the crack beneath the arête up rightwards to the big roof.
3 34m. Take the weakness out left from under the roof (easier than it looks); then finish straight up easy slabs.

★**The Scythe** 61 metres Very Severe (25.5.70)
A way through the overhangs to the right of *Sickle Wall*. Poor protection on pitch 3. Start as for *Sickle Wall*.
1 26m. From the corner, move right and climb the steep little wall onto slabs above, as for *Sickle Wall*. Climb diagonally right up a ramp, the right edge of which drops steeply into the gully, to a stance with a detached triangular block.
2 8m. 4a. Move right; then climb the steep groove to a small stance beneath a roof. Nut belay.
3 12m. 4a. Climb the slab on the left to below the roof (old peg); then traverse left over ribs and grooves to the slabs up to the left.
4 15m. Ascend vegetated slabs to the top.

Tap Ucha Hafn Mawr
A small buttress with a steep chimney-line in the centre (taken by *Apollo*) and a ramp running up its right edge.

Apollo 36 metres Very Severe (25.5.69)
Start at the obvious vertical crack in a groove a metre to the left of and below the steep chimney-line.
1 18m. 4a. Layback up into the crack to good holds above the overhang. Continue up the crack to a large ledge and block belay.
2 18m. 4b. After moving right, make an obvious rising traverse to good holds above the overhang and then a ledge. Climb the overhanging chimney with an awkward move to exit onto another ledge. The next overhanging chimney is also difficult. Tree belay.

Half-Moon Crack   21 metres   Severe   (17.9.68)
A variation start to *Apollo*: the steep curving crack, finishing on the
right-hand end of the ledge under the steep chimney. Start approximately
6 metres right from *Apollo*, beside a man-sized block. Move onto the
block and climb the steep wall above using big holds in a crack. Spike at 3
metres. Reach a small flake and move round to the right into a
corner-crack beneath the overhang. Climb the corner-crack, and move left
to the ledge at the top of pitch 1 of *Apollo*.

Relaxation   36 metres   Very Difficult   (26.5.56)
The easy-angled ramp on the right-hand edge of the buttress. Start at the
base of the ramp, which is the lowest point of the buttress.
1 18m. Move up the slab, negotiating a bulge at 8 metres. Stance with
dubious block belay.
2 18m. Climb awkwardly up a steep section behind the stance to the slab
above; follow this to the top.

The North-North-East Towers
[Diagram page 88b.] Close to the bottom of Hafn Mawr and directly above
the approach track is a short but distinct tower at the foot of Sawdl y Graig.
Just above and left is another, square-cut tower, which is home to the first
three routes.

For Hyll Drem   21 metres   E4 5c †   (18.6.2000)
An exciting line that seeks out the main crack in the tower via some
unlikely, sometimes hollow, ground. Climb the white face left of
Wunderstuff to a large square block hold in the groove on the left. Cut
loose and follow the lip of the slanting ceiling rightwards to pull around a
rock spike. Climb the crack, a little less steeply, to the top.

☆☆**Wunderstuff**   21 metres   E5 6b †   (20.5.90)
A dramatic and improbable pitch which makes an assault upon the grossly
overhanging front face of the tower. Trend rightwards and move up to the
first bulge. Go through the bulges on massive holds (tapes needed for
spike runners) to reach a niche and *in-situ* thread beneath the main roof
(*Friend 1* and 2 placements). Breach the roof (peg runner) via a very
difficult sequence up the unhelpful crack and, from a good block hold
above, climb directly on finger-jugs to the top. Thread belay well back.

☆**Hot House Flowers**   21 metres   E3 5c †   (20.5.90)
Strenuous and spacy climbing up the overhanging right-hand wall of the
tower. Climb fairly easily up the corner below the hanging arête of the tower
until level with a good nut slot on the left wall. Now make an exposed
traverse leftwards past a slot for large cams to reach a resounding spike just
to the right of the hanging arête. Make a hard move up leftwards to reach
the arête (crucial *Friend 1*) and finish up it more easily.

The next four routes are on the lower, right-hand tower (the original
North-North-East Tower).

Shade of Pale (E1) Craig Cywarch
Climber: Jill Sumner   Photo: John Sumner

Keel Haul (E2) Craig Cywarch
Climber: Kurt Sumner   Photo: John Sumner

South Face Crack   18 metres   Hard Severe 4b   (8.8.56)
Start on the left-hand edge at a crack. Climb the crack, then the left-hand
edge of the tower to a ledge below the final wall. Climb the wall just left of
centre, and finish at the highest point.

Don't Even Think about It   18 metres   E5 6a †   (18.6.2000)
The front of the tower: very run-out, with groundfall potential should
strength fail. Reach a hanging block hold, and then blast straight up the
leaning face (low hidden wire under bulge) to a good finger-rail above the
difficulties. Step left onto the arête, and climb its edge to the top.

Bundu   21 metres   Very Severe 4b   (8.58)
Start on the north side of the tower, near the left-hand edge at a diagonal
chimney. Climb the chimney to a grassy ledge and small tree on the left.
An open groove above leads to an overhang; turn this on the right and
gain the arête, which provides the finish.

Wig Walk (21 metres Hard Severe 4a 8.58) takes the obvious overhanging
crack about 3 metres right of *Bundu*.

Sawdl y Graig

[Diagram, photodiagram, and photoplan pages 88a-d.] Sawdl y Graig is
the fine steep nose of rock some 75 metres high, bounded on the left by the
lower right fork of North Gully and on the right by a line of vegetated
terraces leading down to the track beneath the crag.

The descent to the left is by the lower right fork of North Gully and to the right
by the steep ramp known as Llwybr Llywelyn, which descends across the top
of Craig Llywelyn rightwards.

The two main features on the rock nose are the ramp-line of *Charon* on the
right and the inverted V-chimney of *Hades* on the left. Rock left of the steep
nose, where the easier climbs go, is rather vegetated, the only prominent
feature being the rightward-slanting ramp of *Lethe*.

The first two routes start from the large heather terrace above and right of
the lower scrappy pitches of North Gully; this is reached by easy scrambling
just right of the gully.

Phoebus   72 metres   Very Difficult   (12.7.69)
Start at the left-hand end of the heather terrace, where it reaches the gully
at a small slab.
1 24m. Go up the slab to vegetation, and then to the start of another
slab. Large block belay to the right.
2 24m. Crux. Traverse left across the slab to the edge overlooking the
gully. Traverse back right to a break in the steep arête on the right. Move
onto the arête and climb the steep wall directly above on good holds.
Stance and belay on a heather ledge above.
3 24m. Finish straight up vegetated rock.

Lethe   70 metres   Difficult   (7.12.69)
The obvious ramp-line trending rightwards towards the top section of *Styx*.
Start from the right-hand end of the heather terrace. Some vegetation.
1 12m. Climb the corner until stopped by a bulge; then traverse right to a
ledge.
2 6m. Climb the slab above to a stance below a groove leading to the
ramp. Large spike belay high up on the right.
3 9m. Follow the groove to a tree; belay 1 metre past the tree, below a slab.
4 15m. Take the slab, trending right to a small tree at its top. Go past the
tree to vegetation and a large block belay below another slab.
5 5m. Climb this slab to a ledge on the right. Nut belay and a tree up to the left.
6 14m. Follow a groove up left to overhangs; then move right to a stance
in a groove. Spike belays.
7 9m. *Styx* pitch 4.

In view of the extensive vegetation of the standard approach described
below, the first pitch of the next route may provide a preferable means of
access to the upper pitches of *Styx* and *Hades*, as well as to *Technician
Direct*. From the right-hand end of the terrace below the two preceding
routes, scramble up heathery rock to a second terrace (with a row of trees);
tree belay at the right-hand end.

☆☆**Free Aran**   76 metres   E5 †   (18.6.2000)
An exhilarating second pitch: clean, awesomely steep but on good incut holds.
There is a fair amount of heather on the first pitch, but the climbing is easy and
there is good nut protection on the more technical traverse section.
1 36m. 4a. Climb an easy groove on the right, step right into a second
groove, and follow it to a bulge. Climb diagonally right across the top of a
dirty slab, and pull up to peg and nut belays in a scoop below the
Technician corner.
2 15m. 6a. Swing right to a huge jug and pull up onto the arête left of
Hades; arrange good gear. Follow finger-jugs on the left up the leaning
wall to a shake-out. Make hard moves slightly right to bigger holds and a
spectacular position on the arête. Pull over to a stance on the lip (*Friend 2*
and nut and spike belays).
3 25m. 4a. Step left and climb the slab to a heather ledge. Continue up
the slab above, and move right around the prominent roof to gain
scrambling and a tree belay.

Directly below the main 80-metre nose of Sawdl y Graig are two big trees,
below which is approximately 60 metres of vegetation. The trees mark the
start of *Styx*, etc. To pass the initial vegetation, start from a small bay beside a
tree and scramble up first left, then rightwards. Some slabs and a tree on the
left are passed at about 40 metres; this is the start of *AGM*.

AGM   84 metres   Very Difficult   (21.2.76)
A line parallel to that of *Styx* but at a lower level.
1 15m. From the tree, take the easiest line leftward up slabs to a steeper
section; go up this on the left, taking a small rib to a large stance (block belay).

2 20m. Traverse right; then climb the overlapping slabs to a corner beneath a steep wall and climb the corner before moving out right to ledges. Gain the hanging slab on the left and climb it to a large heather ledge.

3 21m. Follow the short ramp on the right and continue up a groove. Then climb the awkward little wall above, moving first right, then left to a stance on *Lethe*.

4 28m. *Lethe* pitches 5, 6, and 7.

Styx 65 metres Very Severe (23.9.56)

Start from the two big trees directly beneath the nose of the buttress.

1 15m. Climb the slab, trending left to a tree.

2 15m. 4a. Gain the next slab in the same line and follow this to a stance and belay at the foot of a short wall.

3 26m. 4b. Climb the short wall; then move left to the edge of a third slab. Continue up the edge until a traverse back right can be made, and move up the slab to its top. Belay in a groove.

4 9m. Climb the groove on large holds to an obvious exit left.

The Technician 44 metres E3 (27.7.68)

The big overhanging corner between *Styx* and *Hades*. Start from the stance at the top of pitch 2 of *Styx*.

1 24m. 5c. Traverse diagonally right, then left across a slab to below the groove. Climb the groove to a decomposed peg (wire above), move left with difficulty to the arête, and then go diagonally up left to a stance.

2 20m. Ascend the easy slabs to a roof, move left round this, and climb an arête to the top.

Technician Direct (36 metres E4 5c 18.6.2000) is best started by climbing pitch 1 of *Free Aran*. Then the overhanging corner is climbed with continuous difficulty until bold and forceful moves lead to jugs at its top. Easier cracks in the slab above are followed to a heather ledge (20 metres so far) and nut belays a little higher. The final slab and roof of *Free Aran* lead to scrambling and a tree belay. Alternatively, to monitor your second's efforts in the groove, take the exposed belay on *Free Aran*, below and right of the heather ledge, and finish by that route's top pitch.

Hades 45 metres E1 (1959)

A compelling line, taking the prominent inverted V-chimney. Start from the stance at the top of pitch 1 of *Styx*.

1 24m. 5a. Follow *Styx* left for a few metres; then climb the steep groove above to a slab below the chimney. Ledge and belays below the chimney.

2 12m. 5b. Climb the overhanging groove to its top and then make a difficult move left to enter the chimney, which is climbed to a ledge on the right.

3 9m. Finish more easily and less steeply.

Hell's Gate 54 metres E2 (11.10.69)

Start from the stance at the top of pitch 1 of *Styx*.

1 27m. 5b. Follow *Stygian Wall* for a few metres; then climb the steep groove above direct, and traverse out right near the top to join pitch 2 of *Stygian Wall*. Follow *Stygian Wall* to the sentry-box belay.
2 21m. 5b. Move left out of the sentry-box and go diagonally up left to the next groove-line right of *Hades*. Make some difficult moves up this to an old peg and some dubious hanging blocks. Traverse right; then go up to gain a heather ledge with a small tree.
3 6m. Steep vegetated scrambling leads to easier ground.

★★**Stygian Wall**   68 metres   Very Severe   (9.7.55)
The old classic of the buttress, taking a weaving line through some intimidating ground up the nose of the buttress. Start from the stance at the top of pitch 1 of *Styx*, below an overhung corner.
1 18m. 4c. Climb just right of the overhung corner via a crack for 2 metres; then take a slight weakness across the wall on the right to the arête, and move round it to belay in a corner.
2 12m. 4a. Climb a slab going up left to a ledge and follow a broken wall to old peg belays in a sentry-box.
3 27m. 4b. Pull out left and step back right to gain a sloping ledge on the right with a dubious quartz wall above. Follow the ledge to a niche, and climb a crack on the right for a few metres; then traverse right round an edge to a groove. Belay at the top of the groove.
4 11m. Climb the wall on the left to reach steep heathery rock.

★★★**Strobe**   85 metres   E3   (8.73/10.6.79)
Sensational climbing: technical and exposed. The line roughly follows the steep nose, first on its left then on the right. Start as for *Styx*, at the base of the nose by the two big trees.
1 32m. 5b. Go up the slab of *Styx* for a few metres to a brown, water-stained slab on the right. Climb this to a big hold, and then the wall to a niche. Go delicately right to the arête, then right again to a groove, which is climbed until moves right can be made to the stance at the top of pitch 1 of *Stygian Wall*.
2 18m. 5a. Climb the short ramp on the right, move right across a slab to a rib, and continue right into a corner with a massive block.
3 23m. 6a. From the block, move back left and climb the rib to the steep wall (thread runner). Difficult moves follow to gain big jugs on the sloping ledge above. Continue straight up the wall to a spike; then traverse left to where a weakness allows a groove above to be gained. Easier climbing up the groove leads to a stance and belays.
4 12m. Move easily out right and finish up vegetation.
Variation
3a E2 5c (20.5.89). From just below the thread, traverse steeply right for 2 metres, and move back left on good holds to rejoin pitch 3 at the big jugs.

Carrion   62 metres   E1   (14.8.76)
Sparse protection on pitch 1. Start beneath an overhanging groove to the right of and 6 metres above the two big trees at the start of *Styx*. Thread belay on the right arête of the groove.

1 21m. 5b. From just left of the thread, climb the right wall of the groove and then a short ramp diagonally right to gain a slab. This leads to the stance at the top of pitch 1 of *Stygian Wall*.

2 41m. 5a. Climb the slab to the sentry-box as for pitch 2 of *Stygian Wall*. Gain a foot-ledge above the dubious quartz wall of *Stygian Wall* that leads to a steep slab (old peg). Climb a groove just left of the peg to a niche above on the left. Step onto a spike on the left, pull over a bulge, and move left into the top section of *Hell's Gate*. Go up this to a small tree, and continue to a stance above.

Trouble Maker   56 metres   E2   (30.8.76)
The ramp-line above the *Charon* ramp. All the quality is in pitch 2. Start a few metres up and to the right of the start of *Carrion*, below a steep corner (normally wet).

1 21m. 5a. Climb the corner and the ramp above to the massive wedged block at the top of pitch 2 of *Strobe*.

2 35m. 5c. Gain the rib on the left of the block and go up to the thread of *Strobe*. Move right to the start of the ramp and climb it to a peg. Climb the wall above the peg to a foothold beneath a good flake, traverse awkwardly left to an obvious large spike, and move left again to easier ground with belays at the top of a groove.

☆☆Tech Noir   24 metres   E6 6b †   (28.7.91)
Beautiful, airy face-climbing up the leaning wall and hanging flake to the right of *Strobe*; well protected after a bold start. Start from big flake belays at the base of the *Charon* ramp, reached easily by traversing 5 metres rightwards from the second stance of *Strobe*. (*Strobe* is by far the best approach.) From an undercut, climb the lower wall slightly leftwards past two poor peg runners (the first marginal) until a reach left gains jugs and a rest on the ramp of *Trouble Maker*. Clip a peg runner above; then use undercuts on the left to gain entry to a tiny groove (hidden peg runner). Move up to the hanging flake on the left and go up it on jugs to easy ground on *Strobe*. Belay and exit right as for *Strobe*.

Charon   57 metres   E1   (10.6.67)
The obvious ramp trending rightwards across the very steep wall right of the nose of the buttress. Start as for *Trouble Maker*.

1 21m. Traverse right to avoid the corner; then go up to vegetation. Stance and belay below a steep little corner leading onto the ramp.

2 24m. 4a. Climb the corner and continue up the ramp to huge detached blocks at the top.

3 12m. 5b. Climb the overhanging groove above.

Pluto   33 metres   E3   (18.5.80)
The top pitch takes a big overhanging groove between *Trouble Maker* and *Charon*. Start below cracks in the wall below the big ramp of *Charon*, which were originally gained by a long vegetated traverse right starting about 15 metres down from the trees at the start of *Styx* (but see over.)

1 15m. 5b. Climb the steep cleaned wall by cracks, making an awkward move to gain a ledge on the left. Climb easily from the ledge to the ramp of *Charon*.

2 18m. 5c. The big left-slanting groove-line is gained by some fingery moves to a dubious flake on the right. Move left to a peg, and continue up left to a thread and another dubious flake; finish strenuously to the left.

Climbers with a good knowledge of the crag (though this would be essential) may find it preferable to abseil in to some of the upper parts of this wall (such as the preceding route) to avoid the tedious and vegetated approaches from below. This is the most practical way to reach the next two routes, and is fairly easy, given the good approach path. From threads in a large boulder 20 metres south of the *Acheron* exit, abseil down a vegetated hollow (that contains a small rowan).

☆**Sweet September**   30 metres   E6 6b †   (9.9.2001)
A dramatic line of increasing difficulty. Start at a small holly tree in a grassy recess below the wall. Step off a pedestal, and take a thin vertical crack and jugs above onto a gangway. Move left 2 metres and, from the right edge of a projecting block (*in-situ* thread on the left), climb through bulging rock onto a narrow sloping ledge (peg runner). Climb the headwall, and then undercut a crack that leads leftwards to easier ground. Follow a flake crack to a rock spike and finish on easy-angled heather.

☆☆**Midsummer's Day Dream**   24 metres   E5 6b †   (24.6.2001)
A hard and varied line of high quality up the right-hand side of the leaning wall. Start on a good ledge, below a flake groove left of the upper *Vulcan* corner. Climb the flake and groove to its end (small cam in pocket on left wall). Gain jugs above directly, and make a long reach to clip a peg runner overhead. Make desperate moves slightly leftwards, before some wild undercutting (two peg runners) leads to an overhang and a committed stretch for a hand-ledge above. Finish in the hollow past a tree-stump and the rowan.

Girdle Traverse   112 metres   E1   (24.5.69)
A rightward traverse of the buttress.
1 30m. 4a. *Styx* pitches 1 and 2.
2 20m. 4a. Traverse right as for *The Technician*; continue right to beneath the inverted V-chimney of *Hades* pitch 2, and right again into the sentry-box on *Stygian Wall*.
3 12m 4a. Reverse pitch 2 of *Stygian Wall*.
4 23m. 5a. Climb the short ramp on the right; then cross a slab rightwards to a rib, and go round it to a massive block on pitch 2 of *Strobe*. Gain the ramp on the right and move up to a corner.
5 15m. 4a. Climb the ramp on pitch 2 of *Charon* to huge detached blocks.
6 12m. 5b. *Charon* pitch 3.

Craig Llywelyn

[Photoplan page 88a; diagram page 96a.] Craig Llywelyn provides the longest and probably the best VS routes at Cywarch. It has a distinct rib and groove structure giving a type of climbing different from that of Sawdl y Graig.

The outstanding feature of the buttress is a 120-metre rib going the full height. This is *Acheron*; and *Doom* takes the big curving groove to its right. Right again the buttress deteriorates into vegetation for its first 60 metres. Above this point there is an overhanging black wall cut by the left-slanting crack of *Northerner*, and the large corner to the right of this is *The Big Cleft*. Right again a series of overlapping slabs are capped by an overhanging rock barrier. The last obvious feature on the right side is a V-groove with a sharp-looking arête to its right: *Jugs Groove*.

Ways off are as for Sawdl y Graig (see page 81).

The large grassy terraces that divide Craig Llywelyn from Sawdl y Graig merge into a vegetated section of rock at the extreme left-hand end of the buttress. The first two routes brave this section, finishing below the steep wall right of the nose of Sawdl y Graig. The way off is down to the left to the trees under the crags.

Trend (104 metres Very Severe 4a 4a 4b 30.8.64) starts on the extreme left-hand side of the buttress at a small slab at the foot of the largest rib. Pitch 1 has a steep corner and leads to two trees. A wall and rib lead to an overhang and another rib.

Troom (110 metres Very Difficult 5.10.69) starts 25 metres left of *Vulcan* and follows a rib, a slab, an arête (junction with *Vulcan*), and an obvious ramp.

Vulcan   146 metres   Hard Very Severe †   (6.6.70)
The big corner just left of the prominent rib of *Acheron*. Vegetated between pitches. Start beneath the corner.
1 27m. Climb the vegetated corner direct to a stance above a small tree.
2 30m. Continue up vegetation to a large stance with a huge flake belay.
3 18m. 5a. Take the steep corner on the right to an exit right, and climb a groove above to another big ledge.
4 23m. Move left from the stance and go up the vegetated corner to an easy-angled groove. Climb this and the steep corner above. Large tree belay higher up.
5 24m. 5b. The groove behind the tree; move right into the steep corner under a line of overlaps. Climb the corner until a traverse right can be made to a small niche. Ascend the groove above for 11 metres to a ledge and a tree belay on the right.
6 24m. Move back left into the groove and go up this leftwards to slabs leading to the top.

★★★Acheron   146 metres   Hard Very Severe   (26.5.56)
A magnificent mountaineering route, finding its way up the huge rib on the
left-hand side of the buttress. Start just left of the corner of *Doom*.
1 37m. 4c. Climb straight up vegetation for 18 metres to an overlap.
Climb a crack in the right end of the overlap onto the slab above, and
then follow the arête to a ledge and belays.
2 27m. 4b. Climb the groove on the left to where it steepens (old pegs).
Traverse delicately right to a nose and climb it to a narrow ledge. Traverse
right into a corner and go up to a peg and nut belay.
3 20m. 4b. Traverse 1 metre left and move up onto the slab; then
traverse left across the slab to the arête. Climb the steep groove just left of
the arête (some dubious flakes) to a ledge, and move diagonally down left
to the gully.
4 18m. 4b. Climb a crack to an overhang, and traverse right beneath it
to the arête; then go up to blocks below a chimney.
5 27m. 5a. Climb the chimney awkwardly to a groove above and then
the groove to a small tree.
6 17m. 4a. Move right to a larger tree and climb the steep wall behind it
to the top.

★★Kaisepakte   78 metres   E1   (30.3.2000)
A superb and well-protected climb, elegantly positioned on the arête
avoided by *Acheron*. Start from the stance at the top of pitch 2 of *Acheron*.
1 30m. 5a/b. Climb the corner above to an overlap. Pull over, climb the
slab to a peg under a steep wall, and follow the leftward-trending ramp to
the arête (junction with *Acheron* above the steep groove). Climb the
right-hand side of the rib for 3 metres; then move left to the edge and
climb it to the stance beneath pitch 5 of *Acheron*. A great pitch.
2 24m. 5b. Move left from the stance to a steep wall beneath the sharp
arête. Climb the wall (good peg runner) and move left to an obvious spike
on the edge. Move up and climb the wall left of the sharp arête, keeping
to the light-coloured rock. (It is also possible to step right onto the arête
above a bulge and climb it direct: E2.) Gain the arête just above a niche
and move up to the stance on *Acheron* at a small tree.
3 24m. 4b. Climb the slab above the belay tree to the left-hand end of
the overhang; then step left to jugs, move up and back right above the
overhang, and go easily to the top. Good nut belays in the corner above.
Variation
3a 18m. 5b. The steep break through the overhangs directly above the
belay. An exercise in layaways. Climb steeply up, then leftwards (good
Friend 1 in slot) to gain easier ground on the left.

The Mule   80 metres   E1   (6.8.75)
Start at the top of pitch 1 of *Doom*.
1 23m. 4b. Traverse 5 metres left to a groove and climb it to vegetation
and the corner stance on *Acheron*.
2 23m. 5b. Climb the slab in the corner to an overhang. Continue
awkwardly up the right wall to a ledge on the right and then into a niche at

FFENESTR Y GRAIG

CRAIG LLYWELYN

SAWDL Y GRAIG

Sawdl y Graig

1 Phoebus   VD
2 Lethe   D
3 AGM   VD
4 Styx   VS
5 The Technician   E3
6 Technician Direct E4
7 Hades   E1
8 Hell's Gate   E2
9 Stygian Wall   VS
10 Carrion   E1
11 Strobe   E3
12 Trouble Maker   E2

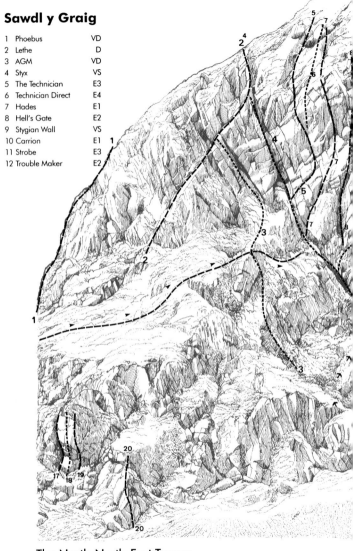

The North-North-East Towers

17 For Hyll Drem	E4	19 Hot House Flowers	E3
18 Wunderstuff	E5	20 Don't Even Think about It	E5

Philip Gibson

| 13 Charon | E1 | 15 Pluto | E3 |
| 14 Tech Noir | E6 | 16 Midsummer's Day Dream | E5 |

Sawdl y Graig

1 Styx   VS
2 The Technician E4
3 Hades   E1
4 Hell's Gate   E2
5 Stygian Wall   VS
6 Strobe   E3
7 Tech Noir   E6
8 Trouble Maker   E2
9 Pluto   E3
10 Charon   E1
11 Vulcan   HVS

the base of a groove. Climb the groove until a move right can be made to easier ground. Belays above.
3 23m. 4b. Move left, go up to gain a slabby groove, and climb it to a tree.
4 11m. Climb the steep wall behind the tree as for *Acheron* pitch 6.

★★Doom   113 metres   Very Severe   (3.11.68)
A classic line, following the big slabby corner right of *Acheron's* rib. Start just right of the huge rib, beneath the corner.
1 37m. 4c. Climb the corner for 27 metres to where it starts to curve left (old peg), move up right to gain a slab in a corner, and climb this before pulling out right over a block to a grassy ramp. Large stance and flake belay above.
2 30m. 4c. Make a slightly rising traverse right, following a ledge to a small arête. Climb the slab above and bear right into the corner. Continue up the corner to an overhang and pull over to an eyrie-like stance below a big curving corner (peg belays).
3 37m. 4b. Make a few moves up the corner until a step left can be made to gain a small niche in the slab. Climb the crack above, and make a traverse left at the top to a spike. Move up and right into the corner, climb it to below a smooth section, and then make a tricky move left across the slab to easier ground. Follow this up to a tree belay.
4 9m. 4a. Finish up the steep wall behind the tree.

★Italia 90   40 metres   E2 5b   (24.6.90)
The prominent arête to the right of the second pitch of *Doom*. A fine exposed pitch on good rock. From the stance atop pitch 1 of *Doom*, move right to a small arête (as for *Doom*), then up to a small bay on the right. Traverse right (peg runner) to a prominent large spike on the arête. Climb directly up the steep arête on good layaways into a recess on the left (large mossy spike for large tape). Gain the slab above the spike and step left onto the edge of the arête, which leads delicately to easier ground. There are poor belays above, from where it is possible to finish up *Guillotine*. Better is to continue for a further 10 metres to a good spike belay beneath a chimney (abseil from here possible – slings required).

Guillotine   53 metres   Very Severe   (10.6.73)
The arête on the right of the third pitch of *Doom*. Start from the corner stance atop pitch 2 of *Doom*.
1 11m. 4b. Traverse delicately right to the arête, and continue right to a stance.
2 30m. 4b. Move up the slab just right of the arête into a wide slanting chimney, and then climb the slab on its left. Pad delicately over some hanging blocks to reach easy ground. Climb an arête past trees to a belay on the left below an overhung corner.
3 12m. From a vegetated groove on the left, climb an arête and then a slab to the top.

Northerner   56 metres   E2 (3 pts aid) †   (19.3.66)
The leftward-slanting crack in the black overhanging wall between the
corners of *Doom* and *The Big Cleft* gives a fierce pitch. Start from the top
of pitch 1 of *Midlander*.
1 9m. 4b. Continue up the groove above to the overhanging wall; then
move right to a rib. Block belay above.
2 23m. 5c. From the block, go out left to an overhanging,
leftward-leaning crack and climb it to a resting-place (peg runner).
Continue up the crack on poor rock with a peg and nut for aid. Move out
right onto the slabs and take a stance on the left below an overhang. Old
peg belays.
3 15m. 4c. Traverse a slab on the right; then go up a little wall to
another slab, and belay below a very steep corner.
4 9m. 5b. Climb the corner using one point of aid. Easier climbing leads
to some protruding rocks and then the vegetated ramp up right.

★Midlander   112 metres   Very Severe   (17.6.56)
A good finish compensates for the rather vegetated start in the next groove
right of *Doom*.
1 37m. 4a. Climb the vegetated groove to a tree.
2 15m. 4a. Move rightwards from the tree over sloping ledges to a cave.
3 18m. 4c. Traverse horizontally right around the arête and move up
over a bulge to a short steep slab. Climb the slab and make a short
traverse right to a small ledge. Thread belay.
4 21m. 4c. Move awkwardly right onto a small steep slab and across it
to a rib. Now climb the slab on the right-hand side of the rib to an old ring
peg, step left, and gain a small ledge below a steep wall. Move back right
above the peg and, with difficulty, gain a good spike on the right. Climb
direct from the spike on good holds to a ledge, and belay in a groove on
the left.
5 21m. 4a. Climb the groove to a slab on the right, and go up this to
easy ground; belay on large detached blocks on the right.

The Big Cleft   92 metres   Hard Very Severe   (13.6.69)
Right of the corners of *Doom* is another large corner. Start approximately
20 metres right of *Midlander*, with the corner directly above.
1 46m. 4a. Climb a short section of rock and then take a line up
vegetation and occasional rock to the cave stance on *Midlander*.
2 23m. 5a. Gain the base of the large corner, and climb it with difficulty
to a slab above. Continue up a slabby groove, first left, then right, to a
flake under a steep crack. Left of this, step onto a slab and climb
diagonally left until easier climbing leads to a belay below the steep corner
on *Northerner*.
3 23m. Go up left; then follow the vegetated ramp to the right.

Man of Kent   90 metres   Very Severe   (9.8.69)
A leftward-trending line over overlapping slabs. There is some vegetation
on the lower pitches. Start at a hawthorn tree in a groove.

1 24m. Climb the groove past the hawthorn for 9 metres and move out right onto easy-angled slabs, which are followed to a large tree on the left.
2 21m. 4b. Work up easily above the tree to a corner, move right, and then gain a ledge below some overhangs. Move left to an undercut slab, and go up this for a short way to a good ledge on the right.
3 24m. 4c. Move out left onto a slab sloping left and climb to join *Midlander* at its old ring peg. Continue as for *Midlander*.
4 21m. *Midlander* pitch 5.

The Magic Dragon   96 metres   Hard Very Severe   (10.5.70)
A climb with some fine situations, but there is some vegetation on the lower pitches, and the second is poorly protected.
1 34m. 4a. As for pitch 1 of *Man of Kent*, but don't go left towards the large tree; instead move up to a ledge on the right. Climb a short steep wall and move up again to a ledge under a large blunt arête.
2 24m. 4c. Climb a broken groove on the left to reach a ledge at 5 metres. Continue up the groove above with the blunt arête on your right to an old peg. Traverse delicately across the wall under the peg to obvious holds on the arête, and climb the arête direct to easier ground.
3 12m. 4b. Climb a steepish wall; then move easily right to a rib which overlooks *Jugs Groove*. Old peg belay.
4 8m. 5a. Climb the weakness in the steep wall above (old peg) to a stance.
5 18m. 5a. Climb a steep groove on the right, and make a thin move right to an exposed ledge. Finish up slabs.

Click   85 metres   Very Severe   (19.7.69)
The leftward-trending line of slabs on the right-hand side of the buttress. There is some vegetation on the lower pitches, and protection on pitch 2 is poor. Start at a groove 25 metres right of the hawthorn tree.
1 21m. Go straight up the slab to a belay under an overhanging wall.
2 34m. 4a. Move right and go up an easy slab to a small tree. Climb the steeper slab above onto the arête at its top. Nut belays.
3 12m. 4b. Move easily up right to the base of a leftward-trending slab, and climb this, a delicate step left to the edge half-way being the crux. A short wall at the top leads to the large ledge and a tree belay.
4 18m. Climb the slabby wall on the left to some large detached blocks on the right, and escape rightwards.

★Jugs Groove   36 metres   E3   (31.5.71)
The groove immediately left of a striking sharp, overhanging arête. Poor protection. It is possible to combine the pitches in one lead. Start from the nut belay of pitch 2 of *Click*. Move a few metres up and right to a small stance.
1 15m. 5b. Climb the overhanging wall on the right to enter the groove, and follow the groove to the overhang. Gain the right arête and climb this for a metre or two; then move back left and go up to a large ledge.

2 21m. 5c. Climb the corner for 3 metres and then move right to gain the arête. Climb it, and move right at its top to a grassy ledge. Steep vegetated scrambling leads to the top.

Mad Ray 27 metres E5 6a †   (6.8.95)
An unquestionably bold interpretation of the glowering dark wall right of *Jugs Groove*. A good route to second. Reach the foot of the wall by scrambling up easy heather/bilbery ledges; a small fir tree marks the start of the scramble. (This approach also gives the most obvious entry to *Jugs Groove*.) Belay on a rock spike 3 metres above the start of *Click's* initial left-trending slab. From the spike, move up right to a ledge and then take a vague line of weakness trending slightly leftwards across shallow slabs until a tentative step-up lands you beneath a huge undercut flake. Make hard moves up the little groove formed by the top of the flake and reach a break. Swing right to the obvious left-pointing flake and make bold moves up a groove before stepping right onto the slab above (crucial *Rock 2* placement). Go delicately back up left; then climb direct to easier ground and a cam/nut belay above the exit of *Jugs Groove*. Scramble to the top as for *Jugs Groove*.

Girdle Traverse 203 metres Hard Very Severe   (9.8.69)
A lengthy right-to-left expedition with some good pitches.
1 21m. *Click* pitch 1.
2 34m. 4a. *Click* pitch 2.
3 21m. 4c. From the left-hand end of the belay ledge, descend slightly and then make a long horizontal traverse for 18 metres to the left, crossing *Man of Kent*. Reverse the awkward first section of pitch 4 of *Midlander* to the small ledge. Thread belay.
4 18m. 4c. Reverse pitch 3 of Midlander.
5 20m. 5a. Climb as for pitch 2 of *The Big Cleft* for 8 metres; then go diagonally left up a slab to a flake. Now traverse horizontally left to small ledges and a stance below an overhang (at the top of pitch 2 of *Northerner*).
6 12m. 4b. Go diagonally left to the arête; climb it for 6 metres to a ledge and then make a traverse left to the stance and peg belay at the top of pitch 2 of *Doom*.
7 26m. 5a. Step down and traverse 6 metres left to the lower extremity of the prominent overlap (exposed). Move onto the slab and climb diagonally left up the slab past a high flake runner (stance on *The Mule*). Continue traversing left and go down slightly to a stance below pitch 5 of *Acheron*.
8 27m. 5a. *Acheron* pitch 5.
9 24m. Traverse left into a groove, climb it, and then move up left to a slab below an overhang. Move left again to finish.

There is an isolated route up the wall at the right-hand end of Craig Llewelyn, beneath the descent ramp (page 81).

Pick n' Choose   20 metres   E4 6a †   (9.9.2001)
One of a genre of routes that fights for an identity. Typically, the climbing is
good. Start at the lowest point of the wall. Climb a flake crack up and
leftwards, and then pull up to a break. Step left, and make bold moves up
a steep and narrow groove to a rock spike on the right (thin tape
required). Climb leftwards across the headwall to positive holds on the lip.
Either pull over onto terrifyingly precipitous heather, or lower off solid wire
runners at the lip (and recover them after by abseil).

Ffenestr y Graig
[Diagram page 96b.] A steep area of rock above and to the right of Craig
Llywelyn extends from the steep rake (the descent ramp from the top of Craig
Llywelyn) to a vegetated gully on the right which contains the tower of Dinas
Llywelyn.

The way off is not obvious: first traverse left past all steep rock; then descend
bilberry ledges to gain the huge rightward-descending ramp mentioned
above.

The first routes start from the top of a very wet gully descending from the
large quartz wall, an obvious feature of the face. This gully develops a a little
to the right of the lowest point of the huge ramp.

Hope Street   42 metres   Severe   (22.10.55)
Exposed, with some unsound rock. From the top of the wet evil gully below
the large quartz wall, ascend the grass slope on the left to its top. Start at a
short chimney right of some blocks.
1 6m. Climb the chimney to a belay block.
2 24m. 4a. Right of the block, make an awkward step onto a perched
block; then traverse right below an overhang with a wide crack. Surmount
the crack and steepish rock above, and move left at the top to a belay
block in a small niche.
3 12m. Go up left, then right to a grassy ledge, from where scrambling
leads to the top of the crag.

★Learning to Fly   34 metres   E3 5c   (28.7.91)
Bold and technical climbing in a fantastic position, taking the centre of the
compact slabby wall above and to the left of the large quartz-streaked wall
of Ffenestr y Graig. Start from the horizontal tree on pitch 3 of *Hopsit*
(better reached by abseil from a 3-metre spike directly above the route;
this is situated just left of the grassy exit from the top of *Quartz Buttress* and
Keel Haul). Protection is rather spaced, but good when it arrives. From the
tree, move up to gain a huge flake on the left. From the top of the flake,
step right and move up to a small ledge (good *Rock 4*). Continue straight
up to good holds beneath a slight bulge (perfect *Rock 7*), and pull directly
over the bulge to a peg and good holds. Move diagonally left beneath the
top headwall to a niche, and exit right to gain the top.

Hopsit   78 metres   Hard Severe   (31.3.56)
A vegetated route, with some dubious rock, taking the obvious
chimney-crack in the wet corner to the left of the large quartz wall. Start
directly below the corner.
1 9m. Climb the wall immediately to the right of the corner, and move
right to another corner with a spike belay.
2 24m. 4b. Enter the main corner by a grassy ramp up left (old peg),
and climb its wide crack awkwardly to the vegetated rake on the left.
3 27m. 4b. On the right wall is a tree growing out at right-angles: gain
this by traversing out right via a crack. Climb a grassy ramp rightwards to
a corner, gain the top of a pedestal, and move up and then right to steep
heather which leads to another corner.
4 18m. Climb a vegetated groove to a grassy rake on the left, which is
followed to the top. Chockstone belay.

The Whisper   82 metres   Hard Very Severe   (30.9.69)
Very poor rock on pitch 1. Start as for *Hopsit*.
1 23m. 5a. Follow *Hopsit* and use the spike as a runner; then climb the
groove above on poor rock to an old peg. Gain a ramp rising leftwards, and
and ascend steep grass to a good stance in a corner.
2 23m. 5a. Move right to the arête, step right around it, and make an
airy rising traverse across the wall to the small stance and peg belay on
Quartz Buttress.
3 21m. 5a. Climb the chimney-crack to a quartz overhang. Pull over it
and immediately move right for 3 metres to an old peg below a quartz
corner. Climb this corner to a good ledge and belay below an
overhanging corner.
4 15m. 4c. Take the right arête of the overhanging corner to a grassy
ramp, which leads to the top.

Quartz Wall   118 metres   E1   (21.9.78)
The obvious diagonal weakness onto the big quartz wall from the corner
on the right.
1 21m. *First Visit* pitch 1.
2 21m. 5a. Follow pitch 2 of *First Visit* to the move left onto a ledge,
where there are good nut belays.
3 17m. 5a. Climb a wide corner-crack above until a line leftwards across
the big quartz wall can be followed to a small stance on *The Whisper*
traverse. Nut belays.
4 35m. 5c. Make a slightly rising traverse left to the arête, move round
into a groove, and climb the good rock on its right edge to a ledge where
the arête steepens. Gain a scoop on the right and make a difficult move
over a bulge above. Easier ground follows, finishing left of a
chimney/crack. Stance in a corner on the right.
5 24m. Go left to a groove and climb it to the top.

First Visit   84 metres   Hard Very Severe   (22.10.55)
The obvious corner immediately right of the big quartz wall. Start as for
The Whisper and *Hopsit*.

1 21m. Follow *Hopsit* and use the spike as a runner; then make a vegetated descending traverse rightwards below the steep quartz wall to the corner.
2 30m. 5a. The corner groove is gained by a steep entry from the right. Climb the groove until the right wall steepens; then make a difficult move left onto a ledge. Climb the chimney above the ledge, overhanging at first, to a large grassy ledge on the right.
3 24m. Follow vegetated ledges to their right extremity. Stance shared with *Plankwalk* and *Keel Haul*.
4 9m. 4a. Climb up and right, taking the line of least resistance, to the arête. Descend steep vegetation on the right.

☆☆**Quartizone** 39 metres E6 †   (9.6.95)
An extremely impressive route, taking a merciless line up the centre of the quartz wall. A must for the connoisseur of the sombre, high-grade Welsh classics. Scramble up the gully; then climb a short wall (good wire belay on the left).
1 24m. 6b. Climb a thin line of weakness in the wall centre (small spike runners) until a long reach gains a downward-pointing flake and a peg runner. Proceed direct up the leaning wall (bold) to pull over onto a glacis. Climb the definite crack above (good gear) before tackling the committing wall. Good spaced holds and plenty of nerve should lead to the traversing ledge of *Quartz Wall* and its nut belay on the left.
2 15m. 6b. Climb up for 3 metres onto a ledge beneath a bare wall. Fix plentiful runners; then execute a very difficult sequence to grope up into the niche on the left. Move up (junction with *Quartz Wall*), swing right, and pull up to take a belay in the slanting break above. Either abseil from here, or scramble up leftwards to exit as for *Hopsit* or *Quartz Buttress*.

The next seven routes start roughly level with the start of *Hopsit*, but from a large grass ledge on the right of the evil wet gully. This ledge is approached from the right up steep vegetated terraces starting in the gully which contains the striking tower of Dinas Llywelyn. The ledge is identified by a large cave-like opening just above it.

Cat o' Nine Tails 34 metres E2 5c   (10.6.79)
The arête immediately right of *First Visit*. Start at the left-hand extremity of the grassy ledge. Climb the wall, 2 metres right from the arête, to a niche (peg runner). The arête is gained with difficulty in 3 metres via a ledge. Go up left to another ledge and, still with difficulty, traverse right around a bulge. Climb slabs and make a final hard move up the arête. Go up easily to the large grassy ledge atop pitch 2 of *First Visit* and *Quartz Buttress*, and finish as for the latter.

Quartz Buttress 72 metres Hard Very Severe   (24.9.66)
Some dubious rock. Start from the grassy terrace, 8 metres left of the cave.
1 12m. Climb diagonally up right to a grassy bay and belay at its top.
2 15m. 4c. Climb the left edge of the bay and then the wall above to a large grassy ledge.

3 9m. 5a. From the left end of the ledge, step left and climb the steep wall and then a quartz corner to a small stance and old pegs.
4 21m. 4c. Climb the chimney crack above, over a quartz overhang, and follow in the same line up a ramp to nut belays below a steep crack.
5 15m. 4c. Climb the crack above to easy ground.

★**Powder Monkey**   70 metres   E2   (29.8.78)
Left of *Plankwalk* pitch 1, an obvious crack slants leftwards. Pitch 2 (only fair protection) is a corner topped by a small overhang below the crux of *Plankwalk*.
1 32m. 5b. Follow *Plankwalk* to below the overhang, and move left to a ledge below the left-slanting crack. Climb the crack with difficulty to a sloping ledge, and continue to an awkward exit. Belay on the grassy terrace above on the left, below two steep corners.
2 38m. 5c. Climb the left-hand corner to a peg (out of sight from below), from which difficult moves follow to gain the slab on the left. Continue with steep sustained climbing up the wall above to the block on *Plankwalk*; then finish as for *Plankwalk* via the fingery wall diagonally up left to the gully on the left.

★**Hard Rain**   80 metres   E2   (12.7.78)
A fine finishing-pitch up the wall between *Plankwalk* and *Keel Haul*.
1 34m. 5a. Climb to below the overhang as for *Plankwalk*. Follow the steep groove continuation through the overhang to a big terrace, and move left to the foot of two steep corners.
2 17m. 4c. Climb the right-hand corner until it fades; then move right and go up to a ledge at the foot of the awkward ramp on pitch 2 of *Keel Haul*. Good spike belay.
3 29m. 5c. Move left onto the block of *Plankwalk*, gain a thin crack in the wall above, and climb it to a peg below an overhang. Gain a shallow niche above, and move out left with difficulty to easier ground.

★**Plankwalk**   74 metres   Hard Very Severe   (24.9.66)
The big smooth wall is an outstanding feature of Ffenestr y Graig, and this fine route takes the line of least resistance across it. Start just right of the cave, at a ramp formed by a huge flake.
1 34m. 4c. Climb the ramp and then the continuation groove above, which slants right beneath an overhang, to a grassy ledge. Go up easy vegetated ground to a sloping terrace.
2 40m. 5b. Take a weakness on the right; then go up left until a long, slightly rising traverse left can be made to gain a prominent small squarish block in the centre of the wall. Make some delicate moves left and up, then left again to reach the left edge of the wall. Move leftwards, and then climb an easy gully/groove to the top.

★★★**Keel Haul**   70 metres   E2   (27.9.69)
[Photo page 80b.] A classic of great character, which ploughs a line through the overhangs right of *Plankwalk*. Start at an arête to the right of the start of *Plankwalk*.

Craig Llywelyn

1 Vulcan   HVS
2 Acheron   HVS
3 Kaisepakte   E1
4 The Mule   E1
5 Doom   VS
6 Italia 90   E2
7 Northerner   E2
8 Midlander   VS
9 The Big Cleft   HVS
10 Man of Kent   VS
11 The Magic Dragon   HVS
12 Click   VS
13 Jugs Groove   E3
14 Mad Ray   E5

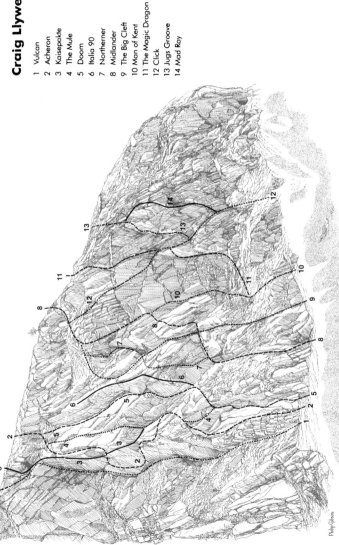

Philip Gibson

Ffenster y Graig

1	Hope Street	S
2	Hopsit	HS
3	Learning to Fly	E3
4	The Whisper	HVS
5	Quartizone	E6
6	Quartz Wall	E1
7	First Visit	HVS
8	Quartz Buttress	HVS
9	Powder Monkey	E2
10	Hard Rain	E2
11	Plankwalk	HVS
12	Keel Haul	E2
13	Sybarite	HVS
14	Spartan	E2
15	Heretic	E2
16	Quartz Vein	VS

Dinas Llywelyn

17	King Edward's Army	HVS

Philip Gibson

1 30m. 5b. Move just right of the arête and climb a leftward-slanting crack to a ledge on the arête. Climb the steep arête above to gain a shallow groove, and follow this to the large grassy terrace on *Plankwalk*.
2 40m. 5b. Take a weakness on the right; then climb up left until a slightly rising traverse left can be made to a good spike runner beneath a short rightward-slanting ramp (5 metres to the right of the squarish block of *Plankwalk*). Climb the ramp awkwardly to a small corner beneath the small roof, swing out right beneath the roof to some old pegs, and make a long reach to the spike above the overhang. Climb for 2 metres above this and move left to a good nut runner. Climb directly up the wall above to a ledge and continue to a large block overhang. Traverse up left to the arête and gain the ledge above.
Descent is by traversing grassy ledges to the left until bilberry ledges lead down to the ramp.

Gornik 39 metres Severe (24.5.69)
A poor climb, but the second pitch is the easiest escape from the big sloping grassy terrace. Start beneath a corner to the right of the arête of *Keel Haul*.
1 30m. 4a. Go easily up grass to a steep ramp which forms the left wall of the corner. Climb the ramp to a grass ledge at the top, move a few metres right, and continue up the wall above to reach the big sloping terrace.
2 9m. 4a. *First Visit* pitch 4.

About 60 metres above and to the right of the preceding routes is a distinctive wall marked with bands of white quartz. Left of this wall is a corner, with overhangs above, reached by steep scrambling with the odd V Diff move to the right of *Gornik* (or, perhaps less worryingly, by abseil from above). The corner can be quitted easily by moving out left above *Keel Haul* etc. This escape is known as *Highway*. The corner marks a starting-point for the next five routes.

Ceramic Chimney 21 metres Severe (10.11.57)
An obvious chimney on the left of the corner, formed by a precariously balanced tower of blocks.
1 12m. Climb the chimney to a stance.
2 9m. Move up right until clear of the overhang; then follow easy rocks above.

Sybarite 40 metres Hard Very Severe (5 pts aid) † (18.4.74)
The overlapping corner to the left of *Spartan*. Climb the corner using two pegs; then go up free into a niche with a downward-pointing flake on the right. Use a sling to place a small thread on the right-hand rib, and use this to gain the chimney/groove on the right. Climb the groove to stepped overhangs (peg runner); go over the first step, and traverse left to a ledge on the left arête. Finish up the wall (sling used to rest near the top).

Spartan   45 metres   E2   (4.6.66)
A strenuous and technical line up the reddish wall beneath a roof a little to
the right of the corner.
1 27m. 5c. Awkward moves lead upwards and rightwards to a corner
under the left-hand side of the roof. Traverse right under the roof to its end
and move up with difficulty to a small ledge (old peg). Traverse delicately
right to a spike runner. Go right again and move over a bulge to gain a
chimney.
2 18m. 4c. Climb the chimney to the top.

☆**Crimea**   40 metres   E5 6a (1 pt aid) †   (9.6.95)
Probably *the* line of the *Spartan* slab. After a problematic entry, the route
takes on the obvious crack in its upper centre. Climb rightwards for 3
metres beneath roofs, as for *Heretic*, but move up to a poor spike runner.
Above in the roof is a small pod. Use a *Friend* in the pod for aid (this pod
could readily take a handjam — but there would be no other runners!), and
so reach better holds and a good spike on the wall above. Bear slightly
rightwards to small ledges on the slab (stance possible). Climb the slab
above to the leftward-trending crack and climb this strenuously, and then,
where it widens and becomes mucky, the difficult wall on the right to gain
easier slabs and soon the top.

Heretic   43 metres   E2   (20.9.78)
1 23m. 5c. Traverse right below loose overhangs to the arête. Climb the
arête (difficult); then follow a groove diagonally leftwards to a foot-ledge
just below the *Spartan* slab.
2 20m. 5c. Up to the left is a blank groove with a sideways spike in it.
Climb the groove and the overhang above, and move right to finish up a
crack.

Quartz Vein   39 metres   Very Severe   (5.10.69)
A climb which breaches the large quartz band to the right of *Spartan*. The
rock in places is appalling. Start about 30 metres down and to the right of
Spartan. Belay on a large block below an overhanging chimney on the
right.
1 12m. 4b. Climb rightwards past the chimney; then go up and back left
to beneath a steep groove.
2 27m. 4c. Climb the groove, and move across right to a small ledge.
Climb steeply for about 3 metres, move left to gain a grassy ramp leading
to a small cave, and then follow the groove on the right. Finish up a
chimney.

Dinas Llywelyn
A striking tower in the gully between Ffenestr y Graig and Creigiau Sawdl
Efa.

King Edward's Army
                        46 metres   Hard Very Severe (3 pts aid) † (25.4.75)
A line up the front edge. Often wet. Start at a smooth slab below the tower.

1 23m. 5a. From a point 3 metres right of the slab base, climb up left to the arête, and follow it, via a grassy ledge, to an old peg. Continue straight up to the top of the slab, using a peg for resting. Boulder ledge above.

2 23m. 5b. Take the overhanging wall above using two aid pegs. Go up left to a quartz rib, climb the overhanging rock above, and move right to a chimney that leads to the top.

Creigiau Sawdl Efa

An area of short steep walls to the right of the tower of Dinas Llywelyn. *Bubble Wall* follows the highest of the steep walls on a level with the Dinas Llywelyn tower. An obvious horizontal grassy ledge runs under this wall.

Bubble Wall 24 metres Hard Severe 4b   (27.5.56)
Start from the extreme left of the grass ledge and climb the wall, trending up right to a break.

From the large boulder on the right of the horizontal grassy ledge a corner leads up to the top: this is **Ronkle Boot Chimney** (9 metres Difficult 1.3.58).

The lowest of the steep walls, near to the stream, has a very prominent large overhanging section of rock, forming a huge cavern. A rib and chimney-line to the left of this is taken by:

The Little Red Helmet 67 metres Severe   (18.7.70)
A vegetated route 60 metres left of the huge cavern. To the left is an open grassy gully. On the right of the rib is a slab that the route takes to the bilberry terrace above. Above this, a chimney and an arête are followed to the top.

Where Eagles Dare 30 metres Hard Very Severe   (17.5.70)
An obvious groove with a small tree at the top, immediately right of the large overhanging section of rock. Start from the stance at the top of pitch 1 of *Whirligig*.
1 18m. 5a. Climb to an arête starting from the left-hand end of the ledge; then make a rising traverse left to below the obvious groove guarded by a bulge. Move awkwardly over the bulge and climb the groove above to the tree.
2 12m. 4c. Climb up left and follow a steep crack to finish.

Whirligig 62 metres Severe   (20.9.69)
An obvious weakness weaves around the front of the buttress. Start at the lowest point of the buttress, on the right of a grassy ramp that goes up to the overhangs.
1 21m. Climb, trending right at 9 metres; then return left to a ledge below the overhangs (good spike belay).
2 23m. 4a. Gain the arête on the right and traverse right to a grassy bay. Move down to the base of a grassy ramp on the right and make a tricky

step onto a slab. Continue moving right to vegetation; then go up left to a small stance in a niche.
3 18m. Climb the steep corner behind the belay, move right to avoid bad rock, and then climb direct up a chimney to the top of the buttress via a chimney-crack.

Creigiau Camddwr
The hillside opposite Ffenestr y Graig and Craig Llywelyn is dotted with small buttresses and crags. These provide immense potential for boulderers who can cope with the risk of a 150-metre roll down the mountain. One of the more obvious crags, a tower opposite *Plankwalk*, supports two routes.

Whistling in the Dark 9 metres E3 5b †   (9.9.2001)
Take fingerholds straight up the centre of the face of the tower to a small expanding flake. Trend leftwards and finish steeply. Unprotected.

Strolling in the Park 9 metres E2 5b †   (9.9.2001)
The right-hand arête of the tower; more technical than it appears and with rock beneath.

Aran Fawddwy   Mawddwy Height   OS Ref 863 224

There is just one recorded route, which is quite good and entertaining, ascending the east face overlooking Craiglyn Dyfi. The route takes a line up the best of the broken buttresses directly beneath the summit of the mountain. Please refer to the access notes on page 35.

★**Christmas Retreat** 160 metres Very Difficult   (26.12.65)
At the base of the most continuous buttress is a large overhang approximately 60 metres above the south end of the lake. Start just to the right of the overhang.
1 30m. Follow the easiest line onto the slab on the right. Climb up the right edge of the slab, with a tricky move at the top, to a grassy stance with block belay.
2 24m. Climb rightwards to blocks and go over these to take a stance between two massive boulders.
3 27m. Go over a hole on the left; then work diagonally left over easy ground to below a steep tower.
4 27m. Climb a crack on the right edge of the tower; then move left to the top of the tower. Go up right to a wide crack in yet another tower above.
5 15m. The crack is taken with increasing difficulty to a grassy ledge with a spike belay below a slab.
6 37m. Climb the left edge of the slab and then easy ground to the top of the buttress.

Aran Benllyn   Lake-end Height   OS Ref 866 243

The east face of Aran Benllyn comprises sound rock walls separated by steep vegetation. Two of these stand out. The first is a clean, compact, 30-metre-high wall, which tapers towards its base and faces predominantly east, though its northern (right-hand) end backs to the north-east. This wall is situated 90 metres below the summit and is known as Citadel Wall. The second, about 20 metres high, is to the right and below Citadel Wall, and consists of overhanging arêtes and grooves; this is currently unclimbed. Please refer to the access notes on page 35.

Citadel Wall

[Photodiagram page 104a.] An arête with a noticeable niche close to the top defines the boundary between the east and north-east-facing sections. Features on the east-facing wall consist of vague cracklines, the left-most one starting half-way up from vegetation.

The bottom of *The Grey Citadel* is reached by gaining the great vegetated ramp which cuts diagonally up leftwards across the east face of the mountain. Follow the ramp for approximately one-third of its height until directly beneath Citadel Wall at a small cairn.

The other three routes all start from ledges at the top of pitch 4 of *The Grey Citadel* and this route could be used to reach them. However, the better approach is by abseil from directly above: go approximately 75 metres south along the ridge from the summit of Aran Benllyn; then descend the east face easily for some 75 metres to a grassy area and a cairn. There is a good abseil rock spike below the cairn.

★**681 Troop**   30 metres   Hard Very Severe 5a   (6.8.95)
A sustained route following the central cracklines. Good protection. Start at the short steep corner on the left at the base of the wall. Climb awkwardly up the corner to easy ground, and then the steep crack in the wall above to a horizontal break. Move left to gain a rightward-curving crack, and follow this with an awkward exit onto a big ledge. Nut belays. An easy horizontal traverse left leads to the top.

★★**King's Squad**   37 metres   Hard Very Severe 5a   (22.7.95)
A direct line up the wall about 5 metres left of the niche on *The Grey Citadel*. Good, sustained climbing with good protection. Start from the lowest point of the wall at a crack with a peg. Climb the crack to big holds. Continue up the crack until it finishes and the wall steepens; then step right to gain a little groove. Climb this and trend slightly left to a horizontal break. Take the wall above to a ledge, step right, and climb steeply on good holds trending up rightwards. Then go straight up to a good ledge at the top of the wall. Nut belays. Finish by taking the little quartzy wall above to the abseil spike.

★The Grey Citadel   106 metres   Hard Very Severe   (27.12.69)
The last pitch takes Citadel Wall itself; the climbing beneath this is much easier and is just a pleasant way up to the wall using the best of the rock available. Start approximately 60 metres below the wall on the great ramp, at a small cairn.
1 18m. Climb a small rib; then go diagonally right over vegetation to a grassy ledge with a spike belay.
2 15m. Above on the right are two corners. Climb the first one, exit right at the top, and then climb up to a grassy ledge.
3 15m. A steep pleasant wall leads to a flake belay.
4 21m. Follow a steep little wall and a wide chimney to beneath Citadel Wall. Belays on the left.
5 37m. 5a. Climb a short way up left to a ledge. Work back right taking the obvious traverse-line to a short crack. Climb this to a good pocket and make a difficult move right; then go up to better holds and continue direct to a vague horizontal ledge. Go right along this to a niche on the arête. Climb the crack above the niche to a ledge, and then continue up a groove to the top.

★★Final X   37 metres   E1 5b   (23.9.95)
The edge between the east and north-east faces gives technical climbing in a fine position. Start below the steep groove just right of the start of *King's Squad*. Climb the groove to big holds beneath the right edge of the wall, and then delicately up the edge (peg runner) to the niche on *The Grey Citadel*. Climb the crack above, but avoid the groove on the right by taking the leftward-slanting crack in the wall on the left. Finish on good holds direct to the big platform at the top of the wall. Good nut belays. Finish by taking the little quartzy wall above to the abseil spike (as for *King's Squad*).

Gist Ddu[1]   Black Chest   OS Ref 873 255

Character and Topography
A high mountain crag, facing east and overlooking Llyn Lliwbran. It is vegetated in places and takes some time to dry out, but the rock is some of the best in the region. The crag has a remote feel to it and will appeal to the climber who wants to get away from the crowds while still enjoying routes of great quality. The main section of the crag, Central Buttress, has an impressive series of corners and arêtes on the right, finishing with the huge clean arête of *Aardvark*. To the left are quite distinct leftward-slanting grooves and slabs finishing with the deep *Souwester Gully*. On either side of Central Buttress are vegetated areas of rock named the Left and Right Wings.

1 The name by which climbers have always known this crag. However, it is clearly shown on the OS maps as Craig y Llyn. Moel Ddu and its crag are more than a kilometre to the north, on the far side of Craig y Geifr.

Approach and Descent

Only the permitted path along the Aran ridge route may be used. This is described on page 35. The shortest approach is from the north end, from Llanuwchllyn on the B4403 (approximately five kilometres). When level with the crag below, descend to its foot keeping well clear of the steep areas.

Ways off Central Buttress are not obvious. The safest is by traversing left until a descent into *Souwester Gully* can be made, crossing this above its first hard pitches to vegetated ledges on the left, which lead to the bottom of the crag. Descent for the Left Wing routes is made by the next gully left of the one containing *Monolith*. A possibility on the right-hand side of the buttress, but recommended only when the crag is very dry, is to make two 45-metre abseils down *Sloose*: the first from the tree at its top, and the second from the jammed boulder; dubious abseil tapes are usually found under the boulder.

Left Wing

In a wide gully, the next one left of *Souwester Gully*, is a prominent, sharp-looking rib. This is *Monolith*. Above it, forming the right wall of the gully, are several slabs: the first (lowest) is grassy, but the rib at its left edge is clean and gives the line of *High and Dry*. The next slab is taken by *Jambiri*, which follows it on its right, just left of the grassy corner-chimney.

Stiff Lower Lip 55 metres Very Difficult (29.8.76)
Start at the left-hand end of the slab taken by *Jambiri*, below a large block.
1 46m. Climb a groove, first on the right, then on the left. Traverse to the right of the block to gain a ledge. Go up and leftwards to gain a rib and climb to its top. A slab leads to a ledge.
2 9m. Large blocks lead up to easy ground.

Stiff Upper Lip 46 metres Severe (29.8.76)
A line up the centre of the slab. Start just left of the start of *Jambiri*. Gain the right end of the small overhang above by zigzagging up the centre of the slab. Move left; then go up to climb a groove in a steeper wall above to finish.

Jambiri 45 metres Severe (24.9.72)
Start at the right-hand end of the slab just left of the grassy corner-chimney.
1 15m. Climb slabs, and make a move right over a block in the corner to gain a large ledge and belays.
2 15m. Go up slabs left of the corner; then move up left to a (once) cleaned area through vegetation. Belay in the corner.
3 15m. Climb the slabs and the ramp below an overhang to gain a cracked corner. Move back right, and take the slab above the overhang to finish.

High and Dry 52 metres Severe (24.9.72)
1 20m. Climb the rib on the right of the main slab to the overhang, move right, and then go up to vegetation. Just above this is a belay ledge.
2 20m. Take the slabby rib to the right. The small overhang is climbed direct. Pinnacle belays.
3 12m. The overhang with a crack in it has good holds. Finish easily.

Monolith   84 metres   Difficult   (6.9.70)
The striking knife-edge arête rising out of the base of the gully left of
Souwester Gully. Start on the left at the bottom of the arête.
1 34m. Trend rightwards along a break, and climb the arête to its top,
passing a small tree.
2 23m. Climb the broken wall on the left, trending left to a big pinnacle.
Climb a huge flake on its right and then go up to a wide ledge. Flake belay.
3 27m. Move 6 metres left to a huge detached block. Climb this by its right-
hand side, and then follow a groove which overlooks the gully. Belays above.

Monolith Direct   55 metres   Hard Severe   (1976)
Above the sharp arête, which is the start of *Monolith*, are two ribs.
Monolith Direct takes the right-hand rib. Start below the rib.
1 34m. 4b. Take the easiest line upwards to a slot on the ridge. Make an
awkward move left to the rib and climb it to a ledge.
2 21m. Climb a slab, then the right edge of a pinnacle, and finally the
crack and slab above.

Central Buttress   [Photodiagram centre-spread overleaf.]
Souwester Gully   90 metres   Severe   (1941)
The vegetated gully bounding the left side of Central Buttress usually has a
small stream down it and difficulties are mainly near the bottom.

Slab and Arête   61 metres   Very Difficult   (1941)
Steep vegetation just right of the gully bed leads up to a wall with a crack in it.
1 11m. Work awkwardly up the crack to a stance.
2 17m. Move up left to a large tree; then go right to the base of an arête
and belay in a crevice.
3 27m. Climb the arête to a grassy ledge.
4 6m. Finish up the arête.

On the left-hand side of the buttress is a large horizontal terrace, which can
be gained from either end by steep scrambling.

Abdication   61 metres   Severe   (8.6.63)
At the centre of the terrace there is a slight change in level. Start at a
groove just to its right.
1 14m. The groove leads to a small overhang. Cross a slab on the left
and climb the corner to a grassy ledge above.
2 14m. Take the slab in the corner; then move left to a short chimney,
climb its left wall, and follow vegetation to a tree.
3 24m. In the wall behind the tree is a niche with a prominent flake. Gain
the niche and climb it for a way; then make a rising traverse left to the
arête of *Slab and Arête*.
4 9m. Finish straight up the arête.

★Box Trick   54 metres   Very Severe   (30.5.70)
A vague crackline slanting leftwards to the left-hand side of a scoop under a
large overhang. Start on the terrace, 5 metres right of the groove of *Abdication*.

Aran Benllyn

Citadel Wall

1 681 Troop   HVS
2 Kings Squad   HVS
3 Final X   E1
4 The Grey Citadel   HVS

Gist Ddu

Central Buttress

Philip Gibson.

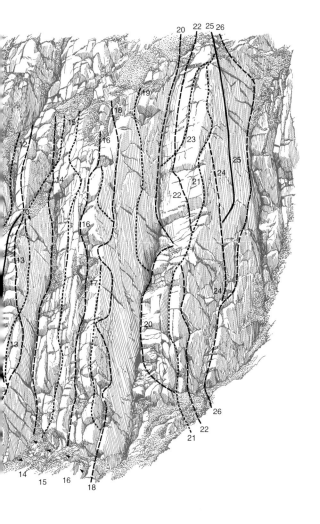

Voie Suisse (E1) Gist Ddu
Climber: Ian Warner   Photo: John Sumner

1 15m. Climb the wall, following the indefinite crackline, to a ledge with a triangular wedged block.
2 21m. 4b. Move up and then go delicately right across the scoopy slab beneath the overhang. Climb a corner, pull awkwardly over an overhang, and continue in the same line to a second overhang, which is surmounted with the aid of a small spike. Good ledges and belays above.
3 9m. Climb a steep groove behind the ledge to another ledge (tree belay).
4 9m. Follow the corner above the tree to finish.

Steel Breeze   55 metres   Very Severe †   (6.9.80)
Start on the terrace, 6 metres right of *Box Trick*.
1 15m. 4a. Climb the slabs direct on good incuts, past a clean V-niche, to a belay in a slanting groove-line, 5 metres below the overhang on *Box Trick*.
2 40m. 4b. Swing right across the right-hand wall and make an awkward move up the slabs. Move left, and climb the increasingly obvious thin crack trending diagonally up and left to a ledge. Step right up a short groove and scramble to a niche.

★★Obvious   66 metres   Severe   (29.8.70)
Pitches 2 and 3 take a long leftward-slanting groove above an overhang just beyond the right-hand end of the terrace. Start from a tree at the right-hand end of the terrace.
1 6m. Traverse right from the tree, just above the large overhang, to gain the base of the groove.
2 15m. Climb the groove (good holds keep appearing on the right wall) to a small ledge with nut belays.
3 18m. Continue up the groove, negotiating two overhangs, to a good ledge; a ramp comes into it from the right. Stance shared with *Devious* (pitch 3).
4 27m. 4a. Then, as for *Devious*, continue up the groove-line, which becomes more of a chimney. Finish up the short wall above.

Curl   63 metres   Hard Severe   (16.5.65)
A natural line, starting at the foot of a clean slab below an overhang, near the top of a steep vegetated ramp slanting up left to the horizontal terrace on the left-hand side of the buttress.
1 12m. Climb the steepening slab, working up right to a large flake belay.
2 24m. 4a. Move up to a chimney, and climb it with a difficult initial move to the ledge of *Devious*.
3 27m. 4a. *Devious* pitch 4.

Devious   67 metres   Severe   (1941)
Belays are difficult to find. Start a little to the right of *Curl*.
1 23m. Climb rightwards over ledges until under a light-coloured overhang. Gain the base of the chimney on the right by a delicate traverse, and climb it to a grassy ledge on the left. Old peg belay.
2 5m. Climb the slab above, or follow the wide crack on the right, to a chimney. Climb the chimney to a stance above.
3 12m. Go left along the terrace and climb to an open groove. Good ledge.

4 27m. 4a. Continue up the groove-line, which becomes more of a chimney. Finish up the short wall above.

★The Wing   39 metres   Hard Severe   (2.5.63)
A climb with some exciting moves through an overhang. Start from the stance at the top of *Devious* pitch 1.
1 30m. 4b. Climb the slab above on the right, as for *Devious*; then traverse right, following a ledge, until below a hanging edge of rock. Climb the corner to just below the hanging edge, and then take the narrow chimney on its right to a ledge. Finish up the chimney above, and move left along a large grassy ledge to belay.
2 9m. Move back right and continue in the same chimney-line to easier ground.

Grad   106 metres   Severe   (30.8.64)
A vegetated groove-line running the full height of the crag. Start down from and to the right of *Devious*, below the groove-line.
1 15m. Climb the groove to a stance on the right.
2 27m. Go up on the right of a large block to its top, and move left into a niche. Climb up to the foot of the chimney on pitch 1 of *Devious* and climb it to a stance on the left (old peg).
3 5m. *Devious* Pitch 2.
4 29m. Continue up the groove-line to an overhang, from where a move up to the right gains a grassy slab under another overhang. Climb the narrow chimney on its left to a grassy stance.
5 21m. Move 1 metre left and go straight up to a grass bay.
6 9m. Scrambling leads to the finish.

Black Eyes   119 metres   Severe   (9.3.73)
A wayward line following a weakness between *The Wing* and *Piledriver*. Some vegetation. Start at the base of the steep vegetated ramp that leads up to *Devious* and *Curl*, where a cleaned rib juts out of the vegetation directly below the weakness between the steep upper sections of *The Wing* and *Piledriver*.
1 40m. The rib leads to a large vegetated ledge (spike belay above under the overhangs).
2 21m. Traverse 8 metres left to a crack going diagonally left. Climb the crack and the groove above to a small ledge with nut belays.
3 14m. Climb a metre up the groove, move right, and then go down to gain a corner. Move right again to a small ledge and climb a short wall to a good belay ledge in a groove.
4 18m. Climb the groove and move right onto the face. Follow a line first right, then left, and go up to a belay ledge under an overhang.
5 26m. Move right for a short way and then go straight up to the foot of a steep wall. Make awkward moves left up a short groove to gain a slab (crux). Climb the slab to easier ground above and finish up a little wall. Jammed block belay.

The next seven routes are best gained from an easy traverse-line starting from the wet base of the big chimney/corner-line of *Sloose*.

Piledriver   78 metres   Very Severe   (2.5.63)
Two corners can be seen above a vegetated wall, the right-hand of which is immediately left of the clean arête of *Moai Man*. Start below and just left of the left-hand corner.
1 18m. Climb the vegetated wall to the base of the left-hand corner. Thread belay in the corner.
2 15m. 4b. Climb the corner, and make a move out to the left edge after a metre or so. After a move up, return to the corner and climb it to a flake belay on the left.
3 15m. 4c. Return right again to an undercut groove and climb it to a grassy ledge.
4 30m. Climb the corner above to finish.

☆☆**Blood of an Englishman**   30 metres   E4 6b †   (25.8.90)
The finely-structured, square-cut, right-hand corner provides a clean, highly technical, but very safe problem, reputedly a last great line! Start from the top of the first pitch of *Piledriver* (or *Moai Man*). Sustained and very thin bridging leads past a peg runner to some good finger-slots where the corner seam opens out a little. Continue more easily to a roof, surmount it, and climb the groove above to another bulge and a grass ledge on the left 3 metres higher. Work up easy cracks to ledges and a two-peg belay. A 50-metre abseil enables the deck to be reached.

★★**The Scarecrow**   73 metres   E1   (3.9.84)
Excellent climbing.
1 12m. 4a. *Moai Man* pitch 1.
2 20m. 5b. Go up and left to climb a steep groove to a ledge on the arête. Climb a short steep wall directly above the ledge (crux of *Moai Man*) and then step down right to a large flake.
3 20m. 5a. Directly above the flake is a thin crack. Climb this, after gaining it by an awkward move from the left. Follow the crack to a big vegetated ledge above.
4 21m. Climb the vegetated corner, and move out right, then back left.

★★**Moai Man**   73 metres   E1   (26.8.72)
A good climb up the left arête of *The Trench*. Start directly below the arête.
1 12m. 4a. Follow the arête to a ledge and a good nut belay in a horizontal crack.
2 43m. 5b. Go directly up the slab above to a small ledge on the arête. Move rightwards round the arête and make an awkward move up to gain a small ledge (old pegs). Climb a crack which trends back left to a ledge on the arête (good runner). Above is a wall; climb this with difficulty, trending slightly left. Continue up the arête with the odd awkward bulge to a large vegetated ledge. Old peg belays high up in the corner.
3 18m. 4b. Reach the arête left of the corner and climb its left wall to the top.

The Trench   78 metres   Very Severe   (1.5.63)
A vegetated route in the big corner left of *Sloose*. If vegetation runs up the
length of the first pitch the grade would be much higher. Start by
scrambling up grassy ledges to the base of the corner.
1 21m. 4c. Climb the undercut base of the corner-crack and continue up
until it disappears. Make awkward moves on dubious flakes, and pull over
a final bulge using a pocket hold above. Move up to a ledge.
2 27m. 4b. Continue up the vegetated corner-crack via two large
overhanging blocks. At the top of the corner, traverse out left to a large
vegetated ledge.
3 30m. Ascend vegetation to an overhanging corner. Climb this on the
right and belay above.

★Die Fledermaus   91 metres   Very Severe   (26.10.85)
The big groove-line on the right wall of *The Trench*. Start a few metres right
of the corner, from where scrambling leads up right into a corner below
the right-hand of two chimney-lines. Huge flake belay.
1 35m. 4b. Climb the steep chimney on big holds to its top and step left
to gain the left wall of the groove-line, which is climbed to a small ledge
under an overhanging block.
2 21m. 4c. Go over the block to a ledge under an overhanging wall.
From the left end of the ledge, climb a crack for a short way to a loose
block and move out right to a rightward-slanting groove going through an
overhang. Pull awkwardly up it and move up to a good ledge.
3 35m. 4b. Continue up the broken chimney-line above to a niche.
Traverse left, and climb the centre of the clean wall with a difficult move over
a bulge and a move left at the top. Scramble up heather to good belays.

Grass   87 metres   Hard Severe   (1963)
A fairly direct line with some vegetation (though not as bad as it sounds!)
up the buttress between *The Trench* and *Sloose*. Start below a small corner
above some steep heather, 6 metres left of the start of *Scimitar*.
1 9m. 4b. Climb the corner, awkward, and then a groove on the right to
a stance above vegetation below a steep corner. Thread belay.
2 21m. 4a. Move left past the corner and climb to a grassy ledge below
a steep wall. Step right onto a large foothold; then go up and climb a slab
on the left, and continue direct to a stance below a corner (nut belay).
3 24m. Climb the corner to vegetation, traverse right easily, and return
left to a stance and a large spike belay in a corner below an overhang.
4 18m. 4a. Move to the left of the spike; then go up and left again to a
vegetated crack, which leads to a stance with a spike belay.
5 15m. 4a. Move right and climb to a ledge. Climb the steep little wall
above and scramble up heather ledges to a good nut belay beneath a
little wall.

Live Is Life   93 metres   Hard Very Severe   (29.9.85)
Start as for *Scimitar*, below the overhung corner on the arête.
1 40m. 5a. Climb the corner for a few metres and then the left wall to
some large flakes below a short undercut arête. Gain the arête with

difficulty and follow a crackline up its left-hand side to a ledge. Climb the bulging arête above to sloping ledges. Good nut crack.
2 27m. 5a. Continue up the arête for a few metres to the roof, move onto the right wall, and climb to an old peg below the start of the curving flake of *Scimitar*. Traverse left to stand on a small ramp on the arête, and climb the arête for a metre to small ledges and nut belays.
3 26m. 4c. Continue up the steep arête above to a sloping ledge, move left, and climb a steep little wall to finish up vegetation.

★★Scimitar   82 metres   Hard Very Severe   (17.5.70)
Bold climbing on the huge slabby wall left of *Sloose*. An extremely fine fourth pitch (when dry). Start at the bottom left edge of the wall, below an overhung groove.
1 6m. Climb the groove to a stance, and belay below the roof.
2 27m. 4b. Continue to the roof; then move right and climb a vague crackline up the wall before trending left at the top to a ledge on the arête.
3 9m. 4c. Step back down right onto the wall and climb a crack until it is possible to move back left onto the arête. Belay on sloping ledges.
4 34m. 5a. Continue up the arête to the overhang. Step rightwards round the arête to a crack in the wall. The crack soon disappears and a line of weakness is followed to the base of a curving flake. Climb just right of the flake to a small ledge, and move up with difficulty to gain the big ledge above.
5 6m. 4a. Follow a ramp to the right and so reach the top of the wall.

The next five routes are reached by scrambling up steep grass on the right of *Sloose*'s initial wet gutter to some jammed blocks under an overhang.

★Deadline   37 metres   E1 5b   (30.9.72)
A fine thin crack in the impressive wall between the upper sections of *Sloose* and *Scimitar*; often wet. Start from the huge jammed boulder at the top of the first pitch of *Sloose*. From the top of the boulder, gain the thin crackline in the wall on the left and climb this over two small overlaps. Slightly easier climbing follows, continuing in the same line to the roof at the top of the wall.

★★Sloose   73 metres   Hard Very Severe   (3.4.63)
A route of quality, and its final pitch, when dry, must rate as one of the great corner pitches of Wales. Avoid the initial, very wet, 18-metre gutter by coming in from the right beneath an overhang by some jammed boulders.
1 27m. 4a. Gain the chimney in the corner by traversing left under the overhang. Climb the chimney, and move up behind the huge jammed boulder to a ledge on the right.
2 46m. 5a. Make an easy rising traverse up left and climb the chimney in the corner over a bulge (dubious blocks) to the corner-crack above. Climb this on good holds to where it becomes off-width and holds diminish. Persevere with the crack to better holds on the right wall and continue up the corner with slightly easier climbing to the tree at the top.

Lifeline   46 metres   E1   5a   (29.8.76)
Start below the top pitch of *Sloose* and follow it to just above the dubious
blocks; then take a traverse-line out right to a groove and crackline in the
middle of the wall. Climb the crack to the top.

★★★**Aardvark**   82 metres   Hard Very Severe   (25.9.66)
A superb route, a Meirionnydd classic, taking the great arête right of
Sloose. Start, as for *Sloose*, from some jammed blocks under an overhang
above its initial wet gutter.
1 37m. 5a. Gain the niche on the right using a small wedged block as a
foothold. Make some difficult moves up the steep crack above to gain a
sloping ledge. Move left to the base of a groove, and climb it to a move
right at its top; then go up to the large grassy ledge.
2 30m. 5a. Climb the slabs, trending right to a spike on the arête under
the big overlap. Move rightwards round the arête and climb an awkward
crack before moving back onto the arête at a small ledge under a bulge.
Climb the bulge and the groove above to perched blocks.
3 15m. Move leftwards and finish up the arête.
Variation
Shadow of Doubt   Hard Very Severe †   (5.96)
2a 30m. 5a. Pull through the first overlap as for *Voie Suisse*; then go
slightly right to join *Aardvark* at the second overlap. Instead of moving up
the groove, go directly up the arête to twin cracks and then climb easier
ground leftwards to the abseil tree.

★★★**Voie Suisse**   83 metres   E1   (21.7.84)
A brilliant route, one of the best of its grade in the area, the top pitch of
which takes the fine clean wall between *Sloose* and *Aardvark*.
1 37m. 4c. Climb the stepped groove and arête a few metres right of the
start of *Aardvark* to the big ledge.
2 46m. 5b. Move up the slab to the break in the first overlap, pull over to
the left, trend slightly left, and go up to a peg. Make some delicate moves,
again slightly up left, to reach good holds beneath the second overlap.
Step left (3 metres from the corner of *Sloose*) and pull over the second
overlap to the right through a weakness; then move up to a flake/block.
Move up a metre from the block; then step left and climb a thin crackline
to the top.

Adrenalin Trip   49 metres   E1   (6.9.80)
A direct line up the left-hand side of the big wall to the right of *Aardvark*.
Protection is rather poor on the upper section of the first pitch. Start from
the top of pitch 1 of *Ethical Voyage*, below a (once)-cleaned area of wall.
1 34m. 5a. Climb the wall with increasing difficulty, following a vague
weakness which gradually gets closer to the arête and joins *Aardvark*'s
second pitch for the final metres.
2 15m. *Aardvark* pitch 3.

★★Hungry Hearts   46 metres   E5 6a   (18.8.84)
A bold and sustained wall climb; superb when clean. Climb the first 9
metres of *Adrenalin Trip*; then make a rising traverse right to the centre of
the wall (thread and peg). Climb the wall direct past a ledge and finish up
easier ground.

Ethical Voyage   63 metres   Hard Very Severe †   (6.78)
The crack on the right-hand side of the big wall to the right of *Aardvark*.
Start at the base of a vegetated, stepped ramp rising rightwards just round
the arête from *Aardvark*.
1 15m. Ascend the stepped ramp to a good ledge beneath a steep
corner.
2 15m. Start in the corner; then climb its right edge to a ledge in the
middle of the wall. Go rightwards along the ledge to belay in a cave.
3 15m. 5a. Move back left to the foot of a crack in the wall above, and
climb this to another cave belay.
4 18m. Go back to the wall; then ascend the gully.

A girdle traverse of the main crag has been done at Hard Very Severe. Its
main interest is in the section crossing the *Scimitar* slab and *Sloose*. The rest
is of a much easier standard with a fair amount of vegetation.

Right Wing
Looked at from below the big arête of *Aardvark*, a clean arête stands out
from the steep vegetation and slabby walls which constitute the Right Wing.
Tamburlaine takes the clean arête. Descent is to the right, over the top of the
crag and down easy vegetated slopes, then scree to the base of the crag.

Tamburlaine   69 metres   Hard Severe   (30.8.70)
Gain water worn slabs leading up to the arête, which is undercut at its
base.
1 21m. Ascend wet slabs to a clean, steep crack. Follow the crack to a
grassy ledge on the left.
2 14m. Climb a rib for 6 metres to a corner, traverse right to a break in
the arête, and move round it to a grassy cave.
3 34m. 4b. Move back left to the arête and climb steeply on good holds
for 10 metres; then gain the left flank of the arête via a weakness using
holds on the left. Climb the arête to the top.

Craig y Geifr   Crag (of) the Goats   OS Ref 874 270

Another east-facing crag lying on the north end of the Benllyn Ridge. It does
not exceed 30 metres in height but is of sound compact rock with strangely
little vegetation. The crag is approached as for Gist Ddu (see page 103).

Descend from the main ridge path three kilometres south of Llanuwchllyn.
Access from the Cwm Croes road is strictly forbidden.

☆**The Highlander**   17 metres   E1 5b †   (25.8.90)
The obvious diagonal crack at the far left end of the crag, just right of the
stone wall.

Tilt   18 metres   Severe 4a   (11.4.71)
On the left-hand side of the crag is a horizontal ledge, above which is a
very steep smooth wall. Start below the right-hand end of the ledge. An
awkward scoop on the right leads to the ledge. Move left along this to the
ramp-like corner, and climb the ramp to finish.

The Nest   12 metres   Severe 4a   (11.4.71)
The hanging slab on the right of the horizontal ledge. Start at a large
flake. Gain the top of the flake and then the ledge on the right. The
smooth slab above leads to the arête.

Left-Hand Break   21 metres   Very Difficult   (11.4.71)
The first obvious weakness to the right of *The Nest*.
1 12m. Climb over the undercut base; then go up to a stance below an
overhanging block.
2 9m. Move left below the block until an escape can be made.

Thin Man   36 metres   Difficult   (28.2.71)
A worthwhile climb, taking the next easy break right of *Left-Hand Break*.
Start by some massive jammed blocks.
1 12m. Climb up 6 metres to a vertical chimney in a corner (chockstone
runner at its base). Climb the chimney to a ledge and a boulder belay.
2 9m. Move right to another boulder belay on a ledge.
3 15m. Gain a wide horizontal crack in the slab on the left and follow it
to the top.

☆☆**Jake**   21 metres   E1 5b †   (25.8.90)
The excellent, clean, overhanging crack left of *Grit* gives dynamic climbing
on good holds.

Grit   15 metres   Hard Very Severe 5b   (11.4.71)
On the right-hand end of the crag are three obvious cracklines in a steep
wall. The middle crack is followed strenuously, with the crux in the middle.

☆**Allanon Lives**   20 metres   E2 5c †   (25.8.90)
A direct line up the middle of the wall right of *Grit*. Difficult initial moves
lead to a bold middle section and then a faint crackline.

☆**Elwood**   20 metres   Very Severe 4c †   (25.8.90)
The obvious crack right again gives positive climbing to an interesting exit
at the top.

Pardon Me for Breathing (E2) Craig y Mwn
Climber: Graham Iles   Photo: Jennifer Tweedy

Waterworld (E3 ~ first ascent) Pistyll Rhaeadr
Climber: Martin Crocker   Photo: Carl Ryan

Y Berwynion   The Snow-dusted Peaks

Craig y Mwn   Crag (of) the Buzzard

Lying on the southern slopes of the Berwynion, the Craig y Mwn complex is home to the famed Pistyll Rhaeadr, the largest waterfall in Wales. In summer, this superb feature attracts droves of sightseers and walkers, and it was a notable spot long before George Borrow went there and it was singled out by Palmer as the finest falls in Britain. There is a good café beside the waterfall with car-parking and toilets, and an ideally-situated campsite on the left just before the parking-area is reached. Approach to the waterfall valley is by narrow roads and lanes from Chirk (B450), Oswestry (B4580), or Shrewsbury (B4396), all of which converge upon the village of Llanrhaeadr-ym-mochnant.

Climbers should note that the whole cliff complex is home for some delicate and uncommon plant life, and are asked **to take the greatest care not to disturb or damage this**. The rock is volcanic and on the whole very sound.

Col Crag   OS Ref 077 282
An interesting small crag with easy access, and good rock and routes. The crag is above a little wood in a col one kilometre left of the waterfall, and is visible from the Pistyll approach road. It is south-east facing and in a very sheltered position.

Walk left from the waterfall along a public footpath for one kilometre until a farm track which zig-zags up the hillside is intercepted. Follow the farm track to a sharp right-hand bend at the col; the cliff is immediately below and on the left, just to the right of a waterfall in the wood.

North Winds Blow   6 metres   Very Severe 4b †   (10.9.2001)
The arête of the isolated block on the left of the crag.

So Lay Low   7 metres   Hard Severe 4b †   (10.9.2001)
Flake cracks in the right wall of the isolated block lead to a judicious step left to avoid a terminally rocking block on the cliff edge.

☆**Liberation**   12 metres   E2 5b †   (10.9.2001)
Superb climbing on the left-hand arête of the main face. Climb a short corner on the right, and then swing left onto a hanging flake right of the arête. Cruise up the flake, and make use of the arête for the final 3 or 4 metres.

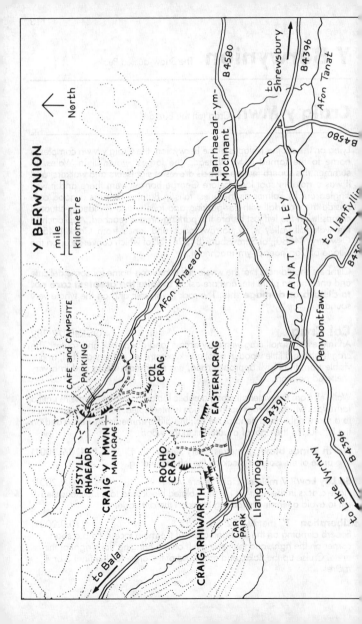

The next four climbs start from a gangway and ledge below the rippled and overhanging main face, 4 to 5 metres above the ground.

Fall Out   10 metres   E2 5b †   (10.9.2001)
From the left-hand end of the gangway, pull over a bulge using a thin left-facing flake. Better holds in the scoop above lead to an easy and exposed exit on the right.

☆**Touch Too Much**   10 metres   E5 6b †   (10.9.2001)
Intricate and committing, with a very bouldery crux. From a large undercut, reach fingerholds above a bulge. Rock-up ferociously to the left, and gain a small rock spike beneath a tiny left-facing corner. A finger-flake above leads to the exit of the preceding route.

☆**Much Too Much**   10 metres   E6 6b †   (10.9.2001)
Strenuous, with gear that is difficult to place and none-too-reassuring. In the centre of the main face there is a leftward-rising flake crack. Gain the flake crack and fight up it, trending leftwards to a sloping hand-ledge. Undercut direct onto the ledge, and step up left to finish.

Head First   10 metres   E1 5c †   (10.9.2001)
A powerful move over a bulge gains entry to the obvious break in the right-hand side of the main face. Climb the break more easily, and step right to finish.

The final climb takes the crack-system in the north-west facing wall that ends the main face.

☆**Gerbil Street**   12 metres   E4 6a †   (10.9.2001)
Pure quality. Climb a flake crack to a small overhang. Reach two good handholds above, and use these to step right into the crackline: hard and bold. Follow the crack above, past two good flakes (and runners), to the top.

Main Crag   OS Ref 074 291

The Main Crag sports an unexpected concentration of fine climbs, some of them 'state-of-the-art'. It faces north-east and receives sun until midday in summer. The crag being steep, well-drained, and quick-drying, most of its routes stay lichen-free, though some (like *Mwnchild*) may need a re-brush from time to time. The approach necessitates a very steep slog up the hillside, but this is amply rewarded by the breathtakingly exposed climbing.

Cross the bridge beneath the waterfall, and make a rising traverse leftwards through woods before the tough bit up to its distinctive, undercut base. The crag reaches a height of 40 to 45 metres and an obvious feature in the left-hand half is the corner of *Pardon Me for Breathing*.

Carboxyhaemoglobin   20 metres   E4 6a †   (20.6.98)
In the slabby wall 10 metres left of the corner is a shallow groove. This provides a welcome, if committing, retreat from the customary roof routes.

Craig y Mwn

Main Cliff

1 Legionnaire's Disease		HVS
2 Pardon Me for Breathing		E2
3 Meisterspringer		E2
4 Big Cigar		E5
5 Pole Rider		E4
6 Mwnchild		E5
7 Dovercourt Special		E2
8 Foundation and Empire		E1
9 Brothers in Arms		E3
10 State of the Union		E3
11 Jack Frost		E4
12 Techtonoc		E6
13 Arian		E5
14 First Blood II		HVS

Start up the left arête of the shallow groove with difficulty to reach a good hold (and crucial *Friend 2½* placement) at 6 metres. Continue up the groove on positive holds to its close. Climb the easier slabby wall above and move left to retreat by abseil from a tree.

Legionnaire's Disease   40 metres   Hard Very Severe 5a   (31.3.85)
Follows cracks and then a groove a short way left of the corner. Gain a ledge below a steep flaky crack, climb the crack (crux), and move left to a groove, which leads to the top of the crag.

★Pardon Me for Breathing   40 metres   E2 5c   (9.3.85)
[Photo page 112a.] The obvious corner gives excellent sustained climbing with a hard move at 5 metres; step right at its top, and climb the steep continuation groove on big holds to a vegetated groove that leads to the top.

☆Xelation   40 metres   E6 6b †   (20.6.98)
A superb and sustained eliminate up the leaning wall that forms the right wall of the *Pardon Me for Breathing* corner. Perfect rock, high in the grade. Climb the corner for 4 metres (to a vertical slot in its initial crack). Move right onto the steep face and reach a pocket above. Now take a direct, yet intricate line up the leaning wall, keeping just to the left of a straight, very thin crackline (gear) until a good pocket is gained (*Friend 3* placement). Pull through bulging rock slightly left to a rest above at the foot of the top corner of *Pardon Me for Breathing*. Move up; then – spectacularly – finish up the right-hand side of the capping arête on good holds.

★Meisterspringer   40 metres   E2 5b   (2.6.85)
The arête to the right of *Pardon Me for Breathing*: elegant and airy climbing. Start, as for the preceding routes, at the foot of the corner. Gain a ledge on the right overhanging wall by a traverse from the left. Move up right onto the arête at a ledge and climb its right-hand side to reach a short overhung groove in the arête (peg). Continue up its right edge to easier ground and another ledge; then go up over some detached blocks and finish out left.

☆Big Cigar   40 metres   E5 6b †   (29.4.90)
The dominating line of the impressive undercut buttress to the right of *Meisterspringer*; a 2½-metre roof at the start contrasts with bold face-climbing above. High in the grade. Start below the arête of *Meisterspringer*. From the ledge beneath the roof, place cams for protection and then launch out rightwards to gain a quartz-lined crack (peg runner) and good pockets on the right leading to a half-height resting-ledge. Step right to a weakness on the face (good wires in short crack on the right) and climb it past a spike runner (thin tape) to a roof (peg runner). Make reachy moves diagonally leftwards to meet good holds leading quickly to easier ground, and finish up *Meisterspringer*.

Pale Rider   40 metres   E4 6a   (26.10.85)
Start about 10 metres right of the *Pardon Me for Breathing* corner, below
an overhung niche. Gain the niche (peg) and step left to a flake (thread).
Continue up the wall to the top.

☆☆☆**Mwnchild**   40 metres   E5 6a †   (29.4.90)
Sustained and sometimes bold climbing up a brilliant piece of rock. The
route takes a direct line up the Pant Ifan look-alike buttress of overlapping
slabs between *Pale Rider* and *Dovercourt Special*. Surmount the bulge past
a thin overlap and downward-pointing peg runner, and step boldly up
leftwards into a V-groove (peg runner immediately). Sprint up the groove
(peg runner) to jugs and a spike runner (thin tape) between the two main
overlaps. Reach over directly to a large pocket (bombproof *Rock 5* in a
small pocket), and proceed up the thin crack in the upper slab to the foot
of a wide corner-crack. Climb the crack and exit easily. Belay on the fence.

★**Dovercourt Special**   40 metres   E2 5c   (29.9.85)
In the centre of the crag, there is a weakness in the overhang with a
groove above. Gain a large dubious hold from the right (peg runner).
Move left and go up to the overhang (second peg); pull over rightwards
and climb the bottomless groove. Then trend slightly left to the top.

Foundation and Empire   39 metres   E1 †   (19.10.85)
The obvious overhanging chimney/crack in the centre of the crag. Start as
for *Dovercourt Special*.
1 24m. 5b. A steep layaway leads to a ledge on the right below the large
overhangs (two pegs). Swing boldly out right and go up to gain a good ledge.
2 15m. Continue up the crack to the top.

★★★**Brothers in Arms**   43 metres   E3 5c   (9.3.85)
A superb route taking the overlapping wall just right of the large
overhangs. Start below a weakness in the lower band of overhangs. Move
up right to gain the wall below the weakness in the first band of overhangs
and go through awkwardly to attain a large pocket in the wall below the
second band. Avoid these by moving right, then left to a delicate slab
(peg). Climb the slab and move out left to finish up a short juggy wall.

★★**Jack Frost**   40 metres   E4 6a   (25.4.89)
Some very good climbing, though escapable in places, on the wall to the
right of *Brothers in Arms*. Start as for *Brothers in Arms*. Move up and step
right onto the slab. Traverse right past the big slanting crack and move up
to a peg in a bay. Climb the shallow groove and continue up the rib to a
deep hole. Move up to an obvious flake (runners); then go diagonally right
up a steep slab to another flake and a small ledge. Climb up slightly left to
a groove leading to the top.

☆☆**State of the Union**   40 metres   E5 6b †   (29.4.90)
Some gymnastic roofwork and technically sustained wall-climbing force a
direct start to *Brothers in Arms*. Start 6 metres to the right of *Brothers in
Arms*, below a step in the path. Go up shaky holds to the roof. Overcome

the roof (*in-situ* thread) and take the wall above via a thin vertical crack (crucial *Rock 4* – carry it in your teeth!) to a jug beneath an overlap. Step up to the right and back left past a peg runner to a junction with *Brothers in Arms* below its fissure. However, now bear rightwards over bulges (*Hex 8* in pocket) and then back left to rejoin *Brothers in Arms* above its delicate slab. Finish as for that route.

In the wall above the large roof between *State of the Union* and *First Blood II* there are two opposite-facing, slim corners.

☆**Techtonic**   20 metres   E6 6b †   (20.6.98)
A wonderful test-piece that also happens to be the hardest route in the Berwynion – to date! Start below and left of the left-hand, left-facing corner and 3 metres right of *State of the Union*. Clip a peg (hero-looped; also advisable twisted wire in pocket immediately above); then work through the bulge strenuously (peg runner) before fingery and intricate climbing leads up the wall just left of the slim corner to a semi-resting-position beneath a bulge. Climb the bulging rib (*in-situ* thread), and trend right to ledges and a flake and thread. Abseil from here or finish leftwards up *State of the Union*.

☆**Arian**   20 metres   E5 6b †   (20.6.98)
A powerful entry, with fine climbing on the wall above the roof. Start below and right of the right-hand, right-facing corner in the wall above the roof; a taunting hanging flake on the lip shows the line. Extend for the hanging flake (questionable flake: questionable cam placement, but small wire immediately above), and power over to good holds on the wall. Move up; then follow a series of incuts leftwards into the slim corner. Climb the corner and easy rock above to the flake and thread (possible) abseil point on the left.

★**First Blood II**   37 metres · Hard Very Severe   5b   (14.9.85)
An obvious clean-cut corner at the extreme right-hand end of the crag. Climb the groove with a difficult move low down and a traverse to the arête just below a ledge. On the left of the overhang above the ledge, climb the wall past a peg. Steep moves lead up and right to the prow and then the top.

Pistyll Rhaeadr   OS Ref 073 296

Hosting one of the most impressive waterfalls in Wales, this cliff is also one of its most atmospheric places in which to climb. Though the number of routes is limited, a day's climbing here, so close to the waterfall, will be no ordinary day. Please refer to the conservation note on page 113. The cliff-top is approached by a signed path to its right.

There are two routes on the face to the left of the waterfall. Unfortunately, this section is often monopolized by abseiling groups, who obediently throw themselves into the pools beneath. Parties wishing to climb these routes will have to wait until they finish their fun. Abseil in from a tree on the edge.

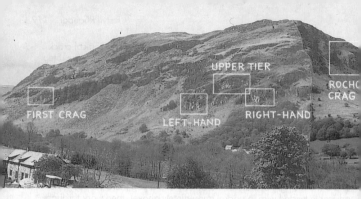

FIRST CRAG   LEFT-HAND   UPPER TIER   RIGHT-HAND   ROCHO CRAG

Craig Rhiwarth

Eastern Crag

1 Full Body Transplant   E2
2 Huggy Bear Goes to School   HVS

CRAIG RHIWARTH

EASTERN CRAG

4	Old as You Feel	E3	7	Class 87/2	HVS
5	Spare Parts	E3	8	Rust in the Machine	E5
6	Cloudwaltzer	HVS	9	Forty and Falling Apart	E2

★Riparian   15 metres   E1 5b   (8.98)
Spectacularly perched next to the waterfall, this delightful pitch has an
ambience all of its own. Abseil to a twin-peg belay at the foot of a
V-groove in the face. Technical climbing up the groove (two peg runners)
leads to a roof. Swing right onto a wall and follow good pockets straight to
the top.

☆Rhythms of the Planet   18 metres   E3 5c †   (9.94)
A line that seems curiously attracted to the waterfall. Move up the groove
of *Riparian*, and traverse right to a grass-covered ledge. Take a
committing narrow groove above, and climb a fine pocketed wall to join
the exit of *Riparian*.

There are two recorded routes on the groove-seamed face right of the
waterfall. Both start from a grassy ledge reached from the right, or by abseil
from the cliff-top. Note that the waterfall has a habit of throwing itself around
in windy conditions.

★Aquatonic   20 metres   E3 6a   (5.8.98/8.9.2001)
Fine, clean climbing when dry. Take an umbrella. Start 4 metres right of
the waterfall. Climb a strenuous corner to an overhang. Swing right and
pull up onto a rib. Gain the groove on the left as soon as conditions allow
(peg runner low left), and follow it past pockets to its close. Trend leftwards
up the headwall (old peg runner out left), finishing with your left foot
scarcely out of the waterfall. It is also possible to climb the pocketed left
arête of the upper groove – if the waterfall permits.

Waterworld   20 metres   E3 5b †   (8.9.2001)
[Photo page 112b.] Delicate and sustained, with sparse protection in places.
Start 8 metres right of the waterfall, next to a shrub at head height. Pull past
the shrub and climb diagonally leftwards (wet rock) to an overhang (old peg
runner). Gain the shallow groove overhead, and climb it and the rib on its
right to the top. Some grassy rock at the top adds to the commitment.

Craig Rhiwarth   Ridge Slope crag   OS Ref 055 265

Standing above the village of Llangynog on the B4391 in the Tanat valley,
this crag and the hill fort just above mark the most southerly point of the
Berwyn mountains. Cars should be parked in the village car-park and not in
the minor road under the crag. The First and Second Crags belong to Miss
Lloyd, who lives in the village, and she has been kind enough to allow
climbing. Please respect this permission and obey the country code at all
times.

Rhiwarth actually comprises half-a-dozen or more small crags some 20 to
30 metres high dotted around a kilometre or so of the hillside, and most

have now been developed. The rock is compact and flawless on many of the
First and Second Crag routes. The crags dry quickly and these first two in
particular have a sunny aspect, making visits worthwhile during the winter
months and when the higher-altitude crags are out of condition.

First Crag

As its name implies, this is the first crag to be seen on the approach from
Llangynog along the minor road, and lies above and to the right of the last
cottage. There is easy-angled scree below and a slate ramp to its left. The
routes start on the very steep wall of the steep, squarish buttress just right of
the trees.

Sledgehammer   24 metres   E2 5c †   (12.6.86)
A line of pockets to the left of *Mismael*. Move right along a break, make a
long reach to a good hold, and then follow a line of good holds, trending
right at the top to finish as for *Mismael*.

★Mismael   24 metres   E3 5c   (8.6.86)
The pocketed crackline just left of centre of the wall. From the block, step
left to the crack. Hard moves gain better holds, which lead to a ledge and
easier climbing to an oak tree.

★★Wingeing Pom   34 metres   E1 5b   (26.5.87)
A rising traverse from right to left, finishing up the obvious stepped crack at
the top of the crag. Low in the grade. Start at a groove on the right-hand
side of the crag, just left of a vegetated gully. Go easily up the groove to
the overhang and traverse left below it to a peg. Move left round an edge
to the base of the stepped crack. Climb this strenuously, take a horizontal
hand-traverse left, and finish up to a small tree.

Bionic Woman   24 metres   Very Severe 4c   (26.5.87)
Climb the groove of *Wingeing Pom* to the overhang. Then make an
awkward move up and right to easier ground leading to the top.

Second Crag

The three buttresses are grouped together about a quarter of a mile right of
First Crag. There is a small wood directly below the Right-Hand Lower Tier.

Left-Hand Lower Tier
Phase Shift   18 metres   Hard Very Severe 5b   (8.87)
Start just left of the diagonal line of *Silwood*. Climb the short pillar with a
difficult groove (peg).

Silwood   20 metres   Hard Severe 4a   (8.70)
Climb the obvious right-slanting weakness.

Craig Rhiwarth
Left-Hand Lower Tier

1 Silwood	HS	4 Eden	HS	7 Rose Corner	HVS
2 Ivy	VS	5 Melangell	VS	8 The Scwp Dragon	E3
3 Charisma	E3	6 The Slide	E3	9 Ivory Tower	HS

Ivy 24 metres   Very Severe   (10.84)
The groove on the left of a smooth slab. Start below an oak tree. Climb through the oak tree to gain the groove and climb this and a steeper continuation groove in the wall above.

Charisma 24 metres   E3 6a   (10.84)
High in the grade. As for *Ivy*, climb through the oak tree; then traverse the base of the smooth slab (peg) to a shallow groove. Take this and the steep continuation groove above.

★**Eden** 24 metres   E2 5c   (10.84)
Climb an obvious crack splitting the small overhang at 6 metres and the continuation groove above.

Melangell 27 metres   Very Severe 4b   (8.70)
Take the leftward-rising flake crack to a ledge at half height; then climb a short wall up and right to an arête. Finish up *Rose Corner* on the right.

The Slide 27 metres   Very Severe 4c   (10.84)
[Photo page 128a.] The left arête of *Rose Corner*. Climb the steep, leftward-slanting ramp awkwardly to gain a ledge on the left; then finish as for *Melangell*.

★**Rose Corner** 26 metres   Hard Very Severe 5a   (1962)
Easy for its grade. Climb the obvious corner, starting at a rose bush on the right. Move right below an overhang at the top of the corner and go up a short groove to finish.

★★**The Scwp Dragon** 24 metres   E4 6a   (17.9.89)
The obvious scoop between *Rose Corner* and *Ivory Tower*. Bold, though high runners can be placed first in *Ivory Tower*. Climb up to a ledge below the scoop. Enter the scoop and move up to a triangular pocket (poor peg runner). Leave the scoop to climb the right arête (poor spike); then traverse left above the scoop, mainly on layaways, to a shallow groove with numerous pockets. Climb easy ground to finish as for *Ivory Tower*.

★**Ivory Tower** 24 metres   Hard Severe 4b   (1962)
The crack forming the left edge of a huge flake on the right edge of the buttress. Take the crack to the top of the flake. Continue up the broken groove above, and move left near the top.

Right-Hand Lower Tier
Sven 18 metres   Very Difficult   (18.3.90)
The rib and huge block left of *Bramble Pie*. Climb the rib directly under the huge block and gain the top of the block via cracks on the left. Tree belay.

Bramble Pie 20 metres   Hard Very Severe 5a   (12.10.86)
To the left of *The Cheshire Cat* wall there is an easy-looking scoopy slab leading to an obvious left-trending crackline under a steep wall. Start below the scoopy slab. Poor protection in the lower crux section. Gain the

Craig Rhiwarth
Right-Hand Lower Tier

1	Sven	VD	4 The Cheshire Cat	E2
2	Bramble Pie	HVS	5 The Gargoyle	HVS
3	Clark the Toothless Shark	E4	6 Tanat	HVS
			7 The Hud	E1

scoop from the right (crux), and pull over a small overhang to the base of the left-trending crackline, which can be followed easily to a tree belay on the far left of the crag.

Clark the Toothless Shark   21 metres   E4 6a/b   (4.5.96)
The sinuous pod just left of *The Cheshire Cat*. Climb the slab left of *The Cheshire Cat* to intersect a right-to-left ramp at 5 metres. Reach a monster jug in the foot of the groove; then make a long reach up the left wall of the groove and gain big holds leading to a blocky ledge. Take the front of the arête above to an abseil tree.

★★The Cheshire Cat   21 metres   E2 5b   (19.10.85)
The thin crackline which starts half-way up the largest unbroken wall; sustained. Go up steep rock directly below the crackline, and move slightly left to a resting-place. Step back right to a hold in the small overhang (peg) at the start of the crack itself. Pull over the overhang and continue up the crack, keeping to its left-hand side. Belay to the oak tree on the right. Abseil off.

The Gargoyle   20 metres   Hard Very Severe 5a   (19.10.85)
The obvious corner/chimney-line direct to an oak tree. Climb the steep corner to gain a niche below the huge chockstone. Pull over and continue direct to the oak tree. Abseil off, or climb the continuation groove at 4b and belay a long way back.

★Tanat   21 metres   Hard Very Severe 5a   (1962)
Excellent rock, though protection is rather sparse. Start at the lowest point of the crag. Step off a block and make a thin move left to the arête; climb this, and move slightly right to good holds below a steep wall. Take the wall direct to a ledge and move left to the oak tree. Abseil off.

★The Hud   20 metres   E1 5b   (29.11.86)
Start to the right of *Tanat*, below a short groove capped by a small triangular roof: there is an orange mark on the rock at the base of the groove. Go easily up a chimney and step right to gain the groove. Pull over the roof on big jugs (peg) to the left. Reach the traverse ledge of *Quartizone Injection*, move up to a peg in the wall above, and finish directly up the little groove. Abseil from the tree on the left.

Quartizone Injection   30 metres   Very Severe 4c   (12.85)
Quite good, if meandering, climbing. Start at a detached slab leading up to a corner. Climb the slab and start up the corner before breaking out left. Reach a traverse-line above the overhangs on the right and follow it to a tree belay. Move back left across a mossy slab and go up a vague crack leading to a ledge; continue up the steep arête above, first on its right, then on the left. Finish up the arête direct on big holds.

★Paper Lace   30 metres   Hard Very Severe 5b   (15.9.84)
On the right-hand side of the crag is a gully separating an overhanging section from the main buttress. This route is just left of the gully and makes for

a slab in a corner with a large pinnacle directly above. Go up and climb the slab, and move up into the corner. Make an awkward move to its right edge and climb this to a belay on the right-hand side of the pinnacle. Step left from the pinnacle top to a ledge below an arête and climb its right edge to the top.

Upper Tier

The routes are described from **right to left**. At the right-hand end of the upper tier is a prominent tower with a groove-line running up its centre; this is *King of Maybe*. *Cavalier Attitude* takes the right-hand edge of the arête to its right.

Cavalier Attitude   24 metres   Hard Very Severe 5a   (10.85)
Step onto the edge and climb slightly rightwards; then go back left to gain the edge again, and climb directly to the top.

★★**King of Maybe**   26 metres   Very Severe 4c   (1962)
Sustained. Gain a crack from the left (peg), go up into the groove to a bulge, and traverse left on big handholds. Go directly up to the summit block and climb its short overhanging groove. Metal spike belay.

★★**Queen of My Soul**   21 metres   E6 6b   (5.5.96)
The fingery and sequency thin crack just left of *King of Maybe*. Superb rock, and a fine test of skill. Amble up to the foot of an off-fingers crack. Traverse right along a sloping break to the thin crack and follow it quickly (peg runner) to massive holds above on *King of Maybe*. Continue to the capping tower and, from a wide crack, belt up the front arête to the top.

★**Thunder Road**   24 metres   Very Severe 4c   (1962)
Well to the left of *King of Maybe* is a chimney/groove-line running the full height of the crag. Climb this, and move out left near the top, just below a small tree. Metal spike belay well back in a small outcrop.

★**Remember Bob Brevitt**   30 metres   E1 5b   (18.3.90)
Climb *Thunder Road* for 6 metres; then follow a weakness in the steep left wall to a peg. Continue up and left again to a ledge. Climb a broken groove on the left edge of the wall and then move back right to climb the centre of the upper wall to finish. Belay spike well back from the top.

☆**No More Lives to Lose**   24 metres   E3 5c †   (5.5.96)
The bulging wall left of *Thunder Road*; strenuous in its bottom half. Start 5 metres down and left of *Thunder Road*. Crank through a bulge to a jug in a broad white scoop. Traverse right for 2 metres (good wire low right) to a flake-line which leads up to a hand-ledge. Move left to a white ledge; then pull up onto the slab crossed by *Remember Bob Brevitt* (peg runner). Continue direct (*in-situ* thread) to big holds and up slabbier rock to the top.

The Slide (VS) Craig Rhiwarth
Climber: Martin Whitaker   Photo: Pat Cocks

The Rocho Machine (E1) Craig Rhiwarth
Climber: Steve Cameron   Photo: John Sumner

Fifty and Rising   30 metres   E2 5c   (3.85)
Strenuous and technical. Climb the overhanging crack to an oak tree. Step
right from the tree and climb up diagonally right to reach an easy slab
above. Tree belay just below the top of the crag.

Stickle Back Man   27 metres   Very Severe 4b   (10.85)
The undercut chimney/groove-line starting half-way up the crag. Start by
gaining an easy ramp below a large tree at the top. Follow the ramp
rightwards; then go up directly to the chimney-line and climb it to the top.

Chacmool   27 metres   Very Severe 4b   (10.85)
Start as for *Stickle Back Man*. Follow the ramp rightwards; then go up to
gain and follow a leftward weakness crossing a slab and a groove to a
ledge on the right of another groove. Climb this groove to a large tree at
the top of the crag.

Luddites Demise   21 metres   Hard Very Severe 5b †   (6.85)
A direct first section to *Chacmool*. Starting as for *Chacmool*, climb direct up
steep rock to the groove.

★Buzzard's Nest Crack   24 metres   Hard Severe 4b   (8.70)
The big leftward-trending ramp-line below a steep wall. There is a large
tree at the top of the crag just to its right. Climb a crack in a corner to gain
the ramp and go up it to a steep little wall. Climb this awkwardly to a
ledge and tree belay. A shallow groove on the right leads to the top.

Rocho Crag[1]   OS Ref 061 272
An east-facing crag high up on the slopes of the side valley immediately east
of First and Second Crags. It has two very different sections, the left-hand
side being steep with overhangs, the right (with no routes at present) an
easier-angled columnar structure of grooves and arêtes, but capped by a
prominent black band of overhangs.

Bleeting a Retreat   27 metres   E3 6a   (2.6.96)
A very worthwhile eliminate, with some nice features, up the centre of the
slab taken by *Blitzkrieg*. Start 1½ metres left of that route. Climb a sinuous
pocketed crack to the obvious layback edge. Follow the edge to a small
roof at the top of the slab. Bear left over the roof, climb direct for 3 metres,
and then step right into the final long groove of *Blitzkrieg*.

★Blitzkrieg   30 metres   E2 5c   (5.5.96)
The clean steep slab on the left-hand side of the crag between a detached
pinnacle and a large holly tree. Climb cracks on the right-hand side of the
slab, and make a difficult move to enter a groove through a band of
overhangs. Continue up the groove to exit onto vegetated slabs. Good
block and nut belays beneath a short wall.

1 Probably a vocalization of Yr Ochor – Side Crag

Rocho Crag

1	Bleeting a Retreat	E3	4	Stew the Orthodox	E3	7	The Rocho Machine	E1
2	Blitzkrieg	E2	5	Experimental	E5	8	Experiential	E5
3	Cougar	E5	6	Man with a Mission	E5			

★★Cougar 24 metres E5 6b (5.5.96)
A wild route on a radical feature: the great prow towards the left-hand side of the crag. Climb an obvious groove to a good ledge beneath the prow. From the right arête, a sort of overhanging ramp leads up leftwards to a capping roof: attack it with an initial lunge (peg runner); then follow a series of amazing buckets to the roof (hidden peg). Battle through the off-width in the prow to the top (good finishing-jug on the left).

Stew the Orthodox 24 metres E3 5c (2.6.96)
In need of adventure? – then embark on this. A spacy excursion onto the right-hand edge of the overhanging black prow of *Cougar*. Start as for *Cougar*. Climb an obvious groove to a good ledge below the prow. Step right and climb the steepening groove right of the prow until it closes and forces a swing left to a crack. With cam protection in the crack, move down left to a line of good handholds on the very edge of the prow. Cut loose across these to a hollow-sounding ledge; then finish direct more easily.

The next four routes start from an obvious pedestal ledge, gained by a scramble from the right.

☆Experimental 21 metres E5 6a † (2.6.96)
A satisfying test-piece that would be equally at home at Tremadog. From the pedestal, go up and climb the left-hand of two striated inverted-V grooves to a bulge. Pass the bulge with precision to reach the foot of the groove of *The Rocho Machine* (*Friend 2*). Swing left immediately to a steep flake-line and take this on big holds to a step left to exit.

★★Man with a Mission 27 metres E5 6a/b (5.5.96)
Solid three-star climbing on a super-sustained and varied line through the complex of slabs and roofs, right of the second broken groove right of the prow. Bear rightwards from the pedestal, move up a groove, then a rib rightwards to a good jug beneath a gap in the first roof, which underlies a prominent green slab. Go over the roof onto the slab (junction with *The Rocho Machine*); then step right across the slab (peg runner) to the second small roof. Pull up and over with a thin move direct to the third roof (*in-situ* thread). Surmount this roof, and follow cracks above through the fourth and final roof to exit direct via a short wall.

☆Experiential 30 metres E5 6a † (2.6.96)
A big pitch full of technical interest, which takes the crack rising through the overlapping slabs right of *Man with a Mission*. Climb diagonally right from the pedestal for 8 metres to the right-hand end of a green slab. Reach a crack above the overlap and follow it over a second overlap, using a good hold or two on the left, to a resting-place on the slabby ramp beneath a leaning wall. With sole protection from a – nevertheless good – twisted wire in a pocket on the right, launch straight up the leaning wall following increasingly large holds to the top: somewhat committing.

★★The Rocho Machine   32 metres   E1   (18.5.96)
[Photo page 128b.] The obvious green slab and right-slanting groove
accommodate a somewhat easier but nonetheless impressive voyage
through the overhangs.
1 8m. From the pedestal, make an easy traverse right to spike and nut
belays close to the vegetated gully/groove.
2 24m. 5b. Move up to the right-hand side of the green slab via a short
groove. Go diagonally up left across the slab using good side-pulls in the
overhang above, to a niche on the left (peg on the slab just before the
niche). Move up to another peg and step right above an overhang. Climb
the broken, right-slanting groove above to the top.

★★Redstart   36 metres   E1   (15.6.96)
At the back of the amphitheatre which lies between the two sections of
Rocho Crag there is a rightward-curving corner with a clean wall above
between two mossy sections.
1 18m. 5b. Climb the corner to an *in-situ* thread and peg runner. Move
left and go directly up the clean wall to a second peg. Then climb a groove
to a horizontal break beneath the black overhangs. Old metal spike
belays.
2 18m. Traverse easily leftwards along the break to finish.

Eastern Crag   OS Ref 068 268

[Photodiagram page 120.] There is a section of worthwhile rock on the
continuation of the Rhiwarth escarpment on the hillside to the east of the
valley holding Rocho Crag. Towards the right-hand end of this there is a
prominent arête with a blank overhanging wall to its left, which forms the
right wall of the striking corner-crack of *Class 87/2*. Near the left-hand end
of the crag there is a large bulge below and to the left of an oak tree at the
top. The first two routes take the arête and groove beneath the oak tree.

Full Body Transplant   21 metres   E2 5c   (4.5.96)
Bold climbing up the left-hand arête: a nice line. Start as for *Huggy Bear
Goes to School*. Climb the bottomless corner-crack for 6 metres, step left
onto the arête, and follow it increasingly steeply to the top.

Huggy Bear Goes to School   23 metres   Hard Very Severe   5a (20.3.88)
Start by some reddish rock with a bottomless corner-crack leading into a
deep V-niche. Climb the corner-crack and move up into the V. Step right
and climb the obvious slot in the steep wall above. Easier ground leads to
the top. Good spike belay.

Old as You Feel   21 metres   E3 6a   (4.5.96)
Twelve metres left of the corner of *Class 87/2* is a blunt arête. Climb the
left edge of the arête, past a hard section at 6 metres (*in-situ* thread); then
continue more easily to a stout bush above. Either retreat from the bush,
or continue slightly rightwards to the top with care.

Spare Parts   24 metres   E3 5c   (4.5.96)
Deceptively difficult and tricky-to-protect climbing up the black left wall of
the *Cloudwaltzer* groove. Start as for *Cloudwaltzer*. Climb direct, just left of
the groove, to a ledge and flakes at 8 metres. Reach a small niche above
a bulge, and go straight up, then left slightly to jugs in the base of a big
black scoop. Cross rightwards beneath an overlap, step back left above it,
and finish direct over a small roof. High in the grade.

Cloudwaltzer   24 metres   Hard Very Severe 5b   (29.8.87)
The groove immediately left of *Class 87/2*. Gain the base of the groove
from the right and climb it direct, passing a peg at mid height.

Class 87/2   24 metres   Hard Very Severe   (17.10.87)
The obvious corner-crack.
1 15m. 5b. Climb the corner-crack with increasing difficulty to a large
ledge.
2 9m. Follow the right edge, then easy ground rightwards to a tree.

Rust in the Machine   24 metres   E5 6a   (4.5.96)
The overhanging arête right of *Class 87/2*. Protectable and just making
the grade. Climb the left-hand of two grooves in the arête; then follow a
more definite thin crack with more exertion to jugs slightly left of the arête.
One final steep move up its left-hand side leads to slabbier rock and the
belay of *Class 87/2*.

Forty and Falling Apart   18 metres   E2 5c   (4.5.96)
Steep and shaky above half height. Start below an obvious crack 5 metres
right of the arête. Go up the crack in the leaning wall; then follow good
handholds above it rightwards before pulling over onto a slab. Take the
groove on the right with care to a large tree on the right.

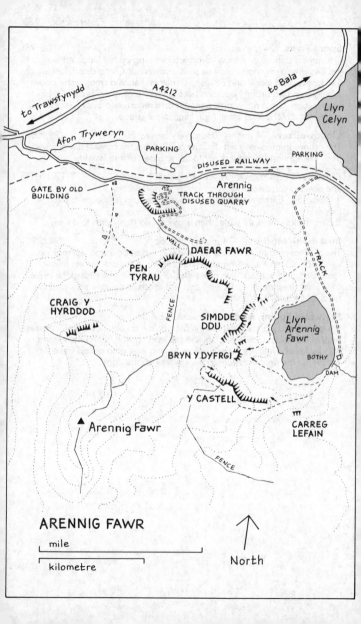

Arennig Fawr   Greater Upland

South of the Moelwynion and west of Bala is the Arennig.[1] Like the other groups in the region, there is a greater and a lesser peak of the name, but unlike the others they do not form a chain, and the two are separated by a major river, road, and (once) rail valley. The crags described in this guide are all situated on the southern peak, Arennig Fawr, the north-east spur of which is truncated abruptly at point 697 by a semi-circle of bristling, terraced crags on its north and east sides. These crags overlook Llyn Arennig and some areas catch the sun for most of the day. The rock is mainly clean and solid with excellent friction. Many of the routes were first climbed without pre-inspection or cleaning. Belays are easy to find and some routes have *in-situ* thread belays. Large perched blocks sit along the top of the crag at the top of the odd route, and some care is needed topping out on certain routes.

Approach
From Bala, head north on the A4212 and, after one mile, turn left for Rhyd-Uchaf on a minor road. Follow this for seven and a half miles to the Dŵr Cymru road gate which appears on the left shortly before Arennig village. If coming from the north, turn left off the A474 south of Ffestiniog, heading for Bala on the A4212 eastbound. Eventually a right-hand turn signposted to Arennig appears.

Park at the old quarry for Daear Fawr (see page 163) or continue on to the gate mentioned above for the main complex, where there is limited parking by the roadside. After the stile, follow the gravel road to the lake; then contour around by its north shore via a sheep-trail well below the crag: a pleasant 30 minutes (20 minutes at reasonable pace) or so. The temptation to take the direct line up the boulder-slope from the path to the crag should be avoided. It is better to follow the path as it contours around the lake and turns down its western shore. Cross a slabby boulder by the lakeside and continue along the track to a larger boulder on the shore. The track now turns away from the lake and up the slope straight to Bryn y Dyfrgi and the boulder-field at the left of Simdde Ddu. See map overleaf.

There is an alternative approach to the northern end of Simdde Ddu (40 minutes). Follow the reservoir track for one kilometre to where the angle eases and the low col hiding the lake is seen (the ridge to the right of the col passes over two knolls to the shoulder of Gelli Deg, screening the cliffs). Here, an old path leads towards small spoil-heaps, a ruined hafod, and the col. Before or at the first excavation, cross the marshy area to reach a further boulder (200 metres). From the boulder, a narrow sheep-path, continuous but easily lost, leads up the depression. At the top a ruined wall is crossed

1 The correct spelling, although a single n is more commonly found in current usage.

and the ridge is gained. Continue up to rocks by a dead tree and immediately past it cross the left ridge, descending slightly, to see the north end of the face and 'the amphitheatre'. Pass below a dripping wall and descend to the faint track along the foot of the east face.

The main climbing area is Simdde Ddu: this consists of the extensive south-east and east-facing terraced cliffs, with a large slabby area on the far left. [Photoplan page 144a.] The second area lies between its left end and Llyn Arennig and comprises the independent Craig Bryn y Dyfrgi and a smaller neighbour. The terraced walls of Y Castell are on the west shore of the lake, up and left of Bryn y Dyfrgi, and are best approached by the walkers' track past the bothy. On the north side of the mountain are the three areas of Daear Fawr, Pen Tyrau, and Craig yr Hyrddod (approaches are described under their respective headings).

Simdde Ddu   The Black Chimney   OS Ref 840 380

Far South Wall
Left of the open scree gully bounding the left of the South Buttress is an extended 12-metre-high wall running along the top of the slope. At its extreme left end, left of two capped corners, is a leftward-facing groove.

Pink-Headed Warrior   11 metres   Severe †   (30.3.98)
Follow the groove to the left end of a large ledge; then take the short wall above.

The Colour Turtle   11 metres   E2 5c †   (22.9.98)
The first capped corner has a short arête on its left leading to the roof. Take the left side of the arête from the shelf below and pull through the roof on small pockets to better holds and an easy finish.

☆**Red-Headed Warrior**   9 metres   E2 5c †   (2.9.98)
Start at the crack right of the second capped corner and gain the sickle crack in the roof above. Jam strenuously up this to exit leftwards.

☆☆☆**Spider Blood Pump**   12 metres   E5 6a †   (7.5.2000)
Fun climbing up a good feature. Start up the corner right of the arête next right. Traverse out left on the break to the small lodged flakes. RPs in the thin crack above protect the burst of power needed to get to the next break. Fight on up the twin grooves directly above. Leans all the way.

☆**Ghostrace**   11 metres   E2 5c †   (7.5.2000)
The next slim groove to the right leads to a small roof where a tricky sequence allows a long leg stretch right onto the ledge. Balance back up and left into the stepped groove.

Next right is a slim tower between two grass ledges.

Simdde Ddu
Far South Wall

1 Pink-Headed Warrior	S	
2 The Colour Turtle	E2	
3 Red-Headed Warrior	E2	
4 Spider Blood pump	E5	
5 Ghostrace	E2	
6 Jump out of Your Skin	E1	

Jump out of Your Skin 11 metres E1 5b † (7.5.2000)
Take the wall on good flat holds to the small ledge up and right. Good open climbing directly above, passing a small recess on the left.

Towards the right-hand end of Far South Wall is a neat and steep leaning wall with a thin forked crack in its left-hand side.

Blue-Headed Warrior 9 metres E3 6a † (22.9.98)
[Photo page 144b.] Climb the crack to the fork. Follow the left fork across the wall to a sustained and difficult section to gain the left arête, which is taken directly and easily to the top.

Purple-Headed Warrior 10 metres E3 5c † (30.3.96)
Gain the fork as for the preceding route, but continue directly up on good but spaced holds. Much steeper than it looks.

Purple Haze 9 metres E4 5c † (22.9.98)
A thin vertical seam 2 metres right of *Purple-Headed Warrior* leads to a horizontal break. A hard start off the right end of the little ledge below the seam gains the break. Pull out up and right via good sharp pockets to large flat holds above. Pass a peg and follow the holds, now smaller, directly up to the top and a mantel finish.

☆☆**Policing the Shadows**   9 metres   E4/5 6a †   (7.5.2000)
On the extreme right of this crag is an innocent looking arête, but it is
perplexing and totally sustained. Good small wires protect at half height,
but keep an *RP3* for the last difficult move.

South Buttress

The slabby South Buttress begins immediately right of the scree slope
dividing it from Far South Wall, but at its extreme left end is a tall, narrow,
diamond-shaped slab facing west with one route at its centre.

Venusian Walkway   15 metres   Very Severe 4c †   (25.8.93)
Start at the lowest point and climb the slab up its centre, trending leftward
to a corner. Finish just right of the corner. Nut belay 5 metres up. (An
earlier, easier variation started up the right edge of the narrow slab before
traversing left into its centre. After a short way the line escaped rightwards
to the edge again. Superseded by the central line.)

There is now a collection of terraced walls before the great, dark, rightward-
facing corner forming the left side of the main section of the buttress. A
couple of metres down and right of the narrow diamond slab is a series of
easy stepped ledges which form a useful descent (Moderate).

Recant   18 metres   Hard Severe 4b †   (25.8.93)
Two metres right again the rock is steeper, and a short spike can be seen
at 8 metres. Gain the spike, step left, and continue up to large ledge. Nut
belay a further 5 metres up. Spaced protection on solid rock.

☆**Gwyfyn Melyn**   30 metres   Hard Severe †   (16.6.92)
1 20m. Start as for *Recant* and gain the spike. From here, step up and
right to gain a clean bay via dubious flake holds. Reach a narrow ledge
above, and then climb a steep slabby wall.
2 10m. 4a. *Monolith* pitch 2.

Monolith   30 metres   Very Severe †   (5.90)
1 20m. 4b. The next feature to the right is a large flake leaning against
the cliff. Climb direct to the top of the flake and then take the wall just left
via a vague rib. Follow this and trend leftwards to gain a heather terrace.
2 10m. 4a. Take the obvious corner-crack to broken ledges.

☆☆**Incantations**   37 metres   Very Difficult †   (27.5.91)
Start further right where broken flakes form a plinth at the foot of the cliff.
From the top of the flake, stride right to gain the steep wall. Then, either
move left for 3 metres and climb directly up the wall on perfect rock; or,
easier, climb to the right of the crackline which splits the face. From the top
of the central heather-field a corner-crack rises. Finish up the slab between
this and the easy stepped crack on the right.

(Bryn y Dyfrgi)

1	Morris Minor	HS
2	Superstring	E2
3	Take a Pig's Head…	E6
4	Lurkio	E5
5	Fighting Spirit	E2
6	Sooth Slayer	E2
7	50 Dead Men…	E2
8	Fiend Two	E2
9	Milkman's Daughter	E1
10	The Coming War	E1
11	Dorothy's Wall	HS

South Buttress

12	Vestigial Tale	VS
13	Sole	VS
14	Spectator Groove	E1
15	Gyllion	HVS
16	Madryn	E1
17	Triathlon	E3
18	Shoka	E1
19	Emperor's New Toes	HVS
20	The In of the Sixth…	E4
21	Stormin' Norman	E2
22	Bed of Roses	E5
23	Drop in Squad	E2
24	Automedon	VS
25	Iron John	HVS
26	Ladies First	D
27	Brimstone	VS
28	Aja	VS

The terraced walls now end at the large dark and damp right-facing corner, but two routes start here and take a line going back leftwards via a ledge to a shattered pinnacle.

Line   30 metres   Severe †   (6.94)
1 · 10m. 4a. From the dark right-facing corner a ledge runs back left for 7 metres to a shattered pinnacle. Follow the ledge and descend the far side of the pinnacle. Move up awkwardly onto a clean inclined shelf (take care to protect your second) and cross this to stand in the corner. Beware loose rock here.
2 10m. 4a. Step left onto the nose, climb a short slab, and cross the heather slope to a corner-crack.
3 10m. 4a. Climb the corner and finish up another short slab on the right.

Sinker   35 metres   Severe †   (6.94)
1 20m. 4a. From the pinnacle on *Line*, climb into a dark recess with a sapling, swing around the left arête, surmount a bulge, and then go up the heather terrace to a corner.
2 15m. 4a. Follow the weakness up the slabs just right of a corner.

The next series of routes take the slabs right of the big right-facing corner. A great ledge rises leftwards from bottom right of the slabs and continues, slanting upwards to the top of the deep zigzag crack of *Madryn*. A step interrupts the ramp at this point but it continues on leftwards to the left side of the slabs with a third level of rock face rising above it. There are thus three tiers.

Vestigial Tale   17 metres   Very Severe 4b †   (3.9.93)
Start 3 metres right of the dark right-facing corner. Climb the slab direct for 6 metres before stepping up and left, heading for an area of clean white rock. Finish up this and belay on the pinnacle.

☆☆**Sole**   18 metres   Very Severe 4b †   (4.90)
Climb the slab as for *Vestigial Tale* but head rightwards to a small triangular niche. Step up and right; then continue directly to a large grass ledge and belays on the middle tier. Walk down rightwards or continue up pitch 2 of *Gyllion*.

Skookum Wall   40 metres   Hard Severe 4b †   (16.6.92)
Start 3 metres right of *Sole*, by a short, flaky pinnacle and below a zigzag crack (thinner than the deeper crack of *Madryn* further right).
1 20m. 4b. From the top of the flake, traverse diagonally left to the triangular niche on *Sole*, and follow *Sole* to the belay.
2 10m. 4a. Step back left around the corner to gain a rib, and continue to a stance beneath the second ramp.
3 10m. Ascend heather for 5 metres; then climb a groove, the third from the right, to the top.

★Spectator Groove 15 metres E1 5b   (25.8.93)
The cleaner area to the right on the same slab has a clean vertical crack
up its centre. Left of this is a groove facing rightwards. Start just left of the
crackline and boldly gain a small roof. Step right into the groove and
follow it delicately to its end, where it is possible to step left onto the steep
face. Finish directly and belay 4 metres back.

★Gyllion 38 metres Hard Very Severe   (5.90)
A fine long slab route taking the full height of the face. A safe and
worthwhile line.
1 15m. 5a. Climb the fine thin crack in the centre of this part of the slab
to gain the ramp of the middle tier and a flake belay.
2 6m. 4c. Take the centre of the short slab to the right of the flake, with
gear in the high crack on the left.
3 17m. 4c. From the belay at the top of this middle tier, walk left for 3
metres to below the crack in the final upper section of the slab. Take the
excellent crack to the top of the crag.

★Madryn 37 metres E1   (5.90)
Another very good line, finishing at the top of the cliff and taking in some
of the most obvious features.
1 17m. 5a. The large, deep, leftward-trending crack to the right of the
slabs. Starting 5 metres left of the crack, climb up, and then traverse right
into it. Follow the crack past an old peg until 4 metres from the top; then
traverse out left on thin horizontal cracks to finish up a short corner.
2 8m. 5a. The middle tier has a series of grooves/corners – take the
arête between the lower two to gain the grass ramp.
3 12m. 5b. Gain and follow a thin flake straight up to a short groove.
Gain the groove with difficulty, and step right into the final crack.

Unknown Soldier 25 metres Severe 4a †   (1994)
This line starts from where the rising ramp/ledge ends above the crack in
pitch one of *Madryn*. A scramble up the ramp from its right-hand end
gains the twin cracks behind the top of the *Madryn* crack. Step up and
right from the ramp to the cracks, which are followed up and rightwards to
a groove. A short chimney above this groove then leads to a giant
protruding block.

Triathlon 18 metres E3 6a †   (21.9.97)
An independent start to the slabs above the first tier, which, combined with
the top two pitches of *Madryn*, provides an excellent outing. Start at the
overhung, heathery, white niche about 15 metres left of *Emperor's New
Toes*. The short crack gains the recess on the right. Follow a flake-groove
above to its close (peg); then span left and up to a finger-flake. Walk up
the terrace to belay as for *Madryn*.

Psychopop 18 metres E4 6a †   (21.9.97)
The groove left of *Cyclops*. Start as for *Cyclops*; then follow the groove
(small wire on the right, 3 metres up *Cyclops*) with a hard move over the

bulge to the sloping hand-ledge on the left. Grasp the break above and exit more easily up the short face.

★Cyclops   18 metres   E1 5b   (3.3.90)
The top tier has a large white wall left of the huge arête leading up to a cyclopean hole in the boulders on top. Climb the left edge of the white wall, via a thin corner, to the hole. Abseil off slings in the hole; or, better, go into the hole and pull out onto the top of the cliff.

Argonauts   18 metres   Hard Very Severe 5a   (3.3.90)
Start as for *Cyclops* and gain a traverse-line after 5 metres. Traverse right past a thin thread until above the bulging overlap of the arête. Step up to the thread belay of *Emperor's New Toes*, and then traverse back left below the top boulder-line to *Cyclops*. The route has been superseded by *Shaka*.

☆Shaka   27 metres   E1 5a †   (21.9.97)
An extremely pleasant and direct way of climbing the white slab left of *Emperor's New Toes*, although protection is well spaced (if not absent). Climb the left-hand arête of the front of the buttress to join *Emperor's New Toes*. Trend slightly leftwards for 7 metres to a flake ledge and good nut runner. Proceed straight up the white streak in the slab above to a horizontal break at its head. Pull up and left past a roof; then finish up the face of the block.

★★Emperor's New Toes   21 metres   Very Severe 4c   (6.9.93)
[Photo front cover.] Good direct climbing, taking the left edge of the rounded arête. Start from the right-hand end of the middle-tier ramp, just before the arête. From the base, climb direct to a grassy ledge. Continue straight up the left edge of the arête to a bulge. Pull through this using good holds on the arête, and finish direct to a thread belay on the huge blocks above.

★★The In of the Sixth Happiness   18 metres   E4 5c   (31.10.95)
This bold wall-climb on very good rock, and with just enough gear, takes the centre of the tall narrow wall right of the slabs area. Start the route from the big ledge by climbing directly on small positive edges to a little horizontal slot at 5 metres (peg runner, small wires, and cam). Continue direct with difficulty (small hidden holds) to the next placement at almost another 5 metres. Gain a narrow ledge below the overlap; then cross the overlap on the right on big holds. Sustained in its lower section.

Stormin' Norman   18 metres   E2 5b   (31.10.95)
The right-hand arête of the wall, compelling and poorly protected. Start on the right-hand side of the flake ledge and pull strenuously up to good flakes. The crux then involves a long reach for good holds and a small niche on the right. Move back up and left onto the arête to below a narrow V-groove, and climb this to the top ledge. Pull up easily leftwards to the *in-situ* belay threads.

East Face

[Photodiagram page 146.] This extensive and terraced face has routes on the top walls that are generally best approached by abseil. Various lines find their way the full height of the crag and may involve passage across the grass and heather terraces. To the right of *Stormin' Norman* a vegetated terrace extends rightwards for a short distance and provides a difficult approach to the first two routes on the dark grey wall. An obvious feature is the huge perched block up and right, the Trojan Horse which is the centre-piece for several routes.

The crag is broken and heather-filled until the next big feature, the leaning tower on the top wall (*The Jump over the Shadow*), which forms the left edge of the big bay above the large scree slope. At the back of the bay ('the amphitheatre') is the deep, dark chimney, Simdde Ddu. The walls to the right of the chimney are broken and dirty between here and a great tower with a distinct arête on its left side (*Graveyard Gates*) forming the right-hand side of the amphitheatre. An orange stepped and terraced wall reaching the full height of the crag is next. Finally, on the top wall, a face with a striking, vertical finger-crack (*Prizewinner*) sits high above a buttress (*Chrysalis*) at the foot of the crag. Some shorter walls and boulders make up the remainder of the crag.

Routes at this northern end can be reached directly from the lake shore by a difficult scramble up the boulder-field leading to the crag but it is easier to approach as for Bryn Dyfrgi and contour along the foot of the east face. The alternative approach described on page 135, past Gelli Deg, is a good way to the north end.

The first climbs on the top tier of this face can be approached by a steep scramble across the grass balcony right of the flake ledge below *Stormin' Norman* to reach a good grassy ledge below the steep, grey face. An easier approach is to abseil in from the top of the cliff. The first route starts 2½ metres from the left-hand edge of the face.

☆**Bed of Roses**   20 metres   E5 6a †   (10.8.98)
Very technical, with the gear spaced enough to facilitate full enjoyment. (Spare a thought for the first ascensionist, solo, on a single backrope.) Climb direct to a slot and a pocket in an incipient horizontal break. Reach fingerholds in the wall above and step left to place *RPs* in a hairline crack. Then move back right to fire confidently up the wall using a thin ragged flake. Lots of slopers on exiting provide a delicate 'sting'.

Drop In Squad   20 metres   E2 5b †   (10.8.98)
A classic-feeling climb using the flake-line in the centre of this wall. Start 3 metres right of the left-bounding corner. Climb diagonally rightwards to a good spike runner at the left end of a ledge. Move right 2 metres. Pull up onto the flake and follow it with a heave over a cracked roof, which gives a good finish.

The next feature right is the great perched block called the Trojan Horse. Below this are a series of routes on the lowest tier. A slabby whale-backed spur descends to form the toe beneath the South Buttress and East Face. The cracked slab at the foot of this spur is Jigsaw Slab, and any of its routes, followed by a rightwards scramble up vegetated slopes, gives the simplest approach to the Trojan Horse area.

Iron John   30 metres   Hard Very Severe 5a †   (25.2.98)
Start at the foot of the main rib 6 metres left of Jigsaw Slab. Scramble up for 9 metres to a stance right of the blocks. Move left onto the rib and traverse to a wide undercut crack. Pass a flake insert to reach ledges, step left onto the arête, and climb to the top.

Ironside   21 metres   Very Severe 4b †   (18.3.98)
Start as for *Iron John* but climb the rib direct.

Ladies First   24 metres   Difficult   (7.8.97)
This is the main chimney/crack in the left side of Jigsaw Slab. The initial crack leads to a ledge at 8 metres. Follow the chimney/crack directly above and exit right.

Close Second   15 metres   Very Difficult †   (2.98)
Take the initial crack of *Ladies First* to the ledge, and then step right to the next crack. Finish over a bulge.

Fire   18 metres   Very Severe 4b   (2.98)
Start 2 metres right of the initial crack of *Ladies First*, and go rightwards up the slab, then back left to a tree. Take the slab behind the tree and finish in a crack.

Brimstone   21 metres   Very Severe 5a   (2.98)
One short hard section. Start 3 metres further down and right from the start of *Fire*. Climb rightwards up the slab to a short edge (flake hold), from where a shallow crack leads up to the right-hand tree on the ledge. Right of the tree is a block with an arête above. Climb the arête to the heather terrace.

Aja Direct   25 metres   Very Severe 4c †   (12.12.2001)
Start at the lowest point of Jigsaw slab, below the flake on *Brimstone*, and follow lovely clean edges directly to the flake. Finish as for *Brimstone*.

Aja   30 metres   Very Severe 4c †   (25.3.98)
This reaches the short edge with the flake hold on *Brimstone* but starts on the undercut section of the same slab 10 metres further right. Gain the slab, move up to the corner, and traverse the 10 metres back left to the flake. Finish as for *Brimstone*.

The Incline and Wall of the Norman Empire
                    15 metres   Hard Very Severe 5b †   (12.12.2001)
Start as for *Aja*, below the left-facing corner, but at 2 metres step right onto the steeper part of the slab. Pad carefully up to the crack above and follow

SIMDDE DDU

FAR SOUTH WALL | SOUTH FACE SLABS | EAST FACE | THE AMPHITHEATRE

Jigsaw Slab

The Trojan Horse

The Jump...

chimney (Simdde Ddu)

Blue-Headed Warrior (E3) Simdde Ddu
Climber: Norman Clacher   Photo: Terry Taylor

this more easily to the massive belay block on the grass terrace. Walk off left easily along the ledge with the trees and scramble down the initial chimney of *Ladies First*.

☆The Story of O   15 metres   E4 6a †   (12.12.2001)
A superb slab climb, bold but protectable with microwires. Start in the overhanging corner next right, which is wicked to pull through, and gain the steep slab. Continue directly above the corner to reach the 'O', a 10-centimetre circle nature has indented in the rock. More hard moves up and right on very small edges deposit you on easier ground. Belay on the big block and walk off as for the preceding route.

Every Step a Lotus   15 metres   E2 5b †   (12.12.2001)
Pass the large corner next right to the huge block with the rounded arête. The face immediately right of the corner is taken direct with very spaced protection. The holds are initially generous but thin out towards the top, which is a perfect flat ledge. To belay, scramble up the easy slab above (5 metres); then disappear into the chasm behind the block to some monster chockstones.

☆Gravity Depravity   15 metres   E3 5c †   (12.12.2001)
The excellent round arête next right is approached from the left via a short ledge. A real barn-door via a small inset block gains the arête, which is skipped up to gain the blocks on the three-quarter ledge (3 metres below the finishing-ledge of *Every Step a Lotus*). Step right on the ledge to finish up the arête with a balancing act. As for *Every Step a Lotus*, romp up the easy slab to the chocks in the chasm to belay.

Animal Watching Without 'im   15 metres   E2 5b †   (12.12.2001)
The right side of the great block has a groove leading to a crack. The groove is steep to start; then tricky moves out on the steep slab follow to gain the crack. The crack is good and takes you all the way to where the angle increases at the top. Pull onto the easy slab and belay as for the preceding routes.

The next routes are on the wall by the Trojan Horse. There is a route each side of the huge block and these are reached from the top of the 9-metre tower above a tree below and left. Gain the foot of the tower by climbing *Ladies First*, and then scrambling up rightwards for 45 metres.

Left Flank   49 metres   Hard Severe †   (7.94)
1 9m. Start below and left of the large perched block and climb the 9-metre tower above a rowan tree.
2 20m. 4a. Pull up from the little gap behind the tower and climb to ledges below a V-groove. Move right, step down 2 metres, and traverse to the foot of the large block. Follow the fissure back left to a stance.
3 12m. Climb easy slabs and a chimney to the top of the block.
4 8m. 4b. Climb the steep groove above and finish rightwards.

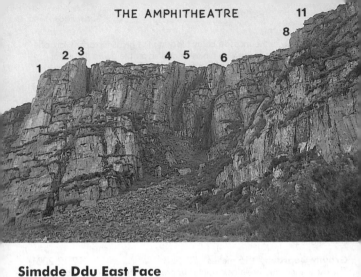

Simdde Ddu East Face

1	The Sound of One Hand Slapping	E2/3
2	The Jump over the Shadow	E5
3	Limelight	E5
4	Left Aisle	VD
5	Night Howl	E4
6	Heart of Darkness	VS

7	Ordinary Route
8	Graveyard Gates
9	Via Dolorosa
10	Right Aisle
11	Jac Codi Baw
12	Road to Anarchy (pitch 4)

Right Flank   48 metres   Hard Severe †   (7.94)
1 9m. *Left Flank* pitch 1.
2 21m. 4a. Continue as for *Left Flank* to the foot of the block; then move
right onto the large ledge to belay at the foot of a chimney.
3 12m. The clean classic chimney leads to the top of the block.
4 6m. 4b. Finish up an awkward little groove above the chimney.

Automedon   83 metres   Very Severe †   (8.7.97)
Below the left side of the Trojan Horse and about 30 metres above the foot
of the cliff, a 9-metre-long block overhang is supported by a pillar left of
centre. The route takes this pillar and finishes up *Left Flank*, straightening
its third pitch. Start in the bay below the left side of the block overhang.
1 11m. 4b. Climb the wall between the stepped corner and the mossy
ramp on the right. Or take the easy stepped corner and then descend
rightwards to:
2 17m. 4a. Follow the left-slanting weakness and ledges to a stance at
the left side of the pillar.
3 20m. 4c. Gain the top of the pillar and make a hard move onto the
block on the left. Step right into a groove and up onto the nose.
4 27m. 4b. This pitch is reached by a 9-metre scramble left to the second
pitch of *Left Flank*. Climb up beneath a V-groove and move right to a
shorter groove. Climb this onto a slab past a perched pillar, move right,
and rejoin *Left Flank* on top of the Trojan Horse.
5 8m. 4b. *Left Flank* pitch 4.

Achilles Heel   30 metres   Very Severe †   (11.7.96)
The big grass balcony right of the Trojan Horse offers a direct and
independent start to *Right Flank*. Scramble 40 metres up thick vegetation
and awkward rock steps to start at the foot of the wall near the left-hand
end of the base ledge. Pass bulges by short rising traverses up steps.
Engaging climbing on compact rock with spaced protection and the crux
to finish. Exit directly above the start.

In the centre of the upper tier of the extensive and terraced East Face is the
great dark chimney that gives the crag its name. The walls on either side of
the chimney form a wide bowl, 'the amphitheatre'. This is bounded 25
metres left by a tall leaning tower with a frontal arête and a shorter hanging
arête on its right-hand (north-east) side. The platform below this leaning
tower can be gained by abseil or a scramble up via the easy-angled scree
below the black chimney. It is a straightforward stroll leftwards for 25 metres
along the left wall to reach the leaning tower.

The Sound of One Hand Slapping   24 metres   E2/3 5c † (14.8.96)
Start on the platform, 3 metres left of the arête, and gain the first ledge via
the centre of the short wall. Then take the faint groove just left of centre on
good holds. A bold and confident approach brings more good holds until
a mantel can be made onto the next ledge. Continue direct via a vague
crack (peg on right shared with *The Jump over the Shadow*); then make

strenuous moves up and left to a pillar on the left arête. Pull around this to the little ledge on the left and finish up the short corner, clapping.

The next two routes take the right edge of the pillar on the arête and give wild exposed climbing.

★★**The Jump over the Shadow**   24 metres   E5 6a   (1.11.95)
Exhilarating climbing up the tower in a wonderful position, committing and strenuous. Take the centre of the short stepped wall to the wide clean ledge (as for the preceding route), and then step right to the arête. Very hard moves and long reaches past little gear gain the next ledge. Step left and up to a peg; then continue up and rightwards almost back to the arête. Finish direct via a short friendly crack.

☆**Life in the Shadow of Death**   24 metres   E5 6a †   (27.9.97)
Effectively a direct version of *The Jump...* – but harder. The start is seriously nasty and will beg the question 'do I really want to do this?' From the platform below the tower, take the edge of the white wall awkwardly and with great commitment to the ledge above (bomber *Friend 2*). Swing right into the leaning white groove and follow it – no piece of cake – to the right-hand limit of a second ledge. Now press on direct over a rickety bulge to finish up the arête. Tempted?

☆**Limelight**   15 metres   E5 6a †   (27.9.97)
A wild 'little' route with a big psychological impact: the short, hanging, north-east (right) arête of the tower. Approach the isolated ledge beneath its right-hand side by abseil. Go up the see-through crack (!) to a break which leads left onto the arête. Implant gear in the break, and with no second thoughts take the edge of the awesomely-angled arête to the big ledge above. A short wall remains. (A 'High Noon' apprenticeship may prove valuable.)

At the very top of the crag, but about 40 metres back from its edge, is a short isolated wall with two routes.

Lather in My Tights   8 metres   Hard Very Severe 5b †   (14.8.96)
Two metres left of *Out of the Night*, at the entrance to the cleft, is a vague groove. Make hard moves to gain a jug on the right, and then a difficult pull up left to reach some more good holds. Finish direct and belay well back.

Out of the Night   8 metres   Hard Very Severe 5b †   (14.8.96)
The crack on the right which starts out of the recess. Strenuous and well-protected.

☆☆**Left Aisle**   21 metres   Very Difficult †   (14.5.96)
Between the leaning tower and the black chimney is a leftward-trending crack dividing the steep walls. Climb the crack, which is steep to start but has good holds throughout. Impressive situation and one of the best routes of its grade here.

Night Howl 27 metres E4 6a † (27.9.97)
Dark, direct, and demanding. Start at the foot of *Left Aisle* and climb the
scantily-protected runnel right of the crack to an incut ledge (good nut
runner). Teeter rightwards around the bulge to a prominent right-to-left
slanting groove. Climb the groove for 2 metres and, at the level of a slot
on its right arête, launch right to a jug right of a thin crack. Follow the
crack steeply to an exit groove.

☆**Heart of Darkness** 36 metres Very Severe † (24.6.96)
The black chimney itself (simdde ddu) looks unappealing but has character
and atmosphere. The first pitch is within the darkness of the chimney, while
the second takes the open wall up and right.
1 24m. 4a. Follow the right-hand crack and get onto a half-buried
chockstone 3 metres below the roof. Traverse the right wall, or bridge out,
to reach a good stance in the corner.
2 12m. 4c. Move down right 6 metres to a comfortable grass ledge.
Starting on the right, climb the bulging wall and follow the groove to the top.

Thirty metres right of the black chimney is a 30-metre-high tower with a
good arête forming its left-hand side. Just left of the tower is a steep chimney
in a corner. The routes here are reached by a scramble up from the scree
below and then a further scramble up two heather terraces.

Ordinary Route 39 metres Very Difficult † (19.5.98)
The chimney gives the easiest exit from the amphitheatre. Start 3 metres
right of the cave formed by its first chockstone.
1 12m. Climb the short corner and go left over ledges to the foot of the
rib.
2 27m. Follow the rib, then the chimney to the summit terrace, passing
the second chockstone on its left.

The left-hand arête of the tower is:

☆**Graveyard Gates** 27 metres E1 5a/b † (27.9.97)
A captivating line, very generously graded. Start at the left end of the
heather ledge below the arête. Climb a small corner on the left to gain the
tower's arête. Follow nice, positive holds up the left side of the arête until
just below the top. A swing right into the groove in the arête provides a
quite spectacular finish.

These next three climbs have a common start at the right foot of the tower. A
3-metre-high pillar with a thread at its top leans against this wall.

☆**Via Dolorosa** 27 metres E1 5b † (23.9.97)
A good, steep line, with just enough gear, takes the weakness just right of
the centre of the tower. Start at the right-hand edge of the tower and go
leftwards to a groove; step up left, then back right to a grass ledge. Climb
a V-groove up left to a hard exit onto a ledge. Take the final weakness on
the right with strenuous, airy moves. If you've carried a cam size 3 all the
way up here, now's the time to use it.

Right Aisle   27 metres   Very Difficult †   (23.9.97)
Start at the same 3-metre pillar, but take the next corner along before the
arête of *Jac Codi Baw*. Climb it directly past two ledges to finish up the
chimney/crack. Take care with perched blocks on the second ledge.

Jac Codi Baw   27 metres   Hard Very Severe 5a †   (29.7.97)
The prominent arête of the pillar forming the extreme right boundary of
the headwall area of the amphitheatre, though a good feature, has
doubtful rock which required heavy gardening initially (hence the name).
Gain the pillar by climbing up and rightwards from the stance shared with
the two preceding routes. Gain a V-groove out to the right. Climb carefully
up this and then trend leftwards to the edge of the arête. Continue steeply
to the big perched block on the rib.

Fifteen metres right is the next wall at the top of the terraces. Approach from
the top of the cliff. An easy scramble down its south side gains the foot of the
wall.

Punks without Pace   17 metres   Very Severe 4c †   (19.10.97)
The right-hand side of the big flake in the centre of the wall. At its top,
continue directly to the rounded finish at the top of the cliff.

Sunk without Tracey   17 metres   Hard Very Severe 5a †   (19.10.97)
The blunt arête and groove at the right edge of the flake wall. Reach a
ledge directly, make hard moves up the hanging groove above, and gain
the rounded finish at the top of the cliff.

The Road to Anarchy   60 metres   Very Severe †   (29.7.97)
The orange-tinted slabs to the right of the scree outfall of the
amphitheatre. Start at the indefinite angle between the foot of the cliff and
the amphitheatre, a short way right of a broken groove.
1 21m. 4c. Pull over a bulge and follow the slabs leftwards to reach a
terrace.
2 15m. 4c. Climb the short corner at the right edge of the next tier. Move
left to a ledge by a steep nose, pull around this to the slab, and continue
up to the next terrace.
3 Walk left along the terrace and belay below the mossy slabs to the right
of the arête of *Jac Codi Baw*.
4 24m. Climb the left side of the slabs to finish above *JCB*.

Ten metres further right of the scree outfall, the cliff rises in short, steep steps
to an open rightward-facing corner in the headwall. This natural drainage
channel requires a period of dry weather, but has good clean rock and
sound ledges. The corner is:

☆☆**Zalamander**   45 metres   Very Severe †   (14.5.96)
A good line with positive holds that can be climbed in damp conditions.
1 18m. 4c. About 15 metres above the foot of the cliff a big block
projects from a ledge. Below it is a leftward-slanting terrace. Start 18

metres up this, by a boss of rock, and follow the wall direct to the big
platform below the corner.
2 27m. 4b. Follow the obvious cracked corner to a ledge at half height.
From there, make some layback moves (crux) to gain a narrow ledge
beneath a small overhang; then go direct to finish.

Ziggurat   37 metres   Very Difficult †   (19.6.96)
Start at a step at the foot of the left-slanting terrace. (There is a wide crack
over to the right.)
1 11m. Climb onto the terrace on the left and immediately move up right
into a corner with a big perched block.
2 11m. Pull out of the corner, step right, and take the short crack through
the bulge.
3 15m. Move up a little, and then leftwards to the big rock platform at the
foot of *Zalamander*.

At the far right-hand side of the East Face are some more terraced walls. The
next route starts at the lowest point on the right, below a tower with a crack in
its centre.

★★Chrysalis   20 metres   E2 5c   (30.3.96)
From the open groove, pull up onto a ledge on the right; then struggle up
the finger-crack. A steep ramp leads up leftwards to the final short wall
and a pull onto the heather terrace on the right.
Variation
From the top of the finger-crack, bear rightwards onto the arête for an
exhilarating finish.

A Midge Too Far   17 metres   E2 5b †   (23.7.96)
Climb *Chrysalis* for 2 metres and make a hard hand-traverse left onto the
nose. Pull up and follow the ramp to a grass ledge. From this, finish
directly up the final short wall.

Right of this tower is a vegetated corner-system with a protruding arête on its
right.

The Inverse Pleasure Principle   17 metres   E3 5b †   (9.8.98)
With gear in the dirty corner on the left, take pockets in the arête to a
ledge. Boldly trend up and right on the arête to a rest and good nuts.
Traverse left to a crack and follow it up past a small chockstone.

Above the *Chrysalis* tower is a face with a striking finger-crack directly up its
centre.

☆Prizewinner   15 metres   E5 6a †   (28.9.97)
Climb the perfect crack past a peg at the crux. Excellent sustained
finger-jamming up the steep and unrelenting crack.

At the extreme top right-hand end of the crag is an impressive leaning
buttress with a fine wide vertical crack (*Fern's Climb*) up its centre topped by a

huge wedged flake. There are three routes on the steep wall left of *Fern's Climb*. The first is the dog-leg crack at the left side of this steep wall.

Nerve Trap   18 metres   E2 5b †   (9.8.98)
Follow the dog-leg hand-crack past *Friend 2½* placements. Safe and satisfyingly strenuous with no hard (yet no easy) sections.

☆☆**Black Power Salute**   20 metres   E5 6b †   (9.8.98)
Rising from the dog-leg crack is a thin crack in the alarmingly leaning sheet. Unfortunately, a blind *Rock 1* placement on the first crux will necessitate an abseil inspection of this powerful climb. From the top of the lower limb of *Nerve Trap*, crank into the thin crack on the right and blast up it past a technical-to-use fist-pod to a ledge (*in-situ* thread). Finish direct.

Ali Baba   14 metres   Hard Very Severe 5b †   (30.3.96)
Three metres left of *Fern's Climb* is a steeper, thinner crack. Difficult to start, then easing as a series of flakes allows the top to be gained directly. Excellent protection.

Sitting Flake Arête   18 metres   E2 5c †   (9.8.98)
The line of the left arête of *Fern's Climb*. Start from a large ledge below a 4-centimetre crack just left of that route. Climb the crack to a ledge below a corner. Swing right to the obvious handhold; then make airy moves up the top of the arête to exit behind the sitting flake.

☆☆**Fern's Climb**   14 metres   Very Severe 4c †   (30.3.96)
This is the fine vertical crack in the centre of the wall leading to the top of the crag. The crack provides a good challenge with a final difficult section in the chimney formed by the sitting flake.

To the right the wall degenerates into broken ledges, but below is a detached pinnacle.

☆**Army of One**   25 metres   E4 †   (9.8.98)
1 8m. 5c. Start on the left shoulder of the detached pinnacle. Swing left into a straight thin crack, which leads onto the large ledge above.
2 17m. 5c. Climb the groove from the right-hand end of the ledge to a jug at 6 metres. Pull into the very steep crack on the left. Good holds lead steeply to the exit above, just right of a bound-in block.

Above and to the right on the skyline is a wide, short slab. Its routes are described under *Daear Fawr*, which can be easily approached from here.

Bryn y Dyfrgi   Hill (of) the Otter   OS Ref 841 378

Between Simdde Ddu and Llyn Arennig is a tiered buttress, with its 20-metre-high, white South Face marked by an obvious horizontal break and two cracks forming a large wigwam shape in its centre. The East Face, overlooking the lake, has a 12-metre-high, leaning wall on the lowest level, and a top tier above a heather-covered, slabby middle section with several small trees. Both South and East Faces have good collections of hard routes, mainly on steep and leaning walls. The rock can be a bit lichenous in places, but dries quickly after rain and gives excellent friction on sound holds.

South Face

★Mabinogion   17 metres   Hard Very Severe 5a   (19.6.96)
The crack and flake at the left extreme of the wall, below a sapling. Climb on good edges to a small roof. Pull around to the right to gain the horizontal break. Continue through directly, using layaways on the left and small pockets on the top wall. A good line.

☆Sounds Like Drums   20 metres   E4 5c †   (20.9.97)
The rounded rib just right. Technically reasonable but a bit bold. Climb direct to a pothole at 5 metres. Move up (*RPs in flake*), reach comforting finger-pockets in the bulge, and then extend right to a small flake, and so gain the horizontal break above. Climb straight up the exit moves of *Shamanic Voices*.

★★Shamanic Voices   17 metres   E5 6a   (3.9.93)
Start at the left end of the large ledge by stepping up onto a pillar. Step off the pillar rightwards onto the wall and pull up boldly to a large pocket (large cam) and a peg runner of sorts. Make a hard sequence (those voices in your head will help) with long reaches up rightwards to the horizontal break and a thread. Use a flake up on the left to gain the superb pocketed wall above the thread; then continue up rightwards onto the sloping ledge, and finish easily up the wall above on huge pockets. Flawless.

☆Magua   17 metres   E5 6a †   (20.9.97)
The blunt, pocketed rib next right is direct and unforgiving: another of the quality routes here. Place wires in the toe of the *Mohican* corner; then climb the rib past two deep pockets to gain the horizontal break, which slopes here. Continue direct to finish up the top crack of *Mohican*.

★Mohican   17 metres   E2 5c   (1.5.90)
One of the original lines on this wall, and well worth a visit. The centre of the wall has a wide rightward-trending crack (*Wig*), which straightens below the mid-height break and then goes diagonally right again to the top. It is joined at the break by the left-trending crackline (*Wam*). Start 2 metres left of *Wig*. Gain the left-facing thin corner directly above and follow it slightly rightwards to the break at a point about 1 metre left of *Wig*. The good clean wall up and left has a thin crackline about 2 metres left of the *Wam* crack which leads to the second horizontal break. Finish up the short thin crack above.

Bryn y Dyfrgi

South Face

1	Mabinogion	HVS
2	Sounds Like Drums	E4
3	Shamanic Voices	E5
4	Magua	E5
5	Mohican	E2
6	Wig	E1
7	Wam	E2
8	War Cry	E3
9	Spirit from the Cage	E5
10	Speaking in Tongues	E5

Wig 17 metres E1 5b † (14.8.90)
This takes the uncleaned, right-trending crack to the top. Very dirty and unlikely looking.

Wam 17 metres E2 5c (14.8.90)
The left-trending crack is thin and clean on the lower wall but, like its neighbour *Wig*, involves dirty jamming in its final uncleaned section above the horizontal break.

★★**War Cry** 18 metres E3 5c (1.5.90)
About 2 metres right of *Wam* is a good, thin crack leading to the recess in the break. Step up right from the recess and follow another thin vertical crack (hard), which gains the next sloping horizontal break. Continue direct to the top on positive holds. Brilliant.

☆☆**Spirit from the Cage** 18 metres E5 6b † (28.10.97)
One of the most sustained and direct lines on the face. Start at the hairline crack near the right-hand end of the rock platform. Very sustained and thin climbing on small, shallow pockets past a peg runner gains the right-facing recess at the break. Place trust in gear behind the block on the left; then launch up and leftwards to a good pocket. Go up directly above this on solid rock to a thin horizontal break and some much needed protection. Continuous hard climbing directly above leads to the finishing-crack in the right-hand side of the headwall.

☆☆**Speaking in Tongues** 18 metres E5 6a/b † (5.6.96)
Follow the hairline crack of *Spirit from the Cage* to the recess at 6 metres. Pull through the roof on the right and step onto its lip by laybacking the right edge. From the horizontal break, pull up past a large pocket and gain the final right-hand ledge with great difficulty. Finish up the short wall above or the vague crack less than a metre left.
Variation E5 6a (20.9.97). A good line with some excellent independent climbing. Demanding for the grade. Start at the right-hand limit of the underlying rock platform. Step off the platform and follow a line of right-facing side-holds (wire in crack on right), before a swing left and a hard reach gain the resting-ledge on the left in the recess shared with the parent route. Surmount the roof as for that, but once the next ledge is reached, swing back left onto the headwall to take the finishing-crack of *Spirit from the Cage*.

East Face
This long 8-metre-high wall leans alarmingly. At its left end is the steep, heather-choked, narrow gully that leads up the top tier 12 metres higher. The first feature on the lowest tier is an open groove, and next right is a hand-jamming crack with a small tree sticking out from the heather ledge at its top. Several vertical seams break the wall further right; and on the extreme right is a pocketed section below a roof split by a wide crack.

Bryn y Dyfrgi

East Face

1	Leather Boots		VS
2	Third Time Lucky		E3
3	Otters Dreaming		E2
4	The Lizard of Id		E4
5	Chorus of Stone		E3
6	Mouldy Mormons		E1
7	Witch's Tit		E3
8	A Hovis Witness		E2
9	Naomi		E4
10	Generals of Tomorrow		E3
11	Hemispheres		E1
12	The 5000 Fingers of Dr T		E1
13	Brigadoon		HS
14	Brubeck's Cube		E6
15	A Point of Snow Return		E5
16	Radiat Bug		HS

E3	
HVS	
E5	
E2	
E5	

SOUTH FACE

NORTH FACE

Leather Boots 5 metres   Very Severe 5a   (15.5.2000)
The open groove in the left end of the wall, about 3 metres left of the tree.

Third Time Lucky 7 metres E3 6a †   (23.5.98)
The obvious hand-jamming crack is rarely fully dry, but is a worthy
companion to the other short and steep lines on this section. The crack has
good protection but involves awkward finger-jams followed by more
peculiar jams.

★★**Otters Dreaming** 8 metres E2 5c   (3.5.95)
Two metres right, a thin seam provides sustained climbing all the way,
though with a good jug at three-quarters height. Pull through onto the
heather-covered top. Tree belay 5 metres back.

★★**The Lizard of Id** 7 metres E4 6a   (19.6.96)
Right of this again is another crack. Gain good holds just below a peg and
pass this with great difficulty to a short horizontal slot and a second peg.
Above is a short vertical slot (good runner and layaway). There is a thin
thread in the next horizontal break. Then make a long reach for a
finishing-jug and the heather terrace. Leans all the way.

Chorus of Stone 7 metres E3 6a †   (13.7.95)
Sustained climbing up the vague crack past an obvious slot at 3 metres
(*Rock 1*). Hard moves lead past this for a good hold high on the right.
Continue direct into the wider slot, and pull over easily onto the heather
ledge. *In-situ* thread and karabiner.

North Face
The two routes here are on the left-hand side by the rib.

Bald Man's Arête 15 metres E2 5b †   (5.6.96)
Start off easily from the bottom of the rib. Make difficult moves to leave the
first horizontal crack, and gain the short ledge on the rib. A sustained
sequence then gains the final short ledge on the rib. Scuttle right to finish
up *Moon Dog*.

☆**Moon Dog** 15 metres E1 5b †   (23.6.95)
This takes the centre of the wall by a series of cracks and flakes. Finish up
the pocketed wall at its centre and mantel onto the heather top.

Top Tier
This is the level sitting above the *Otters Dreaming* wall and facing east to the lake.
The tier is cut off at both ends, and is reached by the heather and rock scramble at
the left end of the East Face. The first route is a fine crack starting off at the left end
of the terrace above *Otters Dreaming*, behind a couple of large trees.

Mouldy Mormons 14 metres E1 5b †   (4.7.98)
Climb the rightward-rising thin crack to the top of the wall and finish up
the easy slab above.

Witch's Tit   14 metres   E3 5c †   (4.7.98)
The steep wall just left of the rightward-facing corner is taken directly. An *in-situ* hex and a cam placement protect until the wall joins the slab above and the easier finish of *Mouldy Mormons*.

A Hovis Witness   14 metres   Hard Very Severe 5a †   (4.7.98)
The rightward-facing corner left of the deep cleft gets progressively harder and reaches a difficult finish. Protection is adequate.

Next right is a fierce steep wall bounded on its right by a vertical finger-crack (*Generals of Tomorrow*). Two metres left of this crack is the next route.

☆☆☆**Naomi**   14 metres   E5 6b †   (7.8.98)
Steep and fingery, with just enough gear. Start below a wide slot and go direct to another slot. Pass this using small edges to gain a third slot and another cam placement. About a metre higher is a perfect mid-size nut placement. From the slot pull up leftwards and continue on pockets to the ledge and the short, easy rightward-facing corner. Belay 4 metres back on the slab above.

★★**Generals of Tomorrow**   14 metres   E2 5c   (19.6.96)
This excellent crack runs up to a narrow ledge before pulling onto the exposed slab above. After an easy start, it quickly steepens until a combination of layaways, bridging, and fingerlocks passes the central crux. Belay in small cracks 4 metres back from the edge.

☆☆**Hemispheres**   14 metres   E5 6a †   (4.7.98)
The overhanging groove just right of the crack is desperate to start and involves a powerful reach for the holds up and right. Pass these and move up the short slab to the steep arête directly above (and just right of the *Generals…*). Climb the arête to the top.

☆**The 5000 Fingers of Dr T**   12 metres   E1 5b †   (19.6.96)
The thin corner right of *Hemispheres* and just left of *Brigadoon*. Bridge up, popping the odd cam into the crack on the left, until it is possible to pull onto the ledge on the right using a pocket on the right wall. Step across to the back of the ledge and finish up the fine short crack in the right wall.

Brigadoon   14 metres   Hard Severe 4c †   (3.9.93)
Between the corner and the square leaning wall is a narrow, steep, white wall with a crack bounding its right side. Pull up directly onto the wall and, using holds on its left edge, climb it to the ledge. Walk to the back of the ledge and disappear into the chasm on the right. Chimney deliriously out of this.

☆☆☆**Brubeck's Cube**   15 metres   E6 6b †   (28.9.97)
This perfect square wall, which draws the eye from the lakeside, has just left of its centre a compelling hairline crack, unquestionably impeccable. Several peg runners facilitate an onsight approach: once the topmost is clipped, this route is safe enough with good, but spaced, *Rock 3* and *4* placements.

Follow pockets (peg runner) and the thin crack intricately past two reasonable pegs (advisable to hero-loop the top one) to a superb shake-out jug in a pocket where the wall rears out. A very powerful, or dynamic (or a combination of a bit less of both) should lead to the lip and a short crack to pull over. Prepare for a 'belter' if rejected from the top move.

☆**A Point of Snow Return** 12 metres E5 6a † (15.4.2000)
[Photo page 176b.] A good line up perfect rock, and considerably easier than its companion. Make cunning moves to the small right-facing ramp just right of *Brubeck's Cube*, and then take small edges up right to gain a good slot. Improving layaways lead to the top. Wild.

Radiat Bug 12 metres Hard Severe 4c † (5.6.96)
Right of the square block is a wide crack almost at the end of the terrace. Entertaining and worthwhile; difficult to finish.

Sooth Slayer Wall

[Photodiagram page 139.] Forty-five metres back up the hill to the right is another independent buttress, with an obvious roof/arch across a leaning wall and a goblet-shaped crack on the right. At the left side of this wall is a slim corner just right of a tree.

Morris Minor 12 metres Hard Severe 4c (15.5.2000)
Climb the slim corner to the niche and then an easy finishing slab.

★**Superstring** 12 metres E2 5b (3.5.2000)
This starts on the pedestal just left of the right-facing corner. A thin start leads to a series of jugs trending left to where the groove is finished directly.

☆**Take a Pig's Head, Add One Spoonful of Medium Rage**
14 metres E6 6b † (21.7.2000)
A line that demands total attention from the very first move. The right-facing corner (small thread) is thin and difficult, and continues strenuously to the roof (good gear here). Wicked moves through the roof onto the wall above lead to some good holds and an easier finish.

☆**Lurkio** 15 metres E5 6a † (20.9.97)
Like its left-hand companion, this should not be approached with complacency: a particularly uncomfortable landing awaits. Start below the ramp in the lower wall 3 metres right of *Take a Pig's Head…* Continuing off-balance moves up the ramp, past a sling on a weak spike and an indifferent peg runner, should (the gods willing) lead to the overlap and good gear. Crank over the roof and follow the crack on good holds directly to the top. Tough for the grade.

★**Fighting Spirit** 12 metres E2 5b (15.5.2000)
The slim groove next right leading to the jamming crack of *Sooth Slayer*.

Sooth Slayer   12 metres   E2 5b †   (18.8.93)
Take the wide crack next right by a series of jams. Follow it leftwards to
where it becomes vertical, and struggle on up. Unrelenting, strenuous, and
just a bit dirty.

★★**50 Dead Men Walking**   11 metres   E2 5b   (3.5.2000)
[Photo page 176b.] Start as for *Sooth Slayer* but continue up the
right-hand crack equally joyfully.

☆**Fiend Two**   12 metres   E2 5c †   (25.8.93)
This is the arête and groove at the right end of the buttress. Gain a flat
spike on the arête from the left. A second spike takes a sling. Strenuous
climbing on good holds up the steep groove on the right gains the top.

☆**Milkman's Daughter**   11 metres   E1 5b †   (19.4.2000)
The fine clean wall right of the arête has a hard start that is worth solving
for the easier wall above.

The Coming War   9 metres   E1 5c †   (5.6.96)
Further right of the arête is a wide crack running up to a short steep
groove below a tree. The difficulties are in gaining the groove and
bridging up it. A week of dry weather needed.

Dorothy's Wall   5 metres   Hard Severe 4b †   (15.4.2000)
The short leaning wall on the extreme right.

Y Castell   The Castle   OS Ref 842 374

This is the large, broken, terraced cliff up and left of Bryn Dyfrgi with a scree
gully (Bwlch Blaen y Nant) forming its right limit and the shoulder of the
walkers' spur its left. Approach can be made via the path from the bothy by
the lake, which will provide access to the routes on the top tier and allow
abseil from this to the lines directly below. For the two routes on the extreme
right of the crag: either walk up the scree slope from Bryn Dyfrgi; or, from the
hillwalkers' path from the bothy, gain the very top of the crag, and walk all
the way along its top (path) to the top of Bwlch Blaen y Nant, from where you
can scramble back down to the foot of *Rainy Day Women*. This climb takes
the edge and striking arête on the right-hand end of y Castell and runs the
full height of the cliff. *Jenga* starts 30 metres left, where a broken corner with
a ledge at its base leads onto a low-profile buttress.

Jenga   39 metres   Hard Severe †   (20.7.96)
1 9m. 4a. Climb the corner to ledges, step right, and move up to
another corner just right.
2 12m. 4a. Climb the short corner to wide cracks and the foot of a slab.
3 18m. 4b. The slab is split by a groove leading into a crack. Move up
right and then traverse left for 6 metres to cross the groove. Climb direct
and step into the top of the crack to reach the top terrace.

☆**Rainy Day Women**   51 metres   Very Severe †   (25.8.93)
A good long line with generally sound rock.
1 12m. 4a. The route starts at the right-hand end of the dark wall at the lowest point of the crag. Climb the rib, bearing left past good horizontal breaks. Belay on huge boulders on the ledge below a shattered tower.
2 9m. 4a. Take the broken tower above until able to step right into a corner, and climb the corner to top out on the great wedged boulders just left of the arête. Belay on good threads.
3 15m. 4c. Step right onto the arête by a tricky move; then continue direct in an excellent position. Gain a faint corner on the right, and follow this to a ledge.
4 15m. 4b. Above the belay ledge is a tottering tower. Escape this by immediately stepping right and gaining the back of the gully. Climb the back of this easily and scramble up onto the heather terrace above.

Top Tier

This is best approached by following the main water-track around the lake and the walkers' path up the shoulder of the mountain. A large grass platform sits below the top tier and is easily accessed via a sheep trail. The walls of the top tier are about 18 metres high whilst the tier below drops for 40 metres at its highest point, which is the central tower.

Magwitch   18 metres   E3 5c †   (30.8.98)
The first corner along the trail is difficult, sustained, and bold until the first runner slot at over 6 metres. Continue up the corner until able to step left onto the ledge. Finish more easily up the stepped ledges directly above.

Charlie Spitkid   18 metres   E3 5c †   (30.8.98)
The thin crack 2 metres left of *The Path to Redemption* is followed for 6 metres to where a step right into that route allows a semi-rest. Pull back up and left (hard) to gain the grass recess. Step up right again to finish as for *The Path to Redemption*.

The Path to Redemption   18 metres   E2 5c †   (8.8.98/30.8.98)
The hand-jamming crack 6 metres right of *Magwitch* is followed easily to the top of the huge flake and the recess. Pull through the bulge above with difficulty but good protection, and follow the thin layback groove above. Finish easily up the short corner.

Spandexterity   18 metres   E2 5c †   (30.8.98)
The next rightward-facing corner is reached from the right before good pockets lead to the sloping ledge. Continue up the smooth corner past two pegs until it is possible to gain the holds at the top of the left-hand wall. Pull up, and climb over good short ledges to the top.

The tiers immediately below, dominated by the long central arête of *Cosy Powell*, are best approached by abseil from the boulder-field at its top. Six metres left of *Cosy Powell* is an isolated route in the centre of a distinctive red wall. Although its start can be reached by scrambling up from below, a long abseil is probably easier. The abseil point for *Cosy Powell* is from the lowest point of a small boulder scree on the top-tier platform. That for the first route is 12 metres left, and for the white wall routes 12 metres right.

☆The Delicate Side of Thunder   14 metres   E4 6a †   (1.8.99)
A very good route, well worth setting up the abseil for. Start in the centre of the pocketed red wall below a thin groove. Climb the groove and scrabble about for some pockets which enable the wall up and right to be reached. This is climbed directly on good holds. Leans all the way.

☆Cosy Powell   40 metres   E3 6a †   (8.8.98)
An outstanding line, with fine climbing on the staggered arête of the tower. Start at the toe of the arête and gain a ledge easily. Step right to the thin crack, which leads to a wider crack. Make a long reach to a good edge and move up to the next ledge. Span up and right around the arête, and go directly and boldly up to a sloping ledge. Finish the still steep final arête on large holds.

☆Drive like You Drum   40 metres   E2 5c †   (8.8.98)
An excellent pitch up the right-hand wall of the tower. Leave *Cosy Powell* after 5 metres by stepping rightwards into a short corner leading to the break. Further up and right a difficult crack and flake are climbed to the second break. Step right and follow the well-protected thin crack up the centre of the wall to the steep final arête of *Cosy Powell*.

☆All Fingers and Thumbs   14 metres   E7 6c †   (1.8.99)
The fine, white wall right of the final crack of *Drive Like You Drum* harbours this gem, which requires great finger strength and a positive approach. Start from the grassy ledge below the wall at its right side. Pull up and left (with savage, crimping, gear in the thin slots) and make a long reach for a finger-pocket on the left edge of the white wall. Try to leave this by continuing directly up past a peg and a preplaced *Rock 1* before yet more hard moves allow better holds up and left to be reached. From the big ledge above, finish easily.

Caught in the Crossfire   18 metres   E1 5a †   (1.8.99)
The right edge of the white wall provides a welcome respite between its hard companions. Pull up directly to a good horizontal cam slot and past a more shallow pocket to gain a groove. Pop up onto the ledge above and finish as for *All Fingers and Thumbs*.

Enemy of the Earth   14 metres   E4 6a †   (8.8.98)
The next arête to the right gives good climbing with an exciting crux. Either scramble down easily 30 metres to the right of *Cosy Powell* and contour back, or find a good abseil point. Take a short, hard groove to a break (*Friend 1½*). Reach finger-flakes and bear left to a foot-ledge on the arête. Climb the safe, thin crack to the top.

Carreg Lefain   Echo Rock   OS Ref 847 374

This small narrow slabby crag faces south and is just below the shoulder on the south shore of the lake. Two routes are recorded here:

Ou Est le Soleil?   17 metres   Very Difficult †   (1990)
At the left of the slabby wall is an obvious crack – wide, and sporting some fronds.

Ghostown   17 metres   E1 5a †   (4.90)
Start in the centre of the slab above an old ruined house. Thin climbing up a vague crack gains easier ground and a direct finish.

Daear Fawr   Big Ground   OS Ref 836 386

This wonderful collection of sharp arêtes and corners holds a concentration of good-quality routes that are most appealing on a summer's day, the north side being a bit dark and cold in the winter. Approach is possible from the private, old, fenced quarry in Arennig village: a good track winds through the quarry and finishes just below the crag after 15 minutes' walk. However, the recommended approach is via the gate (826 393) and cattle grid 200 metres west along the road from the quarry car-park. Go through the gate and follow the track along the stream-side. Once the brow of the first hill is reached the crag complex of the northern slopes can be seen. On the extreme right is Hyrddod, on the left is Pen Tyrau, and on the very far left is the first white wall of Daear Fawr across the pleasant moorland. This is only slightly longer than the quarry track, and far more enjoyable. Approach can also be made from the Dŵr Cymru track as for Simdde Ddu, but it is a lot rougher and probably longer.

This extensive collection of terraced walls faces north-east and is heavily vegetated in places. In fact, the vegetation includes patches of interesting and varied flora where there is localised nutrient enrichment. This should be recognisable by the herbs and ferns present and **every effort should be made to avoid damaging or disturbing it**.

There are, however, some fine arêtes, corners, and walls which provide excellent climbing. It is the most accessible of the Arennig crags and deserves to become popular as it offers routes of all grades.

Except for the few scattered routes at the very end of the section, the climbs are described from **right to left**, as the approach path leaves you at the right-hand side of this crag. A clean, white, north-facing wall with a short roof on its left has some very good routes. The great east-facing wall, which starts at the left edge of the white wall, has eight clear arêtes, an amazing

Daear Fawr

1	Tick Teaser	HVS
2	Hands-full	E5
3	A Pair of Clydesdales	E1
4	Rapscallion	S
5	Scorpion	VS
6	Mystic peg	VD
7	Dig for Victory	E1

8	El Magnifico	E5
9	Umbrella Head	E2
10	Stretchmark	E5
11	Screaming Wet Arête	E1
12	The Outhouse Effect	E4
13	World's Gone Green	E2
14	Kyoto	E5

sight, all begging to be climbed. To the left of the eighth blade arête is a broken, dirty wall with no routes. Left of this are the great left-facing corner of *Redneck Olympics* and two routes just to its right. Left again is the large *Prey* wall, with a distinct V-groove at its base and a large old nest pile on a ledge up left.

The first routes are on the fine, clean, white wall facing the quarry, on the extreme right of the crag.

☆**Tick Teaser**   14 metres   Hard Very Severe 5a †   (31.7.96)
Start below a short left-facing corner. Climb up to a huge flake and continue direct past good wire placements to a difficult finish just right of centre at the top.

☆**Hands-full**   14 metres   E5 6a †   (23.5.98)
An eliminate up the headwall. Follow *Tick Teaser* for 7 metres before easing out left to a left-facing groove and a finger-jug. Limited *RP*s protect the smooth wall above until the finishing-jug.

★★**A Pair of Clydesdales**   14 metres   E1 5b   (31.7.96)
A wonderful clean straight line 2 metres right of the roof. Start on the ledge by a thin crack. Gain the overlap and pull through to a wide vertical slot (good cam). Go direct through the next overlap (protection just left) and finish direct.

★**Rapscallion**   14 metres   Severe 4b   (14.7.90)
One of the best routes of its grade in the area, it takes the thin crack at the right-hand side of the obvious nose. Start below the nose, by the narrow groove. Climb the groove to the left end of the ledge; then pull through the right-hand side of the nose before stepping up left onto it. Finish direct.

★**Scorpion**   14 metres   Very Severe 4c   (14.7.90)
Begin 2 metres to the left of the preceding route. Straightforward Severe climbing leads directly up the steep, slightly loose wall to a V-corner forming the left border of the nose. Exit the corner with difficulty to finish.

Mystic Peg   11 metres   Very Difficult †   (31.7.96)
The first arête, 3 metres left of the roof. Follow this to a broken ledge before finishing carefully up the gully left of the *Scorpion* corner.

Dig for Victory   30 metres   E1 5b †   (31.7.96)
A good long pitch, slightly marred by a break and possible (but not recommended) escape at half height. Start in the groove below the next roof, 4 metres left of *Mystic Peg*. Bridge briefly up the groove and then step left onto the arête. Follow this, passing the left end of a small roof by a large chockstone. Continue up the broken arête on the left until a hard sequence gains the final slab, and belay on a huge wedged boulder.

☆☆**El Magnifico**   18 metres   E5 6b †   (12.10.97)
A magnificent feature, with positions normally reserved for great arêtes. This is the fourth arête (from the right), which forms the right edge of an open corner beneath a huge projecting roof. Fix some runners at the level

of a small overhang 7 metres up the crack of *Umbrella Head* and descend
again. (It may feel like overhead protection to start but will feel far from it on
the crux section of the arête!) Follow a series of small footholds rightwards
above the lip of the overhang and, with long reaches to and then from a
narrow pocket, grasp the arête and a jug above. Take the sharp edge
dramatically to a ledge and retreat by abseil from the tree on the right.

☆Umbrella Head   18 metres   E2 5c †   (12.10.97)
The open corner has a crack/groove in the centre of its right wall. Climb it
to the ledge (and abseil from the tree as for *El Magnifico*).

☆☆Stretchmark   30 metres   E5 6a †   (12.10.97)
A pumpy and very sustained lower half, but all of the climbing is good.
This, the fifth arête from the right, has a bulging, face-like profile (if the
imagination can be stretched like the body). Hard moves up the initial
arête lead to a bulge (awkward wires). Go up right under the bulge
(crucial *Rock 4* placements) and crank over on good pockets up the
left-hand side of the arête to an easy ramp. From the top of the ramp,
continue up the pleasant arête, keeping left of the vegetated corner
bounding the left side of the projecting roof, to the top.

Screaming Wet Arête   24 metres   E1 5b †   (12.10.97)
The sixth arête is inset in a little bay and has a give-away crack in its left
wall. The first ascent was made in waterfall conditions with the bonus of
one dry hold; in good weather this will be a safe and enjoyable climb.
Climb the arête, using the crack, to a ledge. Follow the wide crack, then
the rib above to a belay on a huge jammed boulder. Abseil or walk off left.

☆The Outhouse Effect   24 metres   E4 6a †   (12.10.97)
Superb climbing on good holds up the left side of the penultimate arête.
Take the left side of the arête to pockets (*in-situ* thread). Bear right along
the roof via the right-hand end of a hand-ledge (small wire on left) to the
arête. Continue more easily up the arête to belay on the jammed boulder.

World's Gone Green   12 metres   E2 5c †   (23.5.98)
Fairly inconsequential. Start beneath the groove right of the final (eighth)
arête on this section. Pull into the groove, bridge up, and then transfer left
onto the slab formed by the right wall of the arête. Stretch up for the top of
the arête, surmount a bulge, and climb more easily to a tree. Scramble
out, or abseil off (with care for the tree).

☆Kyoto   12 metres   E5 6b †   (23.5.98)
The superb blade arête which is the final (eighth) arête of this section.
Arrange protection 3 metres up the scruffy corner on the left; then step
right above the overhang to the foot of the arête. Grope around right to
clip a low peg runner on the right wall (to curtail a possible/probable
body-crunching swoop) before powering up the left side of the arête
(*Friend 2½* in pocket) to a break. Surmount a bulge and climb more easily
to a tree (as for *World's Gone Green*).

About 50 metres further left is a big, striking, left-facing corner with a grassy ledge at one-third height. The short steep wall to its right has two routes.

Mandolin Wind   15 metres   E2 5c   (2.8.96)
The vertical crack just right of centre of this wall, below a wedged flake. Using some holds on the left, struggle into the crack and gain good undercuts just right. Follow the crack to where it breaks left and belay as for *Supermodel*.

★Supermodel   15 metres   E3 5c   (2.8.96)
The pocketed wall right of the corner. Start at its centre and gain the overlap directly using the superb pockets (good gear below the overlap). Pull up strenuously leftwards and gain the sloping ledge above. Good but widely-spaced holds lead boldly to a good wire in the faint left-facing groove. Make difficult moves past this to the ledge on top. Up and right is a grass recess with good cracks in the wall behind. Belay here. A short steep scramble up gains the pinnacle and the walk off.

☆Redneck Olympics   23 metres   E2 †   (2.8.96)
The large, left-facing corner is a delightful challenge with varied climbing.
1 8m. 5b. Take the middle of the three short corners below the ledge: layback and bridge up the wide crack in the back of the corner past a chockstone or two to a problematical and strenuous finish. A bit dusty topping out.
2 15m. 5c. Climb the corner by wide bridging to some jammed blocks. Escape out left to a big undercut crack below the overlap. Pass this with difficulty and continue up the leaning corner past good wire placements to big finishing-holds. Belay on a ledge to the right behind the pinnacle.

Further left is a big wall with a dark, V-shaped groove on the right. Up on the left there are two large left-facing corner-ledges with ancient nest remains.

☆Hunted   36 metres   E4 6a †   (23.5.98)
A very good climb, well up in the grade, but very protectable.
1 24m. 6a. Pull up to finger jugs in the V-shaped groove. Climb the cracks in the leaning wall above until a very fierce move up and left gains a sloping ledge and the break. Step up onto the undercut slab above, swing left, and take a groove to a grassy ledge and the junction with *Prey*.
2 12m. 4b. *Prey* pitch 2.

★★Prey   36 metres   E4 5c   (4.8.96)
1 24m. 5c. The crack a few metres left of the groove is hard to start, but as it rises leftwards the holds get better. At the top of the crack, pull rightwards into the recess (good thread on the right). Compose yourself before launching up on flat holds. Gain and hang the ledge (a thin vertical crack swallows some much-needed runners), and then pull up right onto the wall. Good holds lead to a small grass ledge. A 3-metre wall is then taken easily to a long grass terrace and a horizontal crack to belay.
2 12m. 4b. Walk right to a mossy corner; follow this easily for 9 metres to the next ledge. Belay here; then walk left across the terrace to the 3-metre-high boulder and stroll up its left side.

Irish Eyes   15 metres   E3 5c †   (23.5.98)
The excellent blunt arête left of the *Prey* wall is much steeper than it looks.
Climb the right-hand side of the arête and step left into pockets. The arête
above rears up, so rear up with it, taking its left-hand side until a step out
to the right gains the top.

The last rib on the left of Daear Fawr has the appealing:

Apricot Man   14 metres   Hard Very Severe 5a †   (4.8.96)
Take the rib direct on good pockets until it steepens and a hard move
gains the ledge up on the left. Continue up the arête above on big holds,
until a committing move, using a hold on the left side of the lip, gains the
grass terrace above.

Wisecrack   14 metres   E5 6a †   (23.5.98)
The leaning brown-streaked wall around to the left of *Apricot Man* has a
thin crack just right of centre. The crack is strenuous and hard to protect
until some pockets enable holds on the arête on the right to be reached.
Grasp a ledge and exit up a short rib. Somewhat unassured!

Upper Daear Fawr
Up and left of this continuous wall is a series of buttresses. To reach the first,
follow the stone wall for a few minutes to a huge, flat-topped, heather-
covered boulder. The buttress directly above this has three routes.

☆**Boutros, Boutros**   24 metres   Hard Very Severe 5a †   (3.8.96)
At the right of the crag are two ribs. Take the left one to a ledge at 9
metres. Make difficult moves up into the scoop. Follow this to the overlap;
then delicately traverse right. Pull up and finish via a wide crack.

☆☆**Dreaming in Colour**   21 metres   E1 5b †   (3.8.96)
One of the best routes of its grade in the area. The fine diagonal crack in
the hanging slab just left of the centre of the crag. Start below the white
slab just left of a tree and below the roof. Difficult moves at 5 metres lead
to easier climbing to a point below the crack. Enter the crack with difficulty;
then sail up past abundant protection to finish on the sloping ledge above.
Belay there or 5 metres back.

Red Drag   21 metres   E2 5c †   (3.8.96)
A left-hand partner to *Dreaming in Colour* but nowhere as good. Start
below the white slab 4 metres to the left. Easily gain the break. Make
difficult moves up and left to the bottom of the reddish wall and climb this
delicately on tiny edges (very small wires) to reach a short left-facing
corner, which is climbed to a precarious finish onto the sloping final ledge.

Further up and left of this buttress is a smaller, slabbier buttress about another 200
metres along, reached by a short scramble up steep heather. At its right-hand side
is a leaning wall and a short steep corner, and at its left, a rounded rib.

Cian's Wall 12 metres   E2 5b †   (31.7.96)
Start below the rib and climb up a short triangular niche (good thread)
before pulling up onto the wall left of the rib. Step back right and continue
directly on small pockets. Lovely rock.

Cian's Crack 14 metres   E1 5b †   (31.7.96)
Left of the rib is an obvious crack. Step up into this – the big flake opposite
the wall can be used to bridge up for a metre or two before it runs out; the
crack then gets harder. Pull onto the short slab below the final rounded
hump and take the centre of the hump on good pocketed rock.

On the skyline above and behind is a collection of easy, pleasant slabs, the
most obvious of which is a 9-metre pocketed slab on the left, which can be
seen from the track which leads to the lake. **Left-to-right** order is now
resumed.

Left Arête 9 metres   Difficult †   (10.8.98)
As the name says.

First Crack 9 metres   Difficult †   (10.8.98)
Again, as it says.

Second Crack 9 metres   Difficult †   (10.8.98)
Yes, it's the next one.

Below and left of the slab is:

A Step in the Right Direction 6 metres   E3 5b †   (10.8.98)
The distinctive, stepped left-hand arête. Wicked landing.

Implantation 5 metres   Hard Very Severe 4c †   (10.8.98)
The easier and safer, broad, right-hand arête.

Further down and right of the above, by the sheep trail, is a collection of ribs
and arêtes, the largest and most obvious of which has a finger-crack
running up its left-hand side. This is:

Five Finger Ecstasy 12 metres   Hard Very Severe 5a †   (22.9.98)
Follow the crack to where it is possible to pull up right onto the rounded
rib, which is followed rightwards to the corner belay.

Glint in the Flint 12 metres   Hard Very Severe 4c †   (22.9.98)
A solo up the unprotectable pocketed face between the rib and the damp
left-facing corner to its right.

About 9 metres back left on the same trail is a very short rib:

A Short Walk 5 metres   Severe †   (22.9.98)
As it says.

Pen Tyrau Top (of) the Towers OS Ref 833 386

This is the collection of walls and blocks strewn along the 600-metre contour on the northern side of the mountain. The rock is generally clean and provides excellent friction. And, despite its aspect, it catches most of the afternoon sun.

Approach as for Daear Fawr – across the moorland via the gate west of the car-park. The lines of broken buttresses stretching westwards can be easily accessed this way and quickly become visible once the first slope is ascended. West of the rebuilt stone wall, is an 18-metre, tower-like buttress with a big detached block perched on its top and a blind gully runnning up just to its left. The left side of this gully has a narrow, overlapping, slabby rib, which offers the first of the climbs.

Tower Buttress

Tara   21 metres   Very Difficult †   (3.3.97)
A pleasant climb up the slabby rib through a series of short overlaps. Escapable at several points.

Next the tower itself:

Shadowfax   12 metres   Very Severe 4c †   (28.7.97)
The steep wall and upper crack just to the left of Y Crac Ddu.

Y Crac Ddu   15 metres   Very Difficult †   (7.7.97)
The left-hand side of the tower has a chimney-crack opposite the slabby rib of Tara. The crack leads up to a tree on the ledge. Finish up the left edge of the tower.

Mojo Rising   15 metres   Very Severe 4b †   (7.7.97)
Begin in the bay at the foot of the tower and take the left crack to a grass terrace. Climb the staggered crack up and left, and move back half-way to gain the niche on the right. Go back left again to the tree on Y Crac Ddu and take the latter's finish.

The next route begins on the pocketed wall on the right of the bay on the front of the tower.

Zyco   18 metres   Severe 4a †   (3.3.97)
Climb the right wall to gain a heather ledge; then go around the right wall of the tower and ascend on a rightward traverse into the gully (belay possible). Continue up the cracks above to reach a ledge below the square-cut block, and step across the gap to finish. (A direct variation takes the rib on the left of the heather ledge.)

The White Wall

Sixty metres above Tower Buttress is a line of buttresses which are based on two prominent gullies. The gully on the right runs alongside *Ridge of Sighs*. The gully on the left runs along the White Wall area.

White Slab   18 metres   Severe †   (28.7.97)
Climb the left side of the slabby White Wall following a line between two overlaps. Pull through a bulge at the top to a grass terrace. Finish direct up the short wall above.

The Big Yin   30 metres   Severe †   (7.7.97)
This goes up to join the right-hand side of the White Wall area. Approach by a scramble up the steep heather above Tower Buttress on a leftward diagonal line to reach an obvious layback crack 6 metres above a tree.
1 5m. 4a. Take the layback crack to a grass bank.
2 10m. 4a. Climb the deep crack at the back of the bank and exit left.
3 15m. Climb a system of grooves on a leftward-rising line.

Ridge of Sighs Area

Further right is the final gully, with a wide boulder-field at its base. The next route takes the long ridge forming the left side of the gully.

Ridge of Sighs   100 metres   Hard Severe †   (7.4.97)
This involves scrambling between pitches and requires some determination to follow. Scramble up the gully for 30 metres before moving out left at the grooved tower. Above a bay on its left is a large chimney with a block lower down. Traverse up to the block, move out left onto the slab, and go up to a ledge. The ridge is now just right: belay there. Moderate climbing for 18 metres up the left side of the ridge leads to a short steep wall, where there is an optional belay before taking the 5-metre crack just right of centre. The crack is loose at the top. Belay again before scrambling left for 30 metres to where the ridge loses itself in the hillside. Continue leftwards to a boulder in a bay at the foot of a groove below a crack in the slabby wall. Belay before finishing up the 6-metre crack.

Near the bottom of the gully and out to its right is a jumble of massive blocks. Just up a bit from these is a good pocketed wall, bordered right by a grassy gully and left by a short steep face with a thin crack in its left side. This crack is:

Pseudognome   14 metres   E1 5b †   (24.10.97)
Go easily up the wall below the crack and enter it with difficulty. Climb the crack; then pull right below the big block before surmounting it.

☆**Spooked by Time**   14 metres   E1 5b †   (24.10.97)
The wall immediately right with a bilberry ledge at 4 metres. Start just left of the rib, move up, and mantel easily onto the ledge. Climb the wall on good pockets past two horizontal breaks before it is possible to step right onto the top of the rib. Belay boulder well back in the heathery top.

☆**Hooked on Passion** 14 metres Hard Very Severe 5b † (24.10.97)
Start just right of the rib with the small tree on it, at the bottom of the wall.
Gain and follow the flake crack on the left to the next thin crack. Climb
boldly up this crack and the pocketed wall above, and mantel onto the
cleaned ledge. Finish as for *Spooked by Time*.

☆☆**Sour Milk See** 14 metres Very Severe 4c † (24.10.97)
Start as for *Hooked on Passion*, but at the first flake crack pull up right and
follow the easy ramp to another flake crack on the right. Finish rightwards
and belay, as for the two preceding routes, on the boulder well back.

☆**Hobo Jungle** 12 metres Severe 4a † (1.2.98)
Half-way between the rib and Arrowhead Buttress is is an area of rock with
some trees just to the right. Begin in the overhung bay and climb the steep
crack in the wall on the right to a ledge. Go straight up the steep wall
above to the final ledge.

Arrowhead Buttress

The next routes lie 15 metres further right in a jumble of walls and blocks.
The great block perched on the right can be likened to an arrowhead. The
left wall of the second steep gully left of this jumble contains a classic deep
crack with a large flake insert (*Hat Full of Hollow*). An isolated curving arête
about 10 metres left has a block at three-quarters height. This is:

☆**Rock It Up** 14 metres E3 5b (24.5.98)
Take the arête to a break at 7 metres – the first protection. Negotiate a bulge
and, from the huge block above, finish up the short final arête on the left.

★**The Judith Rose** 17 metres E4 5c (9.7.97)
Left of *Hat Full of Hollow* is a fine slabby wall. Start at its left side below the
overhang and climb a short steep crack to a ledge. Step right to place
gear high in *Stone Cold Crazy*. Make committing moves back left and
climb the vague rib on the left. Then, using a series of small edges on the
left, gain the rounded finish. Leave the recess leftwards to big belay
boulders further back.

☆**Snicker** 15 metres E4 6a † (24.5.98)
A harder variation start to *The Judith Rose*, starting directly and with no
side runners. Start 2 metres left of the ledge and pull rightwards over the
short roof to the pockets. Climb the rib as for *The Judith Rose*.

Stone Cold Crazy 15 metres E1 5b (24.10.97)
A good line if it stays free of growth. The leftward-trending thin crack is
gained from the ledge. Pull up into the crack and follow it with increasing
difficulty to the rounded finish of *The Judith Rose*.

Tongues Up 15 metres E2 5b (24.10.97)
Easier than it looks. The fine vague rib just left of *Hat Full of Hollow*. Start
below the small triangular roof at the base of the rib. Pass the roof on its

left, and step up right onto the rib. Good pockets thin out past a good small wire placement at two-thirds height. At the top, step up right to the *Hat Full of Hollow* finish.

Hat Full of Hollow   12 metres   Severe 4b   (11.3.97)
This is the deep crack in the left wall with the large flake insert. Take the crack direct on perfect holds and good protection. Pass the flake with bated breath. Belay in the recess or 5 metres higher.

☆**Viridian Groove**   12 metres   Hard Very Severe 5b †   (21.5.98)
The steep groove immediately right. Climb past the chockstone at half height to gain the downward-pointing flake. Pass this to top out.

The steep wall to the right has two routes.

★**Hostile Ground**   17 metres   E1 5c   (20.10.97)
The amazing pelvis-wide crack at the left side of the wall has an overhanging start, but once the first chockstone is gained, the difficulties ease a bit. After the second chockstone, enter the chimney below the huge flake and climb directly up inside to finish right of the small opening. Excellent squirming.

★★**Pricked by a Pulse**   17 metres   E4 5c   (9.7.97)
The fine wall right of the cleft has a poorly-defined rib in its centre. This is undercut at the base so is best started by pulling up just right of the rib, then immediately stepping back left to gain the first small ledge for handholds. Climb directly up the rib on superb pockets to the next set of flat holds. Arrange gear on the left before committing moves directly up the rib on small holds gain a deep horizontal crack. Pass this on more pockets to the next horizontal crack; then layback up the flake to the rounded ledge and finish up the short wall above.

The narrow gully just right is:

Crow Road   12 metres   Very Difficult †   (22.10.97)
Entertaining. Climb the stepped groove/gully to the cave, and belay. Climb up the back of the cave to exit through the chockstone gap in the roof.

Right of the narrow gully is the collection of immense blocks. The deep overhanging crack on the left provides a strenuous and gymnastic problem:

★★**Gay Abandon**   12 metres   E4 6a   (9.7.97)
Step off the shattered blocks below the crack into its recesses by a perplexing series of moves. Slap some gear in before swinging wildly out on jams and continuing up the unrelenting crack to gain the ledge. It is best to belay here and enjoy watching your second twist in the crevice below. Finish easily up the continuation crack on the left, which also forms the second pitch of *Tuff Gong*, or walk off rightwards on the ledge.

★Tuff Gong   14 metres   Very Severe 4b   (11.3.97)
Continue around the corner past the huge arrowhead to the pocketed wall
5 metres left of a small tree. Gain the ledge direct, then the massive block
above. Traverse up and leftwards to the ledge below the arrowhead, and
belay. At the left edge of the ledge is a steep crack above *Gay Abandon*.
Step out into this and climb it for 6 metres to its end.
Variation   Very Severe   4b (9.7.98). Climb the wall directly below the
arrowhead; then pull up onto the head to gain the top.

Twilight Wall   15 metres   Severe 4a †   (28.7.97)
At the extreme right of this crag is a slabby rib. Climb the slab to the
second ledge. Move right and climb the cracks before pulling out left at the
top. Walk right to the next wall and climb its thin crack, finishing
rightwards.

Kali   15 metres   Very Severe †   (3.3.97)
The final detached giant flake lying against the hillside has an off-width
crack in its centre. From the top, step left and breach the overlapping walls
by moving right past the corner and up to belay beneath another massive
perched block.

Looking for a Rainbow   9 metres   Very Severe 4c †   (20.10.97)
The centre of the slab itself has no gear and is a good solo. Finish on the
right shoulder.

Craig y Hyrddod   Crag (of) the Rams   OS Ref 826 378

[Photoplan and diagram page 176a.] Far off to the right and facing north-
west is the collection of buttresses of perfect solid rock called Craig yr
Hyrddod. Approach as for Pen Tyrau. There are three crags; first is Slabby
Buttress, in the middle is the split Central Tower, and to the right is Square
Buttress.

About 30 metres left of Slabby Buttress is another, smaller slab with a long
capping roof.

☆Shin Splint Roof   18 metres   Hard Very Severe 5b †   (22.10.97)
Although the difficulties are reserved for the final roof, this prominent
feature is a worthy challenge. Start at the foot of the wall left of the
pinnacle. Go direct to the ledge and move up right using the flake to gain
the wide ledge beneath the roof. Pull through the roof 2 metres left of its
right-hand end via some shallow pockets – hard and shin-scraping.

Visions of a Melon   18 metres   Severe †   (19.10.97)
Start 5 metres right of the foot of the wall by a flake crack. Use this to gain
the break and continue directly to the stance at the right of the roof. Finish
direct.

Slabby Buttress

This has an (unclimbed) vegetated crack at its left side.

Creepshow 12 metres Very Severe 4b † (16.4.97)
The left-hand of the two slab climbs starts just left of the vegetated crack
and overlap. At one-third height, cross the crack and follow its right edge
to the scoop on the left. Finish direct up the short scoop above.

The Shootist 12 metres Very Severe 4b † (16.4.97)
Start 2 metres right of the vegetated crack and climb the slab direct to the
overlap. Pull through onto the short scooped slab above, right of the wide
slot in the top.

Leprechaun 12 metres Hard Very Severe 5a † (22.10.97)
The right edge of the slab at its steepest part. Start just left of the edge;
then follow the horizontal crack out right to it. Continue direct with no gear.

Pixie Wall 9 metres E3 5c † (16.4.97)
The right-facing wall above the grass ramp is taken direct up its centre on
shallow pockets and small edges. Finish precariously onto the easy-angled
slab above. Sustained with little gear (i.e. a solo).

Central Tower

☆**Pagan Wall** 21 metres Hard Very Severe 5a † (10.4.97)
Start just right of the tower in a bay below the overhang. Take the steep
crack in the left wall. Traverse out left; then mantel onto the ledge on the
left of the tower. Step right and gain twin cracks. The crux is passing these
to reach a sloping ledge. Move up and left to exit the V-groove formed by
the giant leaning flake and the final tower. The final short crack leads to a
perfect stance.

Between the tower and Square Buttress is a wonderful isolated rib:

★**Aoife's Rib** 12 metres E3 5c (16.4.97)
Start at the bottom left edge of the rib. It is steep and difficult to start but
positive small edges gain the overlap and the first gear. Pull through onto
the easier-angled rib above, and finish onto the heather terrace.

Square Buttress

This fine steep wall has numerous cracklines running its full height, giving
mainly sustained, protected climbing on solid rock.

Ariadne in the Maze 15 metres Hard Very Severe 5a † (16.4.97)
The fine crackline in the arête forming the left edge of the face. Gain the
crack by pulling past the tree, and follow it up the arête to a small flake.
Pull up and left to a short crack and a rounded finish.

★★Hurricane Wall   18 metres   Hard Very Severe 5a   (9.4.97)
Start at the small tree at the left of the face and follow the break out right to its end to below some shattered small blocks. Pull directly up past these with difficulty to gain the scoop. Bridge carefully up the final short wall.

Dearg Doom   18 metres   Hard Very Severe 5a †   (16.8.97)
The next crackline along. The crack is fist-wide as it bisects the slab but is a bit lush, so it is easier to go up the slab just left of it to a small collection of whitish blocks. A thinner crack then continues direct to a horizontal break, from where a long reach left gains the wider crack going directly to the top.

The right-hand side of Square Buttress is considerably steeper and has a whitish slabby wall below it. Another, larger tree is rooted in the centre of the slabby wall and provides a base for some lush plantlife.

Sparta   18 metres   E3 5c   (16.8.97)
This takes the thin crackline leading up to the right edge of the huge triangular flake in the centre of the wall. Start, as for *The Last Asp*, up the slab left of the tree to the hanging garden. Avoid this by pulling up and left via the thin crack to gain the triangular flake. Step up right onto the wall above (bold) to reach the horizontal break and welcome gear. Follow the crack above to join *The Last Asp*; then pull out leftwards to a clean vertical crack leading direct to the top.

The Last Asp   15 metres   E2 5c   (15.4.97)
The tree at the bottom of the face on the right has a crackline either side. Start at the left-hand one and bounce up over the lush start onto the slab between the two cracks to gain a grassy niche below a thin crack. The thin crack rapidly steepens, taking any number of wires, and then reaches a thin horizontal break. A tricky sequence gains the next crack up. This is followed rightwards to where it finishes direct onto the slab above.

★★Elegant Gypsy   15 metres   E4 6a   (16.4.97)
This tackles the wall at its steepest point, giving elegant, intricate climbing. Bounce up past the greenery right of the tree to gain the slab below the thin crack immediately right of *The Last Asp*. Pull through the overlap with difficulty and follow the thin crack past a small lodged block to a larger lodged block at the horizontal line. Step up and right, following the seam rightwards past a peg, until a series of pockets on the steep wall above gain a short thin crack, which finishes direct onto the slab above.

The Hazel Iris   18 metres   E4 6a   (19.10.97)
The wall just left of the blunt rib is approached by the easy slabs to the right of the tree. Stand on the small blocks below the wall and, with gear in the flake on the rib, pull up into a thin crack (poor peg). Pass this with some microwire backup and good grip factor, and follow the hairline crack directly to the top. It is possible to use the ledge on the rib once the crux is passed.

Craig yr Hyrddod

Point of Snow Return
(E5) Bryn y Dyfrgi
Climber: Terry Taylor
Photo: Taylor col.

50 Dead Men Walking
(E2) Bryn y Dyfrgl
Climber: Norman Clacher
Photo: Terry Taylor

★★J and the Silver Shower   14 metres   E4 5c   (15.4.97)
The rib forming the right-hand side of the face has no gear and provides
an exciting, but serious solo. Climb easily to the flakes, above which small
edges on both sides of the rib allow the small ledge to be gained. Once
on this, finish easily up the slab above. The difficulties are short, but high
enough to cause concern.

Nob Direct   9 metres   E1 5c †   (16.8.97)
Above Square Buttress wall is a shorter tier. At the right end of this is a
short roof above a large flat ledge. Gain the ledge from the left via a
corner; then struggle mightily through the roof to follow the finger-crack to
the top. A pleasure for crack-climbers.

A variation on *Nob Direct*, **October Grooves** (Severe † 22.10.97) takes a
steep crack left of the roof.

Just right of Square Buttress is a fine short wall of perfect pocketed rock. The
crack at the left side of this is:

Battle on the Hill   11 metres   Hard Very Severe 5a †   (22.10.97)
Follow the hand-jamming crack to a difficult pull onto the small ledge up
and left. Finish direct up the scoop.

★★The Dark Mirror   12 metres   E4 5c   (16.4.97)
A bold, but rewarding line. Start at the centre of the wall and pull up on
the pockets to a faint left-facing groove. Continue direct until a hard
sequence gains the crack in the overlap above and the first gear
placement. Finish easily up the wide crack onto the large rock ledge.

Keys to Ascension   11 metres   E1 5c   (19.10.97)
The fine thin crack just right of *The Dark Mirror* is hard to start, and
sustained to the ledge, but well protected. Pull up and left, and finish on
the rib.

Y Moelwynion

The Moelwynion are a collection of many crags, mainly on the eastern side of the Moelwyn ridge, which runs roughly south to north in the rugged country between Beddgelert and Blaenau Ffestiniog. The area has suffered the ravages of slate quarrying, a hydroelectric power scheme, and more recently the extension of the Ffestiniog Narrow Gauge Railway. With the exception of Craig y Clipiau, Craig Holland, and Moelwyn Bach, the most important crags are found above the Llyn Stwlan dam service road.

From the town of Blaenau Ffestiniog, head for the hydroelectric power-station at the small village of Tanygrisiau. From here, go up the hill on the right, crossing the narrow gauge railway, until you eventually reach a gate and a bridge across the river on the right (Cwm Orthin track). (The private service road for the storage scheme carries on past the usually locked gate.) Cross the bridge; then go left and on up to a small parking-area beneath a quarry tip (OS Ref 683 454). Alternatively, there is another space for cars on the left just before the bridge. **Beware**: there has been a spate of thefts from cars parked at both these car-parks! All the crags can be reached from here by a short walk.

The climbing here tends to be pockety and usually on excellent rough rock. The main attraction of the area is its plethora of mostly easier-angled classics – however, there are also some excellent modern test-pieces. Protection is generally excellent – but cunning is often needed on the harder routes, where the ability to use small hexentric-type nuts in pockets pays dividends.

There are no known access problems in this area. However, most cliffs are on private land, and access is by the kind permission of landowners and occupiers. Please ensure that this situation is maintained by considerate behaviour towards those who have to make a living from the land. In particular, please ensure that dogs remain on leads at all times, and avoid damaging any boundary walls or fences.

The main cliffs are described from left to right as you approach the massif from the south, and all are reached in 30 minutes or less.

Craig Stwlan Difficult Crag OS Ref 667 446

This small, broken, and rather scrappy crag has a nicely situated south-west facet directly above the northern shores of Llyn Stwlan, and a south-east facet overlooking the lower reservoir. Follow the service road to its end – the cliff is a short scramble above the dam.

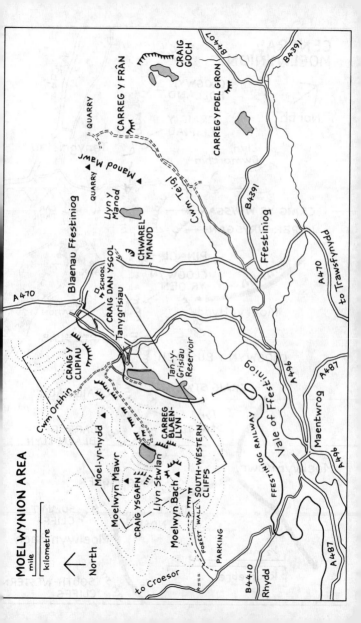

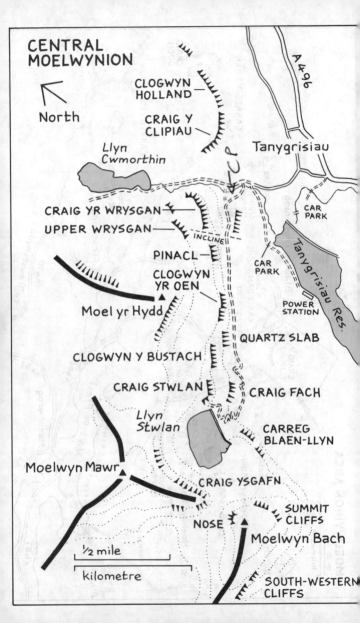

Birthday Route   45 metres   Very Difficult   (25.1.67)
Start in the corner left of a nose and just left of the prominent steep face of
Pocked Wall.
1 9m. Climb the corner; then traverse right, round the arête, to a stance
on a grass ledge in a corner.
2 27m. Take the wall left of the corner until level with the overhang on the
left, traverse slightly right, and then go left over the bulge to easy rock,
which leads straight up to a large ledge.
3 9m. Climb the wall to the top.

Pocked Wall   30 metres   Very Difficult   (12.12.53)
The prominent steep face right of a chimney. Start at a little corner left of a
quartz rib.
1 12m. Climb the little corner; then move left onto the main face, step
right, and go up to a large heathery ledge.
2 18m. Move left up a gangway to the edge of the steep face; then
traverse right to the right edge and climb this to the top.

Brassington Wall (Difficult 1953) takes a steep wall above heathery slabs, 12
metres to the right of the lowest point of the central nose. **Easter Parade**
(Moderate) starts from a big square block at the northern end of the south-east
facet. It has three pitches: the crack on the left of the block, an arête, and a slab.

Craig Fach   Little Crag   OS Ref 669 444

This is a small slabby crag, about 45 metres high, standing above the third
hairpin bend of the upper part of the service road. The climbing is very
pleasant, on slabby rock in the easier grades. There is a boulder-field-
cum-gully on the left, at the top of which a ledge runs back down to the right
across the short overhanging wall bounding the left edge of the main face.

Top Plate (Moderate) is the easy slab on the left of the buttress. It finishes up
the chimney at the top right-hand corner.

Milky Way   49 metres   Difficult   (9.32)
A pleasant route with a choice of finishes. Start under the overhanging left
edge of the slab, near its foot.
1 12m. Swing up onto the slab edge and go up the crack; then trend
right to belay on the slab edge.
2 15m. Climb the knife-edge above, and continue up the slab to a grassy
ledge. Belay in a niche round the corner on the left.
3 22m. Walk round the corner and climb a small chimney; then climb the
pitted slab, heading towards the notch on the summit dome.
Variations
3a 16m. Step right from the niche; then ascend slabs and the nose on
the right to the top.

3b 18m. Climb straight up the nose, and pick your way up the slab above. Slightly harder, but better than the original.

Mars 45 metres   Very Difficult   (4.12.60)
Another pleasant climb up the clean slab in the middle of the crag. Start at a cairn below a pedestal at the lowest point of the crag.
1 15m. Climb the slab; then bear left to a perched flake and a heather ledge.
2 15m. Move across onto the slab on the left and go diagonally left on good holds to its top. Follow the weakness in the little wall above and then climb the slab to a grass ledge.
3 15m. Climb diagonally right to finish up the steep crack. There is a thread belay in a grass corner on the right.

Andromeda 37 metres   Very Difficult   (23.6.57)
A reasonably interesting climb up the rocks on the right of *Mars*. Start 12 metres right of *Mars*, at a flake cairn.
1 10m. Climb the purple slab to a long grass ledge. Belay by the crack in the bulge above.
2 15m. Move left a little and then go on up slabs diagonally left to a heathery groove, which leads to another ledge.
3 12m. Climb the wall just left of the belay to finish.

Orion 97 metres   Difficult   (4.12.60)
An enjoyable traverse – visiting a galaxy, two constellations, and a planet! The launch pad is by two cairns on a ledge 6 metres below and to the right of the foot of *Top Plate*.
1 17m. Launch out and up onto the rib to a good ledge; then take the obvious line rightwards across the quartz slab until it is possible to descend a knife-edge to a good stance (top of pitch 1 of *Milky Way*).
2 12m. Descend the little crack behind the stance, and cross the next slab to the detached flake (top of pitch 1 of *Mars*).
3 21m. Continue right below the flake for 5 metres to a thread on the edge of a shallow gully. Cross this and climb the slab on its far side, ascending slightly to a stance in a corner.
4 17m. Descend below the nose and cross the next slab to a grassy corner. Continue across the right wall and go up to easy ground on the rib.
5 30m. Descend the easy rib by a diagonal line to the right-hand end of the crag.

Craig Newydd New Crag   OS Ref 667 445

This small, newly-discovered crag lies above the service road, between Craig Stwlan and Craig Fach. It is directly above a small parking-bay and is approached in a couple of minutes from the road. The buttress is composed of a short, steep wall, flanked by two heathery groove-lines. Descent is via either side of the buttress.

Pigdog Doc 15 metres Hard Very Severe 5a † (2000)
Climb the obvious left-hand crack: a perfect hand-jamming test-piece.

Dog Days 15 metres E4 6b † (2000)
Take the clean central wall directly until forced leftwards to finish more easily up the final slab.

Reservoir Pig 15 metres E2 5b † (2000)
The right-hand crack gives a short, entertaining struggle until easier moves up the slab gain the top.

Clogwyn y Bustach Cliff (of) the Bullock OS Ref 672 448

This short but steep crag can be found just beyond, and a little higher up the hillside than, Clogwyn yr Oen. It has a vertical main face split by several cracks, with a line of chimneys on the left-hand side. The rock is very compact, making protection difficult to arrange, particularly on the front face. At the base of of the crag and just right of centre is a large detached flake, the start of *Flake Wall*.

Floating Rib (44 metres Difficult) follows the rib running up on the left of the line of chimneys. **Fork** (37 metres Difficult) is an artificial line up vague cracks and chimneys 5 metres left of *South Chimneys*.

South Chimneys 42 metres Difficult (7.10.51)
Start below the chimneys defining the left side of the steep face.
1 21m. Climb the shattered face to a ledge at the foot of the chimney proper. Climb it past several perched blocks to a large grass ledge.
2 21m. Continue in the same line up to the top, finishing over a block.

Southern Cross 48 metres Very Severe 4c (1974)
A slight, but photogenic route that traverses right from *South Chimneys* to climb a groove and then an arête. Start 21 metres up *South Chimneys*. From the grass ledge, take the obvious traverse-line across the right wall to the main face (via an unprotected long reach). Follow the groove to an arête, which leads to the top.

Dal y Twrch 27 metres E3 5c (8.83)
Bold climbing on suspect rock. Climb the arête left of *Groan* to a flake (peg runner). Finish direct up the finishing-groove of *Southern Cross*.

Groan 27 metres E2 5b (1970)
A strenuous route up the jamming cracks on the left-hand side of the main wall. Start 5 metres right of *South Chimneys*. Climb up the wall to a

rightward-trending thin crack. From this, gain a jamming crack, which leads to a large ledge (junction with *Flake Wall*). Finish up the short wall above.

★Titus   30 metres   E2 5c   (1969)
Very good climbing with a short fierce crux. Start below the cracked wall 5 metres right of *Groan*. Climb up the cracked wall for 8 metres to a rightward-sloping thin crack. Follow this to a large flake, and move up to a small niche. Step left into the square bottomless chimney, and finish up the short wall.

Gormenghast   30 metres   E2 5b   (11.80)
The bulging crack and wall between *Groan* and *Titus*, reached by a rising leftward traverse. Start just left of the large detached flake (start of *Flake Wall*), beneath a ramp-line. Climb leftwards up the ramp-line, crossing *Titus*, to gain the bulging crack. Climb the crack and wall to reach a short jamming crack just left of the open chimney. Finish up the short wall.

★Acoustic Flake   34 metres   E2 5b   (15.7.81)
The wall just left of the detached flake gives some good, if serious, climbing. Start as for *Gormenghast*. Move up the ramp a short way; then climb straight up the wall to the 'Acoustic Flake'. Creep silently over this and move up to the traverse of *Flake Wall*. Go up the wall to finish up the groove splitting the bulge.

★Flake Wall   36 metres   Hard Very Severe   (21.9.55)
The classic route of the crag. Start at the large detached flake in the middle of the crag.
1 30m. 5a. Climb the left edge of the flake to its top. Step left off the flake, and climb up to a shallow V-groove. Follow it, using holds on its left, to an obvious foot-traverse. Boldly follow the traverse leftwards to a short crack, which leads to a large ledge.
2 6m. Finish up the short wall.

Going Straight   27 metres   E1   (5.78)
Start behind the detached flake.
1 12m. 5b. Step onto the wall behind the flake, and move diagonally leftwards on hollow-sounding flakes to a groove. Climb this to belay at the start of the foot-traverse of *Flake Wall*.
2 15m. 5b. Go diagonally rightwards to gain a sloping ledge (peg runner), move right, and then finish directly up the bulging wall.

Mr Flibbertigibbet   30 metres   E2 5b   (16.7.81)
A poorly-protected bottom groove leads to the obvious curving gash above the detached flake. Climb the wall behind the flake to a small ledge below a shallow leftward-slanting groove (poor peg runner). Climb the groove and trend leftwards to the curving line of flakes. Traverse these, and finish via the final bulge of *Acoustic Flake*.

Clogwyn y Bustach

1 South Chimneys   D
2 Groan   E2
3 Titus   E2
4 Gormenghast   E2
5 Acoustic Flake   E2
6 Flake Wall   HVS
7 Fiddler on the Dole   E1
8 Creeper   VD

Clogwyn yr Oen

1 Crossover	HS
2 Orange Outang	HS
3 Pinky	VS
4 Skerryvore	E2
5 Ectoplasm	HV
6 Remembrance	E
7 The Widowmaker	E

Clogwyn yr Oen

Remembrance   E3

2	The Widowmaker	E4	5	Block		S
3	Kirkus's Climb Direct	S	6	Thumbelina		S
4	Cuckoo Waltz	VS				

Clogwyn yr Oen

South-East Face

1 Kirkus's Climb Direct   S
2 Block   S
3 Thumbelina   VD
4 Chic   VD
5 Bent   VS
6 Slick   VD
7 Slack   S
8 Pied Piper   S

Fiddler on the Dole   30 metres   E1 5b   (25.1.78)
Start 6 metres right of *Flake Wall*, below an obvious triangular overhang. Go up to the small triangular overhang. Traverse leftwards to a foot-ledge below a cracked groove, and climb the groove to a difficult move left at the top.

Creeper   30 metres   Very Difficult   (5.4.53)
Start below the crack on the right of the steep face.
1 21m. Scramble up to and climb the wide crack to a ledge.
2 9m. Finish up the continuation crack.

The short parallel-sided chimney on the right gives an absorbing back-and-foot exercise – **North Chimney** (23 metres Difficult), which has been described as being easier (or faster?) in descent!

★**The Ebb Tide**   36 metres   E2   (14.7.81)
An interesting left-to-right girdle across the main face gives some very fine climbing. Start by climbing up *South Chimneys* to the first of the ledges.
1 21m. 5b. Bridge across to an obvious foothold, traverse right, and move up to below the jamming crack on *Groan* (crux). Move up this; then traverse rightwards rising slightly to above the groove of *Flake Wall*.
2 15m. 5a. Move diagonally rightwards to the sloping ledge (peg runner), and carry on rightwards to the finish of *Creeper*.

Another girdle, **Barbarillo** (Hard Very Severe), has been climbed at a higher level. It is, however, not as worthwhile as the above.

Clogwyn yr Oen   Cliff (of) the Lamb   OS Ref 673 449

This is the largest and most accessible crag in the area. The skyline of the crag, the line of *Kirkus's Climb Direct*, can be seen by looking up the reservoir service road from the car-park beneath the slate tip. The crag has two facets. The left-hand side is the south-west face, which is split at half height by a terrace. The wall above this terrace (the headwall) has a concentration of the harder climbs. Just to the right of the bottom half of the face is a huge prominent perched boulder. Directly above the service road is the south-east face and although it appears very broken, it contains some wonderful gems in the lower grades. The left-hand side of the crag gives a quick and easy descent. The first three routes described are those which lie on the south-west face, and start below the terrace.

Crossover   51 metres   Hard Severe   (26.5.68)
Nice climbing on good rock. Start below a short, left-facing, white groove.
1 24m. 4a. Climb the short wall to a large ledge. Follow the white groove and continue up to a niche belay.
2 27m. 4b. Traverse right and then climb the steep wall direct, avoiding the easy ground on the left. Scrambling remains.

★Orange Outang   76 metres   Hard Severe   (12.4.53)
Another steep, pleasant climb. Start by scrambling up to the foot of the
orange patch.
1 21m. 4a. Step onto the orange wall, and climb directly up, past the
orange streaks, to a niche belay (junction with *Crossover*).
2 18m. 4b. Climb the wall above until forced to the left; then climb the
little overhang to a ledge and block.
3 37m. Walk up to the rib on the right and follow it to the top.
Alternatively, scramble off to the left to join the descent route.

★★Pinky   58 metres   Very Severe   (15.4.53)
Technically more interesting than its two neighbours. Start at the foot of a
recessed pinkish wall, 6 metres right of *Orange Outang*.
1 37m. 4b. Climb the wall, passing a bulge at 8 metres. Continue up
large pockets to a final steepening, which leads to the terrace. Cross the
terrace to the foot of a grassy corner containing some trees.
2 21m. 4c. Climb the corner to a good ledge; then climb any of the
cracks to finish, the right-hand one being the better.

The next nine routes climb lines on the headwall above the terrace; all are
worthwhile on excellent rock.

Saline Solution   27 metres   Hard Very Severe   5b   (7.8.78)
A good climb up the large flake left of the final corner pitch of *Pinky*. Climb
the wall, first leftwards, then rightwards, passing one hard sequence, to the
top of the large flake. Finish up any of the cracks in the short wall above.

Skerryvore   24 metres   E2 5b   (5.79)
The thin crack right of the final pitch of *Pinky*. Start beneath a blunt arête a
little to the right of the corner of *Pinky*. Steep moves up the blunt, undercut
arête lead to a good resting-place beneath the thin crack, which is
followed in its entirety to finish.

Scaryitis   37 metres   E1 5b †
Very little independent climbing, but the route ventures onto some nice
parts of the wall. Follow *Skerryvore* to the good resting-place; then traverse
rightwards, passing the crack of *Ectoplasm* and joining *Remembrance*
above its steep lower section to finish.

Ectoplasm   24 metres   Hard Very Severe   5b   (10.64)
The obvious jamming-crack right of the thin crack of *Skerryvore*. Start
below a good spike 3 metres right of the start of *Skerryvore*. Gain the spike
by some hard moves, and then follow the crack to the top.

Plasma   34 metres   Hard Very Severe   5a   (11.64)
Start as for *Ectoplasm*. Climb up to the spike and step rightwards, down
and around the nose. Move up to a block; then move left via a horizontal
break to a jamming-crack. Finish up a rightward-leaning ramp.

★★Remembrance 26 metres E3 5c (1972)
[Photo page 192a.] A brilliant, steep line giving good climbing. Start at the overhanging V-groove to the right of *Plasma*. Climb the V-groove, passing a poor peg runner, and make a hard move out. Continue up the wall to the block. Move up and right to finish up a blind crack.

★The Widowmaker 24 metres E4 6a (4.81)
A harrowing climb up the green wall to the right of *Remembrance*. Technical and poorly protected, but nevertheless a fine route. Start just right of the V-groove of *Remembrance*. Step right onto the wall and climb directly up to a bulge (*RURP* runner). Move left to a layaway; then trend rightwards up the wall to the horizontal break. Finish up the obvious groove.

Badger by Owl-light 26 metres E3 6a (1982)
Start by the prominent groove up and right of *The Widowmaker*. Climb the groove to a small ledge and move left over the bulge. Climb directly up to the obvious final groove.

★Erewhon 45 metres E1 (8.78)
A fine girdle of the headwall. Start just left of the tree-filled corner (pitch 2 of *Pinky*).
1 15m. 5b. Climb up the front face of the large flake, going leftwards first and then rightwards, to belay on top of the large flake (pitch 1 of *Saline Solution*).
2 30m. 5b. Climb straight across the wall on small pockets to the wide crack of *Ectoplasm* (hanging belay possible). Step down and traverse across to the block on *Plasma*. Follow the thin crack across the green wall to finish, with difficulty, up an undercut groove.

Hole and Corner Climb (67 metres Difficult) climbs up behind the left side of the huge boulder (head-torches optional!) and then follows the terrace leftwards.

The following three routes are all based on the prominent large boulder between the two facets.

Slate 36 metres Hard Very Severe (8.7.62)
Start at the left side of the large perched boulder on the south-east face.
1 18m. 4c. Climb a short wall, then a crack and the continuation face on the left-hand side of the boulder.
2 18m. 5a. Scramble across rightwards into the corner, beneath a flake below the corner groove. Climb the side of the flake and enter the prominent groove. Continue to its end.

Welsh Insurrection 15 metres E3 5c
The obvious thrutch up the crack in the front of the buttress.

The Wee Bat 18 metres E3 5c
A bold line up the right-hand side of the large boulder.

The next two climbs are based on the rib that defines the two facets of the crag:

★Kirkus's Climb   64 metres   Very Difficult   (1928)
Good climbing, usually overlooked for the more obvious attraction of its *Direct*. Start by the stone wall at the toe of the buttress.

1 15m. Climb the chimney immediately left of the stone wall to a pillar. Step down right and climb the deep-cut chimney, via large flakes, to a cave-like belay.

2 11m. Climb the left-hand crack and the slab to its left, and move right at the top to belay at the foot of a steep arête split by a groove.

3 24m. Start up the arête, but move round left after a couple of metres into a large groove. Climb the groove and then go leftwards on slabs. Finally move back to the crest and climb a short crack to a triangular stance.

4 14m. Traverse rightwards until an obvious leftward ascent of the slab leads to a large ledge with a block belay. Scrambling remains.

★★Kirkus's Climb Direct   64 metres   Severe
This route takes as direct a line as possible up the arête. A very good climb, steep and interesting. Start by the stone wall at the toe of the buttress.

1 18m. 4a. Climb the steep wall – it soon eases to a slab, which leads to a pillar. Step from the pillar and climb the slab to its top. Move right to a cave-like belay.

2 11m. 4a. Climb the right-hand crack above and make an ape-like swing out onto the front face, where further slabs lead to a belay at the foot of a steep arête split by a groove.

3 23m. 4a. A fine pitch. Climb the arête, via the groove, until a short rightward traverse enables easier slabs to be gained and followed to a triangular stance.

4 12m. Climb the right-hand groove above the belay to a large ledge with a block belay. Scrambling remains.

Cuckoo Waltz   110 metres   Very Severe   (21.5.88)
Start at the undercut pillar between *Kirkus's Climb Direct* and *Block*.

1 37m. 5a. Climb the right-hand side of the pillar and then the left arête of a slabby wall, passing a small overhang, to belay as for *Kirkus's Climb Direct*.

2 55m. 4b. Walk up a grassy ramp to the headwall on the right. Climb this direct, right of a corner, and go up grass to a thread belay.

3 18m. 4b. At the back of the grassy bay is a steep wall split by two horizontal breaks and a crackline. Climb the lower half of the crack to a step right, and finish up a pockety crack.

Variation

Flyover   18 metres   Hard Very Severe
3a 5a. Take the wall direct on small pockets, just left of a cream-coloured patch.

Block 70 metres Severe (19.7.53)
Start just right of *Kirkus's Climb Direct*, below a jutting block 18 metres up.
1 37m. 4a. Varied climbing leads to 'the block', after which a groove
and steep slab are followed to a large sloping break. Walk up to belay
beneath the corner on the left.
2 15m. Climb the corner to a ledge with a bollard belay.
3 18m. 4a. Climb the short steep crack in the left wall to a sloping ledge.
A further thin crack with a leftward exit leads to the finish.

Thumbelina 68 metres Severe (29.5.67)
Start 4 metres right of *Block*.
1 21m. Climb the slabby ramp leftwards for a metre or two; then go
steeply up to an overlap and up a mossy slab above. Move rightwards to
the foot of a stunted rib.
2 14m. Gain the rib and follow it to a heather ledge. Step left and climb
cracks to the large break.
3 15m. Climb straight up to the right of a wide crack, to a further long
grass ledge.
4 18m. *Chic* pitch 3.

In Memoriam 58 metres Hard Very Severe (8.8.76)
A very direct line up the cliff. Start 3 metres left of *Chic*.
1 29m. 5a. Climb leftwards to beneath the stunted rib of *Thumbelina*. A
step left, followed by direct climbing to a bulge near the top leads to the
large break.
2 21m. 4c. The wall left of the corner ahead is climbed up its centre to a
sloping ledge. A bold pitch, almost devoid of protection.
3 8m. At the right-hand end of the sloping ledge there is a
leftward-slanting chimney with a groove on its left. Either climb the groove,
which is overhung at the top, or struggle up the chimney.

Chic 68 metres Very Difficult (13.12.52)
Quite a good climb, taking the left edge of the large quartzy slab. Start at
the broad rib just left of a heathery gully.
1 26m. Climb the easy rib and its harder continuation to a ledge below a
steep wall.
2 24m. Climb the steep wall to a ledge and corner, traverse left, and then
go diagonally left to the left edge of the large slab. Continue, to reach
large perched blocks on a long grass ledge.
3 18m. Climb the rightward-slanting crack; then go straight up an easy
slab to another grass ledge. The obvious 3-metre corner provides a finish.

★Bent 74 metres Severe (12.4.53)
A pleasant climb with a finish by the prominent pinnacle above the centre
of the face. Start at a flat slab midway between *Chic* and the pillar leaning
against the face on the right.
1 21m. Climb the slab, finishing just left of a crack.
2 21m. Continue in the same line to the foot of a short wall, which is
ascended diagonally rightwards to the foot of the big slab.

3 20m. 4a. Climb the slab for a couple of metres, and then traverse into the corner on the right. Climb the corner, passing a sort of cave midway, to the foot of a steep crack splitting the right wall. This leads to the foot of a very large pinnacle.
4 12m. 4a. Climb the chimney behind the pinnacle, and finish up the left edge of the steep rib.

Slick   66 metres   Very Difficult   (5.4.53)
Another very pleasant climb, crossing *Bent* to climb the big slab. Start at the pillar leaning against the face, forming a sort of rib.
1 18m. Climb the rib to a ledge with a flake on the left.
2 24m. Step off the flake and go up the little wall above to an easy scoop. Traverse left for 5 metres; then go up again to another short wall, which is ascended diagonally rightwards to the foot of the big slab.
3 15m. Climb the slab just right of a dubious spike to a grassy rake.
4 9m. Climb the steep crack on the left to the much easier continuation, which leads to the top.

Slant   72 metres   Very Severe   (26.12.71)
A good route with an amazing well-positioned finish. Start to the right of *Slick*, below a mossy slab.
1 21m. Vegetated slabs lead to a belay on the left of a detached flake.
2 27m. 4b. The steep groove on the left is taken to a ledge. Step left round the corner and go diagonally up the slab towards the cave midway up pitch 3 of *Bent*.
3 15m. 4a. Continue up the corner to a stance above the right edge of the slab.
4 9m. 4b. The steep left-hand crack in the wall on the right is awkward to start and gives surprisingly exposed climbing to easy ground.

Late Appointment   20 metres   E1 5b †   (1990)
A well-positioned eliminate up the headwall between *Slant* and *Bent*. Approach by either of those routes or by moving left under the roof of *Slack*. The headwall is taken direct and gives thin exposed climbing.

★Slack   71 metres   Severe   (13.11.60/5.66)
A great climb with a good finish. Start at the foot of a two-tier slab beneath a large detached flake on a ledge.
1 21m. Climb the slab to the flake.
2 20m. Climb the right edge of the flake. Step onto the wall, move left at its top to a short crack, and climb this to belay beneath the overhangs.
3 12m. 4a. Traverse left until beneath the nose overlooking the big slab. Climb this (exposed) to a good thread belay.
4 18m. Climb the corner, and exit left to another, shorter corner, which is taken to finish.
Variation
3a 11m. Hard Very Severe 5b. Climb directly above the belay to a weakness in the overhangs; a swing left then enables a steep slab to be followed to a large belay.

Tight 66 metres Severe (1968)
Start as for *Slack*.
1 21m. Climb the slab to the flake.
2 18m. Step right onto a steep wall and climb up, moving right where it becomes steeper, and then back left to a small tree. Block belay to the left.
3 27m. From the block, climb up the slab towards a crack just right of the overhang. Climb the crack, and continue to a ledge. Finish up the short walls above.

Pied Piper 63 metres Severe (12.4.53)
Another pleasant route in the same style as its companions. Start at the foot of the quartz-streaked slab below the broad rib on the right-hand side of the face.
1 21m. Climb the slab into a bay, continue up the corner, and then follow the crack rightwards onto the face.
2 21m. Climb the rib direct until a corner on the left edge is reached.
3 21m. 4a. Climb cracked blocks and mossy slabs to a terrace. Cross this, and climb straight up onto the quartz-covered face of a huge block. Traverse left and finish up the crack behind.
Variation
3a 12m. From the terrace, go to the right of the huge block and climb a harder quartzy slab to the foot of a crack with a chockstone. Climb over the chockstone to finish.

One for the Road 100 metres Difficult (11.4.53)
A bit scrappy on the whole, but with some good climbing. Start beneath a left-facing corner, 6 metres right of *Pied Piper*.
1 15m. Climb the easy slab up to the corner.
2 14m. Climb the corner and the right-hand rib. Scramble up to a cave at the foot of a crack.
3 26m. Climb the crack and the slab above to a belay on the terrace.
4 15m. Follow the cleanest quartz slab above, finishing to the right of the spiky rocks on the skyline. Finish here, or walk right to the foot of the final face.
5 6m. Go up a left-sloping gangway to a stance beneath a crack formed by a flake slanting up left.
6 24m. Climb the crack; then move right to finish up the centre of the face.

Waspie 116 metres Very Difficult (10.10.59)
A worthwhile expedition. Other girdles are possible, but this is the best line. Start at a large grassy corner above the perched boulder on the south-west face.
1 15m. Step up onto the top of a large flake, cross the mossy wall, and go up to a triangular stance (top of pitch 3 of *Kirkus's Climb Direct*).
2 18m. Descend diagonally rightwards to the top of a big flake, and follow the stepped edge of the flake to a large grassy bay (junction with *Thumbelina*).
3 15m. Cross the right wall of the bay; then go over the top of another flake and down its right edge to a little ledge in a corner (on the traverse of *Chic*).

4 15m. Continue rightwards and then climb the rounded nose to some large blocks.
5 20m. Move across to the blocks on the right, and traverse the big slab to the cave stance of *Bent*.
6 9m. Move out round the rib and descend a little to a small ledge.
7 24m. Traverse right to reach easy ground.

Pinacl   Pinnacle   OS Ref 678 453

This small recessed buttress, high on the hillside just before the waterfall on the way to Clogwyn yr Oen, has only three routes. The broken rocky ridge gives a poor route in three distinct steps starting from a bottomless crack – **Weep** (Very Difficult).

The Tumor   21 metres   E2 5b   (2.9.81)
Start below the thin crack in the wall to the left of the obvious corner. Climb the crack on slightly loose holds to finish directly.

Cancer   21 metres   Very Severe 4c   (19.3.63)
Climb the obvious corner.

Moel yr Hydd   Red Deer Hill   OS Ref 672 453

For lovers of solitude the cliffs of Moel yr Hydd offer short steep routes on sound Moelwyn rock with a commanding view. They are best approached by starting up the Cwm Orthin track, then taking the path left up through the quarries to reach the left side of Upper Wrysgan. From here continue south-west almost horizontally along a good grassy path and past a small lake to below the cliffs.

These are extensive but very broken. The first area reached on the right-hand side of the crag is characterized by a steep quartz-streaked slab with a small cairn at its foot. A number of relatively easy lines are visible and this is probably the area pioneered in the 1950s. Centrally placed are several short but very steep buttresses of excellent if often lichenous rock, while the biggest but most discontinuous area lies to the left and features several grassy gullies, one of which contains the prominent pinnacle of the Huntinghorn. This left side of the crag is too scruffy to be of interest to today's climbers, but the central section offers worthwhile, if short outings.

Buttress One
The right-hand section of this buttress rises from a comfortable heather terrace and features two steep, parallel cracklines. The left section begins at

Non Dairy Creamer
(E4) Craig y Clipiau
Climber: Mel Griffiths
Photo: E Edwards

Remembrance
(E3) Clogwyn yr Oen
Climber: Elfyn Jones
Photo: Mel Griffiths

Nosferatu (E3) Craig yr Wrysgan

Sickle Cell (E5) Carreg y Foel Gron
Climber: Tim Emmet   Photo: Nick Dixon

a lower level and consequently gives slightly longer climbs. Left of the buttress a narrowing grassy ramp/gully slants up right above the crag and provides the easiest means of descent.

The Arête   23 metres   Severe †   (31.7.99)
The left edge of the crag is formed by a fine arête of perfect rock. Not too difficult, but protection is sparse. At the top of the arête, move right and climb the upper wall right of the edge by a steep but easy crack. Continue right up the gentle slabby ridge to a belay.

Playing the System   20 metres   Very Severe 4b/c †   (21.8.99)
Unusually, the rock on this route is a little suspect in the lower section, but very good high up. Well protected. Start at the lowest point of the crag to the right of *The Arête*. Climb up on the left for 5 metres to a small overlap. Cross it on big but slightly dubious holds; then move up and right with an awkward move to get established in a jamming-crack. Follow this and its continuation directly to the top.

Saving Grace   15 metres   Severe †   (31.7.99)
A pleasant route starting from the left end of the heather terrace below the right-hand section of the buttress. An obvious hand-crack slants left up the slab. Climb this and then go straight up the slab to a grassy ledge on the right below a short steep corner. Climb the corner to the top.

Quizzical Sister   12 metres   Hard Very Severe 5a †   (21.8.99)
A good route starting from the heather terrace below the right-hand section of the buttress. Climb the left of two prominent vertical cracklines. This gives good finger-jamming with a strenuous pull or two at half height, but the upper section is easier.

Roman Road   12 metres   Very Severe 5a †   (31.7.99)
Another good route, taking the right-hand crackline. Hard for the grade but well protected. The lower section is quite steep but relatively straightforward. The crux is the steep hand-jamming crack to finish.

Buttress Two
A little to the left of Buttress One. There is a green, left-slanting ramp/corner towards the left side of the crag and several prominent cracklines on the steep wall to the right. From the top of the crag, descend right (facing out) via a grassy gully.

Animal Instinct   17 metres   Hard Very Severe 5a †   (31.7.99)
The left-hand crack begins in an undercut niche, reached by a very steep but short grassy scramble. It runs diagonally up right onto the front face of the buttress where a pointed jammed flake, which seems precariously positioned but is actually quite sound, protrudes conspicuously from the crack. Climb the crack strenuously on good jams, passing the flake, and continuing via a wider section to the top of the crag.

Initiation Test   15 metres   Hard Very Severe   5a †   (31.7.99)
On the right of the preceding route is another fairly wide crack, and right
again a steep smooth wall with a thin vertical seam. A direct line up this
seam is not climbed. Instead, take the wide crack formed by a big flake on
the right. Then, from the small ledge at the top (where an escape right is
possible), traverse about 4 metres left into the upper section of the seam.
Continue more easily to the top.

Craig yr Wrysgan   Crag (of) the Bushes   OS Ref 679 454

[Photodiagrams page 200a,b.] This crag is easily identified by a prominent
incline, which begins at the service road and passes the left-hand side of the
crag to enter a short tunnel (one of the descents). The easiest approach is to
follow the Cwm Orthin track until it is possible to cross the stream, at the first
level ground, just below the first ruined building. Easy grass terraces then
lead up leftwards to the boulder-field below the crag. A prominent feature of
the crag is a large quartz-streaked slab below a short summit tower, which is
split by the obvious line of *Honeysuckle Corner*. Beneath this is a large grass
ledge, y Borfa (the Pasture). Towards the centre of the crag is a prominent
V-corner, *Dorcon*. To the right again and higher up is a large enclosed
recess, The Green Wall. The rock is generally good and gives varied and
pleasant climbing. A long easy descent can be made down the right-hand
side of the crag. An alternative descent is by means of the incline.

The first three routes are now very vegetated and difficult to follow.

Y Taith   60 metres   Hard Severe   (25.7.78)
Start at the vegetated leftward-facing corner on the left-hand side of the
crag.
1 21m. Climb the corner; then pass two rowans and go rightwards to a
ledge and stance overlooking the grass funnel.
2 21m. Cross the funnel to the quartzy slab and move rightwards via the
horizontal traverse-line to a grass ramp below the tower. Step onto the
narrow slab beneath the tower and follow this to y Borfa.
3 18m. Go diagonally right across the right wall of y Borfa, and finish up
a steep little groove (the Black Corner), thus completing 'The Trip'.

Y Drafel   33 metres   Very Difficult   (2.6.53)
The broken ground left of the quartz slab. Start 8 metres right of *Y Taith*, at
a large pointed spike.
1 24m. Climb rightwards, move left via an undercut flake onto a slab,
and climb the slab, passing a perched block. Carry on to a belay
overlooking a grassy gully.
2 9m. Climb straight up the arête (y drafel) to finish. Various scrambles
off.

Agog   39 metres   Very Difficult   (20.6.58)
Worthwhile only as an approach to the *Tower Finish*. Start between the
easy way to the grassy bay and *Y Drafel*.
1 6m. Climb the short wall and crack to a perched block and large
ledge.
2 18m. Scramble leftwards to belay beneath a narrow gangway just left
of the grass gully. Move across and climb the slab and a shallow chimney.
3 15m. Take easy rocks to the foot of a steep tower, but avoid it on the
left. Climb the steep wall to the arête and finish up this.
Variation
Tower Finish   15 metres   Hard Severe   (1961)
3a 15m. 4b. Follow easy rocks to the tower and finish up the steep front
face.

★Daufaen and Honeysuckle Corner
                              48 metres   Hard Severe   (1958/4.61)
A good climb following 'two slabs', which is only Severe if *Honeysuckle
Corner* is avoided by traversing right along y Borfa. Start at the short
vertical corner in the grassy bay.
1 15m. Climb the crack and then the slab, making for some blocks and
a ledge.
2 15m. Move out right onto the slab and follow pockets to y Borfa.
3 18m. 4b. Climb the corner (*Honeysuckle*), which gives an excellent
pitch.

★The White Streak   48 metres   Hard Severe   (5.7.58)
Good slab-climbing on small pockets, bold in places. Start in the recess
below the large slab, at a large spike.
1 15m. 4a. Climb up leftwards; then traverse diagonally rightwards to a
triangular corner breaking the right edge of the slab.
2 15m. 4a. Step left and boldly climb the slab to y Borfa.
3 18m. Move right along y Borfa to an easy escape – or, much better,
finish up *Honeysuckle Corner* on the left to give a memorable
combination.

The White Streak/Honeysuckle Corner is probably the best (★★) combination
here and gives an excellent way up the cliff at a sustained grade.

★★Y Gelynen   70 metres   Very Difficult   (27.7.53)
An exhilarating climb on superb rock. Start just left of the V-groove of
Dorcon (approached by an easy scramble).
1 37m. Traverse left and go up the blunt rib to the eponymous holly tree
(prickly belay possible). Step left and climb the rib to below a steep little
wall. Good nut belays behind a flake.
2 15m. Step left and go up to and over the overlap, and climb the slab to
y Borfa.
3 18m. Go diagonally up the right wall of y Borfa, passing a steep
groove on the left.
Variation Finish (Severe): the steep corner on the left gives a better finish.

Bad Reputation   37 metres   Very Severe 4c   (24.4.85)
A barely independent line between Y Gelynen and Condor. Climb directly
up to an overhang; step left and then back right to continue more easily to
belay as for Y Gelynen.

★★**Condor**   37 metres   E1 5b   (5.78)
The fine crack in the left wall of Dorcon's V-groove. Start below the
V-groove. Make some hard moves up the centre of the wall on the left to
gain the crack. Follow this and the rib above to a stance (nut belays) as for
Y Gelynen. Finish by its top pitches.

Conrod   37 metres   E3 5c   (24.7.85)
A poorly-protected eliminate. Climb the thin crack between Condor and
Dorcon.

★**Dorcon**   45 metres   Hard Severe   (17.4.60)
Escape is possible at each stance, but the climbing is good. Start below the
V-groove.
1 12m. 4a. Climb the V-groove to exit right, and go up to a grass ledge
below some overhangs.
2 15m. 4a. Move leftwards and climb the rib left of the overhangs; then
move back right above to a large grass bay.
3 18m. 4b. Climb the corner and crack (crux) to another ledge. Finish up
the short wall.

Taith y Pererin   76 metres   Difficult   (2.6.53)
A rather rambling route. Start as for Dorcon.
1 23m. Traverse right along the ledge into a large corner.
2 17m. Climb diagonally leftwards, passing a ledge, and carry on
leftwards to the nose above the V-groove. Move up into the corner.
3 9m. Traverse rightwards along the ledge and move round the rib into a
niche.
4 12m. Follow the corner-crack and scramble up the groove to a good
ledge.
5 15m. Step onto the slab on the right and continue up ledges to finish
the 'Pilgrim's Progress'.

Remus (43 metres Severe 1956) is a poor line, which is essentially a direct
version of Taith y Pererin.

Grey Slab   44 metres   Hard Severe   (1953)
Start in the corner at the end of pitch 1 of Taith y Pererin.
1 21m. 4a. Go straight up the rib on the left, cross a gangway, and
climb up a short wall to a sloping stance.
2 23m. 4b. Climb above the stance and follow the groove until a
traverse left leads to the crest of the buttress, which is followed to finish.

Mistral   38 metres   Very Severe   (19.7.64)
A harder variation on Grey Slab. Start at the lowest point of the crag, by
the huge overhanging boulder.

1 8m. 4b. Climb the overhanging nose on the left of the boulder; then make strenuous moves via flake holds and go rightwards and up the slab. Scramble up to a belay.

2 30m. 4b. Climb the wall to the left of the stance, cross the gangway, and go up the steep slab to the overhang, where a hard move up leads onto a slab. Climb up its centre, bearing left at the top; then go up the rib and short crack.

Hot Pants 43 metres Very Severe (18.4.71)
1 8m. 4b. *Mistral* pitch 1.
2 21m. 4b. Go up a faint depression in the slab; then trend left to the corner and move up to a small ledge. Climb over the block overhang to another ledge.
3 14m. 4b. Traverse right and finish directly up the slab.

The next climbs start in the recess dominated by the overhanging *Green Wall*.

★Swallowed by Amazons 20 metres E4 5c (21.5.97)
The challenge posed by the nose left of *The Green Wall*. Start 2 metres left of *The Green Wall*, by a slim groove and crack-system. Strenuous climbing leads to a large flake, which is passed on the right to the sloping traverse-ledge. Step up and right to a spike, then back left following a line of small flakes to the blunt nose (good wire below the obvious small pocket). Finish directly on small holds.

★★The Green Wall 26 metres E3 5c (14.8.72)
Strenuous and spectacular climbing, with poor protection in places, up the left-hand side of the wall. Start below a short corner. From the ramp, climb the leftward-facing corner; then move boldly up the wall to a scoop below a thin crack. Climb this, and trend slightly left to a steep finish.

★★Nosferatu 26 metres E3 5c (11.80)
[Photo page 192b.] Another spectacular climb, taking a line parallel to and to the right of *The Green Wall*. Start below a shallow groove just right of the start of *The Green Wall*. Climb the shallow groove and then go straight up to the obvious crack. Continue strenuously up the crack to finish direct. A superb pitch.

Gethsemane 24 metres Hard Very Severe 5a (14.8.72)
The large, obvious corner to the right of *The Green Wall*. Start below the large corner and climb it to the second overlap, where steep moves right lead to easier ground and the finish. Unfortunately, often dirty and vegetated.

Scallywag 24 metres E5 6a (5.9.84)
A hard and worrying eliminate between the corner and *Bing the Budgie*. Climb a thin crack in the wall left of *Bing the Budgie*, and move left to a good hold. Move right above the overlap; then go straight up to the obvious overhang. Pull over and exit right at the top.

★Bing the Budgie   24 metres   E4 6a   (16.10.77)
A serious pitch, giving enthralling climbing up the smooth impressive wall
right of *Gethsemane*. Start 3 metres right of the corner. Climb the crack;
then foot-traverse left until it is possible to climb up, passing a good
pocket, to an overlap. Move slightly right and then climb straight up to
finish rightwards.
Variation 24m. E3 5c (1981). Start as for *Bing the Budgie*, but carry on
up the crack in the wall to an overlap. From here, either move right to the
arête, or continue over the overlap (harder) and then on up the arête to
finish – almost but not quite a route in itself!

The Wanderer   33 metres   Hard Very Severe   (15.8.72)
A traverse of *The Green Wall* area. Start as for *Space below My Feet*.
1 12m. 4c. Climb the crack diagonally left to a ledge in the corner – or
climb direct to the same point.
2 21m. 5a. Move up and leftwards to follow the obvious traverse-line
across *The Green Wall*. Descend slightly to the foot of a gangway, which
leads to the top.
Variation
2a 15 m. E4 5c. Climb *Space below My Feet* to the arête and move
onto the wall of *Bing the Budgie* just above the overlap. Traverse
horizontally left across the wall to the ledge on *Gethsemane* – a worrying
pitch for both leader and second.

★Space below My Feet   30 metres   Hard Very Severe 5a   (9.6.61)
An enjoyable pitch, taking the left-hand of the three ribs right of the recess.
Start at a boulder beneath an overhanging groove right of *Bing the
Budgie*. Climb the groove, strenuous at first, to the ledge. Go up the wall,
and move left to the arête, which eventually eases off to easy slabs.
Variation 30m. Hard Very Severe 5a (1972). Start as for *Bing the
Budgie*; then toe-traverse along a diagonal crack immediately right to the
arête, and climb the arête to finish.

Romulus   30 metres   Very Difficult   (15.6.58)
1 9m. *Babylon* pitch 1.
2 21m. Take the middle of the three ribs.

Babylon   30 metres   Very Difficult   (1958)
This climb takes the right-hand of the three blunt ribs right of the green
recess. Start by easy scrambling to a large block beneath the nose of the
buttress.
1 9m. Step right and climb up the slab, before moving leftwards to an
earthy ledge.
2 21m. Climb the corner behind the sapling, and move right onto the rib,
which is followed to finish.

Y Lloer   24 metres   Very Severe 4c   (8.81)
A poorly-protected pitch, which starts just left of *Y Gilfach*. Climb directly
up the left wall of *Y Gilfach* on small pockets, finishing directly.

★Y Gilfach 24 metres Very Difficult (22.7.58)
The V-groove on the right-hand side of the crag. Classic Moelwyn climbing. Start below the V-groove, at a 'nook', approached via a grassy scramble. Climb the easy slab, then the steep corner to finish directly.

Stained Class 18 metres Hard Very Severe 5b (1985)
The rightward-slanting crack between *Y Gilfach* and the short corner on the right is gained by steep moves on large holds.

Little Corner (24 metres Very Difficult) gives a vegetated route.

Gangway 21 metres Very Difficult
The quartzy gangway on the right, starting from a perched block.

Upper Wrysgan
OS Ref 676 455

[Photodiagrams page 200c,d.] The upper cliff lies beyond the quarry buildings and behind the main cliff. It is approached easily from the top of the main cliff, or by walking up the track from the car-park, then breaking left from the first level and following a path leftwards and up from the quarry tips behind Craig yr Wrysgan for some 300 metres.

The cliff is in several sections on two different levels, and there are many old mine openings along its base. The left-hand side is quite broken and extends leftwards for some 100 metres from an obvious large collapsed opening, which is on the same level as Craig yr Wrysgan. Above this opening are some steep walls (the *Peachstone* area). Immediately to the right are some mossy slabs which curve round into a short gully (*Central Gully*). The cliff continues rightwards to a final steep clean wall (Auction Wall), which tapers down to the old tramway line. A small isolated buttress with three routes lies directly beneath Auction Wall, on the next level down.

The first routes are found on the extreme left of the cliff, directly above a disused level, about 100 metres from the large collapsed opening.

D.Y.W.A.M 30 metres Very Difficult
Start at the extreme left end of the cliff above an old mine-opening leading into the cliffs. A fine little route.
1 12m. Step onto the wall and climb the steep crack to a ledge below the obvious corner.
2 18m. Bridge up the corner until a hand-traverse leads out rightwards onto the final arête of Cave Arête – at this point: 'Do you want a medal?'

Cave Arête 31 metres Difficult (4.10.67)
Start as for D.Y.W.A.M.
1 11m. Climb the wall to a chimney and on up to a large ledge.
2 20m. Go directly up the arête in a fine position.

Headcross   30 metres   Difficult   (22.6.68)
Start about 9 metres right of *Cave Arête*.
1 15m. Climb a large groove and take the left-hand crack to a ledge.
Follow a break left onto *Cave Arête* and up to another large ledge.
2 15m. Step around the block on the ledge and go across the slab on the
right. Follow the wall and the short arête to finish.

Percy Thrower (30 metres Difficult 1968) is a poor line which starts as for
Headcross and finishes left of the wide crack of *Cat Walk*.

Cat Walk   30 metres   Severe   (1964)
Start below a triangular overhang 9 metres left of a square cave, which is
midway between the large collapsed opening and the extreme left of the
cliff. Climb up the groove and the flake cracks to a ledge. Continue up
vegetated slabs to finish.

Twelve Monkeys   15 metres   E1 5b †   (31.8.99)
Above and left of the square cave is a blunt rib. Scramble up heather
ledges to the flake crack and two chockstones before stepping right onto a
ledge. Take the left edge of the rib above on amazing pockets with
adequate protection. Finish on a good clean platform.

Yoghurt Miscellaneous   21 metres   Very Difficult   (7.7.68)
Start below some overhangs to the right of the square cave.
1 9m. Climb the groove to a large ledge with a perched block.
2 6m. Go directly up the shallow chimney.
3 6m. Climb the short wall to finish.

The next two routes are on the wall above the large collapsed opening and
left of *Peachstone*. Approach by abseil or by a scramble in from the heather
gully on the left.

☆**Eat the Peach**   15 metres   E1 5b †   (17.8.99)
The fine finger-crack is hard to start, though well protected, and eases
towards the top.

☆**Ecology of Fear**   15 metres   E5 6a †   (31.8.99)
Hand-traverse right from the belay at the foot of the crack to the bulging
wall. Gain big pockets and a foot-ledge before climbing the centre of the
wall. Steep and sustained, though there are some surprising pockets.

★★**Peachstone**   24 metres   E4 6a   (1.7.88)
A fine route up the overhanging prow above the collapsed opening. Well
worth the tricky approach. Start on a small ledge by a small rowan tree
above the cavern – approached by a vegetated pitch from the right or from
above by abseil. Climb leftwards above the lip of the cave to a peg. Hard
moves past this leads to good pockets. The bulge above is climbed by a
long reach to more pockets and another peg (missing). Climb the wall left of
the (missing!) peg to a vague break and a third peg and finish directly. The
peg runners are very rusty and the slate fangs below are very sharp indeed!

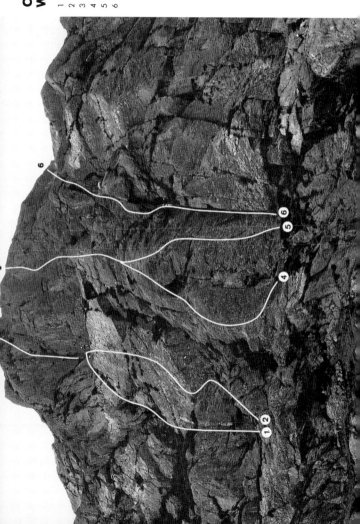

Craig yr Wrysgan

1	Defauen	S
2	White Streak	HS
3	Honeysuckle Corner	HS
4	Gelynen	VD
5	Condor	E1
6	Dorcon	HS

Craig yr Wrysgan

1	Taith y Pererin	D
2	Mistral	VS
3	The Green Wall	E3
4	Nosferatu	E3
5	Gethsemone	HVS
6	Bing the Budgie	E4
7	Space below My Feet	HVS
8	Babylon	VD
9	Y Gilfach	VD

Upper Wrysgan

1 Yoghurt VD
  Miscellaneous
2 Eat the Peach E1
3 Peachstone E4
4 Peach Melba E3
5 Ash Tree Slabs VD

Upper Wrysgan
Auction Wall

1 Chim Chu Roo   HVS
2 Sasquatch   E3
3 The Thin Flim-Flan Man   E3
4 Dislocation   HVS
5 Cuchlain   E4
6 Louis Wilder   E5
7 Wall of Ghouls   E3
8 Gremlin Groove   E1
9 Elf Wall   E3

Peach Melba 20 metres E3 5c (1991)
Start as for *Peachstone*. Climb directly above the stance following a vague flake-line. Finish directly up a pockety wall.

Ash Tree Slabs 26 metres Very Difficult (1964)
Start at a short wall just right of the large opening.
1 9m. Climb the short wall to a ledge, and then the slab to the ash tree.
2 8m. Climb the slab and scramble left to a good belay.
3 9m. Climb the slab on the right, and then the crack to finish on a grass ledge. Scramble off.

The dirty slabs to the left of the next route have been climbed – **Llaregub** (Very Severe).

Dentist's Debut 24 metres Hard Severe (7.7.66)
Start 9 metres left of *Central Gully* at the obvious flake crack. Climb the crack, move right, and go up a short slab to a small ledge overlooking the gully. Gain the sloping grassy gangway, follow this leftwards, and climb the shallow groove above.

Central Gully 21 metres Very Difficult (7.7.66)
Start below the obvious gully which splits the crag. Follow the gully and the slab on its right to exit through a hole.

Buzby 21 metres Hard Very Severe 5a (7.78)
Start below the right wall of the gully, at a large flake. Climb up the flake and enter a groove; trend left to a small sapling. Finish up the short groove above.

Hailing the Alien 31 metres E2 † (4.9.99)
1 8m. 5b. The slim groove in the shield below the upper wall leads to a flake belay.
2 23m. 5c. Belay in the corner 2½ metres right of *Buzby*. Pull directly up to a horizontal break, from which long reaches gain the pockets above. Finish directly up the centre of the wall on endless pockets. *Friends* useful.

Kiss Kinky Boots Night Night 31 metres E1 † (4.9.99)
1 8m. 5b. *Hailing the Alien* pitch 1.
2 23m. 5b. There is a ramp-system starting 2½ metres right of pitch 2 of *Hailing the Alien*. Climb a good crack and then trend right to a sapling. Pass left of this to pad onto the left-trending ramp. Follow the ramp easily but boldly up to the finishing wall, which is climbed passing left of a second sapling.

The Ailing Alien 31metres E2 † (4.9.99)
The wall just left of *Chim Chu Roo* has two thin cracks.
1 8m. 5b. The left end of Auction Wall, just left of the black streak, is a good start to this strenuous route. Fortunately, the last and hardest move (leaving a big pocket) can be protected.

2 23m. 5c. From the belay on the huge boulder below the cracks, step up and left to the steep right-trending ramp. At the top of this, make hard moves into the bottom of the right-hand crack, which is followed via a niche to the top.

Chim Chu Roo   21 metres   Hard Very Severe 4c   (7.78)
Climb the wide chimney 15 metres right of *Buzby*: slightly loose to enter.

The next section of the crag is an unbroken 24-metre-high wall called Auction Wall; it gives some excellent short routes on good rock.

Neusk Prospect   9 metres   E3 5c
The steep bouldering wall on the right has been climbed (and claimed!) by several parties and gives a fine extended boulder-problem, albeit a rather bold outing.

Sasquatch   23 metres   E3 5c   (6.78)
Start at the second thin crack left of the square-topped boulder 10 metres left of the obvious groove on the right-hand side of the crag. Climb the crack – poorly protected – and its continuation to a sloping ledge. Move up the wall to a series of converging short cracks. Climb rightwards to a horizontal break; then finish directly.

The Thin Flim-Flan Man   23 metres   E3 6a   (28.6.95)
An eliminate between *Sasquatch* and *Dislocation*. Climb the first thin crack (left of the boulder) to a narrow sloping ledge, and then up to a flake (poor *RPs*). Step right until below the left side of an overhang (peg). Arrange side runners on the left before climbing direct on poor pockets to a step right to finish.

★Dislocation   23 metres   Hard Very Severe 5b   (15.10.67/1978)
Start at the square-topped boulder 10 metres left of the obvious groove on the right-hand side of the crag. Climb the flake and thin crack to a ramp. Climb the continuation crack to a ledge on the right. Finish direct up the short slab.

★Cuchulainn   23 metres   E4 6a   (18.5.94)
The thin discontinuous crack on the right of the boulder gives hard, but escapable climbing – once the crux is climbed there is good small nut protection! Gaining the crack proves trying – further hard moves lead to better holds and a junction with *Dislocation* below the ledge.

Louis Wilder   23 metres   E5 6a   (9.81)
A serious but fine route left of *Wall of Ghouls* with a very hard start. Start between *Dislocation* and *Wall of Ghouls*, below a very shallow groove. Step off a large boulder and climb the shallow groove (good wire at half height in a pocket). Finish directly, past a long reach.

Wall of Ghouls   23 metres   E3 6a   (1980/1986)
Technical climbing up the wall left of *Gremlin Groove*. Start 2 metres left of the groove – now much harder since the demise of a large flake. Boulder

out the wall immediately left of the groove. Trend slightly leftwards up past narrow ramps; then move right to finish up the thin crack directly above the groove.

Gremlin Groove   23 metres   E1 5b   (8.4.74)
Climb the obvious V-groove on the right-hand side of the crag to the thin crack, move right, and climb the short wall and slab to finish.

Elf Wall   23 metres   E3 5b   (24.5.87)
The bulging wall on the right gives good but scary climbing. Climb the wall (poor protection) to a small ledge. Further trying moves lead steeply leftwards to a heather ledge. Finish easily up the slab above.

The bulging wall tapers to the right. **Friendly Pockets** (Hard Very Severe 5a † 30.6.84) starts part way along this and slants up left via a couple of breaks and pockets (cam placements) to the top.

Directly below Auction Wall there is a short buttress approached down the old incline. There are three worthwhile routes.

Aftermirth   15 metres   E1 5b   (28.5.94)
Start below a short groove on the left. Climb the groove and overcome a bulge to finish up a blunt nose.

Fir Bolg   15 metres   E2 5b   (28.5.94)
'The Sackmen'. The thin groove on the right of the buttress. A hard start leads to the horizontal break. Step left and continue directly past a good flake/thread.

Witchfinder   15 metres   E2 5c †   (26.6.95)
Start just right of *Fir Bolg*. Strenuous pocket-pulling gains a peg at 5 metres; then more pockets up and right lead to the horizontal break. Continue to a second break and then keep right up a fine wall above.

Craig y Clipiau   Crag (of) the Cliffs   OS Ref 683 458

[Photodiagram page 208a.] The cliff is best approached by going directly up the Cwm Orthin track from the car-park. Break right from the dilapidated buildings on the first level section above the steep rise from the car-park. Skirt rightwards up a vague path, and then up the final slate-tip until the crag is reached.

On the left is an obvious easy-angled gully (one of the descent lines). Immediately to its right is a short, steep, south-west-facing wall (*Johnson's Wall*), which is separated from the imposing *Vestix* buttress by a blocky depression, the line of *Depression Direct* (of course!). The main, south-east face lies to the right of a vegetated and broken area. On the left of the south-east face is an obvious large quartzy slab (White Slab). The prominent V-groove above and right of this is the line of *Mean Feat*, approached from the grassy funnel on the right. The narrow slabby wall and steep corner give the line of *Double Criss* before the cliff looses height and adjoins another descent gully.

To the left of the descent gully on the left-hand side of the cliff, several very short routes have been recorded. High up is a short wall above jumbled boulders; there is an obvious crack on its right, which is taken by **Tetse Fly** (8 metres Very Severe 4c). **Johnson's Creek** (10 metres E1 5a) takes the blanker left-hand side of the wall direct with a difficult start and no protection until well up. **Barfly** (10 metres Very Severe 4c) starts up the crack until it is possible to step out leftwards on a rising diagonal to cross the wall and then finish direct on *Johnson's Creek*. (All three 15.4.94). The others are left to be rediscovered yet again!

The next routes to be described are on the south-west spur.

Johnson's Wall   21 metres   E3 6a   (10.80)
The pocketed wall and slabs on the left-hand side of the buttress. Climb up the centre of the wall, via layaways and pockets, and move right at the top. Go directly up the steep slab to finish. Rather bold since the demise of a peg runner.

Jones's Crack   21 metres   Very Severe 4c   (21.2.59)
The obvious cracks to the right of *Johnson's Wall*. Climb the first crack, then the continuation, and finish up a blunt nose.

Betimes   37 metres   Difficult   (9.34)
A pleasant route. Start by scrambling up to the foot of an obvious square-cut depression.
1 20m. Follow flakes, then sloping ledges to a platform at the top of the depression.
2 17m. Escape leftwards and climb a rib to finish.

Depression Direct   29 metres   Hard Severe   (16.8.53/1965)
Start at the foot of the crack starting the depression.
1 20m. 4a. Climb the crack; then go up the depression to a stance on large blocks.
2 9m. 4b. Step right onto the pointed block and climb the crack strenuously.

The next three climbs follow lines up the steep barrel-shaped buttress right of the depression – *Vestix* buttress.

★Thin Wall Special   32 metres   Very Severe   (6.9.53)
Fine climbing in an exposed situation. Start as for *Depression Direct*.
1 27m. 4c. Climb the crack and move right onto some flakes. Climb up the thin crack; then move rightwards and up the nose to a good stance.
2 5m. Move right, and go straight up to finish.

★The Emerald   30 metres   E5 6b   (10.80)
[Photo page 208b.] A direct line up the front face of *Vestix* buttress. Hard
climbing and poor protection make this a tough lead. Start 10 metres left
of the arête of *Vestix*. From a loose spike on the left, make some hard
moves up the groove and go right onto the ramp, using some pockets.
Move up to an obvious undercut and then up a groove just left of the nose.

★Vestix   32 metres   Hard Very Severe 5a   (9.10.65)
A strenuous route, taking the diagonal crack from right to left. Start below
the prominent diagonal crack on the right of the buttress. Follow the crack
to the arête; then continue up the crack, or go up the arête to finish up the
blunt nose.
Variation
True to Form   30 metres   E5 6a
The arête left of *Vestix*, starting just left of it at a thin crack, is climbed to the
right side of the ramp on *The Emerald*. Then climb directly to join *Vestix* at
its wide crack.

Melonmania   21 metres   E2 6a †   (16.8.97)
Start as for *Vestix* and follow it to the sentry-box; then one hard move gains
the wall above, and easier climbing leads to the top.

Reptile Route   37 metres   Very Difficult   (7.55)
A poor route up the broken area between the two main buttresses,
finishing slightly leftwards.

The remaining climbs lie on the main face.

★Africa Rib   37 metres   Very Difficult   (16.8.53)
The left edge of the White Slab can be climbed by many variations and,
although escapable at any point, is well positioned. Start below two
parallel chimneys formed by a block pinnacle, at two iron stakes.
1 12m. Climb either of the chimneys or the pinnacle face to reach a
ledge with a rowan tree.
2 20m. Step left, go straight up the edge of the quartzy slab onto a large
block, and eventually move right to a large stance. Alternatively, from the
block, move left and climb the layback crack.
3 5m. Finish up the corner-groove on the right.

★Usher's Dilemma   37 metres   Hard Severe   (16.8.53)
A variation on *Africa Rib*, which gives good climbing. Start at the slab just
right of the chimneys of *Africa Rib*.
1 12m. Climb up the slab to a small sentry-box, and then go up to the
stance of *Africa Rib*.
2 20m. Move right and make some thin moves up the slab to a junction
with *Africa Rib* at the block. Step right and up to the overhangs, and then
move back left to a rib and heathery ledge.
3 5m. Finish up the corner-groove on the right.
Variation

★Eagle Finish   Very Severe   (4.61)
3a 18m. 4b. A gem. From the block on *Africa Rib*, traverse right beneath the overhangs to the corner of the slab. Step right onto a block (the Eagle) and gain the slab. Either continue up this to finish; or, better, a short way up move right and cross the exposed nose.

Brys   41 metres   Hard Very Severe   28.9.78)
1 21m. 4b. Climb straight up the middle of the White Slab, and go right to a stance (on *Asahel*).
2 20m. 5a. An exciting pitch. Climb up the slab to beneath a groove in the overhangs. Climb the groove and exit left on a good hold.

★Asahel   43 metres   Severe   (7.55)
A good route, keeping close beneath the overhangs to the right of the White Slab. Start at the corner at the extreme right-hand end of the slab.
1 23m. 4a. Climb the slab near the corner, passing a good quartzy thread, to a small stance.
2 15m. 4a. Continue above the stance to the overhang, where a traverse is made to join *Usher's Dilemma* at the large stance above the overhangs. (A very good finish is to move right here and take the *Eagle Finish*.)
3 5m. Continue up the corner-groove to finish.

Great Feet   40 metres   E1 5b   (23.4.67)
A steep and devious route. Start 6 metres right of *Asahel*, by a sapling in a grassy bay. Climb leftwards over a bulge, then up (past quartzy holds) to a groove. Move left and up until directly below the obvious V-groove of *Mean Feat*. A trying few moves leftwards leads to a grassy funnel. Continue over some blocks to finish.

★★★Crimson Cruiser   40 metres   E5 6a   (12.80)
A superb route, strenuous, bold, and in an incredible position, which takes the obvious groove in the overhanging headwall above the traverse of *Mean Feat*. Follow *Great Feet* until past the quartzy holds, where that route moves left. Move right and climb directly to the ledge below the steep groove. Climb up to the green ledge just right of the groove. Move left and climb the groove to the ledge on *Mean Feat*. Step right and make some sensational moves up the overhanging prow to finish.

★★Mean Feat   33 metres   Hard Very Severe   (7.57)
Excellent classic climbing up the prominent hanging V-groove. Start at the top of the grassy funnel beneath the right-hand side of the headwall.
1 15m. 4b. Climb the obvious diagonal traverse leftwards to a stance beneath the V-groove.
2 18m. 5a. Climb the V-groove to a good ledge. Make a high step right to another good ledge. Finish up the short awkward wall.

★★Purple Paradise   37 metres   E5 6a
A bold eliminate in a fine situation, up steep rock right of *Crimson Cruiser*. Start as for *Mean Feat*. From part way along the traverse, climb the shallow groove to a poor peg runner. Hard moves up and right lead past

another poor peg to a ledge (junction with *Non Dairy Creamer*). Finish up the wall above, moving right to join *Non Dairy Creamer*.

★★**Non Dairy Creamer**   20 metres   E4 5c   (1980)
[Photo page 192a.] This excellent climb takes a line up the right-hand side of the overhanging headwall, reached by an exposed traverse from the right. Superb climbing on small pockets. Start from the ledge and corner at the top of pitch 1 of *Double Chris*. Make an exposed leftward traverse along ledges to a resting-place beneath the overhanging pocketed wall. Climb directly up the wall, passing a good flake hold, to finish up a crack. A superb, but poorly protected pitch.
Variation

★★**Non Creaming Dairy Start**   17 metres   E4 5c   (6.81)
A snappy direct start to *Non Dairy Creamer*. If combined with the parent route this gives an excellent pitch directly up the headwall. Follow the traverse of *Mean Feat* to the first spike. Climb the steep shallow groove and wall above rightwards to join the start of the traverse line of *Non Dairy Creamer*. Traverse right to belay in the corner or, better, continue directly in one pitch up *Non Dairy Creamer*.

The next two routes girdle the headwall in opposite directions.

★★**Return of the Horsemen**   48 metres   E3   (4.81)
An excellent left-to-right girdle of the headwall. Start at the bottom of *Asahel*.
1 21m. 5b. Climb up to the thread of *Asahel*; then move right to the second of two holly trees. Move right onto the steep slab and up to the bottom of the V-chimney of *Mean Feat*.
2 27m. 5c. Climb up the V-chimney; then traverse right onto the wall to a sloping foothold. Make some hard moves up; then keep on traversing right to a diagonal flake jug. Climb this to its end (junction with *Non Dairy Creamer*), and climb the crack above as for *Non Dairy Creamer*.

★**The Muleman**   33 metres   E2   (7.81)
An exciting and very exposed right-to left girdle of the headwall. Start at the corner of *The Liquidator*.
1 27m. 5b. Go up the corner, and then move left into the open square-cut chimney. Climb up the slab to the obvious traverse left (*Non Dairy Creamer*). Committing moves (a 20-metre pendulum is possible for the second!) lead leftwards until a resting-place is reached. Move slightly up and leftwards to the final ledge on *Mean Feat*.
2 6m. 4b. Climb the short wall to finish.

The Liquidator   21 metres   Very Severe 4c   (12.2.78)
A start for *Straw Dogs Finish*, or an alternative first pitch for any of the routes crossing the large ledge. Climb the prominent corner to a hollow tree, and continue past blocks to the ledge.

Variation 24m. Very Severe 4b. Climb the crack in the wall right of *The Liquidator* to swing round onto the main face of the slabby wall. Continue up to the ledge.

★Straw Dogs Finish   12 metres   E3 5c   (3.11.77)
The left-hand of the overhanging cracks which, like the film of the same name, gives a needlessly violent experience. Start on the large ledge and move across left to below the small roof and overhanging crack. Climb the crack.

★Double Criss   33 metres   Very Severe   (6.9.53)
A nice start with a 'traditional' finish. Start below the left edge of the slabby wall.
1 27m. 4b. Follow the left edge of the slabby wall more-or-less directly to the ledge and corner.
2 6m. 5a. Climb the corner-crack. Brutal.

Overhanging Cracks   33 metres   E2   (1961)
A pleasant first pitch with a strenuous sequel. Start just right of *Double Criss*, below the middle of the slabby wall.
1 24m. 4b. Climb the wall until a traverse leads left to the edge. Continue up to the ledge.
2 9m. 6a. Finger-jam the overhanging cracks to a niche and finish.

Phidl   37 metres   Hard Very Severe   (1958/23.7.73)
The corner at the right-hand end of the slabby wall, and a bold finishing-pitch. Start below the corner.
1 26m. 5a. Enter the corner via the right wall, and continue up to the ledge.
2 11m. 5a. Take the obvious traverse-line across the right wall, and finish up the slab right of the arête.

★Special K   23 metres   E3 5c   (1.7.84)
The overhanging arête right of *Double Criss*. Climb a groove just right of *Phidl* to a bulging wall and step up to a short rightward traverse to creaking flakes. Follow the arête directly past two peg runners to finish right of a boulder.

Inverted Staircase   23 metres   Very Severe   (7.9.58)
The obvious inverted staircase right of *Special K*. Start below the staircase.
1 6m. 4a. Climb the groove to a stance.
2 17m. 4c. Climb the steep left wall of the groove and the easy slab to finish.

Peth Bras   21 metres   Hard Very Severe 5b   (1981)
Start as for *The Mole*. Climb the corner on the left to a short steep crack. Go up this to a diagonal crack leading onto the final easy slab.

Craig y Clipiau

1 Africa Rib — VD
2 Usher's Dilemma — HS
3 Asahel — S
4 Eagle Finish — VS
5 Great Feet — E1
6 Crimson Cruiser — E5
7 Mean Feat — HVS
8 Purple Paradise — E5
9 Double Criss — VS
10 Overhanging Cracks — E2
11 Straw Dogs Finish — E3
12 Phidl — HVS
13 Special K — E3
14 Inverted Staircase — VS

The Emerald (E5) Craig y Clipiau
Climber: Elfyn Jones   Photo: Terry Taylor

The Mole   21 metres   Hard Severe 4b   (16.9.61)
Start just left of a large boulder 7 metres right of *Inverted Staircase*. Climb up to a flake, traverse right to a short crack and follow this and the final slab.

Sixty metres east of Clipiau, a V-gully has a large west-facing wall with an obvious niche half-way up. **Crab Nebula** (18 metres Hard Very Severe 5a † 18.6.94) gains the niche and then climbs the curving crack above with difficulty to the top and a belay well back.

Clogwyn Holland   Holland Cliff   OS Ref 689 461

This large and fairly complex crag (named after Samuel Holland, one of the nineteenth-century pioneers of the slate industry) stands high up on the flanks of Craig Nyth y Gigfran, overlooking the village of Tan y Grisiau. It can be approached either by traversing round from the base of Craig Clipiau for some 500 metres, or more directly (and steeply!) by a line of old quarrymen's steps leading from a footbridge across the narrow-gauge railway at OS Ref 692 459, and then bearing left to the base of the crag.

The recent development of some fine routes has tranformed this once-neglected cliff into one of the most important hard-climbing areas in the Moelwynion.

The cliff is split into several distinct sections. The west wing is a very steep, clean buttress high up on the left side of the cliff, and is approached either by a tricky scramble up broken rocks or via a diagonal rake which slants down from the top of the cliff. To the right, and running the full height of the cliff, are two prominent blunt ribs (the lines of *Septentrionale* and *Raspberry*) separated by a central recess, and high up above this is the prominent forked crack of *The Hump*. To the right of *Raspberry* are some mossy, easy-angled slabs, and above their apex are three parallel chimney-cracks, beyond which the crag merges into the obvious grassy gully on its right edge.

☆**The Birthing**   24 metres   E5 6a †   (17.7.94)
The obvious curving overhanging corner-crack on the left side of the west wing. Start below the crack, on a small slab. A sustained fight up the lower part of the crack leads to an easing. Follow a jamming crack beneath the roof until wild moves over this lead to easy ground.

☆☆**Holland Groove**   24 metres   E6 6b †   (7.94)
The obvious left-facing groove left of the prow gives a tough challenge. Start directly below the groove. Climb the steepening groove past good wires to a poor peg runner below the bulging upper section. Pull up right past the peg and power through the bulging headwall.

☆☆☆**Memory of a Butterfly**   27 metres   E5 6a †   (7.94)
The prow provides climbing in a spectacular position. Start right of the
undercut prow, at a small slab. Move easily up the slab, and then make
difficult moves to a thin crack and pod (peg runner). Launch out leftwards
onto the prow and make bold moves up its centre to a fine finish.

☆**Changrilah**   18 metres   E2 5c †   (15.6.94)
The broken groove on the right of the prow. Start as for the preceding
route, and move right over an overlap via a crack to gain a short slab.
Balancy moves leftwards gain an open groove, which leads awkwardly to
an easy slab.

Septentrionale   69 metres   Very Difficult   (9.32)
Pleasant, well-situated climbing. Start at the foot of the left-hand buttress.
1 9m. Climb the front of the buttress to a grass ledge.
2 15m. Follow twin cracks to a groove, traverse right, and go up a short
corner to another ledge.
3 18m. Follow the chimney, passing ledges, to a blocked groove. Climb
the groove to a terrace.
4 6m. Climb the steep slab right of a heathery corner to a long ledge.
5 21m. From the right-hand end of the ledge climb up the exposed rib.
Scrambling remains.

Both *Strawberry* and *Raspberry* are, unfortunately, now very vegetated.

Strawberry   60 metres   Very Severe   (18.6.78)
The prominent left-facing corner on the right-hand buttress. Start at
vegetated slabs below it.
1 18m. Climb the slabs to the foot of the corner.
2 30m. 4c. Climb the vegetated corner, passing horizontal spikes low
down and a niche three-quarters of the way up.
3 12m. 4b. Scramble across to the forked crack and climb its wider,
right-hand fork to finish as for *The Hump*.

Brewing up with TT   18 metres   E3 5c †   (17.7.94)
A good line, despite the convoluted approach, taking the thin crack in the
right wall of the large corner of *Strawberry*. Either approach via its first
pitch, or abseil from ledges above. Traverse out right past a huge block to
the crack. Follow the crack on small positive holds (slightly bold in its
middle section) past a small overlap to the top of the rib.

Raspberry   60 metres   Very Severe   (1973)
The left edge of the right-hand buttress. Start at the lowest point of the
buttress.
1 12m. 4a. Climb the short crack; move left, and pass a small tree.
Scramble up and belay among boulders.
2 12m. 4a. Climb the short wall behind the belay to the horizontal break
and the start of the buttress proper. Move left to a poor stance.
3 27m. 4c. Go directly up the short overhanging groove on good holds
and follow the tower to the large terrace.

4 9m. 4b. From the right-hand side of the final tower, climb the obvious crack, which is gained from the right.

The Hump   42 metres   Hard Severe   (13.5.67)
Vegetated climbing leads to a good top pitch up the obvious compelling forked cracks. Start by scrambling up a grassy gully on the right-hand side of the crag to beneath the central of three vegetated cracks above the triangular mossy slabs previously mentioned.
1 18m. Climb the crack to a ledge (the Crows Nest), and then a crack in the short wall to a grassy terrace.
2 12m. 4b. Climb a slab below a steep wall behind the terrace to a grassy groove on the left.
3 12m. 4b. Scramble up leftwards for about 20 metres to below the twin forked cracks on the final tower. Climb the wider, right-hand crack to a difficult finish.

The next four routes are variations on the last pitch of *The Hump*, and can be approached either by scrambling onto the grassy terrace or by abseil.

Robinson Clusoe   15 metres   Hard Very Severe 5b †   (14.6.94)
The wall left of the forked cracks has a faint crack. This is climbed with increasing difficulty to a widening near the top.

The Bump   15 metres   E1 5b †   (14.6.94)
A bold line up the blunt rib to the right of the forked cracks. Climb easily to a ledge; then step right to a poor peg. Shaky moves lead to a horizontal break and a short wall.

Man Flyday   18 metres   Hard Very Severe 5b †   (14.6.94)
The wide crack to the right of the blunt rib. A difficult start and then easier climbing lead to a chockstone. Step right to a slabby wall, which is followed directly to a belay on a quartz slab.

Return of the Sackmen   24 metres   Hard Very Severe 5a † (14.6.94)
A rising diagonal line on the slabby wall to the right of the preceding route. Start below a very easy-angled slab. Walk up the slab to a short vertical crack. Step up left onto a wall and follow a diagonal line to a nose high on the left. Pick your way up this to belay on the quartz slab.

The Beak (60 metres Difficult 1934) starts as for *The Hump*, but takes a poor line of grooves to its right passing 'the beak' at half height, before traversing right beneath an overhang to finish.

Moelwyn Bach   Lesser White Hill

Summit Cliffs   OS Ref 663 438
The crag beneath the summit on the east side is 45 metres high and gives a few climbs of Difficult to Very Difficult standard.

Summit Nose   OS Ref 660 440
The prominent nose seen on the Moelwyn ridge is about 27 metres high, and can be climbed almost anywhere at about Difficult standard. The overhanging section is apparently much harder, giving a short strenuous problem.

Southern-Western Cliffs   OS Ref 655 434
These scattered outcrops are situated on the south flank of the west ridge of Moelwyn Bach and catch the sun all day. There is a good parking-spot at the highest point of the Croesor to Rhyd road (OS Ref 635 434), just outside the forested area on the Rhyd side and directly below a prominent electricity pole. Follow the path up Moelwyn Bach for about 25 minutes to where the ridge begins to steepen. Skirt round to the right to reach a small col adjoining the forest, and follow the wall until the crags appear.

In the middle of the large Ogam Buttress is an obvious perched block. Some 50 metres to the left and above half height are two square-cut blocks separated by a gully.

Arberth   30 metres   Hard Very Severe †   (27.5.90)
A disjointed route, worthwhile only for the upper pitch. Start at a lower buttress slightly left of twin cracks in the upper wall.
1 12m. 5a. Climb into the corner, swing out left onto a loose flake, then move right underneath an overhang and pull up onto a huge jug.
2 18m. From below the right-hand crack, make an awkward move over a small roof and follow the crack above to the top.

☆**They'll Never Keep Us Down**   10 metres   E4 6a †   (2.5.98)
A compact line of contrasts; this is the undercut grooved arête of the right-hand block. Get established in the groove and escape onto the easier but less well-protected arête.

☆**Moonrazor**   15 metres   E2 5c †   (2.5.98)
The razor-sharp arête some 20 metres left of *Igam-Ogam*. Follow the somewhat mossy introductory rib to a tree at the foot of the arête. Make a powerful move to start the arête; then follow its edge to ledges and belays quite well back. Scramble down left.

Tir Na Nog 44 metres   Hard Very Severe †   (12.5.90)
Start at the middle of the slab immediately below and left of the huge
perched block.
1 26m. 5a. Follow cracks to the foot of the obvious corner; then climb
the corner and a short slab to a cave belay.
2 18m. Step up right onto a rib and climb it until 10 metres of scrambling
lead to the top.

☆☆**Man in the Moon** 25 metres   E5 6a †   (2.5.98)
[Photo page 216a.] Archetypal arête elegance. The concave edge of the
great 'man-in-the-moon'-shaped block provides a sustained test of nerves.
Climb grassy slabs and a crack to the base of a corner below and left of
the arête. Transfer right into a wide slanting crack underneath the block.
Move up and step right onto the edge (crucial *Friend 2½*). Follow the arête
with sustained interest, past limited wire placement potential in a thin crack
on its left, to a big recess at the top. Belay here, and then scramble out
right as for *Bryan's Chimney*.

Strictly for masochistic contortionists is ★**Bryan's Chimney** (43 metres †
12.5.90); a grade would be meaningless! Climb the groove below the
block, and move right to enter the depths of the chimney. Struggle up the
chimney, and then climb easy slabs to the top.

★**Igam-Ogam** 39 metres   E1   (31.3.90)
Start just right of the slabby corner in the middle of Ogam Buttress.
1 12m. 5b. A steep crack gains a sloping slab which leads to a stance
below a fine-looking crackline.
2 27m. 5b. Climb the crack to the overhang and make a difficult move
right to gain the arête. Climb the arête to a final grassy section and reach
a good spike belay.

Non Welsh-Speaker's Conundrum 40 metres   E4 5c † (2.5.98)
A not insubstantial right-hand variant of *Igam-Ogam*. Positive holds, but
committing. From 2 metres up the crack of *Igam-Ogam*, traverse right
along the lip of the roof on pockets before making bold moves diagonally
right to the arête and the sanctuary of a sloping ledge. Step right onto an
easier rib to join *Igam-Ogam*, which is followed to the top.

The Dogs Dinner 21 metres   Hard Very Severe 5a †   (12.5.90)
This is the first arête right of *Igam-Ogam*. Climbed directly with poor
protection.

About 100 metres to the right of Ogam Buttress is a fine-looking pillar. The
outside face of this is taken by *Maen Twr Og*; the impending left face and
arête is:

☆**On Easter Island** 20 metres   E4 6a †   (2.5.98)
Typical Moelwynion twisted-wire territory. A demanding climb for the
grade. Spring up a line of pockets in the centre of the wall to a sloping
ledge and a good break above on the left. Make a fierce move on

finger-pockets up the face and step left onto the arête (good *Rock 5* placement just left of the arête). Proceed to a series of larger but widely-spaced handholds, and exit slightly left.

★★★**Maen Tŵr Og**   20 metres   E2 5c   (12.5.90)
[Photo page 216b.] Climb the crack just right of the base and swing left. Step right onto a ledge and move up past a good hold to an excellent pocket. Move left past the arête and make a final tricky pull over the top.

Further right, just past a wide grassy gully and set at a higher level, is a slender buttress split by a wide crack.

☆**Yr Holltalluog**   21 metres   Hard Very Severe 5a †   (3.9.99)
Start just right of the foot of the slender buttress. Swing up left to gain the arête and climb it to a jammed flake. Continue up the almighty crack, passing a welcome thread on the right arête.

Another 30 metres right there is a shale-like vegetated section with a prominent 5-metre pinnacle just above.

Beneath the Underdog   46 metres   Hard Very Severe 5a † (3.9.99)
Scramble in from the right to the pinnacle. Climb twin cracks formed by a flake to the overhang. Struggle up the narrowing and continue up a wide crack to a belay. Scramble up and take the slabby wall on the right.

Right again, and some 15 metres left of a prominent wide vertical crack (*Expel to Air*), is a clean buttress with an obvious scoop in its upper part.

☆☆**The Misfortunes of Elphin**   23 metres   E2 5c †   (14.4.95)
Start below the scoop. Gain the arête, swing onto the face, and reach a small pocket (*Friend 2*). Fingery moves lead to good pockets and an *in-situ* thread. Swing up right onto the scooped section and climb the arête on the right.

Expel to Air   15 metres   E4 5c †   (3.5.98)
The unmistakable and unforgiving off-width. It's everything it looks and more! Mega-cam owners are barred from entry and, besides, some thin wire protection is available both inside and outside the crack. Overcome the crack by traditional or technical means, and escape with a bold layback for the top. Scramble off.

The next buttress to the right, at a much higher level, has an obvious right-to-left-slanting crack.

☆**Cyw Haul**   18 metres   Very Severe 4c †   (19.10.99)
Start below the slanting crack. Overcome some initial vegetation and climb a rib to a ledge. Pull right into the crack and climb it with superb jams and perfect protection.

☆**Sundance Kid**   18 metres   Hard Very Severe 5a †   (19.10.99)
Follow *Cyw Haul* until it is possible to step right onto an obvious foothold. Climb the front of the buttress boldly on good pockets. Large thread lower-off.

Right again, now about 30 metres right of the off-width, is a leaning white wall split by a rightward-rising finger-crack.

The Slot Machine 20 metres E4 6a †   (3.5.98)
Deceptively strenuous climbing up the finger-crack. Battle up the crack past an unaccommodating slot to a welcome hand-jam. Continue up the crack to a large ledge, and finish up the easier groove in the headwall.

☆☆**Exposé** 15 metres E4 6a/b †   (3.5.98)
A gem of a climb, taking a rising line of jugs to nothingness across the leaning white wall right of the finger-crack. Adequately protected. From the ledge below the finger-crack, reach the rising hand-ledge and follow it across the wall to a thin crack just short of the right arête (peg runner). Make hard moves into and up a short groove to a large block sitting on the ledge. Belay and exit as for the preceding route.

To the right is a square-cut arête with twin cracks on its left.

☆**Agenda** 24 metres E1 5b †   (13.10.99)
Using the flake in the left-hand crack, launch into the right-hand one and grovel up to a large ledge. Follow the obvious line up leftwards and climb the wall to a small ledge. Climb the thin finger-crack on excellent locks to the large capstone, and exit right.

On Impulse 6 metres E5 5c †   (3.5.98)
[Photo page 216c.] Teeter up the square-cut arête: a 6-metre route with 60-metre fall potential – a thrilling solo!

Towards the right-hand end of the crags above two huge boulders is a prominent thin crack, *Loki Crack*.

☆**Thor's Wall** 20 metres E5 6b †   (3.5.98)
An extremely taxing and fingery wall climb up the hairline crack in the face left of *Loki Crack*; add on a grade for an on-sight effort since the small wire and *RP* protection is difficult to secure. Pad out left onto the mossy slab and step up to a sloping ledge beneath the hairline crack. Climb the wall in line with the crack past one good slot and a couple of good pockets to a semi-rest at two-thirds height. Continue direct on rather better holds (small *in-situ* thread) to an exit slightly right. Pumped?

☆☆**Loki Crack** 18 metres Hard Very Severe 5a †   (1.4.90)
Good climbing and excellent protection. Start in a small bay just left of the arête. Move left and then enter a corner on the right. Stand on the block on the left to gain the fine strenuous crackline.

Fifth Anniversary 18 metres E2 5c †   (3.5.98)
Escapable climbing up the right arête of the *Loki Crack* face. The finish should set the pulse racing. An overhanging crack leads to a large ledge below the arête. Take the arête direct to flakes and scarily power up its very edge to the top.

The next buttress right has only one route (to date), taking the obvious corner in the left side of the recessed bay:

Penbwl Corner   37 metres   Very Severe 4c †   (13.10.99)
Start at the lowest point of the slabs. Climb a vague groove and an easy slab leftwards to the foot of the corner; then climb the corner and the wall above.

Craig Ysgafn   Light Crag[1]   OS Ref 657 443
The small crag on the connecting ridge between Moelwyn Bach and Moelwyn Mawr offers short routes on friable rock.

Blaenau Ffestiniog Area

Chwarel Moel Ystradau   Straths Hill Quarry OS Ref 682 437
This granite quarry lies on the southern shore of Llyn Ystradau (Tanygrisiau Reservoir) and is approached by a public footpath from the A496 road at a footbridge at OS Ref 688 447, just south of the junction for Tanygrisiau.

There is only one route and its name and first ascent details are unknown (20 metres E5 6b 7a+): climb a stepped wall, passing several bolts, to a desperate final move.

Craig dan Ysgol   Under School Crag   OS Ref 701 456
This cliff is found below the secondary school, and is approached by driving past the school and turning down a cul-de-sac past the swimming pool. Park at the end and follow a path for 50 metres down through the woods until the cliff is reached.

Dunces' Corner   12 metres   Very Severe 4c   (1979)
Start below a small roof in a corner on the left-hand wall. Climb to the roof, traverse left, and go up into the groove. Follow this boldly to the top.

Vertical Playground   12 metres   E2 5c †   (20.4.89)
The right-hand side of the wall capped by an overhanging groove. Climb steeply up the wall and stretch up to an obvious fingerhold. Climb into a niche and swing boldly up the overhanging groove past a peg to a tree belay.

Chwarel Manod   Manod Quarry   OS Ref 708 448
Another recent development has taken place on the concave wall on the right-hand side of a large quarried face above the Manod part of Blaenau

---

1 In contrast to Craig Stwlan.

Man in the Moon (E5) Moelwyn Bach
Climber: Martin Crocker Photo: Don Sargeant

Maen Tŵr Og (E2) Moelwyn Bach
Climber: Martin Crocker   Photo: Don Sarge

On Impulse (E5) Moelwyn Bach
Climber: Martin Crocker Photo: Don Sargeant

Tears in Rain (E7) Chwarel Manod
Climber: Mel Griffiths   Photo: Terry Taylor

Ffestiniog – some very loose routes have been climbed on the main face but are not worth describing. However this short concave wall some 200 metres to the right has some technical gems. Park on the main road below the cliffs, by some large gates, opposite the cemetery (where you may end up if tempted by the large loose face on the left!). Approach via a lane 100 metres back from these gates, which leads to open ground and a scramble up to the crag.

All the routes finish at an in-situ belay/lower-off point. There is an obvious thin crackline just left of centre of the wall – this is *Black Percy*.

★Steel against the Sky   18 metres   E5 6b   (18.7.97)
The rising crackline left of *Black Percy*. Start below the crack, as for *Black Percy*. Gain the left fork of the crack, and make powerful moves to a break. Pull directly through the roof (thread and peg runner) onto a steep finishing-slab.

★★Black Percy   18 metres   E5 6a   (28.5.94)
Climb the thin crackline in the centre of the wall, taking the right fork past peg runners to a break below an overlap. Pull over this to finish.

☆Tears in Rain   18 metres   E7 6c †   (9.97)
[Photo page 216d.] A very hard and committing eliminate, up the centre of the wall. From beneath a small overlap, climb direct to the right-hand side of a short, black, horizontal slot. Small edges on the right lead through the bulge to the thin break. Finish directly.

★Pistachio Man   18 metres   E5 6a   (29.5.94)
Climb the wall right of *Tears in Rain* on pockets, passing a good cam-slot. Hard moves right (peg runner) lead to a small blunt flake. Follow the break leftwards until it is possible to pull up onto the finishing-slab.

Primal Scream   18 metres   E4 6a   (18.7.97)
As for *Pistachio Man*, climb direct to a diagonal break. Then step up and right via a thin crack and sharp pockets to gain broken rock at the right-hand side of the wall. Pull up and move leftwards to a short finishing-slab.

Spindoctor   18 metres   E3 5c †   (20.7.97)
A traverse across the obvious break at three-quarters height. Start at the extreme left side. Gain the horizontal break and hand traverse right along the break to its end. Step up onto the finishing-slab of *Primal Scream*.

Moors North-East of Ffestiniog

The vast area of heather moor and blanket bog to the north and east of the village of Ffestiniog has a scattering of small, often broken cliffs. The quality of the rock is very varied, from excellent rough clean walls and arêtes to crumbling vegetated choss. The whole area has a different character from the Moelwynion massif, being reminiscent of some gritstone outcrops – but in a much grander setting!

Carreg y Frân   Rock (of) the Crow   OS Ref 735 449

Carreg y Frân lies south-east of Blaenau Ffestiniog and faces south in a majestic situation overlooking the Cwm Teigl valley. The easiest approach is from Ffestiniog by a well-surfaced road leading up Cwm Teigl to Chwarel Manod. Take the first road on the left on entering Ffestiniog from the direction of Blaenau Ffestiniog, and follow this past several gates to reach some parking-areas below the cliff.

In the past the cliff has had a reputation for loose rock; however, some stunning recent additions are well worth seeking out. The westerly buttresses are vegetated and are bounded on the right by a deep gully, Gashed Gully, the upper reaches of which has a steep right wall.

The crag has some rare plants so please **refrain from gardening** here.

Tykes Wall   36 metres   Very Severe   (9.8.67)
A good route, taking the right wall of Gashed Gully. Start at the foot of Gashed Gully.
1 12m. Scramble up mixed grass and rock in the gully to a peg belay on the left.
2 15m. 4c. Descend slightly and climb the wall on its left side to a sloping slab. Step up left to an overhanging crack, and climb this to a sloping ledge at the foot of a leaning corner.
3 9m. 4c. Climb the overhanging corner to a good ledge, and continue directly up the short wall to finish.

Nazgul   36 metres   Very Severe   (19.3.66)
A pleasant climb with an exposed finish. Start in a corner between the arête right of Gashed Gully and a red wall.
1 18m. 4a. Move onto the top of a large block and step left into a corner-groove. Climb this to exit left and continue up a short wall to a stance on the arête.
2 18m. 4c. Climb the arête by a shallow groove on the left, and continue steeply up to the top of the gully wall.

Red Wall Crack   42 metres   Hard Very Severe   (12.6.69)
The crack splitting the red wall gives an awkward and insecure climb. Start at the foot of the crack.
1 18m. 5a. Climb the crack to a large ledge.
2 24m. 4c. Climb a short wall and a corner, which leads to another short wall and the top.

The broken vegetated ground to the right of the red wall gives two poor climbs which are not worth describing in detail – **Sting** (Very Difficult 1966) and **Orc** (Severe 1966) climb the vegetated walls and rib to the right.

Tŵr 38 metres Very Difficult (1.9.57)
Worthwhile. Start at the foot of an arête composed of blocks.
1 20m. Climb the arête to a stance.
2 9m. Follow the corner above to a grass ledge.
3 9m. Climb the wall to finish.

On the right is a prominent corner bounded on both sides by clean steep walls – the harder routes are approached by scrambling up easy rocks between the starts of *Little Plum* and *The Corner*.

★**Little Plum** 34 metres Very Severe (12.6.69)
The clean corner on the left-hand side of the steep smooth wall gives a very pleasant outing. Easier than it looks. Start to the right of *Tŵr*, at the foot of the lowest section of the corner.
1 15m. 4c. Climb the corner to a stance below the upper section.
2 18m. 5a. Finish up the clean-cut corner.

☆**Parsimony** 21 metres E6 6b † (1996)
A fine, but poorly-protected start leads to the thin crack left of *Psycho*. Climb the wall (gear in the crack) and make steep moves over the small roof (peg runner) on the right to slightly loose finishing-jugs.

★**Psycho** 21 metres E4 6a (7.5.67/1980s)
The obvious crack splitting the steep wall gives a fierce challenge. Start at the short wall directly beneath the crack. Climb the crack, steep and strenuous, but easing towards the top.

The Sack Thrower's Association 21 metres E4 6a † (17.5.98)
[Photo page 224a.] Start below the overlap right of *Psycho*, and use a small pocket to gain the centre of the wall above strenuously. Thin moves lead to better holds and a step left to finish up the easier top section of *Psycho*.

The Corner 32 metres Hard Very Severe
The corner right of *Psycho*. Start at the foot of the system of grooves left of the overhanging nose in the centre of the crag.
1 9m. Climb the grooves for 3 metres and then traverse left to the foot of the corner.
2 23m. 5a. Climb the overhanging corner-crack to where it relents a little at 8 metres, and continue more easily up the corner above. Ignore the easy way off just below the top and traverse left under the final overhang to finish.

★★**Wee Laddie** 18 metres E6 6b (1997)
The right wall of the corner overhangs alarmingly. This fine pitch climbs the centre of the wall by discontinuous cracklines. Climb the wall, trending left

at first, then slightly rightwards past good hidden incuts. Well protected if you have the strength to place the gear!

★★Big Boy!   15 metres   E7 6b   (28.7.97)
[Photo page 224b.] The right arête gives a demanding lead with poor protection. Move right to the arête with trepidation and boldly climb its left side past some alarming moves to a good pocket near the top. Step right (don't slip now!) and onto easier ground.

Pigtail Grooves   30 metres   Severe   (2.1.58)
Slight, but quite enjoyable. Start as for *The Corner*. Climb the system of grooves, forming a rib to the right of the prominent arête of *Big Boy!*

The rock in the area of the nose gives a loose and dangerous climb: **The Nose** (38 metres Hard Very Severe), and the steep undercut wall to the right is climbed by **Chamber of Horrors** (30 metres Very Severe).

Strider   30 metres   Very Severe   (19.5.66)
Start by a cairn beneath the obvious groove right of the steep undercut wall.
1 24m. 4b. Climb the groove to grass ledges, and continue up a vegetated crack to another grass ledge.
2 6m. 4b. Climb the short slab to the top.

A number of short climbs (not described) start from the grassy bay on the right before the final buttress; the latter gives two pleasant climbs:

Gay   30 metres   Severe   (2.7.67)
Start at the foot of the arête forming the left edge of the buttress.
1 12m. Climb the shallow groove just right of the crack.
2 18m. Go straight up onto the wall above, cross it to the right, and continue up a steep groove to the top.

Deceiver   30 metres   Severe   (5.66)
Start directly below a large pinnacle, at the foot of a shallow groove.
1 12m. Climb the groove to an awkward landing and a belay at the foot of the pinnacle.
2 18m. Climb the right-hand side of the pinnacle and go straight up the wall above.

Craig Goch   Red Crag   OS Ref 752 441
This is a half-mile line of broken crags east-south-east of Blaenau Ffestiniog. Many climbs have apparently been made here but are now lost in the heather and vegetation.

Carreg y Foel Gron   Rock (of) the Round Hill   OS Ref 745 427
This small crag is seen from the Ffestiniog to Penmachno road. There are a number of routes here ranging from 30 to 50 metres long. The main merit of

the crag is as a training-ground for novices; however, a number of new additions (especially on the hidden, upper tier) are far more testing.

Access is from the small parking-area on the southern shore of Llyn Dubach, the small lake just off the B4407. The cliff is approached directly by a short path across marshy ground. The upper tier lies to the left of and behind the main cliff, just beyond a disused quarry.

There are several sections to the cliff. Little Slab (no lines described) is on the left of the main section and can be climbed in several places at about Difficult standard. The Main Slab is obvious in the centre and is the highest section. The routes are not described in detail and first ascent details have long been forgotten.

Cracked Slab   24 metres   Very Difficult
The most continuous crackline on the left. Start from the base of an inset slab and pass the right-hand side of a small overlap.

Tiger Feet   24 metres   Very Severe
A poorly-protected slab on the right.

Elephant's Crawl   24 metres   Very Difficult
Climb the inset slab and the more difficult corner above.

To the right is a huge detached pinnacle:

Inspiration   24 metres   Very Difficult
Climb the left side of the pinnacle – a bold leap is needed to gain the top of the main crag.

Chimney Sweep   24 metres   Very Difficult
Unsurprisingly, this takes the chimney on the right, with difficult moves over the chockstone.

To the right again is a prominent double buttress with some modern additions.

Sickle Cell   15 metres   E5 6b †   (1990s)
[Photo page 192b.] The left arête gives a bold test-piece.

Crads Wall   15 metres   E3 6a †   (1990s)
Climb the front of the left-hand block directly.

Indecision   18 metres   Very Severe
The right-slanting chimney between the two blocks has an awkward move at two-thirds height.

Interesting Drug   18 metres   Hard Very Severe 5a †   (1997)
Climb the stepped ramp-line right of the chimney. Interesting moves round the arête lead to a slabby wall. Make thin moves back left near the arête to the top.

To the left of and behind the main cliff, immediately to the left of some abandoned quarry-workings, is a smaller but much steeper face. This is the Upper Tier and gives climbing which, according to one activist, 'is a cross between the positive jugs and pockets of limestone and the delicate balance and friction of gritstone and is unequalled by any crag in Snowdonia'. Nevertheless, it is a good venue on a sunny afternoon! Many of the routes have been climbed and claimed by several parties, and first ascent details are very confusing. The names given are not necessarily those of the first ascensionists, but are used for convenience and simplicity.

☆The Crack   12 metres   E5 6a †   (1996)
Take the obvious wide crack splitting the fiercely overhanging wall on the left of the cliff.

☆Toxic Haste   12 metres   E5 6a †   (1998)
The thin curving crack immediately right gives a well-protected fight (peg runner).

The Rambler   12 metres   Difficult †   (1995)
Starting on the right, climb easily along the lip of the overhanging wall to finish up the wide crack.

Quiet Introductions   12 metres   Very Severe 4c
Climb the crackline right of the slab until it peters out; then go diagonally left over a slight bulge.

Slab Direct   12 metres   E1 5b
Guess where this (boldly) goes!

Half Height Fright   12 metres   Very Severe 4c
Climb the centre of the wall right of a shallow corner on good pockets and edges, avoiding the loose flake at half height (and the point of the route?).

The Shark's Fin   12 metres   Hard Severe 4b
The arête on the right is gained from the left and is climbed direct.

Josh's Corner   12 metres   Very Severe 4c
The obvious corner capped by boulders; exit onto the right arête.

Dead Tree Arête   12 metres   Hard Very Severe 4c
The arête right of *Josh's Corner*.

To the right is a clean wall above a small roof.

Sweet Summer Evening   12 metres   E4 6b
Powerful moves through the overhang on pockets and crimps lead to easier climbing up the clean wall.

Too Many Children   12 metres   Very Severe 4c
Take the obvious crackline to the right of the small overhang.

Not Enough Babes   12 metres   E1 5c
The thinner crack 1 metre to the right.

To the right is a big broken corner; the following routes are based on the arête to its right.

Perygl   12 metres   E1 5c
Powerful moves gain jugs on the arête. The upper section is unprotected.

Finding a Job   12 metres   Hard Very Severe 5a
Awkward moves up the crack 2 metres right of the arête.

The right-hand side of the cliff, directly above the quarry workings, is green and slimy with loose rock and there are no recorded routes.

Cwm Lledr

Cwm Lledr runs west from the Crimea Pass above Blaneau Ffestiniog to the confluence of the Afon Lledr and the Afon Conwy between the Fairy Glen and the Waterloo Bridge in Betwys-y-coed.

The valley is less densely populated and less frequented than others in Snowdonia, making it a tranquil place in which to climb. Although everything is on a relatively small scale, there is a great variety of climbing here: a high mountain route leading to a summit ridge; the friendly easier climbs of Craig y Tonnau; the hard roadside problems of Pont-y-pant; and, at the centre of the valley and in the centre of the grade-range, the traditional Carreg Alltrem. The valley is densely forested along much of its length, often rendering some of the approaches complex, especially as the forests are continually being harvested and replanted.

The crags are gained from various points on the A470 trunk road (formerly the A469), which winds along the valley floor. At the time of writing the A470 between Dolwyddelan and Betws-y-coed is being widened. This will result in many of the current bends disappearing, together with the already limited number of parking-spaces. Please take note of the parking and access information relating to each crag.

The westernmost three crags, all south-facing, Clogwyn yr Adar, Craig y Tonnau, and Craig Ddu are reached by turning off the A470 along the minor road towards Roman Bridge and then to Blaenau Dolwyddelan. There is limited parking along the minor road, but be aware of farm traffic and please take note of the parking advice for each section. After driving through Pen y Rhiw farm with its many barking dogs, there are two gates on the road before a bridge over the Afon Lledr is reached, where the road becomes a track and it is possible to park four to six cars.

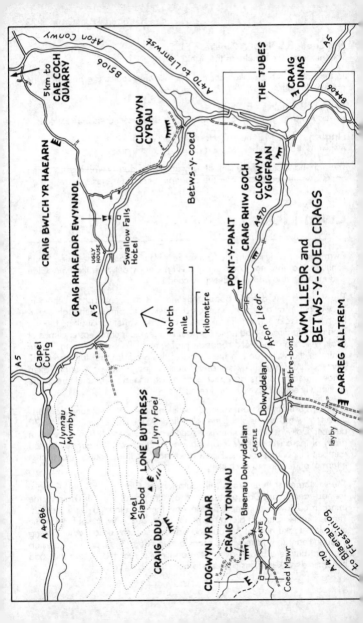

CWM LLEDR and BETWS-Y-COED CRAGS

The Sack Thrower's Association
(E4 ~ first ascent) Carreg y Frân
Climber: Andy Cave   Photo: Terry Taylor

Big Boys (E7 – first ascent)
Climber: Mel Griffiths   Photos: Terry Taylor

Clogwyn yr Adar   Cliff (of) the Birds   OS Ref 693 516

This 25-metre crag can be seen behind Coed Mawr farm. It has some excellent routes for the higher-grade climber. Access to the crag was threatened some years ago after climbers visited the crag and ignored requests to ask permission of the landowner before climbing.

Four to six cars can be parked by the bridge mentioned above, which is 200 metres beyond where the farm track leaves the minor road. Access is along this track, which is a public footpath that passes through the farm but that does not continue directly to the crag. Please ask for permission to climb at the farm. The farmer is at present prepared to allow up to four climbers at a time on the crag, provided that respect is shown for the property. The crag has been visited since the 60s but details were withheld until the blitz of 1988 when locals 'discovered' the crag.

In some years protected birds nest in *The Cheshire Cat* area. This can result in a temporary **restriction** to this part of the crag.

The crag is split into three buttresses divided by areas of vegetation. The left-hand buttress has a superb route, which gives the best climb on the crag.

★★**The Cheshire Cat**   30 metres   E5 [r]   (7.4.88)
The route takes a direct line into a small cave and then the continuation groove above.
1 21m. 6a. Climb past a block on good holds to 'the grin'. Enter this and pull over the roof to a thread. Go straight up; then walk right (two pegs) to belay at a small thread.
2 9m. 5c. Climb the groove (peg on the right) and continue direct, using holds on the left.

Seven Hunters   30 metres   E1 5a [r]   (1990)
On the wall to the right of *The Cheshire Cat* is a hanging flake crack. Some care is needed with the rock in the upper part. Starting just left of the crack, climb up and right to gain it, and then follow the flakes to the top.

Tarantula   36 metres   Severe [r]   (19.8.72)
Start at an S-shaped crack.
1 9m. Traverse leftwards up a gangway to its end, avoiding the huge *in-situ* spiders.
2 15m. Make a bold move over the bulge on the right; then traverse right past the crack up a short wall to some loose blocks.
3 12m. The obvious sloping gangway on the left is followed on small holds to the top.

The next routes lie on the central buttress

Mabel's Route   21 metres   Very Difficult   (19.8.72)
Start just to the left of central vegetation by a boulder-field.
1 9m. Follow a low shelf that slopes up to the right, climb the corner, and move right at its top to a large ledge and trees.

2 12m. On the left is an overhanging wall. Climb the wall to the right of this, and then an arête to the top.

Bimbo   20 metres   Hard Very Severe 4c   (1989)
This poor route lies on a small wall between the two main sections of the buttress. Start at a rusty spike in a crack. Climb the shattered flakes and cracks to finish up the slab by a sapling.

Gringo   24 metres   Hard Very Severe   (19.8.72)
Start to the right of a section of vegetation.
1 15m. Climb the left edge of a green slab, and then a curving crack. Hand-traverse left and gain a niche. Go left round the rib to a stance.
2 9m. Take the bulging wall above via a crack.

The remaining routes lie on the right-hand buttress, above an area of often boggy ground. There is an abseil-point above *Bloodbank*; alternatively, descend via the right of the buttress. This rhyolite crag has a bulge which guards entry onto the face at 5 metres.

Genericon Limits   30 metres   E5 6b   (4.88)
From a good peg on the lip of the bulge, move right; then go straight up to good holds. Head straight for a porthole and finish directly over the bulge.

★★★**Bloodbank**   30 metres   E5 6b   (7.4.88)
A superb left-trending line. Start just right of a rust streak. Move up (two pegs) to a block on the left. Gain the left-trending crack, and climb through the centre of the overlap. Climb the wall to a break; then move left and go up a flake to another break (thread runner on the right). Continue up past an undercut to a jug (peg) and finish leftwards to a ledge (thread) and the top.

Boss Talkers   30 metres   E5 6b   (6.4.88)
From the block on *Bloodbank*, swing right to jugs (peg) and climb the fine wall to a break (old peg and thread). Continue through a niche and climb a wall to a finishing-crack.

Noble Horse   30 metres   E2 5b   (22.5.88)
Climb the wall to a pink thread; then step left and go up to a peg. Climb the groove/crack above to the break, and then the flake above to finish up the crack of *Boss Talkers*.

★★**Hustlers, Beats, and Others**   30 metres   E2 5b   (7.4.88)
Climb straight up to a pink thread; then trend right up the wall on good holds.

John Damocleese   30 metres   E4 6b   (4.88)
Climb the wall below the holly and move left to a thread. Make hard moves to a peg; then climb a slab to the break. Continue up the slab and finish leftwards.

★★Enterprise Allowance   30 metres   E2 5b   (6.4.88)
Start up the obvious crack in the right-hand side of the crag and follow it to
where it fades. Finish up *John Damocleese* past a peg.

Whisper of the Axe   30 metres   E4 5c   (5.4.88)
To the right of *Enterprise Allowance*, gain an earthy hollow from the right
and go up to the base of a slab (*Friend 2*). Move right and climb the slab;
then take the wall above (thread) to the top.

Craig y Tonnau   Rippled Crag   OS Ref 700 518
This is a fine little crag with some unusual rock formations, which is all but
hidden by the forest when viewed from the road. It complements Clogwyn y
Adar with a selection of mid and lower-grade climbs. The crag consists of a
steep undulating slab of granular rock.

The crag is situated in a private working forest, but the owners encourage
access. Park in an open area just after the first gate by a track leading into
the forest (OS Ref 704 518). Take care not to block the gate or entry to a
chapel converted into a house to the left of the gate.

Follow the track for some 300 metres to a line of electricity poles that cross
the path into a fire break on the left. Take an indistinct path along the break,
following the poles to their highest point. Forty-five metres further on, cut up
left over the ridge and drop down to the crag via a series of rocky steps.

The crag is about 100 metres long and is divided into two walls. Most of the
routes are on the main, left-hand wall which itself is split by the obvious line
of *Central Crack*. Descent is as for the last part of the approach.

Dentist's Slab   15 metres   Severe   (1997)
Start as for *Robbin's Nest* but move up and left to follow a line of flakes to
the top.

Robbin's Nest   15 metres   Severe   (1990)
Start 6 metres left of *Central Crack* at a large thread. Follow the wavy
striations to the top.

Brewer's Troupe   15 metres   Hard Very Severe 5b †   (1997)
Start midway between *Robbin's Nest* and *Central Crack* below a small
pocket at 2 metres. Make a difficult move to stand in the pocket and
continue more easily to a steep finish.

Robbin's Reliant   15 metres   Very Difficult   (1990)
Climb *Central Crack* for 4 metres until it is possible to move left above a
wave of rock. Follow a series of ripples to the left of the crack to the top.

Central Crack   15 metres   Very Difficult   (1960s)
Climb the obvious feature of the crag with no deviation.

Robbin's Right Hand   15 metres   Severe   (1990)
From just down and right of *Central Crack*, follow an indefinite line of
flakes to half height. Step right and finish steeply.
Direct Finish 7m. Severe (1990). Instead of stepping right, step left and
climb up to finish just left of *Central Crack*.

Diane's Approval   15 metres   Very Difficult   (1990)
Twelve metres right of *Central Crack*, climb another crack, with a holly tree
at one-third height.

Sunday Lunch   15 metres   Very Severe 4c   (1997)
Start to the right of *Diane's Approval*. Pleasant slab climbing leads to the
veg.

Spring Lightning   15 metres   Very Difficult   (25.5.99)
Start directly under the arête forming the right edge of the main wall.
Climb steeply up to gain the the arête. Continue up, and move left at the
top to finish.

The following routes are to the right of the vegetated gully that divides the
crag.

Robbin' a Bank   15 metres   Severe   (1990)
Start just right of the gully and follow the waves to the tree. Finish up the
loose continuation wall above.

To the right of *Robbin' a Bank* is a small overlap; the next route climbs
through this.

Shooting from the Hype   12 metres   Very Severe 4c   (1997)
Climb through the centre of the overlap to follow a very mossy slab to the
top.

Square Block Route   12 metres   Very Severe 4b
Start at the right-hand end of the overlap, and pass it on the right.
Continue via a tricky section to a grassy finish.

Grug Grog   17 metres   Severe   (25.5.99)
Just past the overlap is a vegetated crack which splits the wall. Climb the
crack to gain a rightward break. Follow the break to its end before moving
back left slightly to finish direct.

Alcantata   12 metres   Severe †   (25.5.99)
Climb a left-facing corner just right of *Grug Grog*, and move left at the
top. Continue directly up the steep wall above.

Craig Ddu   Black Crag   OS Ref 697 536
In a solitary situation on the south-west flank of Moel Siabod is a prominent
crag comprised of three buttresses. Only five routes have been recorded, but

there is scope for further development. The rock is mostly excellent, but take care with perched blocks.

Park and approach as for Craig y Tonnau, and follow the forest tracks to a small dammed lake at 697 530 (excellent for mountain bikes). Follow the boundary fence from the northern side of the lake that leads directly to the centre of the crag. Alternatively, an approach can be made from the *Pen y Gwryd* towards Bwlch y Maen, the col on the ridge leading to the summit of Moel Siabod. From here, contour around eastwards to the crag.

The first route is on the left-hand, west buttress.

Brigate Rosso   21 metres   Very Severe 4c   (1998)
Just left of the main arête which separates the two faces of the buttress is an obvious serrated edge. Begin in the groove to the right of the edge. Bridge over the groove and make an awkward mantelshelf to gain a narrow ledge at the foot of the edge below two cracks. Climb the left-hand crack a short way before moving back right to regain the edge. Climb directly up the exposed edge, and move right to finish up a short slab.

The next route picks its way through the steeper, central buttress. The old fence-line meets the crag at a short overhanging subwall to the right of a central prow.

Wysiwig   32 metres   Very Difficult   (7.7.99)
Start 18 metres left of the fence-line, in the left-slanting gully which runs up to undercut the main prow.
1 12m. Climb easily up the gully and belay at the base of a corner that breaks the right wall.
2 20m. Climb the corner, step over perched blocks, and follow the ramp over ledges to the second stance of *Zenturion*.

★Zenturion   66 metres   Very Severe 4c   (18.8.98)
The original route of the crag weaves a devious line through some unlikely terrain. Start 12 metres left of the fence-line, at the right-facing slab in the centre of the buttress.
1 12m. 4a. Climb the slab to the overhang. Move across right onto a parallel lower slab. Continue to the terrace.
2 27m. 4b. Gain the steep wall above the slab with difficulty. Traverse 3 metres left before moving back right to a grassy groove. Climb the groove and scramble up to belay below the broken overhangs.
3 27m. 4c. Walk left to the edge of the slab. Thin moves across the slab gain the steep, slabby ramp above. Continue, passing a large jammed flake on the left, and climb up steeply left to gain the prow on the edge of the face (exposed). From the prow, move slightly right and climb direct to gain the rock terrace. An excellent pitch.
An optional fourth pitch can be taken by climbing the broken wall above.
Variations

3a 27m. 4c. Between the grassy chimney and the corner is an undercut groove. Enter it directly or from the right, and climb to its top. Step left over a large flake to rejoin the normal route.
3b 20m. 4b. Get into the groove as for pitch 3a, and traverse right to reach the top of a chimney. Finish up easy slabs.

The east buttress has a left flank and a steep main face, which is divided by a left-slanting, vegetated gully.

Ghost Dance   27 metres   Hard Very Severe 5a   (1999)
Start on the left of the buttress at the steep crack with a jammed flake at 2 metres.
1 12m. 5a. Climb the crack to a niche. Exit leftwards to gain a steep wall and make thin moves up to a ledge. Traverse right across a smooth slab for 3 metres; then climb up to a small ledge.
2 15m. 4c. Climb up into a sentry-box, from which a long reach beyond the roof gains good holds. Step right across a bottomless groove to gain easier ground, which leads to a grass terrace. Move back left onto the slabby wall and climb easily to a rock ledge to finish.

Two Against Nature   36 metres   Severe (1 pt aid) †   (14.9.2000)
Right of the slanting gully, the centre of the buttress projects as three sides of a gigantic cube. Directly beneath this is a short nose leading to a perched block and a right-slanting ramp. Start 6 metres right of the nose.
1 20m. Climb leftwards to the perched block, and then up the crack formed by its right-hand side. Follow the ramp to a stance at the foot of a short slab below the left-hand of two weaknesses in the little headwall.
2 16m. Make a steep and awkward move up the wall to a shelf. Get into the recess on the left and move out left onto easy ground to reach belays.

Lone Buttress   OS Ref 708 548
Lying higher still, on the eastern slopes of Moel Siabod above Llyn y Foel, is another solitary buttress, cleft by a gully in the centre. Right of the gully is a steep section of rock, with an easy gully (Embryo Gully) right again. The route follows the line of the rib forming a ridge up the steep section.

Llyn y Foel is best reached by the popular walkers' path from Pont Cyfing (OS Ref 734 571) on the A5 just below Capel Curig.

Lone Buttress   60 metres   Difficult   (1939)
A nice route though it has some loose rock. Start at the foot of the rib, right of a pinnacle with an overhang.
1 30m. Gain the rib from the left and go up its edge pleasantly to a grassy stance.
2 30m. Follow the line of the rib to the top.

Flanking the cwm right of Embryo Gully is a ridge of easy-angled slabs, which give simple scrambling. On the left end of the cwm is another rocky ridge (Daear Ddu), a fine scramble in itself which also gives some interesting problems on the side facing Llyn y Foel.

Carreg Alltrem   Steep-looking Rock   OS Ref 739 507

A small crag situated on the eastern side of Cwm Penamnen, the valley which runs due south from Dolwyddelan. Turn off the A470 and take the road towards the railway station. Go over the river and railway bridges, and turn immediately left. Within 50 metres a track on the right leads into the forest. There is parking for four to six cars in the area of the gate or back over the bridges on the road. Follow the track into the forest, fork left at the first junction, and the crag will be seen above and to the left. If the gate is open there is limited parking below the crag, but take care not to be locked in!

This is one of the most beautifully situated crags in the area, with climbing to match. The rock is good; the routes are exposed and very quick-drying. Climbing here is a delight.

Whale takes the groove starting from a small, overgrown cave entrance on the left of the crag; a deep groove to the right is taken by *Leviathan Direct*. For the next 30 metres the wall is split by a series of grooves, with the V-chimney of *Lightning Visit* at the extreme right, and the large corner of *Penamnen Groove* marking the end of the wall. *Civetta* follows the steep tower, the right edge of which is taken by *Lavaredo*. The tower on the right is defined by a rough slab cut off below by a steep bay of greenish rock, the back wall of which is taken by *Green Wall*. The bay ends with a steep broken arête, *Rib and Groove* and, further right, *Pinnacle Gully*, an easy descent. A descent at the left-hand end of the crag is also possible.

Ahab   15 metres   E1 5c   (5.6.88)
Climb the crack at the left-hand end of the crag, which has an overhanging start.

Whale   55 metres   Hard Severe   (28.6.64)
Quite a good route, spoilt somewhat by a break near the top of the first pitch. Start at the groove from the shallow cave.
1 21m. An overhanging start leads into a V-chimney, which is climbed to a grass ledge on the left. Move right onto an arête and climb it to a large ledge.
2 34m. Move left and climb awkwardly to a crack. The crack is followed to the top.

Leviathan Direct   51 metres   Very Severe   (1964)
A very pleasant route. Start at a boulder, below the deep groove right of *Whale*.
1 21m. 4b. Move left off the boulder into the groove, and climb it to gain a thin curving crack. Climb this and vegetation above to the base of a steep crack.
2 30m. 4b. The strenuous crack leads to some hollow flakes. Stride out right into a steep open groove and climb it to the top.

Variation Finish
2a 30m. Very Severe 4b (31.7.83). Climb the crack to the top; then go strenuously up the arête on good holds to the top.

The Last Post   48 metres   Very Severe   (10.6.62)
A steep strenuous route. Start just right of a boulder, at the foot of a short steep wall guarding the entry to a square-cut corner.
1 24m. 4c. Climb the wall and then the difficult square-cut corner to an exit left. Continue up to the highest vegetated ledge.
2 15m. 4b. Climb a steep groove on the left to flake belays.
3 9m. 4b. A shallow crack leads to the top.

Leviathan   54 metres   Hard Severe   (1961)
Not very satisfying. Start below the groove right of *The Last Post*.
1 20m. The groove is steep but easy and leads to the foot of an open chimney. Climb this steeply and on somewhat loose holds; then step left and climb a rib to a good ledge.
2 34m. Continue up to the next ledge and traverse it to its left-hand end. Climb up some large loose spikes; then move left to a steep but easy groove, which leads to the top.

★★Fratricide Wall   44 metres   Hard Very Severe   (23.4.60)
A brilliant route giving steep varied climbing in a good position and at the top end of its grade. Start at a short groove leading to the right end of a grass ledge.
1 21m. 5a. Climb the groove to the ledge, move onto the wall above, and climb a smooth groove. Step round a bulge to the right, and then go back left. Continue left easily to a good stance beneath a steep wall.
2 23m. 5a. A short thin crack leads to a sloping ledge below a steep headwall. Traverse right along this and around a nose until it is possible to move up to another ledge below a steep corner. Climb the corner until heart-stopping moves out right lead to an arête. Climb this to finish.
Variation
2a Midgicide 20m. E2 5c. Climb the short thin crack, and continue directly up the wall, finishing via another thin crack.

★★Rainbow Warrior   66 metres   E3   (22.6.89)
A tremendous traverse line, with a strenuous and sustained pitch in a stunning position.
1 21m. 5a. *Fratricide Wall* pitch 1.
2 21m. 5c. Climb the steep and awkward, stepped wall to the right of the stance to gain the traverse on *Fratricide Wall*. Follow this until below the final steep corner (runner). Then step down and move rightwards (loose spike) into *Lightning Visit*. Hanging belay on a small flake and large nuts.
3 24m. 5c. Step right on undercuts and make a totally committing bridge into *Penamnen Groove*. Climb to the roof, step right, and layback through the roof; then continue rightwards past a steep crack. Step right again into an even steeper green and greasy crack, which is followed to a notch.

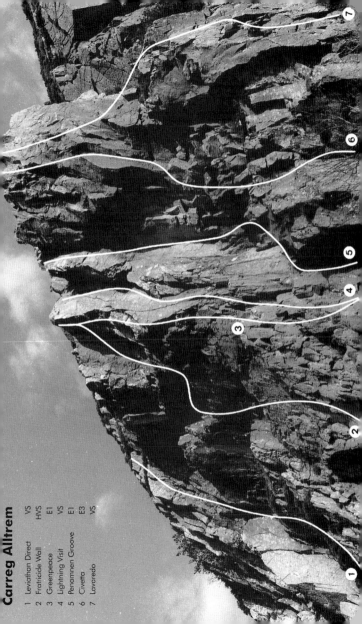

Carreg Alltrem

1 Leviathan Direct — VS
2 Fratricide Wall — HVS
3 Greenpeace — E1
4 Lightning Visit — VS
5 Penamnen Groove — E1
6 Civetta — E3
7 Lavaredo — VS

Lavaredo (VS) Carreg Alltrem
Climber: Mike Rosser   Photo: Simon Cardy

Half a Jesus (E5) Craig Pont-y-pant
Climber: Nick Dixon   Photo: Gareth Dwyer

Craig Pont-y-pant

Swing blindly round to the right and climb the final 3 metres of *Lavaredo*.
A cracking pitch.

★★**Lightning Visit** 40 metres   Very Severe   (6.59)
A delectable route up an obvious line. Start at a groove just left of the
obvious corner of *Penamnen Groove*.
1 17m. 4a. Climb the groove and the wall above to belay on a boulder.
Alternatively, climb the more difficult arête on the right.
2 23m. 4c. Climb up to a good ledge. Step right to a pinnacle, and then
awkwardly into a prominent V-groove, which leads to the top.
Variation
2a Alltrem Arête 23m. 4c. Take the crack in the left wall and finish up
the arête of *Greenpeace*.

Greenpeace 36 metres   E1   (1978)
Some good climbing up the obvious hanging arête. Start at the foot of
Penamnen Groove.
1 9m. 4c. The left wall of the corner leads to a ledge. Continue up and
left, crossing *Lightning Visit*, and take a belay to the left of the latter.
2 27m. 5b. Go up to another ledge, and climb the hanging arête on the
left until a move right is possible just below the top.

★**Penamnen Groove** 37 metres   E1   (18.9.56)
A fine line which proves disappointing on closer inspection; still, a good
thrutch for those in the mood. Start below the obvious groove of a square
corner.
1 14m. 4c. The left wall of the corner is climbed, with a long reach to
finish. Scramble up to a pinnacle belay on the right. The corner can be
climbed direct but is often wet.
2 23m. 5b. Struggle up the corner to the roof with a difficult exit left
around it. A harder exit right is also possible.

Pin Up 39 metres   E1   (7.8.82)
Some excellent crack-climbing.
1 15m. 5a. The shallow groove in the left arête of *Civetta*.
2 24m. 5b. Follow *Civetta* to the niche but continue up leftwards to below
a roof. Pull over, and finish up an excellent jamming-crack.

★**Civetta** 35 metres   E3   (1964/1979)
Some good, difficult climbing. Start at the foot of a steep crack 6 metres
right of *Penamnen Groove*.
1 15m. 4b. The crack leads to a belay above a pinnacle.
2 20m. 6a. Move up to a small niche; then go up again to reach an
uncomfortable ledge beneath a large overhang. Step right and climb thin
strenuous cracks to the top.

★**Original Route** 50 metres   Severe   (12.12.53)
A pleasant route in a good position. Start just left of the edge of the
buttress, where a spike is jammed in a groove.

1 15m. Climb onto the spike; then follow holds up left to the crack of *Civetta*. Continue in its line (more of a chimney) to the pinnacle.
2 9m. A diagonal traverse right over detached-looking blocks leads to a ledge on the arête.
3 18m. Cracks in the slab above lead to a spike belay.
4 8m. A tricky slab in the corner above is followed to finish.

Lavrol   37 metres   E2 5c   (8.77)
An eliminate with some difficult moves. Start up *Original Route* and continue up the crack to a large ledge. Move up detached blocks; then get into a rightward-slanting groove gained from the right. The groove is climbed to an exit left. Continue into *Civetta*, and climb this until a crack, on the left of the finish of that route, can be climbed.

Lavaredo Variations   42 metres   Hard Severe
A poor man's *Lavaredo*. Start as for *Original Route*.
1 21m. Climb the groove on the left of the almost-detached pillar forming the nose of the buttress, and continue to the block belays of *Lavaredo*.
2 21m. Climb the gully for a short way; then move into a groove on the edge of the wall. Step onto the face above its steepest part, and climb to the top via a shallow groove.

★★★Lavaredo   42 metres   Very Severe   (20.3.61)
[Photo page 232b.] The best VS in the valley. Start in the groove on the right of the almost-detached pillar.
1 21m. 4b. The groove leads to a flake on the right. Step left onto a ledge, or go straight up; then follow a rib to a good stance with a block belay.
2 21m. 4b. Pull onto a bulging wall with difficulty and stretch rightwards to good holds. Climb steeply for a few feet before stepping left into a final groove. A sensationally-positioned pitch.

Route II   34 metres   Severe   (12.12.53)
Poor. Start at a thin crack running down to the right from a large holly.
1 11m. Climb the steep wall to the holly, and continue more easily to the stance on *Lavaredo*.
2 23m. Thrust into the crack between the slab and the wall above it, and climb it to perched blocks. Finish up any of several available cracks.

The Falconer   37 metres   Hard Very Severe   (1982)
Start between *Route II* and *Bay Groove*.
1 14m. 5a/b. Climb the wall and thin cracks to a belay on the edge of the slab above the belay of the first pitch of *Lavaredo*.
2 25m. 5a. Continue up, and climb the arête right of *Lavaredo* in a fine position to the top.

Bay Groove   38 metres   Very Difficult   (12.12.53)
Start at the apex of a grass tongue below a groove.

1 15m. Move past a small holly and go up the left wall of a steep, open chimney to belays on the edge of a slab (shared with *Falconer*).
2 23m. Move onto the belay and step across a groove onto another slab. Climb this to finish.

Bavarian Dream 30 metres E3 5c
The crack left of the arête of *Green Wall* is followed to the top.

Green Wall 37 metres Very Severe   (8.7.67)
A steep route and an exposed top pitch. Start at a narrow slab which runs up under the steep back wall of the bay.
1 11m. 4a. A groove and slab lead to the foot of an impending wall. Traverse right to belays on a good ledge.
2 17m. 4c. Move left onto a higher ledge, climb a groove, and then go round left into another groove with a boulder-filled ledge at its base. Steep moves lead onto a white pedestal on the left. Climb the overhanging wall on its left via an awkward crack. Belay on a slab.
3 9m. The easy slab leads to the top.

Rib and Groove 36 metres Severe   (19.6.66)
Worth doing for the top pitch. Start at the foot of the ridge on the right of the green bay.
1 21m. Start up the right side of the rib, but step left at 3 metres. Continue up to a ledge with many spikes beneath a prominent V-chimney and go up to a belay.
2 15m. The groove in the green wall is followed diagonally left until a strenuous move gives access to a slab leading to the top.

Craig Pont-y-pant Bridge-(at)-the-Hollow Rock OS Ref 759 540

[Photodiagram page 232d.] For those climbing at E4 and above, this fine little crag is one of the best outcrops in eastern Snowdonia. The top and bottom of the crag are overgrown but the rock is clean and the lines are unbroken.

The crag overlooks the A470, 400 metres east of the turn to Pont-y-pant station, and lies above the old bailiff's cottage. There is no parking on the road below the crag, so it is best to park at the station and follow the footpath into the woods opposite the bridge. The crag is reached in five minutes via some ancient steps. The current road improvements will change the first section of this path.

The lines can be easily identified by the *in-situ* pegs. The hanging groove of *Half a Jesus* at the left-hand end of the crag and the defining angle of *Steve's Arête* help to locate the routes.

★First Impressions 12 metres E4 6c   (1995)
Start 3 metres left of *Half a Jesus*. Slap hopefully up the wall.

★★Half a Jesus   12 metres   E5 7a   (1995)
[Photo page 232c.] Desperately technical. Start to the left of *Ed's Crack* at
the obvious hanging groove above the boulder. A hideous crucifix move
gains a dynamic entry to the hanging groove in the left wall. (Before the
demise of the boulder, this was *No Coaches*.)

★Ed's Crack   12 metres   E3 6b   (1988)
The crack in the centre of the wall gives a 'more tricky than it looks' trip
(peg).

★★Steve's Arête   12 metres   E4 6b   (1988)
The obvious square-cut arête of the buttress past two pegs.

★★★Crisis in Utopia   12 metres   E7 6b   (1988)
The awesome crack in the wall right of the arête gives a short technical
exercise.

★A Gathering of Old Men   12 metres   E5 6c   (1988)
Four metres right of *Crisis in Utopia*, take a line up right; then finger-edge,
layaway, dyno! Follow the line of three old, tatty pegs up the wall.

Wrinkly Old Men   12 metres   E5 6b   (1997)
The headwall above and to the right of *A Gathering of Old Men* is climbed
direct.

The Good Booklet   9 metres   E5 6b   (1988)
The open groove to the right. Steeper and more fun than it looks. Tiny
wires.

Finally, there is a poor unnamed line (E2 5c) up the rib to the right of the
groove.

Craig Rhiw Goch   Crag (of) the Red Slope   OS Ref 767 541
A fine little crag, pleasantly situated, Rhiw Goch is a National Trust property
facing south on the bank of the Afon Lledr, just below the A470. The top of
the crag is easily reached directly from the road by a number of footpaths in
less than five minutes. The bottom is best approached by following a path on
the upstream side of he crag and then the path along the riverbank. Note
the iron ladders in the river bank: they make for an exciting approach but
are private property and used for fishing. Parking is very limited and the
improvements to the A470 could limit them further. Be prepared to walk a
little.

Reign   24 metres   Severe
The left side of the crag is taken with a steep finish.

Megalomania   24 metres   E2 5c   (12.5.86)
Follow *Reign* for a a short way; then step up to a spike. Move right and
climb the bulge (peg) via a crack. Finish up the steep wall above.

Congl 32 metres Very Severe 4c (1965)

An obvious groove-line. Move up into the groove and climb it until a delicate move left leads onto an obvious traverse. Finish on good holds. A much better but harder alternative is to continue up the groove to the top (HVS 5b).

Endgame 30 metres E2 5c (6.8.72)

A poky route giving strenuous climbing on poor rock. Start as for *Congl*. Follow *Congl* until a step left into an overhanging groove is possible. Climb this and the V-groove above, with a move left to finish.

★The Riparian 30 metres E2 5c (4.8.72)

An excellent route with a serious top section. Start at the left side of a large embedded flake beneath a steep slab right of *Congl*. Climb the wall and a narrow groove above, avoiding the cop-out to the left; then step right and climb a steep wall to a short groove at the foot of a gangway. Climb the groove and another steep wall to a good spike. A further short groove leads to the top.

Rip van Winkle 24 metres E3 5c

An eliminate on *The Riparian* with good technical climbing. Start right of *The Riparian* and climb through the downward-pointing flakes to join that route. Follow it to the spike; then step left and climb a faint rib to the top.

The Anvil 24 metres E2 5c (9.5.82)

Start at the foot of a short overhanging groove behind the large flake at the foot of *The Riparian*. The groove is climbed with an awkward exit at its top. A thin crack and face above lead to good holds and the top.

The following two routes are better climbed in one pitch.

Mur Dena 30 metres E1 (1965)

Start on a ledge to the right of the pinnacle flake.
1 12m. 4c. The right edge of the slab above leads to a break in some overhangs. Pull through them and climb to a poor stance amongst large blocks. Alternatively, climb the left edge of the slab.
2 18m. 5b. Traverse left across a steep wall to a crack and follow it to a good spike on the right. Move onto the spike, step delicately right to the edge, and climb it to the top.

Big River 37 metres Hard Very Severe (19.4.81)

Right of *Mur Dena's* starting-pinnacle is a steep rib with the crack of *Smiler's Route* on the right.
1 12m. 5a. Step right into a small niche in the rib and go over steep bulges above to the poor stance.
2 24m. 5a. Layback into the steep crack of *Mur Dena* on the left; then go up and leftwards across ribs and grooves to the direct finish of *Congl*. Follow this to the top.

Smiler's Route   24 metres   Hard Very Severe   5a
Start beneath an obvious flake round to the right of *Mur Dena*. Climb the
steep wall above the flake.

Clogwyn y Gigfran   Cliff (of) the Raven   OS Ref 793 542

Also known as the Giant's Head, it is pleasantly situated overlooking Cwm
Lledr above the A470, about two miles out of Betws-y-coed towards
Dolwyddelan. The most direct approach is rather brambly. Longer, but
more pleasant, is to strike south-west through the pine woods above the
Conwy–Lledr confluence to the railway line. Cross this immediately, and
make a diagonal ascent to the foot of the crag (20 minutes from the road).
The crag is 45 metres at its steep central section, reducing to 30 metres at
the slabby left-hand end. To the right the crag degenerates into broken
vegetated rock. Much of the climbing is rather scrappy and vegetated; and
the friable nature of the rock demands care, particularly on the steeper
routes.

Black Arrow   30 metres   Very Difficult
The slabs at the left-hand end of the crag.

The left-hand end of the central section is split by three grooves above a
grassy bay. All three have been climbed, the right-hand being the hardest,
while the central one is the best and gives the following route.

Titan   45 metres   Very Severe   (22.4.62)
Start below the right-hand groove.
1 15m. 4c. Step onto a slab and make an awkward swing left into the
groove. Step left again into the central groove and climb it to a narrow
grassy ledge.
2 30m. 4b. A thin crack in the steep slab above is climbed to a corner
that leads to the top.

Several other pitches are available and may be combined with the other
grooves.

The Ent   48 metres   E1   (5.67)
A steep and intimidating first pitch. Start at the left end of the rocky ledge
beneath the large roof right of the start of *Titan*.
1 24m. 5b. Go easily along the ledge and climb an obvious narrow rib
that leads to the end of the roof. Take the steep, vegetated crack above.
2 9m. 4c. Step left into the foot of an overhanging corner and climb it to
a grassy ledge.
3 15m. 4c. Climb a corner-crack a short way; then step right onto a rib
and climb it to the top.

Shelob   45 metres   Hard Very Severe   (5.67)
The first pitch is steep and bold, but the finish is poor. Start by scrambling
up unpleasant, vegetated rock to the lower left corner of the grassy recess
in the centre of the crag.

1 24m. 5a. Traverse left and go up to the foot of a steep groove just right of *The Ent*. Pull over the bulge in the groove (bold), and then follow a line of holds out right until it is possible to climb direct to a grassy ledge.
2 21m. 5a. A rib on the left of the corner behind the stance is climbed to a small ledge. Traverse right onto overhanging rock; then climb the wall above with difficulty, past a small tree on the left, to exit onto a final easy-angled slab.

Cyclops   48 metres   Hard Severe   (22.4.62)
A good route with some steep climbing. Start at the right-hand end of the crag, beneath a steep wall formed by a flake, with a prominent impending narrow crack leading from a niche above.
1 15m. Climb the steep wall and move left into the niche. The crack then leads strenuously to a grassy ledge and a tree belay beneath a recess.
2 12m. Climb the steep right wall of the recess on big flake holds to a ledge under an overhang. Traverse left to a good ledge on *The Ent* and *Shelob*.
3 21m. Climb the corner behind the stance until it overhangs. Step right into an exposed position above a large roof; then continue up slabs above to the top.
Variation
2a 9m. Very Severe. The steep left arête of the recess.

A number of routes are reputed to have been climbed to the right of *Cyclops*, but they are buried under the vegetation.

Betws-y-coed Area

[Map page 224.] There are a number of crags in this section that have been bypassed by recent guidebooks. Their inclusion here should encourage a greater use of what is a very quiet, easily accessible, and interesting area.

Craig Dinas   Fort Crag   OS Ref 808 538
The twin cliffs of Craig Dinas lie on the south-west face of Dinas Mawr and enjoy a fine, open aspect looking out across the beautiful Lledr Valley 2½ kilometres south of Betws-y-coed. Ample parking can be found in the lay-by beneath the cliff on the A5, or in the car-park just beyond the now-derelict *Silver Fountain* inn. Take the public footpath that runs up behind the *Silver Fountain* to a boulder/scree slope, which fans out between the two cliffs. A faint path breaks off the main path here and can be followed through scree and vegetation. In high summer, dense bracken, bramble, and gorse can turn the approach into a bushwhack. Normal approach time is no more than 15 minutes.

The cliffs of Craig Dinas, especially the main, South Cliff, offer an imposing aspect when first sighted from the A5. In the morning sun, the complex face of grooves and overhangs promises a challenging prospect to any climber willing to investigate further. Undeservedly neglected, Craig Dinas has suffered from previous guidebook descriptions that have exaggerated its shortcomings and failed to credit its positive characteristics. The latter will amply reward the climber who chooses to explore the cliff's potential. For those who operate in the lower-middle grades, several fine, steep routes can be found on rock which is generally clean, sound, and in character not unlike the steep pale cliffs of nearby Carreg Alltrem.

Descend from the North and South Cliffs via the obvious broad gully which separates them.

North Cliff
When the twin cliffs are viewed from the approach path the smaller, North Cliff is dominated by a massive roof which overhangs the main body of the rock. A broad rib delineates its left edge, and both routes begin on this rib, below and left of a rowan, which marks the midway belay point.

Sheng   30 metres   Very Severe †   (9.94)
1 12m. 5a. Gain the rib from the left, and continue directly up the left edge, passing through a short overhang with some difficulty (crux). After gaining the top, move across to the rowan stance.
2 18m. 4b. Directly behind is a wall made up of narrow blocks which meet an overhang. Climb the blocks with care and move out right under the overhang to gain a bottomless groove. Climb the groove, move left at the top, and finish directly up the fine hanging slab.

The Wanderer   40 metres   Hard Severe †   (9.94)
An interesting traverse directly across the slab capped by the massive roof.
1 12m. 4a. Start as for *Sheng*, and climb the left edge of the rib before crossing a bottomless groove at 7 metres. Continue on a rightward diagonal line to reach the rowan stance.
2 19m. 4b. Move down from the stance for 2 metres to gain the edge of the slab. Follow a central line across the slab to a heather crack near the right edge, and climb directly up to gain the top right-hand edge of the slab.
3 9m. Climb the wall behind, passing through the overhang on good holds.

South Cliff
South Cliff can be identified by the steep, narrow slab taken by *By-ways*, which forms its left edge. A huge detached pillar, The Boulder, stands at the foot of the cliff, with a deep cracked groove, *Gull's Nest Crack*, on the left and a cave on the right. The right edge of the cliff is bounded by an incipient gully, which is contained on its right by the broad *Moss Rib*.

Crossways 88 metres Very Severe (7.58)
A left-to-right girdle of South Cliff.
1 10m. Climb the crack and slab of *By-ways*.
2 23m. Take the slab left of the groove; then step into it and continue to the overhang. Cross the right wall and continue traversing slightly downwards under the overhangs. Twin spike belays.
3 4m. Step down and scramble up to the next groove (on *Scrub Way*).
4 10m. Go down a step and traverse the wall. Pull up under the bulge and cross it to the top of The Boulder.
5 15m. Step across the void and go up to the roof (as for *The Nurgler*). Continue traversing right, passing a loose block, and climb the steep wall above to a poor grassy belay.
6 4m. Cross the grassy groove to belay on the right.
7 22m. Traverse right under the overhang to finish above *Moss Rib*.

A poor route has been described on the heavily vegetated slabs and short walls left of *By-ways*.

By-ways 42 metres Severe (7.58)
1 27m. Start in the corner behind a small oak tree. Climb the corner to reach a slabby bay and cross the bay to gain the left edge of the narrow slab (belay possible behind block). Continue up the slab to reach a heather ledge.
2 15m. Move across into the bay and climb up and left to gain the slab above. Continue to the top.
Variations
2a 9m. Very Severe 4b. Move left into the corner and make a hard move from the niche to gain the deep crack above. Continue up the steep crack, which eases near the top.
2b 18m. From the slab, move across and climb the broken wall on the right. Finish easily up the slabs.

★Scrub Way 45 metres Hard Severe (7.58)
Despite its unappealing name, a fine, steep route on excellent rock. Bold for its grade.
1 27m. 4b. Begin at the narrow ramp-line just below a small oak. Climb the wall to the groove above (belay possible at the oak-tree ledge just below). Step right and climb the slabby groove to reach a broad steep rib. Continue up the exposed wall, and make some delicate moves onto a short, dirty slab. Climb with care to the small ledge beneath a triangular overhang.
2 18m. 4a. Move across right and climb around the rib. Continue up and move out right at the top onto the hanging slab above. Finish easily.

★Dinas Mawr Eliminate 43 metres E1 (10.9.68)
Strenuous and bold.
1 21m. 5b. Start in the green scoop just right of *Scrub Way*, and climb up the wall above, passing through a bulge at 6 metres. Continue up, and

move back left at 15 metres to cross a rib and reach the stance shared with *Scrub Way*.
2 22m. 5a. Climb up to the triangular overhang via a V-groove. Climb the overhang direct or move out into the right-hand groove, and continue on good holds to easier ground above.

★Main Wall Climb   50 metres   Very Severe   (10.64)
An excellent steep climb, which tackles the main face more or less directly.
1 41m. 4c. Start 2 metres left of the corner and climb steeply up the wall above before moving right at 15 metres onto a slabby area. Make an awkward move through a bottomless groove and traverse back left to join the upper reaches of *Scrub Way*. Cross the rib on the left to a small niche stance.
2 9m. Step across the rib onto the main face and finish as for *Scrub Way*.

Gull's Nest Crack   12 metres   Severe 4a   (10.30)
The obvious corner-crack just right of *Main Wall Climb* proves more difficult than it appears. The route tops out on The Boulder and is now used exclusively as the first pitch of *The Nurgler*.

★★The Nurgler   45 metres   Very Severe   (1953/7.96)
An excellent climb, technically varied and on good rock: traditionally considered the classic of the crag.
1 12m. 4a. *Gull's Nest Crack*.
2 33m. 4b. Step boldly across the void onto the slabby wall beneath the roof. Continue up to the roof and make a rightward traverse passing, with some difficulty, two hanging ribs to reach a chimney/groove. Continue up the groove before moving left at 6 metres onto the slab. Traverse left under the overhang and pull into the defining groove on the left. Climb direct to finish.
Variation
2a 32m. Start as for pitch 2, but at the chimney make an awkward move left to gain the hanging slab. Traverse 3 metres left across the lip of the roof (exposed). Continue delightfully up the steep slab to the overhang above and finish as for pitch 2.

The Bolder Way   41 metres   Very Severe   (7.58/12.67)
A good route with a high degree of exposure.
1 12m. 4b. Begin just right of the corner taken by *Gull's Nest Crack*. A steep move gains a heathery crack. Continue into the niche and pull out near the top. Easier climbing leads to the brow of The Boulder.
2 29m. 4c. Step across the gap and pass a rib on the left. Continue traversing under the roof, making a long step left to a small ledge. Cross the slab to its edge, and make steep moves up a broken rib to a groove-system. Traverse 3 metres right, and either climb the short corner, or move out right and climb the wall. At the top of the corner or wall, move right again, and finish more easily up the hanging slab. (Rope drag can be a problem on this pitch but, unfortunately, there are no good intermediate belays.)

Variation
1a 12m. 4b. From 3 metres right of *Gull's Nest Crack*, climb a short overhangimng corner on the edge of The Boulder to reach a left-slanting crack. Follow this diagonal line to the top.

Freeway 40 metres Hard Very Severe † (1976)
1 14m. Follow the shallow groove on the right-hand edge of The Boulder.
2 26m. Climb around the huge roof above, just left of centre.

Desire 48 metres Hard Severe † (11.96)
1 21m. 4b. Four metres right of The Boulder there is a detached rib which rests against the main face. Climb the rib and move right into a broad, slabby depression. Go up slightly before climbing out of the depression on the left and continuing on a rising leftward line to a small stance just right of *The Nurgler* chimney.
2 27m. Move back right from the belay and climb directly up the broken ground above. At 12 metres a slab on the right is taken to the top.

★Groove Slab 40 metres Very Severe
An excellent climb with an interesting history: it had been omitted from previous guidebooks despite having been identified on a crag diagram in *Snowdon East* (1970) as a V Diff! Start 2 metres left of the groove contained on the right by *Moss Rib*.
1 29m. 4c. Climb delicately and boldly up the slight depression in the slab for 5 metres: at this point, better holds and protection appear. Continue up the slab to the overhang, and traverse left under it to gain the broken groove. Climb directly up the groove and move out right at the top to belay on the left wall of the upper overhang (old peg).
2 11m. 4b. Move off the belay and climb the steep crack in the wall above.

Moss Rib 21 metres Severe (1972)
Start beneath the grooves just left of a quartz block. Climb up into the groove-system and gain a horizontal quartz band. Traverse across to the rib and climb pleasantly up to finish.

Top Buttress
Higher up the hillside, a broad, gorse-filled gully (used for descent) separates the rounded top of South Cliff from a small independent buttress to the right; its left edge is taken by the only recorded route.

White Rabbit 19 metres Severe (6.99)
Start in a depression on the left. Climb up into the depression before moving out onto the slabby rib on the left. Continue directly up the rib and move back right at the top to finish up a short wall.

The Tubes
The Tubes can be found in a gorge section of the River Conwy two and a half kilometres south of Betws-y-coed. Access is best effected from the

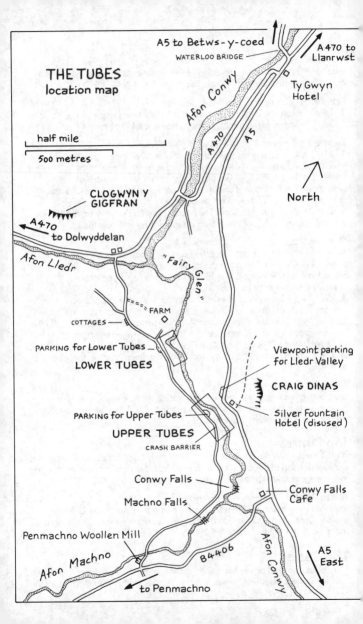

small back road running between the A470 (Blaenau Ffestiniog road), and the Penmachno Woollen Mill. From the *Ty Gwyn Hotel* on the A5, follow the A470 for one and a half kilometres, crossing a bridge over the river to a small group of houses on the right. Here the small back road leads off to the left. At the top of the hill, bear left to pass a row of terraced cottages. Soon, at a dip in the road, the river can be seen on the left; park here for The Lower Tubes. Continue 400 metres further to a lay-by just before the first crash-barrier for The Upper Tubes.

The gorge from the Fairy Glen upstream to Conwy Falls has only recently become a significant climbing venue. Although it was well known locally as an area of intriguing shapes and gorge-hopping possibilities, bouldering and climbing exploration by a keen bunch of locals started only after a reconnaissance for kayaking by Crispin Waddy in 1996. Rumour has it that some lines were first climbed in order to escape after capsizing!

In spate conditions, spectacularly seen perhaps just twice a year, The Upper and Lower Tubes are entirely submerged in a brown maelstrom of standing waves, speeding water, and debris. The features are like those of natural gritstone in size, though the resulting texture is more akin to glass. Surely the most beautiful-to-grasp holds exist here, requiring both palms and all one's finger-surface to produce sufficient friction to allow progress. The climbing is probably unique in Britain. Often the routes are steep and powerful in a whole-body sense, strong fingers being of less use than strong backs and shoulders. The climbing is in its infancy, and the main protagonists feel that they have not yet really mastered it. The future may be here; certainly there is scope for some very hard routes indeed!

An added feature of the venue is that rarely is it in good condition. Many of the routes start off boulders or gravel beaches that are submerged during the area's frequent wet interludes. Equally significantly, some seep badly except over prolonged dry spells. This gives the ascent of some routes a special, rare quality. It is worth noting, however, that even in the hottest weather the river has a cooling effect, which can make climbing pleasant when other areas are too hot and sticky.

Most of the routes in The Tubes are strange and a custom grading-system seems called for. Thus T1, T2, and T3 are given in ascending order of difficulty. Routes are usually either top-roped (saves the feet from a wetting in some cases) or soloed. None has been led placing gear, a good honest ethic to be continued. This is indicated by S (meaning soloed) and NS (not yet soloed). No equipment, no leads, no frigging.

Finally, some note should be made of an extra hazard. Several people have lost their lives in this stretch of water. The features you see above the water exist below also and in some cases form dangerous sumps and shelves; take care!

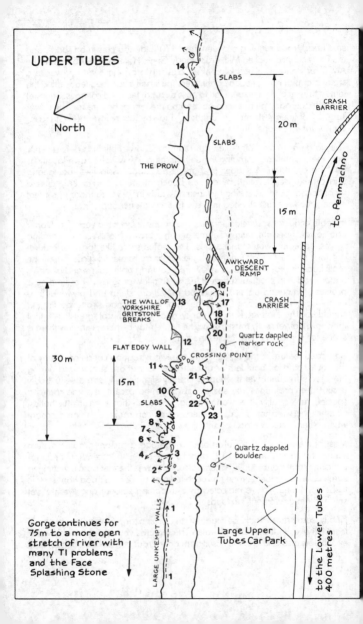

UPPER TUBES

North

SLABS

CRASH BARRIER

20 m

SLABS

14

THE PROW

15 m

AWKWARD DESCENT RAMP

to Penmachno

CRASH BARRIER

15 16
17
18
19
20

THE WALL OF YORKSHIRE GRITSTONE BREAKS   13

CRASH BARRIER

Quartz dappled marker rock

FLAT EDGY WALL   12

30 m

CROSSING POINT

11

15 m

21

10
SLABS   9
8
7   5
6
4   3
2

22
23

1

Quartz dappled boulder

Large Upper Tubes Car Park

Gorge continues for 75m to a more open stretch of river with many T1 problems and the Face Splashing Stone

LARGE UNKEMPT WALLS   1

to the Lower Tubes 400 metres

The Upper Tubes
OS Ref 804 538

Four hundred metres up the back road is a lay-by next to the first crash-barrier. Just down from the lay-by, two white quartz-dappled boulders 25 metres apart make good markers. The following routes on the true right (north-east) bank of the river face you when looking across the gorge. Directly opposite the lower, downstream boulder are the two impressive tubes of *Original Route* and *Tubeway Army*.

1 T1 20m S   **Big Dipper** The long rightward traverse in from the shore on the left; finish up after 10m. [P Pritchard]
2 T1 8m S   **★Belsize Park** Boulder-hop in from the right and climb the small tube. P Pritchard
3 T2 7m NS   **★Left Rib** Obvious prow and rib. [N Dixon]
4 T1 8m S   **★★Original Route** The scoop within the scoop. [C Waddy]
5 T2 NS   **★Barbara Hepworth** The steep central rib on edges. [P Pritchard]
6 T2 8m NS   **★★Down the Tubestation at Midnight** Start up the arête; then edge into the right-hand tube; finish direct. [P Pritchard]
7 T2 8m S   **★★Tubeway Army** The crack starting in the back and trending up the right side of the tube. [A Wainwright]
8 T2 8m S   **★★Monarch of the Glen** A hard pull up to ascend the left side of the arête (great, usually dry). [N Dixon]
9 T2 6m S   **Rodin** The wall right of the arête. [C Waddy]
10 T1 4m S   **Frink** Traverse left round the tube with hands on top. [A Wainwright]
11 T1 7m S   **Tube Left, Tube Right** From crossing-point, layback facing left then right. [P Pritchard]

Further to the right, immediately opposite the higher, upstream quartzy boulder are:

12 T2 5m S   **★Leo's Edge** The centre of the flat edgy wall. [L Houlding]
13 T1 5m S   **Loxton's Dilema** The tube further on the right, gained by getting wet. [T Loxton]

Further upstream again:

14 T1 8m S   **Inner Tube** A unique journey up the S-bend. [P Pritchard]

The routes described next are on the true left bank of the river (south-west side) and are best viewed from *Leo's Edge*. (It may be useful to know that *Inside the Teapot* finishes 16 metres upstream of the higher marker rock.)

15 T3 5m NS   **Impossible Arête** The right side of the sickle. [G Smith]
16 T3 10m NS   **★★Inside the Teapot** Climb the immaculate back of the scoop. Comes into condition rarely, but worth the wait. [N Dixon]
17 T3 11m S   **★★The Ridable Bell** Powerfully à *cheval* the nose and climb the arête above. Stays dry and is one of the best problems. [N Dixon]
18 T2 4m S   **Problem within a Problem** Dyno up left to a jug. [N Dixon]
19 T2 5m NS   **Paul's Ladder** Surmount and stand on a sloper; then left to a jug. [P Pritchard]
20 T2 8m S   **River Ribber** Obvious rib, only climbed from groove on left. [N Dixon]
21 T2 8m NS   **Benvenuto Cellini** The rib left of the 'unclimbable tube'. [J Dawes]
22 T3 6m NS   **Top-less Streaker** The boss and open tube on the right to the break; no finish as yet. [G Smith]
23 T2 4m S   **Aqua Jam** The back of the scoop; exit via hand-jam. [J Dawes]

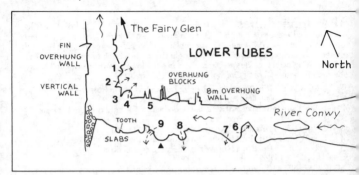

The Lower Tubes   OS Ref 802 539

A major feature is the right-angled bend in the River Conwy as it swings into the Fairy
Glen. At this point the following routes lie on the opposite bank, the first two out of sight
around the bend.

1 T2 6m S   **Tubular Bells** Open sloper scoop, up an arête 7 metres left of
                the bend.
                [P Pritchard]
2 T2 6m NS   **Flamingo Dancing** Slab 3 metres right of the bend. [G Smith]
3 T4?   **The Future** An overhanging prow 6m. upstream.
4 T2 6m S   **Smartie Tube** The crack at the back of the scoop immediately
                right. [Unknown]
5 T1 6m S   **Manuel's Slot** The deep chest chimney 6m. further right.
                [P Pritchard]

All the following routes are difficult to view, being on the true left (south-west) bank.
Forty metres upstream of the bend, below several falls, the river widens appreciably.
Henry Moore faces downstream on a projecting block of rock forming the back of this
pool.

6   T2 8m S   **Henry Moore** [Photo page 272a.] Move into the egg; exit down
                and left; arête finish. [N Dixon]
6a T2 7m NS **Henry Moore Direct** Into the egg and exit up. [J Dawes]
7   T3?   **The Cracks** A very hard project up the wall on the right.

On the left bank, half-way back towards the bend, is a high-point of rock above an
overhanging wall. The next two routes finish here.

8   T3 6m S   **Full Opening Tube** The amazing crucifix of the hidden tube to
                a jug in the back (finishes just upstream of the high-point).
                [G Smith]
9   T2 7m S   **Enter the Bidet** Up the cocoon 6m. further right (finishes
                downstream of the high-point). [P Pritchard]

Clogwyn Cyrau   Cliff (of) Edges   (OS Ref 790 571)

A group of cliffs north-west of Betws-y-coed, from where the three upper
cliffs are visible on the skyline. From left to right these are Main Cliff, Conwy

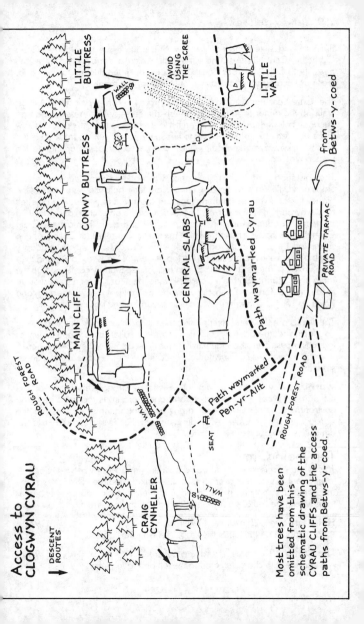

Access to CLOGWYN CYRAU

DESCENT ROUTES

LITTLE BUTTRESS

CONWY BUTTRESS

WALL

LITTLE WALL

AVOID USING THE SCREE

MAIN CLIFF

ROUGH FOREST ROAD

CENTRAL SLABS

Path waymarked Cyrau

WALL

Path waymarked Pen-yr-Allt

SEAT

WALL

CRAIG CYNHELIER

from Betws-y-coed

PRIVATE TARMAC ROAD

ROUGH FOREST ROAD

Most trees have been omitted from this schematic drawing of the CYRAU CLIFFS and the access paths from Betws-y-coed.

Buttress, and Little Buttress. At a lower level there are three more, Craig Cynhelier, Central Slabs, and Little Wall, which are mostly hidden in the trees. Both bands of rock continue to outcrop intermittently to the north; these are ecologically valued and of little climbing merit.

The nearest car-park is across the bridge from the *Pont-y-pair Hotel*. A short walk up the minor road leads to the private Forestry Commission road on the right. Follow this tarmac road until it loops back to the left, passing below three wooden alpine-type houses to become a rough vehicle-track. Take the small, rocky, waymarked path, which can be seen leading uphill into the trees on the right.

The path soon divides. The right branch, waymarked Cyrau, leads to Central Slabs and Little Wall. Routes on Central Slabs lead naturally onto those of the higher tier and various combinations can provide a logical outing. The left fork, waymarked Pen-yr-allt, continues up to all the other cliffs, and after 120 metres a wooden bench on a sharp right-hand bend is reached. Craig Cynhelier lies above and to the left in the trees. After a further 70 metres at a sharp left bend a small vague track leads straight on ahead, gradually climbing between Main Cliff and the top of Central Slabs to Conwy and then Little Buttress. The Main Cliff itself can best be reached by continuing up the main path a further 35 metres and following the near side of a stone wall up to the right. Before the first rocky outcrops, a slight path leaves the wall, and traverses round to the right over rough ground to the base of the cliff.

The climbs are short and steep, with generally excellent rock. Being low lying and facing south-east, they can often provide an alternative venue on wet or overcast days. Even then the views across the Conwy valley, Betws-y-coed and the mountains of Snowdonia, especially from the upper cliffs, can be stunning.

Warning. Any removal of vegetation is to be strongly discouraged. The cliffs are on Forestry Commission land and the area is regarded as being environmentally sensitive. Also, many local inhabitants live close to the Cyrau and are very aware of climbing activities. Misuse could result in difficulties with access in the future.

The Main Cliff
This is the dominating section of cliff when viewed from Betws-y-Coed. A large, centrally-placed overhang, is the striking feature. Descent can be made either steeply from the left edge of the main plateau (slightly higher than where the routes finish), or to the right along a terrace.

Holly Groove   25 metres   Moderate   (1940s)
A floral tribute on the left of the crag, best left undisturbed.

★The Ramp   27 metres   Hard Very Severe   (1960s)
A fine route with character. Start to the left of *Jingling Wall*.

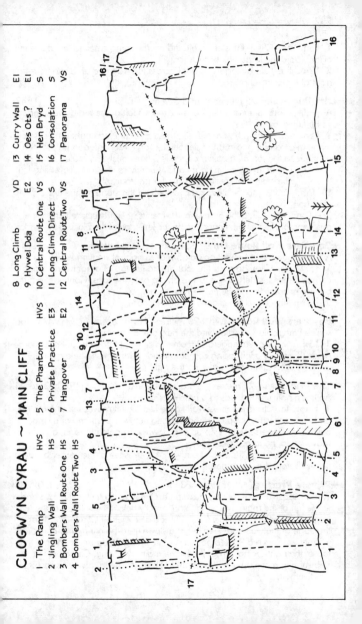

CLOGWYN CYRAU ~ MAIN CLIFF

1 The Ramp	HVS	5 The Phantom	HVS	8 Long Climb	VD	13 Curry Wall	E1
2 Jingling Wall	HS	6 Private Practice	E3	9 Hywel Dda	E2	14 Oes Ots?	E1
3 Bombers Wall Route One	HS	7 Hangover	E2	10 Central Route One	VS	15 Hen Bryd	S
4 Bombers Wall Route Two	HS			11 Long Climb Direct	S	16 Consolation	S
				12 Central Route Two	VS	17 Panorama	VS

1 15m. 5a. Climb the steep wall and overhanging crack to the top of the pillar. Avoid the large oak branch (crux?).

2 12m. 5a. Climb diagonally right across the wall and up a short corner right of the overhang.

★★★**Jingling Wall**   25 metres   Hard Severe   (1947)

A quality climb. Start at a V-groove 12 metres left of the main overhang, at small flakes behind a holly.

1 15m. 4b. Follow the groove. At 7 metres, either step right onto a small ledge in a corner, or climb the steeper section direct on good holds; then continue to the top of the pillar on the left. (Previously the route was described as belaying on the right above *Bombers Wall* and traversing left to finish as for pitch 2 – perhaps better for photographs.)

2 10m. 4b. Climb the steep grooves behind the stance to the top.

Variation

1a 18m. 4b. Climb the groove for 10 metres; then traverse left under the overhang of *The Ramp* before climbing the left edge of the block to the stance.

★**Bombers Wall Route One**   25 metres   Hard Severe   (1947)

A good route. Start behind an oak 5 metres right of *Jingling Wall.*

1 15m. 4b. Climb to a rib (thread) and to the top of a rightward-facing corner. Either step left, or climb straight up onto the face. Continue to nut belays, or cross to a large flake in the corner.

2 10 m. 4b. The steep groove left of the corner.

Bombers Wall Route Two   25 metres   Hard Severe   (1947/1966)

A nice companion. Start behind the next oak on the right.

1 15m. 4b. Gain a ledge at 3 metres. Move right, then back left on large holds. Finish up a left-facing corner to reach a large flake belay.

2 10m. 4b. Climb the corner on the right.

The Phantom   27 metres   Hard Very Severe   (1970s/25.6.94)

An imaginative start leads to a hard finish.

1 17m. 4c. Climb *Bombers Wall Route Two* until it moves left at 6 metres, and continue straight up on good holds to below the left end of a small overhang. Traverse right, step up at a downward-pointing fang, and then move left to the large flake belay.

2 10m. 5b. Climb the steep headwall 4 metres left of the corner by large flakes (before they disappear!).

★★**Private Practice**   25 metres   E3 5c   (20.5.88)

This impressive route follows the thin parallel lines up the wall above and to the left of the main overhang. Start directly below these lines, at the left edge of a wall and next to an oak (thread at 1 metre). Climb directly up the edge of the wall and keep left of a downward-pointing fang of rock at 15 metres. Reach a 'spiked pocket' before swinging up and right into the top of the right-facing corner below the main overhang. Climb out left to a peg runner, move up, and step right to finish. All steep, on well-spaced but positive holds.

Hangover   30 metres   E2 5b   (1960s)
Some interesting situations. Start in the middle of the wall, below the main
overhang. Climb into the small niche overhung by a smooth bulge at 3
metres. Step left and take a straight line up the centre of the face to the foot
of the yellow wall. From the corner, a set of flakes lead awkwardly right to a
tiny ledge in the middle of the wall. Continue traversing to cross the
overhang at its right-hand end on good holds, and reach easier ground.
Variations
Left Variant 32m. E2 5b. Start as for the original route, but climb to the
top of the corner left of the yellow wall. Traverse right immediately beneath
the main overhang to reach the same finish.
Pat's Finish E4 6b † (2.91). A direct finish through the main overhang.
Climb the thin crack and groove-line going through the left-hand side of
the overhang. Strenuous but well protected.

The routes to the right of the main overhang can all be found by reference to
a long, irregular, often grassy ledge at about 6 metres, which is divided into
two sections by a broad, vague rib starting immediately above an alcove.

★**Hywel Dda**   25 metres   E2 5b   (2.91)
Climb to the ledge as for *Long Climb*, and continue steeply with a broken
crack-system on the left and a smooth wall on the right. Avoid an easy
option right at 15 metres (*Curry Wall*) by reaching up to jugs on the left.
Either take the easiest line to the top, or complete the **Good Finish**
(25.6.94) with an idealistic traverse rightwards between the highest set of
overhangs. (It is possible to break the pitch by belaying level with the
traverse.)

Long Climb   34 metres   Very Difficult   (1947)
A pleasant excursion. Start at an oak, to the right of the main overhang
and below the left end of the first section of ledge at 6 metres.
1 24m. Climb up directly to the ledge (or more delicately across from the
left). Steps lead gently up to the right towards a large sloping ledge.
Continue traversing right to a small rounded spike, and climb the steep
wall on the right to an oak.
2 10m. Climb up to the left, then back right onto the next ledge. Finish up
easy ground right of the corner.
Variation
2a 12m. (1956). Climb to the next ledge and then traverse leftwards to
finish.

The next two routes cover common ground, and either start or finish can be
taken as required.

Central Route One   35 metres   Very Severe 4c   (pre-1970)
Climb to the ledge as for *Long Climb*, and then up rightwards into a recess
after 15 metres (below a short, right-facing corner, right of a nose). Step
left round the nose and move up to a ledge. Move across to the left of a
bulge, before finishing just to the right of the top overhangs.

★Central Route Two   34 metres   Very Severe   4c   (pre-1970)
A very good line. Start as for *Long Climb Direct*. Climb up steps and follow
the broad rib and short wall above into a recess (14 metres). Step left
round a nose and move up to a ledge as for *Route One* (or climb the
unprotected corner direct: HVS). Continue up a short corner right of the
bulge on flakes, which leads to a left-slanting groove and then the top.

★★Long Climb Direct   25 metres   Severe   (18.12.83)
Nicely varied. Start at an oak where steps lead rightwards across a wall to
the rib separating the two sections of ledge at 6 metres.
1 15m. Take the steps up to the right and onto the ledge right of the rib at
6 metres. Follow an awkward shallow corner, eventually to reach a small
rounded spike. Traverse out below a wall on the right and climb it to a
small oak.
2 10m. Move up to the left, then back right onto the next ledge. Climb
the corner above to the top.

Curry Wall   35 metres   E1   5a   (13.1.69)
Straightforward apart from the central section. Climb the alcove right of the
start of *Long Climb Direct*. Move leftwards, following a line of weakness
just left of the vague rib into the middle of a steep wall. Climb directly up
onto a ledge below the top overhangs, traverse left to the arête, and finish
easily. (A more demanding finish can be made from the ledge by climbing
up right of the top overhangs as for the top of *Central Route One*.)

Oes Ots?   23 metres   E1
A bit disjointed but still worthwhile. Start right of *Long Climb Direct* at a wall
between an alcove and an oak tree.
1 13m. 5a. Climb steeply up the middle of the wall to a grass ledge;
then move right and climb up to and left of the small overhang. (This
middle section may be damp – a variation takes the shallow corner on the
left until holds can be followed back towards the overhang.) Continue on
the front of the buttress to a small oak tree.
2 10m. 5b. Traverse easily leftwards to a prominent ledge (junction with
Central Routes). A flake above protects the delicate traverse back
rightwards to a small isolated overhang. Climb up the wall and corner left
of the overhang to a little spike near the top. Avoid the easy finish by
moving out to a distant flat edge on the left.

Further right the cliff becomes more broken and vegetated. Many lines have
no doubt been climbed in the past. The two routes described make the best
of what is available.

★Hen Bryd   23 metres   Severe   (1980s)
A pleasing route. Start 10 metres right of *Long Climb Direct*, from a
pointed rock below a short right-facing corner.
1 14m. Climb the corner to easier ground at 5 metres. Move right and
up left of a small overhang. Step right, and continue left of the oak to
reach a large ledge.

2 9m. Step up to the left and climb direct to finish on a slight tower.
Variation:
2a 8m. Climb the wall and small corner further right. Harder.

Consolation   21 metres   Severe   (pre-1970)
Start 12 metres right of *Hen Byrd*, just right of a large oak below a steep
wall.
1 11m. Climb to the obvious break at 4 metres. Traverse left for 2 metres;
then move directly up to a variety of interesting pockets leading to a ledge.
(A direct start is harder at 4b.)
2 10m. Climb the blocks on the left; then move back into the corner on
the right to finish. (The corner direct is VS 4b.)

Panorama   75 metres   Very Severe   (7.6.60)
A fine girdle with good positions. Previously described as starting on top of
the pillar at the first stance of *Jingling Wall*. To get to this point, the
variation to pitch 1 of that route would seem appropriate.
1 18m. 4b. Take the *Jingling Wall* groove for 10 metres. Traverse left
below the overhang and crack of *The Ramp*. Finish up the left edge of the
block to reach the stance.
2 25m. 4b. Traverse down to the right onto the *Bombers Wall* ledges,
and continue easily to a large flake. Move awkwardly under the
overhangs, past the downward-pointing fang, to reach a ledge on the
right below the yellow wall.
3 20m. 4b. After crossing a rib, step down and make delicate moves to a
small ledge. Continue rightwards to the large sloping ledge of *Long Climb*
and traverse to the small rounded spike (belay possible). Step up to the
right, and go round the corner. Avoid the large ledge with a downward
traverse across a vertical wall to reach a corner (junction with *Hen Bryd*).
Move up to belay at the oak tree or on the ledge behind.
4 12m. 4a. To the right, a traverse-line can be taken to the far end of the
cliff, to finish just left of a small corner (junction with *Consolation*).

Some connoisseurs regard a right-to-left traverse as more satisfying. If
Consolation is taken as an approach to locate the start correctly, and the
last pitch of *Jingling Wall* used as the final flourish, **Amaronap** will
provide 90 metres of climbing. Re-interpreting the pitch descriptions will
require some deliberation; a previous outing on *Panorama* would be an
obvious advantage.

Conwy Buttress
This lies east of the Main Cliff across a bramble-engulfed boulder-field. The
vague track, from a sharp left turn on the waymarked path, gradually
wanders uphill to meet the buttress at the prominent *Conwy Corner* and the
heavily undercut arête to its left. Descent can be made on the left, starting
down a small rocky gully hidden in the trees near the top of the next
elevation, or less obviously to the right beyond a prominent conifer opposite
the top of Little Buttress.

Wall Climb   16 metres   Severe   (pre-1966)
A diagonal line across the wall. Start 10 metres up the slope on the left, at
an indefinite groove level with an oak. Pull up to a ledge (hidden spike,
tight up against the rock face). Traverse right to reach a smaller ledge with
some difficulty (a move up and step across is easier). Continue rightwards
to finish up the easing arête.

Wall Street   12 metres   Severe
A more direct route. Start from the middle of a ledge 3 metres further
right. Climb the wall on pockets to a small overhang, the base of a large
block. Move right, avoiding any possible 'crash', to finish more easily.

Walnut   18 metres   Very Severe   4c
A delectable morsel. Start below the overhang on the arête. Climb to the
ledge just left of the overhang. Step right to reach holds on a rib and
continue direct, keeping left of the arête.

Waterloo   18 metres   E3 6a/b †   (13.8.60/1989)
The arête direct. Originally given as Very Severe with one point of aid to
surmount the overhang. Now largely superseded by the *Swing* routes.

★★**Swing High**   20 metres   Very Severe   4b   (1.10.86)
Bold and exciting. The arête, starting from the corner. Follow *Conwy
Corner* for 7 metres. Hand-traverse left, to reach an exhilarating position
left of the arête, on the lip of the overhang. Finish up the edge.

Swing Low   20 metres   Hard Very Severe   5a
A good pitch. As for *Swing High*, but climb up right of the arête.

Con-Trick   18 metres   E1 5b   (25.6.94)
An entertaining eliminate on the left wall of *Conwy Corner*. Go up to a
starting-ledge at 7 metres, level with the overhang. Climb the left wall.
Avoid using the wall on the right or the arête to the left, especially the small
ledge on it at 12 metres. (E3 without runners in the corner.)

★★★**Conwy Corner**   18 metres   Severe   (1952)
A well-protected classic. The obvious right-angled corner is climbed mostly
on its right wall.

Immediately to the right the cliff is somewhat vegetated, but higher up various
clean ribs and grooves are topped by an assortment of tiny overhangs.

Diagonal Climb   25 metres   Very Difficult   (3.7.60)
A nice outing with exposed positions. Follow *Conwy Corner* for 7 metres
and then traverse out to the right on good holds. Cross a number of ribs
and grooves to finish up a small open corner (just prior to reaching a
sapling).

Caerhun   18 metres   Very Severe   4c
An enjoyable pitch. Start 3 metres right of *Conwy Corner*. Climb steeply up
the front of a bulging buttress. Continue up the groove right of a thin

projecting nose to the top overhang, and finish on the left. (The groove left of the nose is harder and perhaps less worthwhile, Hard Very Severe 4c.)

★Academy   18 metres   Hard Severe 4b   (1960s)
A good climb. Start 6 metres right of Conwy Corner below a short corner and left of a small tree at 3 metres. Move up and then left into the corner, at the top of which is a large thread. Continue rightwards across a rib, and up a shallow groove to a 'crown'-like overhang. Step left and climb the wall to the top.

Daear   18 metres   Very Severe 4c
Worthwhile. Start as for Academy. Climb to below the corner and move out to the right across a difficult section. Continue rightwards up the curving rib, and step left to finish.

Tyrch   18 metres   Very Severe 4c
An independent line, which will improve with use. Start 3 metres further right. Climb steeply up a protruding flake and move left onto a ledge. Continue up the wall above, trending right, and finish up the cracked corner.

The next three routes start below the towering cliff 15 metres right of Conwy Corner.

Hironimo   20 metres   Very Severe 4c   (1970)
A varied and interesting route. Start at some blocks right of the vegetation and left of the tower. Climb steeply rightwards towards the overhang on the tower, and then left up a short wall to easier ground. Finish up the corner in the block above.

Irish Rover   18 metres   E2 5b/c   (1960s)
A demanding route. Start below the tower, at the left of two shallow grooves. Follow the groove to the overhang, avoiding easy options on the left. Get into the hanging corner above, by climbing up the right wall using small pockets, and stepping back left when the main difficulties are over. Finish up the corner. (At one stage, graded HVS. A large flake fell from the first section in 1979, altering its character; even so, it was well undergraded.)
Variations
Direct E2 5c. Climb straight into the corner.

★Wild Rover Arête   18 metres   E2 5b   (1980s)
A stunning variation. Follow Irish Rover to the overhang, where a jammed block provides the key to the left arête, which is climbed on good holds in a superb position.

To the right at the top of the cliff is a very large rightward-facing corner. This is flanked on the right by a steep wall with a line of three pronounced overhangs near the top and two more of a similar size at mid height. The following routes climb this area.

The Artful Dodger   17 metres   Very Severe 4c
Rich pickings? Start below the corner, at a prominent block by an old holly. Long pulls lead onto the wall. Move up, trending leftwards. The wall above

leads to the top overhangs. Climb between the left (slightly lower) and middle overhang. From a large ledge take the centre of the final wall.

Precedent   18 metres   Severe   (1960s)
The traditional ascent route. Start 2 metres right at a slanting rock. Make a few steep pulls (use of old holly or combined tactics?), to reach easier ground. Follow grooves and ledges leftwards into the main corner, which is climbed to the top.

★★**Stripper**   17 metres   Severe   (pre-1970)
A very good outing. Start as for *Precedent*. Climb up for 7 metres and then trend across to the right, avoiding the bottom set of overhangs. Move up a short groove and step back left onto the rounded arête, which provides a fine finish.
Variation
★**Stripper Direct**   17 metres   Hard Severe 4b   (1980s)
An excellent line. Start as for *Stripper* but continue up between the first overhangs to a flake. Follow a broken groove through the top overhangs just left of the arête. Finish up the left-hand side of the rib above.

Side-show   17 metres   Severe   (16.8.95)
Start 3 metres further right at a tree on a block. Climb up to the left and up the rib to an open groove at 7 metres (junction with *Stripper*). Take the groove, but continue straight up to finish just to the right of the arête.

The rock face now becomes unappealing and overgrown. A path continues rightwards at a slightly lower level to reach the next major feature after 20 metres: a large tree growing up over a prominent overhang half-way up the cliff. This is the line of *Tree Climb*.

Knight Time   24 metres   Hard Severe 4b
An elusive route. Start 9 metres left of *Tree Climb* below a pedestal. Swing up onto the initial ledge. (It is possible to belay and start from here.) Step left and continue up leftwards to a tree under an overhang. Traverse rightwards with difficulty, before climbing back leftwards onto the ledge above. Follow the fine open groove, beginning slightly on the left and trending right.

Fatal Attraction   18 metres   E2 5b
A worrying proposition. Start 5 metres left of *Tree Climb*. Climb up the corner right of the huge suspended block. Traverse left onto the face before stretching for more reliable holds. Move across into the large corner and continue to the top. Small tree belays.

Bat in Action   20 metres   Hard Very Severe 5a
A safer way of reaching the large corner. Start as for *The Bat* and continue the traverse leftwards into the top corner of *Fatal Attraction*.

The Bat   20 metres   Hard Very Severe 5a   (pre-1970)
A route with some good positions. Climb directly to the large oak of *Tree Climb* by the awkward crack on the left of the nose. Traverse wildly left

under the overhang into a shallow corner. Either follow the corner on excellent holds to a ledge below a smooth wall, or step right half-way up and climb to the same spot. Move leftwards onto the edge of the wall to finish easily. Small tree belays.

Tree Climb   19 metres   Very Difficult   (pre-1966)
An entertaining outing. Start below the large oak at 10 metres. Climb up to the right before traversing horizontally left to the tree. Scale the tree past the overhang. Continue on the rocks above, finishing via a small chimney. Tree belay.

Wolf Rib   15 metres   Severe   (1970s)
An isolated route, immediately above the path 16 metres further right. Either pull steeply direct onto the rib from below, or traverse in from the left. Climb to a ledge at 11 metres and continue up to a wall (thread). Finish up the corner above, left of some surprising pockets. Large tree belay.

Little Buttress
This is the smallest of the cliffs, and the most northerly of the upper tier. It is best reached by following the vague track to below Conwy Buttress and continuing to Little Buttress further right. Please avoid using the scree as a way of getting to or from the cliff as the erosion caused has already led to problems with the Forestry Commission. An alternative track connects with the base of the scree, though it is somewhat treacherous and perhaps unsuitable for groups. It climbs steeply up leftwards from the base of the scree, passing an old lead mine adit to link with the recommended approach left of *Tree Climb* on Conwy Buttress. Cairn.

This compact rock face is a very popular venue for Centre-based groups and it can get crowded. The top has ample belay points and descent can be made easily on the left.

Most of the routes would have been first climbed during the 1970s, when the cliff was heavily cleaned as a training venue. Only three were mentioned in the 1970 *Snowdon East* guide.

The first four routes ascend a wall on the left flank of the cliff.

Nicw   8 metres   E3 6a   (1980s)
An extended boulder-problem. Start 2 metres right of the tree at a steep wall. Climb up and to the right on tiny holds, then directly up the tapering wall to easy ground.

Sion   9 metres   Severe
Start 2 metres further right at a small pointed rock. Climb the obvious left-slanting crackline and up the weakness above.

Sian   9 metres   Very Difficult
To the right is a large block. Move onto the block and follow the groove above.

Siencyn   9 metres   Severe
Step up onto the front of the block and climb the large corner-crack,
largely on the left wall. Continue easily to the top.

Del   11 metres   E3 5c   (1980s)
An audacious test-piece up the front of the buttress on the right. Climb
easily up the crack and move left to grassy ledges. Climb rightwards onto
sloping footholds, using layaways. A few tenuous, balancy moves enable
good finishing-holds on the left to be gained.

Little Chimney   11 metres   Very Difficult   (pre-1966)
The obvious feature of the buttress. Twin cracks lead past a block into the
chimney. Arduous moves enable holds on the right edge to be reached
and salvation to follow.

The Groove   10 metres   Very Difficult
A pleasant route. Clamber to the base of the groove, in which a
constriction provides the only real difficulty.
Variation
Left Wall Finish Severe 4a. From the constriction, move onto the left wall,
which is climbed on positive holds.

Three unassuming routes are found at a lower level, behind a silver birch.

Morus   10 metres   Very Difficult
The shallow left buttress. Follow the buttress to the left of a crack. Continue
up the wall and rib above.

Ifan   10 metres   Very Difficult
The steeper buttress to the right. Step rightwards onto the buttress and
climb more or less directly up to a finishing-rib.

The Arête   13 metres   Hard Severe 4b   (pre-1966)
A good route. An undercut base leads to easier climbing in a fine position.
Easy Start 10m. Very Difficult. From behind the tree, move rightwards
(using branches?) onto the arête.

The front face is steep, and divided into two sections by a large ledge at 4
metres. The face can be traversed close to the ground from a stone at the
base of the arête to the foot of a large block on the right at 4c. In the middle
of the traverse is a bulging area with a heavily undercut base at 1 metre.

Direct Route   13 metres   Very Severe 4c   (1953)
Climb up left of the bulge, using pockets and positive flakes to the ledge.
Follow the shallow scoop and corner to a ledge. Move rightwards to finish
right of a final block.

Eliminate Start   4 metres   Very Severe 5a
From right of the bulge, follow a number of incomplete cracklines onto the
ledge.

Pryderi 13 metres   Very Severe 4c
Starting just left of the block, climb up past the right-hand end of the ledge, and follow the thin crackline direct to the top.

Gwydion 12 metres   Very Severe 4c
Climb directly and steeply from the top of the block to reach excellent holds that continue into a recess near the top.

★Wanderer 13 metres   Hard Severe 4b
Bits from each of the preceding two routes combine to provide an easier variation. Step left from the block but, just before the ledge, move back across rightwards to reach good flake holds. Continue to the top recess with a leftwards excursion midway to avoid difficulties.

Raining Stones 17 metres   Hard Severe 4b   (1997)
Three metres over to the right is a rib of rock. Climb this (easier from the right), and follow the edge and its continuation to a large ledge. Finish up the steep wall just right of the deep crack.

Other slight routes around to the right are perhaps best left in obscurity.

Craig Cynhelier
From just above the seat on the waymarked path, a scrappy and vegetated rock face can be seen coming down from the right. To the left, an old stone wall meets the cliff, and 14 metres beyond this lies the first notable feature, a large right-angled corner, the line of *Jackdaw Cracks*. The cliff is generally steep and clean. Routes are described in the order they are encountered on the approach from **right to left**. The most secure belays are on trees well back. Descent can be made to the left (facing the crag), although one tricky 3-metre rock step may require roping. Alternatively, a long walk up rightwards eventually leads back to the waymarked path. On the left of the cliff, the descent route and some climbs overlook a nearby farmhouse; disturbance needs to be kept to an absolute minimum to avoid problems occurring with access.

The *Snowdon East* (1970) guide referred to 'a remarkable number of steep, distinct, and interesting lines'.

Jackdaw Cracks 15 metres   Hard Severe   (1960s)
A classic line. Start at the recess filled by an oak below the main corner. Scramble onto the terrace and climb the fine open corner, using numerous cracks and blocks, to a ledge. Continue to the top.

Pecker Rib 16 metres   Very Difficult   (1960s)
Some nice positions. Start as for *Jackdaw Cracks*. Climb to the terrace below the main corner and traverse leftwards to reach an airy position on its left edge. A few moves lead onto and up the rib, leading, as the angle eases, to a ledge above the large corner. Step wildly rightwards out above the corner, or climb more directly to reach the top.

Juggernaut   16 metres   E2 5b
Three metres around to the left is an off-width crack below an immense detached block awaiting departure. Climb the arduous crack, and continue up the corner left of the suspect block. Pull onto the front of the towering rib and finish right of the tree.

★The Keen Haulier   16 metres   Very Severe   4c   (1960s)
A good climb. Start 2 metres to the left, below a conifer at the top of the cliff. Follow the crackline to reach the break. Move round to the right and, from just below a sapling, swing back airily leftwards onto the front face of the towering rib. Finish immediately right of the conifer.

Trucker   16 metres   Hard Very Severe   5b
To the left 4 metres, just before a drop in the base of the cliff, are several small vertical ribs with a ledge above at 3 metres. A hard start (the rest being no more than VS 4c). A crack between the ribs leads up onto the ledge. Continue up left of the smooth wall using other ledges before trending rightwards along a crackline under the overhang. Climb the scoop above to finish left of the tree.

★Cofiadwy   18 metres   E2 5b
An excellent, well-sustained climb. Start at a lower level 2 metres further left at a dank corner. Use the corner to reach an obvious pocket on the wall, and step left to ledges near a large tree. Move up rightwards and climb the steep wall to a horizontal break. Continue left of an arête, and step onto it just before the top for a tricky finish.

Lasting Impressions   18 metres   Very Severe   4c   (1960s)
The variation is a better way up the cliff. Start 2 metres to the left, at an undercut groove below a large oak at 4 metres. Strenuous moves lead up to easy ground near the tree. Continue leftwards onto the top of a large flake, and finish up the corner on the left.
Wall Finish. From the large flake, step rightwards onto the intricate wall and climb directly up, passing left of some small stacked blocks at mid height, to finish at a crack in the headwall.

Achub Ni   18 metres   Very Severe   4c
A further 6 metres across to the left, an ominously undercut detached block can be found. Climb onto the block from the left and continue to the large ledge and corner. Move left onto the front of the buttress and finish directly. Direct Finish E2 5b. A crack in the headwall provides a more arduous finish. Climb past a small overhang to reach two hidden positive holds. Move right into the crackline with difficulty and continue to the top.

Piton Route   18 metres   E2 5b (1 pt aid)   (1970s)
The wall below the overhang and the groove on its left-hand side. Climb the centre of the wall on good holds, trending left to a more difficult area below the groove. Using runners in the corner but keeping to holds on the right wall, reach the fang of rock above and clip the peg beyond. Escape onto a ledge on the right and continue easily to the top.

Dr Mayhead's Idea   18 metres   Hard Severe 4b   (1960s)
An engaging route. Start 12 metres to the left, at a large, irregular corner
containing a few trees. Climb up immediately below the corner and onto
the left wall. Continue up the corner (trees may or may not be used), and
finish either via the cleft above or the wall on its right.

Hiraeth   15 metres   Hard Very Severe 5a
A good climb up the wall left of the corner. Start just left of two oak trees at
a rounded rib. Clamber past the large toppled block onto the rib and
continue to a horizontal break at 8 metres. Move right, then back left to
finish up a short corner left of the overhang.
Variation E1 5b. Step right, and tackle the twin cracks in the final
overhang.

★Way Out West   14 metres   Hard Severe 4b   (1960s)
A neat route. A groove can be found 4 metres left of the two large oaks.
Climb the groove to a ledge at 8 metres, before following a crack through
the top overhang.

Central Slabs

The path meets the cliff at a slabby area 30 metres long, with a steep wall
below it and a very large conifer to the right. The brown streak of *Zip Wall* is
obvious. Tree belays are readily available at the top of the cliff.

Any descent on foot is circuitous. To the left, a vague track leads to a
waymarked path. Going down this to the next path junction (previously
visited when approaching the cliff), loses a lot of height and necessitates a
walk back up to the base of the crag. To the right, a walk uphill to the foot of
Conwy Buttress enables the track down described in the section on Little
Buttress to be located (page 259).

The **left to right** order is resumed. The first feature out to the left is a
15-metre slab/wall, slightly lower and projecting from the main rock face. It
offers two routes, both of which lack protection low down.

Face Climb   15 metres   Very Difficult   (1960s)
A strenuous start leads up the front face just left of the edge. Continue,
trending leftwards, and finish with a traverse back to the right onto a ledge
above the overhang. Alternatively, add to the interest by taking the
overhang direct (Severe 4a).

★Wall and Corner   15 metres   Very Difficult   (1960s)
Short but sweet. Start 3 metres round to the right. Climb up and leftwards
onto the rib. Move up and take the corner right of the overhang, and step
left onto the ledge above.
Variation Severe 4a. Climb the wall direct to the corner.

Last Exit   18 metres   Very Severe 4b   (1960s)
A break in the cliff's defences. Start 15 metres to the right behind a large
holly. Climb up into a recess at 6 metres, and diagonally rightwards to a

second. Move up to the right and through a steepening onto a slabby area above. Trend left to finish easily via a crack in the headwall.

★★Arrowhead   18 metres   Hard Very Severe   5a   (1960s)
A great route with atmosphere. Start 10 metres to the right below an overhung, left-slanting weakness. Climb steeply into a corner at 6 metres (old peg). Move left and climb into the scoop above. Step right onto the rib and finish direct.

YKK   15 metres   Very Severe   4c
The route ascends left of the brown streak. From a rocky outcrop, climb the broken wall left of a nose for 5 metres. Step left, and move steeply over a small curving overlap onto a long ledge. Finish direct.

Zip Wall   15 metres   Very Severe   4c   (1960s)
Starting right of the nose, this ascends the brown streak. Climb onto the wall from the right. Surmount a bulge at 5 metres using a shallow pocket and continue straight to the top.

★Mystery Wall   18 metres   Severe   (1960s)
A reasonable route with positive holds but little protection. Start behind an oak 2 metres left of the large conifer. Clamber up rocky steps below the wall and move diagonally right onto the blunt arête. Step left and continue to a large ledge. Climb directly up the weakness in the slabs above, finishing at a break in the final headwall.

Problem Wall   17 metres   Severe   (1960s)
A variation on Mystery Wall, also poorly protected. Start at the large conifer. Scramble up rounded ledges for 5 metres. A few moves up the steep arête lead onto the wall on the right, which is climbed to the large ledge. Continue up the smooth green slab before finishing to the left as for Mystery Wall.

The next three routes have a common start, 20 metres further right, below the obvious cave-like recesses. The area has its share of loose rock. Scramble up through vegetation and then rightwards to the flaky crack immediately below the right recess.

Depression   25 metres   Hard Very Severe   5a   (1960s)
A circuitous ascent. Climb the cracks and continue up to the top of the lower recess, where there are some loose rocks. Move with difficulty into the upper recess. Continue to traverse left (ancient peg), passing a 'useful' block to a resting-place around the corner. Step left again to avoid the last overlap and finish up the front of the buttress.

Earthworm Direct   15 metres   Hard Very Severe   5a   (1960s)
A fine top section. Follow Depression into the upper recess and climb the obvious jamming-crack to reach good finishing-holds.

Earthworm   15 metres   Very Severe   4c   (1960s)
Quite a good outing. Climb into the lower recess as for Depression. Move rightwards below a dubious block and round the corner to below a small

ledge. After an awkward step up, finish easily to a large ledge. Nut belays or trees through brambles.

Little X   49 metres   Hard Very Severe   (1960s)
An intrepid traverse can be made from *Last Exit* to *Earthworm*.
1 24m. 4c. Follow *Last Exit* up into the second recess. Traverse rightwards above the ivy to the scoop and rib of *Arrowhead*, before taking a line across to the large ledge on *Mystery Wall*.
2 25m. 5a. Scramble up rightwards on grassy ledges for 7 metres to an imposing headwall. Traverse under the overlap and around the corner to reach a square block. Climb down into the cave-like recess and continue into a lower one (*Depression* reversed). Move right under the leaning block and finish as for *Earthworm*. A daunting pitch with some questionable rock.

The next section of cliff is heavily vegetated, but 20 metres to the right the path runs directly below an impending wall, climbed by the following three routes.

★★The Fate of Icarus   20 metres   Hard Very Severe 5a   (1960s)
An excellent varied route. Scramble up leftwards onto the highest ledge. Move out rightwards and climb steeply up, before trending left to the 'cave'. Scale the overhang, and step left into the bay above. Climb the rib on the left to a large ledge. Nut belays. (Avoid the brambles above by escaping leftwards along the ledge.)

Flight of Fancy   20 metres   E3 5b   (17.8.86)
Too easy, then too hard? Climb to the top of the corner on the right, before stepping left to ledges that lead up to a steep wall. Delicate unprotected moves at a slanting ramp allow good holds on the next ledge to be reached. Finish wildly just left of the gargoyle. An easy rib and block lead to tree belays after a further 10 metres.

Loose Connection   25 metres   Hard Very Severe 5a   (10.6.88)
An attractive combination. Follow *The Fate of Icarus* into the bay above the cave. Then take the 'loose connection' rightwards to finish steeply just left of the arête as for *Flight of Fancy*. Tree belays after 10 metres of scrambling.

Further right the base of the cliff runs uphill away from the path and into a wooded area. The next two routes start 10 metres up from the path, at a leftward-slanting weakness.

Illusion   25 metres   Hard Severe 4b   (1960s)
An interesting top section after an enclosed start. Follow the stepped slabs of the weakness up to the base of a steeper chimney-crack at 13 metres. Climb past the large, temporary chockstone with caution. Continue up the crackline and corner above to a finishing-block.

Delusion   24 metres   Hard Severe 4b
Follow *Illusion* for 10 metres onto the large slab. Pull steeply rightwards onto ledges and continue to a tree. Climb the groove behind the tree; then move left to a hidden crack and out onto the nose above. Climb the final block.

Ivy's Rib   21 metres   Hard Severe   4b   (1960s)
Start just to the right, level with a large oak. Climb the broad unprotected
rib and trend right at a steepening onto the edge of a slab. Continue
directly up to the base of a projecting block and step rightwards onto it.
Scramble up to tree belays after a further 5 metres.
Variation 19m. 4b. A shorter but similarly unprotected start can be made
7 metres further right. Take a rising traverse leftwards to the edge of the
slab and move up to join the parent route.

Yellow Peril   16 metres   Severe   (1960s)
Further up to the right is a corner containing a prominent drainage streak.
Immediately right is a steep wall. From the corner, move rightwards up the
wall and back left to a flake crack. Continue to the grassy break. Step left
onto ledges and follow a rib of rock to the top.

Little Wall

After passing below Central Slabs, the path continues across scree. Here, the
buttress of Little Wall can be seen down on the right and a small path
descends to the base of the cliff. The main feature is a long, gently overhanging section at one-third height with a clean wall above. The feature is
defined on the left by a corner and to the right by a shallow crackline/corner
running up past several small overhangs. Descent is made easily to the left.

Snowdon East (1970) referred to 'half a dozen routes of all standards'.

Grug   15 metres   Hard Severe   4b   (1960s)
Pleasant enough. Start 3 metres right of the corner defining the upper wall.
Climb up steeply for 5 metres before trending left. Step right back onto the
wall, to finish just left of a small sentry-box and up easy ground.

★Llys   17 metres   Very Severe   4c   (1960s/1990s)
The middle of the impressive wall. Start as for *Grug*. After 5 metres,
traverse right just above the overhang to good holds on a slight rib. Climb
direct to the top, finishing by a thin crack.
(Direct to the slight rib from below is a bold E3 5c/6a †.)

At a Pinch   15 metres   E5   6b/c †   (1990s)
Reach the slab by way of the obvious pinch-grip, just to the right of the
slight rib.

The Corner   15 metres   E2   5b
A harder central section provides some interest.

The Edge   18 metres   E2   5b
The steep rib immediately to the right, just left of *Osian* provides a tricky
climb.

Osian   18 metres   Very Severe   4c   (1960s)
A good line up the vertical crack, which seeps at the base. Follow the crack
to the top overhangs and escape steeply to the left.

★Nia Ben Aur 15 metres   Hard Severe 4b   (1960s)
A rewarding route. Start 3 metres right of *Osian*. Climb the initially
awkward, slanting crack to reach a slab on the skyline. Continue up, via
the two overhangs, for a golden finish.

To the right after 30 metres, and somewhat set back, is a neat square-cut wall.

All Work 10 metres   Severe 4a
Climb the corner on the left and the wall above.

Forgotten Child 11 metres   Very Severe 4c
A little stunner up the middle of the wall. Start below a big block at 3
metres. Reach a small ledge left of the block and make committing moves
up to the right. Finish past large pockets on the upper wall.

No Play 12 metres   Very Severe 4b
Ascends weaknesses right of the wall. Step up into the corner left of a holly,
and gain the next ledge with some difficulty. Continue up the corner above
to where a hand-traverse left provides a good finish.

Craig Rhaeadr Ewynnol Foaming Falls Crag OS Ref 766 578)
Known as Swallow Falls Buttress from a mistranslation of 'ewynnol': a
similar word, 'gwennol', is the Welsh for a swallow.

The crag overlooks the spectacular Swallow Falls gorge, and from the hotel on
the A5 it is easily visible on the opposite side of the river. It is best reached by
using the footpath from the Ty Hyll (Ugly House) bridge, a kilometre upstream.
Follow the path alongside the River Llugwy to the fall, where it becomes
fenced. After another 200 metres the rockface can be seen above the path.

The cliff, which faces south, is an atmospheric place. The routes described
keep to the steepest and most compact area of good rock. Elsewhere the crag
is more broken and vegetated. Descent is easiest to the left; alternatively, to
return to the Ugly House, a forestry track immediately above can be taken.

★Traditional Route 44 metres   Severe   (25.12.64)
A very pleasant route in a scenic location, best done when the river is a
raging torrent and you can't hear your partner. Allowing for this, and in
line with tradition, the pitch lengths have been kept short. Start on the left
side of a large coffin-shaped block, propped up against the base of a
steep groove, 9 metres above the path.
1 14m. Climb onto the top of the block, step out right into a smaller
groove, and go up this to a ledge beneath the right-angled corner.
2 8m. Get onto the right wall and climb the crack that splits it. Tree belays
on a long terrace.
3 11m. Climb the weakness near the left edge of the wall to reach a
ledge and tree belay below a wall.
4 11m. Walk right for 5 metres to the foot of the right-hand of the
grooves in the big recess; climb it directly.

Variation
4a 5m. Climb the wall, starting just right of the slight nose.

Kreen-Akrore   36 metres   Very Severe †   (30.3.2000/28.6.2000)
A fine, harder alternative to *Traditional Route*, starting 15 metres further
right. From the footpath, an obvious deep chimney/corner can be
observed behind a dead tree. Scramble up to the start.
1 9m. 4b. Climb the deep chimney, with an awkward section at the top.
Continue up to belay beneath the steep wall.
2 9m. 4a. Climb up steeply but on good holds to the groove on the right.
Traverse left and gain a bay beneath the impressive corner.
3 12m. 5a. Climb directly up the corner and escape right at the top.
Scramble up the rib, past a small oak, to belay at the short wall above. An
excellent pitch, quite technical and exposed.
4 6m. Gain the wall by stepping off the block, and climb diagonally left
to the top.

Craig Bwlch-yr-haearn   Crag (of the) Pass (of) Iron
OS Ref 778 599
A minor road runs from the Ugly House on the A5 near Swallow Falls to
Gwydir Castle near Llanrwst. At about mid point the road reaches the top of
a partly afforested moorland plateau at a group of houses known as Nant
Bwlch-yr-haearn.

The cliff is situated overlooking the valley less than half a mile north of this
area, above a point on the road where a private track is signposted leading
up to a house called Ty'n yr Ardd. Please do not park on this track or in its
entrance; other suitable spots exist up and down the public road.

The easiest approach is to walk up the private track for about 100 metres to
where it levels off, and a grilled-off mine entrance can be seen on the left.
Immediately beyond, a small path leads steeply up to the right-hand end of
the cliff. A Forestry Commission track starting from the plateau leads
indirectly to the top of the cliff, where it runs roughly parallel with the edge for
a while about 40 metres back. Vehicle access is barred by a locked gate.

The cliff is in the form of a steep escarpment between 10 and 20 metres in
height. Facing across towards the east, it often provides shelter during poor
weather yet may still receive sunshine until mid afternoon. There are
overgrown areas, and loose rock could be a problem in places, but the
majority of routes described are worthwhile. In addition, the views across the
Nant below and the Conwy valley in the distance are magnificent, as are the
tree belays!

The Northern, Central, and Southern sections can best be distinguished in
winter when some of the trees are bare. The climbs are described from **right
to left** as they are found on the approach.

Northern Section

The approach described above leads directly to this section, where the cliff is perhaps at its most impressive and well used. Descent can be made easily by a gully to the right. An obscure descent of the left-hand side of this section only 30 metres from the top of *Metro* is best located by its proximity to the highest point on the Forestry track above. It can be found just beyond the well-preserved stone wall, which follows the edge in that area, at a spot where it drops down slightly into a small hollow. This depression leads leftwards to a small rocky rake, which finishes just 8 metres from the foot of the *Metro* slab.

The Clock of the Long Now 8 metres Hard Very Severe 5a † (28.4.2000)
Start from a grassy ledge half-way up the descent gully, below and just right of a leftward-slanting ramp. Climb the short wall on positive edges and make a long reach for the base of the ramp; speed up this to finish.

Shamanic Wanderings 20 metres E6 6a †   (28.4.2000)
Superb moves following a fine natural line. Climb *First Encounter* to the break (peg runner). Follow angled edges below a slanting diagonal roof to gain a good pocket level with a peg on the left wall. Trend rightwards up the steep wall on ever improving holds.

First Encounter 29 metres Very Severe   (1960s)
This early route was previously described as traversing even further left before finishing. Start below the crag's highest point.
1 17m. 4b. Climb directly up to large flakes below the headwall (peg runner). Traverse left to a stance in a recess.
2 12m. 4a. Traverse leftwards along a walkway. Then, as for *Bonsai Wall*, climb up just right of the oak tree and into the groove above. A few easy steps lead to the top.

☆**Johari Window** 20 metres E1 5b †   (27.11.99)
An impressive line. Follow *First Encounter* to the break (peg runner). Step up, and swing boldly out left to gain a small ledge (crux). Continue up a corner on the right, via some interesting moves, to finish on large holds. Variation E1 5a † (20.11.2001). Start 3 metres to the left at a slanting pocket. Climb directly up and over a final block to the break (peg runner). Move right to join original route at the flakes and peg runner.

★**Bonsai Wall** 25 metres Hard Severe 4a   (21.9.97)
An absorbing climb. From the slanting pocket, traverse across leftwards and climb to a good ledge at 6 metres. From the left end of the ledge, move up to gain the large walkway at mid height (peg runner to the right). Traverse left and climb up just right of the oak tree and into the groove above. A few easy steps lead to the top.

Gorki Groove 19 metres E1 5a   (1960s)
From just left of the small cave at ground-level, make a problematic start to gain layaway holds. Climb in a direct line to the right-hand edge of the

large walkway at mid height (peg runner). Continue towards the obvious rightward-trending groove-line, and reach it by swinging airily to the right. Clip the peg (crux). One more pull and the rest is easy.

Offcut   19 metres   Hard Severe 4a   (20.11.2001)
On the far left is a ramp of rock. Step off this, and climb up to a nut slot just left of a good ledge (junction with *Bonsai Wall*). Move left above an overhang to gain blocky holds and climb to the walkway. Finish right of the tree as for *Bonsai Wall*.

A path starts at a lower level and gradually gains height over to the left. After 25 metres there appears a clean, wide-open groove, identified by an isolated metre-length block. This is embedded below and just left of the small grassy ledge from where two routes start.

Final Flurry   25 metres   Hard Very Severe 4c †   (20.11.2001)
Keep right of an overhang at 4 metres (peg), and continue up towards the large overhang on the right-hand side of the headwall. From a nut slot, traverse with difficulty under the overhang into the recess on the right. Move up and back left to a ledge. Finish above. (The ledge can be gained direct from the nut slot at E1 5a.)

★Heulwen   22 metres   Very Severe 4b   (21.9.97)
A good route. Climb up left of an overhang at 4 metres (peg). A series of small ledges leads to the headwall, where a step left is followed by awkward moves to gain and leave a good horizontal break (cam placements). Finish on large holds.
Variation Hard Very Severe 5a. Just before the break, traverse left onto the blunt arête. This is followed in a splendid position.

Ten metres left, on a ledge at a higher level, there are a number of large rowan trees grouped below a wall, which has a small slab at its centre.

Ulex   18 metres   Very Severe 4b   (1960s/20.11.2001)
The original upper section (left and up from the recess) is now obstructed by vegetation, but the finish described makes the route a good outing. From the trees, reach the slab and follow it to a horizontal recess. From the break, step right and climb to the overhang (some suspect rock), which is taken towards the right on good holds. Finish up the open groove above.

Seven metres left is perhaps the most readily identifiable feature on this part of the cliff, a leftward-opening flake crack. Two climbs begin here.

Quercus's Route   18 metres   Hard Severe 4b   (1960s)
Follow the flake crack to its top, step right, and climb a little groove. From here, the route originally escaped up an overgrown corner on the right. A much better finish can be made up the small subsidiary corner on the left.

Mistake   18 metres   Very Severe 4c   (1960s)
Follow the preceding route to the top of the flake crack. Climb out leftwards to ledges and then up the prominent large corner to finish. (An

independent start can be made keeping to the left wall, using runners in the flake crack, with a change of grade.)

Provo   20 metres   Hard Very Severe 5a   (1960-65)
Start 6 metres to the left of the flake crack, at a shallow depression below a hanging groove in the skyline. Climb the open groove until a long step left can be made. Continue up blocks left of a small tree; then climb rightwards to an old stump. Step across onto a little slab and move up to another tiny tree. Surmount the bulge to finish in the easy groove.

Man of Haearn   18 metres   E3 5b †   (1970s)
Statistics are approximate! A useless rusting peg under the overhang level with the stump on *Provo* is testament to someone's forgotten labours. Climb *Provo* to the stump and traverse left under the overhang to a small ledge. The rounded rib above has good holds eventually.

Digger   14 metres   Very Severe 4b   (1960s)
Across to the left after a further 8 metres there is a shallow corner. Climb the corner and a rib to a holly at 6 metres. Continue steeply up the groove behind, to an old peg. Escape leftwards to finish on a rib left of the oak.

Thirty metres to the left hides another substantial area of rock, the most obvious feature being a smooth, green wall capped by an overhang. Thirty metres further left, and at a higher level, lies the only real slab route in the neighbourhood.

Metro   12 metres   Very Difficult   (1960s)
Not a straightforward plod!

Eight metres left again is the slanting rocky rake, which provides a good line of ascent/descent.

Central Section
An isolated buttress 60 metres left of *Metro*. From above, it can be located close to the forestry track's highest point, where its top is the only significant area of ground projecting beyond a stone wall. Descent can be made via the hollow on the left (facing out) as described under Northern Section.

Suede Slide   18 metres   Hard Severe 4b   (1960-65)
Start at the lowest point of the buttress at a vegetated bay just right of a rowan. Climb the rightward-slanting gangway to a ledge and finish up the open groove above.

Southern Section
A compact block of rock 150 metres left of the Central Section. It is most easily located from above, where a waymarked path leads to the viewpoint at its top. This makes a junction with the forestry track south of the large turning circle. A steep and tricky descent can be made on the right (facing out) over a wall and down past an oak tree.

Twin Cracks   15 metres   Hard Very Severe   4c   (1960s)
Start at the front of the cliff at two slanting cracklines. Follow the cracks to a
ledge at 4 metres. From its right-hand end, climb the wall to the little
overhangs. Traverse right along a small ledge until a finish can be made
directly above.

On the left of the cliff are two grooves.

Oak Tree Jug   13 metres   Very Severe   4c   (1960-65)
The right-hand groove. Interesting now that the oak has gone. Finish up a
rib on the right.

The A5   12 metres   Severe   (1960s)
The left groove. Quite pleasant. Follow a crack and then trend right to
finish on the arête.

Cae Coch Quarry   Red Field Quarry   OS Ref. 776 649)
The quarry is in the Coed Gwydir. It lies immediately above the Roman Spa
visitor attraction on the B5106, two kilometres north of Trefriw village. The
routes face east and catch the morning sunshine.

The easiest approach, taking twenty minutes, is from where a Forestry
Commission track joins the road 200 metres further north (opposite the old
landfill site). Park here, and walk up the track. At a junction, turn left. On a
sharp bend immediately before a stream, the track cuts through the old
incline. Follow this to the top, go left across the stream, and follow the level
into the upper quarry. The level and the quarry floor are shrouded in small
trees. As the quarry opens, an extensive area of boulders is encountered.
These bear witness to the massive collapse of the 70s. Further over, the
remaining rock-face, largely hidden by the trees, still soars above the quarry
floor. The level eventually narrows before ending at a band of rock. Here
there is a notable raised lip of rock on the left edge. The routes on the Lower
Tier finish at the far end of this lip, where it meets the final rock band. This
much smaller, lower quarry can be reached by descending just before the
rock lip.

The Upper Tier consists of impressively long ribs and walls. The rock, however,
is extremely dangerous, loose both in detail and *en masse*. In addition, ledges
and cracks are heavily vegetated, with many damp areas covered in moss.
The ominous nature of the rock together with the oppressive vegetation,
makes it a sombre place to climb, one where sound judgement and good luck
will be required in equal measure.

The Lower Tier, in contrast, 'represents the ultimate in Conwy Valley granite
slab climbing' (N Dixon, 2001) with two remarkable climbs on micro
gratons following bolt-lines up an immaculate narrow slab.

In all, the place is very formidable, but with potential in excess for those with
a pioneering heart.

Henry Moore (T2) The Tubes
Climber: Nick Dixon Photo: Chris Naylor

Callum (E6 — first ascent) Cae Coch Quarry
Climber: Nick Dixon   Photo: Dave Wrennall

Upper Tier

During the summer of 1967 the following five routes were climbed. Described and credited in *Snowdon East* (1970), they have had few, if any, repeat ascents. Understandably, people were more cautious after the major collapse. The climbing is as dauntingly vegetated and the rock as hazardous as it was then. An ascent of any line should be an epic. Only an outline of each route is given here: it is left for a future guidebook to do them justice or consign them to oblivion. Descent is either by abseil from the tree at the top of *Simply Thread*, or over to the left to the small band of rock at the end of the quarry floor: a narrow rib running directly above the lower quarry requires great caution.

Gwydir Gully (Hard Severe 44 metres † 11.5.67) is a line of grass and trees above the huge scree fan on the left side of the cliff; a buttress to the left was soloed(!); both finished up a quartz wall right of an overhang, before stepping left for an earthy groove near the top.

Transect   67 metres   Very Severe †   (9.5.67)
From half-way up the scree, traverse rightwards along a gangway, passing an arête, to a ledge in the main scoop beyond. Step down right and go up the slab and over a bulge to a ledge. Take exposed rock on the right to an overlap, and climb a groove; walk 4½ metres left to a pine. Climb up across the quartz wall on the right, continue up a groove and over an overhang, and exit via blocks to right; then follow a rib to top.
Direct Start 21m. Very Severe † (1967). Reach the traverse of *Transect* from the toe of the buttress, passing through a small overhang.

Tendency   76 metres   Very Severe †   (20.5.67)
A groove 6 metres to the right. Climb up to a sloping ledge, trend left to trees, start up a rightward gangway, and go up to the *Transect* ledge. Step down right and cross the slab, follow a gangway into a depression, and move onto and up a rib. Continue to the top as for *Embargo*.

Embargo   67 metres   Very Severe †   (23.5.67)
A big corner leads to a large vegetated ledge. From the top, move left, climb a groove, move left again, and climb a slab. Climb a groove, traverse right under shattered bulges, and reach a rib of perched blocks. Continue to the top.

The Nave   75 metres   Hard Very Severe ††   (3.6.67)
Though this was previously regarded as the best route, its first pitch is now buried under the massive jumble of rock debris. The long, tree-filled top groove remains.

One new climb has recently been cleaned; perhaps regular traffic will keep it in condition.

★Simply Thread   40 metres   E2 5a   (9.2.98)
Start on the far left-hand side of the quarry, beyond the scree fan, at the
middle of the obvious wall. Sloping holds lead up to a few thin moves and
the first thread at 5 metres. Follow the line of threads straight up the
improving wall. Good tree belay and abseil point.

Lower Tier
Several routes were climbed in 1967 and documented in *Snowdon East*
(1970).

The Left Arête is not very worthwhile. Two routes climb the corner starting
behind the detached block below the bolted lines. **Slipway** (55 metres Hard
Very Severe 2 pegs for aid † 27.8.67) continues left onto and up the arête,
and moves left at an overhang to climb a wall and slab before going
rightwards to the terrace. **Gangway** (55 metres Very Severe 4 pegs for aid †
9.9.67) continues onto the slab, gains the rightward gangway, and finishes
up the broad arête. The line of **Wendaway** (43 metres Hard Severe †
27.8.67) has not been identified. It was described as the first obvious groove
at right-hand end, and was said to involve 2 metres of chain tied to a tree in
the 'garden'!

Bolted Routes
★★★Callum   40 metres   E6 6c   (18.10.97)
[Photo page 272b.] The left-hand line of bolts.

★★★Untrue   40 metres   E6 7a   (1994/1996)
The right-hand line of bolts.

Y Rhinogau

'We're not talking about discovering a few new lines or a few undeveloped crags here, but a whole new Peak District of gritstone outcrops in the most beautiful and quiet mountain environment imaginable.'
(Guidebook of Revelations, Chapter 1.)

Author's Note

This section on the Rhinogau serves the function of presenting the recently documented climbing here for the very first time to fellow climbers. Some may argue that it might have been completely acceptable for this wonderfully unspoilt and craggy wilderness to remain free of the promotional framework of a guidebook. On balance, however, I feel that once routes are customarily put to pen (and acquire a social identity), their whereabouts should be made reasonably accessible to all. Complementing this guidebook regime, there is a strong case for respecting the freedom of climbers to roam outside literary protocol, particularly of those climbers who have operated here in the Rhinogau and have felt no compunction or desire to record their activities. I apologise to any feeling aggrieved on being surprised to find one or two of their discoveries resurrected in this guidebook. It all seems so immaterial anyway, the 'who has done what', when considered against the broader value of these wild, open, tracts of deserted upland. It is an irony that, for a region so infused with ancient history and folklore (let alone the closeness of Tremadog), climbers should have so little history to offer save the very paradox of their abstinence from a beautiful area of hidden promise.

When reviewing the reasons for the area's neglect by climbers, it is hard to visualise – human nature being what it is – that this guidebook will prompt any sort of environmental effect upon the Rhinogau. While the extrinsics of casual and serious walking are increasingly noticeable across part of the range, it is improbable that climbing here could ever be as popular. First-time visitors will soon appreciate that technical ability in the Rhinogau is very much secondary to mountain-sense and a passion for all the hardships that the wild outdoors brings. In addition, I have endeavoured to respect the individual's right to self-discovery by trying not to be over-prescriptive (of the crag approaches especially) or over-zealous in the numbers and scale of the cliffs presented. Indeed there are countless uncharted lines, craglets and whole crags, to say little of a phenomenal bouldering potential, that will keep those in need of the 'wilderness experience' replete for an unforeseeable future to come.

Introduction

'In 1935 George Garrard and myself found a moderately difficult route by following the south ridge of Rhinog Fach from the screes above Llyn Hywl to the summit, and claimed for it the distinction of being the only rock climb

between Snowdon and Cadair Idris. Since then, however, the most popular climbing-ground in Wales has sprung up at Tremadog Rocks, ten miles South of Snowdon, and climbing of moderately difficult standard is considered to be beneath the notice of a genuine climber.'   Showell Styles

The Rhinogau form the range of mountains which run as a broad and craggy ridge from the Vale of Ffestiniog in the north to the Mawddach estuary in the south. They are an unspoilt, wild, and mysterious outlier of the Snowdonia National Park, little-known by the rock-climber but treasured by the wilderness-walker who beats a retreat from over-subscribed hills to the north.

For the climber, the first glimpse of the Rhinogau is normally from Tremadog, a mere fifteen kilometres from their northern limit. But this prospect gives away little about their climbing potential and nothing of their unique topography and geographical extent. Contrastingly, those who approach Snowdonia from due south, via the A496 Trawsfynydd road, will have a better picture, not only of the ridge (a classic adventure walk) and the singularity of its summits, but also of a number of the range's less secretive crags – if they look carefully. On the western side of the Rhinog threshold lies Cardigan Bay, which harbours some of the most beautiful dune-scapes in Wales, and the historic coastal province of Ardudwy concluded in the north by Edward I's mighty Harlech Castle.

Rhinog geology is completely unlike that of surrounding volcanic mountains, and a welcome contrast. For here is represented the thickest (2000 metres) succession of Cambrian sediments in Britain, which were folded north to south and then folded again west-south-west to east-north-east into one giant dome (or pericline) known as the Harlech Dome. Of this bulging pack of greywackes, grits, shales, and slates, it is the outcroppings of Rhinog and Barmouth Grits that favour climbers: coarse and rugged, or compact and quartzitic greywackes and grits, the properties and texture of which in places resemble very closely the much younger Millstone Grits of the Peak and Yorkshire.

The Harlech Dome, especially the shale sediments around its flank, is also the site of speculative mining for a variety of secondary metalliferous lodes and for manganese. The best-known of the mines is at Bont-Ddu to the east of Barmouth, which yielded gold since, at least, Roman times, and which offers the tourist a chance to pan for the real thing – at a price.

The range is a ridge of two personalities: thin acid and peaty soils of the craggy uplands of the north, where heather, bilberry and bracken conspire to hide, from even the most astute walker, the leg-scraping, ankle-twisting clefts between subterranean boulders; and the gentler rolling grasslands of the highest summits of the south, commanded by the bulk of y Llethr (756m). Lichens (and mosses) abound on many of the northerly-oriented crag-faces but these should be enjoyed as indigenous hosts to climbers, even though some may need to be brushed, albeit temporarily, from hand and footholds. Apart from the Crawcwellt coniferous plantation to the east and the enchanting sessile oak copses and woodland of the western valleys, tree life is minimal and dominated by the hardy rowan, the berries of which provide autumnal nourishment for a bird called the ring-ouzel. This bird in turn is hunted by kestrels, sparrowhawks, and other birds of prey, which may from time-to-time displace climbers from particular lines or crags.

The Rhinogau, especially Ardudwy, is a land of considerable historical interest. Scattered around the region are burial chambers and stone arches as at Bryn Cader Faner (north-west of Foel Penolau) and Llyn Prefed (on the ridge) as well as hill-top Iron Age forts like that of Craig y Dinas (en route to Craig Bodlyn). One enigmatic, yet well-trodden, feature that perplexes archaeologists is the so-called Roman Steps. These are the stone steps, some 500 in total, which tame the wild col and pass of Bwlch Tyddiad, and in medieval times clinched a crucial link in the Bala to Harlech trade route for woollen merchandise. Regardless of whether they were laid by the Romans (as strategic support to their gold-mining operations hereabouts – a theory now disfavoured) or by the minions of Edward I when Harlech Castle was built (1283-1290), climbers will be thankful for 'the Steps' while being conveyed into the craggy heartland in conveyor-belt comfort. Today, the Roman Steps offer the sole sacrifice of the Rhinogau to the tourist who is prepared and able to negotiate the treacherous ten kilometres of minor road between Llanbedr and Cwm Bychan. Notwithstanding the summer influx, Cwm Bychan is still one of the most gorgeous spots in North Wales.

One other striking man-made feature, but really a contemporary affliction, is the square 'white elephant' of Trawsfynydd nuclear power station, which is very evident from Craig y Groes and the north-facing crags of Rhinog Fawr. Built in the 60s and taking cooling waters from Llyn Trawsfynydd (flooded in the 60s as part of a hydroelectric scheme) the station provides a curious intrusion into an otherwise wild landscape, as well as an eerily-lit bedmate to those climbers who cast sleeping bags and weary bodies into the moorland to the east. On a wet day, a visit to the power station is one alternative to the pub; another is to the Maes Artro craft centre at Llanbedr (currently for sale), which is full of RAF memorabilia. Here, in particular, check out the sites of crashed World War Two aircraft in the surrounding mountains (Cadair Idris was a favourite), as well as the antics of some flash fighter-pilots – like taking a Spitfire beneath the Barmouth railway bridge and even living to tell the tale!

Layout and Crag Character
[Drawing page 296a.] The main crags are presented in a clockwise circle, starting in the north, and divided into five natural groupings:

Crags of the Northern Rhinog
This covers the part of the ridge between Cwm Bychan and Llyn Trawsfynydd and includes the crags from Craig y Gwynt to Clip. Almost all of these cliffs face south or west and have reasonable all-year-round climbing prospects.

Crags North of the Roman Steps
This rugged mass is classic Rhinog country; most of the crags are tucked away and north-west facing and are best reserved for the summer months.

Crags of Rhinog Fawr
Easily accessible yet well-elevated on the precipitous northern flank of
Rhinog Fawr, many of the crags here face north or east (and can stream with
water outside summer-time).

Crags of the Southern Rhinog
This covers the big mountain crags of Rhinog Fach and Craig Bodlyn, both
providing good winter sport potential.

Crags of the Western Valleys
A bountiful collection of south or west-facing crags situated in Cwmnantcol
and Cwm Artro ; they are quick-drying, easily accessible cliffs that can be
climbed on all year round.

A final section consists of a peripheral circle of outlying crags.

Notes on individual crag character and conditions that can be expected are
incorporated into the introductions to each crag. All of the climbs are wholly
traditional and require the use of leader-placed protection. As is usual on
gritstone, camming devices are of considerable use. In-situ equipment has
been very strictly rationed: fixed pegs and slings are utilized only as a very
last resort; in-situ belays currently have no place here.

Many routes were first climbed after some prior cleaning on abseil. It is not
unreasonable to assume that four or five years of solitaire may require
repeat ascensionists to administer a light brush-up here and there, com-
mensurate with the unspoilt character of the mountains. Additionally, leaders
may find a nut-tool invaluable in unclogging cracks on some of the more
lichenous crags. Recent developments have yielded a host of micro-routes of
around 6 to 8 metres that offer extended solo-bouldering experience akin to
Peak gritstone. Wilderness soloists will find themselves in paradise.

Some Social Considerations
Terrain This is the roughest country, craggy and complex. Of the footpaths
that do exist, most are animal tracks that, while offering reliable if convoluted
connections between crags, rarely lead the mist-bound explorer back to
civilization. Ownership of a 1:25,000 OS map is essential – if you desire a
fighting chance of locating the crags. Slipping a compass into the sack might
not be a senseless precaution either. Stout walking-boots are also a necessity,
especially for those unexpected trips into the fissures of never-heather land.

Car-Parking Most designated car-parks in the western valleys are pay
car-parks, privately owned and controlled by the local farmers and landowners. Please use the honesty boxes or other arrangements provided. At
other locations park sensibly off the road and away from passing-places.

Camping One civilized strategy might be to camp at the privately-run,
unofficial camp site (which is also the car-park) in Cwm Bychan, from which
many of the crags can be reached on foot. There is also a very nice, but
sometimes busy site on the banks of the Afon Cwmnantcol at OS Ref 608

271. An even better tactic, if you're bringing the family on a summer's holiday, is to book a caravan in one of the many sites along the coast between Barmouth and Dyffryn; take the day with the kids on the beach, then belt up the mountains in the evening when most of the crags will be in the sun. Dossing by the car is a very pragmatic solution on the moorlands to the east, and very much in keeping with the complete Earth-experience. There are superb wild camping spots at Llyn Morwynion and Llyn Du, but these are popular with non-climbers, can get to look a little bit trashed, and consequently best left alone.

Walls Climbers will be gob-smacked by the fantastic lineage of stone walls that enlace the mountainside, obviously at the cost of much hard graft. From time to time, these may need to be crossed. Consider it a technical challenge not to displace any stones, but an obligation to replace any that *are* dislodged. A substantial repair programme, in conjuction with the erection of deer-fencing, is currently being undertaken by the National Park Authority, and gaps that previously existed may now be closed.

Environmental Balance The certainty is that no matter how hard you try, you are going to leave some trace of your visit. One way you can repay your debt, and compensate for these effects is – on each occasion – to bring out with you one or two pieces of other people's rubbish (that now seems a permanent accompaniment to the Roman Steps trade route). Gestures like these will help to sustain climbing in our generation – and perhaps beyond.

General Approaches

1 From the west to Cwm Bychan. Cwm Bychan is the logical starting point for the crags of Clip and some of the crags in the vicinity of the Roman Steps. It is guarded, however, by a tortuous single-track road, which forever challenges the skills of the 'Sunday drivers' and, moreover, the patience of those trapped behind them. When travelling from the north on the A496 Harlech to Barmouth road, turn left at Llanbedr, just before the bridge over the Afon Artro. Take this road for one and a half kilometres to a minor left turn signposted Cwm Bychan (if going to Cwm Nantcol, continue over the bridge and take the first left). Follow the minor road for eight kilometres, along the enchanting banks of the Afon Artro and Llyn Cwm Bychan until forced into the car-park in Cwm Bychan – your honesty will exact the required fee (£2.00 in 2000).

2 From the east to the Crawcwellt forest. This gives free and easy access to the spread of crags around the Roman Steps and Rhinog Fawr, and is by far the best option for climbers motoring up from the south. From Dolgellau take the A470 and, when one kilometre short of Branaber, take an inconspicuous left turn into a minor road. Follow this road past a gate, and continue for three kilometres to a second gate at the eastern edge of the plantation. Park in a restricted lay-by area on the western side of the gate. Do **not** take your car any further into the forest.

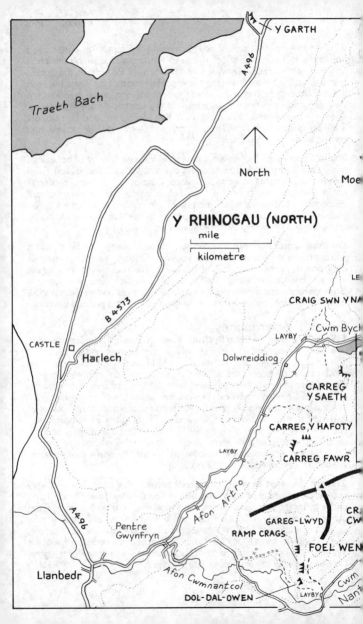

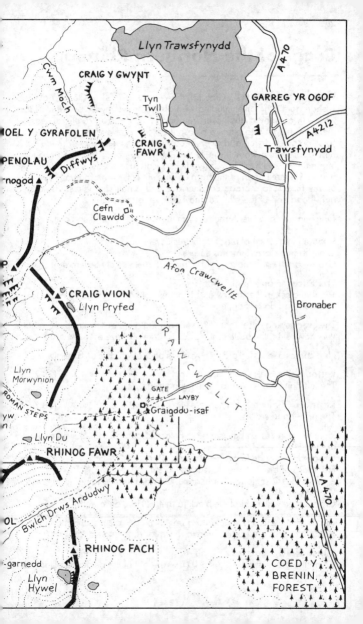

Crags of the Northern Rhinog

Craig y Gwynt   Crag (of) the Wind   OS Ref 669 365
A short northern outlier situated west of Llyn Trawsfynydd, but which faces
west with a sunny outlook over Tremadog Bay. The crag rarely exceeds 10
metres in height and offers a pleasant collection of mid-grade climbs and
solos on quick-drying and clean pebbly gritstone, well away from it all. It is
best approached from the east, via the minor road, the first right turn,
immediately south of Trawsfynydd. Park carefully on the roadside a few
hundred metres north of the farm at Tyn Twll. Follow the footpath due west
up the hillside to a broad col after one and a half kilometres. The upper,
right-hand end of the crag can now be seen on the right.

One hundred and twenty metres from the lower, left (north) end of the crag is
a detached block:
Groove in left arête of block (5 metres Severe 4a).
Crack in front face (5 metres Severe).
Groove and roof 6 metres right of block (5 metres Very Severe 5a).

The Slice   6 metres   E1 5b †   (28.7.99)
The thin crack in the sheer wall 11 metres right of the block. Protectable –
if the landing doesn't appeal.

The overlapping nose right of *The Slice*, using a big quartz knob is 6 metres
Very Severe 4c; the arête of the pillar is 6 metres Severe 4a.

Next comes a recessed grassy bay, at the back of which is an attractive wall.

Leftout   7 metres   Very Severe 4c †   (28.7.99)
The left-hand cracks with a steepening finish.

Righton   7 metres   Very Severe 4c †   (28.7.99)
The right-hand cracks.

Right of the recessed bay is a huge detached quartzitic block with a jagged
right arête.
Groove in left arête (6 metres Difficult).
Front face of block (6 metres Hard Severe 4b).
A micro-classic up jagged right arête. But watch that landing! (6 metres
Very Severe 4b).
Crack in the wall right of the block (6 metres Hard Severe 4b).

To the right the crag rears up to a mighty 8 or 9 metres and the landings
become even more hostile: time to reach for rope and partner!

Sunstroked   8 metres   E2 5b †   (28.7.99)
Climb the green-streaked arête 10 metres right of the detached pillar to a
strenuous exit.

Exothermia 8 metres   E1 5b †   (28.7.99)
The cracks in the face to the right with long reaches between comforting jugs.

Lichen Has Feelings Too 7 metres   Very Severe 5a †   (28.7.99)
The left-facing corner; not unpleasantly lichenous.

☆**Sun Index Seven** 8 metres   E3 5c †   (28.7.99)
The fine arête right of the corner; hard to start. Pretty much a solo (above
an atrocious landing).

Sunscreen? 7 metres   Very Severe 5a †   (28.7.99)
The narrow white corner from a ledge which is hard to get on.

UV for Free 7 metres   Hard Very Severe 5a †   (28.7.99)
Take the line of weakness 4 metres right of the arête to an interesting finish.

Right again is a slightly higher face with three heather-free lines.

Don't Even Think of It 9 metres   Hard Very Severe 4c †   (28.7.99)
Follow blind cracks in the wall left of the central heather-filled groove to the
top.

Rumbling Flake 9 metres   Very Severe 4b †   (28.7.99)
Starting a metre right of the heather-filled groove, saunter up to the left side
of the large flake. Gain the ledge on top of the flake, and finish awkwardly.

Don't Fall! 9 metres   Severe †   (28.7.99)
Climb a crack in the right-hand side of the face to a hollow jug just
beneath the top. Finish direct. Poor protection.

Twenty-five metres to the right, just beyond a little, undercut buttress, is a
square white-pebble wall.

Stone Hail 9 metres   Hard Very Severe 5a †   (28.7.99)
Take the enjoyable, right-hand of two cracks in the wall to a heather ledge;
then finish easily.

Tour de Gwynt 12 metres   Hard Very Severe 4c †   (28.7.99)
The longest route on the cliff! Start 7 metres right of the white-pebble wall.
Move up to obvious, flat hand-ledges, and swing right along these onto an
arête. Go up the arête, and its continuation on the right, to the top.

To the right is an 8-metre recessed wall with two fairly dull routes (the left
arête is Hard Severe 4b, and a central line, Severe). Immediately to the right,
however, is a left-facing corner set in an arête.

On-Sight Delight 9 metres   Very Severe 4c †   (28.7.99)
Gain the corner in the arête from the right. Make an awkward move into
the corner, and exit up a crack.

Moel y Gyrafolen   Hill (of) the Rowan Tree   OS Ref 672 353

The northern-most summit of the ridge harbours many craglets, only two of which support any routes.

Craig Fawr   Big Crag

A modest bank of north-east facing slabs situated a mere 15-minute walk from the road. The rock is beautiful purple grit. Park carefully on the roadside a few hundred metres north of the farm Tyn Twll. Follow the footpath due west up the hillside for one kilometre to the northern end of a small valley; the slabs are clearly visible on the left.

Ness's Back   15 metres   Very Severe 5a †   (25.7.99)
An enjoyable romp up the left side of the main slab. Start behind a large flake embedded in the terrace. A problem move on layaways gains better holds and a spike runner on top of the huge flake. Step up to the right onto the slab proper and take thin cracks to a heather ledge and good belays 3 metres higher.

☆**Purple Reigns**   13 metres   Very Severe 4c †   (25.7.99)
A fine clean slab climb well worth incorporating into a good day's walk. From the higher, and right-hand, of two perched flakes climb direct up the slab to parallel vertical slots in a bulge. Balance up to a good hold and scramble to the belay.

A further line just to the right would clean up nicely at a similar grade.

Rollercoaster   10 metres   E2 6a †   (25.7.99)
An exciting solo. Right of the main slab is a smooth convex section high up. Scramble rightwards past a jammed block to the higher of two heather ledges (a comfortable landing-site!). Mantel onto a finger-ledge; then make thin moves slightly left and up to easier ground.

Bwlch Diffwys   Precipice Col

The col between Moel y Gyrafolen and Diffwys contains a very pleasant, small quartzite crag on its east side. The crag faces south-west and is very quick-drying. (Steeper crags on the west side have less appeal, but hold a few impressive lines.)

At the left-hand end of the crag a wall runs up to fuse with a buttress characterized by an undercut nose.

Pancake Wall   6 metres   Very Severe 5a †   (25.7.99)
Climb the face left of the wall using a tasty pancake hold in its centre.

Humpty Dumpty's Revenge   7 metres   E3 6a †   (25.7.99)
Step left off the wall and make precarious and fingery moves up and right onto the nose. Finish up a tiny groove. A low runner protects: mind that drystone wall!

☆**Mummy's Nose**   7 metres   E1 5b †   (25.7.99)
Step rightwards off the wall, and pull around the right-hand side of the nose on a superb quartzy pocket. An easier arête leads to the top. Good landing.

The next three routes take the buttress right of the wall.

Cross Rock   7 metres   Severe 4a †   (25.7.99)
Climb the little corner and roof at the left end of the buttress.

Squashed Berry   8 metres   Difficult †   (25.7.99)
Climb the cracks left of centre and exit on a huge flake hold.

☆**Dashboard**   8 metres   E2 6a †   (25.7.99)
Reach a finger-crack above a roof and spring for a jug. Top out more easily.

Sloped Off   5 metres   E1 6b †   (25.7.99)
The front of the next block on slopers.

Y Foel Penolau   Last Hill Top   OS Ref 662 348

[Diagram page 296b,c.] Splendidly mounted on the crest of the Rhinog ridge above Llyn Trawsfynydd, this crag distinctively encircles y Foel Penolau (614m) like the ramparts of an ancient hilltop fort. Walkers have been passing the crag since walking the ridge began but, curiously, despite Harold Drasdo's plug in *The Big Walks* (and Tremadog being in the line of sight), no recorded climbs appeared here before 1997. Can walking and climbing be so dissociated? Maybe not; climbers now persuaded enough to don their walking boots will home in on the section overlooking the col between y Foel Penolau and its parent to the south, Moel Ysgyfarngol (623m). Here they will discover some superb face climbing on excellent, clean, and quick-drying Rhinog Grit, all in a refreshingly sunny location. In short, this is one of the best crags in the Rhinogau. All those that visit will be bound to keep it that way.

The easiest means of access is from the east, via a good track starting immediately east of the farm of Cefn Clawdd, two kilometres south-east of y Foel Penolau. The track is probably not a right-of-way, so make sure cars are parked sensibly (or risk being steamrollered by a farm tractor). Longer approaches are possible from the north-east and the north-west.

The first two climbs embark from a broad platform at the left-hand end of the main crag.

☆**Purrfection**   7 metres   E1 5a †   (13.4.97)
[Photo page 288a.] The perfect little grit arête forming the left edge of the main crag (just right of an earlier corner). Bad landing, so stay cool at the top.

Small Wonder   9 metres   Very Severe 4b   (13.4.97)
Climb the obvious right-facing layback crack above the step-down in the platform.

Grach   12 metres   E1 5a   (13.4.97)
Start from the right-hand end of the platform. Bear diagonally rightwards on wobbly holds to a thin crack in the face. Climb direct (difficult gear) to the small roof, and spring over on comforting holds to the top.

★On Secret Sand   15 metres   E3 6a   (13.4.97)
A fine route up one of the crag's most prominent lines: the slim rightward-facing groove in its left-hand side. Start on a square block beneath the groove. Difficult moves gain an undercut (good wire-placement) just below. Make a very long stretch for a horizontal break and so gain and follow the easier groove to the capping roof. Swing rightwards around this to the top.

☆Silence Is Golden   15 metres   E5 6a †   (13.4.97)
The blank face right of *On Secret Sand*. Reliable but spaced protection with reasonable flight potential from the crux. Gain a good foothold at 4 metres (peg runner above). Reach a thin break and, from a positive finger-edge on the left, make some long moves in line with a hairline crack to a narrow finger-ledge beneath the roof. Move up and left and pursue a ladder of quartz nubbins to the top.

★All This and Heaven Too   15 metres   E3 5c   (13.4.97)
Not quite a classic, but the line and holds have got that sort of feel. Start on an enormous block beneath an intermittent crack. Deploy a 'Harrison's move' to get fixed upon a narrow ledge. Pass a misleading angular slot above to reach a thin break. Now climb the crack using jugs on the right to ledges and an easier final wall.

The wall now gets ledgy until, above an ominous trench in the boulders – 'the pit', it steepens again and offers two (sort-of) cracklines.

☆Politician's Wall   15 metres   E4 6b †   (13.4.97)
Deceptive but still satisfying. Start from the pit. Climb over ledges left of the pit and bear right to the foot of the left-hand, disjointed crack. Move up to a hard-to-leave pocket under a narrow overhang (bomber wires). Now make a tricky move to gain the upper part of the thin crack and exit up this smugly.

☆Misunderstood   15 metres   E1 5b †   (13.4.97)
Harder than it first appears and high in the grade. From the pit, scramble to the right-hand crack. Climb the crack to a projecting jug on the right. Proceed strenuously direct and sidle left to top out.

The remaining routes cluster onto the overhanging buttress 15 metres further right. Lovers of Stanage south-end may feel at peace here.

☆Do the Monkey   13 metres   E2 5c †   (13.4.97)
The undercut left-hand arête. Climb easily to the foot of the corner left of the arête. Arrange gear and swing out right to the widest part of the roof (peg runner). Continue right – with redundant feet – to some foot-ledges;

then climb easily up the right-hand side of the arête to the top. It is possible (6a), but less fun, to pull straight up the arête.

★Stanager's Solace   13 metres   E1 5a   (13.4.97)
The central weakness of the buttress; a gift at the grade and wholly spectacular. Climb diagonally right from the start of *Do the Monkey* to a good break under the roof. Ape out right onto the pedestal and follow sinking holds left of the crack to easier climbing above the roofs.

Subterranean Leg Injector   15 metres   E2 5b †   (13.4.97)
Ascend the dusty scoop up the right-hand side of the pedestal to the roof-line. Cast aside custom and follow the deep break above the catastrophically large detached block, using the jug rail over the roof to regain a vertical posture via a small right-facing corner 3 metres to the right. Totally bizarre! Finish traditionally.

☆In Whose Footsteps?   12 metres   Hard Very Severe 4c †   (13.4.97)
The right-hand arête of the overhanging block: much less taxing than it looks. From the foot of the corner, tread diagonally leftwards above free space to the arête. Climb the arête to the top.

☆Greywacke Race   10 metres   E3 6a †   (13.4.97)
An enigmatic flutter with the short arête right of the large corner. Friend 2½ essential. Go up fairly easily to a hanging jug on the arête, but don't assume success until you've bellied out on the platform above.

The remainder of the crags of y Foel Penolau are fairly broken, but there are two climbs on the north-west face (facing Tremadog; OS Ref 662 349). Half-way along the crag is a recess with a jagged arête at its back. The two solos here have good landings initially; but make sure you don't keep on going.

Dehydration   8 metres   E3 6a †   (28.7.99)
Starting a metre left of the arête, crank up to sloping holds in a pink scoop. Continue more easily and exit right onto the top of the arête.

Dry Throat of Fear   8 metres   E3 6a †   (28.7.99)
Make powerful moves up the very edge of the arête, trying hard not to barn-door into oblivion.

Clip   Steep Hill

When viewed from Cwm Bychan, Clip appears a shapely little mountain. Around the hill, rock outcrops plentifully, but perhaps the best cluster of tiers occupies the broad southern flank which stretches down towards the cwm. Accessible, well-drained, and sunny, the upper tiers in particular offer an affable and panoramic venue suitable for clear winter days. Approach the crags by intercepting the Trawsfynydd path from the Cwm Bychan (pay) car-park and following this for about a kilometre to a point just short of the second transverse stone wall. Here, Level One is the crag about 100 metres from the path (not to be confused with the two lesser crags lower down left),

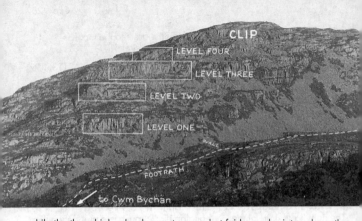

while the three higher levels are staggered at fairly regular intervals on the hillside above and slightly to the right. Those with limited time will head straight for the two upper tiers.

Level One   OS Ref 653 324
A 15-metre crag which might distract the connoisseur for a while. The rock is less than the best Rhinog Grit, however.

Three Front Teeth 12 metres Very Severe 5a †   (9.3.97)
From a triple-toothed, body-scything flake, climb a short angular groove and cracks in the slab at the left-hand end of the crag.

Bychan Slab 15 metres E2 5c †   (9.3.97)
Climb cracks in the centre of the slab left of the prominent corner to finish by swinging right into a tiny projecting corner. Self-discipline is required to stay on line.

Saeson 15 metres E1 5b †   (9.3.97)
Significantly more troublesome than it looks. Ascend the prominent left-facing corner with disappointing protection.

Y Garn 15 metres E4 6a †   (9.3.97)
A sustained and exciting route up the right arête of the corner. Climb the right-hand side of the arête, using the groove on the right, and proceed carelessly direct on resounding flakes to an exit groove. Can be safeguarded with care.

Sargeant Slab 12 metres Severe †   (9.3.97)
Climb cracks in the isolated slab on the broad rib towards the right-hand side of the crag.

Purrfection (E1 ~ first ascent) Y Foel Penolau
Climber: Martin Crocker   Photo: Don Sargeant

Min y Aur (E3 ~ first ascent) Clip
Climber: Martin Crocker   Photo: Don Sargeant

Clip Level Three

		2 Thunderclip Newman	E1	5 Clip Tears	E5
		3 Talking Doughnuts	E3	6 Box'd Ears	HVS
1 Eclipse	E2	4 Min y Aur	E3	7 Gender Crisis	E3

Level Two

OS Ref 652 325

Of minimal interest – even if ticking the mountain.

Uchaf 12 metres Very Severe 4c †   (8.3.97)
A scruffy crack leads to a deeper crack in the left-hand side of the crag.

Isaf 8 metres Hard Very Severe 5b †   (8.3.97)
Towards the right-hand side of the crag is a short sharp arête. Climb the
corner to its left; the steep start is thought-provoking.

Byr 10 metres E3 5b †   (8.3.97)
A nasty landing – if taken short. Confront the sharp arête starting on the
left and finishing on the right. Dubious gear.

Level Three

OS Ref 653 326

The finest crag on Clip, with sound lines on glorious, clean, white grit.

Zero Gravity 16 metres Severe †   (1.5.2000)
Climb a slabby rib left of a short tower near the left-hand edge of the crag.

Shadow People 16 metres E2 5c †   (1.5.2000)
Climb a thin crack in the steep wall right of a capped corner to a small
overlap. Solid undercuts lead up and left into a niche. Curious moves
enable a final gap to be reached.

★Eclipse 18 metres E2 5c   (8.3.97)
Near the left-hand end of the main crag is a right-facing corner; this fine
climb takes the rib to its left. Start up the right-hand side of the rib; then

swing left and up onto a small flat ledge. Go up past a break to a bulge and make a balancy mantel on the left. Trend right to finish easily up the rib.

Thunderclip Newman   18 metres   E1 5b   (8.3.97)
Starting as for *Eclipse*, climb direct to the foot of the right-facing corner and pull leftwards over the capping bulge to exit.

Talking Doughnuts   18 metres   E3 5c †   (8.3.97)
A technical and entertaining eliminate. Start 2 metres right of the left-hand rib. Take a thin groove onto a steep face, and bear right onto the left-hand edge of a niche. Pull up over a bulge to a break and then follow the very thin crack in the headwall right of the corner to the top.

★★**Min y Aur**   18 metres   E3 6a   (8.3.97)
[Photo page 288b.] The plum of the crag, which climbs the central rib on splendid rock. Start at an incipient crack with a minor flake pointing the way. Move up to good handholds and gain the niche above using the crack on the left. Finger-traverse right beneath the roof before reaching over to the lowest of a series of finger-jugs on the rib. Crank up to a short crack at the top.

☆**Clip Tears**   18 metres   E5 6b †   (8.3.97)
Right again is a distinctive overhanging scoop-line which offers a test of both skill and nerve. Stand up on a tall flake and improvise up the scoop past a (grip-clip) peg runner to grasp a break. Pull up a thin crack and follow an easier groove to the top.

Box'd Ears   18 metres   Hard Very Severe 5b †   (9.3.97)
In the right-hand side of the main crag is a box-shaped recess at 6 metres. Climb past a small shelf at 3 metres and step left into the recess. Exit from the recess and move left into the finishing-groove.

Gender Crisis   18 metres   E3 5c †   (9.3.97)
The rounded rib which forms the right-hand end of the main crag. Strenuously, climb cracks and a thin groove passing an obvious vertical slot and a wobbly phallus.

Level Four   OS Ref 653 327
Fashioned in prime grit, coarse and white, this modest crag gives three good crack climbs for the explorer.

Vicious Cycles   9 metres   Hard Very Severe 5c †   (8.3.97)
Gain the top of a big block via a wide crack, and then undercut twin cracks above with no easy options.

Satellite   9 metres   Hard Very Severe 5b †   (8.3.97)
Climb the centre of the blank lower wall and exit up the easier middle crack.

It Hertz   9 metres   Hard Very Severe 5a †   (8.3.97)
Follow the right-hand crack, which leads to a cruel direct finish.

Level Four West   OS Ref 652 328
On the western side of Clip is a collection of short steep buttresses just north of a boulder-strewn gully leading down to a wall that runs east to west. The lower has a large triangular overhang; the upper is broader and houses the following:

Fading into the Sun   6 metres   Very Severe 4b †   (1.5.2000)
The neat layback crack in the left-hand wall.

Twilight People   7 metres   Hard Very Severe 5a †   (1.5.2000)
Climb the overhanging corner and crack, avoiding the wedged flake by using a crack on the left.

Tribal Eclipse   7 metres   Hard Very Severe 5b †   (1.5.2000)
Climb the steep wall right of the corner to a rounded finish.

Craig Swn y Nant   Sound-(of)-the-Stream Rock OS Ref 652/3 323
Below the public footpath running up the south-eastern slope of Clip is a boulder-strewn stream bed. These are the steep buttresses on the left (north-west) of the stream. Approach as for the Clip crags and, after a kilometre, at the level of some old enclosures, break out and contour to the right. The first buttress is 200 metres from the Clip path and has a distinctive roof at just under half height. Both face south-east.

First Buttress
The Finite Pleasure of Swn   10 metres   E4 6a †   (22.6.2001)
The left-hand arête. How can a route that looks E1 be so much harder? Move up into a short groove in the arête – bold. Blast up the arête using opposing layaways, and top-out with a step left.

☆**Cambyah**   10 metres   E4 6a †   (22.6.2001)
Take a short corner in the centre of the buttress to an oppressed position under the mighty roof. Place a large cam in the break above, and span around the lip to reasonable holds. Tall people will now suffer as they attempt to heave their disjointed torsos over the roof. An easy wall awaits those who have managed this feat.

S 'n M is Better than F 'n M   10 metres   Very Severe 4c † (22.6.2001)
Climb the right-facing corner past awkward moves half-way up.

Spotterless Spatter   5 metres   E3 6b †   (22.6.2001)
What would be a convivial boulder-problem above a grassy platform is in reality a climb with serious impact value. Boulder up the right-hand side of the short arête on the right with a bit of the old barn-door at the top.

Main Buttress

Four hundred metres further right is a larger crag, the focal point of which is an arête which divides two walls. Beneath, a stream gurgles merrily under a field of boulders.

The first three climbs start from a raised heather ledge left of the arête.

☆Animals in Suspenders   10 metres   E4 5c †   (22.6.2001)
Beautiful grit. Step off a slightly higher ledge and climb straight up the slab immediately right of a white streak right of a corner. A small undercut 3 metres up shows the line. Unprotected.

Suspended Animation   12 metres   E2 5b   (12.9.99)
Take a direct line up the face 2 metres left of the dominating arête to the left-hand end of a scoop (medium cam placement). Fingery climbing diagonally leftwards leads to the top.

★Animated Suspension   15 metres   E2 5c   (12.9.99/22.6.2001)
Step right and follow good, spaced holds on the arête to the right-hand side of a scoop at three-quarters height. Sidle rightwards to pull out on heather or, much better, take the overhanging crack on the left to finish with difficulty at a square-cut recess at the top.

The Leading Wren   15 metres   E1 5b †   (12.9.99)
This takes a thin line up the wall beneath an obvious pinnacle on the skyline; a bold outing. Climb up the right edge of a large flake and onto a small ledge. Good incut holds in the wall above allow a final V-groove near the top to be reached. Mantelshelf to finish below the pinnacle.

Slick Slidin' Away   8 metres   Very Severe 4b †   (12.9.99)
Solo up the centre of the slabby face right of the steep gully on the right.

Further right past a short leaning face (with potential) is an undercut pillar.

Respect the Spine   12 metres   E1 5c †   (22.6.2001)
Swing right and hang some finger-flakes above the lip of the roof. Power around onto a ledge. Continue up the arête on good holds and exit right. Spotters are softer than the boulders.

A detached tower to the right conceals a delightful south-facing slab. The short rib to its left is a bold 5b boulder-problem, while the slab is Difficult, and the crack and arête on the right, Hard Very Severe 5a (all 22.6.2001).

Craig Wion   *Wion's Rock*

Approach to the crags here is equally possible from east or west via the Cwm Bychan to Trawsfynydd path that runs over the col south of Clip (see page 287). From the col, pick up the main ridge-top path and follow this southwards past Llyn Pryfed to the summit of Craig Wion (566m). A leaning west-facing buttress 12 metres high, the Central Edge, is located 60 metres west of the summit cairn. This gives the steepest and best routes whilst some easier fare is to be found on the Southern Edge 30 metres to the right. The crags are not the best place to be in poor weather, though they do dry quickly. The rock is lichen-free, and solid. The landscape is magnificent.

Northern Edge
OS Ref 661 321

This is a collection of jumbled blocks above extensive scree. Fifty metres from its southern end is a pillar with a small holly tree on a ledge to its right.

Light at the Edge of the World   12 metres   Very Severe   4b † (23.6.2001)
A stand-alone tower near the northern end, right of the final dark, blocky leaning wall.

Tower of Trundle   17 metres   E2 5c †   (23.6.2001)
The continuous line of stacks and blocks left of the pillar leads to a brilliant fingery finish up a culminating pillar.

G   15 metres   E1 5b †   (23.6.2001)
Stagger up the pillars by the holly tree to the white wall. A spindly mantel up the wall via a thin crack on its left gets you to a good finish. Elegant.

Northern Summit   (563m)
OS Ref 664 332

There is a square wall on its southern side just to the east of a stone wall. It is easily visible from the main (southern) summit and from the Central Edge.

★Azura   6 metres   E2 5c   (4.9.2000)
A gem in an open setting right on the Rhinog ridge-line. Climb the square wall in line with a thin crack in its centre. Lovely climbing on positive edges (but pad the landing).

The groove and arête just left have both been soloed at Difficult and Very Difficult respectively.

Central Edge
OS Ref 664 319

★Jigglypuff   6 metres   E3 5c   (4.9.2000)
At the left-hand end of the buttress is a compact, leaning wall. Move up and right to good fingerholds. Swing left and pull up steeply onto a flat ledge. A poor, and hard-to-spot, microwire offers dubious protection, but the route is more enjoyable to solo. Just don't fall into the boulders.

★Burning Time   10 metres   E1 5b   (18.8.2000)
Next right is a short-lived corner formed by a flake. Climb this to reach the roof and some good gear. Steep climbing on spaced jugs above provides a positive finish.

Squirtle Squad   10 metres   E2 5b   (18.8.2000)
Good holds just to the left of a crack on the right gain a break beneath the roof. Power through the roof showing respect for the holds.

Distant Dulcet Tones of Doctor Numb Thumb
                                    10 metres   E4 6a †   (23.6.2001)
Stretch for a jug above an overhang, and make a hard sequence to get
onto it. Continue briskly to the break, and swing right to finish up either of
the next two routes. No gear; bad landing; don't fall.

★A Pitch in Time   10 metres   E2 6a   (18.8.2000)
The well-protected and prominent crack. Strenuous laybacking past a
good slot gains a small spike in the crack. Make a hard move to the break
and finish more easily over the overhang to the top.

Gotta Catch 'em All   10 metres   E3 6a   (4.9.2000)
Start below a short corner right of the prominent crack. Climb direct and
then make a hard crank up to the left (invisible small wire placement) to a
layaway. Climb the seam to a ledge and take the easy corner above.

Mewtwo Strikes Back   10 metres   E3 5c   (18.8.2000)
Start as for *Gotta Catch 'em All*. Climb the corner to side-pulls on the right
(wire placement on *Gotta…*). Complex footwork and a rattling flake help
gain a ledge. Finish steeply up the short leaning wall above.

Team Rocket Blasts Off   10 metres   Severe †   (4.9.2000)
To the right is a short groove capped by an overlap. Take the arête of the
corner to the roof; then finish up the wide crack.

Giovanni Is a Cad   10 metres   Very Difficult †   (18.8.2000)
The corner on the extreme right is followed to the roof, where a short
traverse right gains a finishing-crack.

Southern Edge
Kickus Climb   10 metres   Very Difficult †   (20.8.2000)
The blunt nose at the left-hand edge of the wall is ledgy and blocky and
reserves its crux for the last move.

Splat Race   10 metres   Hard Very Severe 5a †   (20.8.2000)
The wall is climbed on good holds to the sloping ledge up and right.
Continue direct through the bulge above and watch the big block to the
left wobble.

Bone Daddy   10 metres   Hard Very Severe 5b †   (23.6.2001)
A red crack leads to a recess before a direct finish up the short wall above.

Between a step up and a green wall below the roof is a good-looking wall.

Avoiding the Issue   12 metres   Hard Severe †   (23.6.2001)
The obvious roof in the centre of the wall has a corner crack forming its left
edge. Grumble up to the block below the roof before exiting up the crack.
Variation E1 5c. From the block below the roof pull through directly using
a thin crack high and left. Small cams help.

Does My Thumb Look Big in This?   10 metres   E1 5b   (20.8.2000)
The sheer wall next right starts easily enough but blanks out above the thin horizontal break. Take a direct line all the way. Alternatively (HVS), follow the thin break leftwards to the edge of the wall.

Diamox Dreams   10 metres   Severe †   (20.8.2000)
Climb the left-facing corner on plentiful holds.

Fenrir   8 metres   Very Severe 4b   (20.8.2000)
This direct line up the wall at the right-hand end, although well featured, has little in the way of gear.

Loki Walls

Sixty metres downhill and west of upper Craig Wion is a shallow rift that follows the contours of the hill. At its northern end is a small tower.

This Is the End   6 metres   E1 5c †   (23.6.2001)
The left-hand arête of the tower.

Looking for Loki   6 metres   E1 5c †   (23.6.2001)
Finger-edges in the centre of the south face with a long crank for the top.

In the centre of the backside of the rift is a fine rectangular wall of wonderful, clean grit.

★**Loki**   6 metres   E3 5c   (20.8.2000)
A big layaway move just left of centre to a jug. A twin-level landing: miss the higher one at your peril.

☆**Joking**   7 metres   E6 6b †   (23.6.2001)
A remote place for a catastrophe. An even bigger layaway move needing full-on power, just right of centre. No ledge this time; the fall is into boulders.

The next three routes are found by following the *Loki* rift southwards to its end and then continuing, slightly downwards, for 50 metres to a prominent nose. Beyond this is a leaning wall (OS Ref 663 318).

☆**Lock, Stock and One Smoking Bollock**   12 metres   E3 5c † (20.8.2000)
Just right of the (unclimbed) left-hand arête is a roof; pass this on the right to gain a crack above. Pull on a good spike high in the crack to finish more easily.

☆**Wallit and Grimace**   12 metres   E2 5c †   (29.8.2000)
Start 2 metres right of *Lock, Stock and One Smoking Bollock* with a hard sequence to the good thin horizontal break. Follow ledges above to a groove and pull out right at the top. Very steep.

Fifty metres to the right, on the same level, is another steep but dirtier wall. At its right-hand end is a V-groove. The left edge of the groove forms a clean, white tower.

What Goes Down Must Come Up   20 metres   E1 5b †   (29.8.2000)
Take the centre of the tower a bit boldly to the short roof. Step right to
finish up a compact slab.

The *Loki* rift described above provides a modest landmark for finding the
next routes, which are described from **right to left**. From its southern exit go
downhill to the next level. There is a distinctive short, leaning arête on the
right as you go downhill; this is the:

Instankia Tower   8 metres   Hard Very Severe 5b †   (29.8.2000)
Pleasant, steep edge-climbing on the arête.

Fifty metres northwards at this level are some slabs above and beyond a
huge boulder.

Kurst of the Deep   10 metres   Very Severe 4b †   (29.8.2000)
The right-hand edge of the slab.

White Russian   8 metres   Severe †   (29.8.2000)
Five metres left of the lowest point of the slabs, take the seam and crack up
the centre of the slabs.

Further leftwards along this level is a steep buttress marked by three
square-cut arêtes (OS Ref 663 317). The central arête remains a project of a
certain Tywyn GP.

Lacking in Geo-Stability   16 metres Hard Very Severe 5a † (23.6.2001)
The wide crack right of the hanging groove of *West Side Boys* is steep, and
safe until the finishing-blocks.

★West Side Boys   18 metres   E4 6a   (29.8.2000)
An impressive line based upon the hanging groove in the right-hand arête.
Climb the lower wall to the groove (hidden small cam placement left of the
arête). Contortions in the groove bring a wedged block on the left to hand,
before a final battle up a short crack should deposit strong climbers on the
top.

Off the Shelf   18 metres   E3 6a †   (23.6.2001)
The thin corner left of the right-hand arête leans steeply. Enter the corner
with some skill and rock stiffly up onto the sloping ledge to join the top of
the arête for a great finish.

☆So Close to the Monster   18 metres   E1 5c †   (29.8.2000)
Climb the wall directly below the left-hand arête to a ledge. A good hold
high on the arête provides a sensational hang before a finish up a short
wall.

Barn-door Buttress   OS Ref 662 317
One hundred and fifty metres down to the right (facing in) of the preceding
crag is a small buttress characterised by strong vertical cracks, and the
eponymous sensation of being out of control while trying to climb them. The

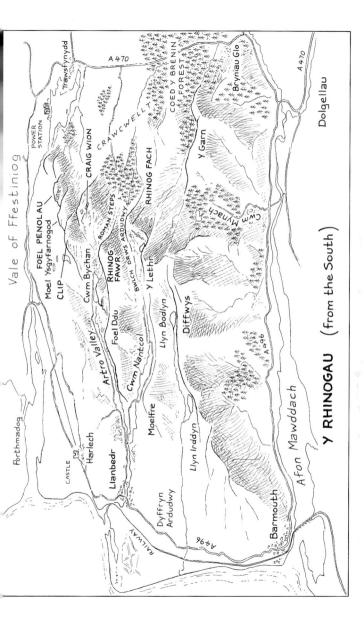

Y RHINOGAU (from the South)

Y FOEL PENOLAU

1 Purrfection — E1
2 Small Wonder — VS
3 Grath — E1
4 On Secret Sand — E3
5 Silence is Golden — E5
6 All this and Heaven Too — E3
7 Politician's Wall — E4
8 Misunderstood — E1

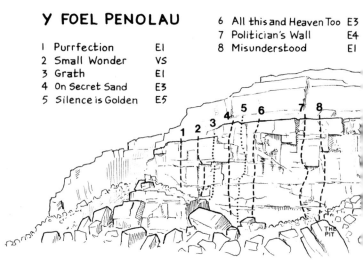

CRAIG Y GROES (The Canyon)

The Rhinog ridge-path

1 Fantasia — VS
2 Tin Town — HVS
3 Hecuba's Camel — E2
4 Crawcwellt Crawl — VS
5 Paradox Sand — E5
6 Y Groes — HVS
7 The Right Unforgiveable — E2
8 Arlog — E1
9 Foggy Dew — E1

Mur y Tonnau

1 Still Virgin — E3
2 Stone Perfect — E2
3 Terry's Old Gold — E4
4 Rippled and satoned — E3
5 Speak of the Devil — E3
6 Home Surf — E3
7 The Seventh Wave — E4
8 The Ebb — E2
9 A Magnificent Thing — HVS
10 Big is Beautiful — VS

buttress can be easily reached from the Mur y Tonnau area, from which it is readily identifiable. **Left to right** order is resumed.

Brace Yourselves!   10 metres   E5 6a †   (27.7.2001)
Graded for a solo or an on-sight lead (but not an on-sight solo). A line of sharp layaways in a tapering wall between two dirty clefts on the left is followed powerfully onto a slab. Escape up the groove on the right.

Twirl   10 metres   E1 5b †   (27.7.2001)
Sprint up the right-hand and widest of four closely packed cracks to a recess. If you must, finish with a grovel through the roof on big dusty holds.

The Biggest Barndoor in Town   12 metres   E2 6a †   (27.7.2001)
Struggle into the widening crack left of a huge wedged flake. Do the layback conversion, and exit pleasantly right of an overhang.

☆**More of a Fridge Door**   8 metres   E1 6a †   (27.7.2001)
Sketch up the thin crack in the face right of the wedged flake, and follow a more positive crack to the top.

Window Shopping   6 metres   Hard Very Severe 5a †   (27.7.2001)
The short-lived crack furthest right, with an exciting pull out on a block lodged in heather.

Crags North of the Roman Steps

The crags described in this sub-section are located at various levels on the south side of the stepped, open valley containing a stream that drains the west side of this part of the mountain mass before running westwards into Llyn Cwm Bychan. (Some of the western-most crags, and the mouth of the valley, are visible when looking due east from the Cwm Bychan car-park.) The valley can be approached direct from the car-park across fields, but there is no right-of-way. A more responsible approach, giving access to the crags in around 20 to 40 minutes, is as follows. From the car-park, follow the Roman Steps footpath (page 305) for half a kilometre to a steepening in the path after a low drystone wall is crossed. Take a slight (descending) track on the left to a stream. Cross the stream and contour left across rocky and wooded ground before ascending over boulders to scree beneath the left-hand end of the 'main crag'. Transfers to succeeding crags are described individually.

Clogwyn Spot[1]   Dog Cliff   OS Ref 652 313
The large rambling cliff that looms over the head of the Cwm Bychan valley, above a wooded slope, lacks the discreet charm of its neighbours, and

1 Shown as Clogwyn Pot on OS map. Spot believed to be correct.

development has yet to reach its zenith. Towards the left end of the cliff, and 150 metres right of an ascent gully, is a good clean wall beneath a terrace at 20 metres. A corner leading to a 1-metre roof aids its identification. The first two routes are located on the wall; a pre-fixed rope is necessary to retreat from the terrace.

☆**The Hatchett**   20 metres   E4 6a †   (31.5.2000)
A shorter version of the more famous arête on Snowdon, yet this is no less fierce and the angle is felt immediately. Follow the stepped wall to the left edge of the roof. Take the arête above precariously, until a pull right to a jug gives access to the terrace.

Wall of Goths   20 metres   E5 6a †   (31.5.2000)
A climb for big shoulders. Start just right of the left-facing corner that leads up to the roof. Gain the corner below a blocky break. Step left above the roof; then continue direct to a final short groove.

The other two climbs here occupy an isolated square wall at the same level, left of the ascent gully.

Invasion of the Booty Snatchers   18 metres   E2 5b †   (29.5.2000)
Climb a short corner formed by a pedestal at the left end of the cliff. Trend boldly up and right to the left-hand end of the central ledge. Follow a line of jugs slightly left to a good finish.

☆**Booty Is Bountiful**   18 metres   E2 5c †   (29.5.2000)
From the foot of the wall pop up onto a small ledge on the right; then reach the right-hand end of the central ledge. An interesting problem must be solved to continue directly up to the easier juggy wall to the top.

On a neighbouring buttress, given OS Ref 655 309, **Ravens on Speed** (37 metres HVS 5a † 4.95) has been reported, but not identified. It takes a break in a lower wall to a terrace, a flaky groove on the right past a spike, and a move back left to finish up a terracotta groove with a loose block.

Mur Cyddiedig   Hidden Wall   OS Ref 653/4 313
Below the extreme left-hand end of the 'main cliff', and 60 metres lower, is an attractive and level hidden bay with three steep, north-west-facing walls up to 12 metres in height. These provide some great climbing in a delightful setting. The first-encountered wall has a vertical crack in its right-hand end.

Rita's Groove   9 metres   Severe †   (10.6.2000)
The roof-capped groove near the left-hand end of the crag. Step right to clear the roof.

Pulling on the Black   9 metres   Hard Severe 4a †   (10.6.2000)
The obvious crack and groove: good climbing.

To the right is a clean, compact wall with a large pedestal block at half height.

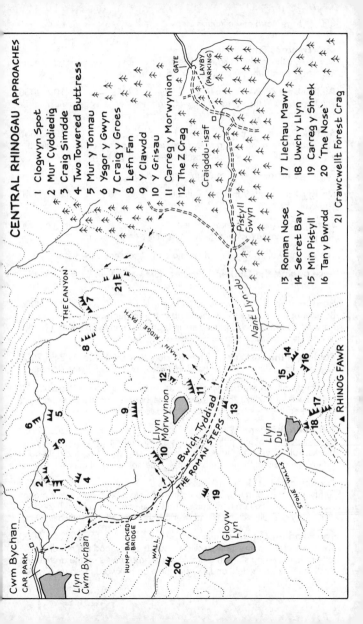

CENTRAL RHINOGAU APPROACHES

1 Clogwyn Spot
2 Mur Cyddiedig
3 Craig Simdde
4 Two Towered Buttress
5 Mur y Tonnau
6 Ysgor y Gwyn
7 Craig y Groes
8 Lefn Fan
9 Y Clawdd
10 Y Grisau
11 Carreg y Morwynion
12 The Z Crag

13 Roman Nose
14 Secret Bay
15 Min Pistyll
16 Tan y Bwrdd
17 Llechau Mawr
18 Uwch y Llyn
19 Carreg y Shrek
20 'The Nose'
21 Crawcwellt Forest Crag

Cwm Bychan
CAR PARK
Llyn Cwm Bychan

THE CANYON

MAIN RIDGE PATH

Llyn Morwynion

Bwlch Tyddiad

THE ROMAN STEPS

HUMP-BACKED BRIDGE

WALL

Gloyw Lyn

Llyn Du

STONE WALLS

RHINOG FAWR ▲

Nant Llyn-du

Pistyll Gwyn

Craigddu-isaf

GATE

LAYBY
(PARKING)

Churchman's End   9 metres   Severe †   (10.6.2000)
Start below the left-hand crack of the pedestal. Take the wall direct to gain
the crack, surmount the pedestal, and finish easily.

All the Best Freaks Are Here   9 metres   E1 5b †   (10.6.2000)
The thin seam in the centre of the wall leads to a large ledge. Finish up the
crack on the right.

Suffolk Punch   9 metres   E2 5b †   (10.6.2000)
The right-hand weakness (a sort of runnel) in the compact wall is gained
via small edges. Follow improving holds to the large ledge.

Past more broken rock to the right is the vertical crack, and to its left:

Dodgy Jammer   9 metres   Difficult †   (10.6.2000)
The broken crack.

Jammy Dodger   9 metres   Severe †   (10.6.2000)
The perfect hand-crack: imagine if it were five times longer!

The second wall, 50 metres left, has a distinct corner on the left.

☆**Race against the Clocker**   12 metres   Hard Very Severe 5b † (24.5.2000)
The corner; strenuous but safe.

☆**Beat the Clach**   12 metres   E3 6a †   (22.7.2000)
Boulder up the rounded right-hand rib of the corner (good landing) to a
horizontal break (*Rock 2* placement in break). Continue up the thin crack
to large holds. Reach right to exit past a nice flake.

☆**Raiders of the Lost Park**   12 metres   Hard Very Severe 5a † (24.5.2000)
Climb the crackline in the centre of the face: well-protected entertainment.

The third wall, an overhanging buttress with a striking off-width crack, is 30
metres left and close to the apex of the bay. An unknown vandal has
hammered the message 'AA groove 5c' below the crack.

Total Commitment   9 metres   E5 5c †   (22.7.2000)
Immediately left of the main buttress is a sharp fin sitting on a jumble of
blocks. Pull up onto the blocks; then make a long stretch up the right-hand
side of the arête of the fin. Finish nimbly. The name says it all.

Snakes and Ladders   10 metres   E3 5c   (24.5.2000)
Terrifying – in its own way. Climb rightwards into a blocky groove 3 metres
left of the arête. Pull up to a break; trust to the gear (in the block!), and
make very difficult moves up and over the short rounded headwall.

★**The Bending Mind**   10 metres   E2 5c   (24.5.2000)
The steep arête; a fine, pumpy climb. Launch up to good flat handholds
left of the arête and so gain a break. Make hard moves up the arête using
the thin crack on the left, and swing right to an awkward finish up a wide
crack.

★Vandal's Crack   10 metres   E2 5c   (24.5.2000)
Also known as *AA Groove*. The off-width crack requires a strong and
confident approach. Some protection can be strenuously arranged on
questionable flakes wedged inside the crack. Whillans would have
appreciated this route.

Stone Graffiti   10 metres   Hard Very Severe 5b †   (24.5.2000)
The pleasant slim corner right of the crack provides a safe crux at mid
height and a good direct finish.

Craig Simdde   Chimney Crag   OS Ref 655 313
From a few hundred metres to the east across the southern slope of the open
valley, a short, steep crag will be visible high up to the right. This is incised by
a deep and unmistakable chimney.

Is It Morning?   9 metres   Hard Very Severe 5a   (29.5.2000)
In the wall left of the chimney is a ledge one move out of reach. Gain the
ledge, and then trend rightwards on good holds to the top.

★★Power Spawn   9 metres   E4 6a   (29.5.2000)
A gem of a route; high in the grade. Start the left arête of the chimney on
the left and gain the first (thin) break. Using the arête, gain a slightly wider
break, and then go for the top. A route with no let-up.

Dwfn Simdde y Rhinog   9 metres   Severe †   (29.5.2000)
The chimney – inevitably.

☆Paraplegic   9 metres   E5 6a/b †   (22.7.2000)
The superb face right of the chimney. A deadly start: take note of the
landing. Reach an undercut at 3 metres, and layback powerfully into the
groove slightly left. Swing out right onto a horizontal break and place
small wires in a vertical crack – the first gear. A final hard move for a
bucket confirms the wisdom of not soloing the route.

There is a long, low wall above Craig Simdde which, unfortunately, doesn't
really get its act together. There is one route at its extreme left-hand end.

☆Dance to the Storm   8 metres   E1 5b †   (12.8.2000)
The centre of the wall leads past some good horizontal breaks. A good
crack appears near the top.

Two-Towered Buttress   OS Ref 652 312
This two-towered crag is 100 metres north-west of 'the hidden walls' of Mur
Cyddiedig and is clean and compact.

☆The Real Thing   8 metres   Hard Very Severe 5a †   (12.8.2000)
The left-hand tower has a crack in its centre-base. Just left of this is a thin
seam which is followed to the short steep wall at the top. A clean but
rounded finish awaits.

☆☆**Why Does It Always Pour on Me?**   8 metres   E1/2   5b †   (12.8.2000)
Climb the central crack to an orange overlap, where long reaches gain a slot. Directly above is a left-facing groove which provides interest all the way to the top.

Daydreaming   8 metres   Hard Very Severe   5a †   (12.8.2000)
The right-hand tower is split by a ramp. From the left-hand end of the ramp, climb a good edge past a big jammed block to a vague crack.

Even Better than the Real Thing   8 metres   E2   6a †   (12.8.2000)
Gain the ramp behind the boulder using a hand-jam crack. The centre of a short white wall above leads to reassuring finishing-holds.

Mur y Tonnau   Wall (of) Waves   OS Ref 657 314
[Photodiagram page 296d.] Two hundred metres east of Craig Simdde is an impressive, north-facing, striated wall. There is a good selection of mid-extremes here, which provide some quality face-climbing as well as refuge from the sun.

The left-hand end of the crag comprises a beautiful runnelled wall of perfect grit that should not be ignored. The first four routes end up on a terrace, escape from which can be made up the groove near its right-hand end (or use a rope pre-fixed to a boulder at the back of the higher terrace).

☆**Still Virgin**   9 metres   E3   5c †   (22.6.2001)
Climb over the right-hand end of a little overhang right of a rounded rib. From a good break, reach a higher break and then exit using a jug at the top of the rib on the left. Good gear after a hard, bold start. E4 to solo.

☆**Stone Perfect**   9 metres   E2   5c †   (22.6.2001)
Take the most obvious seam to a break. Continue over a bulge, and balance over onto a sloping ledge at the top. Protectable all the way.

☆☆**Terry's Old Gold**   9 metres   E4   5c †   (22.6.2001)
Pure pleasure, even as an obligatory solo. Gain a good fingerhold at 3½ metres. Climb direct on texture, and reach the heather above using some sloping holds slightly right.

★**Rippled and Stoned**   9 metres   E3   5c   (29.5.2000)
The best-defined runnel, before the face increases in height. Lovely stuff.

Speak of the Devil   19 metres   E3   6a   (29.5.2000)
Very technical climbing up the thin vertical groove-line gains an incipient break beneath a large left-facing layaway. It is best to swing left to exit as for the preceding route, although the first ascensionists hand-traversed right beneath a huge sitting block to finish up the less interesting upper section of *Home Surf*. Fortunately a good wire protects the crux at 6 metres.

Home Surf 18 metres E3 6a (29.5.2000)
A good, if bold, start leads to disappointing climbing. Start below the huge sitting flake 10 metres up. Take the thin line of weakness to a tough, long move for jugs – no protection to this point, but there is a soft landing. Artificially, climb the thin crack on the left, and swing back right to ledges and a groove. Climb up to exit through a square gap.

★The Seventh Wave 18 metres E4 5c (24.5.2000)
The substantive hard line of the face with gear that's OK if you get the right pieces in. Start up an intermittent finger-crack and step right onto a ledge at the foot of a gangway. Ignore the obvious, and climb the steep wall above (difficult gear in thin crack), past a peg runner, to bigger holds at a deep break. Swing right, and pull up to the top past a good flake.

The Ebb 18 metres E2 5b † (10.6.2000)
Left of the left-hand of two corners is a steep wall with small ledges at 9 metres. Climb thinly to the ledges. Continue up the run-out groove above to meet the right-hand end of a deep break and the top.

A Magnificent Thing 18 metres Hard Very Severe 5a † (10.6.2000)
The left-hand of the two corners; powerful and testing. Pull out on heather – if she doesn't mind.

☆Big Is Beautiful 18 metres Very Severe 4c † (24.5.2000)
The excellent right-hand corner. Finish up the crack in the headwall.

Twenty-five metres right is a lower continuation wall.

Instinct Whip 8 metres E1 5b † (24.5.2000)
Sustained and intuitive climbing up the thin central groove. Tricky to start.

Sunset Wall 8 metres Hard Very Severe 5a † (24.5.2000)
Climb the wall on the right to a scoop, and pad up this past a positive break to the top.

Ysgor y Gwyn The White Rampart OS Ref 656/7 315
Opposite Mur y Tonnau, just above the level of the stream, is a series of white crags, with two rectangular towers on the left. All the routes are good and clean.

Dam the Stream 12 metres E1 5a † (27.7.2001)
The arête right of the square-cut recess in the left-hand tower. A long reach at the top.

☆A Problem Shared 10 metres E4 6b † (27.7.2001)
Very technical climbing on the face right of the arête. Reach a shallow break at 4 metres; and use a faint vein to gain a pocket. Stretch left for a crack, and finish up a short arête above *Dam the Stream*. One good wire placement may be hard to utilize on sight.

☆**Three-Day Wonders**   10 metres   E1 5c †   (27.7.2001)
The left-hand arête of the right-hand tower. A difficult start leads to
jug-hauling. Unprotected.

☆**Slot-in Job**   12 metres   E3 5c †   (27.7.2001)
Climb the centre of the right-hand tower to a slot – first gear. Better holds
lead up to a ledge. Escape left to the exit of *Three-Day Wonders*.

☆**The Mathematician**   12 metres   E3 5c †   (27.7.2001)
Hard moves above a poor landing start the right-hand arête. From the
ledge above, finish scarily on the right; or foot-traverse left to the exit of the
previous two routes.

Fifty metres further right the edge re-emerges in the form of a fine white
pillar, the objective of:

☆**One of Those Days**   6 metres   E4 6a †   (23.6.2001)
Climb the left-hand arête using layaways to either side. Superb. No gear.

☆**Sustainable Energy**   7 metres   E4 5c †   (23.6.2001)
The frontal arête: just go with the flow.

Tros Mur y Tonnau
From the top of the rocky plateau above and to the right of Mur y Tonnau a
further collection of north-facing walls can be seen about 300 metres further
back. Mainly broken and terraced they provide some worthwhile rock and
three routes to date. There is a tall pillar with a short groove in its top centre
and a shallow roof on the left.

☆**Extreme Contact**   15 metres   E2 5b †   (3.9.2000)
The wall directly below the roof on the left has plenty of good (but spaced)
holds leading to the first gear below the roof. Above are more good holds
and an easy finish.

☆**The Art of Communication**   16 metres   E2 5b †   (3.9.2000)
In the bigger wall on the left of *Wings above Water* is a right-facing
groove. Climb the seam left of the groove to the top. Some surprising
holds, but run-out.

☆**Wings above Water**   15 metres   E1 5b †   (3.9.2000)
The blunt arête above a bog pool. Just enough holds on compact rock
lead up the central seam. A good crack on the left lends protection before
a finish can be made up and rightwards.

Craig y Groes   Crag (of) the Cross   OS Ref 666 311
An excellent, clean and solid crag with mainstream appeal and a good
cross-section of quality climbs. Like many of its neighbours hiding in the rock
and heather wilderness of the Craig Wion massif, this crag faces north-west
and, unfortunately, is prone to seepage after prolonged rainfall and is

shaded up to around 4.00 p.m. high summer. Situated about one and a half kilometres north of the Roman Steps it comprises the south side of one of those canyons that laterally incise the ridge and which prove to be of unexpected delight (and consternation) to walkers. It is one of the few crags in the Rhinogau where climbers can expect accompaniment by their fellow species, though rarely to an intrusive extent. Of equal note is the logic of avoiding the crag in conditions of brisk cross-winds when a classic venturi effect can operate and chill the ill-prepared to the bone. A summer crag it is.

There are two standard approaches as well as several expert shortcut variants.

1 From the East (Crawcwellt forest car-park)
1.1 From the car-park (page 279), follow the track eastwards to the farm of Graigddu-isaf, walk south for 100 metres, and pass through a gate; then turn right into a footpath (acorn sign). This path follows the south bank of Nant Llyn-du towards the Roman Steps and offers a view of the crag up on the skyline at about two o'clock. Continuing along the path, and approximately 200 metres beyond the small waterfall of Pistyll Gwyn turn right along a forestry track and follow this northwards across decimated ground to the edge of the heavily cut forest at OS Ref 673 304. Track north-westwards along the stone wall and stream to a fence at its perimeter. Now proceed diagonally right up the hillside in a north-north-west direction (passing a 12-metre crag to its right) to a stone wall. Follow the wall in a similar direction; then bear left to meet the eastern end of the crag (sounds complicated, but getting lost is part of the fun).
1.2 An alternative from the east is to ignore the right turn into the forestry track and to continue to the western edge of the forest. From here, a good track ascends to become the Roman Steps, at the summit of which the main route from the west can be picked up.

2 From the West (Cwm Bychan)
2.1 From the car-park (page 279), take the Roman Steps footpath which starts from a gate at the eastern side of the car-park/camp-site (the footpath has been re-routed since the 1994 edition of the OS 1:25,000 map). Follow the Roman Steps through Bywlch Tyddiad for almost two kilometres to their summit col, with large cairn, at OS Ref 658 299. The idea now is to get established on the 'main' (cairned) ridge-path. This swaggers north-north-eastwards via various strenuous ups and downs and disorienting sidesteps until after a kilometre (that feels like three) it deposits you at the eastern end of the crag.
2.2 An alternative from the Roman Steps summit col is, craftily, to interlock various sheep/people tracks on a zigzag northerly trajectory, passing Carreg y Morwynion (see page 315), passing the north-eastern shore of Llyn Morwynion, passing The Z Crag, and then to contour around level ground to the western end of the crag. This saves a lot of leg work especially when (coming from the west) the approach is made via the crags of Y Grisau and Y Clawdd (see page 313).

The Canyon

[Diagram page 296b,c.] In locating the routes, it will become evident that there are scratched arrows and grades at the base of the routes established in 1992.

Fantasia   18 metres   Very Severe   4b †   (13.6.92)
At the left-hand end of the crag is a prominent corner. Start from a jumble of blocks below the rib on the right of the corner. Climb the rib, passing an overhang at 3 metres to the right, and reach the main horizontal break at 12 metres. Swing right into a hanging groove above a roof and climb to the top.

Tin Town   18 metres   Hard Very Severe   5a †   (13.6.92)
Start beneath the left-hand end of the large overhang in the headwall of the cliff, near its left side. Gain the top of a small low pedestal. Work up the slab above slightly rightwards, then leftwards, to reach the grassy ledge beneath the overhangs. Swing out left and finish up the crack.

Between *Tin Town* and a gully-break 25 metres further right the crag is vegetated and unattractive.

★Hecuba's Camel   18 metres   E2   5c   (7.6.92)
A good, if awkward, face climb that aims for the U-shaped cracks in the wall right of the gully break. Start 6 metres right of the blocks at the foot of the gully, and 2 metres left of *Crawcwellt Crawl*. Climb direct, left of a large grass ledge, to a thin horizontal break at 5 metres. Traverse delicately left to a short flared slot and move up intricately to the base of the U-shaped cracks. Take the right-hand crack and easier ground above to the top.

☆Crawcwellt Crawl   20 metres   Very Severe   4c †   (7.6.92)
Start below the best-defined crack-system in the centre of the crag, 8 metres right of the blocks at the foot of the gully. An interesting route – at this grade! Go up past the large grass ledge and over a small overhang into a short groove. Undercut rightwards beneath roofs for 3 metres and pull around onto the upper face. Climb the right-hand branch of diverging cracks to the top.

☆☆Paradox Sand   18 metres   E5   6a †   (26.5.97)
Unquestionably bold; this superb pitch takes on the blankest central part of the crag midway between the two best-defined crack-systems. Start below the wall, 3 metres left of *Y Groes*. Climb easily to a jammed block. Bear diagonally leftwards into bulges to a rattling flake (your vital wire runner here stops it rattling). Make very committing moves up to a sloper (don't jump!) in a tiny niche below a thin crack. Follow the difficult thin crack, and wall above, to the top.

☆**Y Groes**   18 metres   Hard Very Severe 5a †   (7.6.92)
A fine climb which homes in on the right-hand crack-system on a
religiously direct line. Start beneath the crack, 12 metres from the
right-hand end of this section of the crag. Climb straight up, reaching the
base of the crack with difficulty. The crack leads on with good holds past a
rickety block to the top.

☆**The Right Unforgiveable**   18 metres   E2 5b †   (26.5.97)
The compelling right-trending flake right of the Y Groes crack-system. Start
at the base of the scrappy black corner, 9 metres from the right-hand end
of this section of the crag. Quit the corner after a few metres and force
through the overlying roofs to reach the lower end of the flake. Step right
onto a convex ledge and power up the flake to exit slightly left.

Arlog   18 metres   E1 5b   (14.10.92)
In the face just to the right of the scrappy corner is a thin vertical crack.
Reach and follow the thin crack with difficulty, and careful protection,
before yielding to the attraction of a resting-ledge up to the right. An easier
flake leads to a step up onto a sitting block below an overhang. Finish up
and left or, harder, up and right: neither option should be rushed.

★★**Foggy Dew**   18 metres   E1 5b   (7.6.92)
A safe and soft-touch extreme; a necessary (?) piece of marketing for the
crag. Start at the base of a short right-facing groove 3 metres short of the
right-hand edge of this section of the crag. Climb up to a thin horizontal
break at the top of the groove. Pull up onto a thin crack and take this to
finish on jugs, right of a small overhang.

Isolated Buttress
[Diagram next page.] The main section of the crag is now terminated by a
broad easy gully; a little way further right along the edge is an isolated
buttress of clean grey grit. This is the part that is first in the queue for
sunshine. It is also the only section of the crag that is visible from the west
and north-west ⌐ but coyly even so.

☆**Essence**   12 metres   E3 6a †   (12.4.97)
Proverbial grit. Climb dustily direct to a small roof left of the obvious crack.
Swing over right into a short crack; move up; then step left to a
finishing-flake. Very protectable.

Dr Butt Says You Can't Get More In
                         12 metres   Hard Very Severe 5b † (17.8.99)
Climb the obvious crack slightly left of centre.

☆**'Civilization'**   12 metres   E3 5c †   (12.4.97)
Escapable, but the climbing compensates. Climb up to the right-hand side
of a shaky pedestal at the break. Pull past the break on the right to stand
up on the left end of a sloping shelf. Use flake holds slightly left to proceed
boldly, until a quick exit can be made on the right.

CRAIG Y GROES ~ ISOLATED BUTTRESS

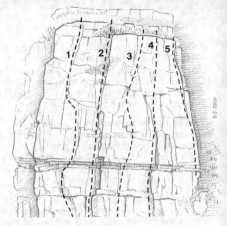

Exiled in the Land of Pickled Fish   12 metres   E1 5b †   (17.8.99)
Climb a left-facing groove 2 metres right of the obvious crack to gain a
thin crack. Pass a small block and get onto the top ledge using good
holds.

Right from Left   9 metres   E4 6a †   (12.4.97)
The right-hand arête of the buttress. Potentially catastrophic if one jumps
off in the wrong direction. Pockets on the left assist the crux at 4 metres.

Opposite the main crag, and through a gap, is a 5-metre wall of crisp white
grit. This offers some bouldering including: the crack left of the arête (5c); the
grooved arête (6a); and the face right of the arête, using the big spike (4b).

Lefn Fan   Smooth Height   OS Ref 664 311
This is the east-south-east-facing slab 250 metres west of Craig y Groes,
from which it is clearly evident. It is best experienced in the summer's
morning sun. Approach as for Craig y Groes: alternative 2.2 (page 305)
passes beneath the crag and may expedite your arrival.

Hail TT   25 metres   E1 5b †   (14.9.97)
A line up interconnected cracks in the centre of the slab with a paucity of
protection. Ascend to a small right-facing flake and somehow get on to it.
Reach right into the cracks, and follow them past miscellaneous dirt to a
simple exit on big holds.

☆**Tall to Order**   25 metres   E2 5b †   (14.9.97)
A promising eliminate that just about maintains its independence. From
the left side of a big flake at 4 metres, climb to a small (in-situ) thread
beneath an overlap. Continue direct on comforting holds to an undercut
(good gear). Keep in line with a hairline vertical crack and exit as for
Eye-Full Crack.

Eye-Full Crack   25 metres   Hard Very Severe 5a †   (14.9.97)
A grotty start; then it warms up. Follow the prominent crack towards the
right-hand edge of the slab, and reach it warily from the right-hand side of
the big flake on *Tall to Order*.

Short Work   9 metres   E2 5c †   (14.9.97)
In short: awesome. Take a central line up the taller of the smaller slabs to
the right, which is distinguished by a roof at half height. Exit on the right.

Three hundred metres west of Lefn Fan is a motley collection of walls. A
striking crackline in a west facing wall can be seen from a distance (OS Ref
662 312).

Eye of the Storm   8 metres   Hard Very Severe 5b †   (12.8.2000)
Climb the crack to a short roof but then deviate left to a good finish.

The large gully running down northwards from *Eye of the Storm* has some
promising north-east facing walls dropping from the rocky plateau which
are home to the next, isolated, route. This gully runs parallel to the more
shallow one that joins the eastern edge of Mur y Tonnau (page 302), from
which the climb could just as easily be approached.

My Feral Heart   15 metres   E5 6a †   (3.9.2000)
Though impressive, the slab is lichenous and remains wet on its left-hand
side. The route lies a few metres north of a rowan tree and is characterized
by very thin twin cracks running up its right side. Gain an overlap using the
right-facing corner. Pull boldly through on the thin cracks to the first gear
(*RP*). A quick shuffle up leads to a perfect finger-and-gear-slot in the
right-hand crack. Continue directly to the top with little more in the way of
gear.

Crawcwellt Forest Crag[1]   OS Ref 668 308
Follow the main Craig y Groes approach (page 305) to the perimeter fence.
Turn right and continue for 20 metres before heading directly up the hill to a
collection of outcrops.

The first crag on the left has a north-facing wall with a sloping ledge at
three-quarters height.

Stone Donkey   8 metres   E1 5b †   (24.6.2001)
The left-hand end of the ledge is reached via the arête below. Continue up
the arête to an easy finish. Minimal gear.

Dead Man's Verve   8 metres   E4 5c †   (24.6.2001)
The leaning wall between the arête and the tree in the corner is a delightful
trip linking small edges. From the ledge, a couple more moves lead
directly past a good spike to an easy finish.

---

1 Crawcwellt means 'coarse grass'.

The next outcrop is located above a stone wall 50 metres rightwards (northwards) at the same level. A finger-crack on the left-hand side of an east-facing wall is unclimbed. To the right is a thin seam rising up compact rock.

☆**Virtual Water**   8 metres   E2 5b †   (17.2.2001)
Start above a large 'shark's fin', which is directly below the seam. ('Don't pop off the good but rounded holds.')

☆**Food for Sharks**   8 metres   E3/4 6a †   (17.2.2001)
The blunt arête to the right is split by a capped groove. Poorly protected climbing gains a good layaway in the groove. Take a fine crack which curls up and leftwards onto finishing slopers.

Sixty metres further right is a tall tower containing a short groove above an otherwise blank wall. The shorter wall to the left has one route.

Banging against Destiny   6 metres   Hard Very Severe 5b †   (24.6.2001)
From bottom-centre, hand-traverse left to the arête and follow this direct via thin slopers at the top.

☆☆**Phallus through the Looking Lass**   8 metres   E4 5c †   (12.2.2001)
The wonderful exposed left-hand arête of the blank wall of the tower. Follow the arête until a ledge above the blank wall can be reached and mantelled. The finish is easier, but a rock-strewn landing and no gear give this edge an extra edge.

Thirty metres to the right is another wall with a wide crack.

☆**Running Like the Red Queen**   8 metres   E1 5b †   (12.2.2001)
The fist-wide crack is excellent and steep, and swallows your arm whole.

Y Clawdd   The Embankment   OS Ref 657 307
[Photodiagram page 312a.] Although this crag has a northerly aspect like most of its near-neighbours, the similarity ends there: this misfit overhangs! Y Clawdd is constructed of a series of leaning sheets rising to between 12 and 25 metres, all seamed with blind and rounded cracks providing uncharacteristically strenuous climbing. Awkward heathery terrain above makes a pre-fixed lower-off rope excusable on most routes and highly desirable on some. If this is a turn-off to securing reasonable access to several high standard gems of the area, then so be it! By far the best time to visit is a fine summer's evening when the sun bends around, de-cloaks the cliff, and brings a shimmer to the sparkling white grit of the Gawr wall. During the average moist winter the crag will remain dank and seeping. When the seepage has retreated, however, most of the routes remain dry and, owing to their steepness, can be climbed even in light to moderate rainfall, particularly in combination with the use of a pre-fixed rope. When the weather forecasters get it wrong, check the place out: it could salvage the weekend. (There again, you may get lost in the mist.)

Y Clawdd is secretively located in a small east-west valley 400 metres due north of Llyn Morwynion, and is only discernible from the north. It is most readily approached from the west. From the Cwm Bychan (pay) car-park (see 2.1, page 305) follow the Roman Steps footpath for one kilometre, passing over the hump-backed stone bridge to the point at which a little stream on the left runs down from a valley beneath the crag of Y Grisau (page 313). Walk up into the valley a short way, contour north and then eastwards, over a wall, and enter the western end of the small valley, in which the crag (virtually hidden) is sited 300 metres further on, and up to the right. An uneducated approach from the east will test navigational skills.

Towards the left-hand end of the crag, a left-to-right break offers an easy way down. Immediately left, and set back slightly, is a 15-metre wall merely vertical, with two worthwhile pitches that are easy to exit.

Loneliness Is Just a Word   15 metres   E2 5c †   (17.8.97)
From a wide flake crack near the base of the descent, move up to a ledge, and strike up the obvious crack to the top.

Eco-Adsorption of the Psyche   15 metres   E2 5c †   (17.8.97)
The 'tower' face right of *Loneliness...*, starting as for that route.
Step up and right onto a narrow ledge; then climb direct past a small spike and jammed block to a niche at the top.

The next two routes are found on the leaning wall 20 metres right of the base of the descent.

Warm Up, Not Burn Out!   15 metres   E3 6a †   (17.8.97)
A crack in the wall slants left to meet the right-hand arête of the dark V-corner on the left. Take the crack, with one peculiar move after another, and either give in to the sub-critical pump, or heave successfully onto the left-hand end of the capping ledge. Exit as for the following route on the right.

'I'm Soloing in the Rain'   15 metres   E1 5b †   (17.8.97)
Climb the modest groove left of the gully on the right to an undemanding exit onto heather terrain slightly right.

Next right, on the other side of the shallow gully, is the crag's showpiece: a leaning sheet of immaculate white grit. The routes here finish on a vegetated ledge 5 metres below the heathery top. From the ledge, scrambling out is one OK option; the other is to use a pre-fixed rope – preferable to abseiling from the solitary tree, which will damage easily.

☆**Gawr**   18 metres   E3 6a †   (8.6.97)
Brilliant coarse grit. There is a prominent V-groove in the upper centre of the wall; start diagonally down left. A highly problematic runnel, but with a good *RP3* placement, may lead up to a ledge. Step up, swing right beneath a small overlap onto the wall, and move up to the foot of the V-groove. Climb the groove with great interest, swing right at its close (thread on the right), and go up a wide crack to the large ledge.

☆☆☆**Gwyllt**   18 metres   E4 6b †   (17.8.97)
Fairly powerful – for the Rhinogau. This is the irresistible direct start to *Gawr*. Sprint up to the overhanging seam (peg runner), and step left into the base of the V-groove.

☆☆☆**Gwen**   18 metres   E5 6a †   (17.8.97)
White gold. From a slender ramp, climb the intricate zig-zag crack-system in the right-hand side of the wall to a ledge and the thread and exit of the preceding routes. Sustained but with one particular stopper move (7a+: dare I?).

Beyond the next leaning sheet is a dominant 25-metre tower cleaved by a crackline. The two routes here finish on a ledge 5 metres below the heathery top; a pre-fixed rope is recommended.

☆**In the Shadows**   18 metres   E5 6a †   (8.6.97)
Probably the most dramatic line on the crag. Follow the unforgiving crack to a rest on a jammed (you hope) block at 7 metres. Continue to a jug beneath a blank-out; then break left onto the arête. Finish up the right-hand side of the arête.

☆**Don't Move a Muscle**   18 metres   E5 6a †   (8.6.97)
A route of character guaranteed to keep you on edge every step of its churlish way. Start below the corner right of the tower. Saunter up the vertical corner to a horizontal break (crucial *Friend* ½). Tackle the corner above with a bold move to gain a very fine hold (and good wire placements) on the slab. Edge up onto the arête of the tower and stretch around for good holds and a **blind** *Friend* 1½ placement in a horizontal slot. Continue up the wall to a wide crack and battle up this and left (crux) to exit onto the ledge immediately left of the small overhang.

Ten metres right, yet another leaning wall hosts a scarcely less fearsome crack in its centre.

Can't Get No Sleep   15 metres   E4 6a †   (8.6.97)
Attack the crack and make committing moves past a flake to a square block, tweezered in by horizontal breaks. A friendlier thin crack now leads to a ledge with big stacked blocks and an obligatory pre-fixed rope that takes one down to ground and consciousness. Bad dream or nightmare?

At the right-hand end of the crag past a steep but broken section, complete with hawk's nest, and past some big piles of ankle-snapping boulders, is an isolated buttress with one special line and a clean top.

☆**Sunset the Scene**   25 metres   E2 5c †   (17.8.97)
The 'come at me' crack in the upper centre of the buttress. Expect little from the indifferent start. Pull into and climb a juggy groove and swing left to a detached pedestal ledge beneath the crack. Finger the crack decisively and stretch for the top: so much for looking like a slab from below!

Y Clawdd

1 Warm Up, Not Burn Out!   E3
2 'I'm Soloing in the Rain' E1
3 Gawr   E3
4 Gwyllt   E4

5 Gwen   E5
6 In the Shadows   E5
7 Don't Move a Muscle   E5
8 Can't get No Sleep   E4

Y Grisiau

| 1 | Jim's Route? | E2 | 3 | Later That Night... | E3 | 5 | Pedestal Arête | E2 | 7 | Man-Twitchers | E3 |
| 2 | Wilderness Grit | E3 | 4 | Looking Down upon the Enemy | E2 | 6 | Araf Nawr | E3 | | | |

Carreg y Morwynion

1 Stranger in the Mirror	E4	2 Green Streak	E3	5 Architect of Chance	E3
		3 Yellow Belly	E3	6 Incognito	E5
		4 Lucky Number	E4	7 Eat Your Words	E2

Lechau Mawr

1 Bebop — E2
2 Rock Steady — E3
3 Splinter — E1
4 Fear Test — E5
5 Peace in Mind — E3
6 Quartz Storm — E3
7 The Collector's Pot — E1
8 Dead Sea Scroll — E4

Just to the west of the main crag, but at a lower level is another crag with a large clean slab in its centre.

Air Guitar   18 metres   E1 5b †   (16.6.2000)
Climb a left-facing corner on the left to a break. Continue direct, and finish up a thin seam in the slabby wall above. Nice climbing that should strike a chord.

☆**On Honeymoon with My Chicken Muscle**
                            18 metres   E2 5c † (16.6.2000)
Classic Taylorism on the centre of the smooth slab. Start just left of a tiny roof at eye-level on a blunt rib. Take a series of slots to a good break below a steep wall. Spaced but positive edges lure to the top.

☆**Helyg Crack**   20 metres   E1 5b †   (16.6.2000)
Climb the thin crack in the right-hand side of the slab to a good slot. The wider crack above gets steeper, but at least the holds get bigger.

Y Grisau   The Steps   OS Ref 653 304
[Photodiagram page 312b.] One of most accessible and public crags in the Rhinogau, poised nobly above the western end of the Roman Steps. There are eight routes here at present; many are excellent, some should not be missed. The crag faces north-west and shares the late afternoon and evening sun (about 4.00 p.m. onwards, high summer). The rock is fine, rugged Rhinog Grit, is predisposed to cracks, and tends to be less affected by seepage after rainfall than many similar adjacent crags.

Approach from the Cwm Bychan (pay) car-park (see 2.1, page 305); the crag first comes into view up to the left from the hump-backed stone bridge on the Roman Steps footpath. Ascend the path for several further hundred metres to the first cross-wall. Turn left at the wall to meet and follow a heather terrace beneath the crag. The best walk-down descent is to the right (west), although it is possible to make a hitch-free abseil from a large block on the terrace to the right of the finish of *Araf Nawr*.

At the left-hand end of the crag is a leftward-rising rake, which can provide a gory descent. Right of this is a crack-seamed wall, the clean penultimate crack of which offers up:

Jim's Route?   18 metres   E2 5b †   (4.10.97)
Quality crack-climbing for big fingers. Start at some boulders near the foot of the rake, and 6 metres left of *Wilderness Grit*. Negotiate a short dirty groove to land on a good ledge at the bottom of a right-slanting ramp. Go direct up the wall to reach the crack. Follow the crack enjoyably, which curves rightwards to sinking finishing-holds.

☆☆**Wilderness Grit**   18 metres   E3 6a †   (26.5.97)
A massif classic that climaxes in a brilliant finger-crack. Twelve metres right of the base of the rake is an off-vertical face with two parallel cracks. Start

below the left-hand crack. Scratch up to good handholds, which lead on past sound cam placements to the upper crack. Surge up this, head-on, to the top. Can be perfectly protected.

☆**Later That Night...**   18 metres   E3 5c †   (30.8.97)
Very pleasant; this is the right-hand of the cracks in the off-vertical face. Climb the crack past a break and a slot to a juggy zone half-way up. A thin crack now leads delicately to a final pull, where care should be taken not to disturb a sitting block.

In the centre of the crag is an obvious large pedestal topped by a heathery ledge at half height; the whereabouts of the remaining climbs are described in relation to this.

Looking Down upon the Enemy   18 metres   E2 5b †   (30.8.97)
The cracks in the wall left of the pedestal. Start beneath parallel cracks immediately right of a pointed flake on the ground. Step off the flake, make one move up the left-hand crack, and then stride right into the right-hand crack. Follow the crack to a break, and beyond to the top. Cams useful.

Pedestal Arête   20 metres   E2 5c †   (4.10.97)
Precariously ascend the right-hand arête of the pedestal, groping left after 5 metres to a thin crack (bold). Easier rock above leads to the heathery ledge. From the highest point of the ledge, climb the short wall on improving holds to the top.

☆☆**Araf Nawr**   18 metres   E3 5c †   (26.5.97)
This is the line that you'll notice first from the steps. Great climbing up the continuous crack right of the pedestal, arguably marred by a serious start. Climb the narrow, left-slanting groove, using good holds on the right, to a small square roof at 6 metres. Now safer, follow the crack past some neat finger-rails on the left to exit just right of a rude spike.

☆**Man-Twitchers**   20 metres   E3 5c †   (30.8.97)
Intriguing and unusual, but with the recurring necky start. Start 10 metres right of the pedestal arête. Take a rightward-rising ledge to a point just left of a V-groove. Now proceed straight up the scooped wall with an exacting long reach for a juggy break – don't cock it up. Swing left and move up to a big ledge at half height. Ascend the arête in the wall above, past an amazing flake, to a curious escape groove on the right.

There are two climbs on a narrow tower to the left of the main crag. From the left end of the crag, continue along and down to a depression with a stream running through a wall. Pass through the gap in the wall; go upstream and then northwards to the tower.

☆**Best of Friends**   12 metres   E3 5c †   (13.6.2000)
The tower is split by a deep corner; start 2 metres right. Pass two good
breaks in the right wall of the corner to gain a short groove. Muscle up
past this to a good ledge and a hand-wide finishing-crack.

Scrambled Legs   10 metres   Very Severe 4b †   (13.6.2000)
The lovely clean arête on the right.

Carreg y Morwynion   Rock (of) the Maidens OS Ref 659 302

[Photodiagram page 312c.] A high-calibre crag having a complement of
tough routes on clean and compact grit, and an uplifting setting above Llyn
Morwynion. The only glitch is a north-north-west aspect and some seepage
after rainfall, making the crag a reliable prospect only from late spring to
early autumn. It is best to come here feeling strong one summer's evening,
when the sun will keep you company from around 4.30 p.m.

The walk-in times from both the east (Crawcwellt) and the west (Cwm
Bychan) amount to around 40 minutes; access is simple using the Roman
Steps. At a point just below and to the east of the summit col of the steps,
locate a good path running northwards up a shallow depression. Follow the
path and – ignoring the big cairn on the hilltop at two o'clock – continue
direct across level marshy ground to intersect the right (west) extremity of the
cliff. (The good path running north from here is a westerly variant of this
portion of the ridge walk.)

Roughly in the (left) centre of the cliff is a face of rock with a prominent green
streak and finger-crack: a useful reference point.

☆**Stranger in the Mirror**   20 metres   E4 6b †   (12.4.97)
The best of the lines left of the green-streaked face. Start below a blank
wall left of a vegetated corner which bounds the green-streaked face.
Climb without difficulty to ledges beneath the blank wall. Organize
protection in the crack (and vivid green slime-mould) on the left and teeter
up the blank wall on tinies (reassuring microwire) to enter the crack above.
Follow the none-too-easy crack straight to the top.

☆**Green Streak**   20 metres   E3 6a †   (12.4.97)
Climb a slim right-facing corner to the foot of the finger-crack in the green
streak. The crack is harder than it looks and more thin moves must be
made to run for the top.

☆**Yellow Belly**   20 metres   E3 6a †   (12.4.97)
Technical and exciting with spaced gear. Link a series of layaways 2 metres
right of *Green Streak* to ledges and a quick break. Step left and pull up to
a second ledge. Continue steeply via parallel cracks to a good break.
Above is a less good break, and beyond is a devil of a scoop, which will
test the brave.

Right of the *Green Streak* wall is a vegetated groove above half height and immediately to its right:

☆**Lucky Number**   20 metres   E4 6a †   (14.9.97)
Start 2 metres right of *Yellow Belly*. A vague crack, containing *RP* placements, leads to flat handholds at the base of the groove. Traverse right for 2 metres past a niche (cam placements), and crank fiercely to a coarse-grained jug. Good holds lead to a sloping ledge beneath the final tower. Ascend the middle of the excellent tower on positive holds (crucial small cam initially), and exit slightly right.

☆**Do the Biz**   12 metres   E5 6a †   (29.7.99)
A gripping solo; if the landing or rock weren't so good the route would rate E6. Start below a small ledge at 7 metres at the base of a shallow groove which leads up to the right-hand end of the heather ledges above half height. Get up onto a narrow ledge. Bear rightwards (sequency) before hard moves leftwards should gain the small ledge. Pull up onto the ledge with a sigh of relief and exit onto the heather ledges. Traverse left and scramble out, or retreat from the rope used to practice the route.

The clean and continuous right wing of the crag sports five climbs, one of which begs recognition.

Architect of Chance   20 metres   E3 5c †   (14.9.97)
Well worth a moment's commitment. Start 2 metres left of an uninviting left-facing corner, which is about 25 metres from the right-hand end of the cliff. Climb a wafer flake in the flat wall; then make a reckless move from a flat hold to a small groove. Continue on more reassuring holds, and spike out left to the right end of a heather ledge. Take the crack in the face above, swing right into a tiny groove-thing, and finish up a perplexing scoop.

☆☆**Incognito**   20 metres   E5 6a †   (12.4.97)
Promotes the left-snaking crack in the best part of the face: superbly sustained, but largely protected by (reliable) *RPs*. Start up the lower wall just to the right of the uninviting left-facing corner, and so gain ledges at 7 metres. Reach the tail of the crack, and wind leftwards along it to a jug and peg runner. Extend for a second jug up and left of the peg and, with protection from a vital *Rock 5* on the left, edge precariously up a short bald slab to finish.

Eat Your Words   15 metres   E2 5b †   (12.4.97)
Inexplicably insecure climbing up the crack next right. From a vegetated ledge at 3 metres, go up the wall (poor to zero gear) to grasp the crack. Follow the crack past a bucket and continue up bulging rock wondering why you got yourself in this position.

Nature Bites Back   15 metres   E3 5c †   (29.7.99)
An interesting route with a bit of a bite. Start 5 metres to the left of a corner near the right-hand end of the cliff. Trend leftwards up ledges and arrange

gear in the vicinity of a block 7 metres up. Traverse left to a large undercut flake and, using this, reach up to good face holds. Stretch up to a niche above; then exit up a short wide crack.

Mighty Midge   8 metres   E1 5c †   (29.7.99)
Reach the obvious crack just right of the arête near the right-hand end of the cliff, and go! An exemplary landing, though very protectable.

The Z Crag   OS Ref 660 304
This is currently a one-route craglet, and the route in question is seriously bold. About 200 metres north of the eastern end of Llyn Morwynion is a short Z-shaped stone wall, with a small north-west facing crag at its northern end. You'll find it if you want to.

One Day I Won't Be Coming Back   12 metres   E6 6b †   (5.10.97)
Take the bulging left-hand arête of the crag to finish via an awkward little groove slightly right. Some small RPs protect the mid-height crux, but then you're on your own.

Roman Nose   OS Ref 657 299
There are many unappealing and vegetated crags on the south side of the historic defile of Bwlch Tyddiad, which houses the Roman Steps. This one, however, is reasonably interesting, and provides a good vantage point from which to surveil the invading legions of tourists and walkers. Be prepared to hold an audience with them.

About 200 metres west of the summit col of the steps, and (on approach from the west) just after a transverse stone wall, there is a broad and blunt nose on the right, about 50 metres above the steps. This stages two (brushed) clean routes; elsewhere, spongy green lichen is best left bountiful.

Celt   20 metres   E4 6a †   (4.10.97)
Technical climbing left of the nose, with one bit needing guts.
Move up into the cutaway beneath the nose; then take a baffling thin crack (peg runner) on the left to a bulge. Pass the bulge boldly to reach big holds. Move left, and up and back right to finish up the easy rib.

Neolith   20 metres   E4 6a †   (4.10.97)
Rugged and raw. The scooped crackline right of the nose. Starting from a higher ledge right of the nose, slip up thin cracks to a sort of rest. Continue strenuously (*in-situ* thread) to a ledge and finish up the rib as for *Celt*. Protectable.

Crags of Rhinog Fawr   Greater Threshold

There is a large number of crags clustered behind Llyn Du on the north slope of Rhinog Fawr. Those described here vary considerably in scale and character, and there is more scope. Especially attractive are the slab routes. Despite the northerly orientation of the mountain face, the crags face in a variety of directions and it is possible to crag-hop and stay in the sun all day in summer. In hot conditions the more adventurous may decide to take to the black waters of Llyn Du, a popular place for the baptism of many a distracted walker. Outside summer, when the rains have set in, seepage can be a problem on many of the crags. On a clear day, the outlook of the higher crags is quite simply stunning, with contrasting panoramas unfolding either side of the main ridge, all triangulating in Snowdon, still in command way to the north.

Apart from Secret Bay and Min Pistyll, and the crags of Rhinog Fawr (West), the crags are best accessed from the shores of Llyn Du. Approach is equally convenient from the east or west via the Roman Steps, the average car-park to crag walk-in time being around 45 minutes. (See approaches 1.2 and 2.1, page 305.) The main Llyn Du path branches southwards from the Roman Steps at a point several hundred metres east of the summit col (and cairn). The crags are described in an east-to-west routine.

Secret Bay   OS Ref 662 294

Impossible to locate from the west, but easily visible on the approach from the east, this is the small, white-streaked (not chalk!) face that can be seen from a point between the two wooden bridges on the Crawcwellt forest path. Make your own way up the hillside below the crag. There are three pleasant pitches here in a secluded bay with a good landing; protection is available below the exits onto heather, so it may be just worth bringing some hardware and a rope.

Strong Heather?   9 metres   Very Severe 4a †   (29.7.99)
Follow a line of good holds in the centre of the slab to an obvious flake at the top and a pull-out onto heather.

A Tomb with a View   9 metres   E2 5b †   (29.7.99)
Starting a metre left of the blocks below the right edge of the slab, work straight up the blankest part of the slab to a jug on the left. Continue past a break and, using a knobble on the right, exit on the right.

Esoterica Hysterica   9 metres   E1 5a †   (29.7.99)
Step off the blocks and take the thin cracks immediately left of the right arête of the slab to the top.

Min Pistyll Waterfall Edge OS Ref 660 294

This is by far the loveliest of the many small crags situated in the valley of the Nant Llyn-du, the outfall of Llyn Du just to the west. It is a 9-metre edge of immaculate grey and rose Rhinog Grit, which becomes sheer on the left where a modest waterfall runs over the cliff. When approached from the east, it becomes visible only some while after the Crawcwellt Forest is quitted. To find it, branch left from the Roman Steps footpath about 200 metres west of the edge of the forest, head south-west over level boggy ground, cross a stone wall, and pick up a sheep-track on the right-hand side of the Nant Llyn-du stream. Follow the stream for half a kilometre, ignoring a few unimpressive short crags on the left, until Min Pistyll, normally complete with waterfall, can be seen 100 metres away on the left.

☆**Sych** 8 metres E1 5a † (18.8.97)
Technically steady but unprotected climbing up the broad front rib left of the waterfall: good holds above a poor landing.

Boil and Bubble 8 metres Hard Very Severe 4c † (29.7.99)
Climb the right-hand arête immediately overlooking the gurgling chimney.

☆**Ffrwd** 9 metres E4 6a † (18.8.97)
The left-hand and most difficult of the trio on the grey sheet right of the waterfall. At low-to-mid water, climb direct just to the right of the waterfall via a narrow sloping ledge and one very thin move. An *RP1* (and nothing else) protects the crux; make sure it's a new one!

☆☆**Cool Grit** 9 metres E3 5c † (18.8.97)
When viewed from the Roman Steps in the morning sun, this is the line that stands out. Climb the incipient central groove past a good little spike and a protectable thin finishing-crack. Requires 'grit cool'.

☆☆**Emilya** 9 metres E2 5c † (18.8.97)
Converge up thin cracks in the right-hand side of the sheet to a pod (*Friend 2½*). Step up (peg runner); then balance up the slab on the right to finish. It would get ★★★ on Peak grit, so why not here!

☆**In an Ideal World** 15 metres E2 5b † (18.8.97)
Near the right-hand limit of the edge, a higher portion of slab offers a good pitch. Start below a thin vertical crack. Climb the crack to a horizontal break. Move up on sidepulls, step right, and then climb slightly rightwards up the purple slab past a generously-proportioned pocket.

There is a lower tier, of sorts, and this has two 'rust stains' up a slab; that to the left being **Left to Rust** (9 metres Very Severe 4a † 18.8.97) and that to the right, **A Right to Rust** (9 metres Hard Severe † 18.8.97). Further right is **Purple Pistyll** (8 metres E1 5a † 29.7.99), the purple slab right of a vertical vegetated break; and **Fisteater** (8 metres Very Severe 4c † 29.7.99), the crack next to the right-hand arête.

Tan y Bwrdd Below the Table OS Ref 661 293

This is the steep west-facing buttress 400 metres east of Llyn Du (and located 250 metres up and behind Min Pistyll). It has but three routes worth reserving for the summer afternoon sunshine (and lots of HVS capability).

☆☆**Airhead** 20 metres E3 6a † (5.10.97)

A varied and improbable route on which plenty of gear can be slung in. It tackles the clean face and obvious roof in the centre of the buttress. Start 4 metres left of a mossy, green left-facing corner. Make a difficult move over a small roof to gain a thin crack curling left. Follow the crack, which becomes a sizeable flake crack leading to the roof. Stretch over for a superb slot and take good holds up the groove above to the top.

☆**Groundpull** 20 metres E4 6a † (5.10.97)

Specific gear placements. Start 2 metres left of the green corner. Climb the sustained thin crack in the left wall of the corner (crucial *Friend 1½* in slot), and move left and up to better holds beneath the roof (thin tape on small spike). Pull right through a gap in the roof to ledges. Continue up the easier groove to the top.

☆**Underfed** 12 metres E2 5b † (24.5.97)

Very Peakish. Start from a high heather platform left of a corner at the extreme right-hand end of the crag. Ascend a slight groove to its close (hopeless *RP*). Make fingery moves up onto the wall and climb its centre on sumptuous grit to the top.

Y Bwrdd The Table OS Ref 661 292

This is the diminutive (but fun) band of rock standing on the large platform atop Tan y Bwrdd; a convivial and light-hearted hour or two replete with lunch of course, can be spent here.

That Panoramic Picnic 7 metres E1 5b † (24.5.97)

This is a right-facing flake with a tiny exit corner near the left-hand end of the band.

Scoop of the Day 7 metres E1 5b † (24.5.97)

The pleasurable clean face and scoop 3 metres right.

To the right of the central descent-chimney are:

Lichen with Everything 6 metres Hard Very Severe 5a † (24.5.97)

Climb the dusty wide crack right of the chimney.

Twopicks 6 metres Very Severe 4c † (24.5.97)

This cleans up the parallel cracks.

Saliva 7 metres E1 5c † (24.5.97)

The thin crack left of the front arête past a quivering 'lower lip'.

Wishbone 7 metres E3 6a † (24.5.97)
The front arête with leg-sprain possibilities.

No Table Manners 6 metres Hard Very Severe 5a † (24.5.97)
The flake cracks over a small overhang right of the arête.

Forked Tongue 6 metres E1 5b † (24.5.97)
The untrustworthy groove above a sitting flake.

Sidedish 6 metres Very Severe 4b † (24.5.97)
The centre of the face on the right.

Llechau Mawr Big Slabs

[Photodiagram page 312d.] As you look look towards the summit of Rhinog Fawr from Llyn Du, a profusion of large and small slabs is evident. These are arranged into two banks of slabs which rise up the mountainside in a south-easterly direction to a level of 100 metres or so below the summit. Although they are of easterly orientation, the lesser angle of the rock allows the sun to make widespread intrusion until around midday, high summer. On both banks climbs are described from **right to left**, as they are approached.

Lower Bank OS Ref 657 292

At the lower end of the bank of slabs, nearest to the lake, is one of the crag's principal selling-features, a 28-metre slab of pristine grit, home for the first two climbs.

Bebop 28 metres E2 5b † (24.5.97)
Rather run-out climbing up the right-hand side of the slab. Follow good holds 2 metres left of a vegetated crack near the slab's right-hand edge and gain a ledge at a break at 6 metres. Take the slab above, right of the overlap, on small holds; then step up left to the upper break. Continue up the slab to a small finishing-corner.

☆**Rock Steady** 28 metres E3 5c † (24.5.97)
[Photo page 352a.] An outstanding slab climb crammed with variety. Start 3 metres right of the vegetated crack on the left. From a ledge, climb direct past a break to a downward-pointing spike (thread). Step right and pass the overlap (peg runner) with difficulty to gain a spike (thin tape) in a short groove. Step left and ascend to the upper break (cams). Follow the long crack above, with interest, to the top.

To the left the crag rises to 40 metres but, apart from the following five climbs, it is heavily vegetated. Approximately 30 metres left of the *Rock Steady* slab is a clean, tapering slab, inset slightly, with a narrow undercut rib on its left.

Mist on the Mountain 40 metres Hard Very Severe 5a † (26.7.99)
Follow cracks in the centre of the tapering slab to ledges at the foot of a left-facing corner. Climb the corner to a second area of ledges. Continue steeply up the rib above, keeping just left of a detached sliver, to the top.

The First Grassfield   20 metres   E2 5c †   (26.7.99)
Start below the narrow undercut rib. Climb up to and over the small roof,
and stretch immediately right to the arête. Follow the arête and crack
above to exit onto grass. Claw up the fifty-degree grass-field to an abseil
retreat from a rock-spike on the right.

The Bridge That Jonathan Built   40 metres   E2 5b †   (26.7.99)
A respectable route of continuous interest. Start 40 metres left of the *Rock
Steady* slab, beneath a smooth slab. Only the start is bold. Climb up over
a tiny roof and link nubbins to reach a good pocket at 6 metres. Follow
faint cracks over a small undercut roof and take a rest on ledges above.
Finish straight up the steep pillar on excellent, but widely spaced holds.

Some 60 metres left of the *Rock Steady* slab is a rectangular pillar that
provides two climbs:

☆**Foreign Object**   25 metres   E3 5c †   (26.7.99)
The delicate right-hand arête; a fine finish. Climb the straightforward lower
arête to a rock-spike. Trend leftwards to a break beneath a roof. With
good wire protection arranged in a thin crack on the left, make hard,
off-balance moves up the arête until easier climbing leads to a large
ledge. Belay; then walk up the ridge.

☆**Splinter**   18 metres   E1 5b †   (16.8.97)
Very elegant positions on the left-hand arête of the pillar. Starting on the left,
cross vegetated ledges to a deep flake crack. Move up the crack to a bulge
beneath the head of the pillar. Take the thin crack in the arête and follow it to
a large ledge. Extremely protectable. Belay; then walk up the ridge.

Upper Bank   OS Ref 658 291
This is the upper series of ad hoc slabs located above a broad grassy rake
which starts from part way up the Rhinog Fawr summit path after leaving the
lake. Seventy metres up the rake (and past a virgin 12-metre slab) is an
isolated, very smooth tapering slab which accommodates the first two routes.

☆☆**Fear Test**   18 metres   E5 6a †   (18.8.97)
A provocative and precise slab climb with just-sufficient *RP* protection. Start
directly below a set of vertical cracks near the left edge of the slab. From a
block jug, rock up right past an always-wet patch, and move up to a break
below the smooth slab. Step left to a good wire-slot at the foot of the
cracks. In the centre of the slab on the right is a shallow finger-pocket;
reach it, transfer onto delicate nubbins, and press on thinly to the top of
the right-hand corner of the slab.

Weeping Wall   15 metres   E2 5b †   (18.8.97)
Ideally this route, which ascends the cracks near the left edge of the slab,
would benefit from a right-hand entry; at present the start is
disproportionately hard. Ascend *Fear Test* to the base of the cracks. Follow
the cracks pleasantly, and with good protection, to the top.

A little distance to the left is a 9-metre slab, the left-hand arête of which is climbed by **For the Record** (9 metres E1 5a † 16.8.97); unprotected. Immediately left is a square slab with three prominent, yet rather grassy, cracks ignored by the following clean but serious climbs.

TLC   15 metres   E3 5b †   (16.8.97)
Reach the flake crack in the right-hand arête directly over a bulge – committing. Continue tenderly up the suspicious flake to the top.

Peace in Mind   15 metres   E3 5b †   (16.8.97)
From the break at 4 metres, step up to the foot of a crackline 3 metres left of the right arête, and place a reasonable wire runner. Swing right above the bulge onto the slab and climb up the centre to exit slightly right. Superb Roaches-like grit and comparably devoid of runners.

☆**Quartz Storm**   15 metres   E3 5b †   (16.8.97)
Refined climbing on wonderful holds but, again, lacking any tangible security. Start beneath the left-hand arête of the slab. Take the sliver of quartz and mostly(!) positive holds above, 2 metres right of the left-hand arête, to a welcome ledge just beneath the top. Finish via a short crack.

Left of a gully, the slabs rear up to a height of around 35 metres (reaching an altitude of about 660 metres; i.e. not that far beneath the summit of Rhinog Fawr: 720m). Some interesting slab climbs can be tracked down here, and there is room for more. Near their right-hand side, at 15 metres, is a prominent semi-detached flake, a useful landmark.

☆**The Collectors' Pot**   25 metres   E1 5b †   (16.8.97)
A good line up the slab right of the flake. From pockets, climb immediately right of a slight seepage line to a small flake at 6 metres. Cross a minor bulge diagonally rightwards on quartzitic protrusions to a crackline. Follow the crack trending a little leftwards to its end (just above the level of the top of the flake). Now, to exit, traverse right just below a chockstone (thread) and curl right around a rib to ledges. Walk off right.

☆☆**Dead Sea Scroll**   37 metres   E4 †   (16.8.97)
Sustained technical climbing on superb rock, left of the flake, with a complementary degree of danger. Start directly below the flake, 2 metres left of *The Collectors' Pot*.
1 12m. 5a. Climb up to gain a thin, leftward-trending crack, which leads to narrow ledges below and left of the flake; good spike belay.
2 25m. 6a. Step up behind the spike to a thin crack (wire), and make an 'impossible' move over the overlap on the right to reach a break. Take a line of weakness in the slab above to a good wire-slot slightly left. Now tiptoe up and rightwards, running it out, and cross a slight bulge (*RP*) to better holds above. Climb up the easier slab and finish on the left.

Don's Cairn   30 metres   E2 5c †   (16.8.97)
The first crack on the left of the prominent flake, which is far from generously protected. Start at a short left-facing corner-crack. Climb the

corner to the ledges and spike of *Dead Sea Scroll* (belay possible). Step up behind the spike to a thin crack (wire) and pull straight up to the main cracks. Steady climbing up the crack leads past a good slot (for a *Friend* 2½) to a heather ledge. A line of weakness straight above gains the exit of *Dead Sea Scroll*.

☆**Disco Bugs**   30 metres   E1 5a/b †   (16.8.97)
The second crack left of the flake; safe once the crack is gained and enjoyable throughout. Start at a slim flake, 2 metres left of *Don's Cairn*. Go up ledges above the flake onto an open wall. Move up the wall on good incuts to the crack. Climb the crack, and step right at its end onto the heather ledge of *Don's Cairn*. Finish as for that route.

Uwch y Llyn   Above the Lake   OS Ref 655 293

Behind the western end of Llyn Du, a little way up the Rhinog Fawr hillside, is a 15-metre buttress featuring twin arêtes.

☆**Min Fawr**   18 metres   E4 6a †   (24.5.97)
Idiosyncratic grit. The steep left-hand arête. Skirt up the crack on the right-hand side of the arête; then shuffle around onto its left-hand side (at an odd peg runner). Make rather spectacular moves up the arête, retiring to its right at a flake. Finish up a scoop.

Mur y Llyn   15 metres   E1 5a †   (24.5.97)
Climb the centre of the steep left-hand wall of the right-hand arête on good finger-ledges to exit right (solitary *Friend* 2 slot at half height).

☆**Min Fach**   15 metres   E2 5b †   (24.5.97)
The square-cut right-hand arête; climb its right-hand side boldly to a straightforward finish.

Twyll y Llyn   15 metres   Very Severe 4c †   (24.5.97)
The prominent crack with a tricky move onto the heather ledge.

Around the hillside above the lake are a whole variety of 3-to-5-metre strips of perfect grit that offer scenic bouldering. Somewhat more substantial are some short solos on a small edge overlooking the south-west shore of Llyn Du:

Grab Some Holds and Pull on Them   7 metres   E1 6a †   (26.7.99)
The leftmost arête with a bit of a nose. A perfect micro-arête, rescued from an E5 death-landing by one good wire placement.

White Wind   7 metres   E3 5c †   (26.7.99)
The rectangular arête in the centre of the edge; bold moves above an indifferent landing.

There are other possibilities; the left arête of the right-hand block is one of them (5a).

Rhinog Fawr (West)

The remaining crags on Rhinog Fawr occupy the area between Llyn Du and Carreg y Saeth, just to the south and west of the western half of the Roman Steps. The approaches are described from Cwm Bychan.

Just before the Roman Nose (page 317) a path from the Roman Steps leads steeply up right alongside a wall towards Rhinog Fawr. Coming into view after a few minutes are two slabs on the left just 30 metres from the path. The smaller, more easy-angled slab has one route just right of centre.

Dr Butt Prefers Them Harder   8 metres   Very Difficult †   (30.6.2001)
Steady and pleasant climbing 2 metres from the right-hand edge.

The next steep slabby wall has two faces divided by a heather-covered pinnacle.

Celtic Tiger   10 metres   E4 5c †   (30.6.2001)
The left-hand wall is a wonderland of small edges with better holds near the top. No protection.

Scarred for Life   10 metres   E3 5c †   (30.6.2001)
Step up right onto a scarred ledge before taking the challenge of the centre of the right-hand wall above. One microwire at three-quarters height protects the last tricky sequence.

Two tier-levels below the preceding crag and about 70 metres eastwards from the path is a larger easier-angled slab marked by a slim right-facing corner in its centre (unclimbed).

Bubbles Burst   12 metres   E1 5b †   (30.6.2001)
The right-hand edge of the slab leads to a rest just right of a downward-pointing flake. The wall above has some good moves and just enough gear.

Dynamo MC   12 metres   Hard Very Severe 5a †   (30.6.2001)
The centre of the slab about 2 metres right of the slim corner leads to a break a comfortable distance left of the flake. The slab is crowned by an excellent crack.

Carreg y Shrek   OS Ref 651 301

On the same level as the preceding crag, but about 500 metres west of the path to Rhinog Fawr, is a fine outcrop with a central arête. The crag is visible from the Roman Steps as the first (metal) gate is passed. Approach by following the steps through the gate in the wall until, just past the next derelict wall, a reddish short slab/wall appears on the right by the steps next to a stream. The crag sits at the head of the small valley from which the stream flows and is visible up on the left after ten minutes' walk up the valley.

Go West with the Wicked   8 metres   E1 5b †   (22.8.2001)
The slim right-facing groove just left of the finger-crack of *Shrek* is entered
direct before gaining and stepping onto the small ledge on the wall just
left. Use the groove to finish.

Shrek   8 metres   Hard Very Severe 5b †   (30.6.2001)
The excellent, steep finger-crack left of the arête.

Viper in Pink Satin   9 metres   E3 6a †   (30.6.2001)
Perfect gritstone arête climbing on the dominating feature of the crag. A
wire in a flake on the right protects the moves to finishing finger-jugs.

Nakedness Is Very Slow   8 metres   Hard Very Severe 5a † (22.8.2001)
The corner and crack just right of *Viper in Pink Satin*. Bridge up to gain the
crack and flow up this directly.

☆☆**Another Leap of Faith**   8 metres   E3 6a †   (22.8.2001)
The superb edge next right features some long stretches. A quartz seam
accommodates some protection.

MiniFrocks Are Best   8 metres   Very Difficult †   (22.8.2001)
The corner to the right of *Another Leap of Faith* is unclimbed but the
stepped corner next right is taken direct.

The Incredible Bounce of Marrow   8 metres   E2 5c †   (13.7.2001)
To the right is a wall with a capping roof. A thin crack leading to the
right-hand side of the roof escalates in difficulty until awkward moves find
a fine finishing-crack formed by the huge wedged flake at the top.

From here some slabs can be seen further up the hillside to the south-west.

Stubborn as an Ass   16 metres   Hard Very Severe 5a †   (13.7.2001)
The centre of the biggest slab, left of the separating gully. Take the thin,
clean slab to a break. Continue directly above via a blind seam.

Ass Landing   15 metres   Very Severe 4b †   (13.7.2001)
The crack in the lower right-hand slab leads steadily up to good holds in
the top wall.

Mowing the Ass   13 metres   Severe †   (13.7.2001)
The vague open seam on the left leads up and leftwards to pleasant
climbing.

Crags North of Gloyw Lyn[1]   Clear Lake

From Cwm Bychan, follow the Roman Steps to the point where a footpath to
Gloyw Lyn branches off right. Take the Gloyw Lyn path as far as a stile in a
stone wall. A prominent nose is visible up to the right (OS Ref 645 304).

---

1 The spelling appears to be correct.

Information Cocoons   15 metres   E1 5b †   (25.8.2001)
Climb the nose to a small overlap and a thin break. Committing moves up
a thin seam lead to an easy finish.

☆☆**Plugs of Muscle**   15 metres   E2/3 5c †   (25.8.2001)
Start below a corner to the right of the nose. Perplexing climbing up the
corner gains a slabby wall. Follow a thin leftward-rising break to the nose.

Elegant in Socks   10 metres   Difficult †   (25.8.2001)
Climb the easy-angled slab and short wall right of the nose.

The remaining three climbs are situated on three leaning towers which are
situated in the col to the west. Reach them by following the stone wall across
rough ground.

Don't Ever Buy Teeth from a Catalogue   8 metres   Difficult † (25.8.2001)
The leaning corner in the first tower past rattling blocks.

☆☆**Serpent Heart**   8 metres   E2 5c †   (25.8.2001)
Climb the committing crack in the face of the tower to a tricky finish.

Serpent Mistress   8 metres   E3 6a †   (25.8.2001)
The striking crack in the third tower: 'hell to gain, fine to climb, devilish to
finish'.

Crags of the Southern Rhinog

Rhinog Fach   Lesser Threshold   OS Ref 665 268 and 665 266
Considering that there is such a lot of rock on Rhinog Fach it is surprising that
there are only two recorded climbs here. But at least one, *The South Ridge*,
has the accolade of being the oldest climb in the Rhinogau – it is also one of
its longest and highest. The other climb is located nearby on the west-facing
slab that dips directly into the waters of Llyn Hywel, which underlies the
south slope of Rhinog Fach. A fine day's mountaineering can be had by
combining both climbs, or maybe incorporating *The South Ridge* in the
Nantcol circuit.

The best approach is from the Nantcol roadhead, where cars may be left at
the pay-at-the-farm pull-off at Maes-y-garnedd, OS Ref 642 269. Follow the
Bwlch Drws Ardudwy footpath for one and a half kilometres towards the col;
then turn right into a short valley which leads south-eastwards to the
north-west shore of Llyn Hywel. *The South Ridge* projects from the boulder-
strewn southern slopes of Rhinog Fach up to the left, while the Hywel slabs
are straight ahead defining the eastern shore of the llyn. A longer and more
tortuous approach is possible from the east, through the Crawcwellt forest.

★The South Ridge   170 metres   Severe   (1935)
This is the great stepped ridge rising towards the summit of Rhinog Fach.
While being escapable to the left, the line described provides a very
interesting climb with an exposed finish and various harder, more direct
options. Start at the foot of the ridge.
1 14m. Climb the right-hand side of the arête, avoiding some suspect
blockwork, and bear left and up to a ledge..
2 13m. Scramble to the obvious cracked block. Go up the block and
short wall to another ledge.
3 8m. Tackle the difficult steep rib behind, to the left of a corner-crack.
4 45m. Scramble up the ridge to a level area which disjoints the ridge.
5 40m. Climb carefully up and right beneath an overhang to a grassy
ledge. Continue right across the top of a gully to gain a projecting flat
ledge in an extremely exposed position. Take the right-hand side of the rib
steeply to easier ground and belays.
6 50m. Scramble easily to walk-off territory. The summit is within spitting
distance.

☆Walking on Water   50 metres   Severe †   (1995)
A unique slab climb above deep, fresh water. Start by scrambling in to the
right-hand (southern) end of the slab and take a belay above the water's
edge. Traverse left just above the water to the centre of the slab (deep
water soloing comes to the Rhinogau!). Climb the centre of the slab, past
an overlap at 20 metres, to the top.

Craig Bodlyn   Crag (of) the Dwelling Lake   OS Ref 649 236
By any standards, Craig Bodlyn is impressive. Towering above Llyn Bodlyn to
a height of 100 metres, it is by far the loftiest of crags in the massif; a sort of
Frêney amongst Fontainbleau. Upon approaching it many will wonder why
they have not been here before, yet with the benefit of experience the unwary
may never return. Alas, this deserving precipice has one huge personal
problem – excess body veg! Forlorned since some big names defuzzed it in
the 60s, the crag has stealthily been re-invaded by vegetation. (The
descriptions of the older routes, rather than being archived, have been
more-or-less reproduced from the 1988 guidebook with the caveat that a
Climbers' Club Health Warning applies.)

This is not to say that some, if not all the climbs are not conquerable (and,
besides, what else but vegetation would you expect on a dormant high
mountain crag?); but to succeed, the climber may have to battle long and
hard against significant odds. Nor will the encounter be any less intense on
the crop of clean big routes of 1997, but here difficulties will be of a more
stylized and technical nature, compliant with modern expectations. On these
climbs, on-sight cleaning tools can be grounded and the delights of the
finest Barmouth Grit prolonged in positions of some grandeur. Perhaps the
cliff's greatest attraction, however, are the year-2000 developments on its
left wing, especially on The Silver Screen. Here lies a state-of-the-art
ensemble of high-standard face climbs on immaculate rough white grit,

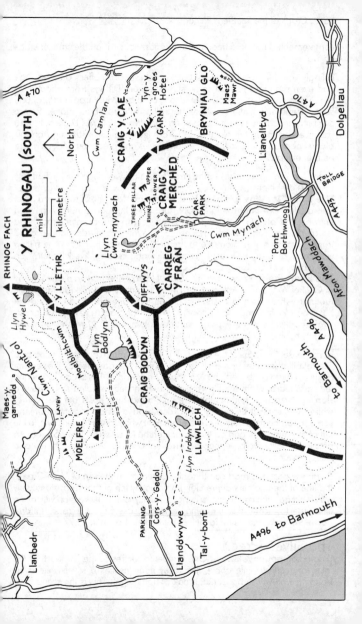

complemented by some beautiful 'wilderness soloing' on the smaller crags above.

Fittingly, the cliff faces north-west but it is not especially affected by seepage and even manages to steal some sunshine from Diffwys from about 4.00 p.m., high summer. A good deal is to grab a big route from Nantcol one sunny summer's evening when the valley will be yours alone. Before climbing, take time to visit the memorial to William Hawes Ledbrook, who sacrificed his life to the place in 1913 at the age of 21. Gaze up from his plaque above the lake to the same dark gullies and precarious ledges where he met his fate.

There are two approaches to the crag, both stocky enough to ward off any frivolous ambitions:

The Long Flat Way From the A 496 Abermawr to Harlech road, at a point half a kilometre north of Tal-y-bont, turn right through a narrow pillared entrance to Cors y Gedol (easy to miss) and dump your car at the roadhead (small car-park on the right: honesty box). Walk eastwards along a good track (passing half a kilometre to the north of the craggy Iron Age hilltop settlement of Craig y Dinas) to Llyn Bodlyn and its crag; five kilometres on foot (shades of the Craig Dubh Loch walk-in).

The Short Steep Way Drive into Cwm Nantcol and park in a small lay-by at OS Ref 629 258. Walk eastwards for 50 metres and pick up the public footpath which rises in a south-south-easterly direction to the broad col between Moelfre and Moelblithcwm. Where the track gives up the ghost, Craig Bodlyn becomes your guide: three kilometres (and with entertaining sunsets behind the Lleyn on your return).

Layout-wise, the focus of the crag is a 100-metre main face dominated by a central pillar (tackled by *Man Is Fauna*), which is demarcated by the verdant gullies of *Inigo* on the left and *The Spade* on the right. The broad face to the left (climbed by *From the Rocks*) holds a large clean striated slab above a slanting terrace at half-height. The right-hand face hosts but one climb, while buttressing it below right is a dark and overhanging crag offering some modern interpretations. The prominent white (silver?) wall down to the left of the main cliff, and on the far side of the lake, is The Silver Screen. An array of smaller walls pepper the terrain above The Silver Screen, left of a steep cascade.

By far the best and most comfortable descent from the top of Main Crag is the line of the heathery depression immediately left of the deep, stony gully which borders the crag mass to its right. The top of the depression will take a little time to locate, despite being very accessible from the rock platform above the crag and being identified with a small cairn in 1997.

The Silver Screen

[Photodiagram page 336a.] One hundred metres to the left (east) of the lake, and only a little above the valley floor, nestles a silver-white over-hanging wall with a horizontal break at half height. This is the scene for a summer's hotspot of desperates, which are unusually steep and powerful for Rhinog gritstone. Some of the routes are of national class; this is probably the best hardman's crag in the Rhinogau, and there is still potential for an E9 or two. The crag faces north-west, receives the summer sun after 3.00 p.m., and is sheltered and relatively well-drained.

In the left-hand end of the crag, facing east, is a striking, wide crack:

☆**Fame Drain**   18 metres   E3 5c †   (12.8.2000)
A very interesting crack, far more pleasant than the tag 'wide crack' would suggest! Climb a short cracked rib to a ledge beneath the crack. Follow the crack, with some pleasant surprises, to a flake where it curls over. Step left onto a slab and finish up a short flake crack.

The next two routes terminate on the large white ledge on the left; it is possible to abseil from here using the chockstones (alternatively, finish up the off-width: looks about Very Severe!).

Stars in Our Eyes   12 metres   E3 5b †   (16.6.2000)
Seriously underprotected; this is the slight groove close to the left edge of the white wall. Make tricky moves into the groove. Using good holds on the left (runner), climb more easily to the break and swing right onto the large ledge. The top pitch of *Anxiety* (E4 6a) would be an appropriate finish.

☆**Silverback**   11 metres   E7 6c †   (30.7.2000)
The immaculate silver sheet – but more off than on. By far the hardest technical test-piece in the Rhinogau. Climb boldly rightwards to a good undercut flake (peg runner). Somehow use the sloping slot on the left (hard-to-place wire) and stretch for a crimp. Gain the hand-ledge above (hand-placed short blade, and *Friend* 1½ on the left) and get onto the ledge direct or with a step to the right.

☆**Anxiety**   25 metres   E6 †   (16.6.2000/12.8.2000)
The first pitch is much harder than it looks, and the gear isn't obvious. One-third distance along the crag a slight and ragged crack leads up to the break. Start at a small cave.
1 15m. 6b. Bridge out over the cave and reach the bottom of the crack using an undercut flake on the left. Sustained, hard moves on difficult holds lead ultimately to the break. Swing left onto the large ledge.
2 10m. 6a. From the right-hand end of the large ledge, gain a small ledge on the headwall, either using flakes on the left, or with a mantel out to the right. Take the micro-thin crack above (peg runner) to a narrow ramp. Foot-traverse the unprotected ramp rightwards to the top. A spectacular, if nervy, finish.

☆**The Silver Usurper**   23 metres   E6 6b †   (30.7.2000)
Possibly the best climb of its grade in the region, which takes on the full height of the centre of the crag. The climbing is beautifully technical and the rock superb; the fixed gear is a little spaced but sound (in 2000). It is possible to take a stance at the break on large cams/hexes, but most

leaders will prefer to drop a line for the belay hardware and the rack needed for the headwall, and lead the route in one pitch. Start at the small cave as for *Anxiety*. Traverse right on widely spaced holds to get bridged up in a narrow, undercut groove (peg runner). Climb the groove to better holds on the right (peg runner). Invent a hard move to reach the foot of a thin, curling flake-line on the left. Follow the flake to the break, and step left to a small ledge (belay possible). Undercut over the bulge to a jug on the right, and then pull up to the base of a crackline in the headwall. Climb the crack on surprising holds, until a desperate move (peg runner) gains big holds and a swing right to exit.

☆R.H. 100%   20 metres   E6 6b †   (12.8.2000)
The central groove, which ends at the break. The easiest of the E6s, but still a bold and powerful lead. Climb the groove with increasing difficulty (peg runner) to a large, sharp side-hold. Muscle up and left to distant holds in a crack (*Rock 2/3* after the crux), and then follow better holds to the break. Ignore the E9 headwall, and hand-traverse the break leftwards (a free girdle thrown in!), to the large ledge.

☆Dynocology   21 metres   E6 6b †   (16.6.2000)
A powerful climb. The start goes without aid at 6c – when drip-free. Start below a hole at 4 metres in the right wing of the crag. Get your hands in the hole (*Friend 4*) using a low peg (or *RP1*) for aid, or a super-hard move. Follow layaways up a slight groove to a break. Forceful climbing above leads to a rest in a larger break (peg runner). Follow good pockets in the headwall, and take the obvious line of holds to a delicate rock-up onto a slab. Finish easily.

☆☆Destiny   24 metres   E6 6b †   (30.7.2000)
Brilliant, varied climbing on perfect rock. The route takes a line up the right-hand side of the wall via the black streaks: wait until they're dry. From a spike, swing left to good handholds and a pocket (cams). Stretch to jugs above and a semi-rest in the break. Move up onto the black-streaked wall using a downward-pointing spike (*in-situ* wire), whereupon an intricate sequence of moves (peg runner, *Rock 2* placement just right) should gain a jug in a scoop. Bridge up into the leftward-leaning groove; then boldly pad up the slab on the left (peg runner), eventually to reach the exit of *Dynocology* on the left.

Streaker   15 metres   E3 6a †   (16.6.2000)
An enjoyable climb with hard opening moves. Start at the right-hand end of the crag. Climb up and left to a good undercut flake. Move left with difficulty (*Rock 7* placement in break-line) to better holds in a rib. Pull up onto slabbier rock, and climb up over a bulge to finish at the right end of a huge flake.

To the left of the crag is a perched boulder containing what may become the most fallen-off route in the Rhinogau.

Gazump   5 metres   E1 6b †   (21.7.2000)
Overcome the boulder's arête. Two rocks protruding from the grass make aiming where to land desirable.

Six-Metre Wall

A small, hidden wall of impeccable clean rough grit which provides four solos mainly above an uncharacteristically soft landing – no need to hoik your designer crash mats up the mountain! Reach the wall by scrambling up heather from the left-hand end of the sloping terrace above the white wall (The Silver Screen).

Not-So-Soft 6 metres Hard Very Severe 4c †   (20.7.2000)
The left arête (above a killjoy-boulder).

☆**Get Laid Twice** 6 metres E2 6b †   (20.7.2000)
Forget *Tierdrop* on Ramshaw, this is the quintessential gritstone micro-route. Reach a left-facing layaway, power into the second layaway, and finish direct or with a step left.

☆**Silence Can Speak** 6 metres E2 6a †   (20.7.2000)
A technical delicacy up the thin central seam.

Wall-to-Wall Sunshine 5 metres E1 5c †   (20.7.2000)
Leap up the right-hand arête, and use a projecting jug to the fullest extent to exit.

Bad Teeth Wall

So named because of the man-made row of skewiff stones overhanging the left end of the crag; reach it either by walking up from the Six-Metre Wall or by taking the third heather terrace from the cascade to the right of the crags. The crag faces north-east; only early-risers will climb in the sun here.

The first three routes take the quartz-flecked wall under the teeth; all were soloed on the first ascents. (Protection is extremely limited, and the landings are soft – but not soft enough to be tested from this height.)

The Wild Around 9 metres E1 6a †   (20.7.2000)
Climb the smooth face right of the arête to a flake hold. Continue more easily to the top.

The Wild Within 11 metres E2 6a †   (20.7.2000)
Trend left on foot-ledges and climb the quartzy wall right of a slight V-groove to bigger holds. Pass a large quartz hold and then trend delicately leftwards to the exit of the previous route.

And Janet Street Porter Walked By 12 metres E4 6a † (20.7.2000)
Unprotected; at least the climbing only rates 5a above half height. Start at a square quartzitic pedestal. Work straight up blind, incipient cracks until a swing right gains a narrow flat ledge below a small roof. Pull over the roof and exit incisively.

Twenty metres right is a taller slab with a hand-crack in its base.

Duck!   20 metres   E2 5c †   (20.7.2000)
Grovel up a dirty flake crack to a heathery niche 7 metres up. Pull over a
small overhang to gain the base of an obvious thin crack. Using
good holds on the left, reach a break (*Friend 2½ placement*). Continue up the
thin crack on improving holds to the top.

☆**Boys in Toys**   20 metres   E1 5b †   (20.7.2000)
Climb the hand-crack to a narrow ledge and step left. Follow a crack to a
wide sloping slot on the left (*Friend 3 placement*). Move up delicately just
left of the arête, and step left to exit.

Forked Lightning Conductor Buttress
This is the buttress a little above and to the left of Bad Teeth Wall. It has a
prominent arête on the left. The rock is delightfully clean and rough grey grit.
The crag faces west, and dries quickly.

The Arête   15 metres   Very Severe 4a †   (20.7.2000)
Climb the arête, easily at first, and then more delicately via a scoop on the
right.

☆**Receding Hairline**   12 metres   E4 5c †   (20.7.2000)
Left of the (unclimbed) corner is a vertical hairline crack in a vague rib.
Climb the rib in line with the crack, with a technical move to reach a jug
and a long move from it. Finish on good finger-holds. Superb rock but the
prospect of 'decking it' is enough to make your hair fall out.

Forked Lightning Conductor Crack 8 metres E1 5c †   (20.7.2000)
Right of the (loose) right-hand arête of the corner is an off-fingers crack. Very
safe to lead (but prepare for a shock if you pull too hard on the sharp flake).

Ten metres right of the corner is an upward-pointing flake embedded in the
ground.

Watch the Point   11 metres   Very Severe 4c †   (20.7.2000)
Climb the disjointed corner left of the flake and slabby rock above.

Impale Face   11 metres   E1 5c †   (20.7.2000)
Step right off the flake and overcome the sheer wall on surprising holds.
Finish up easier rock.

The Curl
A 10-metre cliff of beautiful rough grit tucked right out of harm's way. It is
located 250 metres south of Forked Lightning Conductor Buttress (i.e.
behind and to the left – east – of the summit of the Main Crag). The crag has
an easterly aspect and gets the summer sun all morning. Note that this is
soloing country; there is no protection on any but one of the climbs, and
landings are level and soft. Leave your hardware in the car!

The main event is a steep, horizontally-banded wall on the left with a purple
(water) streak. Six metres left of the streak is:

Gaardevarre 10 metres Severe † (21.7.2000)
Climb the purple face on lovely fingerholds to an easier slab.

Finnmark 10 metres Hard Very Severe 4c † (21.7.2000)
Follow the leftward-trending grooves left of the steep wall to an easier slab.

☆☆**Purple Rain** 10 metres E4 5c † (21.7.2000)
Perfect purple grit. The purple streak with intricate moves at 6 to 7 metres.
High in the grade.

☆**Haircurler** 10 metres E4 5c † (21.7.2000)
Pull over a bulge on obvious shallow pockets, and climb the wall 2 metres
right of the streak to a little rock spike and better holds.

Twenty metres right is a clean white slab above an insubstantial heather
ledge.

☆**The Bodlyn White** 8 metres E2 5c † (21.7.2000)
Attack the centre of the white slab; hardest moves to start.

Near the right-hand end of the crag is a slab undercut by a roof.

☆**Rail to Oblivion** 9 metres E5 6a † (21.7.2000)
A wilderness gem. Follow a jug-rail leftwards through the roof, and make
an athletic rockover onto the slab. Continue direct up the delightful slab to
the top. (The only route here with any gear; probably E4 to lead.)

Main Crag [Diagram page 336b.]
Porky 78 metres Hard Very Severe (1 pt aid) † (4.71)
A route up the left edge of the Main Crag with a deep wet gully to its left.
Start below an obvious corner at the top of pitch 1 of *Mochan*, where a
large terrace comes in from the gully on the left.
1 18m. Take the easiest line up the corner to a large ledge below a
chimney.
2 15m. The chimney leads to another big ledge.
3 25m. Traverse left from the ledge; then climb a shallow groove to
blocks below an overhang. Climb the overhang (peg for aid) and move up
a groove above to a ledge under another overhang.
4 20m. Go right along the ledge a little and climb a vague groove to
gain a chimney on the right-hand side of a pinnacle. Follow this to the top.

Mochan 108 metres Very Severe † (5.69)
The easiest line up this part of the crag. Start 4 metres right of a small tree
at the lowest point of the slabs (the big obvious corner-line of *Inigo* is on
the right).
1 30m. Go directly up the slabs to vegetated ledges. Block belay at the
foot of the corner above.
2 18m. 4c. From the corner, climb the arête on the right for a while; then
traverse right to a groove, and go up this to a vegetated ledge.

3 15m. 4a. Climb the chimney cutting through the wall above to ledges, and ascend to the highest of these.
4 20m. 4c. Take the wall above to a horizontal crack, and move right to the ledge above.
5 25m. 4b. Climb the wall above, starting on the right, and slant left to finish to the left of a cutaway overhang. Belay above on ledges on the right.

☆**From the Rocks**　80 metres　E4 †　　　　　　　　(25.5.97)
A substantial second pitch taking an unrelenting and taxing direct line up the centre of the large striated slab left of the central pillar. Start from the left-hand end of the first grass terrace gained from the easy grassy gully on the left (the first stance of *Mochan*).
1 35m. 5c. Pull over the small roof 3 metres right of the arête and move up to a good spike runner near the arête. Climb diagonally rightwards for 5 metres to a thin crack. Step right into the base of a slim groove in the face on the right, and follow the groove before a long stretch gains a ledge. From the large heather ledge above, climb the wide crack of *Galium* to the slanting terrace beneath the slab; belay on a spike on the wall behind (with gear 6 metres up left).
2 45m. 6a/b. From the spike, climb up to a thin break at 5 metres. Tiptoe up the smooth slab (peg runner) by very technical moves to gain a deeper, shaly break (*Friend* 2 or 2½ placement). Move up, with difficulty again, to a good ledge. Climb the slab slightly leftwards (peg runner), then direct onto somewhat easier terrain. Take a fairly straight line to a short groove and exit recklessly onto the heather terrace: scary.

Galium　98 metres　Hard Very Severe †　　　　　　　(9.69)
A line which flirts with the large striated slab above half height. Start from the top of a large embedded flake 3 metres left of the vegetated corner of *Inigo*, below the slabs.
1 20m. 4a. Go up the steep slabs directly above the flake to vegetated ledges. Belay as for *Mochan* on the left.
2 18m. 4c. Gain the ledge above the overhang and take a fairly direct line as for *Mochan* to a big ledge.
3 15m. 4c. Ascend the crack to the right of the chimney of *Mochan*, to another big ledge (as for *From the Rocks*).
4 45m. 5a. Climb the wall to a horizontal crack; move right and gain the ledge above. Go right along the ledge to grass; then trend up and back left. Traverse right and climb a groove above to the top.

Inigo　95 metres　Very Severe †　　　　　　　　(8.67)
The obvious big corner-line running the full height of the crag. Vegetated. Start directly beneath the big corner.
1 30m. 4b. Climb the vegetated corner to a bulge, and move right to a large vegetated ledge.
2 15m. 4b. Return left to below the overhang, climb this direct and take the steepening groove on the right to another large ledge.
3 35m. 4b. Ascend the corner above by its easiest line to a ledge below the last pitch.

Craig Bodlyn

The Silver Screen

1	Fame Drain	E3
2	Stars in Our Eyes	E3
3	Silverback	E7
4	Anxiety	E6
5	The Silver Usurper	E6
6	RH 100%	E6
7	Dynocology	E6
8	Destiny	E6
9	Streaker	E3

Craig Bodlyn

Main Crag

1 Porky — HVS
2 Mochan — VS
3 Galium — HVS
4 From the Rocks — E4
5 Inigo — VS
6 Nardus — VS
8 Man Is Fauna — E4
9 Mass Extinction — E5
10 The Spade — VS
11 Strictus — E1
12 High Girdle — E1

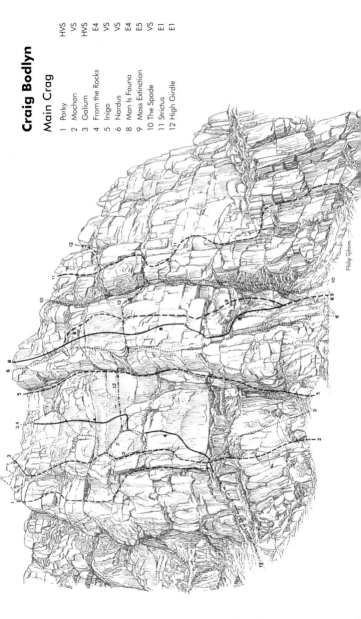

Philip Gibson

4 15m. 4c. Climb the corner above to a bulge; then go directly over this to the top.

Nardus   100 metres   Very Severe   (5.66)
Open and interesting and still occasionally climbed. Escape is possible at many points to *Inigo* (or vice versa!). Start left of the start of *The Spade*, at a cleaned groove.
1 35m. 4b. Climb the groove to a ledge, and the wall above to a big ledge, which goes left under an overhang and meets the corner-line of *Inigo*. (A much cleaner approach would be to use the first pitch of *Man Is Fauna*.)
2 25m. 4c. Climb a shallow groove to the right of the overhang, and move left to a ledge on the arête. The easy arête is taken for a few metres; then climb a groove on the right, capped by an overhang. Step left at the overhang and ascend to some small ledges with nut belays.
3 12m. 4c. Climb the arête direct via a groove to good holds; then move right to vegetated ledges.
4 28m. Take the easiest line above over vegetated ledges to finish just left of a large pointed spike.

☆☆**Man Is Fauna**   95 metres   E4 †   (25.5.97)
Magnificent; the climb strikes a central line up the central pillar of the crag. Start below a white, right-facing corner just right of *Nardus*.
1 20m. 4a. Climb up into the corner and follow it to a large pedestal ledge on the left. Belay below a corner on the left.
2 30m. 6a. Ascend the corner to a break. Negotiate a tricky little groove and stride right onto the obvious foothold above the roofs. Now reach a hairline crack above (peg runner) and follow this delicately before swinging left into a slanting crack which leads to a good little stance at a horizontal break (crossed by *High Girdle*).
3 45m. 5c. Step right and pull up and right to the foot of a left-trending crack. Climb the crack to a grass ledge (belay possible). Scramble up to the base of the final pillar. Take its left-hand edge and then its front face to exit just right of the large pointed spike.

☆☆**Mass Extinction**   100 metres   E5 †   (7.6.97)
Extremely sustained face-climbing above the roofs in the right-hand side of the central pillar. Big lead stakes, though only just meriting the grade. Start as for *Man Is Fauna*.
1 25m. 4c. Climb the white corner, as for *Man Is Fauna*, almost to the top; then step right into a narrow corner leading to a fine stance below the roof stack.
2 30m. 6a. Pull up into a quartz niche, reach over a roof to a handrail (*in-situ* thread), and hand-traverse left to the arête. Pass the final roof at a short left-facing flake, and balance up onto the face. Climb a thin crack above and, from a peg runner, continue boldly direct to a rest below some small overhangs. Make extending moves over the overhangs to reach a finger-slot (*Friend* 1½ placement) and, without missing a jug on the left, move up past a sloping ledge to a good belay at the horizontal break.

3 45m. 5b. Follow the cracks in the right-hand arête to grass ledges (belay possible). Finish up the left-hand arête of the final pillar, as for *Man Is Fauna*.

Tenuous (95 metres E3 5c 1pt aid † 6.69) wandered painfully up the central pillar and has been gridlocked by the preceding two routes, save an excursion on the right of *Mass Extinction* which remains very vegetated.

The Spade   103 metres   Very Severe †   (27.8.60)
The obvious deep chimney/gully line cutting through some large overhangs. Start below the chimney. Vegetated.
1 23m. Ascend vegetation to below the overhangs; then move out right onto a ledge. A step up leads to a grassy ledge beneath a vertical V-corner.
2 6m. Climb the corner to another grassy ledge on the right.
3 15m. Go up delicately back left and move up to below the main overhang. Climb it direct to a small niche; then go up a small overhang above to a stance and belay in a cave.
4 9m. Exit leftwards, mantelshelf, and return to the gully.
5 14m. The 12-metre chimney is strenuous.
6 18m. Move left again, mantelshelf, and go back into the gully. Climb into an overhanging cave making a step left to a large ledge and belay.
7 18m. Trend rightwards easily and follow the continuation line to the top.

Strictus   104 metres   E1 †   (4.67)
Steep varied climbing making for the obvious corner high up the buttress. Start below a heather-infested corner to the right of *The Spade*.
1 18m. Climb the corner to ledges.
2 18 m. 4b. Ascend vegetation, trending left to a chimney cutting through a quartz band. Climb the chimney to the top of a pinnacle.
3 30 m. 5a. Move up, and then go left across the wall to its left edge. Belay beneath a crack in the back of an obvious V-corner.
4 18m. 5b. Climb the corner to a large ledge.
5 20m. 5b. Take the easiest line over vegetated walls above to the top.

High Girdle   118 metres   E1 †   (1972)
The crucial sections appear sufficiently clean, making the route probably worth a bash for a very adventurous team. Start from the top of pitch 1 of *Mochan*.
1 18m. Pitch 2 of *Mochan*.
2 15m. Pitch 3 of *Galium*.
3 19m. 5a. From the big ledge beneath the horizontal crack, take an obvious line traversing right into the corner of *Inigo*. Belay on the right wall (stance as for *Nardus* pitch 2).
4 28 m. 5a. Reverse a few metres of *Nardus* and move right to reach the obvious horizontal break crossing the steep central buttress. Go right along the break into *The Spade*; belay on the right beneath the V-corner of *Strictus*.
5 18m. 5b. Climb the corner as for pitch 4 of *Strictus*.
6 20m. 4c. Go right along ledges. Climb a crack; then follow vegetated walls to the top.

The following two routes take on the overhanging buttress which constitutes the lower right-hand part of the crag; both stay mainly dry in the rain (and no doubt mainly wet in the sun).

Certificated   25 metres   E4 6a †   (7.6.97)
This takes the flake groove in the foremost part of the crag. Start up a whitish wall left of an easy corner, and bear left to the foot of the flake crack. Ascend the crack on good holds to a precarious-feeling, sloping hand-ledge. Step left and, using holds in the groove on the left, pass the bulge with a hard move. From a break, move rightwards onto the headwall; then escape diagonally leftwards on large holds to the top.

☆**Blacklisted**   25 metres   E5 6a †   (7.6.97)
A varied and power-packed pitch that needs a controlled style. Start at the base of an easy corner which leads to an overhanging black groove. Climb up the corner to a ledge at 4 metres. Now pull straight over a small roof (hand-placed medium knife-blade a little above the roof) and gain good spike holds (and runners) slightly right. Follow jugs up the groove to a short crack where it ends (bomber gear). Strenuously overcome the bulge, and take the easier rightward-slanting crack to a positive exit on the left.

Llawlech   Rocky   OS Ref 636 228
A 25-metre, west-facing crag that provides a day's worth of quality climbs on good rock. The crag is situated in the same valley as Craig Bodlyn, but some one and a half kilometres to the south-east, and it is clearly visible to the right on the approach walk (The Long Flat Way – see page 330). It can receive significantly better weather than Craig Bodlyn.

To approach, park at Cors y Gedol (as for the Craig Bodlyn Long Flat Way approach). Turn right through a gate, and walk down a metalled road to a bridge over the Afon Ysgethin. Cross the bridge, and follow the track and then public footpath (sign-posted 'to the lakes') eastwards to Llyn Erddyn. Continue half a kilometre beyond the northern shore of the lake, and then break right to the crag. (About four kilometres: 40 minutes.)

At the left-hand end of the crag is an isolated buttress with a tower above.

☆**Lawless**   15 metres   Very Severe 4c †   (28.5.2000)
The obvious flake crack in the centre of the buttress; well protected. Start behind a large embedded flake. Step off the flake and bear rightwards to the crack. Climb the crack steeply to a sloping, flake ledge. Finish up a delicate little groove straight above.

☆**One Law for One**   15 metres   E3 5c †   (28.5.2000)
Excellent, technical climbing, but fairly bold. Start at a tall jammed block. Climb straight up to a small niche. Keeping left of the right-hand arête, make hard moves direct to a slanting undercut, and use this to gain a narrow groove in the arête. Follow the arête to the terrace.

☆**Tower of Libel**   24 metres   Hard Very Severe †   (28.5.2000)
Enjoyable and exposed. Start below the right-hand arête.
1 15m. 5a. Climb the lower arête to ledges. Move up the continuation arête on its right-hand side to reach the terrace.
2 9m. 4c. To the right is an undercut tower. Step right to a jug and pull up onto the tower face. Climb a shallow scoop, using the right arête, to the top.

The next two routes take the main face, which has a distinctive overhang. Both start from the huge block.

☆☆**The God Summons**   24 metres   E4 6a †   (30.5.2000)
Uplifting and absorbing; but the hand of God may be needed on the upper run-out section. Climb direct from the top of the block to a large undercut. Swing left to a small V-groove; then pull up and right into a short left-facing groove. Pull boldly out onto the face above, and get onto a ledge on the left (good runner). Exit rightwards over steep ivy and heather.

☆**A Roof over Head Makes Home**   18 metres   E2 5c †   (30.5.2000)
The compelling line through the roof: much easier than it looks. Swing right from the block to a jug and pull up to a ledge in a corner (good nut). Move up the right wall of the corner to the roof. Make a long and powerful stretch to a big hold (harder than 5c if you fill the slot with a cam), and take the flake above to a good spike. Abseil off.

There is potential for more climbs to the right.

Down to the right of the main crag is a 9-metre bluff with three solos to kill time; they take steeper rock between the more broken and vegetated lines.

Turn Vertical When Life Is Flat
            8 metres   Hard Very Severe 4c † (30.5.2000)
Take the slabby wall right of the left-hand rib to the top.

Dr Irish Watches   9 metres   E2 5b †   (30.5.2000)
Left of centre, a purple streak shows the way. Worse landing than E2 suggests.

The Tywyn Weird Route Name Society Bolt-less Competition Climb
            9 metres   E1 5a † (30.5.2000)
Make your way up the steep wall at the right-hand end of the crag, using spaced flake holds and a leftward-pointing spike at the top.

The Western Valleys: Cwmnantcol

The following three climbing sites are situated in Cwmnantcol, the quiet, open valley that curls eastwards from Pentre Gwynfryn into the Rhinog heartland. A minor road runs as far as the farm of Maes-y-garnedd, near the head of the valley, beyond which a footpath heads through the ancient pass of Bwlch Drws Ardudwy between Rhinog Fawr and Rhinog Fach.

Moelfre Bald Hill

Unlike most of their immediate neighbours the crags of the huge rotund mass of Moelfre face north or north-west. To climb in the sun here you are going to have to get up at some ungodly hour or choose an evening during high summer. As upon many a Rhinog hillside the crags are of a modest size and scattered. An eclectic range of micro-routes should find modernistic appeal.

The access used to date (but which crosses a small stretch of farmland) is from one of two off-road parking-spots at OS Ref 622/5 258. Walk due south via the one or two gates respectively; then strike upslope to the crags.

The main batch of climbs take the barrel-shaped buttress left-of-centre in the craggy hillside (OS Ref 624 254). Their quality far outweighs all expectations.

☆☆**Just a Little...Please** 9 metres E3 6a †   (23.7.2000)
Superb rock and climbing, with protection where it's needed. Start at the foot of a shallow groove immediately right of the cave at the left-hand end of the buttress. Boulder up the groove to bigger holds under a bulge (flake runner). Traverse left across a sloping ledge until it is possible to step up into a scoop (good wire). Step left and finish up the pleasant slab.

The next two climbs are located on the slabby-looking sidewall to the right.

Farmers' Union 10 metres E3 6a †   (23.7.2000)
From the undercut, move up past a tiny sapling to reach and follow a thin crack in the left side of the wall. A hard move at half height perplexes for a while.

☆**Soldier On** 11 metres E3 5c †   (23.7.2000)
Excellent, but with spaced protection that is not immediately obvious. Start at a small triangular niche in the break. Follow a series of rounded ledges rightwards onto the wall. Take thin, blind cracks above to a slight break. Now reach a jug in the base of a little groove on the right, and exit right.

☆**Pick White** 12 metres E4 6a †   (23.7.2000)
Forceful climbing up the overhanging white (quartzitic) rib in the front of the buttress. Pull up onto a tiny ledge; then climb strenuously past a hidden wire placement up a slight flake to easier-angled ground. Continue direct for 2 metres; then exit right.

☆**Right of White** 12 metres E2 5b †   (23.7.2000)
A close, but safe, companion to the former route. Move up into a narrow groove and climb it and the crack above to comforting holds. Make a long move to get established onto a sloping ledge, and then exit direct.

To the right, past two unclimbed flake cracks (the right-hand of which looks good) is an overlapping rib.

☆☆☆**Underpower**   12 metres   E5 6b †   (23.7.2000)
An absolutely brilliant climb that requires spirited climbing. Climb the overlapping rib (questionable *RP3* and *1* placements, hard to place) and bust a gut to gain good holds on the slab above. Pursue a direct line up the face, in line with a thin crack, and exit delicately with a final heave on the capping block.

Lower down the hillside, to the right, and 20 metres upslope of a wall, is a solitary arête behind a large flake.

The Habitual Segregation of Fear   10 metres   E1 5a † (23.7.2000)
Pull onto the arête using the rounded undercut spike; then follow its left-hand side until it is possible to surface on the arête and finish easily. No protection above an appalling landing.

Fifty metres right again is a short, leaning blade of rock, with an unclimbable arête.

Parting Shots   6 metres   E3 6b †   (23.7.2000)
Scratch desperately up the sheer slab right of the arête and above a soft landing. Deliciously obscure micro-extremism.

Right again is a boulder-strewn gully, with a slabby arête at its head. The next two climbs occupy the short wall left of an isolated stone wall, below a pinnacle on the left-hand side of the gully.

Rowan Asskisson   6 metres   E1 6b †   (29.7.2001)
Right of a wide flake crack, boulder up a leaning arête using layaways to both sides, and finish on the right. Mind the rowan!

Grip Rip Bones   7 metres   E3 5c †   (29.7.2001)
The right-hand arête of the wall; delicate.

Male Spiff   10 metres   E1 5a †   (29.7.2001)
Follow the slabby arête at the head of the gully. Not too taxing, but needing bravado.

At a similar level, 30 metres to the right, is a convex slab identified by a huge flake at its base.

No Smear... So Disappear   12 metres   E2 5b †   (29.7.2001)
Pull up the face of the flake to its top. Keeping a wary eye on the intervening chasm, move up into a slight scoop on the slab, and finish easily.

The next two climbs are situated on the small set of slabs just beneath the level of the stone wall, and beneath *Parting Shots*.

☆**The Moelfre of Kabul**   10 metres   E1 5b †   (28.7.2001)
Jam the centrally-positioned hand-crack. Strenuous but safe.

☆☆**Son Watching**   8 metres   E6 6b †   (28.7.2001)
Rhinog's own *Piece of Mind*. Beautiful climbing, with a friction crux above a
substantial drop. Enter the slim groove in the right-hand slab, and rock into
the scoop at its close. Step into the friction ledge on the left, and shuffle
leftwards with faith to an exit. Note the boulder waiting below the final move.

Two hundred metres right is a north-east-facing wall overlain by a terrace
with an arête at its left-hand end (OS Ref 621 255).

Peach on the Beach   10 metres   E2 5b †   (29.7.2001)
Take a central line up the wall past a thin crack, with delicate moves up
and left at the top. There is a wire placement for the crux.

☆**Showtime**   8 metres   E2 5c †   (29.7.2001)
An improvised route on the arête above the terrace. Start to its left; go up a
wide flake crack and then rock up from a jug to the arête. Take the arête
and hand-crack to the top.

Foel Wen   White Hill
The west face of Foel Wen is laced with small crags, the most substantial of
which are described here. Elsewhere, plenty of scrambling and bouldering
potential exists – but don't expect good landings. Most of the crags are
low-lying, sunny, and unaffected by seepage.

Gareg-lwyd   Grey Crag   OS Ref 627 272/3
These are the two low-lying buttresses on the same level behind woodland.
They face mainly west and are clean and very quick-drying. Some easier
new routes await. Approach from Cwmnantcol by turning east into the
minor road at OS Ref 616 269; follow this road for several hundred
metres, turn right (straight on is marked private), and find a place along
the track to park carefully. Walk along the track below a farm on the left
until the track fades immediately in front of the left-hand crag.

Towards the left-hand end of the crag is a smooth, undercut slab.

★**Slab Solo**   21 metres   E3 5c   (1990)
Move up over an overlap into the centre of the slab. A tricky move on
small edges gains an obvious hold. From the break above, reach easier
ground, and then wander up huge flakes on the rib above to the top.

Tricks   21 metres   Severe 4a †   (13.6.2000)
Climb the prominent flake crack right of the undercut slab, starting with a
difficult groove.

Del   21 metres   Severe †   (13.6.2000)
The corner-crack that bounds a sheer wall in the centre of the crag: 'a
classic delight'.

High Man Slapper   23 metres   E4 5c   (13.6.2000)
Only slightly more serious to solo. Start below the right-hand arête of the
sheer wall. Climb the arête (of *Jason's Corner*) for 5 metres. Hand-traverse
the jug-rail leftwards to its end, and then make a very delicate mantel
using a thin flake. Step up onto a second ledge; then continue direct up
the tapering slab to big flake-holds and an easy finish.

★Jason's Corner   21 metres   E2 5c   (1990)
A good, if problematic, climb. Start at the foot of a corner below a roof 8
metres up. Move up the corner and then transfer into a fine finger-crack in
the left wall. Follow the crack and make a difficult move to pass the roof
and gain the top of a huge jammed flake. Scramble up easier slabs.

At the left end of the right-hand crag is a short wall behind a small,
stone-walled enclosure. This provides **Engage** (6 metres E2 5c † 6.8.2000)
up its delicate left arête.

False Sense of Insecurity   8 metres   E3 6a †   (6.8.2000)
The narrow tower at the right-hand end of the stone wall has some holds
on its right-hand side which allow the top to be gained. Small and peculiar
wire placements.

Confessions of an Irish Opossum Eater   12 metres   E1 5b † (6.8.2000)
The wall to the right has a small oak tree in its top-centre. This line takes
the compact white wall down and left of the tree to a ledge, from which
the corner formed by the huge block/flake is reached. From the top of the
entertaining corner, follow a crack to the top.

Gold Fever   13 metres   Hard Very Severe 5a †   (6.8.2000)
The tallest part of the wall just right of the tree is climbed 2 metres right of
the right-facing corner to an overlap. Pass this on its left before striding
back right into the wide crack. Up and left is an easily gained crack which
leads to the top.

A gully topped by a stone wall divides the crag centrally. To the left of the
gully is a large oak tree, and:

☆The Thing Licker   12 metres   E4 6a †   (6.8.2000)
Fine climbing up the finger-crack in the south-facing wall. Start behind the
tree. Gain a ledge at 5 metres. Move up a short groove to reach a
downward-pointing spike. Swing right, and fight up the deceptive crack to
jugs and an easy exit.

☆Scratchless   14 metres   E3 6a †   (6.8.2000)
Clean and bold. Start beneath a blunt pillar up and to the right of the oak
tree. Climb the arête of the pillar to a vertical slot (small cam). Hard moves
up and slightly right gain a ledge. Move up onto another ledge, and finish
up the left side of the sharp upper arête.

At the right-hand edge of the front of the crag is an arête left of trees.

Scoop-a-Million 6 metres E1 5a †   (5.8.2000)
Balance up the neat white scoop 6 metres left of the arête.

☆☆**Lottery** 9 metres E6 6a/b †   (5.8.2000)
The superb, crisp arête; no gear, crux at the top. Follow its edge, with a
blind rock-up for a good hold at the right end of the ledge. Swing right
onto the nose to scramble 10 metres to the top. A body-scything flake in
the ground should be capped before setting out.

The right-hand end of the crag is intersected by a stone wall, and to the right
of the wall are the following four climbs.

Back against the Wall 7 metres E3 5c †   (5.8.2000)
A short excuse for a route that wanted to go to the top (stacked blocks
preclude). Step off of the wall, and take the blunt arête and ramp on the
right to a holly tree. Abseil off. Unprotected.

☆☆**Snaz** 12 metres E3 5b †   (29.7.2000)
The blunt overhanging arête 5 metres right of the stone wall. Good holds
abound, but the climbing is steep and there is no protection below
two-thirds height: a confident approach is required. Start the arête up a
scoop, and make an off-balance move left to a jug (not too bad for 5b).
Follow good, spaced holds above and pull onto a large flake to top out.

Curiosity's Small 12 metres E5 5c †   (29.7.2000)
A complete absence of protection and a high fall-factor, make setting up a
top rope well worthwhile! Step into the scoop of *Snaz*, but pull up to the
right onto little ledges. Make very committing moves on layaways in line
with a thin blind crack to a ledge. Get onto this using holds on the left, and
finish easily.

Mindless Trivia of Man 6 metres E3 5c †   (29.7.2000)
The not-so-trivial little tower at the right end of the wall packs a big punch
(and possibly a boulder up the backside). Climb a little groove to slopers
and finish with trepidation.

Vague Dome
Two hundred metres up and to the right of Gareg-lwyd is a sort-of dome of
west-north-west-facing slabs, which provide some fine and attractive climbing
as well as a solo test-piece of the area.

On the left is a scooped slab, undercut by a leftward-arching gash.

The Lure 8 metres E3 6a †   (5.8.2000)
E1-escapability, but with an E5-fall if you get it wrong! Climb the lower
slab easily; and work out the fall-free sequence on slopers in the scoop to
gain the top.

Behind a large holly tree on the right is a short slab: **Slab Route** (7 metres
Difficult † 5.8.2000). Right again is the main slab.

The Web   12 metres   E3 5c †   (5.8.2000)
A direct and delicate line up the left edge of the slab. Pull up onto the slab
above a small cave with difficulty. Continue direct to finish up the good
crack. Protection is available after 7 metres.

☆**The Net**   15 metres   E3 5c †   (5.8.2000)
Very little protection to catch you, but straightforward above half height.
Climb flake cracks in the green slab right of the cave; then make tenuous
moves leftwards to stand on the obvious small ledge. Now climb straight
up to finish on sinking holds.

☆**The One**   12 metres   E7 6b †   (5.8.2000)
A super-cool solo, quintessentially grit. A crack slants left and divides the
slab; start at its base. Move up the crack 2 metres, and step right onto a
blind break. Move up to a small overhang, gain marginal holds on the
ramp above and, using a layaway high left, make a precarious move over.
Smear up the ramp, with tiny edges for fingers, to the top. (Cheat runners
in the wide crack up to the left will reduce the grade and character.)

Thirty metres right is a recessed, north-facing wall left of a small ragged
pinnacle. The obvious finger-crack is **6-metre Crack** (Hard Severe 4a †
5.8.2000), the start of which gives:

The Catch   9 metres   E3 5b †   (5.8.2000)
Climb the finger-crack almost to its top. Finger-traverse the horizontal
break leftwards, and rock-up leftwards twice, using thin cracks. Pull out on
better holds.

At the right-hand end of the crag is a convex, purple-coloured slab.

The Three Words   9 metres   E1 5c †   (5.8.2000)
Start at the lowest point of the slab, left of a flake, and follow finger-nail
edges direct to proper holds. Continue steeply, but more easily, to the top.

Dol-dal-Owen   Crag (of) Owen's Holding   OS Ref 627 264
One of the most curious of Rhinog crags; those who enjoy their climbing
accentuated by pain will have fun here. Behind a derelict farm building is a
jumble of boulders and bluff at the base of the hillside, visible from the valley
road to the south. There is an unmistakable off-width crack bisecting the
south face of the bluff. A public footpath strolls directly under the crag.
Approach is quickest from the east after parking as for the Ramp Crags.

The Incision   8 metres   E4 6a †   (6.8.2000)
Slip awkwardly rightwards into the sloping niche, and grapple with the
narrowing crack. Exit all mangled.

The Derision   10 metres   E5 6a †   (6.8.2000)
Slip into the sloping niche of *The Incision*, and finger-traverse the hanging
rail rightwards (difficult gear) until a trying move gains the ledge on the
right. Swing left to exit up a groove.

Ramp Crags
OS Ref 629 266

The next two crags are situated close together half-way up the great wide ramp that rises right to left (south-east to north-west) up the rocky hillside. Park in a lay-by at OS Ref 633 262 and either take the public footpath that rises above the crags and drop down at a suitable point, or walk directly up the ramp (past a 25-metre buttress high up to the right with potential). The crags are set at the back of a widening in the ramp, the right-hand of which is a clean bulging slab with cracklines.

Flaky Pastry 8 metres E2 5c †   (29.7.2000)
Climb up flakes in the left arête to a break. Continue straight up the arête on tiny holds to scrambling terrain.

Grit-Severe 8 metres Very Severe 4c †   (29.7.2000)
Right of an unpleasantly wide crack, climb a short but fine hand-jam crack.

☆**The Story Unfolds** 12 metres E2 5c †   (29.7.2000)
Delicate slab-climbing right of the two cracks. From flakes, move up boldly into a scoop and gain a good hold (and runner) in a break. Get established on the slab above with difficulty, and finish direct.

☆**The Chocks** 12 metres Hard Very Severe 5b †   (29.7.2000)
Climb a groove left of the arête and reach good holds in the crack above a small overhang with difficulty. Pull up on chockstones, and take the easier crack to the top.

Arête de Tête 12 metres E3 6a †   (29.7.2000)
The sharp right-hand arête; nice and balancy. Swing left onto the arête, and climb it to a ledge (wire runner on left to start; climb *The Chocks* first to find out where it is). The upper arête leads to good holds.

Thirty metres left is a slab set back in a widening in the ramp.

☆**Le Mort Solitaire** 12 metres E4 5c †   (29.7.2000)
Technical climbing up the centre of the sheer slab. No protection until the undercut. Start at the lowest point of the slab, and work up and rightwards on sidepulls to a large undercut on the right (cam possible). Step back left and take thin cracks to a swing right to ledges. Easy climbing leads to the top.

Cornered 12 metres E1 5a †   (29.7.2000)
Climb the corner at the right-hand end of the slab with difficulty; then step right onto a slab. Climb easily leftwards to the top.

Craig y Cwm Nantcol Crag (of) the Wooded Vale OS Ref 647 277
This crag may be small, but the steepness and quality of the rock more than compensate. Some hard test-pieces on perfect quartzite pack the punch. Facing south-south-east, the crag is a particularly good morning venue. It is low-lying, very easy to reach, and suitable for the winter months.

Approach from the end of the Cwm Nantcol road via the Bwlch Drws Ardudwy path, in 15 minutes. The farmer levies a small fee for parking; hand it in at Maes-y-garnedd or (for Royalists) sign your death warrant!

☆**Death Warrant**   12 metres   E3 6a †   (2.9.97)
Right of the stone wall abutting the left-hand end of the crag is a projecting pillar face. This harbours a menacing little route. Gain the top of a pedestal flake from the right. Take the tense thin crack above to a break of sorts, and grapple into the little groove overhead. Climb up this to easier ground and a thread belay in boulders.

A wide ramp extends up and rightwards beneath the main crag; the next route starts 2 metres right of a corner below a break containing a large oak tree.

Colonel Jones   12 metres   E5 6a/b †   (2.9.97)
Climb steeply past a small spike, up a thin crack, to a protruding block-hold at a thin horizontal break. Make very hard moves up the leaning wall above (good wire in thin crack slightly left) and swing left from a hand-ledge to exit. Strenuous.

☆**Smoking Limbs**   12 metres   E3 6a †   (2.9.97)
A dynamic little number; satisfying and safe. Start from the left-hand side of a large flake embedded in the ramp. Climb flakes to an angular brown and black niche. Teeter left and launch up past a peg runner to a crack. Follow the line of the crack on outlying jugs, and bear right to the top.

☆☆**Hanged, Drawn and Quartered**   12 metres   E4 6a †   (2.9.97)
Superb, fingery, and unrelenting climbing up the leaning right-hand side of the main crag. Start from the right-hand edge of the large embedded flake. Climb direct to a right-slanting line of slots (good cams). Make a balancy move up to a good spike on the right, step left (peg runner), and move up and left on excellent fingerholds to the top.

The Western Valleys: Cwm Artro

Carreg Fawr Big Crag   OS Ref 627 293
This is a beautiful west-facing crag set adjacent to ancient mature oak woodland on the east side of the Afon Artro valley leading to Cwm Bychan. The rock is a perfect, very clean and quick-drying quartzite which lends itself to some rather nice finger-jugs. The crag is low-lying, very accessible, and hence a pretty good bet for the winter months. Environmentally, this is likely to be a sensitive site, and visitors are entrusted to behave impeccably.

Park very carefully in a restricted lay-by on the Cwm Bychan road at OS Ref 617 290 and follow the Gloyw Lyn public footpath eastwards over Pont

Crafnant into the wood (a nature reserve). Continue along the path for half a kilometre to the eastern edge of the wood. Now turn left through a gate and follow a wall northwards to a boggy level and a short scree slope leading to the foot of the crag. The routes are described from **right to left**.

At the extreme right-hand end of the crag is a rectangular blank face right of a corner (containing an unimpressive holly tree), the target for the first route.

☆**S.M.A.R.T.**   15 metres   E3 5c †   (4.9.97)
Cautious analytical techniques required. Climb the corner for 4 metres to beneath the holly tree clump. Using a finger-jug on the right wall, reach for another and so gain a couple of good hand-ledges on the face – some uninspiring small wires can be wriggled in here. Balance up the centre of the face with two just-out-of-reach moves, and finish up a short flake crack.

☆**But Fear Itself**   15 metres   Hard Very Severe 4c †   (4.9.97)
In the arête left of the corner containing the holly tree is a fine groove. It is not over-protected. From the foot of the corner, stand up on a flake on the left and follow the grooved arête to the top.

Behind the left-hand of the three oak trees is a ledgy buttress, which could support some easier routes, and – left again – a square face with a disjointed thin crack slightly right of centre.

Seeds of Suspicion   12 metres   Very Severe 4b †   (4.9.97)
The corner right of the square face. Some hollow-sounding flakes add interest.

☆**Leave No Trace**   12 metres   E2 5c †   (4.9.97)
A great little route with nice surprises. Climb up to the disjointed thin crack in the square face (bombproof wire); then make a hard move to a bucket. Swing left to exit up a short crack.

Left of a gully housing an oak tree is a small buttress with two ribs.

Post-Urban Species   9 metres   E2 5b †   (4.9.97)
Ascend the right-hand rib, which leans worryingly at the top and forces a committing swing left to top out. Short but sweet.

Smacks of Insanity   9 metres   Severe †   (4.9.97)
Climb the broad left-hand rib via the undercut crack.

Twenty metres left is a tower with a south-facing crack behind an oak tree.

☆☆**Sylvester**   12 metres   E1 5b †   (4.9.97)
A wonderful pitch, on great rock. Climb the leaning crack on amazingly solid flake holds to a small niche where it veers right. Proceed straight up the wall with a long reach to a good finger-jug and a Stallone-like stomach-flop onto the top of the tower.

Carreg y Hafoty Rock (of) the Summer-Dwelling OS Ref 630 293
Noticeable only from Carreg y Saeth, this is an isolated sheet of rock on the
northern flank of Carreg Fawr. The crag faces north-west, and can be
lichenous in its raw state, but the intrinsic quality of the slab climbing
matches these limitations. There is still potential – but bring a big wire brush.

Park at Pont Cwm-yr-afon (honesty box), and follow the Gloyw Lyn public
footpath for a kilometre. Eventually the crag comes into view high on the
hillside and a short traverse right (over a stone wall) reaches its left-hand
end. Alternatively, a visit to this spot can be easily combined with Carreg
Fawr.

The first two routes take on the big, sheer slab. Owing to an ungardenable
heathery exit, both require a pre-fixed rope to retreat; organize the lower-off
point to coincide with a break 3 metres below the top.

☆**The Perfect Bust** 21 metres E3 5b †   (31.5.2000)
Deliciously sustained but with two huge run-outs either side of half-height
protection. Pull over a small roof under the left side of the sheet, and
follow small holds up the smooth slab slightly rightwards to better holds
next to a diagonal slot on the right (cam placements). Move right to step
onto a narrow quartz ledge. Climb up in line with a short, blind crack, and
follow this to the break.

☆**Make or Break** 20 metres E1 5a †   (31.5.2000)
Climb up the right-hand side of the slab direct to a step left to the break
near the top. The route boasts twice the quantity of protection of its
neighbour!

Thirty metres right is a clean arête.

☆**A Home Called Pandy** 18 metres E5 5c †   (31.5.2000)
Immaculate climbing on perfect white quartzite. There doesn't appear to
be any protection. Climb the left-hand side of the arête until standing on a
narrow foot-ledge. A very delicate section above should lead to jugs and
straightforward climbing to the top.

Carreg y Saeth Crag (of) the Arrow   OS Ref 638 307
Follow the narrow road up Cwm Bychan, and one kilometre after
Dolwreiddiog farmhouse park on the left where a track and public footpath
lead up to an isolated cottage. Walk along the road in the direction of the
lake for a few hundred metres past a left-hand bend where an old trackway
can be made out in the field on the right. (This is just after a gap in the wall
on the left.) Hop over the fence carefully, and follow the trackway across a
dilapidated stone bridge over the river to the edge of a small wood. Enter the
trees and locate a vague path on the left-hand side of a slight valley that
leads into an extensive boggy area (an old peat cutting). Negotiate the bog
on the left to reach a bluff of rock (Distraction Bluff) or traverse rightwards to

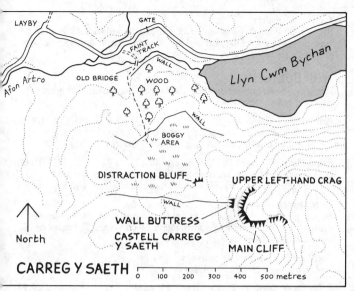

CARREG Y SAETH

North

0   100   200   300   400   500 metres

reach and follow a stone wall to avoid the bog. Above and behind the bluff of rock is a huge scree slope beneath the main crags.

The climbing is in four distinct areas. The Upper Left-Hand Crag is clearly seen from the road. Wall Buttress is also clearly visible, and above and to the right of this is Castell Carreg y Saeth with a prominent corner in its middle. The Main Cliff is around to the right of Castell. See photodiagram opposite next page for crag layout.

Descent
From the top of Castell and the Main Cliff, scramble up to a col and descend a goat track down right. From the base of the Main Cliff an easy scramble up left behind a large block leads back to Castell. There is currently an *in-situ* abseil station above the finishes of the climbs on Castell.

Upper Left-Hand Crag
This proves disappointing on closer inspection and the only two climbs at present are at the extreme left-hand side. They are a short corner and a steep slab just to its right.

Y Grug   12 metres   Hard Very Severe 5a †   (6.9.97)
Start at the foot of the vegetated corner. Climb a left-facing layback crack forming the left edge of the slab, swing right onto the slab, and finish easily.

★Ysgor   12 metres   E3 5c   (6.9.97)
The slab on the right gives some nice moves on good rock. Gain a jug on
the right-hand side of the slab and pull onto the slab. Follow some cracks
to a heathery finish.

Wall Buttress

This is the lowest buttress and has a stone wall running up to its middle. The
left-hand arête is taken by:

☆Artrodeco   15 metres   E4 5c †   (1.9.97)
Committing. Gain a pedestal ledge. Move up to a small overhang, and
continue up the arête to finish up a thin crack just to its right.

Fynci Mynci   14 metres   Very Severe 4b †   (20.10.85)
Start in a bay at the left-hand side of the buttress. Go up to a small
overhang, move left, and climb the obvious shallow groove to the top.

First Choice   14 metres   Hard Very Severe 5a   (20.10.85)
Start as for *Fynci Mynci*. Climb up right to a ledge, and continue up the
wall just right of the arête to a small ledge. Step up right and make an
awkward mantelshelf to finish.

Cod Peace   14 metres   Severe †
The corner-line immediately above the wall.

A Climb of Contrasts   15 metres   E1 6a †   (1.9.97)
Start below the left-hand of two cracks in the front of the buttress. Make a
hard move up the crack to a break; move up, and then reach good holds
on the arête on the left. Ascend the arête easily to the ledge of *First Choice*.
Make a delicate step up to a massive bucket and go up the crack on the
right to a leftward exit.

Holly Direct   14 metres   Very Difficult †
The obvious line to the right of the wall. (The holly has gone.)

Only Fools and Asses   12 metres   E2 5b   (16.7.97)
Start just to the right of the corner of the preceding route. Move up some
flakes and then step up right into the obvious groove. Climb this to the top.

Castell Carreg y Saeth

This buttress is west-facing and dries quite quickly. The rock is clean and
solid, and the climbing is of excellent quality. The first route takes the
left-hand arête.

★Ebill Bob   23 metres   E2 5b   (15.10.94)
Varied and exposed, and bold in one place. Start underneath the arête.
Climb a thin crack to a widening crack formed by a giant flake, and gain
its top. Edge nervously right onto a ledge. Swing left into a groove on the
arête and climb cracks above to the short headwall. An awkward move
reaches good finishing-holds.

Rock Steady (E3 — first ascent) Lechau Mawr
Climber: Martin Crocker Photo: Ben Sargeant

Carreg y Saeth
Main Cliff

1 Lol		4 Maes B	E2	7 Armes Prydein	HVS
2 Haf Bach Mihangel		5 Pip's Present	E1	8 White Tabs	S
3 Seithenyn		6 Something for the Weekend	E3	9 Cymru Rydd	S

CASTELL
CARREG Y SAETH

BLOCK

PINNACLE

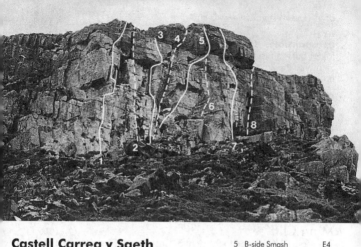

Castell Carreg y Saeth

1	Ebill Bob	E2	3	Ozymandias	E2
2	Ora pro Nobis	E1	4	Koh-i-Noor	E3

5	B-side Smash	E4
6	Irresponsible	E4
7	Going Going Gone	E4
8	Gwyddno	HVS

★**Ora pro Nobis** 23 metres E1 5b   (16.8.97)
Start just right of a spike at a small heather bush. Gain a block just above
the bush and move up the wall to reach an overhanging corner
immediately left of a large overhang. Climb the corner to the top.

★**Ozymandias** 23 metres E2 5b   (24.8.97)
Superb climbing with an exhilarating finish. Start 2 metres right of a tall
unstable flake. Climb flake cracks slightly rightwards above a spike to a
narrow jammed block just left of the foot of a black V-groove. Take the
groove to a large overhang. Move out right to the arête and climb the
hanging slab diagonally leftwards to the top.

★**Koh-i-Noor** 23 metres E3 6a   (6.11.94)
The central overhanging corner – a magnificent and classic line. Start as
for *Ozymandias*. Climb the corner steeply to a good resting-place and
chockstone thread. Move up right to a spike hold and make strenuous
moves up the overhanging headwall. Continue to the top.

☆**B-side Smash** 18 metres E4 6a †   (5.9.97)
A diagonal line across the wall right of the corner. Start as for *Ozymandias*
and *Koh-i-Noor*. From the right-hand arête of the corner, climb a thin crack
and a layaway fin to a good hold above the bulge. Bear rightwards to an
undercut crack and follow this around right to a niche. Pull out to the top.

Irresponsible   12 metres   E4 5c †   (5.9.97)
Minor but menacing. Start from a tall standing flake on the highest ledge.
Step onto the flake and take thin cracks to a bulge and peg runner. Move
up to the niche of the preceding route and pull out to the top.

☆☆**Going Going Gone**   18 metres   E4 6a †   (6.9.97)
Takes the narrow pillar just right of *Irresponsible*. Start from the latter's tall
standing flake. Lean out to an open slot (large cam) in the wall right of the
flake and move up and right into a small niche. Power up the crack rising
from the right-hand side of the niche to a rest beneath the projecting roof.
Finish up the crack splitting the roof.

Gwyddno   30 metres   Hard Very Severe †   (24.2.85)
1 15m. Climb the open-book corner to the roof. Swing out left onto a
good spike and go up a short groove to a tree belay in a large bay.
2 15m. Climb the central cracks in the back wall.

Main Cliff
The Main Cliff is round to the right of Castell and is reached by a diagonal
climb rightwards up the extensive scree. It is south-facing and can be a
sun-trap even in mid-winter. There is a huge leaning pinnacle below the
left-hand side which is a useful reference point. The Castell (upper) cliff can
be reached from here by scrambling up behind the pinnacle. The area
immediately right of the pinnacle has three distinct groove-systems underneath a prominent prow of rock. The left-hand groove is taken by:

☆**Lol**   39 metres   E2 †   (30.8.97)
Start in a corner just left of some large blocks.
1 24m. 5b. Climb up and move left to enter the groove. Climb the
groove to a ledge. Move leftwards up to the overhang and then right
below it. Climb back left above the overhang and go up to a small tree.
Move left to a large ledge and tree belay.
2 15m. 5c. Gain the top of the block. Swing right to the foot of the wide
crack. Climb straight up, and swing out right near the top.

★★**Haf Bach Mihangel**   40 metres   E1 5b   (21.9.97)
Start in front of the leaning pinnacle. Climb over the blocks to stand on the
top, pointed one. Move up to a yellowish streak (sometimes wet) and make
a move right. Go up to the base of a large pedestal (thread), and climb its
left-hand side to stand on its top. A steep but well-protected move leads up
to a niche. Swing out left in a nicely exposed position and climb to the top.

☆**Sais Invader**   36 metres   E5 †   (29.5.2000)
Superb face-climbing followed by a hard move in space. Start by the
blocks as for the preceding route.
1 21m. 6a. Climb as for *Seithenyn* for 3 metres, but follow the thin and
very technical crack in the face above to a niche on the left (perched flake
inside). Climb leftwards more easily up a white groove; then swing left to a
thread belay underneath an enormous sitting pillar (on *Haf Bach Mihangel*).

2 15m. 6b. Gain the top of the pillar from the left. Swing left beneath a hanging arête to a block ledge. Move back right onto the arête (crucial *Rock 2* placement), and desperately grab a jug a little way above a roof. Pull up and head for terra firma.

★★Seithenyn 46 metres E3   (20.10.85)
The route has an impressive finish through the prominent overhang. Start as for *Haf Bach Mihangel*.
1 15m. 5b. From the blocks, move up right to an overhang. Traverse right to a good foothold and go up to a ledge. Climb the corner to a stance.
2 14m. 5b. Move up right to the foot of a clean V-groove. Climb the technical groove and then a bulge, passing a small tree, to a good stance.
3 17m. 6a. Climb the arête on the left until level with the overhang. Swing out left and climb the crack in the overhanging wall with a difficult finish; well positioned.

Four Arêtes 39 metres E5 †   (29.5.2000)
The series of crisp arêtes. Contrived in places; bold throughout. Start below the arête that forms the right edge of the sheer wall containing the start of *Seithenyn*.
1 27m. 6a. Climb the left side of the first arête to a recessed ledge on *Maes B* (a spike on the right can be lassoed after the first few moves). Move up the groove (as for neighbouring routes) and step right below the second arête. Follow the left side of the arête, trying to avoid the use of holds on *Maes B*. Now the route perks up. Work up over a small roof and layback the third arête on its left-hand side (crucial *RP5* placement) to gain a ledge. Drop down right 2 metres to a good belay on *Seithenyn*.
2 12m. 5a. Climb the cracks in the rib and pull up onto a ledge below the final arête (number four!). Stretch left for the sharp edge of the arête, and link jugs to the top: exposed.

The next route takes the leftward-slanting groove-line.

Maes B 46 metres Very Severe 4c †   (18.9.97)
Start 6 metres right of *Seithenyn* at a large block in the corner. Climb leftwards past the block to a ledge, and make an awkward move past the bulge to a ledge (the *Seithenyn* belay). Continue up the fine groove to the overhang. Move out left and go carefully up to a ledge on the right. Climb the arête (as for *Seithenyn*) for 6 metres; then move right to a rib which leads to the top.

Pip's Present 48 metres Severe †   (27.12.63)
Start just to the right of *Maes B*, underneath the rib.
1 34m. Start the rib on the right and climb up before moving left onto the front of the buttress. Go up until a move gains the nose of the rib. Move up to a tree belay.
2 14m. 4b. The V-chimney right of the crest leads to the top.

Something for the Weekend   48 metres   Very Severe †   (21.9.97)
Start as for *Pip's Present*.
1 34m. 4c. Climb the initial moves of *Pip's Present* but swing out left on
some flakes to the front of the buttress. Move up and step up right onto a
gorse-covered ledge. Continue up the right-hand side of the rib until some
flaky holds give a nice move onto the crest. Climb to trees.
2 14m. 4b. *Pip's Present* pitch 2.

The next routes start at a large corner 15 metres right. To the left of the corner
are some blocks and a cracked wall.

Armes Prydein   45 metres   Hard Very Severe †   (24.2.85)
Start on the blocks.
1 15m. 5b. Step off the blocks and climb the cracked wall with an
awkward finish. Continue up to an upper ledge.
2 30m. 4c. Scramble across the gully and climb a short rib to a ledge.
Follow the obvious crack on the right of the arête to the top.

White Tabs   45 metres   Severe †   (27.12.63)
1 15m. Climb the corner and exit left to a ledge.
2 12m. A series of short steep walls trending right lead to a tree belay
beneath two obvious grooves.
3 18m. Layback into the right-hand groove; then step out right. Follow
the arête for a short way; then regain the groove and continue to the top.
Variation
3a 18m. The left-hand groove.

Cymru Rydd   47 metres   Severe †   (24.2.85)
The name is more a comment on the rock than a political statement. Start
below the wide crack in the right-hand arête of the corner.
1 15m. Climb the crack past some chockstones to a ledge.
2 9m. Take the edge direct.
3 23m. Climb the shallow groove, and move left, then back right to the
arête. Continue up to the small rectangular overhang, step left, and finish
over some dubious blocks. An intimidating pitch.

Gully Wall Route   37 metres   Severe †   (5.10.97)
Start about 10 metres up right from *Cymru Rydd* at a spike. Climb up
rightwards and move up the wall just right of a small oak to a bulge. Step
up left, move up and, using the edge, move up right onto the face of the
buttress. Continue up to easier ground and over some large blocks to the
terrace.

The next three routes are on the buttress to the right of the heather-filled gully.

★★Ymryson y Geifr   21 metres   E2 5b   (22.9.97)
Good climbing. Start at a corner at the foot of the buttress. Climb the
corner and move up leftwards to the foot of the left-hand of two shallow
corners. Climb it steeply on good holds until a move right can be made
onto a small ledge. Continue to the top.

Oes Gafr Eto?   21 metres   E1 5c †   (24.9.97)
Start as for the preceding route and move up left to the foot of the
right-hand shallow corner. Climb it using a flake/block hold to a ledge.
Take the continuation corner on the left to the top.

Edrychiad Cyntaf   21 metres   E1 5c †   (12.9.97)
Start at the foot of the buttress. Climb up using a wedged flake and stand
on it. Move up left onto a ledge and swing back right into a corner. Climb
the wide crack; then move up and take the left-hand corner to the top.

The last route is on the next buttress right with the huge jammed flake in its
middle.

★Hydref Eto   12 metres   E1 6a   (25.9.97)
Interesting, though the key protection (*Rock 5*) is difficult to spot. Start
underneath the pointed capstone. Move up leftwards to the steepening
and pull up rightwards to exit right of the pointed capstone.

Distraction Bluff   OS Ref 637 293

At the head of the level, boggy valley, before the start of the scree slope
beneath the main crags, is a compact bluff of rock with some challenging
morsels to distract the specialist for a few hours. Though hard, all but one of
the routes are underlain by moist and soft landings that permit a ground-up
approach in relative, resonating safety. Just bring a resilient mat to save
embedding your legs in the ground each time you deck out.

To Fly above Water   6 metres   E3 5c †   (28.7.2001)
Balance up the slabby left-hand arête. Throw yourself out of the cutting
range of the knife-edged boulder if you fall.

Good Vibrations   6 metres   E1 5a †   (28.7.2001)
A narrow groove in a rib leads to large but spaced holds.

Five on the Richter   6 metres   E3 6a †   (28.7.2001)
Take the left-hand of two grooves to a triangular roof. Power straight over
a nose using fingerholds to both sides. Hard to grade objectively: the crux
is the last move.

Echoes in the Swamp   6 metres   E1 6b †   (28.7.2001)
Very fingery moves direct up the right-hand groove lead to an undercut
beneath a roof. Layback to a ledge above.

☆Shakes of Success   7 metres   E3 6b †   (28.7.2001)
Pure pleasure. Stretch around the centre of a low-level roof to flat
fingerholds. Teeter over using a prominent layaway hold; then use holds
on the right to top out. (A ledge off-line to the right is not used at this
grade.)

Outlying Crags of the Rhinogau

Llanbedr School Crags
OS Ref 589 271

From the village, take the Cwm Bychan road for 100 metres past the primary school. A small road on the left goes up 400 metres to the forest. Park here and walk back. The crag is easily visible up on the left between the forest and the school.

Abraxas   18 metres   E1 5b †   (6.11.90)
Climb the groove left of the *Prowler* groove to gain the ivy stump below an overlap. Pull through the overlap to below a small pinnacle. Layback up this in a great position.

Prowler   18 metres   Hard Very Severe 5a †   (6.11.90)
The central groove below the obvious groove. Step up and left below the groove, and traverse back right along it to gain the arête. Finish directly up the overhanging groove.

Dance on a Volcano   18 metres   E1 5b †   (6.11.90)
The groove right of *Prowler*. Gain the slab behind the tree. At its top, pull up on blocks on the left through the overhang and continue steeply on big holds to the top.

Y Garth   The Enclosure
OS Ref 619 379

This collection of crags runs along the roadside to the toll bridge and reach up to 40 metres in height. Most are broken and heavily wooded with oak and ivy but, as at Tremadog, there are some excellent clean walls, corners, and grooves. Two great diagonal cracks are the obvious features. As some of the names suggest, more than a suspicion exists that many of the routes were climbed long ago. The first crag is on the extreme left, above the small lay-by at Llandecwyn station, and is excellent for beginners.

'Done a Thousand Times Before'
8 metres   Very Severe 5a †   (25.6.2000)
The left-hand edge of the short wall is taken to the ledge. Climb the leaning wall above. Crux near the deck.

Repeating History   10 metres   Very Severe 4b †   (25.6.2000)
Climb the crack next right to the right-hand end of a ledge. A lovely crack above and just left awaits.

The Power of Peach   12 metres   Very Severe 4c †   (25.6.2000)
Start as for the above, but climb the wall directly.

Peachless   12 metres   Very Severe 4c †   (25.6.2000)
Climb a short groove to the clean wall. Finish up a crack just right of the oak sapling.

I Know This Line 12 metres   Hard Very Severe 5b †   (25.6.2000)
The speckled wall just right of the first diagonal crack is taken direct to the wide slot. Continue in a straight line to the top.

This One Too 12 metres   Hard Very Severe 5b †   (25.6.2000)
Follow a direct line, just right, to a circular break in the diagonal crack. Again the line continues direct – to a fine crack in the top of the wall.

☆☆**As Old as Time** 12 metres   Very Severe 4c †   (25.6.2000)
The perfect diagonal crack.

Peach Maker 12 metres   Very Severe 4b †   (25.6.2000)
Climb the next crack to a holly tree. Continue up another crack to the top.

☆☆**The Peach** 12 metres   Hard Severe †   (25.6.2000)
The blunt arête is an excellent climb of the grade.

Fifty metres further right and partially hidden by a knoll is a tower with a striking crackline in the leaning wall facing the road. (There is a peg in the wall further right.)

☆☆**The Passage of Hands** 14 metres   E2 5c †   (25.6.2000)
The wonderful crack leads leftwards up the leaning wall to a niche just left of a roof and a holly tree. A tailor-made line.

Deep in the woods and opposite the double gates on the roadside is a corner with a tree at 5 metres. Approach through the gates along the track to the stream. Follow the path upstream to a flagstone, and cross beside a black pipe. Straight ahead among the leaves is the corner.

A Wild Sheep Chase 18 metres   E2 5c †   (25.6.2000)
The left-facing groove left of the corner is followed to the overlap. Interesting moves through this gain the ramp. Wobble onto the right-hand edge of the short wall above and finish up the corner of *Oak Corner*.

Oak Corner 18 metres   Hard Very Severe 5a †   (25.6.2000)
A difficult start gains the tree, after which easier climbing leads to a strenuous finish rightwards at the top.

Craig Galch Lime Rock   OS Ref 632 387
Drive west and south from Maentwrog (A496) for three miles to the gateway described below; or cross the short toll bridge from Penrhyn, continue past Y Garth (on your left) to a T-junction, and turn left (onto the A496). At the first right-hand bend there is a gateway on the right: park here or at the lay-by 30 metres further north. Pass through the gate and go up the steep track to the holiday cottage, with the crag now visible over to the left (north of the cottage). Either follow the ridge from the cottage to the crag, or drop into the wet valley and take a path along its left side to the crag; each has its merits.

A short leaning wall appears on the left with no recorded lines. The main crag has two sections: a left-hand zone comprising a steep wall capped by a roof, and the huge right-hand zone with steep grooves and corners and roofs.

Left-Hand Zone

Norah Batty   15 metres   Very Severe †   (3.98)
Belay at the base of the main crack on the left side of this zone. Start up the crack and take an obvious line left along a ledge. Climb a small corner to the top.

☆☆**Bat Capers**   15 metres   E3 5c †   (3.98)
The cool crack and wild yet easy roof next right. *Friend 1* and 1½ useful.

☆**Bat Attack**   18 metres   E3 5c †   (3.98)
Another good, if strange line up the wall right of the crack – 'bold but fairly easy'. Start at the right-hand end of the ledge below the face. After 2 metres, follow a line of holds trending up and leftwards until just below the roof. Traverse out rightwards to where the roof ends; then finish direct.

Right-Hand Zone

In the centre of this imposing section is a large wedged flake.

First the Worst   25 metres   E4 5c †   (3.98)
Gain the large loose flake. Scary. Pass it and finish direct (or don't bother).

☆☆☆**Frank Zappa RIP**   25 metres   E4 6a †   (3.98)
The best line on the crag. This is the fierce-looking corner next right. Pass some choss to gain the corner. Despite appearances, the corner has bomber gear and is shockingly easy. Gain the small hanging slab below the roof. Climb the slab rightwards, rock around the arête, and top out. To avoid rope-drag it is possible to take a belay below the roof by going leftwards to the raven's nest.

☆☆**The Kneebar of Eternal Justice**   25 metres   E5/6 6a †   (3.98)
Start up the easy corner (*Subservient Elephant*) next right, and at the first available opportunity traverse left along a tiny slab cum massive block. Make kneebar moves up to the larger flake and continue boldly to the ledge. Rejoin *Subservient Elephant* but climb direct up a short wall to the roof. Arrange and extend gear (many cams), surmount the roof, and finish direct. Belay as for *Frank Zappa RIP*.

☆☆☆**Subservient Elephant**   25 metres   E1 5b †   (3.98)
The obvious way up this piece of rock, which both this and the next route climb. Start up the easy corner at the right-hand end of this section, and continue to a large left-trending ledge. Go along it and up the nice flake at its end. Move around the arête and finish as for *Frank Zappa RIP*.

Craig y Merched

Three Pillar Buttress

1 Call Me Wernage	VS	
2 Pas de Chat	S	
3 Colonel Chinstrap	E1	
4 Alien	VS	
5 Magic Mushroom	S	
6 The Haw Lantern	E1	
7 Sunset Arête	HVS	
8 General Schwarzkopf	E1	
9 Bleating about the Bush	E2	

7 Sunset Arête	VD
8 General Schwarzkopf	HVS
9 Bleating about the Bush	VS

Craig y Merched
Rhino's Buttress

1	Naked Dissent	E2
2	Alchemist's Stone	E2
3	Zig Zag	HS
4	The Flourish of Strumpets	E1
5	Horn of Plenty	VS
6	Endangered Species	VS
7	Velvet Revolutions	VS
8	Rhino's Corner	VS
9	The Tusk	HVS

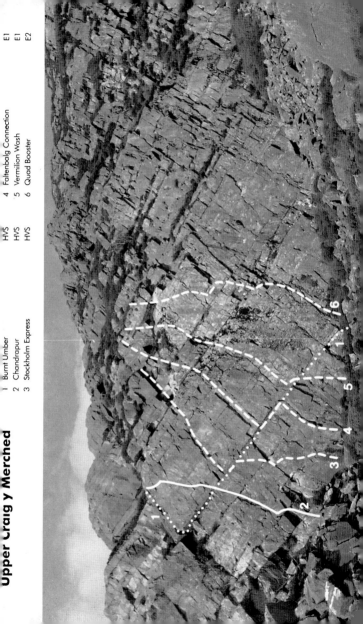

Upper Craig y Merched

1 Burnt Umber	HVS	
2 Chandrapur	HVS	
3 Stockholm Express	HVS	
4 Fallenbolg Connection		E1
5 Vermilion Wash		E1
6 Quad Booster		E2

The Haw Lantern (E2) Craig y Merched
Climber: Alex George   Photo: John Sumner

☆**Fearsome Worrier** 25 metres E1 5b † (3.98)
Start as for *Subservient Elephant*, but continue direct, avoiding loose rock, to a large flake above the overlap. Hand-traverse right on the obvious ledge to finish easily.

Garreg yr Ogof[1] Rock (of) the Cave OS Ref 704 356
A fine and quick-drying west-facing crag on the eastern shores of the lake behind the church in the village of Trawsfynydd. Routes are described from **right to left** (i.e. south to north).

Far for the Fledgling 15 metres Very Difficult † (20.8.2001)
The slab on the right leading to a deep overlap. Step left below the overlap to a good crack directly above.

☆**The Wrath of Cian** 15 metres Hard Very Severe 5a † (20.8.2001)
The excellent wall next left between *First Flight* and the wide unclimbed crack forming the left edge of the slab. Good edges lead steeply to the blunt flake; pass the break and take the right-hand edge of the wall above.

☆**First Flight** 15 metres Very Severe 4c † (20.8.2001)
A crack in the top face is reached directly via the wall below, which contains a short vertical crack.

☆**Training Spotters** 15 metres E1 5b † (28.8.2001)
Climb the open corner on the left to a roof. Pull rightwards and follow a seam in the top wall.

Toxic Texan 15 metres Very Difficult † (28.8.2001)
Climb a rib to a grassy terrace, which accommodates a huge wedged block on the left. Take the corner on the right to finish.

Alive Enough to Spawn 15 metres Difficult † (28.8.2001)
A vague crack in a stepped slab leads to the wedged block. Climb the crack in the left-hand side of the back wall to the top.

☆**Children of Lir** 15 metres Hard Very Severe 5a † (28.8.2001)
A delightful route. Climb the obvious tower, moving rightwards from the highest horizontal break to the top.

First Fright 15 metres Very Difficult † (20.8.2001)
Start 6 metres left of the tower. Climb a layback flake above a grass recess and then a short finger-crack to the top.

Below and to the right of the cliff, in the direction of a farmhouse, is a plethora of small-scale rock faces, lots of bouldering, and four described routes.

On top of the level area behind the farmhouse is a prominent block with a fine arête, which forms part of a low crag.

1 'Ogef' on OS map. This must be wrong.

☆**Bloodscream**   6 metres   E2 6a †   (29.8.2001)
Take the arête of perfect grit.

The Slap of One Hand Sighing
                         5 metres   Hard Very Severe 5b † (29.8.2001)
Climb the block with a bulge left of a short corner to the left of
Bloodscream.

Spreading Mischief   5 metres   Hard Very Severe 5b †   (29.8.2001)
The leaning face left of the next corner on the left.

The final route is located on a north-west-facing cutaway below the left-hand
end of the crag.

☆**When the Rock Crows**   8 metres   E4 6a †   (29.8.2001)
Bring a spring in your step. Climb the thin flake groove in the centre of the
wall. Microwires protect a long reach from a spike to a ledge on the left.

Carreg y Frân   Rock (of) the Crow   OS Ref 670 232
[Map page 329.] This south-facing crag is approximately 15 metres high
and situated on the east slopes of Diffwys. Approach as for Craig y Merched
as far as the parking-place; then take the left-hand forestry track towards
Llyn Cwm-mynach, before branching off it towards Diffwys along an old
engineered path.

White Man   15 metres   Hard Very Severe 5b   (6.5.95)
A direct line up the smooth wall, following a vague crackline with an
overhang at 5 metres. Start on the left-hand side of the crag, just left of a
large flake. Make technical moves to reach the overhang (RP protection),
and then follow the vague crackline to exit via twin cracks onto a ledge.
Continue up the short corner to the top.

Aderyn Halt   15 metres   Hard Very Severe 4c   (6.5.95)
From the lowest point of the crag, about 3 metres right of *White Man*,
climb directly up to an obvious corner beneath a steep wall at the top of
the crag. Climb the right arête of the wall to the top. Poor protection.

Crack of Tears   15 metres   Hard Very Severe 5a   (6.5.95)
Start 4 metres right of *Aderyn Halt*, beneath a left-slanting crackline
through the three tiers (or walls) that make up the right-hand side of the
crag. Sustained, with adequate protection. Climb the first fingery wall (peg
runner) to gain the slanting crack in the second. Climb this, starting on the
right, and continue up the continuation crack in the third tier. Finish as for
White Man. There is an alternative finish (at E1 5a) with no protection:
from the top of the last crack, step boldly right beneath a little overlap onto
the steep wall. Climb the wall and move out right at the top.

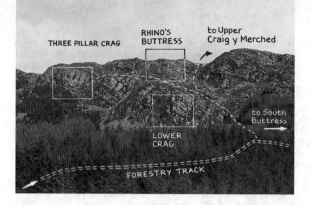

THREE PILLAR CRAG   RHINO'S BUTTRESS   to Upper Craig y Merched

to South Buttress

LOWER CRAG

FORESTRY TRACK

Craig y Merched   Crag (of) the Maidens   OS Ref 690 233

[Map page 329.] This crag is situated at the head of the quiet Afon Cwm-mynach, which drains into the Mawddach estuary, and consists of many small buttresses close together above forestry. Most of the routes are on the buttresses on the far left in three tiers, with the central tier, Three Pillar Crag, probably the best. The rock is a rough, hard Barmouth Grit. The crags, which dry quickly and face south-west, vary in height from 12 to 20 metres, and protection is on the whole good, with cams being especially useful.

Approach from the A496 Dolgellau to Barmouth road by turning off it at a small minor road opposite the toll bridge road over the Mawddach Estuary at Pont Borthwnog. Continue along this road for about two and a half miles, crossing the Afon Cwm-mynach to park just before the road finishes and forks into two gated tracks. Take the right-hand fork, which goes through an open area between forestry. Keep to the track, crossing a small stream, until just before a cottage, and take the stile on the right into the forest. The crag is on the right above the forestry level.

North Walls

To the left of and slightly down from Three Pillar Crag there are three clean walls separated by vegetated gullies that form a natural extension to it. The first of these, on the far left, has an undercut base with a sharp overhanging arête to its right. There are large blocks at the base. Approach as for Three Pillar Crag, over the top of the Lower Tier.

A Good Spoon Full   9 metres   E1 5c   (4.11.90)
From the top of a large block, step onto the wall and climb directly up to a peg. Difficult moves above reach jugs to finish.

The next wall is the highest of the three and has a fine crackline running up its centre.

★★The Gadgie   18 metres   E2 5b   (6.5.91)
The left edge of the wall. Low in its grade. Climb boldly up the wall to the overlap, undercut up, and make steep moves, using layaways and a small pocket, to better holds in a horizontal break. An awkward move above the break gains the fine slabby arête, which is climbed to the top.

★The King of Sunset Town   18 metres   Hard Very Severe 5a   (21.10.90)
The obvious crackline in the centre of the wall. From the top of a block just right of centre of the wall, make some awkward moves up and slightly rightwards to jugs; then follow these back leftwards to the base of the crack. There are difficult moves to start the crack, then more jugs before an awkward finish.

Right again is a short compact wall with fir trees very close to its base. Descent is by following the sloping ledge down to the right.

★Andy's Initiation   15 metres   Very Difficult   (11.8.91)
The left arête of the wall. Climb to the top of a large layback flake, move up, then right to the arête, and climb its left side to ledges (good thread belay on the highest ledge above).

The Three Mosquitoes   15 metres   Hard Severe 4b   (7.8.91)
Start at a groove at the left end of the wall about 2 metres left of a central groove. Climb directly up the groove, which gets easier near the top.

Midge Attack   18 metres   E1 5b †   (7.8.91)
Climb the central groove and continue direct to the highest part of the wall.

Rhythm of the Drones   15 metres   E1 5b †   (7.8.91)
Overcome a difficult bulge two metres right of the central groove, and follow a thin crack to the top.

Lower Tier
The lowest crag to be encountered is also the largest, but has a large vegetated band at mid height.

Brief Encounter   24 metres   E2 5c †   (30.8.91)
Beneath the Lower Tier are two stone walls, and just before the left-hand one there is a roof above a grass ramp. Scramble up to the grass ramp. Climb direct to a large block at the right-hand end of the roof. With long reaches, pull through to good holds and finish easily up to heather and a belay on boulders.

Helical Spiral   30 metres   E1   (11.8.91)
Roughly half-way along the Lower Tier is a steep leftward ramp-line running through the most continuous piece of rock on the lower part of the buttress. Start beneath this, at a short V-groove with overhangs above.
1 15m. 5b. Bridge above the V-groove to reach a large dubious flake hold, step left, and move up to a peg runner (good *Friend 3*). Make a

difficult move up and left to a sloping ledge in a corner, and go straight up from the corner to a heather ledge under a wall. Nut belays.
2 15m. 5b. Walk left along the heather ledge to a chimney. Climb this and move left to a huge jammed square block. Move up, then left again to make a gymnastic effort up through a break to a good hold, and then climb easily to the top. Good spike belay.

This Jug Ain't Big Enough for the Both of Us 36 metres E1 † (30.6.93)
The groove and capped corner 8 metres right of *Helical Spiral*.
1 21m. 5b. Climb the groove directly on good holds to a bridging-position below the roof. Pull through with long reaches for good holds and continue up to the right. Belay well back.
2 15m. 5b. *Helical Spiral* pitch 2.

Three Pillar Crag

[Photodiagram page 360a.] This is the centre tier crag and the most northerly of the three. Approach from the right, over the top of the Lower Tier.

Call Me Wemage 15 metres Very Severe 4c (21.9.91)
Above a heather terrace up and left of the start of *Alien* are two cracks with a vegetated groove just to their right. Two metres left of the cracks is a short groove. Climb delicately up into this groove; step left, then up left again to a ledge. Move up to a small line of overhangs, and traverse left beneath these on good handholds to an edge. Climb the edge and the slab above to the top.

Pas de Chat 15 metres Severe (21.9.91)
Start at the two cracks with a vegetated groove just to their right. Climb the cracks; then step left and go up to a groove just left of a pointed overhang. Climb the groove; then move diagonally right to a block belay.

★Colonel Chinstrap 21 metres E1 5c (24.8.91)
The left arête of *Alien*. Start under the strange tree-stump below *Alien*. Gain the top of the huge block on the left, below a shallow corner leading up to the arête, and climb the corner to just below a vegetated ramp coming down from the left. Step right and climb the crack just left of the arête to a peg. Then continue directly above the peg to a ledge, and climb the slabby scoop on the left to the top.

★Alien 21 metres Hard Very Severe 5a (16.3.91)
The obvious curving corner-line under an overhang: there is a strange tree-stump below. Climb easily up the corner to a large block, move onto the steep left wall (peg), and use a dubious flake to gain a good layback edge above the overhang. Move up to a ledge and continue up the crack above a thin spike to the top.

★★Magic Mushroom 21 metres E1 5b (9.3.91)
Look for the obvious niche two-thirds of the way up the central pillar, and start at a mossy corner about 2½ metres to its left. Climb the corner,

traverse right across a slab until below the niche, and move delicately and directly up the wall to it. Then pull straight over a bulge to the top of the crag.

★★The Haw Lantern   21 metres   E2 5c   (10.3.91)
[Photo page 360d.] Start below a weakness in the steep wall directly below the niche of *Magic Mushroom*. Make difficult moves to a peg at 6 metres, and go up and right to ledges beneath a steep wall. Climb the centre of the wall to a good *Friend 1* slot, gain a good hold in the small overhang above, and make some fine moves up and left to the top.

★Sunset Arête   21 metres   Very Difficult   (17.11.90)
An obvious rightward-slanting arête has a narrow slab on its left. Gain the arête from the left, go up a short groove, and then climb the arête, using the slab on the left, to a final little wall, which is taken on the right to the top.

General Schwarzkopf   21 metres   Hard Very Severe 5a   (17.3.91)
Start as for *Sunset Arête*. Move up and right to an overhang, then awkwardly up and right round its right edge to easier ground. Go right again and then up steeply to the top.

Bleating about the Bush   18 metres   Very Severe 4c   (7.8.91)
Start beneath the dark niche in the wall. Climb directly up to the niche (good nut protection), and pull out to gain the last section of *General Schwarzkopf*.

Rhino's Buttress
[Photodiagram page 360b.] Up and right of Three Pillar Crag, the top tier has a distinctive rock feature on its right-hand end in the shape of a rhino's head.

Naked Dissent   18 metres   E2 5c   (4.7.91)
Start at the left end of the buttress, at some slabs below an overlap. Climb directly up to the overlap at 6 metres (first runner), pass this by reaching a tiny pod above, and then take the left-trending break to finish up the blunt arête.

Alchemist's Stone   18 metres   E2 5c †   (4.7.91)
Start a little to the right of *Naked Dissent*, and 1½ metres left of a ledged crack, and climb direct to an overlap. Pull up and left to a second overlap and reach a horizontal break; move leftwards, and then go direct up the final wall.

The Flourish of Strumpets   12 metres   E1 5c †   (4.7.91)
Start right of the central crackline below a very thin crack in the top wall. Climb directly up via ledges to below the thin crack (*Friend 1½*). Pull up this with difficulty to the top.

Zig Zag   15 metres   Hard Severe   (24.8.91)
The obvious zigzag line left of *Horn of Plenty*. Climb the wall to the right of the groove. Step left to gain the arête and then the ledge. Traverse left along the ledge (crossing *The Flourish of Strumpets*) to a corner, which leads direct to the top.

Horn of Plenty   14 metres   Very Severe 4b   (4.5.91)
The obvious right-facing corner in the centre of the crag. Climb directly up
the corner to its top.

★Endangered Species   18 metres   Very Severe 4c   (4.5.91)
Start a short way left of *Rhino's Corner* at a ragged, left-slanting crack.
Climb the crack all the way, with the crux in the middle.

★Velvet Revolutions   18 metres   Very Severe 4c   (20.4.91)
A sustained route. Start as for *Endangered Species*. Climb the crack for 6
metres, and then move right along a good foot-ledge. Make some delicate
moves up a slab into a corner below a slot in the roofs. Make awkward
moves to gain the slot (good chockstone) and climb it to the top.

★Rhino's Corner   18 metres   Very Severe 5a   (20.4.91)
The main feature of the crag is a big corner topped by roofs. Difficult
moves at the start of the corner over a little overhang lead to pleasant
bridging up to the roof. Step out right, and up and right again; exposed,
but easier than it looks.

★The Tusk   18 metres   Hard Very Severe 5b   (28.7.91)
The right arête of *Rhino's Corner*. Start 2 metres right of the corner. Get
easily onto the top of a huge block, step left (thread), and make a difficult
move up to gain a groove. Climb the groove to the arête, then the arête
direct over a bulge, using good sidepulls, to the final move of *Rhino's
Corner*.

Pinnacle Buttress
On the same level as Rhino's Buttress and approximately 300 metres right is
a crag with a huge leaning pinnacle. There is only one recorded route so far:

The Stunt Club   21 metres   Very Severe 4b †   (27.7.91)
Climb the left-hand arête of the pinnacle; then cross the chasm and finish
up the wall.

South Buttress   OS Ref 690 224
This is the buttress comprising three pillars set just above the tree line on the
east side of the valley. It is due east of the small derelict building on the side
of the approach track to Blaen-cwm-mynach and a kilometre south of the
main crags. One of its routes is well worth seeking out.

Monday Morning Mizzle   10 metres   Hard Very Severe 4c † (4.5.98)
Step off right from a large pointed flake, and climb the left-hand rib to the
top. Unprotected.

☆Weather or Not   13 metres   E2 5c †   (4.5.98)
Elegant and safe climbing up the prominent central rib. Move up onto the
face of the pillar via a short angular groove. Climb the technical left side of
the arête, gain a thin crack over a slanting edge, and mantel to exit.

The Weatherman's Yarn   9 metres   Very Severe 4c †   (4.5.98)
Climb the square-cut right-hand rib. Protection available.

Upper Craig y Merched   OS Ref 694 233
[Photodiagram page 360c.] Higher up the slopes of Y Garn than the crags
described above is another line of small buttresses. Approach by gaining the
top of Rhino's Buttress and crossing a large flat bog area. The crag is the
lowest of the buttresses It is about 15 metres high and faces south-west; the
rock is excellent.

★**Chandrapur**   14 metres   Hard Very Severe 5b   (22.9.96)
From a small overhang on the left-hand side of the crag, climb up to a
slight niche beneath an overlap and go directly over to the large diagonal
break. Climb the fine-looking wall above to its highest point. Small wires
needed for protection.

Stockholm Express   15 metres   Hard Very Severe 5a   (22.9.96)
Sustained climbing. From the lowest point of the wall, climb diagonally up
left to an *in-situ* tape in the large diagonal break. Gain a spike on the wall
above and then climb a small rightward-leaning overlap. Move back left
to gain the top.

★**Faltenbalg Connection**   15 metres   E1 5b   (22.9.96)
From the lowest point of the wall, move up to a huge flake. Gain its top;
then step left along the break and get established in the base of the
obvious rightward-leaning overlap. Climb this and the wall above,
trending left to a niche just beneath the top. Go easily out left and up
vegetation to belays.

★**Vermilion Wash**   18 metres   E1 5b   (17.5.97)
[Photo opposite.] A line of paler-coloured rock just right of the flake on
Faltenbalg Connection runs up to the inverted-V overhang at the top of the
crag. Climb up to a peg under a small slanting overlap and make delicate
moves up and right to a small sloping ledge. Move slightly back left to
gain a groove under the overhang, and pull over rightwards via a crack.

Burnt Umber   23 metres   Hard Very Severe 5b   (17.5.97)
The lower diagonal fault-line running across the crag from right to left.
Most of the climbing is at 4b/c but the final pull over the finishing
overhang is much harder. Climb the fault-line to its finish under an
overhang, and pull over rightwards (good *Rock 4* where it is needed).

Quad Booster   18 metres   E2 5b   (22.9.96)
Climb up to a recess beneath overhangs. Pull directly out of the recess
(good cam cracks), move up, and step left to immediately below the centre
of the headwall. Climb this to the top.

Vermilion Wash (E1) Upper Craig y Merched
Climber: John Sumner   Photo: Alex George

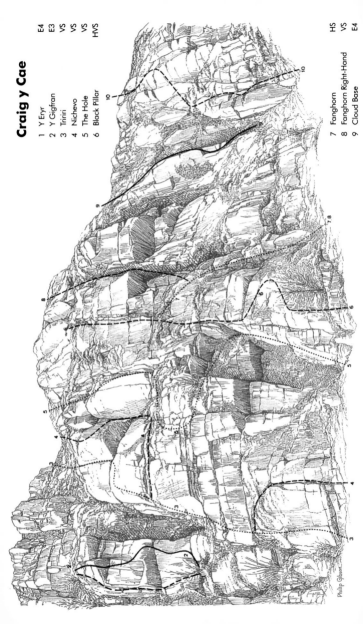

Craig y Cae

1	Y Eryr	E4
2	Y Gigfran	E3
3	Tiriri	VS
4	Nichevo	VS
5	The Hole	VS
6	Black Pillar	HVS
7	Fanghorn	HS
8	Fanghorn Right-Hand	VS
9	Cloud Base	E4

Philip Gibson

Craig y Cae   Crag (of) the Field   OS Ref 708 235

[Map page 329; photodiagram opposite.] From Dolgellau, take the A470 Trawsfynydd road for about 4 miles to the *Tyn-y-groes Hotel*. On the left just past the hotel, a single-track gated road is followed to the edge of the forest; there is plentiful parking on the verges (National Trust land). The crag can be seen above the forest on the left. A short way into the forest, a track rises south-west to emerge at the Nant Las watercourse. Keep to the right of this and go up rough-and-tumble ground to boulders under the crag.

Situated under the north-east ridge of Y Garn, Craig y Cae is about 400 metres above sea-level and faces east. The crag is some 50 metres high, but the worthwhile clean and climbable rock is much shorter than this. There is a lot of vegetation, and the rock is less sound than it may seem on first inspection.

The Central Buttress is the main attraction. Immediately to its left is South Gully, steep and vegetated, though with a tall, narrow, striking-looking roofed buttress set in it. Left of this is the vegetated and unclimbed South Buttress. Right of Central Buttress is the deep easy North Gully with the fine arête of *Cloudbase* in its back. Right again is the also-vegetated North Buttress.

Descend by a wide terrace down over South Buttress.

South Gully Buttress

The narrow roofed buttress at half height near the left-hand side of the crag, and immediately left of *Tririri*. Gain the ledge and good tree belay at the foot of the buttress by a 35-metre abseil from a large tree on the heather terrace (the way off) near the top of the crag.

Y Eryr   25 metres   E4 5c †   (9.5.98)

The exciting left arête of the buttress; bold at the top. Climb a shallow groove to the left-hand end of the first large roof. Step up into the continuation groove, but make a controlled fling right to a good spike on the arête. Take the arête on jugs and make balancy unprotected moves to finish.

☆**Y Gigfran**   25 metres   E3 6a †   (9.5.98)

Plenty of character and a spectacular upper roof; very protectable once the start has been negotiated. Climb a shallow groove in the right-hand side of the buttress to a crack that pierces the first roof. Pull around and follow the crack leftwards to a friendly area beneath a corner. Move up, stretch left for a jug on the lip of the roof on the left, and one-arm over (*in-situ* sling) to exit easily.

Central Buttress

Tririri   60 metres   Very Severe   (28.5.66)

The left edge of Central Buttress. Start on the left-hand side of the buttress, under South Gully.

1 15m. 4b. From the gully bed, go over a small bulge and move right along a ledge for a metre; then climb direct on sharp little holds to a large vegetated ledge below a wall (stance shared with *Nichevo*).
2 21m. 4c. *Nichevo* pitch 2.
3 24m. 4c. Pull over the bulge above the tree to reach a steep slab and climb it direct in the line of a thin crack to a horizontal crack below a bulge. Go right and make an awkward move into the bottom of another crack, which is climbed to a large ledge. Take the vegetated wall above easily on the left.
Variation
3a 18m. 4c (29.3.97). Climb as above to the horizontal crack; then step left and continue up the arête to easier climbing above.

Nichevo   69 metres   Very Severe   (23.3.58)
A climb of character following the line of least resistance up the left-hand side of the buttress. Start to the right of South Gully below an obvious crack in a fairly clean wall.
1 15m. 4a. Climb the crack to a large vegetated ledge on the left below a wall.
2 21m. 4c. Go right and climb the wall above by a series of mantelshelves, trending left to land on a ledge at the edge of the gully. Follow the vegetated gully before moving back right to a tree on the arête.
3 12m. Traverse right from the tree on all fours along a slot through nests to a stance below a large chimney.
4 21m. 4a. Climb the chimney, and then go up a short vegetated wall on the left to the top.

The Hole   63 metres   Very Severe   (17.11.74)
The climb gains the deep recess in the centre of the buttress and then leaves it by an interesting traverse out left. Vegetated in the lower half. Start below the deep recess to the left of a large holly tree.
1 18m. 4a. Climb easily up the right wall of the recess and fight through a tree under the roof. Stance on the tree.
2 24m. 4c. Move delicately across the steep slab on the left to a holly; then take the obvious traverse-line left on good holds to a crack. Go left again across a slab under a small overlap to the edge, and then up with difficulty to reach a crack in a steep slab that slants leftwards above the overlap. Climb the crack a short way before making a move right to good handholds and the large vegetated ledge under the chimney pitch of *Nichevo*.
3 21m. 4b. From the right-hand end of the ledge, climb a groove up the right edge of a steep wall to the top.

Black Pillar   60 metres   Hard Very Severe   (7.73)
Start in a little corner 1 metre left of the large holly.
1 30m. 5a. Go up the right edge of the corner to a ledge. Traverse across the wall to its right edge; climb this for a metre, and then traverse back left to a ledge on the left edge. Take the steep groove directly above the ledge (crux) to a large grassy stance.

2 30m. 4b. Go right and climb the slab to a groove (large pointed overhang on the right). Take the groove to the top.

Fangorn 51 metres Hard Severe (24.11.74)
Start below a narrowing slab in a corner, just above and a little to the right of the large holly tree. Flake belay.
1 21m. 4a. Climb the slab over widely spaced ledges to just below the top; then move right to vegetation. Pointed block belay on the left above the slab.
2 30m. 4b. From the top of the block, step left and move delicately left across a slab to a ledge (large pointed overhang 6 metres above). Move left again and climb the steep groove of *Black Pillar* above to the top.

Fangorn Right-Hand 27 metres Very Severe 4c (1.12.74)
A line following the break between two big roofs above the first pitch of *Fangorn*. Start by the pointed block at the top of pitch 1 of *Fangorn*. Go up easily into the corner above. Pull over the initial overhang, climb a steep ramp above to ledges, and go up these to the corner with an overhang on the right. Climb the right wall of the corner, using a dubious flake, to easier ground and the top.

North Gully
☆**Cloudbase** 35 metres E4 6a † (9.5.98)
An excellent arête on good white grit, unfortunately subsumed by its gully surrounds. Scramble up the gully and belay below the arête. Climb fairly steadily up the groove in the arête to a smoother section beneath a roof. With protection from *Friend* 1/1½ placements on the left, move right to a thin crack rising above the right-hand end of the roof and follow the fierce thin crack to better holds. Positive holds lead up the arête until a tricky move over a bulge gains a small slab on the right under a jammed block (thread). Follow a line of good holds in the easier wall above, past an *in-situ* thread, to an exit onto heather.

North Buttress
Tribarfau 63 metres Very Difficult (19.9.71)
The arête just right of North Gully. Start on the right of the arête below a vegetated chimney.
1 9m. Go a short way up over ledges to the right of the arête; then climb a little chimney and move left onto a heathery ledge below a small overhang on the arête. Nut belay in a horizontal crack.
2 12m. Step right onto a steep little wall, and gain a hold above with difficulty. Climb the corner behind the tree on the right; then move left across another small wall to gain the arête. Block belay.
3 12m. Easy ground leads to the foot of the wall above. Large spike belay.
4 21m. Traverse horizontally right across a steepish wall to a large flake, and go round into a niche above an oak tree. Climb a left-slanting chimney to gain the arête again.
5 9m. Climb slabs above to finish.

Bryniau Glo   Coal Hills[1]   OS Ref 727 214

Just north of the town of Dolgellau on the A470 is a farm on the left called Maes Mawr. Behind the farm is a vegetated escarpment of mainly poor rock, although there are two good lines on solid rock. On the skyline above this is a slabby wall which appears to lean out over the hillside: there are three routes here, also on mainly solid rock. The farm owner is at present well-disposed towards climbers and allows parking by his house. It is appreciated if a check is made with him each visit.

There is a large crumbling wall facing the road at the bottom of the escarpment. Up and left of this is a clean rib of rock reaching 15 metres.

Weevil Fish   15 metres   Hard Very Severe 5a †   (3.3.96)
Start below a short wall with the rib above on its left. Climb steeply to a spike and continue up, laybacking the arête, to reach the top slabby wall with a short overlap. Belay up on the ledge by the holly tree.

Double Take   15 metres   Hard Very Severe 5a †   (3.3.96)
The groove to the right of the rib. Start down and right of *Weevil Fish* just left of the ivy-covered wall. The stepped wall below the groove is very steep and strenuous. Once the groove is gained, the climbing eases and holds improve. Follow the right side of the rib to belay as for *Weevil Fish*.

The upper buttress on the skyline has an obvious nose just right of centre.

Hair-Ball   15 metres   E2/3 5c †   (30.7.96)
Gain the ledge on the left and pull up rightwards onto the wall. Climb the wall until a long reach up and left gains the left-hand ledge by a difficult mantelshelf. The clean pale shield of rock above has some good holds and protection. Climb it directly to the final ledge.

Hair-Brain   14 metres   E3 5c †   (30.7.96)
Start in the centre of the wall just left of the nose, and gain a small quartz thread placement; then, using small sidepulls and undercuts on the left, make long bold moves for a good horizontal slot and a bomb-proof placement. Some good holds above allow a pocket up and left to be gained. Strenuous. Finish directly more easily.

Black Narcissus   14 metres   E1 5b †   (3.3.96)
Start below and right of the nose, and below a thin overhanging groove. Gain the small recess with difficulty; then traverse out left until standing on the nose. Pull up and finish directly.

---

1 This probably refers to charcoal made from burning the wood..

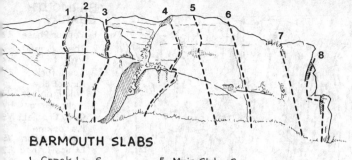

BARMOUTH SLABS

1	Crack 1	S	5	Main Slab	S
2	Xebec	HVS	6	Crack 3	VD
3	Crack 2	D	7	Crack 4	D
4	Zig Zag	VD	8	Crack 5	D

Barmouth Slabs

OS Ref 619 165

These pleasant slabs are situated about one mile north of Barmouth Harbour, and can be approached via the public footpath starting from the harbour below Barmouth Quarry. They lie on the north-east slopes of Garn Gorilwyn (213 metres) close to the summit, and are some 20 metres high. The rock is good, giving mainly easy climbs often used by outdoor centres in the district.

The crag looks smooth and rounded from a distance, but on closer inspection it is found to be seamed with cracklines. Starting on the left:

Crack 1 Severe. Crux near the top.

★Xebec Hard Very Severe 5a (1.1.81). Go up the middle of the slab between the two cracklines with a left-slanting crack to finish.

Crack 2 Difficult.

Zig Zag Very Difficult. Only fair protection.

★Main Slab Severe. Climb the middle of the slab into a scoop; then go directly to the top.

Crack 3 Very Difficult.

Crack 4 Difficult. Not a definite crackline.

Crack 5 Difficult. Make for the wide crack on the arête.

Stevie's Jamming Crack Severe. This is the crack behind the large boulder over the back of the crag at the north end.

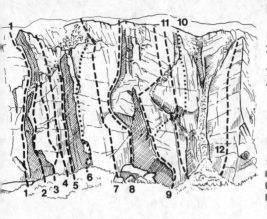

Barmouth Quarry
OS Ref 617 157

This slate quarry faces south-east and overlooks Barmouth Harbour. There is a public footpath leading up steps to it from the main road out of the town. The quarry is owned by the local council and climbing here is **strictly forbidden**.

A dozen routes, many of considerable quality, were climbed in the early 80s before the restriction was imposed. The full descriptions are preserved in the 1988 *Mid-Wales* guide, and in the (unlikely) event of the access situation changing for the better would be republished immediately on the Climbers' Club website. Meanwhile, an outline impression of the routes can be formed by comparing the the diagram above with the statistics below.

★★★**Vapour Phase** 52 metres E2 (27.12.80)

★**The Poisoned Dwarf** 37 metres E2 5c (27.12.80)

Southfork 34 metres E1 5b (1.1.81)

★**King of the Wild Frontier** 46 metres Hard Very Severe 5a (20.12.80)

Broken Arrow 52 metres Hard Very Severe (28.3.81)

Davy Crockett 46 metres Very Severe 4b (27.12.80)

It's Looking Good Houston 43 metres Very Severe 4b (20.4.81)

★**Ethical Cruise** 54 metres E2 (28.3.81)

★★**Columbia** 52 metres E1 (10.5.81)

★★**The Floater** 61 metres E3 (14.2.81)

Slipscream 52 metres E1 † (9.82)

★**Total Perspective Vortex** 46 metres E1 5b (7.6.81)

Cadair Idris   The Chair of Idris

Although a few metres lower than Aran Fawddwy, Cadair Idris completely dominates the landscape for miles in every direction; on a clear day, almost the whole of Snowdonia is visible from its summit, as is Pumlumon Fawr to the south and well beyond towards the Brecon Beacons. Almost uniquely amongst the high mountains of Wales, though there are satellites on its ridges, it is principally a single peak rather than just the dominant peak of a chain. The main ridge runs west-south-west up and across it from Cross Foxes and then down to the sea north of Tywyn. The 'chair' is a large hollow just to the north of the main summit, and its sedent, Idris, was a legendary giant.

The main crags are described in a clockwise circle, starting low down on the south-eastern slopes, rising above Llyn Cau to Cyfrwy, and so across the summit and along the east-north-east ridge over Mynydd Moel. The outlying crags are described anti-clockwise from north to south around the western half of the ridge.

Cwm Rhwyddfor   Big Open Valley   OS Ref 734 122

Turn off the A487 Dolgellau to Machynlleth road at the lay-by a half a kilometre north of the junction with the B4405. Take the short road down to Cwmrhwyddfor farm (good campsite) and follow the track that winds up the hillside between the two crags. Craig y Cwm is on the left and Craig Cwm Rhwyddfor sprawls away to the right.

The path is not a right-of-way, but good relations with the farmer have long existed, and courtesy and good behaviour are requested to maintain this situation.

Craig y Cwm   Crag (of) the Valley
This east-facing crag, previously referred to as Craig Rhwyddfor, is about 35 metres high. Situated at relatively low altitude and well drained, it may be a good choice in questionable weather.

It is rectangular in appearance, and steep with an undercut base. The rock is reasonable. The main features are the overhangs, the most obvious one being a large butterfly overhang at the base. Just right of this is the only weakness in the very steep base, giving access to a slight ramp-line crossing the wall to the right. This is taken by *Ice Man* and its right-hand neighbours.

Descent is by the gully on the left of the crag.

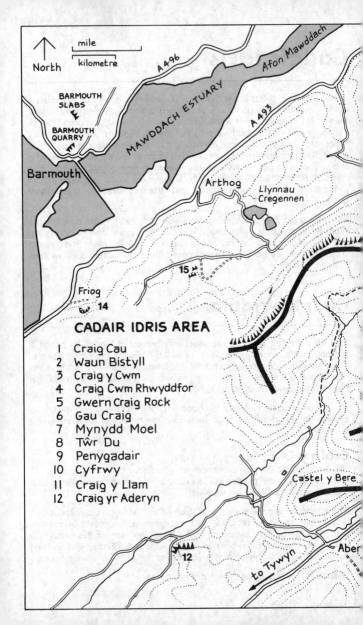

CADAIR IDRIS AREA

1 Craig Cau
2 Waun Bistyll
3 Craig y Cwm
4 Craig Cwm Rhwyddfor
5 Gwern Craig Rock
6 Gau Craig
7 Mynydd Moel
8 Tŵr Du
9 Penygadair
10 Cyfrwy
11 Craig y Llam
12 Craig yr Aderyn

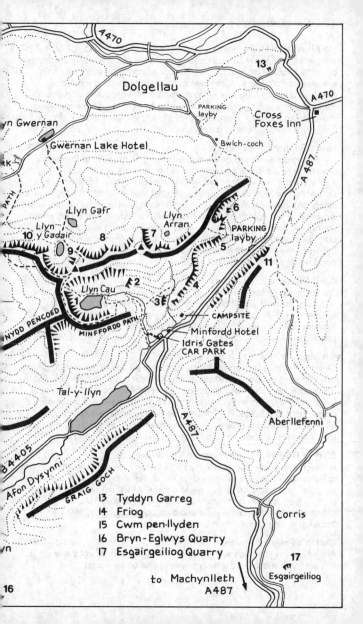

A 470

13

Dolgellau

PARKING layby

Cross Foxes Inn

A 470

yn Gwernan

Gwernan Lake Hotel

Bwlch-coch

A 487

PATH

Llyn Gafr

Llyn Arran

6

10
Llyn y Gadair

8

7

PARKING layby

5

9

11

Llyn Cau

2

4

3

NYDD PENCOED

MINFFORDD PATH

CAMPSITE

Minfordd Hotel
Idris Gates
CAR PARK

Tal-y-llyn

Aberllefenni

B 4405

Afon Dysynni

GRAIG GOCH

13 Tyddyn Garreg
14 Friog
15 Cwm pen-llyden
16 Bryn-Eglwys Quarry
17 Esgairgeiliog Quarry

Corris

17
Esgairgeiliog

16

to Machynlleth
A487

yn

Ice Man Direct   34 metres   E2 5c   (15.4.79/14.7.80)
The big central groove directly above the centre of the butterfly overhang
at the base of the crag; some hollow rock to start. A 2-metre roof bars
entrance to the groove. Ascend an easy vegetated wall to the roof. Pull
over with difficulty (peg runner) to the base of the groove, and strenuously
work up it to a resting-place. Continue up the groove with a final tricky
move to join *Ice Man*. Then, as for *Ice Man*, go up and left to a slab and
finish by a steep groove to a tree.

★**Loki**   34 metres   E1 5b   (10.5.80)
The next groove, barred by a small overhang, to the right of *Ice Man
Direct*. There is a small tree growing out of the base of the crag just right of
the foot of the groove. Start below the groove and gain it from the right
above the tree (nut runner can be arranged high in a crack on the right to
safeguard the initial moves over the overhang). Pull over the overhang on
big but dubious holds and climb steeply up the groove past a peg. Move
out right to a resting-place, then up to the roof, and up left for 1 metre
onto a sloping ledge. Climb directly to a large spike and make an
awkward move up right to gain a steep ramp. Continue straight up on
good holds, finishing airily out left.

April Blizzards   27 metres   E3 5c   (24.4.89)
Start at the small tree between *Loki* and *Ice Man*. Pull up into an overhung
niche and gain the right-hand of two thin cracks going through the bulge.
Pull steeply leftwards, and then up past the right-hand side of a roof
(crossing the traverse of *Ice Man*), whence steep climbing up and leftwards
gains a small ledge. Continue diagonally right and up a buttress to the top.

★**Ice Man**   40 metres   Hard Very Severe 5a   (14.4.79)
Good sustained climbing up the steep central section of the crag. Gain the
open groove, the only weakness in the undercut base, from the left. Go up
the groove for a short way and make some difficult moves right to small
ledges. Move up left to the line of small roofs and traverse horizontally left
below them to a bulge. Pull left over the bulge and go left to a groove.
Make a move up the groove and then go left again to a slab. Climb up
the steep groove above on big holds to a tree belay at the top of the crag.

Bird in Flight   34 metres   Hard Very Severe 5a   (24.2.80)
A direct line up the crag above the large tree. Follow *Ice Man* up and right
to the small ledges. Move up and go slightly left to a small roof, pull over
on good holds, and go up steeply to a niche. Move out steeply leftwards
using big underpulls, and reach a small groove capped by a small
triangular overhang. Move right and then up on big holds; then move
back left to reach easy ground.

Blatch's Folly   41 metres   Hard Very Severe   (14.4.80)
A right-slanting line across the wall on the right-hand side of the crag. The
first section is much harder than anything else on the route.

1 30m. 5a. Follow *Ice Man* up and right to the small ledges. Move up right, and follow the obvious diagonal line across the wall to the edge. Climb the edge a short way and then traverse right to a large tree.
2 11m. Climb easily rightwards, then leftwards to the top.

★Girdle Traverse 54 metres E1   (20.4.80)
A left-to-right traverse between the roofs. Go up easy rock on the left of the crag to a vegetated ledge with a tree and a gorse bush. Level with this ledge, a short horizontal ramp cuts into the very steep undercut wall on the right.
1 20m. 5b. Traverse right along the short ramp and make a long reach up to holds above an overhang; pull over and move up to a larger horizontal ramp-line with a big roof above (peg). Traverse right along the ramp and move up to a small ledge (nut and spike belays).
2 34m. 5a. Climb down 3 metres; then traverse right under a line of small roofs (*Ice Man* in reverse) to small ledges. Continue the traverse rightwards, rising to follow a weakness; then move up and right again to a large tree just under the top of the crag.

Craig Cwm Rhwyddfor Crag (of) the Big Open Valley
This line of broken buttresses runs parallel to the main road. The only recorded routes lie on the buttress closest to the road and directly above the farm, and on a section about a third of the way along the escarpment, the Central Area. The buttress above the farm has a large shield-like face with a descent gully.

Shield Buttress
Rituals of a Pagan 37 metres E2 5b †   (9.4.96)
A direct line at the left end of the wall, unremitting and technical, with spaced protection. Follow *Gwyth o' Wynt* for 5 metres onto the ramp. Move up directly onto the steep slab above and continue to the overlap. Pull straight through and finish up a vague left-facing groove.

Gwyth o' Wynt 40 metres Hard Very Severe 5a   (18.9.82)
Start 2 metres left of the lowest point of the wall, and climb a short steep section to gain the obvious ramp running diagonally up right across the wall. Climb this to a peg and then the ragged crack above to the top. Large boulder belay well back.

Virtual Reality 37 metres E3 5c †   (1.3.91)
A direct line through the centre of the crag. Starts 2 metres right of the lowest point of the wall. Trend up rightwards to an overlap and pull through on its left. Cross the diagonal ramp and go direct up the wall above to the small roof. Pull through to the right of this.

A Pagan Place 37 metres E2 5b †   (1.3.91)
Start 4 metres right of the lowest point of the crag, below some overlaps. Climb directly up to the overlap and pull through on the right. Continue up to below a large broken tooth of rock on the right of the crag; then step back left into the ragged crack of *Gwyth o' Wynt* to finish.

Trick in the Tail   37 metres   Very Severe 4c   (18.9.82)
A light-coloured groove on the right-hand side of the wall, with a small
holly tree at the top. The first 9 metres are rather artificial. Climb the slabs
directly below the groove for 9 metres, and then make a step left to gain
the groove. Climb it, with an awkward move over the final overhang to
reach the holly. Large boulder belay well back.

Just down and right from Shield Buttress is an isolated buttress with an
orange-tinted corner on its right.

Biohazard   15 metres   Very Severe 4c †   (2.11.92)
Although the rock is not brilliant the corner is entertaining. After a hard
start, easier climbing directly up the corner leads to an overlap. Pass this by
stepping out left onto the face, and finish straight up.

Central Area
This section of crag is probably the most significant of the long escarpment
crags of Craig Cwm Rhwyddfor, being some 45 metres high and 90 metres
long. The outstanding feature is an arête starting half-way up the crag,
which is taken by *Giotto*. The first route starts up a crack in the mossy slab to
its left.

Tri-Grainian   30 metres   Very Severe 4c   (7.86)
Climb the crack on the right-hand side of the slab to a niche under the
overhangs. Traverse left to a ledge on the left-hand side of the slab, move
up, and then go left to tree belays. Abseil from trees.

Giotto   45 metres   Hard Very Severe   (23.8.86)
Start to the left of the arête-line below a chimney leading up to overhangs.
The left-hand side of the chimney forms the right-hand side of the slab of
Tri-Grainian.
1 24m. 4c. Climb the chimney to the overhangs (some dubious rock);
then traverse right to a hanging slab. Climb the slab diagonally right to the
arête, go up this a short way, and then traverse left to a stance below the
arête.
2 21m. 5a. Move up to the bulging arête on the right (peg). Step right
and climb its steep right edge on good holds to a ledge. Continue directly
up the arête above to easier ground and a peg belay in a slab well back.
Descent is by a gully on the left.

Waun Bistyll   Waterfall Moor   OS Ref 725 129

A 25-metre-high, south-east-facing, leaning wall situated on the north side
of the valley leading up to Craig Cau, midway between the upper limit of the
woods and Llyn Cau. It lies about 90 metres above the valley floor and is
reached easily from the Minffordd Path. It catches the sun until midday.

Waun Bistyll

1 Awaken the Monster   E1
2 Sundew City   E3
3 Bilberries   E5
4 Professor Phibes   E5
5 Phantom   HVS

Descent is to the left, by steep bilberry and heather slopes and then a short easy gully.

★Sundew City   27 metres   E3 6a   (20.6.92)
[Photo page 408c.] On the left of the crag is a steep wall. The route takes its left edge, starting from the obvious overhanging corner at the start of the slanting undercut base. Protection is adequate. Climb strenuously up the corner, and make a difficult move to gain the ledge on the right. Climb the wall above (thread) and trend back slightly right up the broken arête to a steeper section (peg in horizontal crack on the right wall). Climb the bulging arête on the right until a step left can be made onto a slab (peg). Move delicately left to gain the left edge of a bulge, pull over, and climb the short wall above to the top.

★Awaken the Monster   27 metres   E1 5b   (23.8.92)
A rising right-to-left line making for the hanging slab on the left edge of the wall. Good protection. Start as for *Bilberries*, 4 metres right of the obvious overhanging corner of *Sundew City*. Pull over the overlap to juggy holds on a steep wall. Move up and left to a peg; step left to a notch on the arête, and left again to a ledge. Climb the left wall of the short steep corner on the left, and move left on good holds to the mossy slab. Finish up this and follow the ridge up rightwards to belay well up the heather.

☆Bilberries   24 metres   E5 6b †   (24.5.92)
A devitalizing pitch up the smoothest and steepest part of the main face. Protection up to half height is good; thereafter difficulties ease. Start 4 metres right of the obvious overhanging corner of *Sundew City*. From the deep slanting break at 3 metres, climb straight up the wall (peg runner) to meet a thin left-slanting crack. Follow this strenuously, eventually rocking-up to a resting-ledge on the left. Continue on the right (peg runner), and then direct to reach better holds in a slim groove, which leads to the top.

Professor Phibes   24 metres   E5 6a/b †   (24.5.92)
A good line, but scary and with marginal gear in places. From a recess in the slanting break, pull up to jugs at the base of the obvious flake-line. Follow the flake past a good pocket on the left wall to a spike. Grope up the awkward leaning groove above (peg runner) and pull over to small ledges (*Friend* 2½). Continue up a slim groove, then swing left to exit as for *Bilberries*.

Phantom   18 metres   Hard Very Severe 5a   (10.10.92)
A steep, well-protected route taking the fine crackline in the wall right of the break with the huge block. A good warm-up route with quite sustained climbing. Climb the crack, with an awkward start and a strenuous finish, to enter a V-groove. Climb easily up this to finish on steep heather. Good nut belays well back.

Craig Cau   Crag (of the) Enclosed[1]

'I find it difficult to imagine any modern Hard Man tackling its wet lichens in the sort of footwear now considered correct for serious climbing. It will need a coalition of old and new, tricouni nails with slings and pitons, before Craig Cau yields its full quota of climbing routes.'   Showell Styles.

After two intensive phases of exploration – one in the 70s and one in the 90s – Craig Cau now shines as a Mecca for high-standard climbing in Meirionnydd. It is also the home for a number of established mountain classics. Craig Cau is not just one cliff but, properly, the whole east face of Mynydd Pencoed, an appreciable sub-summit of Cadair Idris, which rises 300 metres above the dark and sometimes mysterious waters of Llyn Cau. There is a vast acreage of rock and a considerable variety of climbs to investigate quietly at one's own pace across the mountain's many different faces and buttresses. The rock is volcanic, and mainly sound.

Normally, most of the mountain will come into condition by May, even after a wet winter; and at other times, even after rain, it is not difficult to locate climbs that will be in a palatable condition. Seepage is not that great a problem, especially in relation to the upper walls.

As on many of its neighbours, lichens (and to a lesser extent mosses) enjoy the freedom to thrive on Craig Cau. Their presence, together with that of prevalent wide-bladed grasses and heather, is an integral characteristic of this crag environment – which is a nature reserve and the preserve of rare ferns, wild flowers such as the starry and purple saxifrages, and curiosities like the *hairy greenweed*! While most climbs embark on inherently clean and steep rock, some, nonetheless, will have been conceived after various degrees of wire brushing. But lichens are very quick to recolonize rock and, in the absence of repeated ascents, abseil inspection (possibly with re-cleaning) of the more serious routes may be a prudent precaution – say, three, four, or five years down the line. To launch out on, for example, *Brass Butterfly*, a bold and (at the time of writing) unrepeated E6, would correctly qualify as foolhardiness, whereas not to do so on *Lord of the Flies*, a well-worn classic of similar difficulty, would simply be cheating!

Most of the routes are unrepeated as at 2001, and it would be naïve to expect – in this day and age – any but the finest and cleanest routes to attract more than a handful of ascents each year. On the older vintage climbs vegetation can be copious, though testing of the peripheral skills and motivation of the climber. I would recommend *Pencoed Pillar* as a compulsory step in any bolt or indoor climber's career development(!).

1 Llyn Cau, the 'enclosed' lake below, lends its name to the crag.

I have tried to take a pragmatic approach to the question of approach to the various cliffs, substituting abseil access to some of the upper crags for often belabouring or dangerously vegetated ground-up assaults from the lakeside. An independent 50-metre or 60-metre abseil rope will be required in prescribed circumstances. On some of the 70s routes, carrying a few pegs and a hammer may be a wise insurance.

While the mountainside faces east, many crags shoulder south or south-east oriented facets; the author – a devout sun worshipper– will endeavour to optimize climbers' stay in the sun where he can.

Approach and Descent
The only feasible approach is to utilize the popular Minffordd Path, which starts from the (free) car-park next to the *Minffordd Hotel*, OS Ref 732 116 (or the fairly adjacent small campsite at Doleinon; there is a second campsite one kilometre to the north at Cwmrhwyddfor Farm). Take the sign-posted track from the north-west corner of the car-park, which bears left to a gate on the right at the foot of the wooded Nant Cadair Valley. Follow the zigzag path strenuously up along the west side of the stream until it levels out, and then a gentler walk of one kilometre leads to a split of the paths about 300 metres before the eastern shore of Llyn Cau. For climbs recommended to be accessed from the Minffordd Path above them, take the main – cairned – track up the ridge on the left and follow the ridge to the appropriate destination. For climbs reached from the lakeside, continue straight on past a *roche moutonnée* on the right and use either of the lakeside tracks. Further access (and descent) information is provided in the crag sections.

There are two standard means of descent for climbs which start from the lakeside and finish on the ridge-top. Either: (i) descend the south ridge of Craig Cau summit to the top of the third gully beyond Pencoed Pillar (the first is *East Gully*, the second *Little Gully*), which provides a scramble on the left (north) side down to slopes above the lake; or, (ii) descend the ridge north of Craig Cau summit beyond any steep rock to a col and the top of a rough but well-trodden track that leads straight down to a point right of Whale-back buttress and the northern shore of Llyn Cau.

A Whirlwind Crag Tour   [See also diagram pages 392b,c]
Rest for a while by the eastern shore of Llyn Cau, let the early morning summer mists dissolve, take the photo-diagrams to hand, and study the mountain... The most distinctive interruption of the main face is the deep incision of Great Gully, left-centre. Overhanging the gully, to its left, is the lofty sentinel of Pencoed Pillar. The precipitous gully left of the pillar is East Gully, at the top of which are a number of faces offering a clutch of climbs accessed from the ridge. The large north-east face of the pillar is broken and vegetated while the *pièce-de-résistance*, the sheer 70-metre west face, is partially hidden in the gully confines, and only appreciated upon closer acquaintance or contact.

Pencoed
Pillar

EAST GULLY WALLS

Great
Gully

WHITE LADY WALLS

BIRD OF TIME AREA

SOUNDS OF THE SIXTIES COMPLEX

IDRIS CORNER CRAG

WHALE-BACK BUTTRESS

Craig Cau

East Gully Walls

1 Missing *Friends*   E1
2 Thumb Wall   HVS
3 Millennium Bug   E3

White Lady Walls

4 Alone in the World   E3

To the right of Great Gully, a south-to-north diagonal banding is evident, which produces four main layers of rock outcrops rising up across the mountainside to the northern ridge of Craig Cau. Between them, huge grass and heather ramps provide natural lines of access to some of the crags.

At the foot of Great Gully, some 100 metres above the lake, is a buttress with three (or four, depending on the light) eye-catching arêtes – this is Idris Corner Crag. Right again in the very centre of the main face is Sounds of the Sixties Buttress, a 60-metre-high zone of walls and ribs below a steep ridge – *Central Rib* – which soars up towards the summit of Craig Cau. To the right of the top of Great Gully is a series of grey and white, banded faces – the White Lady Walls – which are best approached from the ridge. Returning to the lakeside, in the lower right-hand corner of the main face is the conspicuous slabby mass of Whale-back buttress. Directly above this, and immediately below the crest of the northern ridge of Craig Cau, is the Bird of Time Wall, which extends leftwards past the major vertical crackline of *Crack of Cau* towards *Central Rib* in the form of a less inviting 100-metre-high cliff of overlaps and ribs above a heathery bowl.

Little Gully   135 metres   Very Difficult
The gully to the left of East Gully. The final overhanging chimney pitch is normally avoided, but if this is climbed direct the grade is Hard Severe.
1 45m. Scramble up the gully bed to the first obstacle – a huge wedged block.
2 10m. A tight chimney on the left of the block is climbed to vegetation.
3 45m. Vegetation leads to an overhanging chimney.
4 35m. Take an easy groove at the start of the overhanging chimney until just below a large chockstone. Move out left to a small grassy bay on the left wall and climb up to a large spike on the left. A move down from the spike and a long stride left leads to a big foothold. Continue traversing left to easier ground.

East Gully   180 metres   Severe   (19.5.1895)
The gully immediately to the left of Pencoed Pillar. It is very wet and vegetated in its lower section but improves towards the top.
1 30m. Scramble up vegetation on the left to enter the gully; then go up a short grassy section on the right wall.
2 45m. The gully continuation is normally wet, so ascend a chimney on the left, traverse right at the top (back into the gully), and climb a wet gutter to where the gully narrows.
3 45m. Climb the groove above and then over a mossy slab and a jammed rock. Continue easily to follow a clean groove.
4 30m. Climb the groove, with three steep sections, until an easy traverse right, crossing an arête, leads to a shallow vegetated groove.
5 30m. Go straight up the groove to the top.

Pencoed Pillar
East Gully Walls
[Photodiagram page 384b.] At the left-hand corner of Pencoed Pillar, overlooking the upper reaches of East Gully, is an attractive and fairly sunny wall, distinguished by a slim, rectangular, 50-metre-high pillar at its left-hand side. All of the routes can be approached by some subtle scrambling via the top of the pillar, but it is far easier to get to them by selective abseil.

☆☆**Missing *Friends*** 50 metres   E1 †   (7.7.96)
A really enjoyable climb which takes the left rib of the slim rectangular pillar. Start just above the bed of the gully below the lower point of the rib.
1 25m. 5b. Climb fairly directly via ledges to a crack in the rounded left arête of the pillar. Follow the crack (peg runner) and pull up on a jug to belay on a large sloping ledge.
2 25m. 5b. From the left end of the ledge, step left and climb the right-hand side of the arête to another ledge. Take the strenuous crack above, and finish more easily up the rib.

Millennium Bug 20 metres   E3 6a †   (4.9.99)
The striking crackline between *Missing Friends* and *Uncensored*. Make a 40-metre abseil to the base of the route. Climb the pocketed wall just left of the crack; then move into the crack with difficulty and climb it to a ledge (*in-situ* thread). Climb the left-slanting groove to the second of two ledges, and finish up a steep wall on the right to heather ledges.

☆**Uncensored** 20 metres   E5 6b †   (22.9.96)
Fierce pocket-pulling up the centre of the leaning wall 25 metres right of the *Missing Friends* rib. Start from a raised heather ledge midway between a crack on the left (*Millennium Bug*) and a corner on the right. Take a central line on pockets to a big shake-out jug. Continue up the open left-slanting groove, using sumptuous finger-pockets on the right, and so reach a resting-ledge. Finish direct up the easier headwall.

☆**Thumb Wall** 20 metres   Hard Very Severe 5a †   (8.9.96)
Short-lived, but pleasant. Start below the overhanging arête 30 metres right of *Missing Friends*. Climb the fine pocketed wall just right of the arête, passing a peg runner at 8 metres. Thread belay.

North East Face
The next two climbs are located on the massive vegetated front face of Pencoed Pillar. A left-to-right rising heathery ramp truncates the foot of the pillar (and recontinues beyond *Great Gully* in the form of a wider ramp to the top of Sounds of the Sixties Buttress). Scramble up above the lake shore to the left-hand end of the ramp and follow it to a point just left of *Great Gully* where the routes start.

★Pencoed Pillar   210 metres   Severe   (7.1903)
A historic mountaineering route, providing many climbers' sole encounter with Cau. There are good stances and protection in its upper reaches, but some considerable vegetation lower down requires aptitude. Start by some quartz-flecked rock below vegetated and often wet slabs.
1   35m.   The initial slabs. Trend 4 metres right to some vegetation; then step left and climb the slabs above on good holds to more vegetation. Ascend this directly to a dubious spike and veer right to a small rowan.
2   50m.   Wander up vegetation to the left, passing beneath a steep grey wall on the right until a broad chimney is reached.
3   35m.   Climb the broad chimney and the short wall above, before moving out left to more vegetation. Above is the pillar itself. Move right and gain the base of a left-slanting groove with some chockstones wedged in a crack near its top. Belay beneath the groove.
4   15m.   Climb the wall with the aid of the chockstone; exit left and ascend more easily straight up to a stance and a fine thread belay on the right.
5   15m.   Go up the wall on the right, taking a rising traverse-line on big holds to a good stance and huge block belay on the arête.
6   30m.   Climb directly up the wall above on good holds, keeping just left of the arête, and so gain a long, narrow, vegetated ledge under a steep wall. Nut belay in a crack in a little corner on the left.
7   20m.   Take the corner; then go up a short ramp on the right to a wall (chimney on the left). Climb the wall slightly rightwards and make a final awkward move to a hidden hold on the edge. Move easily right and go up to a ledge. Good nut and spike belay.
8   10m.   Climb a short groove on the left, and scramble to the narrow summit of the pillar.

Pamplemousse   130 metres   Hard Very Severe   (27.8.73)
A vegetated and rarely repeated route up the front of Pencoed Pillar, making for an obvious groove at about half height. The upper section weaves through the large overhangs at the top of the pillar, giving an exposed finish. From part way up the second pitch of *Pencoed Pillar*, scramble up a vegetated groove (steep grey wall on the left) which leads to the base of a ramp rising diagonally left to the bottom of the main groove.
1   23m.   5a.   Climb the left-slanting ramp (peg runner) to a small quartz cave (thread). Move awkwardly over the bulge above the cave (peg runner) to a slab beneath the groove. Peg belay on the slab to the right of the bulge.
2   17m.   4c.   Climb the groove to a big grassy ledge.
3   12m.   Continue in the line of weakness diagonally left to a huge block.
4   48m.   From the block, move up a short way and climb a grassy ramp on the right. Climb a slab to an overhang formed by a large wedged flake. Go over this and move right to a good crack. Climb the crack until just below the roofs, and move right around the arête of *Blame It on the Gods* to belay above a mossy bottomless groove.
5   30m.   4c.   Traverse right beneath the overhangs to the obvious weakness through them. Take this, moving slightly right, before stepping back left and climbing the slab to the top of the pillar.

West Face

[Diagram page 392a.] This is the towering right-hand wall of Pencoed Pillar, which makes for some sensational positions, best appreciated in the summer afternoon sun. All of the climbs are most readily accessed by abseil. Take the Minffordd Path along the ridge until, about 250 metres short of the summit of Craig Cau, you arrive at a vantage point at the top of the yawning depths of *Great Gully* on the right. For a good view of the west face and its abseil approach, continue a little further.

An approach from the lake shore is perfectly feasible – for the adventurous – though the original starting-pitches of *Darker Angel* (which can give access to a common belay) are now vegetated. This, and a fairly easy section of *Great Gully*, should not, however, present a problem to climbers committed to this ground-up methodology.

The following climbs start from a small foot-ledge at a break at the bottom of a ramp in the centre of the lower part of the west wall. The ramp evolves into a crack leading up to a sizeable roof (this is the line of *Darker Angel*). Abseil 45 metres from the edge of the pillar (extension required, unless using 60-metre rope), going down the west side of the finishing slab, and over the east (left, facing in) side of the roof, eventually swinging in to nut belays at the base of the ramp. (Those prone to getting these sorts of things wrong should take some means of prusiking out.)

☆☆**Blame It on the Gods**   55 metres   E5 †   (4.8.96)
[Frontispiece photo.] Downright spectacular. The flying left-hand arête of the wall provides an inspirational route in a gob-smacking environment.
1 30m. 6a. Traverse left along the lip of the bulge on downward-pointing spikes (high flake runner) to a step down left onto a small slab on the rounded arête. Grope up over the bulge and pull up left to a good rest below a small roof – this move is far harder than anything else on the route. Climb the right-hand side of the arête, generally on positive holds, to a good spike runner after 12 metres. Move left and, avoiding cop-outs to the left, climb the very edge of the arête to a fine foothold stance below bulging rock.
2 25m. 5c/6a. Climb straight up the rib to a gap in the roof. Improvise through; then proceed direct up the clean slab, and step left at its top to exit over a small undercut slab.

The Gods Themselves   55 metres   E3 †   (4.8.74/1996)
Immediately before the arête of *Blame It on the Gods* is an open bottomless groove, normally occupied by unclimbable mats of lurid green moss. Start from the common stance.
1 30m. 5c. Go up the ramp for 3 metres to an overhang. Traverse leftwards into the foot of the groove, and climb it until it is possible to move left to the foothold stance of *Blame It on the Gods*. Serious.
2 25m. 5c/6a. *Blame It on the Gods* pitch 2 (some variants are possible).

☆Preacher Man 50 metres E5 †   (6.7.96)

Two contrasting pitches on a line that crosses *Darker Angel*. Start from the common stance.

1 25m. 6a. Go up the ramp for 3 metres to an overhang. Pull leftwards into an open groove (*in-situ* thread) and move up to a small undercut flake. Climb up with difficulty; then bear right to twin flakes. Take the delicate thin seam above, which slants right to the ledge and final belay of *Darker Angel*.

2 25m. 6a. Climb the corner to the large capping roof. Traverse right for 2 metres, and extend monstrously for a hanging flake above the lip. Grapple over, wishfully, and then trend left up the slab to a grass ledge. Step left and finish up a low-angle rib.

★★Darker Angel 113 metres E2   (30.5.74)

While not quite making the status of 'one of the great Welsh classics' predicted by the previous guidebook, this climb is nonetheless a very fine outing. It does get a little dirty from time to time, but this should not pose a problem to competent climbers. The ground-up approach is described, which is rather vegetated but – equally – the route could be commenced from the common stance, reached by abseil, below pitch 3. Approach from part way up the second pitch of *Pencoed Pillar*, going up a vegetated groove on the right and then mastering more vegetation to reach an obvious rightward-rising ramp.

1 45m. 5a. Follow the ramp rightwards until a traverse back left, past a block, leads to the foot of a groove. Move up to a spike belay underneath a fang of rock.

2 18m. 5a. Traverse right along another grassy ramp, cross a slab, and climb rightwards and up to the small stance at the bottom of a ramp.

3 25m. 5c. Go up the ramp for 3 metres to an overhang. Continue up the narrowing ramp, before steeper moves up the crack lead to an awkward landing on a good stance beneath the large capping roofs.

4 25m. 5c. Climb the corner (with ferns, normally) to the roof. Traverse left with difficulty to a rib; then break through the roof and move up to a grass ledge. Step left and climb the right-hand side of the slab and low-angle rib above to the top. (With expert rope-work it is possible to combine the top two pitches into one super run-out.)

★Messiah 50 metres E5 6a   (17.5.80)

A superb pitch when clean, but be warned: the crucial peg runners were in a worrying condition as long ago as 1992. For the entrepreneur, linking the main body of the pitch with the upper two-thirds of *Holy Cau* would provide an exceptional challenge. Start from the common stance, reached by abseil. Traverse rightwards across the bare wall for 5 metres. Trend right to a crack, which leads up to a rest beneath a bulge (peg runner). Make a very hard move up onto the sandwiched slab overhead (peg runner); then, using layaways on the right, pull up onto the steep slab and continue to a small ledge on the arête. Step left, surmount the roof using the obvious leftward-slanting crack, and then climb the easier slab to a grass ledge. Finish up the broken groove, or step left and follow *Darker Angel* to the top. (For those lured by the *Messiah–Holy Cau integralé*, pull up onto the small ledge on the arête and step right to the lower set of downward-pointing fangs on *Holy Cau*.)

☆☆**Holy Cau**   30 metres   E3 5c †   (9.6.96)
An outstanding climb, replete with character, which navigates the overlapping slabs and fang-like undercuts in the upper right-hand section of the West Wall. Take a belay above the chockstones in the right-bounding corner, gained by making an abseil down the line of the top pitch of *His Satanic Majesty*. Ascend diagonally left to a thin groove and follow this slightly rightwards onto a slab beneath a beautiful undercut fin. Place a trustworthy *Friend 1½/2* on the right; then undercut around left to the unmistakable drooping fang (*in-situ* thread). Step delicately over the overlap (crux) to another undercut overlap, and move left and up to the foot of a narrow groove. Climb the groove, taxingly, to the top.

His Satanic Majesty   130 metres   E3 †   (29.8.74)
An exposed girdle traverse of the wall, parts of which are in poor condition. Start as for the ground-up approach to *Darker Angel*.
1 45m. 5a. *Darker Angel* pitch 1.
2 15m. Climb up, trending slightly left from the belay to a bulge at 8 metres. Traverse right until a move can be made onto a slab. Move left to a poor stance in a shallow depression (peg belays).
3 18m. Move back right into a groove and continue onto a small slab (rotted *in-situ* wire). Follow this line into *The Gods Themselves*. Reverse part of pitch 1 of *The Gods Themselves* to the common stance at the base of the ramp on *Darker Angel*.
4 18m. Climb *Darker Angel* pitch 3 for 6 metres; then take a slab-line rightwards and go down slightly right. This leads onto a larger slab near the gully. Move diagonally right to a small stance.
5 9m. Broken rocks lead to nut belays below a square chockstone – the stance of *Holy Cau*.
6 25m. Pull over the chockstone and go up to a steep wall. Follow cracks to the left over bulges until a move right can be made to a good ledge. Go up and left to finish.

Great Gully Wall

Extending rightwards from the West Wall of Pencoed Pillar into Great Gully is an expanse of rock, characterized by a series of corners rising from the gully bed and a glorious, often sun-lit, rectangular hanging slab at its top. It is an ill-frequented and isolated spot high on atmosphere. All of the climbs are approachable by a not overly arduous scramble up Great Gully, or by means of a 50-metre abseil down the wall.

Demian   95 metres   Very Severe †   (1975)
Start in *Great Gully* just below where it almost closes, some 20 metres below *Abraxus*.

1 35m. Go left to a shallow corner, climb it for 12 metres, and then traverse delicately right to a narrow corner. Climb up to a wide crack; then move out right at the top of the crack on a flat ledge to the rib on the right. Climb straight up to a ledge some 12 metres below an overhang with a half-round break in it.

2 20m. Climb up cracks; then gain a slab beneath an overhang on the right. Ascend a break in the overhang and move left across ledges to below a rib. Peg belays.

3 40m. Take the groove in the right-hand side of the rib, move left 9 metres, and climb up the rib to reach easy ground. A tower with a deep crack is then climbed to the top.

The next four climbs start below a left-facing corner that evolves into a flake chimney higher up. This point is about 70 metres from the top of Great Gully at the base of an unstable chimney.

Bassillades   66 metres   Very Severe   (17.5.75)

1 30m. Go left from the base of the *Abraxus* corner to a slabby ledge. Climb the wall above until an obvious weakness trending up left can be reached. Follow this until a move can be made into a groove. Climb the groove and exit left at the top to a ledge.

2 18m. Move back right and take a crack on the right; then go up slabs and ledges to a small stance.

3 18m. Climb a crack-system close to the left edge of the hanging slab. Continue up the cracks to the top in an exhilarating position.

Here Comes the Sun   65 metres   E2   (5.77)

Quite an interesting route, with an elegant finish up the prominent hanging slab. Start as for *Abraxus* and *Bassillades*.

1 45m. Go 6 metres left from the foot of the *Abraxus* corner, as for *Bassillades*. Directly above is an overhanging corner, leaning leftwards at the top. Climb the corner, and then go straight up easier rock and ledges to a large spike belay below the clean-cut hanging slab.

2 20m. Reach the foot of the slab and climb its centre to the top.

☆**Fantastic Day**   60 metres   E6 †   (22.9.96)

A devastating first pitch in sombre surrounds. A prominent pocketed wall and arête is visible when looking down Great Gully from the ridge: that's the line.

1 42m. 6b. Climb the *Abraxus* corner for 8 metres to the point at which it slabs-out rightwards. Immediately, swing left on finger-pockets to the arête. Balance up the arête to a superb pocket (crucial *Friend* 2½ placement); then make long moves across right to more pockets (good wire). Go straight up the wall with the inevitable committing final move to a big sloping ledge above the arête. Step right (*in-situ* thread); ascend a rib and a short steep wall (peg runner) to pull up onto a pocketed slab, and belay below the hanging slab.

2 18m. 5b. Move up to mantel onto a short leftward-rising ramp. From its top, continue direct up the hanging slab on good holds and finish by stepping left and exiting up its centre.

Abraxus   60 metres   Hard Very Severe   (9.5.75)
The corner and overlying chimney.
1 40m. Climb the corner to a slab at its top. Trend right to avoid two
bulges in the corner, and then traverse back left to the foot of a chimney
formed by a flake. The chimney and more broken ground above lead to a
stance below a short corner.
2 20m. Climb the corner and move right to the base of a shallow steep
chimney. Climb the chimney, go over the overhang above it, and finish up
the cracks above.

Deadpan   60 metres   Hard Very Severe †   (27.4.74)
About 50 metres down from the top of Great Gully is an 8-metre chimney
in the gully bed. Just below and left of this is a chimney/groove with a
chockstone at 8 metres. Start below the groove.
1 33m. Climb the chimney and move onto the chockstone. Go up for 3
metres and then move left across a series of ribs and grooves (peg runner)
until a small slab below a prominent roof can be gained. Cross this and
climb up to the left of the overhang to a ledge.
2 27m. Ascend leftwards and go back right to a shattered groove
immediately right of the big overhang above. Climb this for 3 metres; then
go up and left to a smaller overhang to reach a corner-system which leads
to the top.

Great Gully   292 metres   Hard Severe   (18.5.1895)
The huge gully between Pencoed Pillar and the main cliff. An outmoded –
but adventurous – concept in climbing with little in the way of pure rock,
and much in the way of greenery. Helmets are recommended. Start at the
base of the gully above grass and scree slopes.
1 12m. A double chockstone pitch, taken on the right.
2 40m. Another chockstone pitch can be passed on either side; then
scrambling leads up the gully to a wet cave. Avoid this by moving out left up
vegetation to a large grassy ramp coming in from the left – escape possible.
3 40m. Cross the gully and scramble up vegetation on the right to avoid
another wet cave. Move back left up more vegetation to belay.
4 35m. Continue traversing left to gain the bed of the gully. Climb it,
taking a huge chockstone on the right, to a belay above on the right wall.
5 30m. The gully now becomes narrower; climb the vegetated chimney
above to a grassy bay on the right. Nut belay.
6 40m. Go over a chockstone on the left; then move up to another
chockstone which is taken on the right. Nut belay on the right.
7 40m. The 'converging walls' pitch is above. Go up a groove crossing
the gully from right to left. Move right out of the groove; then continue
straight up the gully to ledges. Nut belays. There is much loose rock
hereabouts.
8 25m. Climb the narrowing chimney on the left and go easily to a
chockstone, which is taken on the right. Belay under a steep little chimney.
9 30m. Avoid the chimney by traversing out right up a grassy ramp; then
return left to the top of the gully.

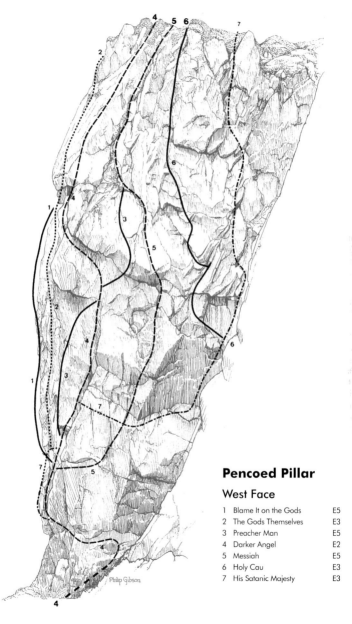

Pencoed Pillar

West Face

1	Blame It on the Gods	E5
2	The Gods Themselves	E3
3	Preacher Man	E5
4	Darker Angel	E2
5	Messiah	E5
6	Holy Cau	E3
7	His Satanic Majesty	E3

Philip Gibson

Craig Cau

| 1 | Little Gully | VD |
| 2 | East Gully | S |

Pencoed Pillar

3	Missing Friends	E1
4	Millenium Bug	E3
5	Thumb Wall	HVS

| 6 | Pencoed Pillar | S |

Idris Corner Crag

11	Leander	E2
12	Idris Corner	E2
13	Artrageous	E5

Sounds of the Sixties Complex

14	Prestissimo	E4
15	Sounds of the Sixties	E6
16	Zabberdack	E5
17	Dreams and Reality Collide	E5
18	Battered Caravanserai	VS

| 19 | Druid's Own Eyes | E5 |

Whale-back Buttress

| 20 | Marsum | VD |
| 21 | Whale-back Groove | E1 |

White Lady Walls

8	Face to Face	E5
9	Come Rain or Shine	E5
10	Central Rib	VS

Great Gully

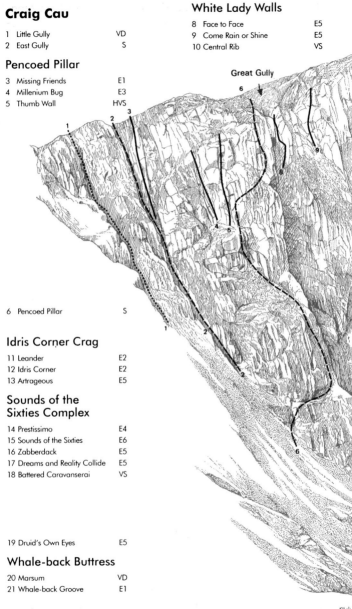

Philip

Black Shiver Area

22 Black Shiver   E2
23 The Baron   HVS

Crack of Cau Area

24 Crack of Cau   HVS
25 Touchstone   VS

Bird of Time Area

26 Highlanders Fling   E6
27 Solo Engagement   E3
28 Moving Finger   E1
29 Bird of Time   E3
30 Dawn Patrol   E4

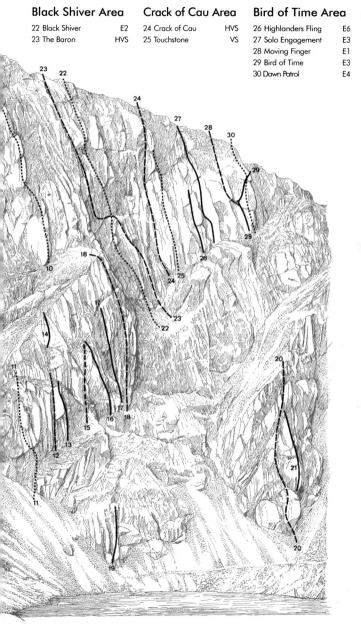

Craig Cau

Idris Corner Crag

1 Leander with Waterwings E5
2 Leander E2
3 Across the Hellespont E6
4 Suicidal Wall E4
5 Time is the Fire in Which We Burn E7
6 Brass Butterfly E6
7 Idris Corner E2
8 Artrageous E5

P Pencoed Pillar VD

Great Gully

Idris Corner Crag

A great crag in its own right characterized by three prodigious columnar arêtes and some world-class routes. It is located just right of the base of Great Gully, about 100 metres above the lake shore. The starts of the climbs are reached from the boulder-scree zone at the foot of the gully on the left, via a rightwards scramble up slabs and a heather rake. Two descents are possible: either by means of a heather ramp on the right with a (normally uncontrolled) slide over a short rock chute; or by reversing leftwards to the foot of the huge heathery ramp above, from which Great Gully can be accessed, and the approach ramp of Pencoed Pillar climbed down and leftwards.

However, the first route described is an isolated pitch up a rib which is beneath the main crag and about 30 metres above the lake shore, where there is an exclusive little rock island from which to swim.

Druid's Own Eyes   20 metres   E5 6b †   (21.9.96)
A nasty climb which feels pumpy and insecure – need it be marketed further? Climb a mossy groove left of the rib and place a wire runner at 5 metres. Reverse a little; then awkwardly cross the leaning wall rightwards to the rib (peg runner). Make strenuous and precarious moves up the rib and enter a small groove (peg runner). Take the arête above to reach a ledge (and metal stake belay: abseil descent possible).

★Leander   45 metres   E2   (9.7.83)
To the left of a prominent vertical black streak (which is just left of the three arêtes) is a slightly less distinct arête; this route largely climbs its left-hand side. Both pitches are E2. Start directly below the arête, beneath a flake-line.
1 15m. 5c. Climb up to a niche below a right-facing corner, or scramble into the niche from the left. Follow the corner for 5 metres to a bulge (peg runner), and exit awkwardly left onto a slab.
2 30m. 5a. Pull up onto a ledge above the belay, and ascend the wall above to another ledge. Follow a poorly-protected line of weakness left of the arête, and step right onto the arête. Take the arête above to a good flake, step right, and bear left again to the top of the arête and belays a fair way back. Scramble off rightwards.

☆Leander with Waterwings   45 metres   E5 6a †   (21.9.96)
A direct version of *Leander*, with impeccable rock but giant peel potential. Start from a belay in the niche below the initial corner of *Leander*. Climb the corner up the steep flake and swing up right above the overhang to a wafer flake. Move up onto two sloping handholds, step right, and then go up the pocketed face to a slanting break with positive gear. Now boldly climb the right-hand side of the arête (twisted *Rock 5/6* placement in a pocket) until thin moves gain a good layaway and the easier upper arête. Continue to join *Leander* at the flake and proceed direct on the arête to the belay. Scramble off rightwards.

☆☆**Across the Hellespont**   40 metres   E6 6a/b †   (25.5.92)
This is the first of the three major arêtes, which provides a nerve-racking
and very run-out pitch. Start from an elevated grass ledge at 12 metres
height, directly beneath the arête. Climb up scrappy rock to a broken
ledge and an enormous spike runner. Traverse right; then pull up onto a
small spike and a peg runner beneath the bulge undercutting the arête.
Make powerful moves through the bulge (in-situ wire), and then traumatic
climbing on tinies leads to a step up left into the foot of the dark-streaked
runnel. Bridge easily up the runnel to a good RP3 placement 3 metres
above. Now traverse right along good footholds towards the arête (crucial
Friend ½ placement on the right). Climb straight up the pocketed slab just
to the left of the arête (peg runner on the left) before trending rightwards
on small but positive holds with no further protection to the arête and an
easy finish. Scramble out.

Suicidal Wall   35 metres   E4 †   (8.6.96)
Good for warming up the mind before engaging the harder neighbours. A
serious lead up the slabby wall right of Across the Hellespont, gained from
the central major arête (Time Is the Fire in Which We Burn). Start from a
sloping grassy ledge directly beneath the central arête.
1 15m. 5c. Traverse left and move up before gaining the foot of a thin
crack on the left. Climb the crack, exit left onto a sloping ledge, and take a
belay 8 metres down the grass tongue beneath the slabby wall. Good nuts
and Friends in the corner (unclimbed).
2 20m. 5c. Above the belay is a faint line of hope left of a dark streak;
climb it past various sloping ledges and unpromising gear to a good
hand-ledge 3 metres below the top. Step left to the arête of Across the
Hellespont and exit as for that route.

☆☆☆**Time Is the Fire in Which We Burn**   30 metres   E7 6b †   (8.6.96)
Where else in England and Wales did lines like this linger into the 90s
unclimbed? A masterful climb on the central, major, right-angled arête of
the crag. All of the protection above the horizontal break is of marginal
holding power. Start from the sloping grassy ledge beneath the arête, as
for Suicidal Wall. Traverse left and move up before gaining the foot of a
thin crack on the left. Climb the crack to a sloping ledge on the left, and a
horizontal break beneath the arête. Ascend the arête directly (two peg
runners) to share the final moves of Brass Butterfly (peg runner). Selected
RPs and microwires can be placed en route, together with a hand-placed
knife-blade a little below the Brass Butterfly peg runner. Scramble out (or
lower off!).

☆☆☆**Brass Butterfly**   25 metres   E6 6b †   (25.5.92)
An immaculate face climb, somewhat reminiscent of a condensed
upside-down mirror image of Lord of the Flies (for the imaginative). This is
the left wall of the main corner of the crag, Idris Corner. Belay at the foot of
Idris Corner. Climb the opening wall 4 metres left of the corner and so
gain good breaks and protection at 6 metres. From a small,
rightward-pointing flake, climb boldly to better holds, a peg runner, and

indifferent wire placements. Traverse left to the foot of a slim, blind, right-facing flake. Move up (peg runner), step left (peg runner), and finish immediately right of the arête.

★★Idris Corner 30 metres E2 5b (16.5.82)
The *Cenotaph Corner*-like feature between the central and third arêtes. A fine test of dihedral technique – and temper. Follow the exponentially trying corner wondering how much further the top can be. Take plenty of big pieces to complement John Sumner's bong.

☆Artrageous 35 metres E5 6a/b † (25.5.92)
A stunning natural sculpture: the third, right-hand, major arête. Start from a high grassy platform diagonally down right of the arête, best approached from the right. Climb an awkward striated rib to a jug-rail at 6 metres (*in-situ* thread). Gain the crack on the left over the bulge and – with cam protection a little higher – traverse left across the steep slab above the huge roof, stepping up to some good footholds (peg runner). Move up and diagonally left to an awesome position on the sharp arête (peg runner). A few abstract dynamic moves up the final arête (peg runner) should leave their impression.

Approximately 35 metres right of the third arête (*Artrageous*) is a continuous sweep of slab. This lies below the left-hand side of the Sounds of the Sixties Complex. A hazardous pitch lurks here:

Long Hot Mid-Sumner's Night 20 metres E5 5c † (3.8.96)
Use a rib in the introductory slab to reach the large heather ledge beneath the main slab. Try to fix some appalling wires; then go straight up for 8 metres, without gear, to a position with a negative outlook. Hunt around for protection before continuing direct and then slightly right to escape.

Sounds of the Sixties Complex

In the very centre of the main face right of, and at a slightly higher level than, Idris Corner Crag is a 60-metre-high zone of rock bounded on its left by a left-slanting chimney-line and on its right by the heathery bowl beneath the Crack of Cau Area. A clean grey face on the left houses many of the routes, while above it is an unmistakable pyramid called The Metronome, which provides two exposed pitches. Right again, beyond vegetated rock, is a loftier area of ribs and grooves. A concentration of tough climbs on excellent rock is on offer hereabouts.

Approach is straightforward from the right, via a choice of heathery ramps. There is a comfortable broad platform below the main grey face on the left. The left-bounding chimney rises from this platform and can be used as a descent for all of the climbs at about Very Difficult standard. The way to reach the chimney from the finishes of the routes on the grey face – *Wheels on Fire* to *The (Heart) Beat Room* – is by traversing left across heather ledges beneath The Metronome, with an exposed but easy step at the end. From the top of the chimney it is also possible to walk out onto the huge diagonal heathery ramp above, from which *Great Gully* can be accessed, and the approach ramp of Pencoed Pillar climbed down and leftwards.

Wheels on Fire   20 metres   E3 6a †   (20.7.96)
A pitch of mounting interest. Start at the foot of the descent chimney bounding the grey face on its left. Follow a rightward-slanting ramp to its end. Reach jugs above a small roof and swing left; then proceed on strenuous holds up a thin line of weakness to exit right and then back leftwards onto heather ledges. Good thread in gully.

☆**God of Hellfire**   25 metres   E5 6a †   (20.7.96)
A superb sustained route which takes the thin right-facing corner at the left-hand side of the grey face. Follow a steep crack rightwards to the foot of the corner and a ledge on the right. Enter the corner – hard – and climb it to a bulge. Surmount the bulge and go up a steep incipient crackline to the exit of *Wheels on Fire*.

Chills and Fever   25 metres   E6 6b †   (20.7.96)
A super-bold eliminate guarded by a ferocious leaning wall. Start 2 metres left of a clean crack. From an undercut flake, climb directly up the wall before committing moves gain the ledge of *God of Hellfire* slightly left. Move up the rib to a good resting-position below an impending wall (poor knife-blade, removed); move left and then power feverishly up the wall to the sanctuary of the exit of *Wheels on Fire*.

☆☆☆**Sounds of the Sixties**   30 metres   E6 6a/b †   (20.7.96)
The strongest line on the face, and certainly its most varied, it heads for the twin-groove-system at half height. Start at a clean overhanging crack left of an obvious vegetated crack. Attack the crack and sprint to ledges. Climb up the twin grooves above (tricky gear) and make a worrying move up to a chockstone (*in-situ* thread). Bear strenuously right to a good ledge, step right onto a slabby rib, and climb this pleasantly to heather ledges. Scramble left to belays.

The next two short pitches terminate at a ledge at 13 metres, which is the first stance of *The (Heart) Beat Room*. To the right of the belay is a good rock spike enabling an abseil descent.

Go – Now!   13 metres   E5 6a †   (3.8.96)
A non-stop direct start to the next route: very strenuous. Start below a slim rightward-leaning corner right of the vegetated crack. Boulder up the corner (knife-blade in undercut flake at 6 metres – removed) to a spike above on the left. Finish direct.

☆☆**Zabbadack**   15 metres   E5 6a †   (3.8.96)
A delicacy on the pristinely textured grey slab at the right-hand end of the grey face. Starting 2 metres right of the leaning corner, trend rightwards to a good finger-ledge at 6 metres (hand-placed knife-blade in pocket, removed). Sweep back left to a blind, right-facing flake and the top of the *Go – Now!* corner and its spike on the left. Finish direct.

Craig Cau

Sounds of the Sixties Complex

1 Prestissimo — E4
2 Hologram — E5
3 Wheels on Fire — E3
4 God of Hellfire — E5
5 Chills and Fever — E6
6 Sounds of the Sixties — E6
7 Zabberdack — E5
8 Go – Now! — E4
9 The (Heart) Beat Room — E3
10 Dreams and
   Reality Collide — E5
11 The lorryman — E6
12 Jin-Go-La-Ba — E5
13 Battered Caravanserai — VS

D Descent Gully

M The Metronome

☆**The (Heart) Beat Room**   40 metres   E3 †   (20.7.96)
In the right-hand rib of the grey face is a long open scoop, Dinas Mot-like, and similarly under-endowed with protection. This provides an elegant climb for steady climbers. Start below a vague leftward-slanting scoop at the right limit of the grey face.
1 15m. 5b. Pad up the scoop and gain the stance above using the crack on the right. Rock spike belay on the right.
2 25m. 5c. Gain the scoop-line on the left and follow it with increasing heart pump until thin crux moves enable heather ledges above to be reached. Scramble left to belays.

The following two pitches are perched on The Metronome, the pyramid of rock immediately overlying the preceding climbs. They can be accessed independently using the descent chimney, or from the huge heathery ramp above.

☆☆**Prestissimo**   25 metres   E4 6b †   (21.7.96)
The striking crack which cleaves the face of The Metronome, gained with subtlety: a Cadair classic. Start from a good thread belay below the left-centre of the face. Climb up for 2 metres; then follow a diagonal line of pockets rightwards to the arête. With protection from a high peg runner on *Hologram*, make a fingery move to start the crack (peg runner), and continue speedily on good locks to the easier wider section and nut belays behind the top of The Metronome.

☆☆**Hologram**   25 metres   E5 6a †   (21.7.96)
The grooved arête of The Metronome, dizzily projected out into the thin air of the cwm. Start from a big ledge beneath the groove. Climb easily up the initial corner to a bulge at 6 metres (peg runner). Enter the tapering groove above and stick with it to its close. Now move up onto the arête and, keeping it together, go for the summit of The Metronome.

The right-hand part of the Sounds of the Sixties Complex comprises some overhanging wet slabs (with the broken rib of *Battered Caravanserai* on the right), and a pair of arêtes on the left. The following route takes the contiguous left-hand arête:

☆☆**Dreams and Reality Collide**   60 metres   E5 †   (21.7.96)
A tremendous climb. A range of difficulties will test the resources of most aspirants.
1 45m. 6a. From quaky moss ledges, take a groove left of the arête (spike runner on the right) to a blank-out at 15 metres. Place some reasonable wires up to the left and gain undercuts using the arête on the right (peg runner). Move up to a recess below the higher arête. Follow a strenuous crack just to the left of the arête but, where it backs left, balance right into a scoop in the arête. Move up the scoop (runner on right) to ledges and nut belays atop the arête.
2 15m. 4b. Climb up behind the belay, following ledges slightly left to a recess. It is possible to abseil (50 metres) from a rock spike here;

alternatively, continue scrambling leftwards across heather ledges to the top of The Metronome.

☆☆**The Lorryman**   60 metres   E6 †   (8.9.96)
The all-out, body-pumping beast-groove between the pair of arêtes. Improvisational.
1 20m. 5a. Follow the initial groove of *Dreams and Reality Collide* to the good spike on the right at 10 metres. Step right into another groove and climb the right-hand side of a big jammed flake to a foothold stance on the right, beneath the groove-funnel.
2 25m. 6b. Climb cracks in the base of the funnel to a bulge where the funnel closes in around. Swim through the narrows – full body pump guaranteed – continuing up the narrow groove above until a final hard pull over a bulge gains the belay ledge of *Dreams and Reality Collide*.
3 15m. 4b. *Dreams and Reality Collide* pitch 2.

☆**Jin-Go-La-Ba**   60 metres   E5 †   (8.9.96)
The hanging blade right of *The Lorryman* – sharp enough to shave the bristles of fear.
1 20m. 5a. As for *The Lorryman*.
2 25m. 6a. Skirt under the foot of the blade and, avoiding a delightful flowerbed, udge up into a small chimney. Step left onto the face at a thin crack, reach left to the arête, and teeter up it to a break and *in-situ* thread. (Rope-slashing prospects will have diminished significantly at this point.) Swing right and then leftwards beneath the capping roof (peg runner) to the final hard pull of *The Lorryman*.
3 15m. 4b. *Dreams and Reality Collide* pitch 2.

Battered Caravanserai   100 metres   Very Severe   (19.4.74)
At the right-hand end of this area is a rib of rock with a weakness in it, and wet slabs below it.
1 25m. 4b. Follow the weakness up and curving left; then move rightwards to gain a grassy chute and belay at its top.
2 15m. 4b. Traverse 6 metres left over slabs and move up to climb a short square chimney. Exit right from its top onto a grassy ledge and climb a short vegetated groove to a flake belay.
3 8m. 4a. Climb the corner above to a ledge.
4 12m. 5a. Continue up the corner, and move out left to a grassy ledge.
5 27m. 4b. Go diagonally right up vegetated rock for 3 metres until the main groove on the right can be gained. Climb the groove for about 6 metres to reach the right wall, which leads to heather. Move left and climb a short crack to a ledge.
6 13m. Climb the corner above to a ledge and peg belays at the right-hand limit of the huge heathery descent ramp.

Great Gully to Central Rib
This is an expansive area of the upper half of the main face between Great Gully on the left and the *Central Rib* on the right. There are two principal

clusters of routes: the Snodgrass Area, where the climbs are accessed from the lake shore; and the White Lady Walls, where the climbs are approached by abseil from the Minffordd ridge above.

Snodgrass Area

Take note of the name: vegetation is plentiful hereabouts and the routes see minimal, if any, traffic. With the exception of *Terraneai Rib*, the climbs are accessed from the underlying huge heathery ramp which rises rightwards above Idris Corner Crag from the lower reaches of Great Gully. The toe of the ramp is reached easily from the left, as for Pencoed Pillar.

The first two routes ascend the large wall above the broad central part of the heather ramp, which is fairly featureless apart from a triangular overhang at 65 metres, and a crackline to its right taken by *Snodgrass Diversification Company Direct*.

Snodgrass Diversification Company 95 metres Hard Severe (25.5.75)
Sods, tufts, and clumps: green fingers obligatory. Start at a rib of rock directly below the triangular overhang.
1 15m. 4a. Climb the rib; then follow grass above, slanting right to reach rock again. Spike belays.
2 20m. 4b. Ascend slightly leftwards until a short leftward traverse leads to a ledge and belays at the start of a conspicuous diagonal groove/chimney.
3 40m. 4a. Go up the groove/chimney diagonally left to a grassy ledge. Nut belays.
4 20m. Climb the wall above onto steep grass; then traverse right to a belay.
Variation
Snodgrass Diversification Company Direct Very Severe (1983)
3a 40m. 4c. A better finish. Climb the crack and groove right of the triangular overhang to grass and belays in a corner above and to the right.

Terraneai Rib 55 metres Hard Severe † (15.5.74)
This is the fairly prominent arête above the *Snodgrass* wall. It could be reached by abseil but it would be best linked with either of the preceding two climbs by means of an intervening steep scramble up precipitous grass. Start below a wide crack formed by a large block on the left-hand side of the rib.
1 30m. 4b. Climb on the left of the rib; then take a crack in the left wall to a small ledge with a little overhang above and pull over to a block belay.
2 12m. Climb the rib to a spike belay.
3 13m. 4a. Move up and left, and climb a crack to the top of the wall. Scramble up onto the ridge.

Central Rib   120 metres   Very Severe   (16.4.74)
The broad rib which falls from the summit of Craig Cau to the right
extremity of the huge heather ramp rising rightwards from the lower
reaches of Great Gully. It could be combined with *Battered Caravanserai*
to provide around 250 metres of serious mountaineering. Care is required
with the rock. Start from a ledge behind and to the right of a short, steep
lower step.
1 20m. 4c. Climb the groove on the right-hand side of the wall until a
move right can be made. Trend rightwards up the wall to gain the arête
and grass at the top. Go up the grass for 6 metres to a stance below the
prominent tower.
2 25m. 4c. Climb a crack-system in the arête of the tower to a narrow
grassy ledge. Traverse left below a small overhang and continue up
leftwards to the top of the tower. Thread belay.
3 40m. 4b. Climb the next step by the right-hand arête.
4 20m. Scramble up to the final wall.
5 15m. 4b. There is a groove to the right of the rib with overhangs at its
base. Surmount the overhang at its right-hand end, step left into the
groove, and climb it to the top, finishing about 10 metres from the summit.

White Lady Walls
Between the upper 50 metres of Great Gully and *Terraneai Rib* is a series of
diagonally-banded white and grey slabby walls. The routes here are
generally quick drying and attract the sun until early afternoon.

Opposite and level with the top of Pencoed Pillar, across Great Gully, is a
two-tier crag comprising a triangular slabby face topped by a shorter,
steeper pocketed wall. The following five routes are to be found here, and
are accessed by means of a 50-metre abseil to the spacious underlying
grass ledge. The upper pitches are interchangeable. In the left-centre of the
lower face is the distinctive thin left-trending groove of *White Lady*.

☆**Markova**   45 metres   E3 †   (7.7.96)
Two nimble pitches on a direct, no-digressions line. Start 5 metres left of
White Lady at a flake crack.
1 26m. 5c. Climb the flake for 3 metres and, where it veers left, go direct
up a hairline crack to a quartz break (good small wires). Continue straight
up the slab on a series of glorious monos and other pockets, trending
slightly left to exit up a thin crack and over a bulge just to the right of a
twin-crack system. Nut belay on the terrace.
2 19m. 6a. Climb straight up the fine pocketed wall 2 metres left of a
slim, left-facing corner to ledges. Step left, and proceed up an intermittent
thin crack to the top (essential *Rock 7/8* placement twisted in a pocket at 4
metres).

Breathtaking Incompetence   45 metres   E5 †   (9.6.96)
Excruciatingly hard in one place. Start left of *White Lady*, beneath a
left-to-right diagonal crack.

1 30m. 6b. Take the crack to the grass ledge at the foot of the *White Lady* groove. Make one move up the groove; then follow another diagonal crack rightwards for 3 metres to a spike. Move back left along an incipient crack and scratch desperately for better holds on a long ramp overhead. Follow the ramp rightwards, using the superb pocket-line and, after 3 metres, go up a crack to easier ground leading leftwards to the terrace.
2 15m. 5b. Four metres right of the slim left-facing corner is an open hour-glass groove. Ascend the groove and the easy rib above to the top.

White Lady   50 metres   Hard Very Severe (1 pt aid) †   (7.4.74)
The prominent right-to-left groove/ramp in the lower face curiously requires a point of aid. Start below the right-hand end of a grass ledge at the base of a groove.
1 30m. 5a. Pull up onto the ledge and step left into the foot of the groove. Follow the groove, rather grassy, and crack above to bulges. Place a peg for aid, and move up and right beneath the bulge until it is possible to climb up onto the terrace.
2 20m. Walk right for 10 metres and exit up an easy groove.
Variation
Bride of Dracula   20 metres   E2 †   (22.9.96)
2a 5b. A natural continuation which climbs the slim left-facing corner in the upper tier: rather poky.

☆☆**Face to Face**   45 metres   E5 †   (9.6.96)
An excellent eliminate taking a challenging line up the centre of the 30-metre face. Start as for *White Lady*.
1 30m. 6a. Climb up to the right-hand end of the grass ledge. Continue direct via a small left-facing flake to the spike runner on *Breathtaking Incompetence* – bold. Proceed up the smooth slab (peg runner), with some difficulty, to emerge on a long ramp. Go up the wall above, skirting immediately below a heather-ledge and exit onto the terrace via a groove.
2 15m. 4c. Climb directly up the face of the pocketed 'tower' behind the belay, and move slightly left to finish up a perfect hand-crack.

★**Dawn's Left-Hand**   50 metres   Hard Very Severe   (7.4.74)
A line based upon the groove in the right-hand side of the lower triangular face. Start below the groove, some 10 metres right of *White Lady*.
1 35m. 5a. Climb cracks to a wide corner with a crack in the back. Move up in the corner, then out left and up the arête, and finally back right into the corner. Continue to a grassy stance beneath an overhang.
2 15m. 4b. Go up rightwards on vegetation to below a small overhang, traverse right to climb a groove, and exit left at the top.

There is a smooth triangular facet of rock above and to the right of the groove of *Dawn's Left-Hand*; the following route can be tracked down here. Approach by abseil.

Craig Cau

White Lady Walls

Come Rain or Shine   25 metres   E5 6b †   (7.7.96)
Obtuse, serious, blind, and strenuous: the penalty of applying traditional
tactics to a blank wall. From the toe of the triangular facet, swing
along a break and ascend the shallow leaning groove into a niche. Place
a good wire 2 metres up in the crack; then traverse left onto the sheer
pocketed wall (good ¾" angle, removed). Make a hard move up to a
slanting break, and swing right, then back left over the overlap (crux) to
finish up flakes.

There is yet another triangular face offering one isolated route to the right;
this one is located approximately 50 metres up to the right of *White Lady* and
constitutes the left-retaining wall of *Terraneai Rib*.

☆☆**Alone in the World**   30 metres   E3 5c †   (6.7.96)
A commendable climb of its grade: varied and airily positioned high up on
the main face. Approach by abseil and belay at the lowest point of the
face beneath a left-slanting break. Climb white quartzitic rock directly to a
heather ledge. Make one move up the left-slanting break, swing right onto
a narrow-grooved rib, and gain a fine crack with difficulty. Climb the
widening crack to a ledge, and finish up a juggy groove in the headwall.

Whale-back Buttress
This is the large slabby boss of rock in the lower right-hand part of the main
face which commences from 50 metres above the north-western shore of
Llyn Cau. It has the capacity for some genuine mid-grade slab climbs,
currently unfulfilled.

★**Marsum**   105 metres   Very Difficult   (27.10.73)
Pleasantly wandering. The main slab is undercut by a leaning wall; start at
its right-hand end below a groove.
1 30m. Gain the groove and climb up onto the slab. Work up the slab
leftwards, and then move right below a steeper section to the left end of
the terrace.
2 25m. From the top of the short corner above the stance, move left, and
follow the broad rib above to a huge block at the top of the main slab
(escape is now possible).
3 50m. Continue up the disjointed ribs above, maximizing time spent on
rock, to the top of the crag. Walk left and descend a broad gully.

Incongruously set in this slabby buttress is a ferocious headwall, the next two
routes on which start from the terrace above pitch 1 of *Marsum*. The terrace
can also be reached by scrambling up the rake from the right.

Made in Wales   18 metres   E6 6b †   (8.6.96)
A secluded horror requiring an extraordinary degree of commitment. Belay
in the corner at the left end of the terrace. Starting 3 metres right of the
corner, reach a pocket at 5 metres. Step left and make a repulsing crank
to flake holds (poor spike at 6 metres, the first protection). Move right
(knife-blade at 8 metres – removed), and commence a protracted series of

snatches to a good flake-line. Take the flake right to a stout rock spike; then pull through the bulge, and scramble to the huge block belay.

Longman 18 metres E2 5b/c   (21.9.96)
Height should help on the ramp in the headwall. Grasp a finger-jug, and follow the ramp before moving 2 metres left along a good break. Overcome the final bulge, just right of *Made in Wales*, and scramble to the huge block belay. Some nice surprises make up for lousy protection.

Whale-back Groove 30 metres E1 5a   (8.6.96)
The groove in the right-hand edge of the headwall, starting from the foot of the rake leading to the underlying terrace. Enter the groove and climb it with minimal gear to ledges. Climb the rib on the right-hand side, and then move back left to a good break. Either finish direct with an awkward mantel over the bulge, or sneak off to the right.

Immediately left of Whale-back Buttress is a thin, wave-like, rising strip of rock that would be more at home in Northumberland; this boasts two micro-specialities.

Ripple on the Mountain 9 metres E4 6b/c †   (21.9.96)
Twin hairline cracks show the line: take nothing larger than an *RP3*, and expect trouble.

Ripple Crack 8 metres E1 5b †   (21.9.96)
Climb the thin crack in the centre of the triangular face towards the top of the strip.

The Col to Central Rib
Effectively, this covers all of the crags in the upper right-hand half of Craig Cau, between the col separating Craig Cau from Cadair Idris and *Central Rib*. The routes are described from **right (north) to left (south)** since, unless abseiling in, this will be the usual direction of approach (access options are noted in each sub-section).

Bleed the Soul Area
This is the rightmost worthwhile section of rock, characterized by the spectacular arête of *Bleed the Soul*, which has a large corner and then a slabby wall to its right. The crag is most quickly approached by using the northern lake-shore footpath to reach the col between Craig Cau and Cadair Idris. The top of the arête is unmistakable from the ridge footpath, several hundred metres south of the col. Descend easy grass slopes to the right (north) of the crag, and pick up a sheep-track that switches back left (south) beneath the routes (and continues on to the *Bird of Time* wall).

☆**Dusk** 20 metres E1 5a †   (27.7.96)
A gentle slab climb, though irregularly protected. Start 2 metres right of the large corner. Start up a narrow, left-facing corner and gain a ledge above. Promptly step left onto the slab, and take the intermittent flake-line,

trending rightwards to a short groove. Move left around a small projecting overhang, and exit direct.

☆**Bleed the Soul**   27 metres   E5 6a †   (1.6.96)
The impressive arête – that can turn red in the summer evening sun. Expect to be challenged. Commence up an overhung groove; then follow a gangway rightwards to a crack-system 5 metres right of the arête. Move up to fix protection before entertaining a loop leftwards onto the slab, which leads to a rising undercut. Step left to a second undercut, and follow the very steep and unremitting right-hand side of the arête to the top. A photographer should be at hand.

Bird of Time Area

[Photodiagram page 408a.] Seventy-five metres left (south) of *Bleed the Soul*, and again readily visible from the ridge footpath, is a second major north-facing arête, with a striking wide crack in the right wall (*Jackknife*). The original classic of these cliffs, *Bird of Time*, takes a circuitous line a little to the left of the arête. There are many other fine routes here, on sound and clean rock, some of which are as commendable as any in the guidebook.

There are three means of access:
• Approach from the col and ridge as for Bleed the Soul Area, but continue along the steep and exposed sheep-track.
• For a more complete mountain experience, branch off left from 150 metres or so up the normal route to the col, picking up a sketchy sheep-track on a heather ramp that leads above craggy ground to a 5-metre pinnacle. From here, scramble diagonally leftwards to the foot of the cliffs.
• If you have carted a spare rope up the mountain, why not abseil in from a chosen point? (A good plan would be to abseil from ledges above the *Bird of Time* arête, which are reached by a short down-scramble, and are removed from any inquisitive tourist traffic.)

Life-sucks   15 metres   E5 6a †   (7.9.96)
Possibly suicidal, given the bleak protection. This is the leaning wall at the head of the gully right of the arête. Scramble up 50-degree heather and slippery grass to its foot (or abseil in!). Step up into the centre of the wall, and grope up and leftwards over a rejecting leaning step to a small, sloping shelf. Move up a vague groove to a jug and – yes – more jugs on the ramp above, and climb out easily.

☆☆**Jackknife**   40 metres   E2 5b †   (7.9.96)
[Photo page 408b.] An unavoidable line: the widening crack in the overhanging right wall of the arête. It provides surprisingly amenable climbing, not even requiring the ability to jam. Start up the white angular groove right of the arête to reach a break; or, if the groove is wet, gain the break from a short juggy wall and a step off the obvious little pinnacle. Ascend steeply to the foot of the crack and follow it briskly to a big chockstone. Continue into a recessed corner above (junction with *Bird of*

Time, stance possible), surmount the roof, and finish up the left-hand arête of the chimney.

☆☆**La Merci Dieu**   40 metres   E6 6a/b †   (1.6.96)
A magnificent climb up the edge of the arête, perilously run-out in its upper half. Start up the white angular groove right of the arête to reach a break; or, if the groove is wet, gain the break from a short juggy wall and a step off the obvious little pinnacle. Climb diagonally left onto the right-hand side of the arête. Pull up into a tiny groove and very delicately relocate onto the left-hand side of the arête, so gaining an incipient break (crucial wires slightly left for left-hand rope). Sustained technical climbing above leads to a jug on the arête, from which an easier, yet unprotected ascent gains a good break beneath a bulge (junction with *Dawn Patrol*). Move left and up a flake crack, and then swing left to finish up the short headwall on nice holds.

☆☆**Dawn Patrol**   40 metres   E4 6a †   (1.6.96)
One of the best extremes on the mountain, offering intricate and absorbing climbing on a direct line up the face left of the arête. Start at the foot of a chimney immediately left of the arête. Climb the chimney for 6 metres to a grass ledge. Transfer onto the right wall and reach a flake under the roof. Pass the roof on the right and step back left into a thin crack running up the face. Follow the crack to a break; step right and move up left into a slim groove, which leads with interest to a commodious ledge on *Bird of Time*. Ascend the bold shallow groove (as for *Bird of Time*) to a good break beneath a bulge. Move left and up a flake crack, and then swing left to finish up the short headwall on nice holds.

★**Bird of Time**   55 metres   E3   (26.5.74)
A very interesting climb of character, with one especially bold section. The key to the climb is the narrow left-facing corner 7 metres left of the arête. Start at the foot of a chimney immediately left of the arête.
1 15m. Climb the chimney to take a belay towards the right-hand end of a long grassy ledge.
2 25m. 5b. Left of the belay, climb a crack to a small ledge. Traverse rightwards to the base of the left-facing corner. Climb the corner to a commodious ledge, and walk to the right-hand end. This is it: try to implant some tiny wires in a shallow groove, and either go up the groove onto the arête, or climb the arête direct; with a steady touch either option should lead to a belay in the recessed corner on the right.
3 15m. 4b. Surmount the roof above the stance, move right into a chimney, and tunnel through its interior to the top.

☆**Lightfoot**   40 metres   E3 †   (1.6.96)
A technical delight that responds to neat footwork.
1 15m. *Bird of Time* pitch 1.
2 25m. 5c. From the right-hand end of the ledge, pull steeply onto a juggy ledge. Climb up a thin crack, crossing the traverse of *Bird of Time*;

then continue direct up the sustained white scoop to the capping roof.
Swing right around the roof, and follow a strenuous crack to the top.

★The Melting Clock   40 metres   E3   (22.6.96)
A steep and protectable route up the prominent kinked crack in the wall
left of *Bird of Time*.
1 15m. *Bird of Time* pitch 1.
2 25m. 6a. Starting as for *Bird of Time*, climb a crack to a small ledge.
Follow the left-slanting crack above until it insists on kinking back right.
Layback up the widening crack to the capping roof. Move left, until an
awkward move right can be made to reach the ledge above the roof.
Follow the strenuous crack of *Lightfoot* to the top.

Moving Finger   45 metres   E1   (25.5.74)
An evasive excursion that needs pointing in the right direction. The finish of
pitch 2 involves serious commitment.
1 20m. *Bird of Time* pitch 1; but belay at the left-hand end of the ledge
below a corner.
2 25m. 5a. Climb the corner to an overhang. Move left onto the arête and
climb up to a tapering ramp on the left. Follow the ramp until it is possible to
rock-up onto the slab above. Belay; then scramble out rightwards.

☆☆Stressed-Out   40 metres   E1 5b †   (4.8.96)
A classic line, prominent from afar, that should appeal to crack-addicts
who have procured some big nuts (*Hex 10* or equivalent required). Left of
The Suffering arête is a deep crack with a left turn at its middle. Start below
the arête as for *The Sufri*. Ascend the corner to the right-hand end of the
ledge, as for *The Sufri* (belay possible, but only one wire placement). Move
2 metres left and climb up to a second, narrower ledge. Swing along
flakes into the crack and take this to the roof where the crack veers left.
Traverse leftwards and pull around onto a ledge below the final, wider
crack. Battle up the crack to the top. Belay; then scramble out rightwards.

☆A Cure for Stress   40 metres   E5 †   (4.8.96)
An issue of focusing the mind: at least the underlying ledges are soft.
1 20m. 4b. As for pitch 1 of *The Sufri* (or abseil, since the protection pegs
need to be placed).
2 20m. 6a/b. Four metres right of *The Sufri* is a modest double-groove
system in the compact wall. Very technical moves up this (two knife-blades,
removed) lead to positive fingerholds in a scoop on the right. Now, with no
further protection, step left onto a rib and coolly attain the traverse-crack of
Stressed-Out and then the ledge above. Should this position be reached,
there is a bonus of an exhilarating finish out to the right across the
headwall to a spike, and an exit just left of *Moving Finger*.

The Sufri   65 metres   Hard Very Severe   (26.5.74)
A substantial diagonal outing, unfortunately with some precarious rock in
its top pitch. Start directly below a discontinuous arête which is the next
arête (20 metres) left of the *Bird of Time* arête.

Craig Cau

Crack of Cau Area

1	Götterdämmerung	E2
2	Crack of Cau	HVS
3	Touchstone	VS

Bird of Time Area

4	Dancing Kukaracha	E4
5	Donsong	E1
6	Highlander's Fling	E6
7	Solo Engagement	E3
8	Tumbling Five Ten	E4
9	A Cure for Stress	E5
10	Stressed-Out	E1
11	The Suffering	E4
12	The Melting Clock	E3
13	Lightfoot	E3
14	Bird of Time	E3
15	Dawn Patrol	E4
16	La Merci Dieu	E6

Jackknife (E2 ~ first ascent) Craig Cau
Climber: Martin Crocker   Photo: John Sumner

Sundew City
(E3) Waun Bistyll
Climber: Steve Burns
Photo: John Sumner

One Swallow
(E2 – first ascent) Gau Craig
Climber: John Sumner
Photo: Sumner.col.

Hyrib (HS) Cyfrwy
Climber: John Ball   Photo: Don Sargeant

1 20m. 4b. Ascend a vegetated corner right of the lower arête to a leftward-rising ledge and a block belay at its left-hand end.

2 15m. 4c. In the face above is a diagonal line of weakness; follow it leftwards, without good protection, to a good ledge, and place carefully-secured belays.

3 30m. 5a. Pull over the bulge to a big spike. Follow a groove leftwards, step left around a rib, and gain the right end of a narrow ledge running beneath roofs. Traverse left for 6 metres, and climb steeply to the top.

The Suffering   40 metres   E4 6a †   (27.7.96)

A troublesome eliminate on the discontinuous arête. Start below the lower arête, just to the left of *The Sufri*. Climb the blunt arête, using a thin crack on the right, and the edge above delicately and boldly to a heather ledge at 13 metres (belay possible, but only one wire placement). Take the scoop on the right to a horizontal break. A thin crack above leads to a line of holds left of the arête, which is followed before an intrepid swing right gains the arête. Move up the arête and exit via the tapering ramp on the left, as for *Moving Finger*.

The next two routes climb an inset wall right of a shallow grassy gully, the base of the gully being about 30 metres left of the *Bird of Time* arête.

Tumbling Five Ten   45 metres   E4 †   (7.9.96)

Demanding; both pitches rate E4. Start from a ledge under the wall, accessed by climbing a ramp in the right wall of the gully (Severe standard).

1 20m. 6b. From a block on the right, pull up direct to a very thin crack, and fight up it to a projecting hold in a niche. Move up right onto a narrow ledge; then follow the easier crack leftwards (crossing *Solo Engagement*) to belay at the left-hand end of the long ledge.

2 25m. 5c. Pull straight over the bulge to a big spike. Follow a groove leftwards, step left around a rib and gain the right-hand end of a narrow ledge running beneath roofs. Go up to the right-hand side of a massive hanging block in the roofs and hand-traverse its top leftwards into an overhanging groove (*in-situ* thread). Creaking holds initially, and then more conventional rock, lead up the groove (*in-situ* thread) to the top.

☆☆**Solo Engagement**   45 metres   E3 †   (27.7.96)

Two excellent pitches and an exposed finish combine to make this a climb of considerable merit. Start from a ledge under the wall, as for *Tumbling Five Ten*.

1 20m. 6a. Reach the base of the left-hand crack in the wall from the right and climb it to a projecting spike. Proceed straight up via a left-facing flake-line to gain a big jug. Cross the crack on the right diagonally rightwards to join the top of a leftward-rising ramp (*The Sufri*), and pull up onto a good ledge.

2 25m. 5c. Climb a crack 3 metres on the right to ledges beneath a short groove and pull over a bulge onto a fine rectangular slab. Ascend the left edge of the slab to the overhanging roof and traverse the lip leftwards to finish up a shallow groove in the arête – the world beneath your feet.

Twenty metres left of the shallow grassy gully is a deeper gully which runs up and leftwards towards an enormous projecting roof – a useful landmark. Between the two gullies are a pyramidal pillar and the following three routes. Descend by means of the gully on the left, or by abseiling from a rock spike.

☆☆**Highlander's Fling**   25 metres   E6 6c †   (27.7.96)
The brilliant seam right of centre. The hardest pitch in Meirionnydd at this altitude. Start at the toe of a left-trending ramp. Ascend the ramp easily for 4 metres, and swing up right onto a tall flake. Clip a peg runner on the left, extend to a good hold below the seam (peg runner), and follow the seam to small ledges. Fix some good nuts in the crack adjacent to the arête on the left, and make some hard, committing moves up and to the right into a shallow niche. Step back left to exit up a short flake.

Donsong   25 metres   E1 5b †   (4.8.96)
Start as for *Highlander's Fling*. Follow the ramp to its close. Continue up the crack-extension and, just before it ends, make a tricky move up and right to the foot of a corner. Climb the corner to spike belays.

Dancing Kukaracha   20 metres   E4 6b †   (7.9.96)
Not to be underestimated: the crux could well leave you in knots. Start at the base of the deep gully. Climb a flake crack to a good horizontal crack under an obvious square-cut roof. Stretch around for one good hold and heave over to a short ramp leading to easier ground.

Crack of Cau Area

[Photodiagram page 408a.] In the face 150 metres left of the *Bird of Time* arête is the unmissable vertical crackline of *Crack of Cau*. This rises from near the foot of the cliff up the enormous projecting roof at the top of the gully that slants left from *Dancing Kukaracha*. The three routes on this wall are accessed as for the Bird of Time Area: scramble down from the foot of the slanting gully, and beneath a 12-metre pinnacle, to heather ledges running beneath the face. A direct approach is also possible on steep mixed ground.

★**Touchstone**   85 metres   Very Severe   (21.10.73)
Start at a leftward-slanting chimney which cuts into the steep wall 12 metres right of the start of *Crack of Cau*, where a ledge comes in from the right.
1 13m. 4c. Go up the cracked slab, which forms the left wall of the chimney, to a good spike; continue more easily to reach a grass ledge with a large belay flake.
2 20m. 4c. Three metres right of the belay, climb to a thread under a big detached spike. From the spike, traverse right around a sharp edge to gain a foothold. Move right, and climb the corner via a crack on good jams to a ledge and a large block belay.
3 20m. 4b. Climb a scoop on the left that slants slightly left to where it steepens. Make a long step across to the right and then ascend steeply on big holds, trending right to the right arête of the buttress.

4 32m. The final tower is above. Climb a broken corner on the right and move back left onto the arête. Gain a wide crack above with a slab on its left to reach a cave. Chimney out to gain a foothold on the right (thread runner); then go more easily up the chimney to a big flake belay. Take the grassy gully with an awkward finish.

★**Crack of Cau**   75 metres   Hard Very Severe   (27.10.73)
The great chimney-crack provides a compelling line. Start at a cracked wall down to the right of the base of the crack, which commences from ledges 12 metres up.
1 12m. Climb the left edge of the wall; then follow grass to ledges below the chimney.
2 13m. The chimney leads to a grassy stance on the right.
3 25m. 5a. Continue up the chimney, take the steep groove above, and follow a slightly left-slanting crack to a good resting-place. The crack, difficult at first, leads to good holds and then a wide crack in an overhang; climb this to a small stance with good belays.
4 25m. 5a. Climb the groove above with three steep sections, finishing just right of the projecting roof.

Götterdämmerung   110 metres   E2   (7.6.75/1976)
The left wall of *Crack of Cau*.
1 12m. *Crack of Cau* pitch 1.
2 40m. Traverse out left for 5 metres and go up the obvious line to a small undercut overhang. Move up left of it for 3 metres; then traverse right to reach a line trending up left, which is followed by a block on a vague arête. Traverse left to a wide crack at the back of a large detached flake, and climb to the top of the flake.
3 20m. 5c. Move right from the flake and then up a shallow groove to reach a horizontal crack. Traverse right for 2 metres and climb up to another shallow groove. From a metre up it, move down right onto a traverse-line level with the base of the groove, go right around a rib, and traverse across a smooth groove to a very small ledge just left of *Crack of Cau*. Nut belays high up to the left.
4 20m. Climb slightly leftwards to a groove with a large projecting block. Move past this and trend left to reach easy ground. Go up grassy ledges to a sharp arête and spike belays.
5 18m. An easy arête leads to the top.

Black Shiver Area
This is the steep area of cliff between *Crack of Cau* and *Central Rib*, below which is a heathery bowl. The climbs are best gained by scrambling up steep heather-covered ground from the top of the boulder-field left of Whale-back Buttress (page 404). A descent from the Bird of Time Area is more tortuous. Though all the routes date from the mid 70s, only the eponymous climb is known to have been repeated.

The Baron   90 metres   Hard Very Severe (1 pt aid) †   (14.4.74)
Start 25 metres left of *Crack of Cau* at a large water-worn groove below a big roof.
1 15m. Take a diagonal line on water-worn rock on the left of the bulge in the groove to a block on the right.
2 12m. Follow the groove to a slab below the large roof. Traverse left below the roof (peg belay, missing).
3 12m. Move left onto the edge of a slab. Climb the slab with a peg for aid to reach a grassy terrace.
4 12m. Scramble down to the left along the terrace to its end.
5 39m. Ascend the groove on the left of the overhang and continue up the gully until scrambling remains.

★Black Shiver   100 metres   E2   (10.4.74)
Start at the base of a line of leftward-trending slabs and grooves 30 metres diagonally down left of the start of *Crack of Cau*.
1 20m. 4c. Ascend a short corner to a slab; then go left and climb up to a block wedged behind a fang of rock. Traverse left around this and go up the groove and slab to a small stance.
2 15m. 5a. Move into a groove up to the left. Climb this until a slab can be crossed leftwards to a rib. Go around the rib and traverse the next slab. Move down to a stance in the groove.
3 20m. 5c. Climb direct over a bulge. Traverse left for 3 metres and use an undercut flake on the right to gain a rib. Step right across a slab into an overhung corner, and go up this to vegetation and spike belays on the terrace.
4 20m. 5b. Go left along the terrace and climb a slabby groove to just below the overhang. Move up rightwards into a niche beneath the right-hand end of the overhang and then out right and up into the groove above with a good hold on the lip. Continue up the groove to an awkward stance below the next overhang.
5 25m. 5a. Climb right around the overhang to continue up the groove. Move left at the next overhang and go back right above to steep grass. Ascend the grass to a stance and nut belays. Move right easily to a grassy gully; then 50 metres of easy climbing and scrambling lead to the top.

Tatham Wife   110 metres   E1 †   (24.5.75)
Start below the right-hand of two grooves, reached by scrambling up and left across steep vegetation from the foot of *Black Shiver*.
1 18m. Climb the groove and move up to a small stance where a traverse-line goes out right.
2 25m. 5c. Move right to a small flat ledge, and make a difficult move right to reach holds on the rib. Climb up and into the groove above (junction with *Black Shiver*). Then move right and climb a rib before moving right again to vegetation and belays.
3 17m. Go back left and climb to the top of a corner. Move left across the left wall; then climb up and left again to a rib. Work up to grass and spike belays on the mid-height ledge (junction with *Mere Gill*).
4 25m. Grass scrambling up to the right leads to a ledge and belays.

5 25m. From just below and left of the belay, take the right-slanting groove to a stance and then scramble to the top.

Mere Gill 130 metres E1 †   (18.5.75)
Approach as for *Tatham Wife* and start below the left-hand groove.
1 35m. Climb the left-hand groove and go up the slab above, trending right to an overhung corner. Climb the corner and move right to the stance at the end of pitch 2 of *Black Shiver*.
2 30m. Climb the cracks straight above the stance; then move left for 5 metres to a leaning corner and a thin flake on the right wall. Trend rightwards onto a rib and right again into a corner, which leads to the grassy mid-height ledge and spike belays. Fifteen metres of scrambling on grass trending right leads to a peg belay just right of a left-slanting slab.
3 20m. Climb the slab to its top; then go left to a very small incut ledge. Cross a bulge leftwards and climb an easy groove to a spike belay.
4 45m. Ascend grass on the right; then move back left and climb the gully to easy ground.

Tremor 135 metres Hard Very Severe †   (8.5.74)
Connects the gully-line of *The Gulch* with *Black Shiver*. At the left-hand end of the wall is a short groove leading up into vegetated rock.
1 25m. Climb the groove to grassy rocks and an earthy chimney, which leads to a stance and peg belay.
2 20m. Trend up left, then back right just above the stance to climb a groove. Move left to a flake crack, go back right again, and climb a slab to its top left edge, where there is a small stance.
3 25m. Traverse right below an overhang to gain the foot of an overhanging chimney. Continue traversing for 5 metres; then move up to a grassy niche (peg runner). Climb diagonally right until easier ground close to the top of *Black Shiver* pitch 3 can be gained. Climb up to the ledge and spike belays of *Black Shiver*.
4 20m. Climb the groove on the left.
5 30m. Move right and climb a slabby buttress, trending left to reach a grassy bay. Belay at its top left, below a deep crack.
6 15m. Climb the crack and a bulge to reach easy ground. Scramble to finish.

The Gulch 150 metres Hard Very Severe †   (30.5.75)
Dank, often wet, yet atmospheric climbing up the major gully/chimney cutting into the left-hand side of the wall, right of *Central Rib*.
1 25m. *Tremor* pitch 1.
2 20m. *Tremor* pitch 2.
3 20m. Move down left; then traverse left to just above the base of the corner. Climb a flake on the left wall to the bulging corner, and surmount the bulge to a small ledge (peg belays on the left).
4 40m. Climb the corner, taking an overhanging section, to a final chimney which leads to a large ledge.
5 45m. Climb the left corner to gain easy ground. Belays are eventually reached on the right.

Cyfrwy   Saddle   OS Ref 703 135

[Diagram page 424-5.] Cyfrwy is a huge, north-facing crag up to 180 metres high and over a kilometre in length, with its base standing at more than 600 metres above sea-level. Its reputation for being loose and dangerous persists, although the routes, with the exception of some of the sub-extremes on Slanting Gully Buttress, especially *Lowrib* and *Squall*, generally follow lines that are solid by any standards. Protection is not abundant owing to the compact nature of the rock. Most of the climbs are quick-drying as the rock is inherently cleaner than on many other high mountain crags, and it is a great place for summer evenings.

The outstanding feature on the approach is the left-bounding arête, *Cyfrwy Arête*. Its jagged profile, with the flat-topped truncated pillar (The Table – y Bwrdd) at its foot, stands out clearly before any other feature is seen. Well below The Table, on the lowest section of the crag, is a fairly clean-looking buttress (Table Buttress) and a gully descends to its right from the gap behind The Table. Right of the gully, two huge ribs run nearly the full height of the crag, the right-hand one being the largest. Right again is the obvious Slanting Gully. A large, impressive rib, *Hyrib*, starts from the upper half of the crag.

Well over to the right is an area of fine-looking, clean slabs known as Slabby Buttress. The best routes on the crag make their way up these. The large, obvious *One Pitch Gully* comes next, and right of this the crag gradually tapers off, although about a third of a mile of rock remains and is known as the Western Wing.

Approach
The trditional approach for the left-hand half of the cliff was via the Fox's Path from the Gwernan Lake Hotel. However, as there is no parking anywhere near the start of this, the alternative used for the Western Wing is now recommended as standard: follow the popular walkers' track up Cadair from the National Trust car-park (OS Ref 698 152) for a kilometre to a multi-junction, and then fork east-south-east to Llyn y Gadair below the crag.

Descent
To descend from the top of main crag (left of *One Pitch Gully*), gain the main ridge at the top of the crag and traverse to the top of *Cyfrwy Arête*. Descend its easy top section for about 20 metres until a traverse can be made to enter the big scree gully on the right of the arête (facing in). Descend the gully to the crag base.

For the Western Wing, descend a wide scree gully roughly half-way along this section. *Claw Mark* is just to its right (facing in).

★Cyfrwy Arête   142 metres   Difficult   (18.5.1888)
The left-bounding ridge of the buttress has a very distinctive stepped
outline; the largest and lowest step, The Table, is in the form of a huge
flat-topped pillar. A fine and very popular mountaineering route, although
the rock in places needs care. Start at a ledge about 35 metres below The
Table, reached by traversing in from the left above Table Buttress.
1 18m. From the lowest rocks 6 metres left of the drop into the gully,
climb an arête, then a corner to the arête above.
2 18m. Continue along the arête to the top of The Table.
3 4m. Descend into the gap off the edge of The Table.
4 9m. Go left to a crack and climb it to a small pinnacle on the left arête.
5 15m. Climb the arête above to a large ledge.
6 18m. Go up two walls with a ledge midway.
7 60m. Scrambling up short walls and spikes leads to the top.

Table Buttress
A clean, sheer buttress about 50 metres high, which forms the lowest section
of rock below The Table on *Cyfrwy Arête*. A gully descends from the gap
behind The Table immediately to its right. An obvious reference feature is the
'leaning pinnacle' of *Pisa* in the short grassy gully slanting up rightwards
from the foot of the buttress.

Steric Slab   40 metres   Hard Severe 4b   (30.6.42)
On the left-hand side of Table Buttress there is an obvious clean edge of
rock, the right-hand side of which is formed by a smooth steep slab, and the
left by a chimney. The route takes the edge and then the upper section
of the chimney. Start with a scramble up to the base of the arête. Go up
diagonally right on good holds to a large pointed flake on the right of the
arête. A delicate rising traverse left leads to the edge of the arête. Climb
up on good holds to a small ledge, step into a chimney, and climb it to a
ledge; then a short wall above leads to a wide terrace.

Steric Arête   30 metres   Hard Very Severe 5a †   (17.5.98)
Climb the right-hand side of the arête in its entirety, starting as for *Steric
Slab*. A photogenic pitch with a just-out-of-reach crux.

Nudging Groove   51 metres   Hard Very Severe   (27.5.74)
In the largest and most prominent arête of the buttress there is an obvious
groove-line. The route takes this groove. Protection is rather poor on the
first 12 metres, which is also the crux. Start by a slab right of an overhang,
below and 10 metres to the left of the 'leaning pinnacle'.
1 30m. 5a. Climb the slab, continue diagonally up left above the
overhang to an arête, and climb this to a peg in a little corner. Move left
and traverse delicately across a groove to a rib; then go straight up to a
V-groove topped by an overhang. Climb the groove, move out right, and
follow the arête. Then trend slightly right to a stance with good belays.
2 21m. 4c. Move up a metre, step left, and climb an obvious groove
direct to the top.

Table Eliminate   60 metres   E4 †   (21.6.98)
Rather contrived overall, although both pitches have merit. Start below a
narrow orange corner containing the 'leaning pinnacle', two metres right
of *Nudging Groove*.
1 35m. 6a. Balance up finger-nail edges, using the arête (crucial *Friend 0*),
to the narrow corner. Enter the corner with even more difficulty and reach the
base of the pillar; then step right to spike runners on a traverse-line (on
Pisa). Climb straight up the smooth face above, just to the right of the corner,
with bold moves to reach a good ledge (belay possible). Climb a slim
groove and hand-crack 2 metres right of a corner-line, past a good flake on
the right, to the large spike belay on *Table Direct*.
2 25m. 6a. Climb a line of weakness in the steep slab left of the corner
of *Table Direct* to the spike runner after 10 metres. Here step right onto the
smoother slab and, ignoring the loose crack on the left, move thinly up
over small overlaps to bigger holds and the top. Walk off left.

Minnie the Minx   60 metres   Hard Very Severe †   (6.96)
Start below a small overhang, 5 metres left of the 'leaning pinnacle'.
1 27m. 5a. Either climb the crack to the left of the overhang direct or join
it above the overhang by climbing in from the right. Continue up to the
wider crack on the skyline and climb it direct to a belay on the ledge
above.
2 33m. 5a. Climb the broken crack of *Table Direct* for about 2 metres;
then follow a line of holds diagonally left to join the central crack of the
main slab, which takes a direct line through the broken overhang to belays
near large embedded flakes.
Abseil off or continue to the arête via *Table Direct*.

Denis the Menace   55 metres   Hard Very Severe †   (6.96)
Start 3 metres left of the 'leaning pinnacle'.
1 25m. 5a. Follow the right-slanting crack, with unexpected and
enjoyable holds appearing where necessary; then easier ground leads to
nut belays below the left edge of the clean slab.
2 30m. 5a. Start up the centre of the slab and trend left to the thin crack
just right of the arête. A fine delicate pitch.
Either finish up *Table Direct* or abseil off.

Pisa   45 metres   Hard Severe   (6.56)
A line of pillars up the wall to the right of *Nudging Groove*. Start at the
'leaning pinnacle' (as for *Table Direct*).
1 15m. 4a. Go horizontally left across the wall for 4 metres and climb a
vertical pillar. Make a move left across a slab into the bottom of a broken
groove (difficult) and climb the groove easily to a ledge on the right. Nut
belays.
2 12m. 4a. On the left of the ledge rises another pillar. Climb to the right
of this until the pillar top can be gained. Make an awkward move into a
corner on the right and climb it to a ledge on the right.
3 18m. 4b. Climb the steep slab above the ledge and move slightly left
to a weakness. Belay on the large terrace beneath The Table.

Table Direct   51 metres   Very Difficult   (19.6.51)
Start at the 'leaning pinnacle' (as for *Pisa*).
1 9m. Climb between the pinnacle and the wall, and belay on a wedged stone at the top.
2 18m. A rising traverse leads easily up right for 11 metres; then go steeply leftwards on good holds to a large ledge.
3 15m. Climb the corner-crack on the right to a ledge.
4 9m. Go to the right end of the stance, which overlooks the gully, and climb leftwards up the wall to the terrace under *Cyfrwy Arête*.

Slanting Gully Buttress
The big rib lines between Table Buttress and Slabby Buttress give some of the longest routes on Cyfrwy. Some are rarely climbed. The routes starting part way up Slanting Gully itself are reached by straightforward scrambling from the left across large terraces.

Quartz Rib   88 metres   Very Severe   (6.56)
The rib just right of the gully descending from behind The Table has a noticeable white quartz-line running down its edge. The lower section is vegetated. Start as for *Rib and Slab*, by an obvious narrow rib just right of the start of the gully.
1 43m. Climb the narrowing rib, which is in two sections. Then go up the vegetation above to a good spike belay just right of a steep arête.
2 18m. Traverse left under the arête; then go diagonally left across slabs to another arête. Climb this until an easy traverse back right can be made to a stance and thread belay.
3 27m. 4c. Go straight up for a short distance, step left, and climb a crack to a scoop on the left under the bulging quartz arête. Pull over onto the arête (crux, hold high on the left). Continue straight up the arête on good holds, and move out right just below the top to a niche stance.

Rib and Slab   141 metres   Very Severe   (2.7.60)
The big rib on the left of the crag with a prominent butterfly overhang at 35 metres gives a good mountaineering route. Protection is rather poor on the lower pitches. There is a bay at the entrance to the gully which descends from behind The Table and a narrow rib runs up the right wall, finishing just to the left of the butterfly overhang. Start below the rib.
1 40m. Climb the narrowing rib, which is in two sections, to grass. Good nut belay on the right.
2 15m. 4b. Climb the steepening slab just left of the butterfly overhang for 11 metres and trend slightly right to the arête. Move round to the right and climb a groove to a small ledge and good nut belays.
3 37m. Move right and go up a slab to steep vegetation, which is taken to the base of the upper slab. Large boulder belay.
4 43m. 4c. A good pitch. Climb the slab by a crack (4 metres from the rib edge) over several small bulges, and move left near the top to the arête. Take a stance on the arête with a good spike belay 6 metres from the top.
5 6m. Dubious rock leads to the top.

Variation
4a. Instead of climbing the slab on the right of the edge, traverse left onto the arête (past a grassy gully with a large chockstone). Climb the left edge for 6 metres; then step right onto the arête and climb directly to *Cyfrwy Arête*.

Sunset Boulevarde   75 metres   Hard Very Severe †   (6.96)
Traverse steep grass, climb broken rocks, or take the first pitch of *Squall* to the obvious clean slab.
1 30m. 5a. Traverse 7 metres of overlapping exfoliating slabs diagonally left to a straight crack just right of the arête. Follow this to the grass and belay as for *Rib and Slab*.
2 45m. 5a. Climb a thin crack just right of the wide crack of *Rib and Slab* with a precarious move through the overhang at 10 metres; follow a thin crack and trend steeply right and then back left to belay on *Cyfrwy Arête*.

Squall   146 metres   Hard Severe   (27.8.74)
A similar route to *Rib and Slab*, but not as hard. Most of the climbing, except on pitch 4, is Very Difficult, but the rock on the lower section is in a dangerous condition. Start at a broken arête below and 10 metres to the right of the main rib of *Rib and Slab*. There is a shallow gully to the right.
1 46m. Go easily up the arête to where it steepens; then climb the groove on the left to grassy ledges back on the arête. Spike belay up on the left.
2 15m. Continue up the arête by its weakness on the left to grassy ledges. Good nut belay high above.
3 27m. Go up right to where the arête steepens again, climb on the right, and then move out left. Continue easily up the arête to vegetation with a large overlapping slab above. Large boulder belay on the left.
4 43m. 4b. A good pitch. Move 1 metre up and right on vegetation; then make a slightly rising traverse right for 6 metres above a small overhang until directly below a slot in a big overlap 15 metres above. Climb directly up to the overlap, passing a flake. Move over the overhang using a good spike, and continue straight up a shallow groove to a small ledge with a large spike belay above.
5 15m. Climb on up, and move leftwards to finish on the upper section of *Cyfrwy Arête*.

Lowrib   142 metres   Hard Severe   (30.8.74)
The big rib just left of *Slanting Gully* that starts from the large terraces half-way up the gully. The climbing is about Very Difficult but some bad rock at the top of pitch 5 has rendered the route rather serious; hence the grade. From the terrace, broken ribs and vegetation lead up to the main rib. Start at a cairn under the most continuous and left-hand of the ribs.
1 37m. Climb the rib direct to its top; good spike belay.
2 12m. Traverse diagonally up right across vegetation to a huge spike. Move right off the top of this to ledges with spike and nut belays.
3 15m. Go up vegetation to a pinnacle. Climb this on the right, and step left off its top to a stance among large detached blocks.

4 18m. Go up the blocks; then move left to a groove forming the right-hand side of a huge spike. Climb the groove to the top of the spike and continue up the short wall above to a small ledge with a good spike belay.

5 23m. Continue up the slab above, taking the easiest line, to a large ledge. The final section of this pitch has some distinctly worrying rock.

6 37m. Above is a smooth steep slab with a crack in it. Avoid this by moving down and traversing into the top section of Slanting Gully, which can then be followed to the final section of *Cyfrwy Arête*.

Slanting Gully Grooves 92 metres E1 (30.8.70)

A line up the steep green slab on the left of *Hyrib*. Start about 30 metres above the start of *Hyrib* in the upper section of Slanting Gully. Gain a subsidiary groove left of the main slab.

1 21m. Climb the groove, grassy at first, and then a good crack to an obvious move out right to a stance and peg belay below the slab.

2 34m. 5b. Move up and out onto the left edge to a cutaway, using the slab and holds round the edge (old peg); then gain a small ledge. Widely-spaced holds on the inset slab above lead to a move left into a grassy corner. Move up to an old peg belay at a small pedestal.

3 37m. 4a. Climb the groove above pleasantly to a steep section, and finish up an awkward corner to a stance on the ridge.

★Hyrib 114 metres Hard Severe (6.60)

[Photo page 408d.] The climb follows the rib on the right of Slanting Gully, starting about half-way up the gully at a water-worn groove just right of the rib.

1 27m. 4b. Climb the groove to nut belays in the gully bed above.

2 18m. 4a. Go diagonally left and climb the edge of the rib to a stance.

3 18m. 4a. Climb the rib on large but dubious holds to a ledge.

4 21m. 4a. Continue up the rib, taking a crack on the right to a steeper section.

5 30m. 4a. Follow the slab on the left; then move round to the left along a grassy rake to a corner (spike runner). Climb the corner, with an awkward move near the top, to the main ridge.

In the buttress below *Hyrib* is a tall and smooth-looking east-facing wall, taken by the next two routes. Easy descent to the left.

Call Yourself a Doctor 40 metres E6 6b † (31.7.99)

The sheer white-streaked face of *Fox Whistle* climbed direct. A very bold lead, entrusted to gear that you daren't even blow on. So keep your doctor on call in case things don't go to plan. Start at the base of the face, left of the pinnacle of *Fox Whistle*. Climb easily up the face for 6 metres and arrange as much gear as possible. Using a good side-pull up to the right, balance up to a blind horizontal break (hand-placed small knife-blade, removed, and poor *RP* here). Move left and make a very thin sequence past a small undercut spike to better holds. Follow the holds leftwards and up to ledges (and a junction with *Fox Whistle*). Take cracks and flares up the clean centre of the face to the top as for *Fox Whistle*.

Fox Whistle   40 metres   E3 5b †   (17.5.98)
A very fine but sparsely-protected face route. Start below the frontal arête of
the block beneath the wall. Climb the arête to ledges beneath the wall (belay
possible). Boldly pull up into a thin groove in the right-hand side of the wall
to gain spikes above (solid nut runner). Trend left using a white foot-ledge,
and pull up to a break. Follow a ramp leftwards almost to its close; then take
the narrow face above, keeping just left of a vegetated crack to exit up a
tricky little groove. Good holds abound most of the way up.

Extremely Silly Arête   25 metres   E3 5c †   (30.7.99)
Enjoyable climbing with a complementary level of commitment; this is the
second arête right of the tall, white-streaked face of *Fox Whistle* (and left of
a slender finger of rock 20 metres up). Follow the tricky lower arête on its
right-hand side to a ledge. Continue in the same line until standing on a
small flat ledge below the smoother upper arête. Step nervously up over a
little overhang and, with protection from good gear in the vertical crack on
the left (including *Friend* 2½), take the edge of the arête to a good ledge
(that supports a small pinnacle). Traverse right to belay; then abseil off a
spike of your choice.

Slabby Buttress
The finest-looking section of the crag takes the form of a huge triangle, the
base of which extends from Slanting Gully to *One Pitch Gully*. The left side is
bounded by a shallow gully starting just above the base of Slanting Gully, the
right side by *North Arête*, and the two meet at the apex of the buttress. The
most apparent features are two smooth, clean-looking slabs, the lower (and
finer) situated just right of the upper.

There is no easy descent. Abseil down *Gwydrin* is possible, and accessible
from other routes in this vicinity; be prepared to sacrifice slings for backing
up *in-situ* tat. Otherwise, go up the shallow vegetated gully that slants
rightwards to the col behind the top of the buttress. Then follow the easiest
line trending right, which is the top section of *North Arête*. There is some 90
metres of climbing at Moderate standard to the summit ridge. Descend as
for *Cyfrwy Arête* (page 414).

Stross   97 metres   Hard Severe   (18.8.74)
A line up the slabs to the left of *Obsession*, making for the chimney formed
by a flake high up the buttress. Start 18 metres right of Slanting Gully and
a short way left of *Obsession*.
1 18m. A short cracked wall leads to a big ledge at 6 metres. From the
left end of the ledge, climb a short groove to a stance on the right with a
good thread belay.
2 21m. Climb, trending left, to an overhang, and move into a groove on
its right. Thread and nut belay.
3 12m. Climb the left-hand groove above to a ledge with loose blocks
below the huge flake forming a chimney.

4 12m. 4a. Climb up between the flake and the wall until the flake looks too unstable. Move out right and climb a groove to a ledge with a leaning block in a corner. Good nut belay above.
5 34m. 4b. Go up the groove above the block to a large thread through its right edge. Climb the steep wall above the thread and make a move right to a wedged flake. Go up 1 metre and move right to ledges. Then, as for *Obsession*, return left and climb a crack, step out right to another crack, and follow it to the top.

The next route was said by the first ascenionist to be 'hard to describe', and it has not been identified or checked. It appears to take a fairly direct line up the buttress, initially midway between *Stross* and *Obsession*, and then between *Then There Were Five* and *Obsession*.

Androsack 80 metres E1 † (7.95)
1 40m. 5a. Take a direct line, avoiding the overhangs, to the corner of the obvious slab.
2 40m. 5b. Step down and left to take the cleaned crack near the left edge of the slab. Follow this and the easier continuation cracks above to reach abseil slings on the ridge.

★★Then There Were Five 71 metres E2 (17.7.83)
An excellent clean and sustained climb. Start at the top of *Obsession* pitch 1 at a large spike belay.
1 24m. 5b. Step left from the spike and climb the steep, clean, blunt pillar to the ledge with a wedged block.
2 17m. 5b. Step off the top of the block and climb up to good holds on the edge of the upper smooth slab. Move a metre left and climb the faint groove in the left edge of the slab to good ledges.
3 30m. 5b. Traverse right and climb the corner to the roof. Pull over and continue up the corner above to a large terrace.

★★Obsession 114 metres Very Severe (24.6.56)
A fine slab route taking an interesting line up the centre of the buttress. Its upper section crosses the big upper slab from right to left. Start directly below overhangs some 7 metres left of the corner with the whitish water-mark, which lies directly under the lower slab.
1 37m. 4b. Go up the cracked slab below the overhangs for 12 metres and step left to gain the top of a large jammed block, the underside of which forms the lowest and most left-hand of the overhangs. Go straight up to a crack and climb it to a stance with perched blocks.
2 37m. 4c. Traverse right for 2 metres, climb straight up, and then move out right to good holds. Climb up to a ledge with a good thread and, from the groove just to its right, traverse diagonally left. Make an awkward step above an overhang and go straight up to a ledge with a jammed block. Step right of the block and climb a step-like groove until a good corner-crack on the right can be gained. Nut belays.
3 40m. 4c. Step back left into the groove at the extreme right of the big slab and climb it to a crack (awkward move to reach a spike). Move left

onto the slab and go up to follow a line of holds crossing the slab to ledges on the left. Go left again and climb a crack; then move right to another crack, which is taken to a large terrace.

★★Gwydrin 57 metres E1 (14.8.82)
The brilliant second pitch takes the centre of the big smooth lower slab. Start at a groove 2 metres left of a white water-mark, directly under the lower slab, and about 5 metres right of *Obsession*.
1 27m. 5a. Climb the groove for 12 metres to a ledge (thread), and then a steeper reddish groove trending slightly right to the traverse-line of *Route 2*. Traverse right to the stance on the right of the slab. Nut and thread belay.
2 30m. 5b. From the thread, step back left onto the slab, move up, and step left again, following a vague weakness in the slab some 2 metres left of the corner until it ends. Make a delicate traverse left (peg), climb a thin crack, and move right to a small ledge. Move up and go back left to follow thin cracks to the top of the slab, finishing close to the arête. Nut belay in a corner 7 metres above. Abseil descent, or finish up *Obsession*.
Variation
Gwydrin Direct 50 metres E3 6a † (19.8.93)
A true straight line up the lower slab. Follow *Gwydrin* to the ledge and thread at 12 metres, and then continue directly up. Hard climbing past a good Rock 4 placement allows a small pocket to be reached. Fight directly upwards to rejoin the parent route at its peg on pitch 2. Very satisfying.

Dena 119 metres Hard Severe (17.5.59)
The main pitch takes the pillar to the right of *Route 2*. Some poor rock. Start below the lower, big smooth slab at a vegetated groove.
1 21m. 4a. Climb the groove with the white water-mark on its left wall to a stance below the big smooth slab. Thread and nut belay.
2 18m. Move round to the right, and climb vegetation before moving back left to a thread belay in perched blocks next to the smooth slab.
3 34m. 4b. Climb the centre of the pillar above to a ledge with a shattered pinnacle. From the top of the pinnacle, move straight up to an overhang, pull over, and climb the slab above to a large ledge (nut belays).
4 46m. Climb the shattered rib above to the top of the buttress.

Route 2 98 metres Very Severe (8.6.59)
Another fine slab route, similar to *Obsession*, but crossing the *lower* big slab. The central section is unfortunately rather scrappy, and protection is poor on pitch 5. Start under the lower slab, in a corner just right of the water-mark groove. Large block belay.
1 24m. 4b. Go up the groove or its arête, grassy at the top, to a ramp under the big smooth slab. Thread and nut belays in a corner on the right.
2 12m. 4b. Traverse out horizontally left across the slab, following the obvious weakness. Go round the rib to a stance at the foot of a groove.
3 15m. 4a. Climb the groove to a ledge and thread belay (junction with *Obsession*).

4 21m. Climb up the left-hand groove to a stance with the upper big slab on the left. Large spike belay high above.

5 5m. Move rightwards round the rib and climb this by a crack for 11 metres to a stance on a grassy ledge 3 metres to the right.

6 21m. 4c. Move back left to the edge of the slab, climb up delicately for 3 metres (crux), and go right to better holds in a small corner. From the top of the corner, traverse back left to the edge; then go straight up to the platform at the top of the slab.

Variation

★Pusher Man Variation   30 metres   Hard Very Severe 5a   (14.9.74)
This very good pitch is a harder alternative to pitches 2 and 3 of *Route 2*. Start at the top of the latter's first pitch, below the big smooth slab. From 3 metres above the traverse-line of pitch 2 of *Route 2*, take a slightly rising leftward traverse across the smooth slab, following a line of awkwardly spaced holds, to the arête. Climb the right edge of the arête with difficulty for about 8 metres to an overlap, go up left to a flake, and then move left into a groove, which is climbed easily to the ledge at the top of pitch 3 of the parent route.

North Arête   152 metres   Difficult   (3.9.1900)
Initially, the left edge of *One Pitch Gully*, higher up becoming lost in mixed rock and vegetation. Start from the scree at the start of *One Pitch Gully* where a steepening rib goes up on the left forming the bounding arête of the gully.

1 30m. Climb the rib until it steepens; then continue on its right on big but dubious holds to a terrace.

2 30m. Follow the arête, keeping to its left, to a ledge and a good spike belay below a steep slab.

3 18m. Climb rightwards to the arête overlooking the gully and continue up two short walls above on the right to a large grassy bay.

4 37m. Easy climbing leads up the line of the arête.

5 37m. Climb straight up to the top of a table-topped pinnacle.

About 90 metres of climbing at Moderate standard leads to the top.

One Pitch Gully (Very Difficult). This obvious big wide gully is of little merit as a summer route, having only a single short chockstone pitch near the top.

Cyfrwy Pinnacle

This is the pinnacle overlooking the entrance to One Pitch Gully and forming its right wall. It has faces to the east and north. The upper section of the east face gets the sun in the summer.

★Red Crystals   103 metres   Severe   (28.8.82)
A pleasant line on the pinnacle's east face. The first two pitches are also taken by *Cyfrwy Pinnacle*. Start a short way up *One Pitch Gully* at a rib with a quartz streak, directly beneath the broken arête below the pinnacle.

1 37m. 4a. From the lowest point of the rib, move first left, then right to reach a ledge at 3 metres. Climb the crack above to the top of the rib.

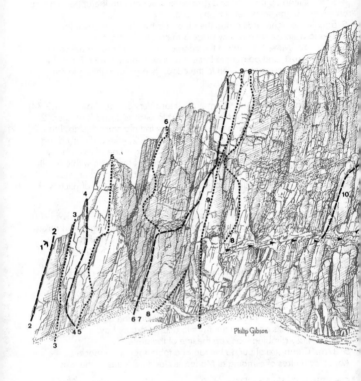

Philip Gibson

Cyfrwy

| 1 | Cyfrwy Arête | D |

Table Buttress

2	Steric Slab	HS
3	Nudging Groove	HVS
4	Pisa	HS
5	Table Direct	VD

Slanting Gully Buttress

6	Quartz Rib	VS
7	Rib and Slab	VS
8	Squall	HS
9	Sunset Boulevarde	HVS
10	Lowrib	HS
11	Fox Whistle	E3
12	Slanting Gully Grooves	E1
13	Hyrib	HS

Approach to Slanting Gully

Slabby Buttress

15	Stross	HS
16	Androsack	E1
17	Then there Were Five	E2
18	Obsession	VS
19	Gwydrin	E1
20	Dena	HS
21	Route 2	VS
21a	Pusher Man Variation	HVS

Continue up easier ground, following the stepped arête below the
pinnacle. Flake and nut belays below a steeper section.
2 21m. 4a. Step right and climb a weakness in the wall to more easier
ground, still following the arête. Stance on a large horizontal ledge below
the pinnacle.
3 21m. 4a. Move 6 metres left along the ledge to a vague crack with a
thread 4 metres up. Climb to the thread, step left, and climb a crack in a
bulge. Move 1 metre left to a ledge and climb the knobbly wall on the left
to a ledge below an overhang. Small spike and nut belays.
4 24m. 4a. Step left onto a spike. Move up the wall above until a step
right can be made to a thin crack; then make some difficult moves up this
to good holds. Step right again; then traverse right for 3 metres to a ledge
and finish up a chimney/crack.

Cyfrwy Pinnacle   101 metres   Very Severe   (3.9.82)
A direct line up the pinnacle, following the arête all the way. An excellent
top pitch.
1 37m. 4a. *Red Crystals* pitch 1.
2 21m. 4a. *Red Crystals* pitch 2.
3 23m. Continue up the line of the arête, climbing a short chimney to a long
narrow ledge below a headwall. Good nut slot round the edge to the right.
4 20m. 4c. Step round the edge to the right and climb up before making
an awkward move left to gain a groove in the arête. Take the groove to a
roof, and traverse delicately right under the roof to a finishing-crack.

Western Wing

To the right of *One Pitch Gully*, the rock tends to be more vegetated than that
of the main crag, although there are areas which are fairly clean. The crag
tapers from about 90 metres high near *One Pitch Gully* to 30 metres at the
far right-hand end. The total base length is over a third of a mile and there is
obviously scope for many more routes. The main features are deep, wet,
cave-like gullies cutting into the crag at regular intervals, some of which give
excellent winter climbing. For descent, see page 414.

Ffion   75 metres   Hard Very Severe †   (6.97)
Start on the clean face left of the gully of *Mochyn*, after scrambling up the
precarious slanting grass traverse.
1 40m. 5a. Follow the obvious cracks trending slightly rightwards,
keeping away from the edge of the gully on the right and contriving to
keep to the cleanest slabs.
2 35m. 5a. The cracks continue until the slabs ease back and large loose
blocks appear. Use jammed blocks as threads to belay, and then make a
two-stage abseil down the gully to reach the grass starting-ledge.

★Mochyn   83 metres   Very Severe   (31.7.83)
An enjoyable line up the clean face to the left of the deep chimney/gully to
the left of *Chinese Poppy*. Start 11 metres up the gully at an obvious ledge
on the left below the intimidating overhangs.

1 30m. 4c. Move left to a recess and climb the rib on its left to steepening rock; then make a rising leftward traverse to a shallow groove, and climb the groove to gain a traverse-line going back right to an exposed ledge above the overhangs. Nut and peg belays.
2 30m. 5a. Step back left and climb on good holds up to a small overhang. Make a short traverse right to a ledge below a corner, climb the corner to another overhang, and then make an awkward traverse right to a ledge on the edge of the gully.
3 12m. 4a. Climb the crack in the arête above to a good stance.
4 11m. 4a. Climb the rib directly behind the belay block to the top.

Chinese Poppy   97 metres   Severe   (11.8.74)
The buttress has a distinctive vegetated ramp running diagonally from right to left, from the mid point of which the gully of *Mochyn* rises. The climb takes a line just to the right of this gully. Start from the ramp, below and to the left of an obvious pinnacle-like block.
1 18m. Traverse right to the base of the pinnacle; then climb the arête on its left on good holds to a vegetated ledge (nut belays on the right).
2 18m. 4a. Climb the leftward-slanting ramp above, keeping to its left edge (which overlooks the gully), to a ledge at its top.
3 21m. Move up and right to gain another ramp trending back left, climb this passing a large doubtful block, and then go out right to a good ledge with flake belays.
4 40m. Climb easily up right to the top.

Trojan   91 metres   Very Severe   (19.5.74)
Well to the right of *One Pitch Gully* is an obvious big water-worn corner topped by a triangular overhang and just to its left, a huge arched overhang. The waterworn corner and the overhang are set back and are approached by entering a small rocky amphitheatre. Start 4 metres left of the wet corner.
1 21m. 4a. Climb the left wall of the corner, trending slightly right up a weakness. Move left to some small ledges. Dubious nut and peg belay (peg removed).
2 40m. 4b. Move back right and continue up the weakness; then move right again to a little ledge in the corner. Follow the corner until an obvious traverse-line out left can be made across the slab, and continue straight up to finish on a ledge just to the left of the triangular overhang. Nut belays.
3 21m. 4a. Take the chimney/crack above for about 20 metres; then move out right to a ledge.
4 9m. Finish easily up broken rock above.

The following three single-pitch climbs occupy the overlapping slabs left of *Claw Mark*, pitch 1. They terminate at a common rock spike belay, from which it is possible (and desirable) to retreat by abseil.

The One and Only Sargeant Scuff

28 metres   Hard Very Severe   4c †   (21.6.98)

Rather run out in its upper reaches, but technically reasonable. Start 4 metres above and left of a solitary tree, beneath an obvious small roof. Climb a slab to a recess beneath the roof, swing out left, and follow the diagonal crack leftwards for 6 metres. Pull up onto the sandwiched slab and move left again to the end of the overlap. Step up onto the next slab, pull straight out over a minor bulge, and continue direct up a slim slab to where it is obstructed by vegetation. Step right onto a heather ledge, and climb easily on the right to the belay.

☆Roberto Zucco   28 metres   E1 5a †   (21.6.98)

The best of the trio, which takes a fairly direct line up a light grey streak; really enjoyable climbing on excellent rock. Start as for …Sargeant Scuff. Climb a slab to a recess beneath the roof. Delicately pull up over the right-hand side of the roof to a higher slab. Bear diagonally leftwards beneath the overlap for 5 metres. Reach over the overlap to good fingerholds and follow a light grey streak before trending left to a right-facing flake. Climb the flake to a heather ledge, and climb easily on the right to the belay.

Death Becomes You   28 metres   E3 5c †   (21.6.98)

Engagingly committing above the roof. Start from directly behind the solitary tree. Climb the orange-pink slab on the right and pull up to beneath a prominent roof at 10 metres (cam placements in undercuts). Pull through the roof onto a compact grey slab and, keeping left of (and not using) the rib on the right, ascend the unprotected slab slightly leftwards to easier ground. Take the easier rib, left of the Claw Mark corner, to the top.

Claw Mark   131 metres   Hard Severe   (4.8.74)

A line up the smooth clean slab well to the right of Trojan. There is a deep cave-like gully just to its right. Pitch 1 gives the best climbing. Start 5 metres up to the right from the toe of the slab, at a weakness trending left.
1 40m. 4b. Climb leftwards and follow a thin crack in the middle of the slab to a corner with a large block on the left. Go directly up the corner to vegetated ledges. Stance on a large ledge with a large flake belay.
2 43m. 4a. Climb rock above the belay to vegetation, and then the wall above, keeping right of a large overhang. Climb a shallow groove, and move right to vegetation and a block belay.
3 30m. Scrambling leads to the top of a pinnacle.
4 18m. Descend into a gap and climb a smooth slab to more vegetation.
Variations
1a Wishbone 40m. Hard Very Severe 5a † (7.5.90). Start 5 metres up and left of the toe of the slab, by a small tree. Climb directly through the overlap (crux). Continue up the slab above on good holds and then move right to Claw Mark at the flake belay.
1b The Direct Start 40m. Very Severe 4c † (7.5.90). From the toe of the slab, go directly up to join Claw Mark at the large block at 23 metres, and continue to the flake belay.

Towards the right-hand end of Cyfrwy, and clearly visible from the approach path, is a smooth, tapering, grey slab between gullies, either of which can be used for descent.

★Turquoise Lady   25 metres   E1 5a   (7.5.90)
Go directly up the centre of the slab and belay on the pinnacle. Blind cracks give good holds but protection is sparse.

Two Spots, One Chance   20 metres   E5 6a †   (30.7.99)
An obligatory solo up the right wall of the slab. There are two landing-spots, but the crux sequence is above neither. Step up to and follow a narrow, angular groove to a jug on top. Make difficult moves diagonally right to slopers on a rib. A quick move up the rib, and easier ground is to hand.

Tŵr Du   Black Tower   OS Ref 719 135

The crag lies midway between Mynydd Moel and the ridge which the Fox's Path takes to Penygadair. It faces north-west and rises to a height of about 120 metres. The rock is good rock in places, but the lower section is scrappy-looking and heavily vegetated. The two lines of *East* and *West Gullies* are obvious, and their upper parts hem in a compact-looking buttress.

Park at the National Trust car-park at OS Ref 698 152. Either pound a kilometre of tarmac and take the Fox's Path from the Gwernan Lake Hotel, break off at Llyn y Gafr, and go south-eastwards for just over half a mile to some huge boulders which lie below the crag; or follow the Cyfrwy approach (page 414) until able to cut up between the two lakes to the crag.

There is no easy descent except by going along the main Cadair Ridge and descending the Fox's Path. The quickest way, but tricky in its lower section, is to descend the first grassy-looking gully to the south-west along the main ridge to Penygadair.

East Gully   132 metres   Very Difficult   (28.8.1902)
The gully to the left of the steep buttress is generally wet, and escapable in most places. Start below a leftward-slanting groove.
1 37m. Follow the groove, avoiding a steep section by climbing the arête on the left to a grassy bay.
2 37m. The vegetated groove at the back of the bay is followed to slabs; move right across these to reach the gully, and take a stance a short way up it, below a steep wet section.
3 40m. This section is avoided by going out left onto the arête. Climb leftwards and up a corner; then move back right into a deep chimney.
4 9m. Climb the chimney, keeping to the left of a hanging rib.
5 9m. Climb the chimney above past a block at the top.
Continue up the gully for another 65 metres with no serious difficulties.

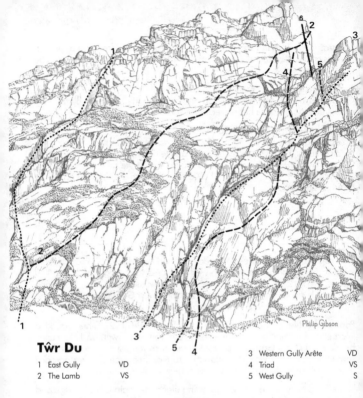

Philip Gibson

Tŵr Du

1 East Gully	VD	
2 The Lamb	VS	

3 Western Gully Arête	VD
4 Triad	VS
5 West Gully	S

The Lamb   151 metres   Very Severe   (23.6.74)
The easiest line up the central rock between *East* and *West Gullies* is taken
to reach the fine top pitches of *Triad*. Start 8 metres up *East Gully*.
1 43m. 4a. Traverse right to the slabs and climb them slightly leftwards;
then go up to a short corner with a steeper, smoother corner above.
2 27m. 4c. Climb up to the base of the smooth corner, go over a small
overlap, and traverse delicately right to a break. Take this and then move
right on good holds to a steep corner with a good ledge below it.
3 30m. 4c. Follow the steep corner and move out right onto the arête.
Climb the wall above for 1 metre; then go right and climb another arête
on good holds on the right to a large ledge under an overhang.
4 30m. 4c. *Triad* pitch 4.
5 21m. 4a. *Triad* pitch 5.

Western Gully Arête   132 metres   Very Difficult   (10.54)
The obvious striking arête some 65 metres up the crag to the right of *West Gully*. Protection on pitch 3 is poor. Start below a rib 1 metre left of *West Gully*.
1 21m. Climb the rib; then go up a grassy groove on the left and move back right into the gully. Belay, as for *West Gully*, on jammed blocks.
2 21m. *West Gully* pitch 2.
3 30m. *West Gully* pitch 3. Crux.
4 12m. Go straight up the arête to a ledge below a steep wall (chockstone pitch of *West Gully* on the left).
5 18m. Move right and climb the right edge of the arête for 9 metres; then go round onto the left side and climb a crack to a small stance with a large block belay.
6 30m. Continue just left of the arête, passing an overhang, to ledges above. Climb easy ground above to a spike belay.
Follow the arête for another 65 metres at Mod/Diff standard to the summit plateau.

West Gully   132 metres   Severe   (29.8.1902)
The gully/crackline with the big steep buttress on the left in the upper section and the striking arête on the right. The upper section is poorly protected and some of the rock dubious. Start below the gully, which here is more of a crack.
1 18m. Move in easily from the right; then go up the crack to an awkward exit. Belay on jammed blocks.
2 21m. The gully now opens out. Climb a corner on the right and continue to the base of some water-worn slabs (nut belay).
3 30m. Climb the slabs, and move up leftwards, then rightwards to gain a vegetated ledge below a steep wall. Move up left and go up the gully for 6 metres. Nut belay in the crack and a spike on the right arête.
4 12m. Continue straight up the gully to a stance below a steep chockstone pitch. Huge spike on the left.
5 30m. Climb the chockstone pitch above. Move out right for 1 metre across a little scoop; then climb straight up until a move left can be made to the bed of the gully at a vegetated ledge. Thread belay in the crack above.
6 21m. The gully now forks: take the right-hand branch, moving left across into a crack; go straight up and step out right to a big ledge. Scrambling leads to the summit.

★Triad   149 metres   Very Severe   (5.5.57)
A line initially just to the right of *West Gully*, then crossing it to finish up a clean section of rock on the right-hand side of the steep central buttress. Start as for *West Gully*.
1 40m. 4b. Follow the gully for 6 metres; then step out right to a small pedestal and go diagonally rightwards to gain a groove. Move up delicately right to a grassy ledge, and then traverse back up left to the arête. Climb this for 1 metre to a large ledge and then go up to the base of the water-worn slabs (nut belay).

2 15m. The water-worn slabs lead to a grassy ledge under a steep wall (part of pitch 3 of *West Gully*). Peg belay removed.
3 43m. 4b. Step left easily into the gully bed. After 1 metre make a slightly descending traverse left on some sloping ledges to grass. Climb an easy broken rib to a weakness in the steep wall above; go up this to grass and soon good holds on the left wall enable some blocks on a ledge to be gained. Climb directly above the blocks on excellent rock to a ledge under an overhang.
4 30m. 4c. A good pitch. Go up right to another overhang. Traverse right under it and climb a right-trending groove to the top of a pinnacle. Move up and then right to a small foothold on the arête. Climb up and traverse right to gain a scoop in a corner. Climb the corner to a ledge.
5 21m. 4a. Step right and move up a slab into a corner. Climb the crack above to the top.

The next two routes take the clean, west-facing gully wall above the upper section of *West Gully*.

★★Storms in Africa   30 metres   E3 6a   (27.8.89)
The thin intermittent crackline on the left edge of the wall. Good protection, excellent rock. Start from the top of the fifth pitch of *West Gully*, at some jammed flakes on the arête (*in-situ* thread). Swing left to the foot of the obvious crack. Make strenuous moves up the crack (*in-situ* thread), and gain a ledge above. Move up a tiny groove (peg runner) with difficulty to another small ledge. Climb the flake crack above and pull left into a groove. Follow the groove and a short arête slightly left to a ledge and good spike (hidden from below). An abseil descent via good rock spikes and threads is the most practical way off.

★Helwriaeth   43 metres   E2 5c   (30.9.89)
Care required with ropework. Start as for *Storms in Africa* and climb to the *in-situ* thread. Move delicately right along a ledge and then up to gain the base of a chimney/flake. Move right to a corner/groove-system trending slightly right and climb to its top. Easy ground leads to good spike belays on the ridge. Descend as for *Storms in Africa*.

Twr Groove   61 metres   Severe   (4.74)
Immediately right of *Western Gully Arête* there is another gully just right of an obvious groove. Start below the groove.
1 40m. Climb the groove by its slabby right wall to a good stance.
2 21m. Continue up the groove to where it steepens; then gain another groove on the left using an obvious big hold on the left wall. Climb the left-hand groove to heather.
Escape is not easy and it is preferable to continue upwards on steep heather and rock for about 65 metres to the summit plateau.

Mynydd Moel   Rounded Mountain   OS Ref 728 138

The impressive high-altitude crag lies just below the 863-metre summit of
Mynydd Moel. It faces east, catching the morning sun, and is about 60
metres high. The rock is excellent. The crag is bounded on the right by a
pinnacle ridge and just left of this is the largest section of the crag, its main
feature being a central band of overhangs, which forms the cruxes of most
of the routes that break through it. The most obvious lines are two grooves
which go up to the overhangs, the left of which is taken by *The Bee*.

Take a minor road south out of Dolgellau alongside the Afon Aran to a spot
about a half a kilometre short of its end at Bwlch Coch (OS Ref 744 159),
where it is possible to park by a forestry track on the left. From the end of the
road, take the right-of-way south and south-west for a kilometre to its
intersection with the Afon Aran, which is then followed to its source, Llyn
Aran. Scramble up rock scree and heather slopes above to the crag.

Immediately left of the crag is a large easy-angled gully which gives the best
means of descent.

☆**Rain of Terror**   47 metres   E3 †   (10.5.98)
Makes best use of the steep walls in the left-hand side of the crag. The first
ascent was made in heavy rain and the grading assessment therefore
probably lies outside the usual standard error range. Start 20 metres left of
the base of the gully left of *Sundog* and directly beneath a large overhang
near the top of the cliff.
1 20m. 5a. Take a central line up a clean, steep wall past some good
spikes; then trend rightwards up easy heather ledges for 9 metres to belay
at the foot of the larger upper wall.
2 27m. 6a. Move up to a crackline left of a tall finger of rock and follow
it to exit onto the right-hand end of a ramp which slopes up to the left.
Climb direct above, make hard moves to reach and pass a small
overhang, and so gain ledges to the right of the large overhang at the top
of the cliff. Belay, and scramble easily to the ridge.

The next two routes climb the slim pillar just left of *The Bee*.

The Sketch Man   55 metres   Hard Very Severe   (5.9.81)
1 40m. 5a. Follow *Sundog* to the rounded crack. Step left onto a small
ledge and climb the left edge of the groove to the left-hand side of the
overhangs. Make a sensational traverse left on downward-pointing spikes
to easier ground and trend right to a good stance.
2 15m. 4b. Step right onto an arête and climb it to ledges.

★**Sundog**   50 metres   E3 5c   (16.8.81)
From the base of the pillar, climb up to a bulge at 12 metres, take this on
the right via a crack, and then move left above an overhang to a short
crack. Climb the crack, avoid a ledge on the left, and climb a wall to a

ledge. Make a delicate rising traverse left to reach a jug below a peg. Move back right using a diagonal crack to below an overhang, pull over to a groove, and climb it to a ledge. Take the groove above to easier ground.

The Bee   60 metres   E1   (15.6.74/1981)
The prominent left-hand groove leading to the overhangs. Go up the first 5 metres of broken rock to a ledge with a big leaning pinnacle immediately right of the groove.
1 15m. Gain the top of the pinnacle and go left into the groove. Climb the groove on big holds to a grassy stance below an overhang.
2 30m. 5c. Move up to a peg under the overhang on the left, and with difficulty gain a large spike on the left under a second overhang. Move left and go up through the break, following the groove, to a ledge. Go straight up from the ledge, keeping to the rock on the left, to a ledge below an undercut crack.
3 15m. Climb the crack to the top.

Twist Grip   67 metres   Hard Very Severe   (17.5.75)
A devious line through the overhangs between *Route Central* and *The Bee*, finishing up the wall left of *Ritander*. Protection is rather poor on pitch 2. Start below the central groove, 3 metres right of the pinnacle at the start of *The Bee*.
1 20m. 4a. Climb easily up the groove to the large recess and take the obvious traverse-line out left to belay at the top of the first pitch of *The Bee*.
2 24m. 5a. Move up right onto the top of a large spike to a weakness in the overhangs. Reach a good little spike which enables the wall above to be gained. Climb up to an overhang made of downward pointing-flakes. Traverse right under the overhang to gain a groove on the right, and move up it a metre to gain easier rock on the right. Good spike belay up to the right.
3 23m. 4c. Move right along a small ramp and up to the right of some large dubious blocks. Climb a steep groove directly above the blocks; then go right and follow an easier groove to the top.

☆**Diamond Lake**   60 metres   E3 †   (16.5.98)
A big-feel route with three hard pitches and a direct, near-independent line up the centre of the crag. Start from high-level heather ledges just to the left of *Route Central*, below an isolated wall.
1 15m. 5c. From the left, swing right along jugs and reach some finger-jugs in the centre of the wall. Move right to a short crack, step back left, and pull steeply to a narrow ramp. Pass the bulge directly; good stance.
2 25m. 6a. From a jammed block on the left (thread), pull up the cracks (*in-situ* thread) to the roof. Break through the roof awkwardly to a broken groove (junction with *Twist Grip*) and follow *Twist Grip* slightly rightwards to nut and spike belays (*Rabble Rouser* stance).
3 20m. 5c. From the left-hand end of the pack of dubious blocks above the stance, step up and follow thin diagonal slots leftwards across the steep wall to good fingerholds on a rib. Climb through a bulge and step left; then finish up a short steep wall and easier ground above.

Mynydd Moel

Route Central   69 metres   Hard Very Severe   (8.6.59/6.81)
Start below the largest of the overhangs, at the base of a
rightward-sloping vegetated terrace.
1 15m. Climb an easy short groove and the vegetated terrace above to a
large flake belay.
2 24m. 5b. Move left and climb a diagonal crack to the overhangs.
Move right to avoid these and climb a steep groove for about 6 metres;
then make difficult moves up left to a ledge. Nut belays.
3 30m. 4b. Trend leftwards, taking the easiest line to the top.

☆**Countdown to the Millennium**   45 metres   E5 †   (10.5.98)
An intricate excursion up the right-hand walls of the crag; the second pitch
is superb. Start by scrambling 20 metres up heather ledges and take a
belay 7 metres right of a deep, right-facing crackline that leads up towards
Route Central.
1 25m. 5c. Go up a few more ledges on the left, and climb a wall with a
step right to gain a crack on the right-hand side of an undercut,
resounding flake. Continue direct past spike runners for a further 7 metres
until it is possible to swing left around a rib onto a slab (good wire
placements). Tiptoe along the upper, and smoother, of two little ramps;
then traverse left to belay on small ledges on the *Ritander* rib, 3 metres
above the first stance of *Route Central.*
2 20m. 6a. On the left is a smooth wall featuring a tantalizing
finger-jug-lined niche. Move left past a peg runner to the niche, stand up
in it, and proceed steeply direct to good jugs and a spike runner up on the
left. From a second spike, enter a short, hanging groove above and
continue to a spike and nut belay.
Abseil off the spike; traverse easily right along ledges to the top of the
crag; or finish via pitch 2 of *Ritander.*

Rabble Rouser   46 metres   E6   (5.9.81)
A testing pitch through the overlaps just right of *Route Central.* Start from
the top of pitch 1 of *Central Route.*
1 26m. 6b. Move leftwards up a ramp and climb a groove to gain a
niche. Continue over the overlap above, moving slightly leftwards. Make a
sustained series of moves to gain a steep groove, which is climbed to an
exit left.
2 20m. 4c. Traverse right along a ledge and go up a wall and chimney.
Step left onto a nose and go over blocks to finish.

Ritander   52 metres   Very Severe   (2.7.60)
Start from the top of the vegetated terrace, above and right of the top of
pitch 1 of *Route Central.*
1 15m. 4a. Climb the pillar and the wall to a grass ledge on the right.
2 37m. 4c. Trend left up the grassy groove and traverse left below the
overhang into a steep groove. Move up to the right, go back left into a
niche, and climb the groove above to the top.

Morning Crescent 50 metres   Hard Very Severe   (23.6.74)
A rather poorly-protected girdle. Start from the foot of the grassy rake on the left-hand side of the crag.
1 18m. 4b. Traverse horizontally right, passing an obvious spike, to join the first pitch of *The Bee* at roughly half height, and climb up to the stance under the overhangs.
2 11m. 4c. Move right past a large spike; then traverse across a scoop on the right (delicate) to some jammed blocks, and continue right to the stance below the big overhang on *Route Central*.
3 21m. 5a. Step down and gain a ledge under a small overhang. An awkward move right reaches *Ritander*'s first pitch: go easily up its last few moves.
Finish up *Ritander* or scramble off to the right.

At the lower right-hand corner of the crag is a small set of slabs which can provide an hour or two's light entertainment.

The Wrath of Idris 15 metres   Hard Severe 4b †   (16.5.98)
Climb the twin-crack-system left of the vegetated groove a third of the way along the slab.

Clipped Wings 20 metres   E1 5b †   (16.5.98)
Very interesting. Start immediately right of the vegetated groove. Reach and follow a thin crack in the steep wall to gain good holds in the left side of a niche. Bear leftwards and step up and left above a roof to exit up a crack.

Dead on Impact 17 metres   Very Severe 4c †   (16.5.98)
Starting 2 metres left of *Jetsam*, wander up to a left-slanting ramp and climb a more delicate hairline crack in the smoother wall above to the top. Very limited protection.

Jetsam 17 metres   Very Severe 4b †   (16.5.98)
From the right end of the grass ledge below the slab, climb a narrow groove and the slab directly above to finish up a short mossy crack on the left. No protection, but good rock.

North Ridge 92 metres   Difficult   (15.6.74)
The arête on the right-hand side of the crag has a fine-looking pinnacle half-way up, but there is some loose rock. Start left of a black hanging chimney.
1 46m. Gain the ridge by an open chimney and follow it pleasantly to the pinnacle.
2 46m. Descend from the pinnacle to a gap and move easily up to a steep nose, which may be climbed by trending left (loose at the top), or avoided by scrambling on the right. Pleasant slabs lead to the top.

Gwern Graig Rock Alder Marsh Crag OS Ref 745 138

This crag is situated high up on the shoulder of the mountain on the south-east side of the long spur sent out by Mynydd Moel and overlooks the highest part of the pass road from Tal y Llyn to Cross Foxes. It is fairly clean and gives some good climbing in the middle to lower grades.

From the parking-place at the top of the pass, go over a stile and take a faint track up the steep hillside, making for the crag high up on the ridge. About half-way, pick up a better track beside a fence and follow it to the right-hand side of the crag.

Descent is by the big open gully to the left of *The Quaker*.

The Quaker   30 metres   Very Severe 4c   (3.8.97)
Steep exposed climbing on big holds up the left edge of the buttress. There is a striking, overhanging, pocketed wall to its left. Care is needed with some of the rock. From the lowest point below the left edge, climb up to a niche beneath an overhanging wall. Move out left to the edge on big holds. Climb up the edge via a slot, then the corner on the right formed by a detached pedestal. Finish up the short crack on the right.

Pilerog   30 metres   Very Difficult   (27.7.97)
Start 10 metres down and to the left of *Gwern Pillar*, at the foot of a leaning pillar/buttress.
1 12m. Climb up easily to a ledge below a slab with overhanging rock above. Flake belay on the right.
2 18m. Climb up the slab on the left and step across a gap into the gully. Climb the gully and rocks above to the top.

★★Gwern Pillar   39 metres   Very Severe   (27.7.97)
[Photo reverse frontispiece.] Superb exposed climbing. The impressive clean pillar situated in the first major gully in from the right-hand side of the crag.
1 27m. 4c. Start from a flake crack at the base of the pillar. Gain the top of the flake easily, move up over a slight bulge, and go slightly right to the right edge (*in-situ* thread). Climb the steep arête above on widely-spaced jugs to a horizontal crack. Climb the next bulge using holds on the right of the arête, move back onto the arête, and climb straight up via cracks to the top of the pillar. Huge thread belay on the wall behind the pillar.
2 12m. 4b. Gain the top of the belay pedestal. Move right beneath an overhang and climb the obvious crack in the steep wall (*in-situ* thread) to the top.

Munchkins   18 metres   Difficult   (2.8.97)
The clean slab between two mossy sections at the top of the gully holding *Gwern Pillar* makes a pleasant way to finish most of the routes on the crag. Excellent rock. From the toe of the slab climb directly up to the top.

Gwyddon   46 metres   Severe   (3.8.97)
The left edge of the buttress immediately right of the gully with *Gwern Pillar*.
1 23m. From the lowest rocks, climb steeply up on big holds to a niche.
Move left and climb up to a small tree. Continue straight up to a terrace
beneath large detached blocks.
2 23m. Climb over the blocks and continue straight up good rock to the
top of the crag.

Gau Craig   Enclosing Crag   OS Ref 746 145

This complex crag lies in the wild and remote cwm on the end of the
north-east spur of Mynydd Moel. There are two independent areas with
different appraoches.

The Plug
The first routes are concentrated on a plug of immaculate rock in the base of
the cwm. It has an overhanging front face looking down the valley and a
striking smooth, steep wall on the left. Take the Gwern Graig approach to
the fence and follow it until the steep upper mountainside is reached; then
contour round to the crag.

Pull the Plug   15 metres   E2 6a   (11.6.95)
The slight but quite testing rib left of *Guangdong GT*. Start on the far left of
the smooth steep wall beneath a small roof at 3 metres. Make a long
reach to gain the roof and an obvious spike runner above. Stand up, bear
very slightly leftwards, and then move easily rightwards to slabs and the
top.

Guangdong GT   18 metres   E2 5c   (2.9.90)
Start beneath a small overhang on the left-hand side of the wall. Move up
and then right to follow jugs past a hole (*Rock 6*) to a fine short crack.
Climb the crack and make a bold move over the bulge to a slab; continue
up more slabs to the top.

A Conversation with JS   18 metres   E5 6a   (11.6.95)
Straight to the point: a direct, no-nonsense eliminate between *Guangdong
GT* and *One Swallow*, with an exacting finish. Follow flake cracks just left of
One Swallow and, from the *Rock 5* slot, climb direct to a thin horizontal
break. Now go straight up the leaning headwall on perfect holds (awkward
but good *Friend 1½* in right-hand slot) to the easy capping slabs.

★**One Swallow**   18 metres   E2 5c   (15.9.90)
[Photo page 408c.] The obvious dog-leg crack. The best route on this wall.
Ascend a short rightward ramp, pull over a bulge to gain the
near-horizontal crack (good *Rock 5*). Move right and climb the steep crack
above with a hard move at the top past a peg runner.

The next three routes lie on overhanging front face.

★★**Exact Science** 15 metres E6 6b (11.6.95)
A top-notch hard, volcanic micro-arête. Impeccable moves for the
specialist. Start below the left-hand arête of the overhanging front face.
Climb a groove in the arête to get established at the obvious jug. Elegant
stretches up the arête gain a good hold and another just above a small
overhang. Pull over and finish rather more easily. Two poor peg runners
and one reasonable, all removed.

Volcanic Cubism 30 metres Hard Very Severe (15.9.90)
The obvious groove in the centre of the face.
1 15m. 5a. Pull onto the top of a huge wedged block, climb the groove
above, and make an awkward move onto the left wall. Continue directly to
a large heather ledge.
2 15m. 4c. Climb the continuation groove to the top. Belay well back on
a large ledge with good nut belays.

Green Diamond 21 metres E5 6a (11.6.95)
The angular arête 8 metres right of *Volcanic Cubism*, which features a
diamond-shaped block at 9 metres. A route with many challenges. Gain
an obvious spike at 6 metres; then flow up the arête on slopers to hang a
good edge which forms the top of the 'green diamond'. Continue,
somewhat nervously, up the arête to a niche. Swing around right onto a
slab and pull through the heather above to exit.

High Crag
This comprises the buttresses situated on the high line of crags directly
beneath the skyline ridge which forms the right-hand side of the cwm. Follow
the Mynydd Moel approach (page 433) to the half-way south-west kink in
the path. Walk left up a steep grass bank, crossing another public footpath;
then follow a long straight wall southwards up to the ridge above the crag.
The routes are reached by descending from obvious points on the ridge.

★★**Bridge of Sighs** 30 metres E2 5b (15.6.97)
There is an obvious corner between a prow and a steep blank wall on the
highest of the climbable buttresses. The route dries very quickly after bad
weather and protection is good. Start left of a grassy niche and directly
beneath the prow. Climb clean rock with a green streak to the base of a
rightward-slanting ramp beneath an overhanging wall. Climb the ramp
(peg and *in-situ* thread), and then the corner itself with increasing difficulty
to its top (two more pegs and *in-situ* thread).

The next two routes lie on the wall about 100 metres right of *Bridge of Sighs*.
There is an easy gully on the left.

Was It a Kestrel? 21 metres Very Severe 5a (6.7.97)
The rounded rib to the left of *Esmerillion*. Climb a short ramp to a bulge,
pull awkwardly over rightwards, and then move straight up to the top of

Gau Craig

High Crag

1 Bridge of Sighs	E2	
2 Was It a Kestrel?	VS	
3 Esmerillion	HVS	

4 The Last Drop	HVS	
5 Pierrepoint	E1	
6 Jack Ketch	E2	

the rounded rib. Climb directly up the headwall with a final hard move, reach easy ground, and belay well back.

Esmerillion   21 metres   Hard Very Severe 5b   (5.7.97)
The obvious steepening crackline in the wall. Reach the crack via mossy slabs (*in-situ* thread) and climb it with increasing difficulty. Easy rock above leads to a belay well back.

To the right of the *Esmerillion* wall is an overhanging wall with roofs at the base, and to the right of this a rather blank wall with a scoop in its centre and a brown-coloured steep section just left.

The Last Drop   24 metres   Hard Very Severe 5a   (12.7.97)
Steep climbing on big holds just left of the brown-coloured section. Good protection (*Friends 1* and 2 and two *in-situ* threads). Climb steeply to the highest thread and go diagonally right to a spike. Step left and climb to a niche. Climb directly out of this to the top. Belays well back.

Pierrepoint   24 metres   E1 5b   (9.8.97)
Sustained, delicate climbing. Start beneath the brown wall. Climb up to a good nut crack at 4 metres, and move slightly down and right using a little ramp to gain the slab on the right. Climb delicately up the left edge of the slab to large holds (brown wall immediately to the left). Climb straight up on easier rock, finishing via the niche on *The Last Drop*.

★Jack Ketch   24 metres   E2 5c   (19.7.97)
A fine route climbing the scoop and obvious diagonal crack above. Start at the right-hand side of the wall at a slight weakness leading up to the

scoop, and just left of a rowan. From a frost pocket, make difficult moves up and slightly right (good *Rock 3* in a slot at 4 metres), move up, then left to good holds in the scoop, and follow this to a ledge. Climb the diagonal crack in the wall above to a difficult exit move.

A Touch Sketchy 25 metres E3 5c † (18.5.98)
A worthwhile companion to *Jack Ketch*; protection is restricted on the upper wall. Climb the compact white scoop of *Jack Ketch*, but where that route steps left continue slightly rightwards to reach the right end of the central ledge (*in-situ* thread). Pull up onto the headwall and move diagonally right along foot-ledges to the arête. Proceed steeply to larger holds and the top.

A hundred metres right of the *Jack Ketch* wall and about 25 metres lower is a squat, thumb-like pinnacle, and above this a steep face.

☆**Thumbs Up** 15 metres E4 6a † (18.5.98)
An outstanding pitch on beautiful holds up the arête of the thumb. The gear, overall, is quite reasonable, yet is placement-specific. From a ledge on the left, pull up to a thin break below the arête. Hang a sloper over the bulge (superb wire slot) and make a powerful move to a big side-hold. Continue steeply up the arête to the top.

Two Fingers   15 metres   E5 6a †   (18.5.98)
Unassumingly good; this is the front of the small steep wall above the
thumb. Protecting the route requires skill. Climb the short initial arête on
'so big they can't be solid' holds to get established in a groove. Move left
around the arête (very thin tape on spike) to a couple of pockets (Rock 5 in
rightmost) and gain a further, larger pocket above. Move up to a bulge,
whence strong moves up the short capping arête lead to good
finishing-holds on its right-hand side.

Cadair Area: Outlying Crags

Cwm-pen-llydan   Wide Head Valley
This complex of short, clean walls sits on a hillside to the south-west of
Cregennon lake in the foothills to the north of Cadair Idris.

Drive westward up Ffordd Ddu from Dolgellau past the standing stone to a
sharp left-hand bend and a gate across the road. Pass through the small
gate in the wall by the main gate, and Crag One is reached in a few minutes
by contouring around the south side of the hill. Crag Two is just beyond,
across a shallow cwm.

An alternative approach to Crag Two is to park at the sharp bend at Trawstir
and take the track uphill between two stone walls to a break in the
right-hand wall. Go straight up the hill from the break, and cross a stile over
another (good) wall to reach the east end of the cwm with the crag on the
right-hand side.

Crag One   OS Ref 645 129
The first wall has ivy at its northern end, but just to its right there is a good,
clean wall with an overhang at its base.

Head in the Thundercloud   15 metres   E1 5c †   (6.8.99)
Pull through the initial overhang using small spaced edges above, and
step left into the thin crack. This is followed more easily to the big cleaned
ledges above and a straightforward finish.

To the right is a holly bush, and to the right again, a clean white pillar.

☆**Time Artist**   16 metres   E2 6a †   (6.8.99)
The wall is taken on good holds to the thin ledge below the final leaning
wall. A hard sequence of moves up left past a peg gains a cleaned, flat
ledge which, once flopped onto, leads to an easy finish.

A short walk up further right there is another compact wall, which has an
unclimbed central groove bounded by two pillars.

Neolithic Span   16 metres   Hard Very Severe 5a †   (30.10.98)
Start up the left-hand pillar 2 metres to the left of the central groove to
reach the shattered overlap. Pull out leftwards and finish carefully and
directly. Not as good as its neighbour.

☆**Monolithic Man**   16 metres   E1 5b †   (30.10.98)
Pull up the leaning short wall 2 metres right of the central groove to gain a
ledge. Continue direct to a committing finish up the rounded left side of
the pillar.

Crag Two   OS Ref 647 132
Never Miss a Chance   10 metres   Hard Very Severe 5a † (10.5.2000)
The easiest route here, but poor compared to its neighbours. The left edge
of the clean wall starts very steeply to gain the sloping ledges. A tough
sequence will lead to a good hand-ledge up and right before a tricky
mantel finish.

☆☆**Sir Killalot**   10 metres   E2 5c †   (10.5.2000)
To the right is a clean sheet of very compact rock with a vague right-facing
groove in its centre. Start via some stacked blocks, and bridge and
layaway up the immaculate rock above past some good runner slots.

Sergeant Bash   10 metres   E1 5b †   (10.5.2000)
Next right is a steep groove with a couple of flakes high in its left side.
Gain these directly and bridge thinly past small wires to an easier finish.

☆☆**Dead Metal**   10 metres   E2 5c †   (10.5.2000)
The pillar left of the right-hand open groove leans all the way. Start in the
recess and labour up the thin seam in the centre of the pillar past spaced
but good protection.

Friog: Blue Lake Quarry   OS Ref 620 123
The Blue Lake Quarry faces north above the small village of Friog on the
Dolgellau to Tywyn road. The walls around the lake itself are unfortunately
friable and of poor quality. However, the level immediately below here has
one very good face and several minor ones. Leave the main track leading to
the lake after reaching the second arch. Follow the minor track down the
stream bed until the walls come into view.

Top Tier
This sits above the old railway line and has three routes.

Route One   9 metres   E1 5b
Pass the home-made bolts to the ledge. Step right and pull up to the next
narrow ledge. The original line continued to the top on shaky rock but it is
now possible to lower-off from the two bolts on *Lilliput's Bane*.

Lilliput's Bane   9 metres   E3 6a   (14.3.93)
At the centre of the wall are two *Petzl* bolts. Start just right of the first and
gain it by a series of thin moves. A very long reach past gains a good
pocket and the short ledge above. Continue up to the lower-off.

Route Two   9 metres   E1 5b
The crack right of the centre takes a couple of good wires to back up the old
home-made hangers. At the top of the crack, step up left to the lower-off.

Main Tier

The routes on this tier are described from **right to left**. At its extreme right,
the fine rock deteriorates. There is one route here.

Sow's Ear   12 metres   Very Severe 4c   (14.3.93)
Gain the slab, passing a peg. Step right and finish direct up the wall,
passing a final peg on its right. Belay on the track.

The clean sweep of slab below the fine steep wall has been well bolted. At
half height there is a break where the slab meets the wall, and only here is
the rock a little scrappy.

★Great Mambo Chicken   15 metres   E2 5c   (27.7.92)
The right-hand side of the fine slab and the right arête of the wall above.
Climb easily up the slab to the break. An easy clip is followed by a
problematical series of moves up the arête to the crack. Follow this back
leftwards to the lower-off.

★★Grips of Wrath   15 metres   E4 6a   (27.7.92)
The lower slab is thin and sustained but now sports three bolts compared
to the original one, making it much safer. From the break, climb the
hairline crack up the steep wall past more good bolts to the lower-off.
Powerful.

☆Bolt from the Blue   15 metres   E3 6a †   (27.8.91)
The fine right-trending crack has good holds once gained. The wall poses
a much harder problem: being fingery and powerful it requires an effort to
pass the bolts and gain the lower-off on the right.

☆Blue Moves   15 metres   E3 6b †   (27.9.91)
Very safe but very hard: the crux moves on the slab are fiercely thin.

The Hard-Boiled Wonderland   15 metres   E3 6a †   (27.7.92)
The steep orange wall left has three bolts protecting a slim groove.
Gaining and passing the first is the crux; there are good holds higher up.
Lower off.

Blue Lagoon Area

Follow the footpath up to the entrance tunnel and take the right-hand fork of
the two tunnels. With the lake on your left-hand side and walls on the right
follow the path until it bends left. The two routes are situated to the right on

the cleanest slab. A short scramble up a rock tier places you at the foot of both lines.

Spanking the Monkey   10 metres   F6b   (5.6.99)
A good jug allows the wall to be gained; continue direct via small edges and a couple of high rockovers past two bolts. Tree belay some way back.

Hole in the E Zone   10 metres   F6c   (5.6.99)
A slightly more sustained route than its left-hand neighbour, requiring precise footwork and balance. Follow crimps and edges past three bolts to the tree belay.

Cae-du Quarry   Black Field Quarry   OS Ref 567 056

The A493 Dolgellau to Tywyn coast-road bends sharply at the entrance to Cae-du farm and caravan site. Drive carefully through the farmyard and park at the caravan site (£1 in 2001). The west-facing quarry walls are 100 metres south of the site and above the railway line. There are three routes here though the main attraction of this area is the expanse of short sea-cliffs below the path. The routes are described from **right to left**. At the right-hand end of the open quarry is a large slab, mainly easy angled.

Out of My Mine   24 metres   E1 5a †   (5.4.96)
Start at the right side of the slab by the huge flake. Follow the obvious leftward-rising ramp for 5 metres; then step up and right to gain a good ledge. Gather your wits (no protection) and continue direct to the overlap 8 metres higher. Arrange protection and pull up right through this to fine thin climbing on the shorter slab above. Belay on an old concrete fencepost.

☆**Mine over Matter**   37 metres   Hard Very Severe 4c †   (5.4.96)
This rising leftwards diagonal from its lowest point to the top left makes full use of the available rock. Start 5 metres left of *Out of My Mine*, at the toe of the slab. Climb easily up and left to a short flake. Continue, rising leftwards to the overlap below the short gully above the centre of the slab. Continue up and left to finish up the obvious groove at the top left of the slab. Fencepost belay.

Seashell Babylon   24 metres   Hard Very Severe 4c †   (5.4.96)
From directly below the finishing-groove of *Mine over Matter*, climb the unprotectable slab until the bottom of the groove and the first wire is reached. At no point is the climbing hard. As with all routes in quarries, top out with care.

The sea-cliffs below the path are used extensively by local outdoor centres and many routes get heavy traffic; these are marked with belay posts. The cliffs are no higher than 10 metres or so and this beautiful setting is an ideal beginners' cliff. Some of the routes are inaccessible one hour either side of high tide. In Ogof Owain (Owain's Cave) there is even an old aid route from over 30 years ago following the roof at its left side from the back of the cave right to the lip. There are also many boulder-problems too numerous to

record. Although many are no harder than 5a there are also some 6b gems
up the overhanging wall left of the entrance to the cave. The steep slab right
of the entrance is also worth noting.

Craig yr Aderyn   Bird Crag   OS Ref 643 069

Craig yr Aderyn rises dramatically out of the flat Dysynni Valley only 7 miles
from the seaside town of Tywyn. Approaching from the inland side via
Welshpool or Dolgellau, make for the junction at the Cross Foxes Inn and go
down the A487, then the B4405 to Tal y Llyn. A mile further downstream,
take a minor road marked signed Llanegryn, which follows the river Dysynni
to the crag.

Although it has a northerly aspect, it is very low-lying at only a few metres
above sea-level, and can make a suitable venue in winter. *The Diamond* wall
on The Bastion dries very quickly, making it an obvious choice when most
other crags are wet.

Eastern Face, the rather vegetated big north-east facing crag above the
quarry, is a cormorants' nesting-site. Apparently, the crag was once a
sea-cliff. Much lower down and practically next to the road is the main
attraction, The Bastion. Between these two is Central Buttress, with its
prow-like overhangs.

Eastern Face and Central Buttress are subject to **bird-nesting restrictions**,
and climbing is not normally allowed from 1st April to 31st July. However, the
restrictions may be reviewed mid season.

Eastern Face

[Diagram page 448a.] Eastern Face, the largest of the Craig yr Aderyn
crags, lies above a quarry and is a bird sanctuary (note the above restriction).
It is heavily vegetated in places and there is some dubious rock. All routes bar
the first are approached from the right.

Safe as Sausages 43 metres   Hard Very Severe 4c [R]   (8.83)
On the extreme left-hand side of Eastern Face is a slim pillar with an
obvious groove-line up its centre. There is some dubious rock. Start at the
lowest point of the pillar, directly below the groove-line. Ascend the pillar
for 11 metres; then step left and climb the groove to a large spike runner.
Step left again to enter another groove and follow this to a ledge on the
left. Finish up the easier continuation groove.

The Talon 88 metres   Severe [R]   (14.6.64)
The pinnacle on the left-hand side of the face (the pillar of *Safe as
Sausages* is round to the left). Some dubious rock. Start at a crack, gained
by traversing above the quarry from the right.
1 40m. Ascend the crack to grass at 5 metres. The crack continues
above, but climb the wall to its right and move right near the top. Continue
more easily above to a ledge in a grassy gully.

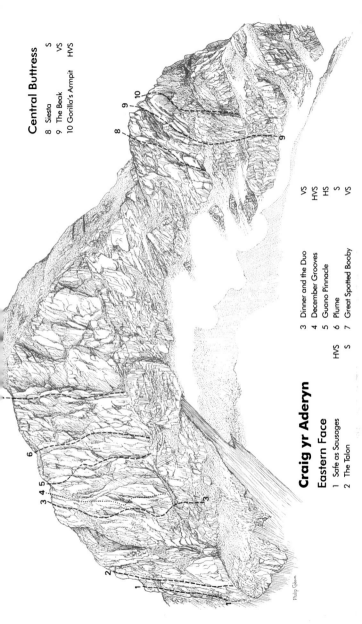

Central Buttress

8	Siesta	S
9	The Beak	VS
10	Gorilla's Armpit	HVS

Craig yr Aderyn
Eastern Face

1	Safe as Sausages	HVS
2	The Talon	S
3	Dinner and the Duo	VS
4	December Grooves	HVS
5	Guano Pinnacle	HS
6	Plume	S
7	Great Spotted Booby	VS

Philip Gibson

Craig yr Aderyn

The Bastion

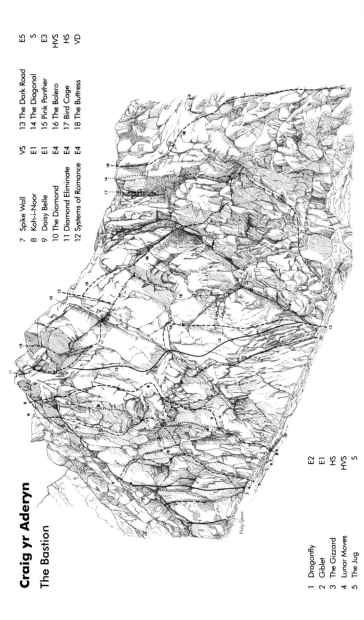

Philip Gibson

1	Dragonfly	E2	
2	Giblet	E1	
3	The Gizzard	HS	
4	Lunar Moves	HVS	
5	The Jug	S	

7	Spike Wall	VS
8	Koh-i-Noor	E1
9	Daisy Belle	E1
10	The Diamond	E4
11	Diamond Eliminate	E4
12	Systems of Romance	E4

13	The Dark Road	E5
14	The Diagonal	S
15	Pink Panther	E3
16	The Bolero	HVS
17	Bird Cage	HS
18	The Buttress	VD

2 9m. Move left across the gully and gain the top of a pinnacle on the left.
3 18m. Take the easiest line up the wall above, first left to an old peg, then right to the arête at some blocks. Climb the pinnacle to its top.
4 21m. Step down from the left end of the ledge. Move round an arête; then go left again and climb another arête.

Dinner and the Duo   94 metres   Very Severe [R]   (22.11.75)
A fairly direct line up the centre of the large buttress to the left of *Guano Pinnacle*. Start at a left-slanting weakness in a lower wall situated directly below the large buttress.
1 20m. Start easily up a vague crack, trending left for a short way. Move left on grass and go up a short wall to a grassy terrace. There is an ivy-covered wall up to the right. Spike belay on the left.
2 37m. 4b. Gain the wall above and move up between two overhangs. Climb steeply up right above the right-hand overhang to easier ground. Move up right to a poor ledge on the edge of the wall; then go leftwards to below a corner-crack, and avoid it by moving up right to the top of a huge spike.
3 23m. Take the easiest line leftwards to ledges; then go directly up on easy ground to a steep wall with a crack. Stance on the right.
4 14m. 4b. Gain the top of a big spike on the left; then climb the steep crack above to a niche, and more awkwardly from the niche to the top.

December Grooves   76 metres   Hard Very Severe [R]   (5.12.75)
The big groove to the right of *Dinner and the Duo*. Protection is poor on pitch 3. Start from the top of that route's first pitch, and move right to a groove just right of an ivy-covered wall. Large spike belay.
1 14m. 4c. From a ledge, climb the groove and move left at the top to another ledge.
2 20m. 4b. Continue up the groove to the overhangs, move left round an edge, and climb to a huge spike.
3 30m. 4c. From its top, step right onto an exposed wall and climb this on large, well-spaced holds to ledges. Continue to a notch between a pinnacle and the wall above.
4 12m. 4b. Finish up the steep groove.

Guano Pinnacle   95 metres   Hard Severe [R]   (5.59)
This mountaineering route has some interesting situations and makes for a large conspicuous pinnacle (cormorants' favourite roosting-ground) in the middle of the crag. There is some dubious rock, and protection is rather poor on pitch 3. Start below the conspicuous pinnacle at a broken groove/chimney-line descending from the right-hand side of the pinnacle.
1 37m. Climb a short wall and then go leftwards up a grassy ramp. Continue up vegetation to a corner on the right, and climb it until a move left can be made to more vegetation, which leads to a steep corner beneath the chimney-line below the pinnacle.
2 24m. 4a. Climb the arête on the left for a short way to a ledge. Climb the steep wall above on good holds and move right to a ledge above the steep corner. Go up the broken wall above (dubious rock) to easy ground leading to the base of the chimney.

3 34m. 4a. Climb the chimney to evil ledges between the face and the pinnacle (large spike on the right). Gain a foot-ledge above on the face behind, and follow it left beyond the pinnacle to a groove. An awkward move across this leads to easier but rather unstable ground and then the top.

Plume   98 metres   Severe [R]   (17.2.74)
The next crackline to the right of *Guano Pinnacle*, and a similar type of route. Start 10 metres right of *Guano Pinnacle*, at a cleaned rib (which leads up directly to large flakes and spikes at the start of the long traverse section into an upper groove-line).
1 37m. Climb the rib; then take a fairly direct line up cracks and short walls to the large flakes.
2 27m. Traverse left to more spikes and flakes, and climb to the highest of these. Move left and make a delicate step down to gain a grassy ramp on the left, and follow it to a slab leading to a small stance in a little corner. A broken spike forms the left wall of the corner.
3 34m. Climb the corner to the top of the broken spike and traverse left into a steep corner. Continue up this to an overhang (steep crack above); then move left to the edge and climb on big dubious holds. Go back right above the overhang and climb the broken crack above to the top.

Great Spotted Booby   70 metres   Very Severe [R]   (3.2.74)
To the right of the crag centre where it is highest, a large wet corner cuts the entire face. The route takes a series of grooves in the arête on the left of this corner. Some unstable rock. Start below a clean steep groove (old peg at its foot) about 45 metres up the vegetated lower section of the face. Ascend this lower section by first taking a large grassy ramp on the right and a little wall, and then following more vegetation to a rock niche on the right. Go up left of the niche to another wall, and zigzag up vegetated ramps to the groove.
1 34m. 4c. Climb the groove, negotiating a small overhang half-way (crux). Step left at the top to the arête and ascend vegetation, passing some dubious blocks, to gain the top of a large pinnacle.
2 24m. 4b. Climb a groove to the right of the belay to the second of two small ledges. Go left, avoiding two pinnacles ahead on the right, and climb a chimney behind the last one to a belay on the left below an overhanging block.
3 12m. 4c. Climb up to the right of the overhanging block (loose rock on the left) and gain a slab. Move right to ledges on the arête and finish easily.

Central Buttress
The buttress has an upper and lower tier. Prow-like overhangs dominate the upper tier, on which the first four routes are situated. Above the lower tier is a track which comes in from the left, ending below the final pitch of *The Beak*. Please note the nesting restriction (page 446).

Barking at the Moon 24 metres E1 5b † [R] (21.5.93)
Start on the steep, orange-coloured slab 50 metres up and left of *Siesta*.
Climb easily up a groove to an overlap (good nut placements). Pull up and
left with difficulty to a peg, and follow the thin diagonal crack up and left
to a second peg. The crux sequence is passing this up direct to a ledge on
the right. Finish up the short wall above, and belay behind.

The Howling 24 metres E2 5c † [R] (1.7.93)
A good exciting climb, taking the right-hand side of the orange slab.
Follow *Barking at the Moon* to the overlap. Then step up and right,
undercutting the overlap to pull over onto the slab on small holds.
Continue thinly up from here (small *RPs*), and gain a large ledge with
consternation. Romp up the short wall above.

Siesta 34 metres Severe 4a [R] (1962)
A favourite with the Aberdovey Outward Bound School. Poor protection on
the crux slab section. The line takes a slanting groove on the upper tier, 15
metres left of the prow-like overhang of the final pitch of *The Beak*. Start
from the track about 15 metres past a fence, just before a huge block with
a rectangular block lying across the top of it. Climb a crack on the left;
then climb rightwards to a small cave (the pitch could be split here). Make
a traverse to the right for about 3 metres to the edge of a slab. Go
delicately up the edge and then follow an easier section to a jammed
block overhang. Surmount this to reach easy ground.

Day of the Tripheads 24 metres E2 5c † [R] (6.7.93)
The steep series of overlaps between *Siesta* and the *The Beak*. Start by the
large flake pinnacle to the right of *Siesta*. Pull up onto the large flake and
surmount it. A rightward-slanting groove is followed strenuously on small
holds to gain a peg and *in-situ* wire. Rock-over leftwards with difficulty to
gain good holds on the lip, pull through precariously, and climb boldly up
the prow (peg). Surmount the prow with difficulty.

The Beak 60 metres Very Severe [R] (10.6.64)
On the lower tier, directly below the prow – a prominent feature of Central
Buttress. The first pitch follows the lower tier at its highest section. There is a
shallow corner to its left and a vague groove to the right. Pitch 2 is merely
scrambling. Start at the cleanest section of rock.
1 21m. 4b. Move straight up the buttress front, and step right at 12
metres to a ledge and a dubious spike; climb on good holds above the
spike to grass. Block belay above on the right.
2 24m. Scramble up over broken rock and grass to a large niche just
above the track. Above are the grooves which slant down from the prow.
3 15m. 4b. Climb the right-slanting cracks, negotiating small bulges until
below the final roof. Either move out right onto the edge of the prow
(exposed) and go up this to the top, or surmount the overhang direct.

★Gorilla's Armpit   38 metres   Hard Very Severe [R]   (22.6.75/4.11.79)
The obvious overhanging groove right of *The Beak*. Start at a steep crack
in a wall just below the end of the track that comes in from the left above
the lower tier.
1 27m. 4c. Climb the crack to a ledge. Step right and climb a steep
cracked ramp to a ledge directly below the overhanging groove.
2 11m. 5a. Finish up the groove.

The Bastion

[Diagram page 448b.] The most popular of the Craig yr Aderyn crags, and
not subject to the nesting restriction. It has two faces, north and west, divided
by *The Buttress*. The rock on the north face is clean, but dubious in places.
The west face is much scrappier, with some vegetation. The main feature of
the north face is *The Diamond* wall, which is slightly overhanging for most of
its 46 metres. To the left of *The Diamond* wall, the rock diminishes in height,
and a large boulder below a pedestal marks the start of *Pedestal Route*. The
first definite feature on the left is a groove with a small narrow slab rising
leftwards below it. This is the start of *The Gizzard*.

Dragonfly   12 metres   E2 5b   (11.89)
Short, but unprotected. Start at the bottom centre of the slab, a metre and
a half left of *The Gizzard*. Move up on pockets to the bottom of a shallow
groove. Finish directly up the groove to the final ledge.

★Giblet   18 metres   E1 5b   (12.10.90)
A direct line above the start of *The Gizzard*, taking the vertical finger-crack
left of the groove. The crack is unrelenting and has some superb
finger-jams.

The Gizzard   18 metres   Hard Severe 4b   (14.6.64)
Climb the slabby corner to enter the groove with difficulty (good hold at its
base). Climb the groove to its top and move out left to a grassy slope.
Scramble up to the descent track to metal belay spikes.

Lunar Moves   34 metres   Hard Very Severe 5a   (11.89)
Start at the base of the *The Gizzard* and take the centre of the wall on its
right to reach the arête. Continue up the arête to the final wall and finish
up its centre.

The Jug   34 metres   Severe 4a   (4.67)
Start a short way right of *The Gizzard*. Climb easily up to a ledge just left of
and level with the large pedestal (belay possible). Go left up a ramp to an
overhanging corner (old peg) and climb the steep wall diagonally right to
a ledge. Then, as for *Pedestal Route*, follow the ledge up left to broken
rocks. Belay on metal spikes by the track.

Pedestal Route   34 metres   Hard Severe 4b   (1962)
Rather poor protection on the steep little wall above the pedestal. Start at
the large boulder below the pedestal and climb steeply to a niche

underneath it; then move right and go up to its top (belay possible). Climb the steep little wall above (crux) to gain a ledge on the left, and follow this up left to grass and broken rocks. Belay on the track.

Spike Wall   40 metres   Very Severe   4c
Follow *Pedestal Route* until just right of the pedestal; then traverse right, passing an old peg. Climb steeply up to gain a slab beneath an overhang (old peg and good nut). Climb up left via a crack to a large spike, pull over a bulge, and finish up the groove to belay on the track above.

The Great Mogul   57 metres   E2   (8.9.79)
A high-level traverse of *The Diamond* wall. Start as for *Pedestal Route*.
1 11m. Climb easily to belay just right of the pedestal.
2 46m. Follow *Spike Wall* to and up its final groove until standing on a sloping ledge. Traverse right with difficulty until a good edge enables a resting-place in *Daisy Belle* to be reached. Step down 2 metres and traverse right to the bottom of the niche. Reverse the traverse of *Diamond Eliminate* and finish up the slab of *The Diamond*.

Koh-i-Noor   40 metres   E2   5a   (24.6.78)
A vague groove-line between *Spike Wall* and *Daisy Belle*. Serious. As for *Daisy Belle*, step up from the boulder and traverse a metre right; then climb straight up the slight groove to join *Spike Wall* at the first peg. Go steeply up to the slab below the overhang (as for *Spike Wall*); then pull out rightwards on layaways to reach a flat-topped spike. Continue straight up the groove using holds on the left, and move right at the top to a slab. Finish leftwards as for *Daisy Belle*.

★Daisy Belle   39 metres   E1   (5.64/1978)
The easiest and most obvious line up *The Diamond* wall. Exhilarating climbing. Start from the large boulder below the pedestal on *Pedestal Route*.
1 18m. 5a. Step up from the boulder and traverse right; then go up and right again to a groove (peg). Climb the groove, and exit right to a ledge.
2 21m. 5b. Climb strenuously up the overhanging groove above the left end of the ledge (old pegs) to a niche. Climb the niche to a small overhang, move out left, and climb a slab with a move left to finish.

★The Diamond   45 metres   E4   (8.5.76/3.78)
The definitive route of the crag, but the crux on pitch 2 is very poorly protected. Start 2 metres right of the large boulder.
1 21m. 5b. Climb up rightwards to a shallow groove with an old peg (not seen from below). Move up and traverse right across the steep wall; then climb up to a belay niche on the central ledge.
2 24m. 5c. Just right of the belay, climb a shallow groove to its end. Move up with difficulty (poor *in-situ* nut) to a resting-place below an obvious slanting slab. Climb the slab to a ledge and finish up the short wall above.

★★Diamond Eliminate   45 metres   E4   (3.78)

The objective, the large central niche in the upper wall, is achieved by some sensational climbing and the same poorly-protected crux. Start at the foot of *The Diagonal*, the lowest point of the wall.

1 24m. 5b. Climb diagonally left for 8 metres, then up for 2 metres to a spike. Climb the obvious leftward-slanting crack into the first pitch of *The Diamond*, and follow this to the belay ledge.

2 21m. 5c. Follow *The Diamond*, taking its poorly-protected crux to the resting-place below the slanting slab. Then traverse delicately left until below the central niche. Move up into it and climb its left-hand slab and arête to finish.

☆☆☆**The Dark Road**   45 metres   E5 †   (29.9.90)

A perfect direct line up the centre of The Bastion, taking in strenuous, intricate, and totally committed climbing.

1 23m. 6a. Start at the foot of *The Diagonal* and pull directly and boldly through the bulge on some dubious-looking rock to a narrow, sloping ledge at 5 metres. Now trend up and leftwards on better rock to place a sling over a flake on the left. The thin, steep section up and right leads to a small hand-ledge and a blessed peg. A tricky rockover and more steep thin climbing up a vague crack gains the belay ledge, but only after a hair-raising mantel.

2 22m. 6a. From the belay (shared with *The Diamond*), traverse rightwards on the big ledge until below a left-facing edge on a big flake (about 2 metres left of *The Diamond* crux). Bold moves on small but very good edges lead to the flake and a peg. The wall continues to lean out as you move up and leftwards to a spike, where some protection may encourage you to gird your loins before going direct up the wall above. A final rockover leaves you on the easier slab in the top recess of *The Diamond*, which is followed to the top.

Systems of Romance   57 metres   E4   (26.5.79)

Rather contrived, and the rock is poor. Start at the foot of *The Diagonal*.

1 23m. 6a. Climb *The Diagonal* for 3 metres; then go strenuously out left over a bulge to a spike. Move right to a horizontal ragged crack (dubious spike runners); then gain a diagonal ramp up right (peg) and climb this to a ledge. Nut and spike belay.

2 11m. Go easily left along the central ledge to the niche belay (peg).

3 23m. 5c. Go back right along the ledge and climb a groove, past an old *in-situ* nut, to the resting-place below the slanting slab (pitch 2 of *The Diamond*). Move down right and round the corner (*Pink Panther* in reverse) to below two thin cracks. Climb the cracks and a steep wall to the top.

★Pink Panther   59 metres   E3   (21.8.78/5.5.79)

Effectively a high-level traverse with little independent, but nevertheless sustained and technical, climbing. Start as for *The Diagonal*.

1 24m. 5b. Climb *The Diagonal* for 11 metres until under a scoop. Gain the scoop and then move out right onto a steep wall. Follow this to a ledge.

2 11m. 5c. Move right and climb a groove/slab to its top. Continue up the steep wall above to a hanging belay on a spike.
3 24m. 5c. Hand-traverse leftwards on ledges until a few hard moves lead to the resting-place on *The Diamond*. As for *Diamond Eliminate*, traverse delicately left and move up into the central niche; then climb the wall out to the right.

The Diagonal   37 metres   Severe   (22.11.64)
The prominent diagonal crack slanting up right from the base of *The Diamond* wall. Protection is sparse on the first 9 metres (normally a peg is *in situ*); adequate above. Start at the base of the crack.
1 26m. Take a line just below the crack on good rock to a ledge. Climb more in the crackline to an awkward final move onto a large ledge (boulder and tree belay).
2 11m. Move easily right to a stance on the buttress; then climb a clean-cut groove on the left to the top.

★The Bolero   36 metres   Hard Very Severe   (10.11.74/24.8.75)
Start at the top of pitch 1 of *Birdcage*, just beneath the black cleft. The upper pitch makes a good introduction to the exposure of *The Diamond* wall and enables an inspection of the harder routes.
1 15m. 5a. Take *Birdcage* for 1 metre to where it overhangs; then traverse left on good holds and make an awkward move to gain the top of a pedestal. Go up left from the pedestal with difficulty to good holds. Make a move up; then go diagonally up left to reach the ramp of *The Diagonal*. Climb this for a short way to the big ledge.
2 21m. 5a. Step back down left across an ivy groove and climb a steep ramp to its top. Continue up the steep wall above until just above a good spike runner; then traverse out left along good foot-ledges and make some steep moves up to a ledge on the left. Climb the final steep little wall to the top.

Birdcage   33 metres   Hard Severe   (4.67)
The 'cage' is the deep black cleft below the belay ledge of *The Diagonal*. Only the wall above the cleft is of interest. Start a little to the right of the fence below a right-slanting slab.
1 12m. Climb the slab and go up easily into the base of the cleft.
2 12m. 4b. Move up the cleft; then swing out left and climb steeply on widely-spaced jugs to the tree.
3 9m. Finish up the vegetated groove above.

The Buttress   41 metres   Very Difficult
The obvious line of the buttress can be climbed as two, three, or four pitches and there are several variations. Protection is rather difficult to find. Start at the lowest point.
1 12m. Climb the left-hand wall of the buttress to a large ledge. Spike belay on the left.
2 21m. Go up to the left of a bulge and climb fairly directly to easy ground. Metal spike under the final steep wall.

3 8m. Climb steeply up the wall on good holds; scrambling above leads to more metal spike belays.

Rockerfeller   21 metres   Hard Severe 4b   (1.4.67)
A rather artificial line. The rock is good but protection is poor on the lower section. Take a direct line up the right flank of *The Buttress* to the right end of the large platform. Finish as for *The Diagonal*.

North Face Girdle   90 metres   Hard Very Severe   (4.67/16.5.76)
There is some good independent climbing.
1 24m. Climb *Rockerfeller* for 8 metres; then move left to a ledge on the arête and traverse left to the black cleft on *Birdcage*.
2 18m. 5a. As for *The Bolero*, move up *Birdcage* to where it overhangs, traverse left to a pedestal, and go awkwardly up left to join *The Diagonal*. Then descend *The Diagonal* for a short way to a ledge.
3 18m. 5b. Strenuously climb the overhanging left wall diagonally left to a good spike (two old pegs). Traverse left to gain the central ledge with a niche stance and peg belay.
4 30m. 4c. Go to the left end of the ledge and move left on good handholds to a slab. Move left to a crack and finish as for *Spike Wall*: go up the crack to a steep wall, pull over to a groove, and climb it to the top.

The Buttress forms the dividing line between the two faces, and the remaining routes are on the west face.

Chouca Rib   60 metres   Very Difficult   (21.1.74)
The first rib to the right of *The Buttress* gives some interesting climbing, although it is escapable at several places.
1 18m. The rib leads to a ledge; continue up a steeper section above on good holds. Belay round the pinnacle.
2 12m. Make an awkward move to gain a ledge on the right, traverse right round an edge, and climb a corner to easier ground. Belay to a large prominent spike on the right.
3 21m. From the spike, make an ascending traverse right to the edge. Move back left up a ramp above a steep wall until a long stride can be made across a slab to easy ground. Climb slabs to a large ledge and belay in a shallow chimney on the left.
4 9m. Climb a steep wall on the right of the chimney.

Picket Line   59 metres   Hard Severe   (17.2.74)
Pleasant though rather artificial climbing on a series of short steep walls to the right of *Chouca Rib*; pitch 2 takes a prominent wide crack in one of the walls. Start about 15 metres right of *Chouca Rib*, at a short vertical corner beside a small black hole.
1 17m. 4b. Climb the corner to a good foothold. Move left and go up to some spikes; then step back right and climb a short slab above to a grassy ledge. Climb the wall just right of the ledge to a corner on the left.
2 12m. Climb the wide crack in the steep wall above, and move left at the top to finish directly up a short tower with large grassy terraces above.

3 30m. Take the clean wall above on the right and move right at the top; then climb easy slabs to finish.

Curly Fringe Frown   39 metres   Very Severe   (17.3.74)
Interesting climbing on the best of the rock hereabouts. The second pitch takes the obvious left-slanting, clean arête. Below this is a black overhang cut by a crack. Start beneath the crack.
1 15m. 5a. Climb up to the crack in the overhang, surmount the overhang by a little rib just left of the crack, and step back right above. Then, as for *The Rockery*, go up the wall above on big holds to a ledge. Small flake belay below the arête.
2 24m. 4c. Climb 3 metres up a short slab directly above the belay, just left of the arête (good nut placement in crack on the left). Traverse right to a good small spike on the arête, and climb the wall right of the arête following a leftward line up the edge to the top. Finish more easily to a sloping grassy ledge and a large block belay.

The Rockery   51 metres   Severe   (1966)
A meandering line, aiming for the clean section of rock to the right of an oak tree. Start a metre up left of the huge block at the start of *Goat Walk* – there is a black overhang on the left.
1 12m. 4a. Follow the weakness leading leftwards over the overhangs to a spike; then climb directly up the wall on good holds to a ledge (small flake belay) below a steep arête.
2 24m. 4a. Go easily right and climb a corner for 3 metres. Make a move left and continue up the steep wall until easier climbing above leads to a large sloping grassy ledge and a large block belay.
3 15m. On the left is a wall with a niche in it. Gain the niche, and move out right over steps to broken rock and then the top.

Goat Walk   42 metres   Moderate
Start by a huge block beneath the rib to the right of *The Rockery*.
1 21m. Climb the slabby edge of the rib to a ledge on the left. Block belay above.
2 21m. Surmount the wall directly behind the belay on big holds to a ledge. Climb the left edge of the smooth wall above to grass (spike belay higher up).

Black Monday   20 metres   Very Severe   4c †   (11.89)
Start around the corner and about 15 metres right of *Curly Fringe Frown*. Climb a black corner and finish directly up the bulging centre of the black headwall.

Col Crag
OS Ref 644 067
This small bouldering crag is found at the eastern side of the saddle which divides the two highest points It has long been used for bouldering and top-roping; a year or two ago, bolt belays were installed (it is thought, by a local outdoor centre), but many have now been removed.

Approach. From the lay-by at OS Ref 649 075, follow the farm track uphill heading southwards; when the track finishes, bear right and continue by path uphill. As the main bulk of Craig yr Aderyn comes into view another path turns left in a southerly direction. After 200 metres the crag is seen on the left. Approach time – 15 minutes.

The crag faces north-west and is a well-sheltered spot. A short walk in and pleasant surroundings with views of Cadair Idris make this an ideal afternoon/evening bouldering area. A good picnic site and safe for the family while you move over stone! The rock is excellent and characterized by fingery edges or good jugs. The protection is only moderate; however, given the height and grade of most of the routes this does not pose much of a problem. All routes were climbed solo on the first ascent.

Lion Bastard   8 metres   Very Severe 5a   (12.8.97)
Step off the boulder at the left end of the crag and take a line up the white slab, utilizing the three horizontal breaks and left and right vertical cracks.

Little Tommy Pickles   12 metres   E2 5b   (11.96)
Start below and right of a large boulder. Without using cracks to either side, follow a series of small edges and crimps, and make a delicate move to gain a standing-position in the obvious scoop. Exit direct to finish on larger holds. No protection.

Ageneration   12 metres   Very Difficult   (11.96)
Start at the prominent rock steps leading to the grass ramp. Climb easily to gain the rightward-trending cleft, and finish as for *St Benet's Rd*.

Roger Rabbit   12 metres   Very Severe 4c   (13.8.97)
From 1 metre right of *Ageneration*, go directly up and pull over the small overhang onto the slab/rib; finish direct.

St Benet's Rd   12 metres   Very Difficult   (11.96)
Follow the crack 1 metre left of *White Streak Rib* until it develops into a series of cracks leading to a finish in the wide cleft above.

White Streak Rib   11 metres   Very Severe 4b   (11.96)
Just right of centre of the crag is a prominent rib with a white streak running down its right-hand side. Pull onto the rib and follow it to the top: precarious moves at mid height.

Chucky Vinster   11 metres   Very Difficult   (11.96)
From the rib, semi-layback the rightward-rising elephant's ear. Follow the faint groove to finish on good holds directly above *White Streak Rib*.

Minor Crags East and South of Cadair

Several small outcrops and quarries lying to the east and south of the main mountain groups have been developed, mostly since publication of the 1988 guide. They are presented here in a north-east to south-west line, starting above the south-west corner of Lake Bala between the extremities of the Aran and Arennig ranges, and roughly following the A494 from Llanuwchllyn to Dolgellau and thence the A487 to Machynlleth.

Creigiau Llyn-gwern   Marsh Lake Crags   OS Ref 848 284

[Map page 34.] This sits on the hillside near Llanuwchllyn and can be easily spotted up on the left as you drive from Dolgellau. Leave the main road by a track south of the crag and follow this down to the railway embankment. Take the embankment through a gate and park carefully on the edge of the bank before the forest below the crag (by a stream crossing). Head off up the hill, contouring around the west edge of the forest to reach a stone wall, which is followed rightwards to a stile. There is some good bouldering below the crag, which lies steeply along the incline of the hill. First seen is the square blank leaning wall at the bottom end of the cliff. The arête just left has one route.

☆**Would the Real Owner Step Forward**   18 metres   Severe   †   (2.7.2000)
Take the arête to the ramp leading leftward and up to the big ledge. A second pitch has been added up the groove in the short wall above.

Roaring Forties   16 metres   Hard Very Severe 5a †   (2.7.2000)
Ascend the hillside across the blueberry bushes to the prow and crack left of the preceding route. Climb the prow and roof direct to belay on a large flake far back on the ledge above.

The final wall at the top of the crag has a rightward-running ramp below it, from which the next two routes start.

☆☆**Being Anita**   18 metres   E2 5c †   (14.2.2001)
The excellent hand-jamming crack in the left of the wall is gained via the ramp. Very steep and sustained. Belay well back by a boulder by a short wall on the hilltop.

☆☆**Face in the Clouds**   18 metres   E3 5c †   (14.2.2001)
The left-facing groove next right is a bolder, yet equally enjoyable route. After a couple of moves up the crack of *Being Anita*, pull out right into the groove. Labour up past a good peg; then run it out to the top on good holds. Very sustained.

Rhobell Fawr   Big Saddle End

The Rhobells form a small north-to-south chain between the Rhinogau to the west and the Aran to the east. The southernmost, and main, rocky peak is easily accessible from the A494; and low on its eastern flank lies a small crag complex on which a few routes have been found.

It is a pleasant sunny location facing south-east that is reached by leaving the road at Aran Hall school near Rhydymain. Turn right where the road divides, pass through a gate on the same road, and then take thr right fork. The track is followed through two more gates into the forest until the rocks come into view up on the left about 200 metres away. A gully stream separates the two crags.

Fridd Craig Fach   Little Crag Intake   OS Ref 794 253

Sentina   18 metres   Very Severe 4b †   (5.7.97)
Begin on the left side of the left-hand buttress. Climb the slabby rib beneath an overhanging block. Carefully ascend the right side of the block and continue up the steep narrow corner to pull out left at the top. Finish up the bottomless groove.

Cherry Picker   16 metres   E2 5c †   (12.7.1999)
The shield of rock on the left of the right-hand crag is reached via the easy slab left of the deep crack. The centre of the shield is hard and bold.

A Hole Full of Cherries   15 metres   Very Severe 4c †   (12.7.1999)
The slab over on the right-hand side of the crag is followed through its centre past good pockets to a tricky finish in a great position.

Tyddyn Garreg   Rocky Dwelling   OS Ref 756 176

The Quakers Burial Ground. This fine lump of rock sits just south of Dolgellau, two minutes drive off the main road with parking by the rock. The owner of Tyddyn Garreg allows access to his land at present, but it is a courtesy to call at the house and ask first.

★An Answer from Limbo   10 metres   E4 6a   (28.8.2000)
At the left-hand side of the left-facing wall is a short right-facing corner below a short roof. The corner is gained directly on tiny holds. Small *RPs* protect the tricky and strenuous pull through the roof to an easier finish.

Quakermass   10 metres   Very Severe 4c   (1.7.2000)
Gain the sloping ledge on the arête next right before tricky balancing up and right leads to a good hold above (protection). Continue up left on large ledges.

★Three Men in an Oat   10 metres   E3 6a   (1.7.2000)
The groove next right is taken direct with the help of a small wedge-shaped block up and right. Follow the groove to a problem finish at the square slot.

Oating for Beginners   10 metres   Hard Severe   (1.7.2000)
The crack to the oak tree is safe and pleasant enough until the camouflaged finish.

★Oat Race 10 metres E1 5c (1.7.2000)
The obvious steep crack leads to a niche and gear, above which the climbing eases slightly.

☆☆X-Man 10 metres E4 6b † (25.8.2000)
The centre of the leaning wall next right is ferocious and fingery. Once the left end of the narrow ledge is reached some more powerful moves above gain the small fault in the big flat ledge. Small *RPs* probable. Finish as for *Oat Race*.

★Wobble to the Ledge of Hedge 10 metres E1 5b (1.7.2000)
The rounded edge forming the right edge of the *X-Man* wall leads to a good spike and, in turn, the perfect finger-crack via a high rockover. Finish leftwards from the large ledge as for *Oat Race*.

Minllyn Quarry Lake-edge Quarry OS Ref 853 139

The junction, two miles east of Dolgellau between the A487 and the A470 is known as Cross Foxes. From here, follow the A470 east (signposted Newtown) for about five miles to the hamlet of Minllyn and park in the large area behind the very old garage on the west side of the road. Take the forest trail north, parallel to the road, until a left exit appears. Follow this up through the woods to where it swings right and a footpath branches off left. The path rises very steeply up to a plateau and some old works buildings, behind which there is a small quarried hole with no worthwhile walls. Continue up the hill to the main quarry, the bottom of which is easily reached by a scree scramble.

The red wall between the two tunnels has two bolt-lines.

Red Dwarf 14 metres E2 5c † (15.6.91)
Climb up past two bolts on the left. Crux passing the first; finish direct past the second.

Dark Star 14 metres E2 5c † (15.6.91)
The bolt-line right of *Red Dwarf*. Crux passing the second bolt; finish up a short groove.

☆☆Zone of Totality 26 metres E4 6a F6c † (7.4.98)
[Photo page 464a.] The long and steep slab facing east has a safe, clean, and fine technical climb which finshes at a double-bolt chain lower-off. The difficulties are mainly in the middle but the route gives interesting climbing throughout.

Obi-Wan 30 metres E4 5c † (20.9.86)
The obvious curving groove in the wall round left from *Borderman* and then the slab just right of the arête. Now woefully overgrown. Climb the groove and then go right to the obvious ledge near the arête. Move rightwards round the arête to a good foothold and two pegs. Technical climbing leads up to a good foothold and another peg in a shot-hole. Go

up and right to a good hold, then back left to the tree. Climb to the ledge; then traverse right past some dangerous rock to finish up *Borderman*.

Borderman   30 metres   E3 5c †   (27.5.86)
The corner-groove with an overhang low down is lost below thick wet green slime.

There are two short routes on a small slab on the front edge of the quarry.

Ah-Ha   11 metres   Difficult   (26.5.86)
Climb the clean, easy-angled slab 5 metres left of *Fringe Benefit* direct to the top.

Fringe Benefit   11 metres   Difficult   (26.5.86)
Climb the obvious thin diagonal crack; then go straight up to finish.

Craig y Llam   Crag of the Hawk   OS Ref 755 135
From Cross Foxes, follow the A487 south for 2 miles to the pass, where the crag appears above. From a car-park on the western side of the pass overlooking Tal y Llyn, walk back up the road a little, and then take a path up and onto the ridge that rises south-westwards above the crag.

Craig y Llam is approximately 90 metres high and faces north-north-west, looking across to the slopes of Mynydd Moel. Its lower 45 metres are heavily vegetated and most routes start above this vegetated band. The most obvious feature is a huge green ramp cutting across the crag from right to left. This is the line taken by *Gate of the Winds*. To its left is a very steep wall undercut at the base. To the right of the ramp the crag is more scrappy, although the top is guarded by a band of overhangs.

All routes on the main cliff except the first and last are easily reached by a 45-metre abseil from the edge of the cliff, which is very close to the top of the ridge and the approach path.

White Rock   91 metres   Very Severe   (5.7.80)
The white slab which bounds the left-hand side of the crag. The rock is dubious in places. Start at a tree on the left-hand side of the buttress.
1 46m. 4a. Climb up to the right to the foot of an arête with a corner on its left-hand side. Move right to the arête and climb steeply to the white slab in a good position. Continue more easily and belay on the left where the rock steepens.
2 24m. 4b. Climb rightwards to the foot of a flake crack. Follow this until able to move right to an overhung stance (nut belays).
3 21m. 4a. Return left; then follow the slabs to the top, finishing on the left at the final tower.

Judge and Two Convicts   37 metres   E1 5b   (27.9.80)
The big groove at the left-hand side of the crag. Start from the ledge at the foot of the approach abseil. Climb the left-slanting groove a metre left of the groove of *Bomber* to a peg. Make some awkward moves, passing a

Philip Gleeson

Craig y Llam

1	White Rock	VS
2	Roumagoou	E2
3	Judge and Two Convicts	E1
4	Bomber	E3
5	Larry the Lamb	E4
6	Tyburn Gate	E3
7	Psyclone	E4
8	Gates of the Wind	HVS

second peg, to exit on a slab on the left (the girdle crosses here). Continue straight up a short steep wall to ledges. Climb the corner above on good holds to the top.

Bomber   37 metres   E3 5c   (5.7.80)
The wide vertical crack running the full height of the crag, from just left of the quartz coffin block of *Tyburn Gate*. Some poor rock. Start as for *Tyburn Gate* and go up to the block. Stretch left and climb with difficulty to the base of a chimney. Climb this and the groove above until a step right can be made to a ledge. Take the steep crack above to the top.

Larry the Lamb   40 metres   E4 5c   (10.6.95)
A direct version of *Tyburn Gate*, on a logical natural line. Some care is required with the rock on its central portion. Follow *Tyburn Gate* to the 'coffin block'. Surmount the bulge (*in-situ* thread and 'bomber' *Rock 4* above the site of the defunct peg runner); then proceed direct over the next bulge to gain the foot of a crack and open groove between *Bomber* and *Tyburn Gate*. Climb the crack and groove direct, crossing the leftward traverse of *Tyburn Gate*. Pull over the capping bulge; then move left to exit up the final easy crack of *Tyburn Gate*.

★★★**Tyburn Gate**   40 metres   E3 5c   (26.6.80)
A brilliant groove-line up the centre of the undercut face; sustained, technical, and exposed. Take the approach abseil to ledges next to a pinnacle which almost reaches the lip of a roof. The pinnacle is topped by a quartz, coffin-shaped block. To the right of this block is a cantilevered block. Reach the 'coffin block' by a traverse in from the left. Above is a 1-metre roof; pull over this (good *Rock 4*) and traverse right on the lip of the overhang to good holds in a niche. Move up right and climb the obvious groove (peg) to a slab on the left. Traverse left across the slab to a hanging rib, gain the rib, and climb this to the top.

★★**Psyclone**   42 metres   E4   (10.6.95)
A splendid route, replete with atmosphere and mountain character. Start 10 metres right of *Tyburn Gate* beneath the large roofs.
1 15m. 6a. Move up the initial easy slab to the roofs. Pull through the obvious line, and bear strenuously leftwards (*in-situ* thread), then back right along a crack to a good belay in a vertical crack.
2 27m. 5c/6a. Climb the crack to a place to ponder beneath a leftward-rising overlap. Move up to the overlap (peg runner); then traverse intricately leftwards across overlapping slabs to jugs and a thread runner. Cross leftwards again around a bulge to join and finish up *Tyburn Gate*.

★**Gate of the Winds**   41 metres   Hard Very Severe 5a   (4.5.80)
The obvious green left-trending ramp is the main feature of the crag. Abseil to the start at the foot of the ramp. Climb the chimney on the right of the slab to an overhang. Traverse left to the edge and climb the steep wall (crux), trending left to reach the upper ramp. Continue left in the obvious line to finish up a short groove to the top.

Zone of Totality (F7a) Minllyn Quarry
Climber: Terry Taylor   Photo: Taylor col.

Choose Life (F7a) Bryn Eglwys Quarry
Climber: Terry Taylor   Photo: Taylor col.

First Ascents

A number of routes, mostly on Craig Cywarch, recorded between 1951 and 1973 were not considered worth describing for various reasons, mainly being very vegetated, very short, or always wet and slimy. Their names alone are unlikely to inspire climbers to spend time 'rediscovering' them but, for the record, these were: **Langwek, The Nose of the Old Man of Cywarch, Garden Path, Pigsty, Capability, Dirty Knave, Van Wall, Solo Crack, Barbican, The Hoe, Flake Wall, Postscript, Gardener's Rib, Mint Cake, Compensation, The Green Sweater, Christening, Odin, Encore, Ace of Spades, Dungeon Flea, Tourist Gully, Oak Arête.** First ascensionists involved included: D Kay, R E Lambe, V Leese, J P Downes, A B Knox, M H Jahn, R E Kendal, P Burden, J A Sennett, S J Salt, F R Edgar, P M Edgar, A J J Moulam, G J Lambe, A C Scott, J G Wilding, P Chalmers, J A Sumner, J P Henrickson, A J Swindale, L Pedrisa. Full details are preserved in the 1988 Climbers' Club *Mid-Wales* guide.

For many routes in this guide, any records there may once have been of the first ascensionists are lost, and these routes are not included in this list. Often it has been possible to identify at least an approximate date, and where this is the case it is printed on the route-title lines in the main text in the usual way.

Certain climbers, most notably but not exclusively the two principal authors, have been meticulous in recording the styles of their ascents – in particular the extent to which prior knowledge of the moves and available protection was gained by top-rope inspection, cleaning, or practice. As fashions change and what in one decade is regarded as cheating, at least when not declared, in the next becomes the norm (and *vice versa*), this always need to be viewed in the context of the period of the climb (and sometimes the nature of the crag). Nothing is to be deduced from the fact that others have not recorded these details; it has in the past not been general practice to do so, and any records that may have been made have probably simply been lost. Indeed, these pages are already numerous enough as they stand, and additional entries would have ensured that the book would never leave the ground. Nevertheless, the details that *are* included contribute to the overall picture of activity, and set an example which others should be encouraged to follow.

'Lead-solo' signifies the use of the USA-built, self-belaying device called *Soloist*; all ascents were made ground-up, all gear being placed as for a conventional lead.

AL and VL, as usual, mean alternate or varied leads.

1888 May 18	**Cyfrwy Arête**	O G Jones (solo)
1895 May 18	**Great Gully** (Craig Cau)	W P Haskett Smith, O G Jones, E L W Haskett Smith
	A section of this climb fell away shortly after the first ascent.	
1895 May 19	**East Gully** (Craig Cau)	W P Haskett Smith, W E Sumpner, O G Jones
1900 Sept 3	**North Arête**	T K Rose, F W Rose
1902 Aug 28	**East Gully** (Tŵr Du)	S Ridsdale, H L Jupp, J Phillips
1902 Aug 29	**West Gully**	S Ridsdale, H L Jupp, J Phillips
1903 June	**Pencoed Pillar**	M Dalton, H G Dalton
1907	**Great Gully** (Cywarch)	Unknown party

1907	**Little Gully** (Cywarch) A H Bramley, P S Minor, C H Pickstone
1907	**North Gully** S Houghton, G T Ewen and others
	All three gullies were climbed over the Easter period.
1928	**Kirkus's Climb** C F Kirkus, C G Kirkus
1932 Sept	**Milky Way, Septentrionale** R Elfyn Hughes
1934 Sept	**Betimes** R Elfyn Hughes
1935	**The South Ridge of Rhinog Fach** S Styles, G Garrard
1939	**Lone Buttress** C W F Noyce
1941	**Devious** R C Evans, E Ker
1941	**Slab and Arête** R C Evans
1941	**Souwester Gully** R C Evans
1942 June 30	**Steric Slab** E L Furness, J H S Gilham
1947	**Bombers Wall Route One, Bombers Wall Route Two** P W W Nock, D Nock, R D S Carpendale
	Pitch 1 of Route Two was added later by A J J Moulam, G D Roberts in 1966.
1947	**Jingling Wall** P W W Nock, F H Keenlyside, J Cairns
1947	**Long Climb** P W W Nock, et al.
	Pitch 2 variation by J R Lees, D W Walker in October 1956.
1950	**Kurzweg** P R J Harding, N L Horsfield
1951 June 19	**Table Direct** R E Davies, H E Chatburn
1951 Oct 7	**South Chimneys** S Styles, H Morris
1952 Aug 30	**Central Route** R E Lambe, M A Ounn
1952 Dec 13	**Chic** A J J Moulam, W R Craster, C W Brasher
	Variations have been done by many people. In particular, R Elfyn Hughes wandered all over this face in the 30s. The theme song for this ascent was 'California, Here I Come'.
1952	**Conwy Corner** S Wignall, H Berkeley
1953 April 5	**Creeper** M J Harris, J Neill
1953 April 5	**Slick** A J J Moulam, J A F Watson, R G Hargreaves
	Some of this had been climbed by R Elfyn Hughes in 1932.
1953 April 11	**One for the Road** A J J Moulam, J M Barr
	Pitches 5 and 6 were added by J Neill, A T Griffith in 1955
1953 April 12	**Bent, Orange Outang, Pied Piper** A J J Moulam, J M Barr
	A line similar to Bent had been climbed by R Elfyn Hughes in 1932.
1953 April 15	**Pinky** I G McNaught-Davies, C W Brasher
	The upper pitches were done on the same day by T F Dawe, D Thomas, E M Herbert.
1953 May 17	**Diagonal Arête** R E Lambe, S H G Taylor (AL)
	The route was originally done by climbing the first three pitches of Central Route. G Jarvis, R J Thorndyke, R Knox added pitches 1 and 2 on 24.8.70.
1953 June 2	**Taith y Pererin** G Williams, D H Jones
1953 June 2	**Y Drafel** D H Jones, G Williams
1953 June 13	**Steilweg** R E Lambe, R O L Clarke
1953 June 14	**Incapability** E Byne, C W Ashbury
1953 July 19	**Block** A J J Moulam, J H Longland, J V Rusher
	Pitches 4 to 6 had been climbed by C Bramfitt a month earlier.
1953 July 27	**Y Gelynen** R Davies, G Williams
1953 Aug 16	**Africa Rib, Usher's Dilemma** R Buckland, J Neill
	The Eagle Finish to the latter was climbed by J R Lees, K C Gordon in April 1961.
1953 Aug 16	**Depression Direct** M J Harris
	The first pitch only; pitch 2 added by E Beard in 1965.
1953 Sept 6	**Double Criss, Thin Wall Special** C J S Bonington, C W Brasher
1953 Sept 26	**Oread** E Marshall, K A Wright, R Simpson
	Pitch 3, which is more in keeping with the rest, added by A J J Moulam, R E Lambe on 1.4.56. The original way took the line of Will-o'-the-Wisp.
1953 Dec 12	**Bay Groove** A J J Moulam, J M Barr
1953 Dec 12	**Original Route** A J J Moulam, G J Sutton
1953 Dec 12	**Pocked Wall** M J Harris, J Neill
1953 Dec 12	**Route II** (Alltrem) C W S Pigott, J M Barr
1953	**Direct Route** W A Trench, G D Roberts
1953	**Grey Slab** D H Jones, G Williams
1953	**The Nurgler** R James, C T Jones
	Pitch 2 variation by J Appleby, D Craig in July 1996.
1954 Oct	**Western Gully Arête** R Handley, B Cook

1955 June 4	**Buzzard's Balcony**	J A Sumner, G F Williams (AL)
1955 July 9	**Stygian Wall**	J A Sumner, D M Adcock (AL; 1 pt aid)
1955 July	**Asahel**	R James, R L Roberts
1955 July	**Reptile Route**	P Langley, R James

Via the nose to the left of Africa Rib.

1955 Sept 21	**Flake Wall**	D D Steward, T Kellett
1955 Oct 22	**First Visit**	H Smith, C T Jones, K J Clarke
1955 Oct 22	**Hope Street**	A B Afford, E Griffin
1955 Nov 27	**Clubs**	R J R Vereker, J D Nicholson
1955 Dec 4	**Cerebos**	J A Sumner, A Mills
1956 March 31	**Black Wall**	W J Finlay, A B Knox

Pitches 3 and 4 were added by W J Finlay and R E Lambe on 3.4.56.

1956 March 31	**Hopsit**	A J J Moulam, R E Lambe

Aid was used to gain the tree on pitch 3.

1956 April 2	**First Anniversary**	R E Lambe, Mrs R E Lambe
1956 April 3	**Sifta**	J A Sumner, D G Chisholm, W J K Finlay, R E Lambe
1956 May 26	**Acheron**	A J J Moulam, R E Lambe

*A fine piece of route finding. Pitch 1 added 30.5.70 by A J Swindale,
A B Knox. The original way took the wet start of Vulcan.*

1956 May 26	**Jungle**	D T Roscoe, A W Newton
1956 May 26	**Relaxation**	A J J Moulam, R E Lambe
1956 May 27	**Bluebell Babylon**	A J J Moulam, R E Lambe
1956 May 27	**Bubble Wall**	J A Sumner, D M Adcock
1956 June 17	**Midlander**	P M Biven, H T H Peck
1956 June 24	**Obsession**	A B Black, H Gartside, S Grantham, G Payne

*A climb called Route 1 done in 1959 followed approximately the same line
by R Handley and W Richardson.*

1956 June	**Pisa**	A B Black, E Swann, J Alexander
1956 June	**Quartz Rib**	A B Black, E Swann, J Alexander
1956 July 10	**Square Chimney, Square-Cut Gully**	A Mills, T Wheeler, R Hancock
1956 July	**Purge**	J A Sumner, D M Adcock

*First complete and continuous ascent. Pitch 1 had been climbed by
D G Chisholm, A B Knox, on 10.6.56, and pitch 2 by J A Sumner,
D G Chisholm on 1.4.56. 'About a dozen pegs required for each pitch. Some
are in place. Some wedges may also be found useful.' A2, mainly on etriers.
Climbed with two points of aid on the first pitch and one point on the second
by N Robertson, D McGonigal in June 1969. Climbed free by J A Sumner,
R Whitehouse on 29.8.79.*

1956 Aug 5	**Thung**	G F Williams, D M Gilbert, A Mills

*Pitch 1 was added by A Ward and A J Swindale 5.7.69. The original way took
to the trees and vegetation on the right.*

1956 Aug 8	**South Face Crack**	B C Roach, W Drew
1956 Sept 18	**Penamnen Groove**	R D Downes, J E M Clark (1 pt aid)
1956 Sept 22	**Jack o' Diamonds**	M H Jahn, R E Kendal (AL)
1956 Sept 23	**Styx**	D M Adcock, G F Williams
1956 Nov 4	**Portcullis**	A B Knox, R E Lambe, K H Higgins
1957 May 5	**Triad**	R Handley, F Allen, J N Millward
1957 May 26	**Knockdown**	A B Knox, J P Downes (AL)
1957 June 23	**Andromeda**	S R G Bray, M Blamey

The ubiquitous R Elfyn Hughes climbed a similar line in 1932.

1957 June 23	**Shady Saunter**	A B Knox, J P Downes, L S Galpin
1957 July	**Mean Feat**	R James, P Vaughan
1957 Sept 1	**Twr**	R Elfyn Hughes, C West, R West
1957 Nov 10	**Ceramic Chimney**	T W Goodwin, G A Martin
1958 Jan 2	**Pigtail Grooves**	T J Fraser, R Elfyn Hughes
1958 March 1	**Ronkle Boot Chimney**	G Martin, T Goodwin, J Downes, N Smyth, A B Knox

*'This poor inoffensive route was beaten into submission very promptly by a
very strong party who gave it no quarter, after being repulsed by a couple of
other lines on the same crag, which were found too steep (i e overhanging).'*

1958 March 23	**Nichevo**	M J Harris, R J Jones
1958 May 31	**S & D**	G A Martin, T W Goodwin, A B Knox, M Andrews
1958 June 15	**Romulus**	G Rees, A F Mason

1958 June 20	**Agog** R L Roberts, E Thomas, G Dwyer, R Dwyer
	The Tower Finish was climbed by J R Lees, R Wilson in April 1961.
1958 July 5	**The White Streak** G Dwyer, R L Roberts
1958 July 22	**Y Gilfach** R L Roberts, G Dwyer, E Thomas
1958 July	**By-ways, Crossways, Scrub Way, The Bolder Way** J Richardson, D Williams
	Pitch 1 variation of The Bolder Way by J F Kerry in December 1967.
1958 Aug	**Bundu** G A Martin, J G Wilding
1958 Aug	**Wig Walk** J G Wilding, G A Martin
1958 Sept 7	**Inverted Staircase** R James, A F Mason, G Rees
1958	**Daufaen and Honeysuckle Corner** R L Roberts, G Dwyer, E Thomas
	Pitches 1 and 2. Honeysuckle Corner was climbed by J R Lees and G Moffatt on 1.4.61.
1959 Feb 21	**Jones's Crack** C T Jones
	The original route up the buttress, Tarry, was climbed by M J Harris, J Neill on 16.8.53.
1959 May 17	**Dena** K A Podmore, G Bailey, R Jones
1959 May	**Guano Pinnacle** C J S Bonington, M White
	Bonington also just failed on The Bastion which was not climbed until 1975.
1959 June 8	**Route 2** (Cyfrwy) D Burgess, J R Allen
	The Pusher Man variation was climbed by G R Herus and J A Sumner on 14.9.74.
1959 June 8	**Route Central** J Brown, H Smith
	One point of aid; climbed free by J A Sumner and N Cauldwell June 1981
1959 June	**Lightning Visit** R James, C T Jones
	Alltrem Arête variation climbed 19.6.89 by W Shakell, G Carter
1959 Oct 10	**Waspie** J R Lees, R H Newby
1959	**Hades** C J S Bonington, I Douglas
	A line which had been attempted many times without success by different parties. Pitch 1 previously climbed by D Adcock and A B Knox in 1958.
1960 April 17	**Dorcon** R H Newby, J R Lees
1960 April 23	**Fratricide Wall** C T Jones, A S Jones, A Daffern (1 pt aid)
1960 June 7	**Panorama** J R Lees, I F Cartledge, R H Newby, K C Gordon
1960 June	**Hyrib** J R Allen, W Hayden, F Allen
1960 July 2	**Rib and Slab** D Burgess, J R Allen
	Variation to pitch 4 C Wells, I Smith 20.8.94.
1960 July 2	**Ritander** D Burgess, J R Allen
1960 July 3	**Diagonal Climb** P R Janney, J R Lees, I F Cartledge
1960 Aug 13	**Waterloo** I F Cartledge, K C Gordon, J R Lees
	With a point of aid. FFA by E Stone 1989.
1960 Aug 27	**The Spade** J R Lees, I F Cartledge
1960 Nov 13	**Slack** I F Cartledge, J R Lees
	The alternative finish was climbed by N Gough in May 1966.
1960 Dec 4	**Mars** I F Cartledge, J R Lees, K C Gordon
1960 Dec 4	**Orion** K C Gordon, I F Cartledge, J R Lees
1961 March 20	**Lavaredo** R James, K Forder, I F Campbell
1961 June 9	**Space below My Feet** J R Lees, D W Walker (aid slings)
1961 Sept 16	**The Mole** K H Forder, E Forder
1961	**Leviathan** C T Jones, G Holmes
	The Direct Finish was climbed by C Knowles, A Bateman on 31.7.83.
1961	**Overhanging Cracks** J Brown, D Thomas (2pts aid)
1962 April 22	**Cyclops** (Gigfran, Lledr) B D Wright, C E Davies
1962 April 22	**Titan** C E Davies, B D Wright, D Alcock
1962 May	Three unrecorded climbs were made on y Foel Penolau by father and son team, son leading, A N Gough and R E J Gough.
1962 June 10	**The Last Post** C T Jones, R F Jones (1 pt aid)
1962 July 8	**Slate** J E Roberts
1962	**Ivory Tower, Rose Corner, Tanat, King of Maybe, Thunder Road** B Phillips, P Hill, J Jenks
1962	**Pedestal Route** R Owen, D Rudder (AL)
1962	**Siesta** F Williams, A N Other
	The start of real activity at Craig yr Arderyn.
1963 March 19	**Cancer** J E Roberts, C Bloor
1963 April 3	**Sloose** J Brown, G D Verity

1963 May 1	**The Trench**	J Brown, G D Verity, G Mansell
1963 May 2	**Piledriver, The Wing**	J Brown, G Mansell
1963 June 8	**Abdication**	G Mansell, G D Roberts, M E McMorland
1963 June 8	**Grass**	J Brown, J Smith, C E Davies, D Alcock
1963 Aug 5	**White Ribbon**	B Wright, D Wright, M Perrin

Pitch 2 was climbed previously by B Wright and J Hunt via the grass terrace in June 1961.

1963 Dec 27	**Pip's Present**	J Murray, N Gough (AL)
1963 Dec 27	**White Tabs**	G Griffiths, E Davies, A Owen

Variation finish J G Trumper, B Grimston on 17.3.85.

1964 May	**Daisy Belle**	L K Forsey, D Davies (AL)

Originally with a lot of aid. FFA probably by J Codling and party 1978.

1964 June 10	**The Beak** (Aderyn)	A Howard, A Green
1964 June 14	**The Gizzard, The Talon**	A Howard, A Waterhouse (the latter route AL)
1964 June 28	**Whale**	H Banner, A J J Moulam
1964 June	**Mother's Pride**	J Wilding, C U Cockshott (AL), C U Cockshott
1964 July 19	**Mistral**	N Gough, W Johnson
1964 Aug 30	**Grad**	D J Steele, A B Knox (AL)
1964 Aug 30	**Trend**	D W Matthews, E J Perrin
1964 Oct	**Ectoplasm**	N Gough, A Hughes
1964 Oct	**Main Wall Climb**	G Arnold, J F Kerry
1964 Nov 22	**The Diagonal**	A Howard, D Davies (AL)
1964 Nov	**Plasma**	N Gough, A Hughes
1964 Dec 25	**Traditional Route**	H Drasdo, N Drasdo, G D Roberts, M Feeley

After three pitches the team left to attend a Christmas lunch. They returned later in the day to add the finishing pitch and a variation.

1964	**Ash Tree Slabs**	N Gough, S Glass
1964	**Cat Walk**	N Gough, A Hughes
1964	**Civetta**	J V Anthoine, R James

With a sling for aid; climbed free by G Tinning in 1979.

1964	**Leviathan Direct**	A J J Moulam
1965 May 16	**Curl**	D J Steele, A B Knox
1965 July 3	**Wright's Route**	B Wright, J Hunt
1965 Oct 9	**Vestix**	R Newcombe, G Ashton

Pitches 2 and 3 had been climbed by R James and E Beard respectively.

1965 Dec 26	**Christmas Retreat**	J G Wilding, R J Thorndyke
1965	**Congl**	R James, B James, R Rowlands
1965	**Mur Dena**	R James, P Fletcher, D Rowlands
1966 March 19	**Nazgul**	D T Roscoe, B D Wright
1966 March 19	**Northerner**	D K Scott, R Gillies

Two points of aid. On the second ascent a block came off with the second below the aid peg. The block was used as one of the main holds for the leader. The route has not yet had a third ascent.

1966 May 19	**Strider**	D T Roscoe, B D Wright
1966 May 28	**Tririri**	J F Murray, C J James

The variation finish was climbed by A D Erskine and S Ramsden on 29.3.97.

1966 May	**Deceiver**	D T Roscoe, B D Wright
1966 May	**Nardus**	M Anthoine, I F Campbell (AL)
1966 June 4	**Sheep's Climb**	A B Knox, J Wiltshire, S Bingham, J Lockett, J Shaw
1966 June 4	**Spartan**	D Cuthbertson, G Caine (AL)

A fierce lead. A peg was placed for protection above the overhang.

1966 June 5	**Flanker**	A B Knox, S Bingham
1966 June 19	**Rib and Groove**	S Tunney, C Osborne, R Poole
1966 July 7	**Central Gully, Dentist's Debut**	A J J Moulam, P F J H O'Donoghue
1966 Sept 3	**Peal**	R Fairbrother, E R Fairbrother
1966 Sept 3	**Recuperation**	J A Sumner, S A Sumner
1966 Sept 24	**Plankwalk**	M Boysen, J Jordan
1966 Sept 24	**Quartz Buttress**	A Nicholls, A Rhodes, D Little (AL)
1966 Sept 24	**The Arch**	J A Sumner, J C I Saxton
1966 Sept 25	**Aardvark**	M Boysen, A Williams, D Little

Shadow of Doubt variation climbed by A Hall, S Roberts in May 1996.

1966	**The Rockery**	W Baker with two OBSS pupils
1967 Jan 25	**Birthday Route**	D J Ashton, B J Blackhall
1967 April 1	**Rockerfeller**	R A Wilson, P Surfleet

1967 April 23	**Great Feet** R Newcombe, G Ashton
	Pitch 2 was climbed by R James, J M Benson, P H Benson in 1958.
1967 April	**Birdcage, The Jug** R A Wilson, P Surfleet
1967 April	**North Face Girdle** (Aderyn) R A Wilson, P Surfleet, P Doncaster
	Two points of aid; climbed free by K Bentham, D W Shaw 16.5.76
1967 April	**Strictus** M Anthoine, I F Campbell (AL)
1967 May 7	**Psycho** D T Roscoe, J M Brailsford
	One peg was used for aid at 20 feet and the crack was climbed mostly on inserted slings. FFA M Griffiths, 1980s.
1967 May 9	**Transect** A J J Moulam, H Drasdo (AL)
	The Direct Start was added later in the year by C T Jones with Moulam and Drasdo.
1967 May 11	**Gwydir Gully** A J J Moulam, H Drasdo (AL)
	A week or so later J Brown and C E Davies soloed the buttress to the left and joining the final pitch.
1967 May 13	**The Hump** A J J Moulam, H Drasdo
1967 May 20	**Tendency** N J Soper, J H Swallow, H Drasdo (AL)
1967 May 23	**Embargo** H Drasdo, R J Holroyd (AL)
1967 May 29	**Thumbelina** B St J Phillips, C Phillips
1967 May	**Shelob, The Ent** J Brown, C E Davies
1967 June 3	**The Nave** C T Jones, A J J Moulam, H Drasdo (VL)
1967 June 10	**Charon** J A Sumner, R Fairbrother
	Originally climbed with three points of aid. Climbed free by J Codling, G Davies 1.9.79.
1967 July 2	**Gay** A J J Moulam, N Drasdo, H Drasdo
1967 July 8	**Green Wall** (Alltrem) A J J Moulam, H Drasdo
1967 July 9	**Rolling Stone** P Treble, D Bone, J Kelley
1967 July 23	**China Shop** D Thornley, B Benson
1967 Aug 9	**Tykes Wall** J Barker
1967 Aug 27	**Slipway** J Ball, H Ball
1967 Aug 27	**Wendaway** A Shawe, J Booth (AL)
1967 Aug	**Inigo** M Anthoine, I F Campbell (AL)
1967 Sept 9	**Gangway** (Cae Coch) D Pownall, M A Reeves, J Booth (AL)
1967 Sept 24	**Lectern Direct** D Thornley, J A Sumner
	Originally climbed taking the vegetated start of the arch, and then known as Lectern, by J A Sumner, R Fairbrother, E R Fairbrother (AL) on 14.1.67.
1967 Oct 4	**Cave Arête** B St J Phillips, D Sneath, J W Morris
1967 Oct 15	**Dislocation** R J Eddington, J F Kerry
	With two points of aid. Climbed free in 1978 by M Griffiths, A Moller.
1968 May 11	**Girdle Traverse (Tap Rhygan Ddu)** D Thornley, J A Sumner (AL)
1968 May 25	**Restoration** J G Wilding, P J George
1968 May 26	**Crossover** B St J Phillips, M Phillips
1968 June 22	**Headcross** D R Headley, S Shallcross
1968 July 7	**Dunsinane** A B Knox, P Cockshott
1968 July 7	**Yoghurt Miscellaneous** S F Gleeson, S Shallcross, D R Headley, B Thomson
1968 July 27	**The Technician** D Thornley, J A Sumner (AL)
	Originally with three points of aid and called Crucifix. The aid (on the crux section of the groove) was whittled down from three pegs to one with shared efforts. Climbed free by J Codling.
1968 Aug 4	**Ring Wraith** R J Thorndyke, J P Downes
1968 Aug 4	**Yggdrasil** R E Lambe, F M Lambe, J C Coppard
1968 Aug 27	**The Gem** J A Sumner, J P Downes
1968 Aug 29	**The Grafter** J A Sumner, G Kirkham (AL)
	Originally climbed with 3 points of aid on the first pitch and two on the second. Climbed free by M Elwell and A Grondowski 12.4.80.
1968 Aug 30	**The Comedians** J A Webster, R J Thorndyke
1968 Aug 31	**The Wizard** A B Knox, H Lawton
1968 Sept 10	**Dinas Mawr Eliminate** J F Kerry, J Roberts
1968 Sept 13	**Sveinstock** D Thornley, D L Walker (1 pt aid)
1968 Sept 14	**Sickle Wall** R J Thorndyke, H Lawton
1968 Sept 17	**Half-Moon Crack** H Lawton, A B Knox

1968 Nov 3	**Doom** J A Sumner, A Gillis (AL)
	Several pegs were used on the first ascent.
1968	**Moss Rib** A J J Moulam, H Drasdo
1968	**Tight** A J J Moulam, E Hammond
1969 Jan 13	**Curry Wall** D G Peers, J E Brittain
1969 April 6	**Surrealistic** A J Swindale, G R Herus (AL)
1969 May 24	**Girdle Traverse (Sawdl y Graig), Gornik** J A Sumner, J Entwistle (AL)
1969 May 24	**Paper Back** R J Thorndyke, J A Lockett
	Three points of aid – all on nuts.
1969 May 24	**Room at the Top** J A Webster, R J Thorndyke (AL)
1969 May 24	**Scourge** G Kirkham, T Thorndyke
	Originally climbed with two pegs and a nut for aid. Climbed free by
	D Beetlestone, P Gibson, G Gibson 17.5.80.
1969 May 25	**Apollo** G Kirkham, A B Knox
	Pitch 1 was climbed the previous day by A B Knox, H Lawton.
1969 May	**Mochan** M Anthoine, A S Hunt (AL)
1969 June 4	**Taranu Crack** R J Thorndyke, L Foden, R D Cryer
1969 June 12	**Little Plum** L Noble, J M Brailsford, D T Roscoe
1969 June 12	**Red Wall Crack** J M Brailsford, D T Roscoe, L Noble
1969 June 13	**The Big Cleft** D Thornley, J A Sumner
	Pitches 1 and 2 climbed previously by G Jarvis and J Tooke Easter 1969.
1969 June	**Tenuous** M Boysen, M Anthoine
1969 July 12	**Phoebus** A B Knox, R E Lambe (AL)
1969 July 19	**Click** J A Sumner, J P Henrickson
1969 Aug 5	**Barad d'Ur** R J Thorndyke, J A Webster .
1969 Aug 9	**Girdle Traverse (Craig Llywelyn)** J A Sumner, D Thornley (AL)
	Pitch 7 added by F Van Den Broeche, J A Webster in August 1975.
1969 Aug 9	**Men of Kent** R J Thorndyke, J A Webster, T Thorndyke
	A peg and nut were initially used for aid to climb the steep wall direct on pitch 3.
1969 Sept 20	**Whirligig** R Thurman, J G Wilding
1969 Sept 27	**Keel Haul** J A Sumner, J P Henrickson
	Led after peg runner on pitch 2 had been placed by abseil.
1969 Sept 30	**The Whisper** J A Sumner, J P Henrickson
1969 Sept	**Galium** M Anthoine, D Alcock (AL)
1969 Oct 5	**Quartz Vein** G Jarvis, A B Knox
1969 Oct 5	**Troom** D Walker, A Ward
1969 Oct 11	**Hell's Gate** G Jarvis, L Nuttall
1969 Dec 7	**Lethe** J A Sumner, J P Henrickson
1969 Dec 26	**Flu '69** I R Tapley, A Ward
1969 Dec 27	**The Grey Citadel** G Jarvis, A B Knox
1969	**Titus** R Newcombe, G Ashton
1960s	**Academy** J Arthy, I Shaw, A N Other
1960s	**Arrowhead, Earthworm, Hangover** J F Kerry and party
	Including Left Variant to Hangover. Pat's Finish climbed by P Littlejohn,
	P Judge in February 1991 (this may well be the line of Justin Kendall's Big
	Burger claimed about the same time).
1960s	**First Encounter** H Banner, H Drasdo, Bill Wynn
1960s	**Gorki Groove** H Banner (1 pt aid)
1960s	**Illusion, Problem Wall** H Drasdo and party
1960s	**Metro** Metropolitan Police Force Team
1960s	**Precedent** A J J Moulam and party
	Whilst President of The Climbers' Club.
1960s	**Quercus's Route** A J J Moulam, H Drasdo
1960s	**The A5, Oak Tree Jug, Provo, Suede Slide** J F Kerry
1960s	**The Fate of Icarus, The Ramp, Irish Rover** J Arthy and party
1960s	**Ulex** H Drasdo, A J J Moulam
	Variation climbed by D Wrennall, C Shaw on 20.11.01.
1970 April 11	**Stronghold** J A Sumner, J P Henrickson, I R Tapley
1970 April 19	**Battlements** J A Sumner, I R Tapley (AL), J P Henrickson
1970 May 2	**Concorde** A Thorndyke, M la Forest
1970 May 10	**The Magic Dragon** R J Thorndyke, I R Tapley (AL)
	Pitch 5 added by R J Thorndyke, P Blatch on 26.5.73.
1970 May 17	**Scimitar** J A Sumner, A J Swindale
	Pitch 3 originally took the arête.

1970 May 17	**Where Eagles Dare** I R Tapley, R J Thorndyke (AL)
1970 May 25	**The Scythe** A B Knox, I R Tapley (AL)
1970 May 30	**Box Trick** J A Sumner, J P Henrickson
1970 June 6	**Vulcan** G Kirkham, J A Sumner (AL)

Pitches 1 to 4 previously climbed by G Kirkham, A Storey on 3.8.69.

1970 June 14	**Delli** A B Knox, R Chapman
1970 July 18	**The Little Red Helmet** R J Thorndyke, T Thorndyke
1970 Aug 8	**Inclination** A B Knox, A J Swindale
1970 Aug 8	**The Archer** A J Swindale, A B Knox
1970 Aug 23	**South West Arête** R J Thorndyke, G Jarvis (AL)
1970 Aug 24	**Oh Calcutta** G Jarvis, R J Thorndyke, A B Knox (AL)
1970 Aug 25	**Porcupine** G Jarvis, R J Thorndyke (AL)
1970 Aug 29	**Obvious** R J Thorndyke, T Thorndyke
1970 Aug 29	**Schnellweg, The Wall** J A Sumner, J P Henrickson

One point of aid on the latter. This route had been climbed by J A Sumner on 10.7.55 with the use of a top-rope on the last few feet.

1970 Aug 30	**Slanting Gully Grooves** D Burgess, J R Allen
1970 Aug 30	**Tamburlaine** R J Thorndyke, T Thorndyke (AL)
1970 Aug	**Buzzard's Nest Crack** D Shone, D Bishop
1970 Aug	**Silwood, Melangell** D Bishop, D Thomas (AL)

Probably climbed before.

1970 Sept 6	**Monolith (Gist Du)** R J Thorndyke, G Kirkham (AL)
1970 Sept	**The Perishers** R J Thorndyke, T Thorndyke (AL)
1970 Oct 18	**Tombstone Blues** G R Herus, R J Thorndyke (AL)
1970 Dec 20	**The Dome** J A Sumner, R Cully (AL)
1970	**Groan** R Newcombe, D Davies
1970	**Hironimo** J Hiron and party
1971 Feb 28	**Thin Man** J A Sumner, J P Henrickson
1971 March 27	**The Yellow Policeman** R Cully, J A Sumner (AL)
1971 April 11	**Grit** J A Sumner
1971 April 11	**Left-Hand Break, Tilt, The Nest** J A Sumner, J P Henrickson
1971 April 13	**Elephant Walk** A B Knox, I R Tapley (AL)
1971 April 18	**Hot Pants (Wrysgan)** J R Lamberstone, R Carrick
1971 April	**Porky** M Anthoine, N A Phillippe (AL)
1971 May 1	**The Overlap** J A Sumner, R J Thorndyke, R Cully

After inspection on a rope.

| 1971 May 2 | **Hot Pants (Gigfran, Cywarch)** D Mason, D Pawson |
| 1971 May 31 | **Jugs Groove** J A Sumner, G R Herus |

Originally climbed with two points of aid on the first pitch and two points on the second. Climbed free by J Codling, D Jones on 5.8.79.

1971 Sept 19	**Tribarfau** A B Knox, C G Powell, R E Lambe (AL)
1971 Dec 26	**Slant** A J J Moulam, G D Roberts
1972 Jan 2	**Mud Slide Slim** G R Herus, R Cully (AL), D Brown
1972 April 4	**Will-o'-the-Wisp** J A Sumner, J P Henrickson
1972 May 7	**The Mekon** A J Swindale, J Bromwich
1972 Aug 4	**The Riparian (Lledr)** J Perrin, A Cornwall
1972 Aug 6	**Endgame** J Perrin, T Clare
1972 Aug 14	**Gethsemane, The Green Wall (Wrysgan)** J Perrin, A Cornwall

One point of aid on the the latter.

1972 Aug 15	**The Wanderer (Wrysgan)** J Perrin, J Balmer
1972 Aug 19	**Gringo** A Green, K Latham
1972 Aug 19	**Mabel's Route, Tarantula** A Green, K Latham, D Hughes
1972 Aug 26	**Moai Man** J A Sumner, J P Henrickson, D Brown

Pitch 3 added by J A Sumner, J P Henrickson, A B Knox on 2.9.72. The peg on pitch 2 was placed by abseil.

1972 Sept 24	**High and Dry, Jambiri** C G Powell, J Powell
1972 Sept 30	**Deadline** J A Sumner, D Shepherd, A Ward (after top-roking)
1972	**High Girdle (Bodlyn)** M Anthoine, D Alcock (AL)
1972	**Remembrance** J Perrin, A Skuse
1973 March 9	**Black Eyes** J A Sumner, I R Tapley
1973 May 27	**Gryptych** A B Knox, P Miles, J Bromwich
1973 June 10	**Guillotine** R J Thorndyke, J A Webster (AL)
1973 July 23	**Phidl** P Morris

Pitch 2 was climbed by R James in 1958.

1973 July	**Black Pillar** M Boysen, D Little
1973 Aug 27	**Pamplemousse** K Bentham, J A Sumner (AL)
1973 Aug	**Delft** F Van Den Broeche, J A Webster
1973 Aug	**Strobe** G R Herus, J A Sumner (AL)
	One point of aid. Climbed free by A Grondowski, C Little on 10.6.79. The variation climbed by J A Sumner, A George 20.5.89.
1973 Oct 21	**Touchstone** J A Sumner, R J Thorndyke
1973 Oct 27	**Crack of Cau** J A Sumner, K Bentham
	A nut and sling were used beneath the major difficulties, left by A B Black and party on an earlier attempt.
1973 Oct 27	**Marsum** B J Marsden, G Summers (AL)
	There were signs that it had been climbed before.
1973	**Raspberry** J C Bucke, J R Mason
1974 Jan 21	**Chouca Rib** J A Sumner, R J Thorndyke (AL)
1974 Feb 3	**Great Spotted Booby** R J Thorndyke, J A Sumner (AL), R F Short
1974 Feb 17	**Picket Line** P Blatch and others
1974 Feb 17	**Plume** J A Sumner, A B Knox, G Summers
1974 March 17	**Curly Fringe Frown** J A Sumner, J P Sumner
1974 April 7	**Dawn's Left-Hand** K Bentham, D W Shaw
1974 April 8	**Gremlin Groove** J F Kerry
1974 April 10	**Black Shiver** K Bentham, D W Shaw (AL)
	A sling was used for aid while cleaning pitch 1, and four points of aid were used on the crux.
1974 April 14	**The Baron** K Bentham, R J Thorndyke
1974 April 16	**Central Rib** D W Shaw, K Bentham (AL)
1974 April 16	**The Sting** (Tap Pant Cae) P Blatch, A B Knox (AL)
	Two points of aid were originally used on the first pitch.
1974 April 17	**White Lady** K Bentham, D W Shaw (1 pt aid)
1974 April 18	**Sybarite** D W Shaw, K Bentham (5 pts aid)
1974 April 19	**Battered Caravanserai** K Bentham, D W Shaw (AL)
1974 April 27	**Deadpan** D W Shaw, K Bentham (AL)
1974 April	**Twr Groove** J A Sumner, I R Tapley
	There were signs that pitch 1 had been climbed before.
1974 May 8	**Tremor** K Bentham, D W Shaw (AL)
1974 May 15	**Terraneai Rib** K Bentham
1974 May 19	**Trojan** J A Sumner R F Short, A Jones, G P Cockshott
1974 May 25	**Moving Finger** K Bentham, D W Shaw (AL)
1974 May 26	**Bird of Time, The Sufri** K Bentham, D W Shaw (AL)
1974 May 27	**Nudging Groove** J A Sumner, M J Cameron (AL)
1974 May 30	**Darker Angel** D W Shaw, K Bentham (AL)
	The aid points were originally used on pitch 4.
1974 June 15	**North Ridge** C P Cockshott, G Thorndyke, T Thorndyke
	Probably climbed before.
1974 June 15	**The Bee** J A Sumner, G Summers
	One point of aid; climbed free by J A Sumner, D Lee in June 1981.
1974 June 23	**Morning Crescent, The Lamb** J A Sumner, A Jones (AL)
	First section of the latter route had obviously been climbed before.
1974 Aug 4	**Claw Mark** J A Sumner, R F Short
	An old peg was found at the top of pitch 1. The Direct and Wishbone starts were added by T Taylor, A Barton on 7.5.90.
1974 Aug 4	**The Gods Themselves** D W Shaw, K Bentham
	Pitch 2 with a peg for aid. Climbed free and on a more direct line as pitch 2 of Blame It on the Gods by M J Crocker and D Sargeant on 4.8.96.
1974 Aug 11	**Chinese Poppy** J A Sumner, G F Jarvis
1974 Aug 18	**Stross** J A Sumner, D Power (AL)
1974 Aug 27	**Squall** J A Sumner, D G Chisholm
	First section had obviously been climbed before.
1974 Aug 29	**His Satanic Majesty** D W Shaw, K Bentham (AL)
1974 Aug 30	**Lowrib** J A Sumner, J P Downes, I Cowan
	Probably climbed before.
1974 Nov 10	**The Bolero** J A Sumner, R F Short
	Top pitch extended by J A Sumner, R F Short on 24.8.75.
1974 Nov 17	**The Hole** R F Short, J A Sumner (AL)
1974 Nov 24	**Fangorn** J A Sumner, I Cowan

1974 Dec 1	**Fangorn Right-Hand**	J A Sumner, R F Short
1974	**Southern Cross**	D R M Bailey, R J Shimwell
1975 April 25	**King Edward's Army**	D W Shaw, K Bentham
1975 April 27	**The Graveyard**	J A Sumner, R F Short
1975 May 9	**Abraxus (Craig Cau)**	K Bentham, D W Shaw (AL)
1975 May 17	**Bassillades**	D W Shaw, K Bentham (AL)
1975 May 17	**Twist Grip**	J A Sumner, I Warner
1975 May 18	**Mere Gill**	K Bentham, D W Shaw (AL)
1975 May 18	**The Steeple**	J A Sumner, A B Knox, I Warner
1975 May 24	**Tatham Wife**	K Bentham, D W Shaw (AL)
1975 May 25	**Snodgrass Diversification Company**	K Bentham, D W Shaw (AL)

The direct variation was climbed by J A Sumner, A N Other in 1983.

1975 May 30	**The Gulch**	D W Shaw, K Bentham (AL)
1975 June 7	**Götterdämmerung**	K Bentham, D W Shaw (AL)

With a point of aid; climbed free by L McKinley, D W Shaw in May 1976

1975 June 22	**Gorilla's Armpit**	J A Sumner, M J Cameron

Direct finish added 4.11.79 by J A Sumner, I R Tapley.

1975 June 28	**Lucy in the Sky**	J A Sumner, R J Thorndyke (AL)
1975 Aug 6	**The Mule**	J A Webster, F Van Den Broeck
1975 Nov 22	**Dinner and the Duo**	J A Sumner, I Warner
1975 Dec 5	**December Grooves**	J A Sumner, D Thornley
1976 Feb 21	**AGM**	J A Sumner, I R Tapley (AL), D G Armstrong
1976 May 8	**Derwent**	G Jarvis, T Lugg
1976 May 8	**The Diamond**	K Bentham, D W Shaw

With 1 point of aid on each pitch; climbed free by D Wiggin, J Codling (AL), M Elwell in March 1978.

1976 May 9	**Sweet Baby James, Tappers Arête**	J A Sumner, D G Armstrong
1976 June 6	**Migraine**	I R Tapley, J A Sumner (AL)
1976 July 28	**Fritz the Cat**	I R Tapley, A H James
1976 July 31	**Flashback**	J A Sumner, E R Fairbrother
1976 Aug 8	**In Memoriam**	D R M Bailey, R J Shimwell
1976 Aug 14	**Carrion**	A Simpson, J A Sumner

Pitch 1 climbed previously by G R Herus, J A Sumner in August 1973.

1976 Aug 29	**Lifeline**	D Walker
1976 Aug 29	**Stiff Lower Lip, Stiff Upper Lip**	C Powell, D Kent
1976 Aug 30	**Trouble Maker**	J A Sumner, D L Walker

Two points of aid. Climbed free by J A Sumner 15.9.79.

1976	**Freeway**	R Hughes, M Whitfield
1977 May	**Here Comes the Sun**	L McKinley, D W Shaw
1977 Oct 16	**Bing the Budgie**	D R M Bailey, M Griffiths

Variation climbed by M Griffiths, E Jones in August 1981.

1977 Oct	**Lavrol**	J Moran, S Horrox, D Banks
1977 Nov 3	**Straw Dogs Finish**	M Crook, D R M Bailey

Probably climbed earlier by several other parties including M G Mortimer.

1978 Jan 25	**Fiddler on the Dole**	D R M Bailey, M Crook, M Griffiths
1978 Feb 4	**A Touch of Class**	J A Sumner, I R Tapley (AL), G Sumner
1978 Feb 12	**The Liquidator**	M Crook, M Griffiths
1978 March	**Diamond Eliminate**	D Wiggin, J Codling (AL), M Elwell
1978 April 23	**Pear Tree Blues**	J A Sumner, I R Tapley
1978 May	**Condor**	M Crook, M Griffiths
1978 May	**Going Straight**	M Griffiths, P Denham
1978 June 18	**Strawberry**	M Crook, M Griffiths, P Denham
1978 June 24	**Koh-i-Noor (Aderyn)**	J Codling, M Elwell
1978 June	**Ethical Voyage**	D L Walker, J Roberts
1978 June	**Sasquatch**	M Griffiths, P Denham
1978 July 12	**Hard Rain**	G R Herus, J A Sumner

One point of aid. Climbed free by T Bristlin, J Codling.

1978 July 25	**Y Taith**	D Johnson, R Griffiths
1978 July	**Buzby**	M Griffiths, P Denham
1978 July	**Chim Chu Roo**	M Crook, M Griffiths, P Denham
1978 Aug 7	**Saline Solution**	D R M Bailey, E Jones
1978 Aug 21	**Pink Panther**	J Codling, M Elwell

Originally climbed with 1 point of aid. Climbed free by D Wiggin, A Grondowski (AL), C Little, 5 May 1979.

1978 Aug 29	**Powder Monkey**	J A Sumner, C G Powell, M S Harris
1978 Aug	**Erewhon**	M Griffiths, A Prellas (AL)
1978 Aug	**Tumblin Dice**	G R Herus, R Bradley (AL)

Pitch 1 climbed previously by G R Herus and G Caine.

1978 Sept 3   **Katmandu**   J A Sumner, R J Thorndyke
The Direct Start was climbed by J Codling, G Davis on 1.9.79.

1978 Sept 20   **Heretic**   J Codling, Jerry Codling
1978 Sept 21   **Quartz Wall**   J A Sumner, G Kirkham
1978 Sept 28   **Brys**   M Griffiths, A Moller
1978   **Greenpeace**   P Gomersall, E Masson
1979 April 14   **Blatch's Folly, Ice Man**   J A Sumner, I R Tapley
1979 April 15   **Ice Man Direct**   J A Sumner, I R Tapley
Originally climbed with 1 point of aid. Climbed free by N Longland and E Murray 4 July 1980.

1979 April 16   **Raindrop**   G Jarvis, G Armstrong, C P Cockshott
1979 May 19   **Baskerville**   J A Sumner, I Warner
1979 May 26   **Systems of Romance**   D Wiggin, A Grondowski
1979 May   **Skerryvore**   M Griffiths, P Elliot, E Jones
1979 June 10   **Cat o' Nine Tails**   J Codling, R Cope, J A Sumner
1979 July 6   **Dancing Man**   J A Sumner
1979 Sept 8   **The Great Mogul, Old Glory**   J Codling, P Gibson
One rest point on a wire on the latter route. Climbed free by M J Crocker on 5.5.90.

1979 Sept 16   **The Fortifier**   J A Sumner, R Fairbrother
1979   **Dunces' Corner**   E Jones (solo)
1970s   **Wolf Rib**   Party from the Towers OEC
1980 Feb 24   **Bird in Flight**   J A Sumner, M Tolley
1980 April 20   **Girdle Traverse (Rhwyddfor)**   J A Sumner, D L Walker, M Tolley
1980 May 4   **Gate of the Winds**   J A Sumner, D L Walker
1980 May 10   **Loki (Rhwyddfor)**   J A Sumner, D L Walker
1980 May 11   **Lost Man**   J A Sumner, D L Walker
1980 May 17   **Bear Cage**   G Gibson, D Beetlestone, P Gibson
1980 May 17   **Messiah**   J Codling, D Jones, T Bristlin
1980 May 18   **Pluto**   J A Sumner, M Tolley
1980 June 12   **Buzzards Groove**   D L Walker, D W Walsh
1980 June 26   **Tyburn Gate**   J A Sumner, D L Walker
1980 July 3   **Right Little Lady**   D L Walker
1980 July 5   **Bomber**   J Codling, J A Sumner, D L Walker
1980 July 5   **Quartzberg**   G Gibson
1980 July 5   **White Rock**   D L Walker, J A Sumner (AL)
1980 July   **Electric Rail**   J Codling, P E Douglas (AL)
1980 Aug 9   **Roumagaou**   P Gibson, J A Sumner (AL)
Pitch 2 climbed previously by D L Walker, July 1980.

1980 Aug 10   **The Crab**   J A Sumner, P Gibson (AL), R F Short
1980 Aug 23   **The Mind's Eye**   G Gibson, P Gibson, J A Sumner
One rest point, eliminated by M J Crocker on 5.5.90.

1980 Aug 24   **Soldier**   G Gibson
1980 Aug 30   **Crozzley Wall**   J A Sumner, P Gibson
Pitch 2. First pitch added by M Elwell, J A Sumner on 24.4.82. The Right-Hand Finish climbed by J Codling, C Seymour on 30.10.82.

1980 Sept 6   **Adrenalin Trip**   D L Walker, J A Sumner, P Gibson
1980 Sept 6   **Steel Breeze**   G Gibson, P Gibson
1980 Sept 27   **Judge and Two Convicts**   J A Sumner, G Summers, J Phillips
1980 Oct   **Johnson's Wall, The Emerald, Wall of Ghouls**   M Griffiths, C J Hicks
1980 Nov   **Frigid Pink**   J A Sumner
1980 Nov   **Gormenghast**   M Griffiths, C J Hicks
1980 Nov   **Nosferatu**   M Griffiths
1980 Dec 20   **King of the Wild Frontier**   D Wiggin, J A Sumner, S Darlington
This line had probably been climbed before by A Hughes, H Boswell in October 1971.

1980 Dec 27   **Vapour Phase, Davy Crockett**   J A Sumner, M Tolley (AL the former)
1980 Dec 27   **The Poisoned Dwarf**   A Grondowski, M Elwell
1980 Dec   **Crimson Cruiser**   R Fawcett, P Williams

1980	**Non Dairy Creamer** R Fawcett, P Williams	
	Non Creaming Dairy Start *climbed by M Griffiths, E Jones in June 1981.*	
1981 Jan 1	**Southfork** A Grondowski, J A Sumner	
1981 Jan 1	**Xebec** J A Sumner, A Grondowski	
1981 Jan 31	**Georg Machine** J A Sumner, M Ridgway	
1981 Feb 14	**The Floater** A Grondowski, J A Sumner (AL)	
1981 March 28	**Broken Arrow, Ethical Cruise** J Codling, T Bristlin	
1981 April 4	**Big River** D Cook, C Hoyland (AL)	
1981 April 18	**Green Wall** (Tap Pant Cae) J A Sumner, I R Tapley	
1981 April 20	**It's Looking Good Houston** J A Sumner, M Cameron, J P Sumner	
1981 April	**The Widowmaker, Return of the Horsemen** M Griffiths, M Crook	
	Pitch 1 of the latter had been climbed by M Griffiths, E Jones in July 1980.	
1981 May 9	**Heist** J A Sumner, C Seymour	
1981 May 10	**Columbia** J Codling, D Astbury	
1981 June 7	**Total Perspective Vortex** J A Sumner	
1981 June 21	**Dream Racer** J A Sumner, R J Thorndyke, N Caldwell	
1981 July 4	**Beggars Banquet** J A Sumner, A B Knox	
1981 July 14	**The Ebb Tide** M Griffiths, E Jones	
1981 July 15	**Acoustic Flake** E Jones, M Griffiths	
1981 July 16	**Mr Flibbertigibbet** M Griffiths, E Jones	
1981 July	**The Muleman** M Griffiths, E Jones	
1981 Aug 16	**Sundog** J A Sumner, D Lee (AL)	
1981 Aug	**Y Lloer** M Griffiths, E Jones	
	First climbed in 'the moonlight'.	
1981 Sept 2	**The Tumor** E Jones, M Griffiths	
1981 Sept 5	**Rabble Rouser** J Codling, J A Sumner	
1981 Sept 5	**The Sketch Man** J A Sumner, R J Thorndyke	
1981 Sept 13	**Lone Ranger** J A Sumner, N Caldwell	
1981 Sept	**Louis Wilder** (solo) M Griffiths	
	In memory of Gordon Tinnings.	
1981 Oct 4	**Little Red Rooster** J A Sumner, S Lewis	
1981	**Peth Bras** E Jones (solo)	
1982 Feb 13	**Tower of Babel** J A Sumner, K D Sumner, G Lambe	
	Pitch 3 climbed previously by A B Knox, P Williams, P Cockshott, I R Tapley on 3.4.72.	
1982 March 7	**Lanchester** J A Sumner, N Caldwell	
1982 April 4	**Lincoln Green** J A Sumner	
1982 April 24	**Rolair** J A Sumner, D Clilvered	
1982 May 9	**The Anvil** A Pollitt, J Perrin	
1982 May 16	**Idris Corner** J A Sumner, I Warner	
1982 May 17	**Short Circuit** J A Sumner, R F Short	
1982 May 30	**Darkness on the Edge of Town** M Elwell, T Bristlin	
1982 June 13	**General Galtieri** J A Sumner, A Green	
1982 Aug 7	**Pin Up** G Gibson, M Lynden	
1982 Aug 14	**Gwydrin** J A Sumner, I Warner	
	Gwydrin Direct climbed by T Taylor on 13.8.93.	
1982 Aug 28	**Red Crystals** J A Sumner, I Warner	
1982 Sept 3	**Cyfrwy Pinnacle** J A Sumner, A Green	
1982 Sept 18	**Gwyth o' Wynt, Trick in the Tail** J A Sumner, G Lambe	
1982 Sept	**Slipscream** J Codling, S Allen	
1982	**Badger by Owl-light** M Griffiths, E Jones	
1982	**The Falconer** M Crook, H Walton	
1983 May 5	**Shade of Pale** J A Sumner, I Warner	
	The Right-Hand variation had been climbed by J A Sumner, I R Tapley on 4.4.81.	
1983 June 25	**Alicia** J A Sumner, A Clements	
1983 July 9	**Leander** J A Sumner, R Cottell	
1983 July 17	**Then There Were Five** I R Tapley, J A Sumner (AL)	
1983 July 31	**Mochyn** C Nunn, J A Sumner (AL), I Warner	
1983 Aug	**Dal y Twrch** M Griffiths, B Skadding	
	'Catch the Mole'.	
1983 Aug	**Safe as Sausages** J A Sumner, I Warner	
1983 Nov	**The Worm** J A Sumner, I Warner	
1983 Dec 18	**Long Climb Direct** D Wrennall, R Mulliss	
1984 May 13	**Thyme** J A Sumner, C Nunn	

1984 June 10	**Chariots of Fire**	J A Sumner, P Harding
1984 June 16	**Baptême de l'Air**	J A Sumner, P Harding
1984 June 30	**Friendly Pockets**	L Griffin, J Solov
1984 July 1	**Special K**	D R M Bailey, W Shakell
1984 July 21	**Voie Suisse**	J A Sumner, P Harding
1984 Aug 12	**Grimbarian**	J A Sumner, D Gale, J P Sumner
1984 Aug 18	**Hungry Hearts**	A Grondowski, J A Sumner
1984 Sept 3	**The Scarecrow**	J A Sumner, S Smith
1984 Sept 5	**Scallywag**	D R M Bailey, F Filzek
1984 Sept 15	**Paper Lace**	J A Sumner, J P Sumner
1984	**Eden**	C Nunn
1984	**Ivy, Charisma, The Slide**	J A Sumner with various partners
1985 Feb 24	**Armes Prydein**	E Davies, M Lewis (AL)
1985 Feb 24	**Cymru Rydd**	M Lewis, E Davies, B Grimston
1985 Feb 24	**Gwyddno**	M Lewis, E Davies
1985 March 9	**Brothers in Arms**	A Grondowski, C W Little, J A Sumner
1985 March 9	**Pardon Me for Breathing**	J A Sumner, C W Little, A Grondowski
1985 March 31	**Legionnaire's Disease**	J A Sumner, C Nunn
1985 March	**Fifty and Rising**	A Grondowski, C W Little, J A Sumner
	D Bishop and D Thomas did first section up to the tree 1970.	
1985 April 24	**Bad Reputation**	P Wright, R Barker
1985 June 2	**Meisterspringer**	J A Sumner, J P Sumner
1985 June	**Luddites Demise**	C Nunn, S Coneys
1985 July 24	**Conrod**	E Jones (solo, next to hanging rope)
1985 Sept 14	**First Blood II**	C W Little, C R Little
1985 Sept 28	**Live Is Life**	J A Sumner, C W Little
1985 Sept 29	**Dovercourt Special**	J A Sumner, C W Little
1985 Oct 19	**Foundation and Empire**	C W Little, I Cowan
1985 Oct 19	**The Cheshire Cat (Rhiwarth), The Gargoyle**	J A Sumner, J P Sumner
1985 Oct 20	**First Choice**	M Lewis, D Carson
1985 Oct 20	**Fynci Mynci**	N Carson, E Davies, J Ells
1985 Oct 20	**Seithenyn**	M Lewis, E Davies
1985 Oct 26	**Auto Man**	C W Little, I Cowan, C R Little
1985 Oct 26	**Die Fledermaus**	J A Sumner, K D Sumner
1985 Oct 26	**Pale Rider**	M Elwell, A Grondowski
1985 Oct 26	**Second Foundation**	C W Little, I Cowan
1985 Oct	**Chacmool, Stickle Back Man, Cavalier Attitude**	J A Sumner with various partners
1985 Dec	**Quartizone Injection**	J A Sumner, R Norris
1985	**Stained Class**	P Wright, R Barker
1986 May 12	**Megalomania**	P Wright, M Barker, M Walker
1986 May 26	**Ah-Ha**	C R Little
1986 May 26	**Fringe Benefit**	M Little, C R Little, E Little
1986 May 27	**Borderman**	C W Little, A Grondowski
1986 June 8	**Mismael**	C Nunn, S Coneys
1986 June 12	**Sledgehammer**	C Nunn, D Gale
1986 July	**Tri-Grainian**	J A Sumner, J P Sumner
1986 Aug 17	**Flight of Fancy**	D Wrennall, P Blain
1986 Aug 23	**Giotto**	J A Sumner, J P Sumner
1986 Sept 7	**Bric-a-brac**	J A Sumner, J P Sumner
1986 Sept 14	**Brick Wall**	J A Sumner, R Norris
1986 Sept 20	**Obi-Wan**	C W Little, C R Little
1986 Oct 1	**Swing High**	D Wrennall, R Teed
1986 Oct 12	**Bramble Pie**	J A Sumner, J P Sumner
1986 Nov 29	**The Hud**	J A Sumner, R Norris
1987 May 24	**Elf Wall**	E Jones (solo)
1987 May 26	**Bionic Woman**	J A Sumner, I R Tapley, J P Sumner
1987 May 26	**Wingeing Pom**	J A Sumner, I R Tapley
1987 Aug 29	**Cloudwaltzer**	J A Sumner, J P Sumner
1987 Aug	**Phase Shift**	J A Sumner, J P Sumner
1987 Oct 17	**Class 87/2**	J A Sumner, R Norris
1988 March 20	**Huggy Bear Goes to School**	J A Sumner, J P Sumner
1988 April 5	**Whisper of the Axe**	S Howe, G Smith
1988 April 6	**Boss Talkers**	S Howe, G Smith, M Crook

1988 April 6	**Enterprise Allowance** S Howe, S Harland
1988 April 7	**Bloodbank** S Howe, G Smith
1988 April 7	**Hustlers, Beats and Others** M Crook, G Hughes, S Howe, E Felson
1988 April 7	**The Cheshire Cat** (Adar) G Smith
1988 April	**Genericon Limits** G Smith, S Howe, P Williams
1988 April	**John Damocleese** G Smith, S Howe
1988 May 20	**Private Practice** D Wrennall, P Blain
1988 May 21	**Cuckoo Waltz** J Beasanty, J McQueen, P Semnar, J Maskis
1988 May 22	**Noble Horse** S Howe, P Kirton
1988 June 5	**Ahab** J Tombs
1988 June 10	**Loose Connection** D Wrennall, R Teed
1988 July 1	**Peachstone** S Howe, G Smith
1988	**A Gathering of Old Men** N Dixon
1988	**Crisis in Utopia** G Smith, M Thomas, N Dixon
1988	**Ed's Crack** E Stone
1988	**Steve's Arête** S Howe
1988	**The Good Booklet** G Smith, E Stone
1989 April 20	**Vertical Playground** W Shakell, D R M Bailey, R Barry
1989 April 24	**April Blizzards** P Littlejohn, M Hardwick
1989 April 25	**Jack Frost** P Littlejohn
	Second too frozen to follow.
1989 June 22	**Rainbow Warrior** D R M Bailey, W Shakell
1989 Aug 27	**Storms in Africa** J A Sumner, I R Tapley
1989 Sept 17	**The Scwp Dragon** S Williams, C Roberts
1989 Sept 30	**Helwriaeth** J A Sumner, A George
1989 Nov	**Dragonfly, Black Monday** T Taylor, E Green, R Jones
1989 Nov	**Lunar Moves** T Taylor, E Green, M Davidson
	Done at night, naturally.
1980s	**Nicw** N Dixon
1990 March 3	**Cyclops** (Simdde Ddu) J Cooper, D R M Bailey
1990 March 18	**Remember Bob Brevitt** J A Sumner, J P Sumner
1990 March 18	**Sven** J A Sumner, S R Sumner, C A Sumner
1990 March 31	**Igam-Ogam** M Lewis, J Yates, B Grimston, E Davies
1990 March	**Ou Est le Soleil** J Cooper
1990 April 1	**Loki Crack** (Moelwyn Bach) M Lewis, E Davies, J Yates
1990 April 29	**Mwnchild, State of the Union, Big Cigar** M J Crocker
1990 April	**Argonauts** J Cooper, M O'Brian
1990 April	**Ghostown** T Taylor, J Cooper
1990 April	**Madryn, Gyllion** T Taylor, J Cooper (both AL)
	The latter climbed during a fall of snow
1990 April	**Monolith** (Simdde Ddu), **Sole** J Cooper, T Taylor
1990 May 1	**Mohican** T Taylor, E Jones
1990 May 1	**War Cry** E Jones, T Taylor
1990 May 5	**Basil Brush Stroke** M J Crocker
	Cywarch's first E6. Brushing caused a huge clean strip that quickly disappeared!
1990 May 7	**Turquoise Lady** T Taylor, A Barton
1990 May 12	**Bryan's Chimney** B Grimston, J Yates
1990 May 12	**Maen Twr Og** M Lewis, E Davies, J G Trumper
1990 May 12	**The Dogs Dinner** W Kyffin, B Grimston
1990 May 12	**Tir Na Nog** M Lewis, E Davies, J Yates
1990 May 19	**Fleet Air Arm** M J Crocker
1990 May 19	**Nicht Schlafen Trauma** M J Crocker
1990 May 20	**Hot House Flowers, Wunderstuff** M J Crocker
1990 May 27	**Arberth** M Lewis, E Davies, J Yates
1990 May 27	**Loon Plage** S Findlay, K Marsden
	Chalk-free lead (the Bristol Clean Hand Gang still crusading!) but with one rest point; eliminated by M J Crocker on 9.6.95.
1990 June 16	**The Devil Within** M J Crocker
1990 June 17	**Tithing Man, Penpushers Groove, The Stud** M J Crocker
	The last so named because Crocker's wife and belayer, Beverley, lost a precious earring in the vegatation.
1990 June 24	**Italia 90** J A Sumner, J P Sumner

1990 July 14	**Scorpion, Rapscallion**	J Appleby, E Fisher

The first of the recorded routes here, but it was to be some years before the vast potential of the north side of Arennig Fawr was realized.

1990 Aug 14	**Wig, Wam**	J Cooper, D R M Bailey
1990 Aug 25	**Allanon Lives**	C W Little, M Little, C Nunn
1990 Aug 25	**Blood of an Englishman**	M J Crocker, J A Sumner
1990 Aug 25	**Elwood**	C Nunn, M Little, C W Little
1990 Aug 25	**Jake**	C Nunn, C W Little, M Little
1990 Aug 25	**The Highlander**	C W Little, C Nunn, M Little
1990 Aug 26	**The Doghouse**	M J Crocker, J A Sumner

A route called Alecto, climbed 10.8.79 by J A Sumner, R F Short using six points of aid, took the section to the niche on Dream Racer. A Grondowski, M Elwell had reduced the aid to one point in April 1980.

1990 Sept 2	**Guangdong GT**	J A Sumner, J P Sumner
1990 Sept 9	**Concorde Direct, The Clilverd Line**	J A Sumner, A George
1990 Sept 15	**One Swallow**	J A Sumner, J P Sumner
1990 Sept 15	**Volcanic Cubism**	J A Sumner, S Cronshaw
1990 Sept 29	**The Dark Road**	T Taylor, A Barton
1990 Oct 12	**Giblet**	Z Filzek, T Taylor
1990 Oct 21	**The King of Sunset Town**	J A Sumner, K D Sumner
1990 Nov 4	**A Good Spoon Full**	J A Sumner, J P Sumner, C A Sumner, S R Sumner
1990 Nov 6	**Abraxus (Llanbedr), Dance on a Volcano**	T Taylor, J Cooper
1990 Nov 6	**Prowler**	J Cooper, T Taylor
1990 Nov 17	**Sunset Arête**	J A Sumner, E Fairbrother, R Fairbrother
1990	**Jason's Corner, Slab Solo**	J Cooper (second route on-sight solo)
1991 Feb	**Hywel Dda**	P Littlejohn, P Judge

The Good Finish by D Wrennall, D Pendlebury on 25.6.94.

1991 March 1	**A Pagan Place**	F Filzek, T Taylor
1991 March 1	**Virtual Reality**	T Taylor, F Filzek
1991 March 9	**Magic Mushroom**	J A Sumner, A George
1991 March 10	**The Haw Lantern**	J A Sumner, A George
1991 March 16	**Alien**	J A Sumner, A George
1991 March 17	**General Schwarzkopf**	J A Sumner, A George
1991 April 20	**Rhino's Corner**	J A Sumner, P Benson
1991 April 20	**Velvet Revolutions**	J A Sumner, K D Sumner, R Martin
1991 May 2	**Slab Dab in the Middle**	T Taylor
1991 May 2	**Stinking Hippy**	J Cooper
1991 May 4	**Horn of Plenty, Endangered Species**	J A Sumner, E Fairbrother, R Fairbrother
1991 May 6	**The Gadgie**	C W Little, E Little
1991 May 25	**Incantations**	J Appleby, S Lloyd
1991 June 15	**Red Dwarf, Dark Star**	T Taylor, M Flannery
1991 July 4	**Bleating about the Bush, The Flourish of Strumpets, Naked Dissent**	T Taylor, F Filzek
1991 July 27	**Sulphur Mountain**	M J Crocker, J A Sumner
1991 July 27	**The Stunt Club**	P Baxter
1991 July 28	**Learning to Fly**	J A Sumner, M J Crocker
1991 July 28	**Tech Noir**	M J Crocker, J A Sumner
1991 Aug 4	**The Tusk**	J A Sumner, J P Sumner
1991 Aug 7	**Alchemist's Stone**	T Taylor, F Filzek, R Hudson
1991 Aug 7	**Midge Attack**	T Taylor, E Green
1991 Aug 7	**Rhythm of the Drones**	T Taylor, F Filzek
1991 Aug 7	**The Three Mosquitoes**	F Filzek (solo)
1991 Aug 11	**Andy's Initiation, Helical Spiral**	J A Sumner, A Tomkins
1991 Aug 24	**Colonel Chinstrap**	J A Sumner, A George, J P Sumner
1991 Aug 24	**Zig Zag (Merched)**	S Keir, P Benson
1991 Aug 27	**Bolt from the Blue**	T Taylor, F Filzek
1991 Aug 30	**Brief Encounter**	T Taylor, D R M Bailey
1991 Sept 21	**Call Me Wemage**	J A Sumner, J P Sumner
1991 Sept 21	**Pas de Chat**	J P Sumner, C A Sumner, S R Sumner, J A Sumner
1991 Sept 27	**Blue Moves**	T Taylor, F Filzek
1992 May 23	**Artrageous**	M J Crocker, J Harwood

Crocker's first contribution to Cau was made on the same day as his second ascent of Messiah.

1992 May 24	**Bilberries, Professor Phibes** M J Crocker, J Harwood
1992 May 25	**Brass Butterfly, Across the Hellespont** M J Crocker, J Harwood
1992 June 7	**Foggy Dew, Y Groes, Crawcwellt Crawl, Hecuba's Camel** M Lewis, J Yates
1992 June 13	**Tin Town, Fantasia** M Lewis, J Yates
1992 June 16	**Gwyfyn Melyn** J Appleby, N Parry
1992 June 16	**Skookum Wall** J Appleby, M Davies
1992 June 20	**Sundew City** J A Sumner, S Burns
1992 July 27	**Great Mambo Chicken** T Taylor, R Hudson
1992 July 27	**The Hard-Boiled Wonderland, Grips of Wrath** T Taylor
1992 Aug 23	**Awaken the Monster** J A Sumner, J P Sumner
1992 Oct 10	**Phantom** J A Sumner, C Jones
1992 Nov 2	**Biohazard** T Taylor, M Flannery
1993 March 14	**Lilliput's Bane** T Taylor, W Metcalfe
1993 March 14	**Sow's Ear** R Hudson, T Taylor
1993 May 21	**Barking at the Moon** R Hudson, T Taylor
1993 June 30	**This Jug Ain't Big Enough for the Both of Us** R Hudson, T Taylor (AL)
1993 July 1	**The Howling** R Hudson, T Taylor
1993 July 6	**The Day of the Tripheads** T Taylor, R Hudson
1993 July 30	**The Changeling, Praise the Lord and Pass the Ammunition** T Taylor, R Hudson (AL)
1993 Aug 18	**Sooth Slayer** T Taylor, R Hudson
1993 Aug 18	**Venusian Walkway** C Taylor, T Taylor, G Lloyd Williams
1993 Aug 25	**Spectator Groove, Fiend Two** T Taylor
1993 Aug 25	**Recant** T Taylor, G Lloyd-Williams
1993 Aug 26	**Rainy Day Women** T Taylor, H Beeston
	The first ascent between torrential onsets. It wasn't until 3 years later that the line was finished with the two top pitches by T Taylor and N Clacher.
1993 Sept 3	**Brigadoon** T Taylor (solo)
1993 Sept 3	**Shamanic Voices** T Taylor, R Hudson
1993 Sept 3	**Vestigial Tale** R Hudson, T Taylor
1993 Sept 5	**Salt Free** D J Power, A Whitten
1993 Sept 6	**Emperor's New Toes** C Taylor, T Taylor
1994 April 15	**Barfly, Johnson's Creek, Tetse Fly** T Taylor, R Hudson
1994 May 18	**Cuchulainn** M Griffiths, T Taylor
1994 May 28	**Aftermirth, Fir Bolg** T Taylor, M Griffiths
1994 May 28	**Black Percy** T Taylor (1 rest pt), M Griffiths (free)
1994 May 29	**Pistachio Man** R Griffiths, M Griffiths (both led)
1994 June 14	**Man Flyday, Return of the Sackmen, Robinson Clusoe** T Taylor, M Griffiths
1994 June 14	**The Bump** M Griffiths, T Taylor
1994 June 15	**Changrilah** M Griffiths, T Taylor, E Jones
1994 June 18	**Crab Nebula** T Taylor, R Hudson
1994 June 18	**The Cywarch Finger Flake, Kangaroo Moon, Higher than the Sun, Pencilhead** M J Crocker, J Harwood
1994 June 25	**Con-Trick, The Phantom** D Pendlebury, D Wrennall
	Pitch 2 of the latter dates from the 1970s, climbers unknown.
1994 June	**Line** H Drasdo, N Drasdo (AL)
1994 July 17	**Brewing up with TT** M Griffiths, T Taylor
1994 July 17	**The Birthing** T Taylor, M Griffiths
1994 July	**Holland Groove** D Towse, M Griffiths
1994 July	**Left Flank, Right Flank** H Drasdo, D. Boston (AL)
1994 July	**Memory of a Butterfly** M Griffiths, D Towse
1994 Sept	**Rhythms of the Planet** C Silverstone, M Boniface
1994 Sept	**Sheng, The Wanderer (Dinas)** J Appleby, S Arraton
1994 Oct 15	**Ebill Bob** M Lewis
1994 Nov 6	**Koh-i-Noor (Saeth)** M Lewis
1994	**Untrue** G Smith, R Drury
	At 6c before the second pulled off vital holds. Repeated by N Dixon, A Popp in 1996 at the new grade.
1994	**Sinker** H Drasdo, K. Richards
1995 April 14	**The Misfortunes of Elphin** M Lewis, J Yates
1995 April	**Ravens on Speed** J Perrin, M Crook
1995 May 3	**Otters Dreaming** T Taylor

1995 May 6	**Aderyn Halt, Crack of Tears** J A Sumner, R Short
1995 May 6	**White Man** J A Sumner, J P Sumner, R Short
1995 June 7	**Sharkfing** M J Crocker (solo, with trailing rope through wires)
1995 June 9	**Live like a King, Peacekeeper, Crimea, Quartizone, All in a Day, Time after Time** M J Crocker, J Harwood
1995 June 9	**Tapdance, Big Boy** (Cywarch) M J Crocker
	Together with a free ascent of Loon Plage, this must rate as one of the most productive days in the area's climbing history.
1995 June 10	**Larry the Lamb** M J Crocker
1995 June 10	**Psyclone** M J Crocker, J Harwood
1995 June 11	**Exact Science, A Conversation with JS** M J Crocker
1995 June 11	**Green Diamond, Pull the Plug** M J Crocker, J Harwood
1995 June 23	**Moondog** T Taylor, R Hudson
1995 June 26	**Witchfinder** T Taylor, M Griffiths, M Flannery
1995 June 28	**The Thin Flim-Flan Man** M Griffiths, T Taylor
1995 July 13	**Chorus of Stone** T Taylor
1995 July 22	**King's Squad** J A Sumner, J P Sumner
1995 July	**Androsack** A Hall, A N Other
1995 Aug 5	**Sci-Fi** M J Crocker
	Climbed as a sports route: redpoint technique applied. A frustrating 10-metre fall was taken from the lip on the near-successful first attempt when a screwgate refused to unscrew.
1995 Aug 6	**681 Troop** J A Sumner, A George
1995 Aug 6	**Mad Ray** M J Crocker
	Named after Ray Chappell, who had long since wilted in the fearsome summer heat.
1995 Aug 16	**Side-show** D Wrennall, H Drasdo
1995 Sept 23	**Final X** J A Sumner, I Warner
1995 Oct 31	**Stormin' Norman** N Clacher, T Taylor
1995 Oct 31	**The In of the Sixth Happiness** T Taylor, N Clacher
	An old peg was found low in the wall but the hand wielding the hammer was never found. Variation finish by M Crocker on 9.8.98.
1995 Nov 1	**The Jump over the Shadow** N Clacher, T Taylor
1995	**Half a Jesus** N Dixon, C Naylor, G Dwyer, W Roberts
	The line of No Coaches, which was climbed in 1988 by G Smith, N Dixon, E Stone and subsequently collapsed.
1995	**First Impressions** C Naylor, N Dixon, G Dwyer, W Roberts
1995	**Walking on Water** D Williams, N Parry
1996 March 3	**Black Narcissus** T Taylor, G Morgan
1996 March 3	**Double Take** G Morgan, G Morgan, T Taylor
1996 March 3	**Weevil Fish** T Taylor, G Morgan, G Morgan
1996 March 30	**Ali Baba, Chrysalis** T Taylor, N Clacher
1996 March 30	**Pink-Headed Warrior** T Taylor (solo)
1996 March 30	**Fern's Climb, Purple Headed Warrior** N Clacher, T Taylor
	A rest point on the latter.
1996 April 5	**Out of My Mine, Mine over Matter, Seashell Babylon** T Taylor, G Jarvis
1996 April 9	**Rituals of a Pagan** T Taylor, G Morgan
1996 May 4	**Full Body Transplant, Clark the Toothless Shark, Old as You Feel, Spare Parts, Forty and Falling Apart** M J Crocker, J A Sumner
1996 May 4	**Rust in the Machine** M J Crocker
1996 May 5	**Blitzkrieg** J A Sumner, M J Crocker
1996 May 5	**Man with a Mission, Cougar, Queen of My Soul** M J Crocker
1996 May 5	**No More Lives to Lose** M J Crocker (solo with trailing back-rope)
1996 May 14	**Left Aisle** H Drasdo, J Appleby
1996 May 14	**Zalamander** J Appleby, H Drasdo
	Pitch 1 added 19 May 1998.
1996 May 18	**The Rocho Machine** J A Sumner, A George
1996 June 1	**Dawn Patrol, La Merci Dieu, Lightfoot, Bleed the Soul** M J Crocker, J Harwood
1996 June 2	**Bleeting a Retreat, Experimental** M J Crocker, J Harwood
1996 June 2	**Experiential, Stew the Orthodox** M J Crocker
1996 June 5	**The Coming War, Radiat Bug** N Clacher, T Taylor

1996 June 5	**Bald Man's Arête, Speaking in Tongues** T Taylor, N Clacher
	The latter, one rest point: FFA. T Taylor 28.10.97. Variation start: M J Crocker, D Sargeant 20. 9.97
1996 June 8	**Made in Wales, Suicidal Wall, Time Is the Fire in Which We Burn** M J Crocker, D Sargeant
	'It seems to me the less you have of time, the more you get in the way of adventure.'
1996 June 8	**Whale-back Groove** D Sargeant, M J Crocker
1996 June 9	**Face to Face, Breathtaking Incompetence, Holy Cau** M J Crocker, D Sargeant
	Last route climbed in the rain.
1996 June 15	**Redstart** J A Sumner, S Cameron
1996 June 19	**Mabinogion, Generals of Tomorrow** N Clacher, T Taylor
1996 June 19	**Lizard of Id, The 5,000 Fingers of Dr T** T Taylor, N Clacher
1996 June 19	**Ziggurat** H Drasdo, J Appleby
1996 June 22	**The Melting Clock** J A Sumner, J P Sumner, S Cameron
1996 June 24	**Heart of Darkness** J Appleby, H Drasdo
	This was first climbed by J Cooper as an ice route the previous winter.
1996 June	**Denis the Menace** A Hall, S Roberts
1996 June	**Minnie the Minx** A Hall, E Chard
1996 June	**Sunset Boulevarde** S Roberts, A Hall
1996 July 6	**Alone in the World** M J Crocker (solo, with trailing back-rope)
1996 July 6	**Preacher Man** M J Crocker, J A Sumner
1996 July 7	**Come Rain or Shine** M J Crocker
	It rained!
1996 July 7	**Markova** M J Crocker, J A Sumner
1996 July 7	**Missing Friends** J A Sumner, M J Crocker
	Somewhere in the gully is a little goldmine of (dropped) Friends.
1996 July 11	**Achilles' Heel** D Craig, J Appleby, H Drasdo
1996 July 20	**Jenga** J Appleby, H Drasdo
1996 July 20	**The (Heart) Beat Room, Sounds of the Sixties, God of Hellfire, Chills and Fever, Wheels on Fire** M J Crocker, D Sargeant
1996 July 21	**Hologram, Prestissimo, Dreams and Reality Collide** M J Crocker, D Sargeant
	On the last route, a Sea King helicopter came so close as to overpower the senses of the leader.
1996 July 23	**Cian's Crack** G Morgan, T Taylor
1996 July 23	**A Midge Too Far, Cian's Wall** T Taylor, G Morgan
1996 July 27	**Solo Engagement, Dusk** M J Crocker (solo, with trailing back-rope)
1996 July 27	**The Suffering, Highlander's Fling** M J Crocker
	The attempts of his partner, Alex, to disable a potent midge population led to the name of the latter route.
1996 July 30	**Hair-Brain, Hair-Ball** T Taylor, R Hudson
1996 July 31	**A Pair of Clydesdales, Dig for Victory, Tick Teaser** T Taylor, R Hudson
1996 July 31	**Mystic Peg** R Hudson, T Taylor
	The ancient remains of what was once a peg were found on a ledge half-way up.
1996 Aug 2	**Redneck Olympics, Supermodel, Mandolin Wind** T Taylor, R Hudson
1996 Aug 3	**Boutros Boutros** R Hudson, T Taylor
1996 Aug 3	**Dreaming in Colour, Red Drag** T Taylor, R Hudson
1996 Aug 3	**Zabbadack, Go – Now!, Long Hot Mid-Sumner's Night** M J Crocker (solo, with trailing back-rope)
1996 Aug 4	**Apricot Man** R Hudson, T Taylor
	The leader had earlier declared 'I'm not an apricot man' when offered the fruit.
1996 Aug 4	**Blame It on the Gods, Stressed-Out, A Cure for Stress, Donsong** M J Crocker, D Sargeant
1996 Aug 4	**Prey** T Taylor, R Hudson
1996 Aug 14	**Lather in My Tights** T Taylor, N Clacher
1996 Aug 14	**Out of the Night** N Clacher, T Taylor
1996 Aug 14	**The Sound of One Hand Slapping** T Taylor, F Filzek, N Clacher.

1996 Sept 7	**Jackknife, Dancing Kukaracha, Life-sucks, Tumbling Five Ten** M J Crocker, S Cameron *A boot was lost to the mountain.*
1996 Sept 8	**The Lorryman, Jin-Go-La-Ba** M J Crocker, S Cameron
1996 Sept 8	**Thumb Wall** J A Sumner, A George *Sumner whacked his thumb hard with his peg hammer.*
1996 Sept 21	**Leander with Waterwings, Druid's Own Eyes, Longman, Ripple Crack, Ripple on the Mountain** M J Crocker, D Sargeant
1996 Sept 22	**Chandrapur, Quad Booster, Stockholm Express, Faltenbalg Connection** J A Sumner, A George
1996 Sept 22	**Uncensored, Bride of Dracula, Fantastic Day** M J Crocker, D Sargeant *The curtain closes on a beautiful summer.*
1996 Nov	**Desire** J Appleby, M Davies
1996 Nov	**Little Tommy Pickles, Ageneration, St Benet's Rd, White Streak Rib, Chucky Vinster** M Hedge (solo)
1996	**Parsimony** N Dixon
1997 March 3	**Tara, Zyco, Kali** J Appleby, L Appleby
1997 March 8	**Eclipse, Thunderclip Newman, Talking Doughnuts, Min y Aur, Clip Tears, Byr, Vicious Cycles, Satellite, It Hertz** M J Crocker, D Sargeant
1997 March 8	**Uchaf, Isaf** M J Crocker (on-sight solo)
1997 March 9	**Bychan Slab, Saeson, Y Garn, Box'd Ears, Gender Crisis** M J Crocker, D Sargeant
1997 March 9	**Sargeant Slab** D Sargeant (solo)
1997 March 9	**Three Front Teeth** M J Crocker (on-sight solo)
1997 March 11	**Hat Full of Hollow, Tuff Gong** J Appleby, H Drasdo
1997 April 7	**Ridge of Sighs** J Appleby, L Appleby
1997 April 9	**Hurricane Wall** J Appleby, H Drasdo
1997 April 10	**Pagan wall** J Appleby, P Livesey
1997 April 12	**Right from Left** M J Crocker (solo)
1997 April 12	**Stranger in the Mirror, Green Streak, Yellow Belly, Incognito, Eat Your Words, Essence, 'Civilization'** M J Crocker, D Sargeant
1997 April 13	**Grach, On Secret Sand, Silence Is Golden, All This and Heaven Too, Politician's Wall, Misunderstood, Do the Monkey, Stanager's Solace, Subterranean Leg Injector, In Whose Footsteps?, Greywacke Race** M J Crocker, D Sargeant
1997 April 13	**Purrfection, Small Wonder** M J Crocker (on-sight solo) *It is likely that the reported activity at this crag embraces the climbs done in 1962 by A N Gough and R E J Gough.*
1997 April 15	**J and The Silver Shower, The Last Asp** T Taylor (the former solo)
1997 April 16	**Aoife's Rib, Elegant Gypsy, The Dark Mirror** T Taylor, N Clacher
1997 April 16	**Ariadne in the Maze** N Clacher, T Taylor
1997 April 16	**The Shootist** N Clacher solo
1997 April 16	**Pixie Wall, The Smallest Show On Earth** T Taylor solo
1997 May 17	**Vermilion Wash, Burnt Umber** J A Sumner, J P Sumner
1997 May 21	**Swallowed by Amazons** T Taylor, M Davies
1997 May 24	**Rock Steady, Be Bop, Underfed, Twopicks, Saliva, Wishbone** (Rhinog Fawr)**, Min Fawr, Mur y Llyn, Min Fach** M J Crocker, D Sargeant
1997 May 24	**That Panoramic Picnic, Scoop of the Day, Lichen with Everything, No Table Manners, Forked Tongue, Sidedish** M J Crocker (on-sight solo)
1997 May 24	**Twyll y Llyn** D Sargeant, M J Crocker
1997 May 25	**Man Is Fauna, From the Rocks** M J Crocker, D Sargeant *The former route takes in a 6-metre section of Tenuous, a climb rendered extinct by Mass Extinction and substantial revegetation of its remaining independent loop.*
1997 May 26	**The Right Unforgiveable, Paradox Sand, Wilderness Grit, Araf Nawr** M J Crocker, D Sargeant
1997 June 7	**Certificated, Blacklisted, Mass Extinction** M J Crocker, J Harwood *The latter route incorporates a 6-metre section of Tenuous on its main pitch, and the first half of Pitch 3 of Tenuous on its final pitch.*

1997 June 8	**Gawr, In the Shadows, Don't Move a Muscle, Can't Get No Sleep**

M J Crocker

Concluded a wild weekend of gales, showers and rain which deprived the hapless (dossing) duo of any sleep whatsoever. Mass Extinction was ascended hastily during a 90-minute weather window.

1997 June 15	**Bridge of Sighs**	J A Sumner, K D Sumner, J P Sumner
1997 June	**Ffion**	J Savage, A Hall
1997 July 5	**Esmerillion**	J A Sumner, D Sargeant
1997 July 5	**Sentina**	J Appleby, H Drasdo
1997 July 6	**Was It a Kestrel?**	J A Sumner, D Sargeant
1997 July 7	**Y Crac Ddu, Mojo Rising, Zyco Direct, The Big Yin**	J Appleby, L Appleby
1997 July 8	**Automedon**	J Appleby, H Drasdo
1997 July 9	**Gay Abandon**	G Morgan, T Taylor
1997 July 9	**The Judith Rose, Pricked by the Pulse**	T Taylor, G Morgan

On the walk-in the leader straddled a fence only to discover it was connected to the national grid. He rose several feet into the air screaming wildly much to the amusement of his partner who had yet to cross

1997 July 12	**The Last Drop**	J A Sumner, J P Sumner, C A Sumner
1997 July 16	**Only Fools and Asses**	M Lewis, J Yates
1997 July 18	**Primal Scream, Steel against the Sky**	T Taylor, M Davies

Both led the former.

1997 July 19	**Jack Ketch**	J A Sumner, J P Sumner
1997 July 20	**Spindoctor**	M Davies, M Griffiths
1997 July 27	**Gwern Pillar**	J A Sumner, D Setterfield, S Bailey
1997 July 27	**Pilerog**	J P Sumner, D Setterfield
1997 July 28	**Big Boy!** (Frân, Ffestiniog)	M Griffiths, T Taylor
1997 July 28	**Shadowfax, White Slab, Twilight Wall**	J Appleby solo
1997 July 29	**The Road to Anarchy**	J Appleby, H Drasdo
1997 Aug 2	**Munchkins**	C A Sumner, J P Sumner
1997 Aug 3	**Gwyddon**	C A Sumner, J P Sumner
1997 Aug 3	**The Quaker**	J A Sumner, A George
1997 Aug 7	**Ladies First**	M Drasdo, H Drasdo
1997 Aug 9	**Pierrepoint**	J A Sumner, B Fyfe
1997 Aug 12	**Lion Bastard**	M Hedge (solo)
1997 Aug 13	**Roger Rabbit**	M Hedge (solo)
1997 Aug 16	**Disco Bugs, Don's Cairn, Dead Sea Scroll, The Collectors' Pot, Quartz Storm, Peace in Mind, TLC, Splinter, For the Record**

M J Crocker (lead-solo; last route on sight-solo)

Disco Bugs was climbed in a pervasive storm of big black flying insects released by the warm summer sun.

1997 Aug 16	**Jac Codi Baw**	J Appleby, H Drasdo

This is the Welsh expression for JCB and refers to the loose rock that needed removing to make the route a bit less unstable.

1997 Aug 16	**Melonmania**	T Taylor, E Jones
1997 Aug 16	**Ora pro Nobis**	M Lewis, J Yates
1997 Aug 16	**Sparta, Dearg Doom, Nob Direct**	T Taylor, G Dunford
1997 Aug 17	**Loneliness Is Just a Word, Eco-Adsorption of the Psyche, Warm Up, Not Burn Out!, 'I'm Soloing in the Rain', Gwyllt, Gwen, Sunset the Scene**	M J Crocker (lead solo)
1997 Aug 18	**Ffrwd, Cool Grit, Emilya, In an Ideal World, Weeping Wall, Fear Test**	M J Crocker (lead solo; the last route after top-rope practice)

Fear Test proved a suitable climax to three days' soloing with zero human contact.

1997 Aug 18	**Sych, Left to Rust, A Right to Rust**	M J Crocker (solo)
1997 Aug 24	**Ozymandias**	M Lewis, J G Trumper
1997 Aug 30	**Lol**	M Lewis, J Yates
1997 Aug 30	**Man-Twitchers, Looking Down upon the Enemy, Later That Night...**	M J Crocker (lead solo)
1997 Sept 1	**Artrodeco, A Climb of Contrasts**	M J Crocker (lead solo)
1997 Sept 2	**Death Warrant, Colonel Jones, Smoking Limbs, Hanged, Drawn and Quartered**	M J Crocker (lead solo)

Colonel Jones was a Parliamentarian, born at Maes-y-garnedd, who was a signatory to the 1660 death warrant of King Charles 1; his fate is duly recorded at this crag.

1997 Sept 4	**S.M.A.R.T., But Fear Itself, Leave No Trace, Post-Urban Species, Sylvester** M J Crocker (lead solo; fourth route on sight)
1997 Sept 4	**Seeds of Suspicion, Smacks of Insanity** M J Crocker (on-sight solo and on-sight reverse solo)
	A scar on Sylvester indicated that it may have been climbed before.
1997 Sept 5	**Y Grug (Saeth), B-side Smash, Irresponsible** M J Crocker (lead solo)
1997 Sept 6	**Ysgor, Going Going Gone** M J Crocker (lead solo)
1997 Sept 12	**Edrychiad Cyntaf** M Lewis, J Yates
1997 Sept 14	**Hail TT, Tall to Order, Eye-full Crack, Short Work, Lucky Number, Architect of Chance** M J Crocker (lead solo)
	Hail TT appears to be a line attempted by T Taylor who, after being thwarted by a cataclysmic hail storm, developed severe flu and didn't return to The Rhinogs until 1999. Tall to Order may well be the (unnamed, unrecorded) route climbed by M Lewis in 1992.
1997 Sept 18	**Maes B** M Lewis, J Yates
1997 Sept 20	**Lurkio, Variation start to Speaking in Tongues** M J Crocker
1997 Sept 20	**Sounds Like Drums, Magua** M J Crocker, D Sargeant
1997 Sept 21	**Bonsai Wall, Heulwen** P Blain, C Blain
1997 Sept 21	**Haf Bach Mihangel** M Lewis, J Yates
1997 Sept 21	**Shaka, Psychop, Triathlon** M J Crocker, D. Sergeant
	A very productive weekend for the team, bringing the Simdde Ddu slab area to completion.
1997 Sept 21	**Something for the Weekend** J G Trumper, M Lewis
1997 Sept 22	**Ymryson y Geifr** M Lewis, J Yates
1997 Sept 23	**Right Aisle** H Drasdo, J Appleby
1997 Sept 23	**Via Dolorosa** J Appleby
1997 Sept 24	**Oes Gafr Eto?** M Lewis, J Yates
1997 Sept 25	**Hydref Eto** M Lewis, J Yates
1997 Sept 27	**Life in the Shadow of Death, Limelight, Night Howl, Graveyard Gates** M J Crocker, J Harwood
1997 Sept 28	**Brubeck's Cube** M J Crocker (redpointed), J Harwood
	This route translates into French 7c and awaits an on-sight.
1997 Sept 28	**Prizewinner** M J Crocker, J Harwood
1997 Sept	**Tears in Rain** M Griffiths, N Dyer
1997 Oct 4	**Neolith, Celt, Jim's Route?, Pedestal Arête** M J Crocker (lead solo)
	The second route was dripping with water and the nearby lichen sponged up and green; the soloist didn't respond well to yo-yoing, and the ascent was made only after jerking down to a semi-rest at 5 metres.
1997 Oct 5	**Airhead, Groundpull, One Day I Won't Be Coming Back** M J Crocker (lead-solo, last route after top-rope practice)
	On that day the second route was a sheet of water, and some frigging about with gear proved necessary. One Day I Won't Be Coming Back was a fitting swansong, near-epitaph, and was climbed in a manic final fling as dark enveloped the hills. The Soloist, normally so reliable, only had to jam in the exit groove…
1997 Oct 5	**Gully Wall Route** M Lewis, J Yates
1997 Oct 12	**Stretchmark, The Outhouse Effect, El Magnifico, Umbrella Head, Screaming Wet Arête** M J Crocker
	The routes were cleaned the previous day in continuous torrential rain, and the only way Crocker could keep dry was by having an umbrella strapped to his head! The last route was climbed in waterfall conditions with the bonus of one dry hold.
1997 Oct 18	**Callum** N Dixon, D Wrennall
	Originally bolted by G Smith in 1994 but never led.
1997 Oct 19	**Punks Without Pace, Visions of a Melon, The Hazel Iris, Keys to Ascension** T Taylor, N Clacher
1997 Oct 19	**Sunk Without Tracey** N Clacher, T Taylor
1997 Oct 22	**Battle on the Hill, Shin Splint Roof, Hostile Ground** N Clacher, T Taylor
1997 Oct 22	**Leprauchaun, Crow Road, October Groove** J Appleby, L Appleby
1997 Oct 22	**Looking For a Rainbow** T Taylor (solo), N Clacher
1997 Oct 24	**Pseudognome, Spooked By Time, Hooked to Passion, Tongues Up** T Taylor, N Clacher
1997 Oct 24	**Sour Milk See, Stone Cold Crazy** N Clacher, T Taylor

1997 Oct 28	**Spirit from the Cage**	T Taylor (after top-roping)
1997	**Raining Stones**	J Appleby
1997	**Wee Laddie**	E Jones, M Davies
1997	**Wrinkly Old Men**	N Dixon, C Naylor
1998 Feb 9	**Simply Thread**	D Wrennall, N Dixon
1998 Feb	**Iron John, Close Second, Fire, Brimstone**	J Appleby, H Drasdo
1998 March 18	**Ironside**	J Appleby, H Drasdo
1998 March 25	**Aja**	J Appleby, H Drasdo
1998 March	**Bat Attack, First the Worst**	T Shelmerdine, N Dyer
1998 March	**Fearsome Worrier**	N Dyer, T Shelmerdine
1998 March	**Bat Capers, Frank Zappa RIP**	L Houlding, M Reeves
1998 March	**Norah Batty, Subservient Elephant**	M Reeves, L Houlding
1998 March	**The Kneebar of Eternal Justice**	L Houlding, N Dyer
1998 April 7	**Zone of Totality**	T Taylor, M Hedge (both led)
1998 April 13	**Choose Life**	M Hedge, T Taylor (both led)

1998 May 2 **Man in the Moon, Moonrazor, Non Welsh-Speaker's Conundrum**
M J Crocker, D Sargeant

1998 May 2	**On Easter Island, They'll Never Keep Us Down**	M J Crocker

1998 May 3 **Exposé, Expel to Air, Fifth Anniversary, The Slot Machine**
M J Crocker, D Sargeant

1998 May 3	**On Impulse, Thor's Wall**	M J Crocker (the former solo)

1998 May 4 **Monday Morning Mizzle, Weather or Not,**
The Weatherman's Yarn M J Crocker (solo)

1998 May 9	**Cloudbase**	M J Crocker
1998 May 9	**Y Eryr, Y Gigfran**	M J Crocker, J Harwood
1998 May 10	**Rain of Terror, Countdown to the Millennium**	M J Crocker, J Harwood
1998 May 16	**Clipped Wings, Diamond Lake**	M J Crocker, D Sargeant
1998 May 16	**Jetsam, Dead on Impact, The Wrath of Idris**	M J Crocker
1998 May 17	**The Sack Thrower's Association**	A Cave, A Perkins, T Taylor, E Jones

*There were several well-known guides at the crag suffering heavily after the
final-night party of the International Women's Meet at Plas y Brenin, and at
one stage a rucksack got dropped down the cliff, narrowly missing the then
BMC Access Officer.*

1998 May 17	**Steric Arête, Fox Whistle**	M J Crocker, D Sargeant

*The name of the latter relates to calls of distress from a walker who had
injured himself on the Fox's Path. They mistook the whistle to belong to a
family who were swimming in the lake. Eventually, however, a Sea King
arrived to pick up the casualty.*

1998 May 18	**A Touch Sketchy, Thumbs Up, Two Fingers**	M J Crocker
1998 May 19	**Ordinary Route**	H Drasdo, J Appleby
1998 May 21	**Viridian Groove**	J Appleby, L. Appleby
1998 May 23	**Third Time Lucky**	N Clacher
1998 May 23	**World's Gone Green, Kyoto, Hands-full, Hunted, Irish Eyes, Wisecrack**	M J Crocker, J Harwood
1998 May 24	**Snicker, Rock It Up**	M J Crocker, J Harwood
1998 May 25	**Barbarism, Tobias**	M J Crocker
1998 May 25	**Shouts in Space**	M J Crocker, D Sargeant
1998 June 4	**Hobo Jungle**	J Appleby, L Appleby
1998 June 20	**Carboxyhaemoglobin, Arian**	M J Crocker, D Sargeant

A similar line to Arian had been led by N Dixon in 1985.

1998 June 20	**Xelation, Techtonic**	M J Crocker
1998 June 21	**Table Eliminate, The One and Only Sargeant Scuff, Roberto Zucco, Death Becomes You**	M J Crocker, D Sargeant
1998 July 4	**Mouldy Mormon, Hemispheres**	N Clacher, T Taylor
1998 July 4	**Witch's Tit, A Hovis Witness**	T Taylor, N Clacher
1998 Aug 5	**Aquatonic**	J Porter, E Hoskins

*The left-hand variation on the upper groove was climbed M J Crocker and
J Harwood on 8.9.2001.*

1998 Aug 7	**Naomi**	T Taylor (after top-roping), M Davies
1998 Aug 8	**Cosy Powell, Drive Like You Drum**	M J Crocker, T Taylor
1998 Aug 8	**Enemy of the Earth**	M J Crocker (lead solo)
1998 Aug 8	**Path to Redemption**	T Taylor (2 rest points), M J Crocker (free)

Taylor led the route free on 30.8.98.

1998 Aug 9	**Inverse Pleasure Principle, Nerve Trap, Sitting Flake Arête, Army of One** M J Crocker (lead solo)	
1998 Aug 10	**Bed of Roses, Drop In Squad, Black Power Salute** M J Crocker (lead solo)	
1998 Aug 10	**Left Arête (Daear Fawr), First Crack, Second Crack, Implantation, A Step in the Right Direction** M J Crocker (solo)	
1998 Aug 18	**Zenturion** J Appleby, H Drasdo	
1998 Aug 30	**Charlie Spitkid** M Hedge, T Taylor	
	Named after the lad who can fit his head perfectly inside a spit bucket, his regular party trick.	
1998 Aug 30	**Magwitch, Spandexterity** T Taylor, M Hedge	
1998 Aug	**Riparian** (Pistyll Rhaeadr) I Deans, J Porter	
1998 Sept 2	**Red-Headed Warrior** N Clacher, T Taylor	
1998 Sept 22	**A Short Walk** N Clacher (solo)	
1998 Sept 22	**Blue-Headed Warrior, The Colour Turtle** N Clacher, T Taylor	
1998 Sept 22	**Glint in the Flint** T Taylor (solo)	
1998 Sept 22	**Purple Haze, Five Finger Ecstasy** T Taylor, N Clacher	
1998 Oct 30	**Neolithic Span, Monolithic Man** T Taylor, G Morgan	
1998	**Toxic Haste** T Taylor, M Davies	
1999 April	**Brigate Rosso, Ghost Dance** J Appleby, P Livesey	
1999 May 25	**Spring Lightning, Grug Grog, Alcantara** J Appleby, L Appleby, H Hobson	
1999 June 5	**Spanking the Monkey, Hole in the E Zone** T Taylor, M Hedge (both led)	
1999 June	**White Rabbit** J Appleby, P Livesey	
1999 July 7	**Wysiwyg** H Drasdo, J Appleby	
1999 July 12	**A Hole full of Cherries** T Taylor, J Thomas	
1999 July 12	**Cherry Picker** T Taylor	
1999 July 25	**Ness's Back, Purple Reigns** M J Crocker (solo)	
1999 July 25	**Pancake Wall, Humpy Dumpty's Revenge, Mummy's Nose, Dashboard, Sloped Off, Rollercoaster** M J Crocker (solo, after top-roping)	
1999 July 25	**Squashed Berry, Cross Rock** M J Crocker, J L V Crocker	
	Seven-year-old junior Crocker's first new routes.	
1999 July 26	**Grab Some Holds and Pull on Them, White Wind** M J Crocker (solo, after top-roping)	
1999 July 26	**Mist on the Mountain, The First Grassfield, The Bridge That Jonathan Built, Foreign Object** M J Crocker (solo)	
1999 July 28	*Craig y Gwynt climbs: M J Crocker (solo, some after top-roping). Other climbers may have visited the crag, and therefore names and dates are excluded from the text in some cases.*	
1999 July 28	**Dehydration, Dry Throat of Fear** M J Crocker (solo, after top-roping)	
1999 July 29	**Do the Biz, Nature Bites Back, Mighty Midge** M J Crocker (solo after top-roping)	
1999 July 29	**Strong Heather, A Tomb with a View, Esoterica Hysterica, Boil and Bubble, Purple Pistyll, Fisteater** M J Crocker (solo)	
1999 July 30	**Two Spots, One Chance, Extremely Silly Arête** M J Crocker	
	The former solo after top-roping, the latter lead-solo.	
1999 July 31	**Call Yourself a Doctor** M J Crocker, T Taylor	
1999 July 31	**Initiation Test, Roman Road** P Bartlett, L Griffin	
1999 July 31	**Saving Grace** L Griffin (back-rope solo)	
1999 July 31	**The Arête (Moel yr Hydd), Animal Instinct** L Griffin, P Bartlett	
1999 Aug 1	**Caught in the Crossfire** T Taylor, M J Crocker	
1999 Aug 1	**The Delicate Side of Thunder, All Fingers and Thumbs** M J Crocker (second route after top-roping), T Taylor	
	The difficulties in the Arennig enter new dimensions.	
1999 Aug 6	**Head in the Thundercloud, Time Artist** T Taylor	
1999 Aug 17	**Dr Butt Says You Can't Get More In, Exiled in the Land of Pickled Fish** P Jenkinson, T Taylor (AL)	
1999 Aug 17	**Eat the Peach** T Taylor, M Hedge	
1999 Aug 21	**Playing the System, Quizzical Sister** L Griffin (back-rope solo)	
1999 Aug 31	**Ecology of Fear, Twelve Monkeys** T Taylor, N Clacher	
1999 Sept 3	**Yr Holltalluog, Beneath the Underdog** M Lewis	
1999 Sept 4	**Hailing the Alien, Kiss Kinky Boots Night Night** T Taylor, N Clacher	
1999 Sept 4	**Millennium Bug** J A Sumner, A George	

1999 Sept 4	**The Ailing Alien** N Clacher, T Taylor
1999 Sept 12	**Slick Slidin' Away** T Taylor (solo)
1999 Sept 12	**Suspended Animation, The Leading Wren, Animated Suspension** T Taylor, M Hedge (AL); *Variation finish to the last route climbed by M Crocker on 22.6.2001.*
1999 Oct 13	**Agenda, Penbwl Corner** M Lewis
1999 Oct 19	**Cyw Haul, Sundance Kid** M Lewis
1999 Nov 27	**Johari Window** M Hedge, A Sneddon *Variation by D Wrennall on 20.11.01.*
1990s	**At a Pinch, Llys Direct Start** N Dixon
2000 March 30	**Kaisepakte** J A Sumner, K D Sumner *Pitches 1 and 2, exiting via Acheron. Pitch 3 added by J A Sumner, G Probert on 19.7.2000. Pitch 3a climbed by J A Sumner, D Renshaw on 24.8.2000.*
2000 March 30	**Kreen-Akrore** J Appleby, H Drasdo *Pitch 1. Pitches 2,3,4 by J Appleby, M Perks on 28.6.00.*
2000 April 15	**Dorothy's Wall** N Clacher (solo)
2000 April 15	**Point of Snow Return** T Taylor, N Clacher, G Morgan *While it snowed.*
2000 April 19	**Milkman's Daughter** N Clacher, T Taylor,
2000 April 28	**Shamanic Wanderings, The Clock of the Long Now** M Hedge, T Taylor (AL)
2000 May 1	**Fading into the Sun** T Taylor (solo)
2000 May 1	**Shadow People, Zero Gravity, Twilight People, Tribal Eclipse** T Taylor, G Morgan (AL)
2000 May 3	**Superstring, Dead Men Walking** T Taylor, N Clacher (AL)
2000 May 7	**Spider Blood Pump, Ghostrace, Jump out of Your Skin, Policing the Shadows** T Taylor, N Clacher (AL)
2000 May 10	**Dead Metal, Sergeant Bash, Sir Killalot, Never Miss a Chance** T Taylor
2000 May 15	**Fighting Spirit** N Clacher, R Jarvis, T Taylor
2000 May 15	**Leatherboots** N Clacher (solo)
2000 May 15	**Morris Minor** R Jarvis, N Clacher, T Taylor
2000 May 24	**The Seventh Wave, Big Is Beautiful, Instinct Whip, Sunset Wall, Raiders of the Lost Park, Race against the Clocker, Stone Graffiti, Vandal's Crack, The Bending Mind, Snakes and Ladders** T Taylor, N Clacher (VL) *The Artists Anonymous responsible for the damage to Vandal's Crack have yet to make themselves known.*
2000 May 28	**Lawless, One Law for One, Tower of Libel** M J Crocker (solo; second route lead solo)
2000 May 29	**Dwfn Simdde y Rhinog** G Morgan (solo)
2000 May 29	**Four Arêtes, Sais Invader** M J Crocker, J Harwood *Later, by accident, the Crocker-Harwood team meet the Taylor-Morgan team in Cwm Bychan: competition in The Rhinogs?*
2000 May 29	**Home Surf, Speak of the Devil, Power Spawn, Is It Morning?, Invasion of the Booty Snatchers, Booty Is Bountiful, Rippled and Stoned** T Taylor, G Morgan (Morgan led the fourth route)
2000 May 30	**The God Summons, A Roof over Head Makes Home, Turn Vertical When Life Is Flat, Dr Irish Watches, The Tywyn Weird Route Name Society Bolt-less Competition Climb** M J Crocker (solo; first two routes lead-solo)
2000 May 31	**The Perfect Bust, Make or Break, A Home Called Pandy** M J Crocker (solo, after top roping)
2000 May 31	**Wall of Goths, The Hatchett** T Taylor, N Clacher (AL)
2000 June 10	**A Magnificent Thing, The Ebb** N Clacher, T Taylor (AL), M Hedge
2000 June 10	**All the Best Freaks Are Here** T Taylor, M Hedge
2000 June 10	**Jammy Dodger, Dodgy Jammer, Pulling on the Black, Rita's Groove** N Clacher (solo)
2000 June 10	**Suffolk Punch, Churchman's End** M Hedge (solo)
2000 June 13	**Best of Friends, Scrambled Legs, High Man Slapper, Del** (Foel Wen), **Tricks** T Taylor (unseconded; latter two routes solo)
2000 June 16	**Anxiety, Dynocology** M J Crocker, J Harwood *The second pitch of Anxiety was added by M J Crocker on 12 8 2000 in the pouring rain and with a knot in the abseil rope for protection in the appalling*

*conditions (about E6 like that). An aid point used on Dynocology was
bouldered past by M J Crocker on 30 July 2000, thus completing a good day out.*

2000 June 16	**On Honeymoon with My Chicken Muscle, Helyg Crack, Air Guitar** T Taylor, N Clacher (AL)
2000 June 16	**Stars in Our Eyes, Streaker** M J Crocker (solo and lead-solo after top-roping)
2000 June 18	**Don't Even Think about It** M J Crocker
2000 June 18	**Technician Direct, Free Aran, For Hyll Drem** M J Crocker, D Sargeant
2000 June 25	**'Done a Thousand Times Before', Repeating History** T Taylor (solo)
2000 June 25	**I Know This Line, This One Too, As Old as Time, The Passage of Hands, A Wild Sheep Chase** T Taylor, N Clacher
2000 June 25	**Peachless, Peach Maker, Oak Corner** N Clacher, T Taylor
2000 June 25	**The Power of Peach, The Peach** N Clacher (solo)
2000 July 1	**Oat Race, Oating for Beginners, Three Men in an Oat** T Taylor, M Hedge
2000 July 1	**Quakermass, Wobble to the Ledge of Hedge** M Hedge, T Taylor
2000 July 2	**Roaring Forties** T Taylor, M Hedge
2000 July 2	**Would the Real Owner Step Forward** M Hedge, T Taylor
2000 July 20	**Not-So-Soft, Get Laid Twice, Silence Can Speak, Wall-to-Wall Sunshine, The Wild Around, The Wild Within, And Janet Street Porter Walked By, Duck!, Boys in Toys, The Arête** (Bodlyn), **Receding Hairline, Forked Lightning Conductor Crack, Watch the Point, Impale Face** M J Crocker (solo, some on-sight; seventh and eighth routes lead-solo)
2000 July 21	**Gaardevarre, Finnmark, Purple Rain, Haircurler, The Bodlyn White, Rail to Oblivion, Gazump** M J Crocker (solo, most after top-roping)
2000 July 21	**Take a Pig's Head, Add One Spoonful of Medium Rage** T Taylor, N Clacher
	After top-roping and with preplaced thread in lower section.
2000 July 22	**Total Commitment, Beat the Clach, Paraplegic** M J Crocker (first route solo after top-roping; last two lead-solo after top-roping)
	With the second route Crocker aims to get his own back on Clacher.
2000 July 23	**Just a Little...Please, Farmers' Union, Soldier On, Pick White, Right of White, Underpower, The Habitual Segregation of Fear, Parting Shots** M J Crocker (lead-solo; fifth and last two routes solo after top-roping)
2000 July 29	**Flaky Pastry, Grit-Severe, The Story Unfolds, The Chocks, Arête de Tête, Le Mort Solitaire, Cornered, Snaz, Curiosity's Small, Mindless Trivia of Man** M J Crocker (solo, most after top-roping)
2000 July 30	**Silverback, The Silver Usurper, Destiny** M J Crocker, J Harwood
	A perfect day; Crocker reckoned Silverback to rate about French 8a.
2000 Aug 5	**Scoop-a-Million, Lottery, Back against The Wall, The Lure, The Web, The Net, The One, The Catch, 6-Metre Crack, The Three Words, Slab Route** M J Crocker (solo after top-roping; last route seconded by J L V Crocker)
2000 Aug 6	**Engage** M J Crocker (solo after top-roping)
2000 Aug 6	**False Sense of Insecurity, Scratchless, Confessions of an Irish Opossum Eater, The Thing Licker, Gold Fever** T Taylor, M J Crocker (AL)
2000 Aug 6	**The Incision, The Derision** M J Crocker (lead-solo)
2000 Aug 12	**Dance to the Storm, Eye of the Storm, The Real Thing, Why Does It Always Pour on Me?, Daydreaming, Even Better than the Real Thing** T Taylor (solo, mostly on sight)
	Someone else was having fun that day.
2000 Aug 12	**Fame Drain, R.H. 100%** M J Crocker, J Harwood
	It was a good forecast, so it threw it down all day.
2000 Aug 18	**Burning Time, Squirtle Squad, A Pitch in Time, Mewtwo Strikes Back** T Taylor, P Jenkinson (AL)
2000 Aug 18	**Giovanni Is a Cad** P Jenkinson (solo)
2000 Aug 20	**Diamox Dreams, Fenrir** M Hedge (solo)
2000 Aug 20	**Loki** (Wion), **Kickus Climb** T Taylor (solo)

2000 Aug 20	**Splat Race, Does My Thumb Look Big in This?, Lock, Stock, and One Smoking Bollock** T Taylor, M Hedge
2000 Aug 25	**X-Man** T Taylor (solo)
2000 Aug 28	**An Answer from Limbo** T Taylor (solo)
2000 Aug 29	**Instankia Tower, Kurst of the Deep** P Jenkinson (solo)
2000 Aug 29	**What Goes Down Must Come Up, So Close to the Monster, West Side Boys, Wallit and Grimace** P Jenkinson, T Taylor (AL)
2000 Aug 29	**White Russian** T Taylor (solo)
2000 Sept 3	**Extreme Contact, Wings above Water, My Feral Heart, The Art of Communication** T Taylor (the first two solo)
2000 Sept 4	**Azura** T Taylor (solo)
2000 Sept 4	**Jigglypuff, Gotta Catch 'em All, Team Rocket Blasts Off** P Jenkinson, T Taylor (AL)
2000 Sept 14	**Two Against Nature** H Drasdo, N Drasdo
	The party set out to celebrate the fiftieth anniversary of its first new route. One point of aid was used while cleaning a greasy crux. The Foot and Mouth restrictions of 2001 prevented a return to free the pitch.
2001 Feb 12	**Phallus through the Looking Lass, Running Like the Red Queen** T Taylor (solo)
2001 Feb 14	**Being Anita, Face in the Clouds** T Taylor
2001 Feb 17	**Virtual Water, Food for Sharks** T Taylor (solo)
2001 June 22	**Spotterless Spatter, S 'n M is Better than F 'n M, Animals in Suspenders, Respect the Spine, Still Virgin, Terry's Old Gold** M J Crocker (solo: second and fourth routes on-sight; others mainly after top-roping)
2001 June 22	**The Finite Pleasure of Swn, Cambyah, Stone Perfect** M J Crocker (lead-solo after top-roping)
2001 June 23	**Avoiding the Issue, Bone Daddy, Tower of Trundle, G, Off the Shelf, Light at the Edge of the World, Lacking in Geo-Stability** P Jenkinson, T Taylor (AL)
2001 June 23	**Distant Dulcet Tones of Dr Numb Thumb, This Is the End, Looking for Loki, Joking, Sustainable Energy, One of Those Days,** M J Crocker (solo: second and third routes on-sight; remainder after top-roping)
	The two teams did not meet that day, but Crocker had his arch adversary in his sights.
2001 June 24	**Banging against Destiny, Stone Donkey, Dead Man's Verve** T Taylor (solo, last route after top-roping)
2001 June 24	**Midsummer's Day Dream** M J Crocker, D Sargeant
2001 June 30	**Bubbles Burst, Shrek, Scarred for Life** P Jenkinson, T Taylor
2001 June 30	**Celtic Tiger** T Taylor (roped solo)
2001 June 30	**Dr Butt Prefers Them Harder** P Jenkinson (solo)
2001 June 30	**Viper in Pink Satin, Dynamo MC,** T Taylor, P Jenkinson
2001 July 13	**Ass Landing, The Incredible Bounce of Marrow** M Davies, T Taylor
	The names commemorate the consequences of Taylor's on-sight attempt at what was later to become Another Leap of Faith.
2001 July 13	**Stubborn as an Ass, Mowing the Ass** T Taylor (solo)
2001 July 27	**A Problem Shared, The Biggest Barndoor in Town** M J Crocker (lead-solo)
2001 July 27	**Dam the Stream, Three-Day Wonders, Slot-in-Job, The Mathematician, Brace Yourselves!, Twirl, More of a Fridge Door, Window Shopping** M J Crocker (solo, most after top-roping)
2001 July 28	**To Fly above Water, Good Vibrations, Five on the Richter, Echoes in the Swamp, Shakes of Success, The Moelfre of Kabul, Son Watching** M J Crocker (solo, most after top-roping)
	Climbing was interrupted by a trip to the beach.
2001 July 29	**Peach on the Beach, Showtime, No Smear... So Disappear, Male Spiff, Grip Rip Bones, Rowan Askisson** M J Crocker (solo, most after top-roping)
2001 Aug 20	**Far for the Fledgling, First Flight, First Fright** T Taylor, A Taylor
2001 Aug 20	**The Wrath of Cian** T Taylor (solo)
2001 Aug 22	**Another Leap of Faith** T Taylor
	An earlier assault was almost fatal as a high hold snapped.
2001 Aug 22	**Go West with the Wicked, Nakedness Is Very Slow** T Taylor (solo)

2001 Aug 22	**MiniFrocks Are Best** T Taylor, D Owen	
2001 Aug 25	**Elegant in Socks, Don't Ever Buy Teeth from a Catalogue** T Taylor, D Owen	
2001 Aug 25	**Information Cocoons, Plugs of Muscle, Serpent Heart, Serpent Mistress** T Taylor	
2001 Aug 28	**Children of Lir** T Taylor	
2001 Aug 28	**Toxic Texan, Alive Enough to Spawn** T Taylor, A Taylor, C Taylor	
	Dr Taylor brings along his 5- and 7-year-old children.	
2001 Aug 28	**Training Spotters, Drinking This Water May Turn You Sane** T Taylor (solo)	
2001 Aug 29	**Bloodscream, The Slap of One Hand Sighing, Spreading Mischief** T Taylor (solo, the first above a mat and pre-inspected on top rope)	
2001 Aug 29	**When the Rock Crows** T Taylor	
2001 Sept 8	**Waterworld** M J Crocker, J Harwood	
2001 Sept 9	**Sweet September, Pick n' Choose** M J Crocker, D Sargeant	
2001 Sept 9	**Whistling in the Dark, Strolling in the Park** M J Crocker (solo)	
2001 Sept 10	**Liberation, North Winds Blow, So Lay Low, Fall Out, Touch Too Much, Much Too Much, Head First, Gerbil Street** M J Crocker	
	The first four routes solo; the last four lead-solo. The penultimate route was named after a head-first fall from the underlying ledge 5 metres up. 'I was chasing around as usual when a hold broke. So I plummeted down head first. Fortunately, out of the corner of my eye, I noticed a slender sapling. I managed to grab it and rectify my orientation into feet-first position. The sapling was only half an inch diameter and I'll never know how it managed not to break as it bent right over with me hanging onto it.'	
2001 Nov 20	**Final Flurry, Offcut** D Wrennall, C Shaw	
2001 Dec 12	**Aja Direct, The Incline and Wall of the Norman Empire, Animal Watching Without 'im** T Taylor (on-sight solo)	
2001 Dec 12	**Every Step a Lotus, Gravity Depravity** T Taylor (solo after inspection)	
2001 Dec 12	**The Story of O** T Taylor (solo after top-roping)	

Index of Crags

Index of Climbs

Accident Procedure

First Aid

If spinal or head injuries are suspected, do not move the patient without skilled help, except to maintain breathing or if this is essential for further protection.

If breathing has stopped, clear the airways and start artificial respiration. Do not stop until the patient recovers or expert opinion has diagnosed death.

Summon help as quickly as is compatible with safety. Do not hesitate or delay.

Rescue

In the event of an accident where further assistance is required, dial 999 and ask for the North Wales Police. The Police are responsible for co-ordinating all rescues and will contact other services as necessary.

- State that you require cliff rescue and report the exact location (six-figure grid reference if possible) and details of the accident.
- Be prepared to give your own name and home address if asked.
- Follow any further instructions or requests issued.

Helicopter

In the event of a Helicopter evacuation, all climbers on or off the cliff should take heed. A helicopter flying close to the cliff will make verbal communication very difficult and small stones will be dislodged by the rotor downdraught. All loose equipment should be secured and climbers in precarious positions should try to make themselves safe.

The people with the injured person should try to identify their location. **No** attempt should be made to throw a rope at the helicopter, but assistance should be given to the helicopter crew if requested. Do not approach until directions are given by the crew. In particular, keep well clear of the main rotor, the tail rotor, and the engine exhaust.

Follow-up

After an accident, a report has to be compiled. Normally the details will be collated at the scene by the Police or rescue team, who will then pass the information to the Mountain Rescue Council Statistics Olfficer.

If unreasonable equipment failure is suspected then the British Mountaineering Council's technical committee may wish to investigate; contact the BMC at 177-179 Burton Road, West Didsbury, Manchester, M20 2BB. In the event of a serious accident, any equipment used by the casualty may be impounded.

Local Hospitals

There are hospitals with small Accident and Emergency units at Dolgellau, Tywyn, and Penrhyndeudreath, where minor injuries can be attended to.

CLIMBING GUIDES TO WALES

1 Gogarth
2 North Wales Limestone
3 Ogwen and Carneddau
4 Llanberis Pass